JEWISH ROOTS IN POLAND

PAGES FROM THE PAST AND ARCHIVAL INVENTORIES

To Harvey,

I know you understand the importance of this book and it is my great pleasure to give it to you.

Miriam Weiner

February 9,
1998

The publication of the book was made possible through a major contribution from

THE JOSEPH S. AND DIANE H. STEINBERG CHARITABLE TRUST

in memory of

Paul S. Steinberg, Sylvia Neikrug Steinberg, Max Steinberg,
Rachela Weinberg Steinberg and Sonia Steinberg

and through the generosity of

HARVEY M. KRUEGER AND CONNIE KRUEGER

and

ALAN FORTUNOFF

THE SEEVAK FAMILY FOUNDATION

WILLIAM H. FERN
MARJORIE AND ALAN GOLDBERG
THE SLOVIN FOUNDATION
LAWRENCE G. TESLER

ERNEST W. MICHEL
LEONARD AND JUDITH POLISAR
THE AARON ZIEGELMAN FOUNDATION

Dr. Arnold W. Baskies; Allen Bildner; Debra Braverman; Michael and Marilyn Brenner;
Jeffrey K. Cymbler; Abraham Gannes; Paul Gass; Martin Heilweil; Iscol Family Foundation;
Michael and Ginger Jacobs; Roman Kent; Eric Kessler; Dr. Samuel LeBauer; Dr. Mark Lester; Herbert C. Lee;
Morton A. Linzer; Michael Maidenberg; Isidore C. Myers; Berta Odnoposoff; Gertrude Prior; Riva Quitt;
Paul Rosenbaum; Sylvia Rosenberg; Harry J. Saal, Jill Sagarin; Edward J. Schifman; Leo Sirota;
Irving I. Stone; Thomas Teicholz; William Ungar; Herbert Weller; Joe L. Williams

JEWISH ROOTS IN POLAND
PAGES FROM THE PAST AND ARCHIVAL INVENTORIES

by
MIRIAM WEINER

in cooperation with the
POLISH STATE ARCHIVES

YIVO Institute for Jewish Research
ייִדישער וויסנשאַפֿטלעכער אינסטיטוט – ייִוואָ

New York, New York

The
MIRIAM WEINER
ROUTES TO ROOTS
FOUNDATION, INC.

Secaucus, New Jersey

Published jointly by

The Miriam Weiner Routes to Roots Foundation, Inc.
P.O. Box 1376
Secaucus, NJ 07066-1376
http://www.rtrfoundation.org

YIVO Institute for Jewish Research
555 West 57th Street, 11th Floor
New York, NY 10019
http://www.baruch.cuny.edu/yivo

Library of Congress Catalog Card Number: 97-60973

Printed by Horowitz/Rae Book Manufacturers, Fairfield, New Jersey

Printing Number
1 2 3 4 5 6 7 8 9 10

Publisher's Cataloging-in-Publication
(Provided by Quality Books, Inc.)
Weiner, Miriam.
    Jewish roots in Poland: pages from the past and archival inventories / by Miriam Weiner in cooperation with the Polish State Archives. -- 1st ed.
    p. cm. -- (Jewish genealogy series ; 1)
    Includes bibliographical references and index.
    ISBN: 0-9656508-0-4

    1. Jews--Poland--Genealogy. 2. Jews--Poland--Archives. 3. Poland--Genealogy--Religious aspects--Judaism. 4. Poland--Archival resources. 5. Holocaust, Jewish (1939–1945)--Registers of dead. 6. Cemeteries--Poland. 7. Holocaust memorials--Poland. 8. Concentration camps--Poland. I. Title.

CS877.J4W45 1998   929'.3438'088296
                      QBI97-40861

FOREWORD

IN MEMORIAM

ACKNOWLEDGMENTS

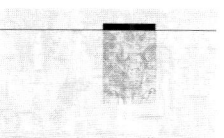

Wall constructed from tombstone fragments in Kraków's Remuh cemetery, 1982

INTRODUCTION

Deportation of Kraków Jews to the ghetto, 1941

ONE

INTRODUCTION TO POLISH–JEWISH GENEALOGICAL RESEARCH

Kraków ghetto, 1941

TWO

CITIES AND TOWNS IN POLAND: *Pages from the Past and Present*

View of the "old town" in Warsaw, c. 1917

TABLE OF CONTENTS

Polish State Archives in Warsaw, 1996

Urząd Stanu Cywilnego Office in Tarnów, 1993

Left: Judaic Library (now Jewish Historical Institute) *Right:* Great Synagogue destroyed by Nazis in 1943

Memorial at Majdanek death camp, 1991

Jewish birth record in Białystok, 1830

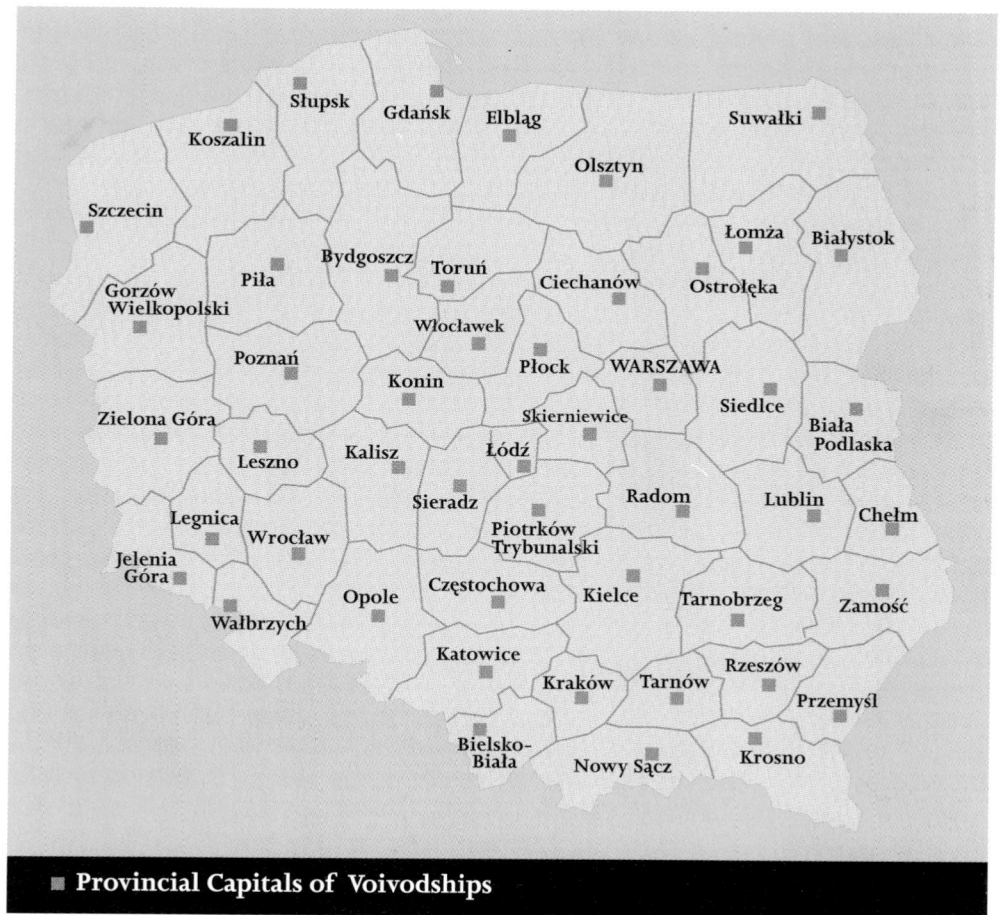

■ **Provincial Capitals of Voivodships**

Voivodships (Current Administrative Districts) of Poland Since 1975   *Map 1*

In the Old Town in Lublin, Jan Jagielski (right), historian at the Jewish Historical Institute, explains local history to Rabbi Sholem D. Horowitz of Antwerp, Belgium, 1988

2

American Jews have long struggled with their European roots. The immigrants from the *shtetls* of Eastern Europe came to America in several waves, with most of them arriving at the turn of the century. They tried, often successfully, to preserve something of the past in a world that was strange to them. They gathered in *Landsmanshaften* with other immigrants from their native towns, to be with someone who remembered the villages, who could sing a familiar song or pray with the proper intonation—someone else for whom the sights and the sounds of the Old World could evoke a sense of nostalgia.

In truth, those immigrants broke with their European roots. They left behind parents and siblings, even spouses and children, to journey forth to an unknown land. Often when they parted with their parents, they knew that this was their last meeting, their final goodbye. They would not return for illnesses or funerals, they would not be there when needed. The break was not without guilt. Separation by an ocean so large was usually final. Communication was confined to letters.

Their children were first-generation Americans, embracing all that was American. Even if they arrived in school speaking only Yiddish, they soon spoke an unaccented English fluently and eagerly absorbed American culture. Bernard Malamud wrote *The Natural*, still one of America's great baseball stories. Chaim Potok began *The Chosen* with a confrontation between Hasidim and more worldly Orthodox Jews on the baseball field— not quite a diamond, but a concrete schoolyard. These first-generation children of immigrants entered the American mainstream. They moved from the Lower East Side and other such Jewish enclaves to less "intense" neighborhoods—more Americanized, less ethnic. They regarded everything American as progressive and their European roots as backward, something to throw off, to abandon and leave behind. Only the future was of interest. The past did not beckon.

The second generation, however, and later the third and the fourth, sought to remember what their parents had chosen to forget. They turned back to Europe in search of something. But it was a different Europe to which they looked back. The fires of the Holocaust had consumed the world that was. Only the ashes remained— abandoned graves, former synagogues and memories. Poland was the home of dead Jews, of graveyards and concentration camps.

The Holocaust, the systematic, state-sponsored anni- hilation of the European Jews, destroyed the world that would have permitted American Jews access to a living past. The Holocaust looms large in American Jewish consciousness, larger in the past decade than when I

Dr. Michael Berenbaum, President and CEO of Survivors of the Shoah Visual History Foundation, Los Angeles; former Director of the Research Institute at the U.S. Holocaust Memorial Museum, Washington, D.C.

was growing up in the fifties and sixties, larger still than in the seventies and eighties. Thus interest in the European roots of American Jews grows as the ties that bind us with our European roots become ever more attenuated.

In recent years, a new ritual has arisen. Or, more precisely, an ancient ritual has been renewed. Pilgrimage is among the most ancient religious acts. One journeys to and one journeys from. Pilgrimage, a part of all religions, is an essential part of Judaism.

The first call to the first Jews, God's summons to Abram, was *Lech lecha*—Journey forth from your land, from your birthplace, from your father's house to the land that I will show you. Hasidic sages offer a different reading: *Lech lecha*—Go unto yourself. We leave everything behind in search of the unknown, yet it is the great unknown, ourselves, that we take along.

Our ancestors journeyed from Egypt to the Sinai Desert to the Promised Land. Save for two, Caleb and Joshua, those who began the journey did not enter the Land. Even Moses could not bring them but to the edge. He then had to cede his position to Joshua, his disciple.

In our generation, pilgrimage has returned as an essential religious act, along with a new path. If our ancestors went from Egypt to the Promised Land, if our parents, grandparents or great-grandparents went from Europe to America, we, their descendants, follow the tortured path of modern Jewish history from Auschwitz to Jerusalem.

We go as pilgrims back to Europe. For many of us, planes, trains and buses provide the means of return. For those of us who cannot make the pilgrimage physically, it is the discovery of documents that allows for the return, for the encounter with the past, for the sense of self-discovery.

Thus, Miriam Weiner's painstaking work, *Jewish Roots in Poland*, is as timely as it is valuable. She has initiated and made available to the public for the first time, in a concise and readable form, the inventories of records relating to the Jewish experience in Poland that are held in archives throughout Poland. She has taken us through these archives and offered us a peek at their treasures. And she has empowered fellow pilgrims—scholars and novices alike—to begin their own searches, to commence on their own journeys.

We travel with Miriam on the path that she has taken. We traverse the cities of Poland with their once vibrant Jewish populations, and we explore their remnants— physical buildings and documents—in a way that permits those of us who trace our roots to Poland to rediscover our past, to touch the generations that preceded those who came to America.

These efforts must be celebrated. Miriam was brave and bold, persistent, disciplined and demanding. She has opened to us an entire world for exploration and saved all of us, even the most informed, months of effort and false starts. She has made a daunting task appear ever more possible, even more beckoning.

This book is not Miriam's first contribution to memory, but it must surely rank as her finest. I first met Miriam when she worked with the American Gathering of Jewish Holocaust Survivors as it was beginning to gather what is now known as the Benjamin and Vladka Meed Registry of Jewish Holocaust Survivors, located in the United States Holocaust Memorial Museum. She worked with skill and dedication. She created order and empowered the survivors, most especially Benjamin Meed, the indefatigable president of the American Gathering, to do so much. I admired her then, and that was just the beginning.

She then wrote on the subject of genealogy. Still later, she became a guide, a mentor and a leading authority. She assisted people to find their past and, in turn, she discovered her mandate, perhaps even her destiny.

Jewish Roots in Poland is Miriam Weiner's singular achievement. Yet she did not work alone and did not write the book on her own. She asked for and received the assistance of the Polish State Archives and of individual archivists in Polish archives throughout the country. From archives large and small, from scholars of distinction and ordinary paper pushers, she received splendid cooperation. Only one who has worked in these archives and with these people can understand the magnitude of her achievement. She must have been cajoling and persistent. She must have persuaded by force of reason and of personality.

Generally, archivists belong to one of two schools. They are hoarders or sharers. The hoarders gather treasures that they deem all the more valuable because they are unknown and unexamined. They recognize the mystery of what they have, and they have a sense of power in knowing its importance and how only a handful of people understand the true value of what they possess. From these men—and they were mostly men—Miriam demanded the ultimate sacrifice, to reveal the concealed, to make known their treasures, to share what they have.

For the sharers, she became the midwife, the vehicle through which their treasures could come to light, their documents explored. Reading page after page, I could sense the depth of their gratitude as well as the anguish of those archivists for whom sharing is so difficult.

Miriam Weiner's book is a gift to all of us would-be pilgrims. The true measure of its value is to be found in the journeys we undertake, the secrets we uncover. These acts of pilgrimage return us way beyond the world of the Holocaust, to the moments when more than 3 million Jews lived in Poland, when Warsaw was the home of Jewish theaters and the Jewish press, when Hasidim and Misnagdim, secularists, Zionists and Bundists walked its streets and the small alleys of the hundreds of Jewish towns, villages and hamlets. With her aid, we return not to the world of destruction, but to a time when the world was whole. We can taste its spiritual richness and be charged by its vibrancy. After all, Jews lived in Poland for a millennium, and their sojourn was not always marked by antipathy and anti-Semitism. The murderous end of Polish Jewry is not all there is to the life of Jews in Poland. We must return not only to the ghettos, the concentration camps and death camps, but also to the towns, villages and hamlets where Jews dwelled for so long.

Such a journey can change our sense of who we are, of where we have come from, and, above all, of what we must become.

Dr. Michael Berenbaum
Survivors of the Shoah Visual History Foundation
Los Angeles, California

This book is dedicated to the memory of Professor Jerzy Skowronek, director of the Polish State Archives, who died in a tragic automobile accident in July 1996. Professor Skowronek was an enthusiastic and dedicated partner in this project, which he first embraced in 1993, shortly after accepting the directorship of the Polish State Archives. His energetic approach to each challenge and his ready smile were known to all those who worked with him. This book would not have been possible without his deep commitment to the project and his ongoing involvement.

Professor Jerzy Skowronek (1937–1996)

Książka ta poświęcona jest pamięci Profesora Jerzego Skowronka, dyrektora Polskich Archiwów Państwowych, który zginął śmiercią tragiczną w wypadku samochodowym w lipcu 1996 roku. Profesor Skowronek był zaangażowanym i oddanym partnerem przy realizacji niniejszego projektu, z którym rozpoczął współpracę w 1993 roku, wkrótce po objęciu przez siebie stanowiska dyrektora Polskich Archiwów Państwowych. Wszyscy, którzy mieli sposobność współpracować z Profesorem Skowronkiem znali Jego pogodę ducha i pełną energii osobowość. Książka ta nie powstałaby bez Jego głębokiego i nieprzerwanego zaangażowania.

When Miriam Weiner first approached me about our joint cooperation in producing a published listing of documents in the Polish State Archives, I was very impressed with her initiative, ideas, goals and recommendations. Ms. Weiner's many resources included a network of knowledgeable and professional researchers and archivists throughout Poland. Her local representative in Poland, Mariola Jeziak, served as Ms. Weiner's translator, administrative assistant and local coordinator. Ms. Jeziak served a vital role in this project.

When Miriam presented her proposal for this project, I was very interested in her methodology of gathering and organizing the data. As a historian and archivist, I completely support the methodology as presented in this book.

Although small segments of the Polish State Archives' holdings have been published or disseminated through the Internet and genealogical journals by others not associated with the Polish State Archives, this book represents the first officially sanctioned comprehensive publication outside of Poland of the holdings of the Polish State Archives, where the material was reviewed and verified by our archivists.

In addition to her work in Poland, Ms. Weiner simultaneously worked in archives in the neighboring republics of Belarus and Ukraine where documents could be found for towns now in Poland.

The gathering and verifying of archival data was truly a team effort. In Warsaw, many of my staff members participated in various levels of this project. I am particularly grateful to Dr. Andrzej Biernat, a vice-director of the State Archives, who was the coordinator between the central archives and the more than 85 archives throughout Poland that were surveyed for this book.

Many relevant documents for this book are located in Warsaw in AGAD (Archiwum Główne Akt Dawnych/ Archives of Ancient Acts), and the director, Dr. Władysław Stepniak, was very helpful in identifying and verifying the material in AGAD and also in preparing material for the video announcement of this book, which we filmed in June 1996.

My secretary and assistant, Elżbieta Kopica, was called upon frequently for her skills in scheduling and keeping track of the many details connected with this project. Her valuable assistance and professionalism are appreciated, as always.

I am grateful to the many archive directors and their staff archivists who reviewed the computerized data for this book several times and made vital additions and corrections to the information. Without their

Professor Jerzy Skowronek, 1996 1

cooperation, we could not have succeeded with this monumental survey of hundreds of thousands of documents in the Polish State Archives. In the archives throughout our system, the staff was asked to review a massive amount of material in order to provide as specific and complete data as possible. This was a difficult job, and I am proud of both the effort and the results.

Through her sheer persistence and focused efforts, Miriam Weiner has produced a book that will surely motivate those who wish to know more about their Jewish roots in Poland and will become a standard reference work for historians, librarians, archivists, researchers and genealogists who have been waiting for a town-by-town guide to the holdings of the Polish State Archives. In addition, the second inventory organized by repository will be of great assistance to archivists throughout Poland as well as those who are researching specific regions.

I am grateful to Miriam for asking me to be a part of this effort, and I look forward to working with her for many more years.

Professor Jerzy Skowronek
Warsaw, June 1996

Kiedy Miriam Weiner po raz pierwszy zwróciła się do mnie z propozycją współpracy w przygotowaniu publikacji i indeksu materiałów znajdujących się w kolekcji Polskich Archiwów Państwowych, ujęła mnie jej inicjatywa, pomysłowość, jak też i posiadane przez Nią rekomendacje. Zaimponowała mi swoją znajomością szeregu profesjonalnych badaczy przedmiotu i archiwistów na terenie całej Polski. Jako Jej przedstawiciel w Polsce, tłumacz i asystent w jednej osobie, występowała Pani Mariola Jeziak, która wniosła nieoceniony wkład w realizację niniejszego projektu.

Kiedy Miriam przedstawiła mi swój projekt, zainteresowała mnie zwłaszcza metodologia, którą zastosowała Ona przy kompilacji i organizacji zebranego materiału, w którą a pełni akceptuję i jako historyk i jako archiwista.

Jak do tej pory jedynie nieznaczna część materiałów zgromadzonych w Polskich Archiwach Państwowych dostępna była zainteresowanym w postaci publikacji rozsianych czy to w czasopismach zajmujących się genealogią, czy też w Internecie. Żadne z nich jednak nie zostały wydane za zgodą i poparciem Archiwów. Niniejsza praca jest zatem pierwszą oficjalną publikacją w Stanach Zjednoczonych zawierającą pełny wykaz archiwaliów znajdujących się w naszych zbiorach i przygotowaną przy współpracy naszych archiwistów.

Poza materiałami znajdującymi się w posiadaniu polskich archiwów Miriam Weiner włączyła do swojego projektu również archiwa Białorusi i Ukrainy w których udało jej się odnaleźć dokumenty związane z historią miast znajdujących się obecnie na terenie Polski.

W zbieraniu i weryfikacji materiałów archiwalnych w Warszawie uczestniczył cały szereg pracowników naszego Archiwum, którym chciałbym niniejszym podziękować za owocną współpracę. Przede wszystkim pragnę złożyć moje serdeczne podziękowania Panu dr. Andrzejowi Biernatowi, piastującemu funkcję wice-dyrektora Archiwum Państwowego, za koordynację współpracy pomiędzy Archiwum Centralnym a ponad osiemdziesięcioma pięcioma archiwami na terenie całego kraju, które wzięły udział w kwerendzie. Znacznej ilości materiałów, które weszły do niniejszej publikacji dostarczył nam dyrektor Archiwum Głównego Akt Dawnych w Warszawie, dr Władysław Stępniak. Za ich udostępnienie, jak i za pomoc w przygotowaniu filmowej zapowiedzi niniejszej książki w czerwcu 1996 roku, składam Mu gorące podziękowania.

Dziękuję również mojej asystentce, Elżbiecie Kopica, której pomoc w planowaniu szczegółów przy pracy nad niniejszym projektem była, jak zawsze, nieoceniona.

Wdzięczny jestem także wszystkim dyrektorom i pracownikom archiwów, którzy poświęcili swój czas na wielokrotną weryfikację zebranych informacji, dzieląc się swoimi uwagami i wprowadzając stosowne poprawki. Bez ich pomocy skompilowanie tak monumentalnego przeglądu setek tysięcy dokumentów znajdujących się w posiadaniu Polskich Archiwów Państwowych nie byłoby możliwe. W przypadku większych archiwów, nasi pracownicy mieli do wykonania trudne zadanie polegające na przejrzeniu ogromnych ilości materiału, celem dostarczenia jak najbardziej szczegółowego i jak najpełniejszego ich przeglądu. Praca jaką wykonali zasługuje na jak największe uznanie.

Dzięki swojej determinacji i staraniom, Miriam Weiner przygotowała pracę, która bez wątpienia stanie się nie tylko motywacją dla tych, którzy pragną dowiedzieć się więcej o swoich polsko-żydowskich korzeniach, ale również wejdzie do kanonu lektur historyków, bibliotekarzy, archiwistów, badaczy i genealogów, którzy już od dłuższego czasu czekali na przewodnik po zbiorach Polskich Archiwów Państwowych. Będzie ona także pomocnym źródłem informacji dla polskich archiwistów oraz dla wszystkich zainteresowanych studiami regionalnymi.

Jestem ogromnie wdzięczny Miriam za zaproszenie mnie do udziału w realizaji niniejszego projektu i mam nadzieję, że naszą współpracę dane nam będzie kontynuować przez wiele kolejnych lat.

Profesor Jerzy Skowronek
Warszawa, czerwiec 1996 r.

Dr. Daria Nałęcz, Director
Polish State Archives

When I accepted the position as director of the Polish State Archives in September 1996, the work on this book, which is a cooperative effort between Miriam Weiner and the Polish State Archives, was in essence in the final stages of its completion. I, therefore, familiarized myself with the finished product. I cannot overemphasize that this book far exceeds anything I could imagine, and I express my full approval of this work. I am pleased to add my endorsement of this publication dedicated to the memory of my predecessor, Professor Jerzy Skowronek, who was tragically killed.

I believe this book will surpass the expectations of the many researchers who are interested in receiving a maximum amount of archival assistance along with an exhaustive list of our collections that takes into account the location of our documents by repository.

■ *Daria Nałęcz, director of the Polish State Archives* 2

This publication is the first effort to present a comprehensive listing of our archival holdings and documents relating to Jewish people together with documents in the Urząd Stanu Cywilnego offices and the Jewish Historical Institute. The book will be very helpful to thousands of people all over the world, including private individuals researching their family history, historians who are researching specific subjects, and archivists throughout Poland.

Warsaw, June 1996

Uwagi Dr. Darii Nałęcz, dyrektora
Naczelnej Dyrekcji Archiwów Państwowych

Gdy obejmowałam stanowisko Naczelnego Dyrektora Archiwów Państwowych we wrześniu 1996 r., prace nad książką będącą owocem współpracy Miriam Weiner z polskimi archiwami były już w zasadzie na ukończeniu. Pozostało mi więc jedynie zapoznać się z gotowym dziełem. Nie mogę ukryć, że rezultat pracy przeszedł moje najśmielsze oczekiwania i mogę się o nim wyrazić z pełną aprobatą. Z dużą satysfakcją przyjmuję też ideę Miriam Weiner o dedykowaniu książki memu tragicznie zmarłemu poprzednikowi profesorowi Jerzemu Skowronkowi.

Myślę, że książka ta wychodzi na przeciw oczekiwaniom wielu badaczy, którzy zainteresowani są otrzymaniem największej ilości pomocy archiwalnych, wyczerpujących wykazów naszych zbiorów także uwzględniających rozmieszczenie zasobów według ich proweniencji.

Niniejsza publikacja jest pierwszą próbą prezentacji wyczerpującego spisu zbiorów archiwalnych i dokumentów odnoszących się do ludności żydowskiej i znajdujących się w Urzędach Stanu Cywilnego i zbiorach Żydowskiego Instytutu Historycznego. Książka ta będzie służyć pomocą tysiącom ludzi na całym świecie, zarówno osobom prywatnym zajmującym się historią swojej rodziny, historykom prowadzącym prace badawcze na ten specyficzny temat, jak i archiwistom w całej Polsce.

Warszawa, czerwiec 1996 r.

Urszula Olszewska, Director
Urząd Stanu Cywilnego
Warszawa-Śródmieście

In 1997, I assumed the position of director of the Urząd Stanu Cywilnego (Registrar's Office) in Warsaw. While I had no direct involvement in the coordination of efforts with our office regarding the publication of this book, I am sure that the book will be of great significance for many people around the world.

It is clear to me this publication is a pioneering effort, since such a vast amount of information relevant to this subject has never been gathered in one publication. It is very important for the documents in our collection to be included in the inventory lists; however, it is tragic that so much was damaged or destroyed during World War II.

The book will also be helpful for our office as it constitutes a guide that can assist not only our staff, but also the many people from abroad who send inquiries to us in search of records about family members.

Warsaw, June 1996

Urszula Olszewska, director, Urząd Stanu Cywilnego 3
Warszawa-Śródmieście

Uwagi Urszula Olszewska, dyrektora
Urząd Stanu Cywilnego, Warszawa-Śródmieście

W 1997 objęłam stanowisko Kierownika Urzędu Stanu Cywilnego w m. st. Warszawie. Nigdy wcześniej nie miałam więc możliwości ani współpracy z Panią Miriam Weiner ani też nie współuczestniczyłam w pracach nad tym opraco-waniem. Nie ulega wątpliwości jak wielkie znaczenie będzie miało to dzieło dla ogromnych rzesz obywateli całego świata.

Dzieło to jest natury pionierskiej ponieważ tak duża ilość informacji na ten temat zebrana w jednym opracowaniu nie miała nigdy dotąd miejsca. Jest to bardzo ważne, że dokumenty w naszym zbiorze także figurują w inwentarzach. Jednak jest to przykre, że tyle ksiąg zostało uszkodzonych lub zniszczonych podczas działań II wojny światowej.

Także dla celów Urzędu Stanu Cywilnego będzie ogromnie pomocne. Będzie bowiem także formą informatora gdzie można próbować szukać aktów stanu cywilnego, i pomaga naszym pracownikom w przygotowaniu odpowiedzi na ogromną ilość listów, które otrzymujemy zza granicy od osób szukających informacji o swoich rodzinach.

Warszawa, czerwiec 1996 r.

Professor Feliks Tych, Director
Jewish Historical Institute

Miriam Weiner took the initiative of preparing an extraordinarily useful publication. I thought of such a publication as one of the most urgent goals of the Jewish Historical Institute even before I knew that such a work was already under way. Ms. Weiner did it before us and she deserves to be praised for it.

A big plus of this work is that it can be used both by professional historians as well as by non-professionals who independently attempt to look for their roots. If one takes into consideration that at least 4 million Jews scattered today throughout the world derive their ancestry from Poland, which once had the largest concentration of Jews in the world, the significance of Miriam Weiner's publication becomes evident.

Surely, it is not a definitive work, but only because it cannot be. Even today, historians and archivists continue to discover new collections relevant to the history of Polish Jewry and the Holocaust. I am confident that the

▌ *Professor Feliks Tych, director, Jewish Historical Institute*   4

new findings will be included in forthcoming editions by the author and Ms. Weiner will keep updating her useful and so much needed publication.

Warsaw, June 1996

Profesor Feliks Tych, dyrektor
Żydowskiego Instytutu Historycznego w Warszawie

Miriam Weiner podjęła inicjatywę przygotowania nadzwyczaj użytecznej publikacji, o której sam myślałem jako o jednym z najpilniejszych zadań Żydowskiego Instytutu Historycznego, nie wiedząc jeszcze, ze praca taka jest już w toku. Pani Weiner wyprzedziła nas i chwała jej za to.

Ogromną zaletą tej pracy jest to, że korzystać z niej może zarówno zawodowy historyk, jak i nie-zawodowiec, próbujący na własną rękę szukać swoich korzeni. Jeżeli się zważy, że conajmniej 4 miliony Żydów rozsianych obecnie po całym świecie wywodzi swoje korzenie z Polski, niegdyś największego skupiska

Żydów na świecie—znaczenie publikacji Miriam Weiner staje się oczywiste. Napewno nie jest to publikacja definitywna bo być nią nie może. Historycy i archiwiści w Polsce odnajdują wciąż nowe kolekcje dotyczące historii Żydów polskich oraz Holocaustu. Nie wątpię jednak, że w miarę odnajdywania tych kolekcji autorka będzie w następnych wydaniach (a nie wątpię że do nich dojdzie) uzupełniała swoją użyteczną i tak bardzo potrzebną publikację o nowe znaleziska archiwalne.

Warszawa, czerwiec 1996 r.

AUTHOR'S ACKNOWLEDGMENTS

This book is the result of the concentrated efforts of a dedicated team, numerous colleagues and many friends in the United States, Poland, Ukraine, Belarus, Lithuania and Israel who have cooperated in helping me to produce this book.

I worked closely with the following repositories in Warsaw: the Polish State Archives, the Jewish Historical Institute and Urząd Stanu Cywilnego (USC), Warsaw Śródmieście. Inventory holdings were also provided by the Majdanek Archives and the Auschwitz-Birkenau Archives. I particularly want to acknowledge the important cooperation of and contributions from the staff at each of these repositories.

Polish State Archives

In mid–1993, I approached the newly appointed director of the Polish State Archives, Professor Jerzy Skowronek, and proposed the idea of a town-by-town listing of documents throughout the Polish State Archives to be published along with inventory lists from the Jewish Historical Institute in Warsaw and the USC Warsaw Śródmieście office, which holds Jewish documents for towns currently within Ukraine borders, but within Polish borders prior to 1939.

From the beginning, Professor Skowronek was excited about this project and promised his full cooperation and efforts to meet the goals of the publication. He kept that promise, and within three short years, he had become a close collaborator in this project as well as a friend.

The cooperation and participation of archivists from more than 85 repositories throughout the Polish State Archives far exceeded what I could have hoped for. In Warsaw, I had long meetings with Professor Skowronek and his vice-director, Dr. Andrzej Biernat, who helped interpret and then transmitted the revised inventories to the archives. Dr. Biernat's interest in this project and the many hours he devoted to it are much appreciated.

Many staff members of the archives in Warsaw also helped in the gathering of information and the administrative details, including Elżbieta Kopica, secretary to Professor Skowronek, and Dr. Władysław Stępniak, director of the Archives of Ancient Acts (AGAD), whose enthusiasm and knowledge were a welcome addition to the team. Also helpful were Marzena Januszewska and Bronisława Witkowska, in coordinating my research visits to the various archives.

Many of the archivists throughout the Polish State Archives returned their corrected inventories with lengthy letters and additional data that significantly expanded the database. Their comments were always insightful and helpful. I am grateful to all those who responded and do understand the time and staff constraints that prevented a few of the larger archives from responding in great depth, as was possible in the smaller archives.

❚ *Miriam Weiner, author*   5

In June 1996, Professor Skowronek and I filmed a video announcement about the methodology and completion of information gathering for the book. The video was shown at a July 1996 annual conference on Jewish genealogy held in Boston. One week after the conference, Professor Skowronek died in an automobile accident in France. I will be forever grateful for his work and, most especially, for his deep understanding of the importance of this book.

In September 1996, Dr. Daria Nałęcz assumed the position of director of the Polish State Archives. Even though the work had been completed on the archival inventories, she has confirmed her support for this project and reviewed Chapter 3. I am grateful for her interest and recognition of the importance of this publication. Her overnight response to our request for additional photographs was much appreciated as we finalized the book. Her ideas for joint cooperation and promotion of the access to documents for family research purposes are refreshing, and I look forward to the development of other projects toward these goals.

Jewish Historical Institute

The Jewish Historical Institute in Warsaw is a unique repository of documents, books and artifacts pertaining to the Jews of Poland, dating back many hundreds of years. In 1993, the Institute's director was Dr. Daniel Grinberg, with whom I had worked for a few years while I was leading group tours to Poland. Dr. Grinberg agreed that it was necessary for an inventory of the Institute's archival holdings to be included in this book. He referred me to Dr. Alina Cala, director of the Institute's archives who assigned Marek Józwik to help in compiling an inventory, town by town, of the Institute's documents. My thanks to Marek for his research, verification, additional material, and attention to detail.

Also at the Institute, I worked with Eleonora Bergman, who became vice-director in 1995. In late 1995, Dr. Grinberg left his position with the Institute, and I turned to Eleonora for assistance. Eleonora is a specialist in synagogue architecture, and she was very helpful in the latter phases of information gathering and verification of data at the Institute. Eleonora has always shared her knowledge and has never been too busy to answer my questions and requests for help. I appreciate her review of Chapter 5 and the corrections she provided.

In 1989, I had the good fortune to meet Jan Jagielski, who was then spending most of his time traveling by bus to various towns and villages in Poland, where he was documenting and photographing the remaining synagogues and Jewish cemeteries. His photo collection and books on these subjects overflowed his apartment. Subsequently, Jan accepted a position with the Jewish Historical Institute as director of Research and Documentation of Monuments. His photographic archives and town files are considered to be Poland's most comprehensive private collection. His willingness to share information and photographs can be seen throughout the town entries in Chapter 2 and in the Selected Bibliography. Whenever I had problems in locating a photograph of a particular synagogue or cemetery, I could almost always find it in Jan's collection. His contribution to this book and to my work is immeasurable. He is a mensch in every sense of the word.

During the course of the years necessary to collect the archival data, all three main repositories represented in the inventories gained new directors. At the Jewish Historical Institute, I had the pleasure of working with Professor Feliks Tych, who became the director in 1996. Professor Tych graduated from the History Department of Warsaw University, and for many years he had worked in the History Institute of the Polish Academy of Sciences. He published six books and 18 volumes of archival sources regarding the history of Poland in the nineteenth and twentieth centuries. His editorial background and expertise are reflected in his review of Chapter 5 and I am grateful for his support and enthusiasm.

In 1994, the Ronald S. Lauder Foundation Genealogy Project was created at the Jewish Historical Institute. I appreciate the cooperation of its director, Yale J. Reisner, who has shared photographs and his knowledge with me over a period of many years.

Urząd Stanu Cywilnego, Warszawa Śródmieście

This office is one of more than 2,500 local USC offices throughout Poland, yet it is unique because of its holdings. Here, we find the Jewish birth, marriage and death records for towns that are currently in western Ukraine, but that were part of Poland prior to 1939.

The recently retired director of this office, Kazimierz Kotlarski, authorized the creation of an inventory of the Jewish holdings specifically for this book. The inventory was periodically updated when books were transferred from this archives to AGAD. Mr. Kotlarski was very cooperative from our first meeting and he assigned his chief archivist, Grzegorz Mucha, to work with me as a liaison. This is the first time that Mr. Kotlarski has authorized publication of this inventory, and I am honored by his willingness to do so.

The new director of the office, Urszula Oszewska, is truly a joy to work with. She reviewed Chapter 4, and her suggestions were both insightful and important.

Majdanek Museum and Archives

At the Majdanek Museum and Archives, many people were helpful to me, including Edward Balawejder, museum director; Janina Kiełboń, archives director, and Henryka Telesz, archivist. Their assistance and cooperation were always prompt and efficient, dating back to our first meeting in 1989. I particularly appreciate their multiple reviews of Chapter 6.

Auschwitz-Birkenau Museum and Archives

For their years of friendship, guidance and cooperation, I thank Teresa Świebocka, museum curator, and Dr. Franciszek Piper, historian at Auschwitz-Birkenau. For more than a decade, Teresa has been a friend and colleague. She has always been available to answer questions and has opened her home to me as well. I also want to thank archivists Barbara Jarosz and Helena Śliż, who wrote the Auschwitz-Birkenau section for Chapter 6 and reviewed it several times. My thanks also to the director of the Auschwitz-Birkenau Museum, Jerzy Wróblewski, who provided the graphic document examples and photographs, including the cover photograph.

Consultants in Poland

In 1989, I met Mariola Jeziak, who was then a tour guide for ORBIS Travel Bureau. She began working with me in that capacity for my tours, and when the research began for this book, her duties increased substantially. During the years of preparation for this book, Mariola wore many "hats," including as translator, administrative assistant, liaison with various archives and institutions, chauffeur and host. Her tireless efforts and patience, along with accommodating so many of my papers, books and office equipment in her home, can never be measured but are appreciated, now and always.

In Lublin, I was fortunate to meet Robert Kuwałek, then working in the Lublin Archives, who was of great assistance in supplying information about the holdings in archives in Lublin and nearby regions.

In the survey process of archives throughout Poland, one individual outside of the Polish State Archives system made extraordinary contributions to the inventory data included in Chapter 7. Stanisław Maczka studied philosophy and history at Jagiellonian University in Kraków and has researched the history of Polish Jews throughout Poland, with a focus on the Żywiec and Oświęcim regions. He is the author of numerous publications on the topic, and his expertise greatly enhanced this project. Mr. Maczka is a sensitive and knowledgeable guide at the Auschwitz-Birkenau Museum and a fine historian. He logged many kilometers on my behalf, traveling to archives throughout Poland and compiling inventory lists for this book.

In Warsaw, Jolanta Kucharska was very helpful in compiling archival inventories in the Warsaw region and in sharing her knowledge about old photographs of Jewish sites.

Illustrations

Choosing the photographs, document examples and maps for this book was perhaps the most enjoyable part of the project for me. While text for the chapters was provided by the named authors, the illustrations wholly were my choice.

Maps

The maps for the town entries in Chapter 2 were reprinted with the permission of Polskie Przed-siębiorstwo Wydawnictw Kartograficznych (PPWK). I am particularly grateful to Alina Meljon, president of PPWK, for her cooperation. A current inventory and price list of maps may be requested by writing to PPWK, ul. Solec 18, 00-410 Warszawa, Poland.

My thanks also to Brian Lenius for sharing his expertise and for giving permission for the reproduction of one of his Galician maps.

Postcard Reproductions

Many of the present-day views of the localities in Chapter 2 were reprinted with permission from Krajowa Agencja Wydawnicza (KAW), a distributor of postcard views of Poland. I want to thank the director of KAW, Leszek Leśniak, for his cooperation, and all the photographers who so graciously agreed to the reproduction of their photographs (see Appendix 6).

Old Photographs

Many fine old photographs of Jewish sites were reprinted with permission of Instytut Sztuki Polskiej Akademii Nauk (PAN), through its director, Professor Stanisław Mossakowski. I am grateful to all the PAN staff, and particularly to Ewa Furmańska, Małgorzata Florczak and Jolanta Kucharska for their guidance and cooperation during my frequent trips to the Institute.

Others in Poland

Also helpful were Mirosław Nalazek, general manager of the National Tourism Promotion Agency; Piotr Kadlcik, director of "Our Roots"; Jacek Żmichowski, publicity manager, and Małgorzata Staniewska, marketing director of ORBIS in Warsaw; Ewa Kortylewicz of LOT Polish Airlines; Wojciech Adamiecki, formerly of the Embassy of the Republic of Poland in Washington, D.C., and now Poland's ambassador in Israel; Joachim S. Russek, assistant director of the Research Center on Jewish History and Culture in Kraków; Bolesław Szenicer, caretaker of the Jewish Cemetery in Warsaw; and Rabbi Chaskel O. Besser and Rabbi Michael Shudrich, of the Ronald S. Lauder Foundation.

Others who shared their knowledge, time and photographs for this book were Kazimierz and Maria Piechotka (Warsaw), Monika and Stanisław Krajewski (Warsaw), Tomasz Wiśniewski (Białystok), and Ryszard Bogdziewicz (Lublin).

The Białystok entry was reviewed by Tomasz Wiśniewski, a local historian of Białystok Jewish history, and I am grateful to him for providing access to and copies from his extraordinary collection of Judaica and old photographs.

I would also like to thank Czesław Jakubowicz and Eugeniusz Duda (Kraków); Władyslaw Fedorowicz (Krasnystaw); Barbara Malek (Łęczna); Josel Honig and Andrzej Trzciński (Lublin); Tadeusz Duda, Szymek Holcer and Kazimierz Opoka (Nowy Sącz); Halina Arczewska (Opatów); Jadwiga Nowicka (Ostrołęka); Janina Gredecka, Barbara Pancielej and Grażyna Kaczmarska (Piotrków Trybunalski); Teresa Balcerzak (Przemyśl); Adam Penkalla (Radom); Ewa Lipko (Rejowiec); Adam Szela, Jan Basta and Zofia Szulc (Rzeszów); Adam Bartosz and Marek Pawlik (Tarnów); Alicja Bukowska and Araksja Sarkisjan (Warsaw); Sara Ader and Maria Łukaszewicz (Włodawa).

Ukraine

The staff at the Central Historical Archives in Lviv (formerly Lvov) provided access to their documents and were very helpful in providing information about their holdings and verifying data, including those relating to towns within the current borders of Poland. My special thanks to Orest Jaroslawowicz Maciuk, director; Diana Ivanovna Peltz, vice-director; and archivists Elizabeta Markovna Stetsev, Galina Ivanovna Svarnik, Maria Emilyanovna Murin, Natalia Tsariova and Nina Shestakova. I am especially grateful to Mark Shraberman, a former archivist, who now lives in Israel, who was my translator and friend during my early years in Ukraine.

Moldova

I am deeply indebted to Vitaly Lukich Chumak, the former mayor of the town of Ataki in Moldova, who assisted me in compiling archival inventories in Belarus and Ukraine for towns now in Poland. Vitaly is my translator, travel coordinator, security guard, photographer and good friend. I thank him for all of this, and more.

Belarus

In Grodno, several people were kind and helpful in providing access to and information about archival holdings. I want to thank Felix Katz, formerly an archivist at the Grodno Oblast Archives and now living in Israel. At the Grodno Oblast Archives, director Svetlana Alexandrovna Kondrashova was particularly helpful. I also want to acknowledge the cooperation of Katrina Petrovna Batrakova, director of the Grodno Historical Archives.

Consultants in the United States

This book resulted from the input of many people, and as the project developed, the team expanded.

From the beginning, Jill Sagarin wore many hats, as a proofreader, researcher, administrative assistant and friend. She was always consistent with her commitment, her expertise and her patience. I could always depend upon her objective comments and relied upon her throughout this project.

When we needed someone to do the computerized production of the book, Jill recommended Stephen Freeman, who worked with me on the particularly challenging layout of Chapter 2, along with the other chapters in the book. His contributions included implementing the page-by-page layout of the book (with the exception of the archival inventories); the scanning and retouching of hundreds of documents, photographs and old postcard images; the adaptation of the typeface to include the Polish characters; and the design of several maps. I will be forever indebted to him for the many hours he spent on this project, at the cost of time with his family. His ideas as well as his skill were a major component in the completion of the project. This project was truly a labor of love for me, and Steve came to understand this in a way that few others did. He continually made suggestions and improvements, which resulted in a much better book.

A vital member of the team effort was Dorcas Gelabert, artist and graphic designer, who developed the conceptual page layout for the book, jacket design and promotional materials. Among the myriad of details involved in the book's preparation, my meetings with Dorcas were most exciting. Each time we met, she brought the latest version of her wonderful vision of the book. She was able to produce something beautiful out of my vague ideas and hopeful dreams.

I am also grateful to Richard White, who guided me through numerous editorial and technical problems during his early involvement with the project.

As the project developed, the team expanded. A valuable addition was Ben Geizhals of Express Printing Company, who served as a consultant.

The printing process of this book was a complicated job and I want to thank Robert M. Rosier and Ron Morris of Horowitz/Rae Book Manufactuers, Inc. and also Rush H. Housel, Jr. of Techniscan Integrated Imaging Systems for their patience and professionalism.

The computer database program for the archive inventories was developed and refined by David Kleiman, a fellow genealogist as well as a computer specialist. David is a computer and management consultant, president of DKI, Inc., and a partner in Up-A-Tree Software, which produces software utilities for genealogical research. He is also co-founder and chair of the New York Computer and Genealogy Special Interest Group. David worked with me for several years on this database. His combined expertise in genealogy and computer programming made his contribution to this book so great that I will always be grateful for his many long hours of work.

In the early phase of this project, I consulted with Jeffrey K. Cymbler, who has researched his Polish-Jewish ancestry for many years. He has also traveled to Poland, where he visited his ancestral towns and worked in the archives. He is one of the most knowledgeable people I know on the subject of Jewish roots in Poland, and he has compiled an extensive bibliography about synagogues and Jewish cemeteries in that country. Therefore, I asked Jeff to write Chapter 1 and to prepare the Selected Bibliography for the book. He has done all I asked, and much more. Jeff spent countless hours re-reading sections of this book. His meticulous reviews and remarks can never be adequately acknowledged. It seemed for awhile that I was telephoning Jeff on a daily basis with questions. His patience and cooperation never waivered, and his efforts went far beyond what I could have envisioned.

Two friends who contributed to this book in many ways are David Rosensaft and Debra Braverman. David designed the initial draft layout for the town entries and provided technical support for computer questions. Debra, his wife, provided access to her library, antique postcard collection and scanning skills.

During the development of this book, two people were always there for me, and I warmly acknowledge and thank Michael and Marilyn Brenner for sharing their ideas, photographs and document examples, and numerous other ways in which they showed how much they cared. Michael spent long hours in libraries verifying bibliographic entries, along with anything else I asked him to do. Their friendship and support sustained me during difficult segments of the book's development.

Over the years, I have come to know and respect Jonathan Shea, who was able to provide a unique contribution to this book. He is fluent in Polish and

Russian, and he is an experienced Polish genealogist—the first to receive permission to take genealogy tour groups to Poland, which included archival access. Jonathan is a professor of Foreign Languages at Central Connecticut State University in New Britain and founding president of the Polish Genealogical Society of Connecticut. He knows the Polish archives very well. I cannot thank him enough for his multiple reviews of the book and response to dozens of telephone inquiries.

Roberta Saltzman, who works in the Jewish Division of the New York Public Library, was essential to this project. I appreciate her thorough and prompt response to my seemingly never-ending queries.

My heartfelt thanks to Ruth Ellen Gruber (author of *Jewish Heritage Travel: A Guide to Central and Eastern Europe*) and Joram Kagan (author of *Hippocrene Insider's Guide to Poland's Jewish Heritage*). When it comes to specialists in travel to Poland, these two people probably hold the record for frequent-flyer miles accumulated during their numerous trips, where they gained a wealth of knowledge, established a network of local experts to help them and in the process, photographed many Jewish sites throughout the country. For many years, they have shared information with me and directed me to additional sources. They have become friends as well. Their publications have been the companion guidebooks for thousands of travelers.

Chapter Authors and Contributors

Although I have acknowledged their efforts elsewhere, I want to thank particularly the following people, who made major contributions to segments of this book, including Jeffrey K. Cymbler (Chapter 1, Selected Bibliography); Dr. Michael C. Steinlauf (Chapter 2), Professor Joachim S. Russek (Chapter 1); Mark E. Talisman (Chapter 1); Professor Jerzy Skowronek and Dr. Daria Nałęcz (Chapter 3); Kazimierz Kotlarski (Chapter 4); and Edward Balawejder, Janina Kiełboń, Jerzy Wróblewski, Barbara Jarosz and Helena Śliż (Chapter 6).

Reviewers and Editors

Many historians and professionals in the United States and Poland reviewed segments of this book. I want to thank Eleonora Bergman and Professor Feliks Tych of the Jewish Historical Institute in Warsaw, for their insightful comments and encouragement.

Especially supportive and helpful was Dr. William L. Shulman, president of the Association of Holocaust Organizations. Bill was very generous with his time and I am grateful for his review of Chapter 6.

I have always been envious of those authors who bestow glowing accolades on their editors. I had long hoped to find someone for the editing process who understood and cared about this book. I was very fortunate to be introduced to Lisa Clyde Nielsen, who had just completed an assignment as editor for an eight-volume series entitled *Holocaust*, geared for young readers. Lisa spent many hours with my manuscript, and her meticulous attention to detail and accuracy of content are reflected throughout. Equally important was her enthusiastic support for the project. She also recommended Joshua Safran, whose careful proofreading and editorial comments gave credence to the expression "fine-toothed comb."

YIVO Institute for Jewish Research

YIVO's director, Tom Freudenheim, understood and supported this project from our first meeting. I am very grateful for Tom's interest and also the enthusiastic cooperation of Bruce Slovin, chairman of YIVO's board of directors. At YIVO, I met with many staff members who were helpful in their suggestions. I am grateful to Zachary Baker, Fruma Mohrer and Marek Web, who reviewed text, offered advice and assisted with the Yiddish, Polish and Hebrew translations. Also at YIVO is a special person who has encouraged me for more than a decade. I want to warmly acknowledge Dina Abramowicz not only for her caring and help on this project, but also for her unwavering confidence and support since our first meeting.

It was important for many people to verify the factual material and review the manuscript. I am very grateful to Dr. Michael C. Steinlauf, senior research fellow at the Max Weinreich Center for Advanced Jewish Studies at YIVO Institute in New York for his review of and input to Chapters 1 and 2. Dr. Steinlauf is a specialist in the fields of Eastern European Jewish history and culture, Polish–Jewish relations, and the history of the Holocaust. As a Fulbright Fellow in 1983–1984, he was one of the first students since World War II permitted to study Jewish history in Poland. Dr. Steinlauf wrote a historical introduction to the town entries in Chapter 2, and my book is better because of his involvement.

Others in the United States

When Dr. Steinlauf suggested that I meet with Jolanta Goldstein, a graduate of Gdańsk University in Poland, I was impressed with her knowledge, professional background and enthusiasm for this project. Her research efforts contributed significantly to the book.

Over the years, one mentor continually encouraged me and was always there with advice and help. When Rabbi Malcolm H. Stern passed away a few years ago, I lost a friend whose guidance and counsel cannot be replaced. Therefore, it is with special feelings that I acknowledge the editing job of his wife, Louise Stern, with her many years of experience as an editor and wife of the "grandfather" of Jewish genealogy. I am grateful to her for her caring and meticulous editing of the Selected Reading lists and Selected Bibliography.

Also reviewing Chapter 2 was Dr. Robert Moses Shapiro, a historian of Polish Jewry. Dr. Shapiro teaches history and Yiddish at the Ramaz School, Yeshiva University and the National Yiddish Book Center.

For many years, I have worked and cooperated with Samuel J. Gruber, former director of the Jewish Heritage Council of the World Monuments Fund and now the president of the Jewish Heritage Research Center. Sam has always answered my questions and shared photographs with me. His *Survey of Historic Jewish Monuments in Poland* (edited with Phyllis Myers) was an important reference for data about the towns included in Chapter 2.

I am also grateful to Barbara Blicharski (ORBIS Polish Travel Bureau in New York), Joram Kagan (LOT Polish Airlines in New York) and Krzysztof Ziębiński (LOT Polish Airlines in Warsaw) for their assistance with my frequent trips to Poland and their friendship through the years.

For many years, Eric Goldman, president of Ergo Media, Inc., has been supportive and helpful in responding to my requests for information.

In Chapter 1, we included an entry for the Judaica Foundation of Poland, and I want to acknowledge the cooperation and assistance I received from Mark E. Talisman, vice-chairman of the Judaica Foundation.

For the intricacies of foreign alphabets, I turned to William F. Hoffman and Jonathan Shea, authors of *Following the Paper Trail: A Multilingual Translation Guide,* who very kindly gave me permission to reprint the Polish, German and Russian alphabets included in Appendix 4.

In 1982, I heard a lecture by Emmy Mogilensky, a Holocaust survivor. Our subsequent meeting resulted in a lasting friendship and I am deeply grateful to her for helping me decide upon a career change.

In 1984, I began working for the American Gathering of Jewish Holocaust Survivors in New York, where I met its president, Benjamin Meed, who became a teacher and mentor. He influenced the direction of my life by sharing his knowledge of the events and impact of the Holocaust. I am indebted to him for all of that, and more.

I wish to thank Gary Mokotoff and Sallyann Sack of Avotaynu, Inc., for permission to reproduce updated and revised versions of the articles by Jeffrey K. Cymbler and Professor Jerzy Skowronek, which appeared previously in *Avotaynu.* I also appreciate their courtesy in allowing some descriptive wording of their reference sources to be adapted for and reproduced in this book.

Some town entries were reviewed by Holocaust survivors who were responsibile for the publication of *Yizkor* books about their towns. I particularly want to thank Alfred Lipson, who reviewed the Radom town entry and shared many of his old postcards. Thanks also to Moshe Kirschenbaum in Israel, who provided copies of Radom photographs. The Piotrków Trybunalski town entry was reviewed by Ben Giladi. The Łódź town entry was reviewed by Marian Turski, born in Łódź and an editor of the *Polityka* newspaper in Warsaw.

I am grateful to Yechiel Geller Katz for his supplemental historical research for several town entries.

At the Leo Baeck Institute, Dr. Frank Mecklenburg was always responsive to my questions and requests for help.

Many colleagues and friends provided information about archival holdings, translations, photographs, document examples and other data. For all of this, I am grateful to Nancy Arbeiter, Michael Brenner, Jeffrey K. Cymbler, Stephen Dubner, Alex Friedlander, Solomon Gluck, Marjorie Goldberg, Janet Greenberg, Lucille Gudis, Estelle Guzik, Claus Hirsch, Eric Kessler, Harvey M. Krueger, Bruce I. Leibowitz, Irene Newhouse, Gary Palgon, Murray Seletsky, Joan and Gerald Sanders, and Steven W. Siegel.

This book would not have been published without extensive financial assistance, all acknowledged on a separate page in the book. Here I wish to add my special appreciation to The Joseph S. and Diane H. Charitable Trust and to William H. Fern, Alan Fortunoff, Marjorie and Alan Goldberg, Harvey M. Krueger, Leonard Polisar, Sheldon Seevak, Bruce Slovin, Joseph S. Steinberg, Lawrence G. Tesler and Aaron Ziegelman.

I am deeply indebted to Dr. Michael Berenbaum for writing the eloquent and moving Foreword to this book. His unique knowledge of so many facets of the Holocaust and Judaism, his experiences in the archives of Eastern Europe and his deep understanding about the importance of knowing one's roots are reflected in his Foreword. During the many years I have known Michael, he has always been an exceptional teacher, a strong motivator and a great inspiration.

The board members of *The Miriam Weiner Routes to Roots Foundation* were asked to serve because of their interest in "roots" and their commitment to this book. They attended board meetings, made important suggestions, and guided the book to its publication. They supported this project in every sense of the word. I want to thank my friends and board members: Michael Brenner, Marjorie Goldberg, Alan M. Fortunoff, Harvey M. Krueger, Ernest W. Michel and Leonard M. Polisar. Each of them contributed something unique from their wealth of experience and expertise.

Finally, I wish to thank my parents, Edward Weiner and Helen Rabkin Weiner, both of whom were involved in the early planning and preliminary research for this book and both of whom passed away before they could hold the book in their hands. Their guidance, financial support, love and faith gave me the strength to finish what I began.

Miriam Weiner
Secaucus, New Jersey
October 1997

INTRODUCTION

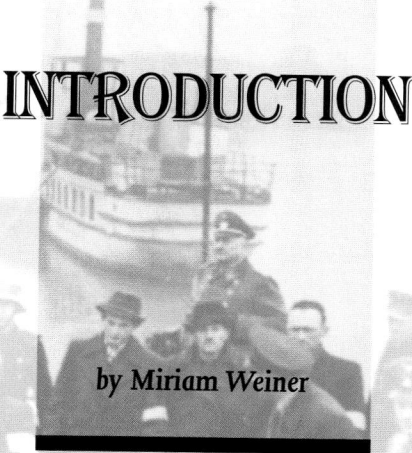

by Miriam Weiner

There has been a strong perception in Jewish communities worldwide that virtually all documents pertaining to Jews in Eastern Europe were destroyed by the Nazis during World War II.

While it is certainly true that many documents were lost, a significant number survived and can be found in archives throught Poland and the former Soviet Union.

The interest in family history is very strong among Jews throughout the world. It is estimated that more than 75 percent of American Jews can trace at least one grandparent to towns within the Polish borders as defined in 1939. The number of Jews visiting ancestral towns in Poland and the former Soviet Union is growing rapidly, and the interest in surviving archival material has brought family historians in pursuit of genealogy into the fold of scholarly research.

With the political changes in Eastern Europe during the past few years, it has become possible to visit places and work in archives that one could only dream of a decade ago. With this access, it became clear that there was a need to identify resources for people who wish to know more about their family history—specifically, what documents survived, for what time period, and in which archival repositories the documents could be found.

I visited Poland for the first time in 1989 and have returned several times each year since then, working in various levels of archives throughout the country. In 1993, I approached Professor Jerzy Skowronek, the newly- appointed director of the Polish State Archives, with a proposal to compile and publish an inventory of the State Archives, accessible by town name and also by repository. He was enthusiastic and had many ideas for the project. For the purposes of genealogical research, it is essential to be able to identify documents by the geographical location in which they were created—that is, either by town or district. The following methodology for

gathering the material was discussed and agreed upon with Professor Skowronek and he as well as key members of his staff have cooperated and assisted me throughout the project.

Synagogue in Sandomierz, early 20th century

1

| Title page of Lwów births in 1881 in three languages: Polish, German and Russian

FOCUS OF THE BOOK

One of the most difficult decisions in producing this book was what had to be omitted. The focus of the book prohibits an exhaustive study of all repositories in Poland. Those associated with this project agreed that the primary purpose was to concentrate on archival holdings in the state and branch (*oddział*) archives. While we have expanded these parameters to include the Jewish Historical Institute in Warsaw and the Urząd Stanu Cywilnego (USC) offices, or local town halls, as well as a more general description of the archives at Majdanek and Auschwitz-Birkenau, the reader should be aware there is material of interest to Jewish researchers in virtually all archives in Poland (see Chapter 3).

METHODOLOGY OF ARCHIVAL SURVEY

Data for the archival inventories came from many sources, including, but not limited to, archival inventories published by various archives in Poland; published lists of Jewish records microfilmed by the Family History Library (FHL) in Salt Lake City, Utah; inventories prepared by contracted researchers; district archivists in Poland who reviewed the compiled inventories at least twice; and a 1984 national survey of local town halls by the Ministry of Internal Affairs (the Ministry has not done a subsequent survey and, therefore, this inventory is based upon the 1984 data with updating as documents were transferred from the USC offices to the State Archives).

A special computer program was designed to accommodate the specific needs of the project. The information gathered from the above sources was translated and then analyzed prior to coding. This was a lengthy process that led to coding by document type, which was subsequently entered into the database. Any conflicts in data as a result of overlapping material in two or more repositories were questioned and resolved at that time.

A computerized listing by repository, based upon the above research, was provided to Professor Skowronek, who then had the data sent to each district archive (*Archiwum Państwowe*)

and the branch or sub-archives (*oddział* archives) of the district archive, with the request that the material be corrected and supplemented where possible. The revisions were then incorporated into the database, and the revised inventories were again provided to the Polish State Archives for a second review.

It was clear from comments received from archivists that, while the bulk of the data was correct, there were entries that had been accurate at one time but no longer were. Due to a restructuring of archives and administrative districts, the material had been moved to other archives. In some cases, an archives closed and the material was moved to another archives after we had entered the data. Every effort has been made to update and include the most current information.

Most archives were very responsive to requests for review of inventory lists and provided helpful additions and clarifications. However, a few larger archives stated that the sheer size of the project was more than they could accommodate and thus did not provide the requested archive file numbers or expand the inventory list we provided. This was particularly true with *spisy mieszkańców* (books of residents), which cover a span of many generations and proved difficult for the archives to include in the inventory list. In

---

Important Note to Remember

The inventory lists provided by the Polish State Archives and Jewish Historical Institute listed the year-span of documents followed by the archives' file numbers. As a result, it is not always possible to identify which archive number corresponds to a particular year or year-span.

Example: 1842–1844;1857;1859–1861;1873
270/2/4,7,9,12;273/1/3–4;279/1/78

Therefore, the archival inventories in this book should be used **in conjunction with** the *zespół/sygnatura* (file name/number) descriptions held in the Polish State Archives and the Jewish Historical Institute in Warsaw.

---

these cases, inventory data came primarily from published archival inventories.

FAMILY HISTORY LIBRARY MICROFILMS OF POLISH DOCUMENTS

Another issue that was difficult to resolve was the lists of Jewish metrical books (vital record registrations) that were microfilmed in the 1960s–1970s by the FHL. Obviously, because it was microfilmed, this material existed; but, in some cases, the current location of these books could not be confirmed. Inquiries were made to the Polish archives where the material *should* be, and sometimes, the books were located. However, in a significant number of cases, the individual archive directors simply crossed out the entry on the verification inventory list and were unable to state where the material might be.

An extensive search of the microfilms in the FHL revealed that more than 90 percent of those books that the Polish State Archives had been unable to locate were filmed in repositories in Germany. Therefore, rather than eliminate this substantial block of data from our inventories, a new repository category was created: "G," designating those vital records that were microfilmed by the FHL in repositories in Germany. The repositories in Germany where the material was located at the time of the microfilming are shown in the inventory, but the current location of the books has not been verified, since the focus of this book is the archives in present-day Poland.

The microfilms of the German-held books can be viewed at or requested from the FHL. The FHL has branch libraries (Family History Centers) throughout the world. Specific microfilms can be requested from the FHL to be sent to any Family History Center.

DOCUMENTS INCLUDED IN ARCHIVAL INVENTORIES

Documents included in the archival inventories can be divided into two groupings:
- Documents created by the Jewish community including metrical books; Jewish school records and Jewish hospital records; *Kahal* documents (including Jewish community and organization records); *pinkassim* (see Chapter 1); and other documents relating to the Jewish community.
- Documents created by local government offices, institutions, organizations and district government offices that include birth, death, marriage and divorce records (in those areas of Western Poland [Silesia] where separate Jewish records were not kept); family lists and books of residents; election and voter lists; documents created during the Holocaust period, including transport lists, property records, lists of people confined in ghettos and concentration camps, and confiscated property lists; immigration records; property records; name changes; police files; public school records; tax lists, bank records; applications for business licenses and occupational lists; notary records; local government records including wills and probate, transfer of property to and from the Jewish community; and many other related documents.

LANGUAGE: TOWN NAME SPELLINGS AND ALPHABET

It is anticipated that the primary readership of this book will be an English-speaking audience and, accordingly, *town names in the archival inventories in Chapter 7 are alphabetized in the alphabetical order of the English language.*

To enable the reader to locate books referenced in the *Selected Bibliography* (Appendix 1) and in the *Selected Reading* lists for each of the 28 towns included in Chapter 2, the entries are in Polish, but the Polish alphabet is not followed anywhere in this book. While this may be disturbing to my Polish colleagues, the decision was made in order to accommodate the primary readership of this book.

NOTES ON THE TRANSLITERATION OF HEBREW AND YIDDISH

Hebrew

A slightly modified version of the American Library Association/Library of Congress (ALA/LC) Hebrew romanization table is used for the transliteration of Hebrew bibliographical information. The ALA/LC Hebrew romanization table uses ḥ for the Hebrew letter *het*, kh for *khaf*, ' (apostrophe) for *'ayin*, and ts for *tsade* (with the exception of ḥ [*het*], diacritical marks appearing in the ALA/LC Hebrew table have been omitted). In other respects, Hebrew transliterations should be straightforward.

Proper names (including place names) are transliterated according to the ALA/LC Hebrew table when they appear *within* the bodies of bibliographical entries (*e.g.*, titles, names of publishers). *Author headings* appearing at the beginning of entries usually employ either Roman-alphabet forms that appear within the works or forms that are found in standard reference sources (encyclopedias, bibliographies and library catalogues). In cases where this information is not available within the works, names are systematically transliterated according to the ALA/LC Hebrew romanization table.

▌*Synagogue in Chełm, pre-1939*   3

Yiddish

The YIVO Yiddish romanization table, found in Uriel Weinreich's *Modern English-Yiddish, Yiddish-English Dictionary* (New York: YIVO Institute for Jewish Research, 1968), is used for the transliteration of Yiddish bibliographical information. The YIVO table uses kh for the letters *khof* (Hebrew *khaf*) and *khes* (Hebrew *het*). Yiddish words of Hebrew or Aramaic derivation (*e.g., matsev*) use transliterations found within entries appearing in the Weinreich dictionary. In other respects, Yiddish trans-literations should be straightforward.

Proper names (including place names) are transliterated according to the YIVO Yiddish table when they appear within the bodies of bibliographical entries (*e.g.*, titles, names of publishers). Author headings appearing at the beginning of entries usually employ Roman-alphabet forms that either appear within the works or are found in standard reference sources (encyclopedias, bibliographies and library catalogues). In cases where this information is not available within the works, names are systematically transliterated according to the YIVO Yiddish romanization table.

TRANSLATION OF TITLES

For all books and articles that are not in English, translations are provided in parentheses. In cases where the works include English translations of their titles (*e.g.*, on added title pages or supplementary tables of contents), those are the versions that are supplied. However, town names are transliterated into current spellings.

JUDAIC DISCOVERIES IN OTHER REPOSITORIES

During my travels in Poland since 1989, I have not only visited archives, but have also made inquiries about Jewish documents and Judaica in other places. Throughout Poland, I have encountered Jewish documents and Judaica in both private collections and several local museums. In the town of

Portion of Torah discovered in local museum in Krasnystaw, 1990   4

Krasnystaw, after a lengthy tour of the local museum exhibit (nothing Jewish in nature), the museum director took me into his private office and, over the next hour, showed me several items, including a Torah, kept in locked cabinets. One can assume this is not a unique situation.

ADDITIONS TO ARCHIVAL DATABASE

The ambitious joint effort with the Polish State Archives to produce the first systematic inventory of holdings focusing on Jewish sources is only a beginning. We know there is much more there and hope the book will motivate archivists and researchers to supplement the material included in this survey.

In a project of this magnitude and as a first attempt, it is inevitable that errors and omissions will occur. The database is being maintained on an ongoing basis and updated upon receipt of new information. Therefore, readers are invited to submit any additions or corrections to the publisher's attention, and the new data will be included in a future edition of the book.

Synagogue in Węgrów, 1918   5

JEWISH HISTORICAL INSTITUTE

I visited the Jewish Historical Institute (JHI) in Warsaw for the first time in 1989. Despite a lack of adequate funding and state-of-the-art-equipment, the JHI continues to be an oasis for those visiting Poland, who tour the JHI Museum with a sense of awe at what survived and despair that so much did not. People from all over the world, Jews and non-Jews alike, visit the JHI, which is located in one of the few architectural remnants of pre-war Jewish Warsaw.

The dedication of the JHI employees to their job of preserving and protecting documents, books and Judaic objects is impressive even to the first-time visitor.

The JHI archival holdings include many unique and interesting documents. New documents come into the JHI on a regular basis, some donated by local Polish residents who found them hidden in their homes or who were holding them for safekeeping for Jews who never returned for them.

In 1994, the Ronald S. Lauder Foundation Genealogy Project was established at the Jewish Historical Institute. Since then, it has become a major resource within Poland for Jews throughout the world who are seeking information about their relatives and heritage. In the last few years, a number of Poles have discovered that they were born to Jewish parents and have come to the JHI for help in learning more about their roots and ancestors.

URZĄD STANU CYWILNEGO OFFICES

The Urząd Stanu Cywilnego (USC) offices throughout Poland, consisting of more than 2,500 local town halls where vital records are recorded, are an important source of surviving Jewish records dating from the late 1890s to 1943. Since this time period covers a substantial number of Poland's 3 million Jews who perished during the Holocaust, it was essential that the records of these local archives be included in the Archival Holdings Indexed by Town (see Chapter 7).

A unique USC office located in Warsaw holds books of Jewish vital records from eastern Galicia, dating from the late 1890s to 1943, when registrations ceased. The Jewish holdings in this archive are subject to access restrictions by law, but research requests for specific records are permitted, and a certified copy of a birth record is often the only official verification available. For those interested in what diseases are common in their family, the death records from Galicia prior to 1918 generally list the cause of death.

THE ARCHIVES AT MAJDANEK AND AUSCHWITZ-BIRKENAU DEATH CAMPS

Archival holdings from these two death camps are not included in the inventories, as the documents are primarily accessible by family name rather than by locality or town name. Therefore, Chapter 6 includes sections written by archivists of both the Majdanek and Auschwitz-Birkenau Museums, wherein they describe the documents contained in their archives. Examples of documents are provided by both institutions. Among the particularly poignant photographs sent to me from the Auschwitz-Birkenau archives was one that I chose for the cover of this book: a photograph of a Jewish couple wearing the yellow Star of David on their sleeves. The identity of this couple is unknown, as are the identities of individuals in thousands of photographs confiscated from Jews upon their arrival at Auschwitz-Birkenau.

The "Auschwitz Complex" (also referred to as KL [*Konzentrationslager*] Auschwitz) included Auschwitz I (in the nearby village of Brzezinka), Auschwitz II-Birkenau and Auschwitz III-Monowitz (on the premises of the Buna factory). Within this book, the terms Auschwitz, KL Auschwitz and Auschwitz-Birkenau are used interchangeably. Both Auschwitz and Majdanek functioned as concentration and forced-labor camps as well as extermination centers.

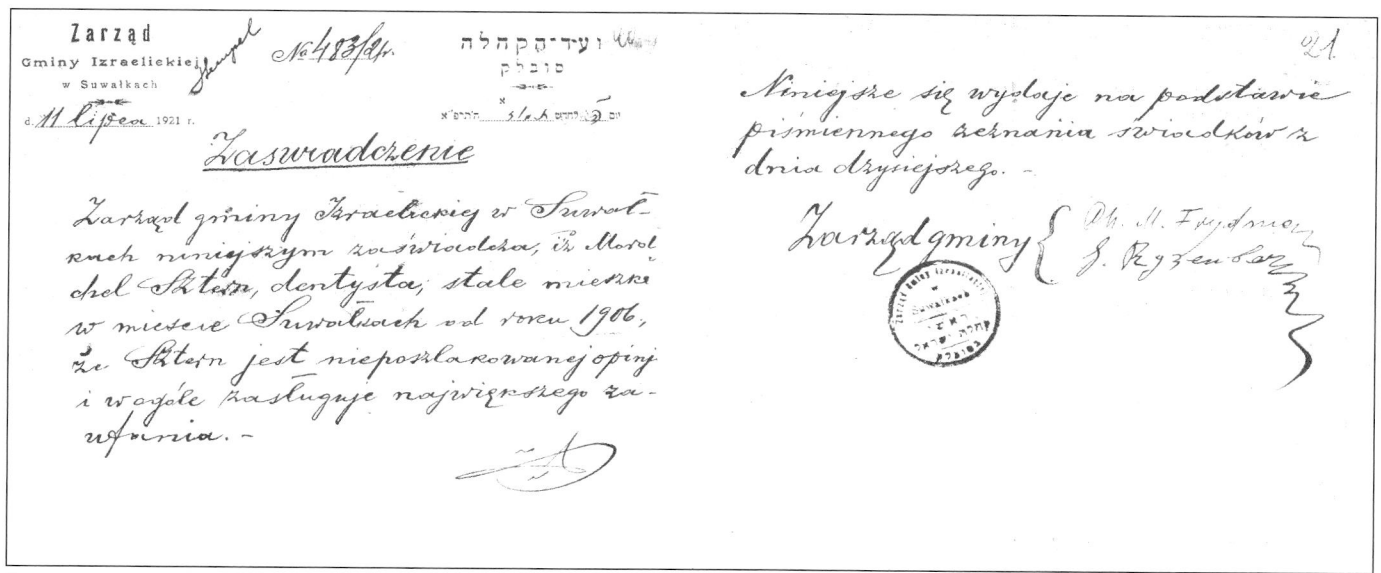

Letter from Jewish community of Suwałki attesting to the professional qualifications of Mordechai Sztern, dentist, 1921

6

PHOTOGRAPHS AND DOCUMENTS

Photographs and documents are numbered sequentially within each chapter (and in Chapter 2, within each town entry). The source of each graphic is reported in Appendix 6, *Photograph and Illustration Credits*.

SELECTED READING LISTS (CHAPTER 2) AND SELECTED BIBLIOGRAPHY (APPENDIX 1)

There are individual *Selected Reading* lists for each of the 28 towns described in Chapter 2 and also a *Selected Bibliography* (Appendix 1). The language of publication is indicated in ( ) at the end of the bibliographic entry, as follows:

(F)	French	(P)	Polish
(G)	German	(R)	Russian
(H)	Hebrew	(Y)	Yiddish

All other books are in English. If a book is in both English and another language, a bibliographic entry of (E) is added to show that the book has an English section.

The current condition (if known) of synagogues and Jewish cemeteries views in the *Selected Bibliography* is shown in ( ). The word "reconstructed" refers to a new site use (another building constructed on the site of the former synagogue shown in the picture) and the word "renovated" refers to renovated synagogue building with a different purpose today.

Because of the vast number of publications about the larger cities in Poland, there are additional bibliographic entries in the *Selected Bibliography* relating to several of the towns entries in Chapter 2.

SELECTED BIBLIOGRAPHY

The *Selected Bibliography* does not include the hundreds of *yizkor* (memorial) books published for localities in Poland (see Chapter 1 regarding major repositories for *yizkor* books). In addition to *yizkor* books, many town and regional histories have been published; however, because of their vast number, they are not included in the *Selected Bibliography*.

The *Selected Bibliography* focuses on publications about localities within the current borders of Poland. Although the *Selected Bibliography* is not an exhaustive compilation, we have attempted within the Cemetery and Synagogue sections of the *Selected Bibliography* in Appendix 1 to compile a list of all known relevant publications; therefore, some entries are duplicated in the *Selected Reading* lists of Chapter 2.

AUTHOR'S NOTES

There are several instances where material overlaps with similar material in another chapter or is actually duplicated. Explanatory information that is pertinent to more than one chapter is repeated in the appropriate place. This is intentional and done to assist the reader so that there will be a minimum of cross-referencing between chapters.

The term *metryka* in various Slavic (and other) languages refers to, among other things, registers of vital statistics. However, in many transliterated English-language versions of material referring to these registers, the registers are commonly referred to as *metrical books*. That terminology is used in this book.

Throughout this book, the Polish city of Warszawa is translated as Warsaw within the text; however, the Polish spelling of Warszawa is used in addresses. All other towns currently within the Polish borders are spelled according to the Polish alphabet.

USEFUL ADDRESSES

FAMILY HISTORY LIBRARY, 35 North West Temple Street, Salt Lake City, Utah 84150 <http://www.lds.org>

Archives in Germany where Polish–Jewish records were microfilmed by the Family History Library in the 1960s–1970s:

> BUNDESARCHIV, Potsdamer Str. 1, Postfach 320, 56075 Koblenz, Germany
> GEHEIMES STAATSARCHIV PREUSSISCHER KULTURBESITZ, Archivstr. 12-14, 14195 Berlin, Germany
> STADTARCHIV AUGSBURG, Fuggerstrasse 12, 86150 Augsburg, Germany
> DEUTSCHE ZENTRALSTELLE FÜR GENEALOGIE, Käthe-Kollwitz Strasse 82,
> (Postal Box address: D-04002 Leipzig, Postfach 274), 04109 Leipzig, Germany

Łuków Holocaust Memorial, 1975

Major Jewish Communities in Poland, 1931 (Above Figures Represent Jewish Population)   *Map 2*

INTRODUCTION TO POLISH-JEWISH GENEALOGICAL RESEARCH

by Jeffrey K. Cymbler

HISTORICAL BACKGROUND

Jews first settled in Poland as early as the eleventh century. By the eve of World War II, the Jewish population of Poland had reached 3.3 million people. By the end of the Holocaust, only 300,000 Polish Jews remained. Most of them subsequently emigrated to Israel or the United States.

Today, estimates of the Jewish population in Poland range anywhere from 5,000 to 15,000, including people discovering their Jewish roots only recently and those who have hidden their ancestry since the war.

The year 966 is generally accepted as the official birth date of Poland. Jewish legend has it that the name Poland— or, more precisely, its Hebrew name, Polin—is derived from the Hebrew po-lin, meaning "here, stay overnight." In 1264, Duke Bolesław of Kalisz signed the first law granting privileged status to Jews living in the western province called Greater Poland. This Statute of Kalisz, as it is known, provided the legal foundation for the rights of Polish Jewry for centuries. From 1264 to 1648, the Jewish community in Poland prospered and rose to become the best organized since the expulsion of Jews from Spain in 1492. In 1569, Poland and Lithuania formally united into the Polish-Lithuanian Commonwealth. At its greatest expanse, the borders of the Commonwealth stretched from the Baltic Sea to the Black Sea. From the end of the sixteenth century until 1764, the Council of the Four Lands (*Vaad Arba Aratzot*), a supreme Jewish communal body, was recognized by the Polish authorities and was granted great power over every aspect of Jewish secular and religious life in Poland.

Beginning in 1648, tens of thousands of Polish Jews as well as non-Jewish Poles were murdered, first at the hands of Cossack armies led by Bogdan Chmielnicki and later during the Swedish and Russian invasions. As a result of these catastrophies, some Jews emigrated to neighboring Silesia and Bohemia. Nevertheless, Jewish communities in Poland revived with surprising speed.

Taking advantage of a weakened state, Poland's imperial neighbors—Russia, Prussia and Austria-Hungary—partitioned the Commonwealth in 1772, 1793 and 1795 (see page 25). After the third partition, Poland was eliminated from the map of Europe. In 1807, Napoleon defeated the Prussians and established the Grand Duchy of Warsaw out of the territories previously anexed by Prussia; additional territories were added from Austria. However, after Napoleon was defeated at Waterloo in 1815, Russia and Prussia divided the Duchy between them at the Congress of Vienna. The Poznań area became the Grand Duchy of Posen, ruled by Prussia. The western provinces of Poland—Silesia, Pomerania, Poznania, West Prussia and East Prussia—were retained by Prussia. Kraków became an independent republic until 1846, when it was annexed by Austria after Austria defeated a Polish uprising in the province of Galicia. The eastern territories of the Commonwealth went to Russia; the semi-autonomous Kingdom of Poland (also known as Congress Kingdom or Congress Poland—it included the Russian portion of the Duchy of Warsaw) was established in the western portion of these territories. After Czar Alexander II defeated the Polish insurrection of 1863, the Kingdom of Poland was abolished when these lands were annexed by Russia.

During the late eighteenth and nineteenth centuries, the Russian imperial government organized and redrew the boundaries of 19 *guberniyas* (provinces) from the lands of the former Polish Commonwealth. These lands, in which Jews were densely settled, became the so-called Pale of Settlement, an area to which Jews were exiled and forced to live except through special permission, until the Russian Revolution in 1917. The 19 *guberniyas* were Grodno, Kalisz, Kamieniec,

Kielce, Kijów (Kiev), Kowno, Łomża, Lublin, Mińsk, Mohyłów (Mohylew), Piotrków, Płock, Radom, Siedlce, Suwałki, Warszawa, Wilno, Witebsk and Wołyń (see page 21).

The portion of southern Poland that became part of Austro-Hungary was known as Galizien, or Galicia. In 1875, Galicia was divided into 74 administrative regions. The two prinicipal administrative centers in Galicia were Kraków in the western portion and Lwów (Lemberg, Lviv) in the eastern portion. Because Poland was no longer an independent geopolitical unit between 1795 and 1918, Jews born during that time period were necessarily subjects of one of the three partitioning powers—Russia, Austria-Hungary or Prussia (after 1871, Germany). Therefore, genealogical documentation from that time period will refer to the Russian, Austro-Hungarian or Prussian (German) Empires; some genealogical records for that time period for areas that are in present-day Poland are held in archives in Germany, Belarus, Lithuania and Ukraine (see Introduction and Chapters 4 and 7).

The independent state of Poland was reborn after World War I, through the Treaty of Versailles. This Poland, however, was much smaller than the Polish-Lithuanian Commonwealth. In 1939, Germany and the Soviet Union partitioned Poland once again; towns in areas annexed by Germany were renamed for the duration of the occupation (e.g., Łódź became Litzmanstaadt and Będzin became Bendsburg). In German-occupied Poland, German laws decreed that every Jewish male be given the middle name "Israel" and every Jewish female be given the middle name "Sara" to identify them as Jews. Indeed, civil vital registers for the years 1939 through 1943 from the western part of Poland occupied by Germany reflect this practice.

At the end of World War II in 1945, Poland was reborn for a third time. This time its borders shifted westward. The formerly German city of Breslau became the Polish city of Wrocław, and the formerly Polish city of Lwów became Lvov, Ukrainian Soviet Socialist Republic (S.S.R.). When Ukraine declared its independence from the former Soviet Union in 1992, the Russian city of Lvov became the Ukrainian city of

Lviv. These are but two examples of changing place names. The renaming of geographical entities, principally restricted to larger urban areas, was relatively common.

EDICTS AND DECREES DURING THE PARTITION PERIOD

With the demise of Poland as a political entity during the period 1795–1918, members of the Jewish community of Poland became subjects of one of three different empires— each submitting its Jewish residents to varying decrees and record-keeping systems. An understanding of some of these laws is useful to genealogists.

In 1787, Galician Jews were ordered to adopt fixed, hereditary surnames. In Russian Poland, Jews were not required to adopt family names until December 1809. Prior to that time, most Polish Jews used their father's given name (patronymic names), such as Moses ben ("son of") Abraham or Moses Abramowicz. (The Polish suffix owicz and its similar variations in other Slavic languages [ovitch] mean "son of.") For an exhaustive discussion of the adoption of surnames by Jews in Poland, see Beider, Alexander, *A Dictionary of Jewish Surnames from the Kingdom of Poland* (Teaneck, NJ: Avotaynu, Inc., 1996). As for Prussia, the 1790 Law of Breslau Concerning Jews and an 1812 edict in Silesia proscribed the adoption of surnames. Jews in Posen, however, were not required to adopt surnames until 1830. See Brilling, Bernhard, "Adoption of Family Names by Jews in Prussia (1804)," in *Avotaynu*, vol. 1, no. 2 (July 1985): 23–26.

The adoption of surnames makes it easier to trace family group in vital records once one finds the ancestor who first adopted a last name. However, it may be impossible to identify one's ancestor's siblings, since they may have adopted different last names. One thing to keep in mind is that spellings of surnames and given names may vary in documents. Prior to the twentieth century, names in Eastern Europe were not always spelled in a standard way. For example, Birnbom, Birnbaum, Birenbom and Birynbaum are all forms of the name Birenbaum.

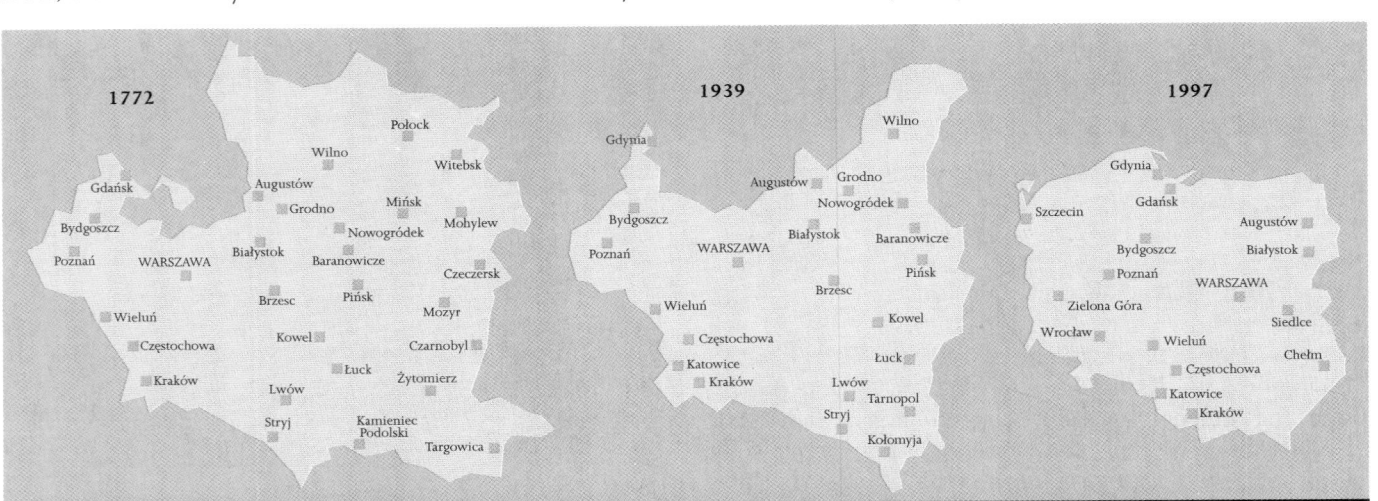

Poland's Territorial Boundaries: 1772, 1939, 1997

Map 3

In Austro-Hungarian Galicia, according to civil law, only one son in each Jewish family was allowed to marry. In addition, only those couples who possessed between 500 and 1,000 florins and who paid 10 percent of their wealth as a marriage tax could marry. Galician Jews who had less than 500 florins could not even apply for permission to marry; those with more than 1,000 florins had to pay a higher marriage tax. The result was that most Galician Jews were married only in a religious ceremony by a rabbi. The marriages were never recorded nor recognized by the civil authorities. The children of such unions were recorded by the civil authorities as illegitimate, and they were required to adopt their mother's maiden name as their own surname. Frequently, a mother's maiden name was followed with her husband's surname listed as "*vel*" or "*v.,*" meaning "also known as."

In the Russian Empire, during the period 1825–1855, the tsars decreed that young Jewish males ages 12 to 25 were to be inducted into the army for up to 25 years (Jews in Congress Poland were exempt from this decree from 1827 to 1843). As a result, a variety of strategies were adopted to avoid recording the births of sons (birth records provided the tsar with a list of the names and ages of Jewish boys eligible for conscription). Because the eldest son was exempt from the draft in Russia, subsequent sons often were assigned the names of relatives who had no boys. In Galicia, "only" sons (no other sons in the family) did military service just in times of emergency. A second son often assumed his mother's maiden name, thereby pretending to be an only son, to avoid army service.

CIVIL VITAL RECORDS

Except for those who descend from rabbinic families, most Jews of Polish descent cannot trace their Polish ancestry further back than the eighteenth century. As discussed above, fixed hereditary family names were not customary among Polish Jews until required by the civil authorities—1787 in Galicia, c. 1808 in Prussia, 1812 in Prussian Silesia, 1830 in Posen and 1809 in Russia. The family names that existed before those periods tended to be found in rabbinic families, who also were more likely to maintain genealogies and family trees.

Vital Records Registration in Poland

After the partitions of Poland, the three empires that controlled Poland required the church to record Jewish vital records and make copies of the church records for the benefit of the state. These vital records are called "civil transcripts of church records." Eventually, Jews were permitted to maintain their own civil records. Many synagogues also maintained their own records of births, marriages and deaths.

In 1808, civil registration began in the Duchy of Warsaw, using the Polish language and the Napoleonic paragraph format of record-keeping—a format established by the Napoleonic Code. In a given year, all birth entries are followed by all the marriages and finally the deaths. Birth records provide the date of birth; the father's name, age and occupation; the

mother's name, age and maiden name (in earlier records, this may just be a patronymic); names of witnesses; and the house number where the birth occurred (which is important in establishing possible interrelationships). Marriage records state the bride's and the groom's ages; whether they were previously widowed; and their parents' names, including mother's maiden name. Death records provide the age of the deceased and, at times, parents' names or surviving spouse's and children's names. Each town's records tend to vary somewhat in the type of format and completeness of information.

An index often is found at the end of each set of records (*e.g.*, births), or at the end of all the year's entries. Even if there is an index, it is advisable to scan each record, since women's maiden names are often listed within the record. In addition, one may wish to locate documents wherein ancestors appeared as witnesses to other births or deaths. Sometimes an ancestor's occupation or birth year may be determined from these tangential records.

Prior to 1918, Russia utilized the Julian calendar. Therefore, many records from the former Russian Poland contain two dates, 12 days apart. The first date is the Julian calendar date, and the second date is the Gregorian date used by much of the rest of Europe.

Jewish records in Russian Poland were interspersed with Catholic and Evangelical records in the same metrical books. Beginning in 1826, the Russian government allowed Jews to maintain their own separate ledgers. After the unsuccessful Polish insurrection in 1863, the Russian government began an intensive program of Russification in all former Polish territories and decreed that all government business had to be conducted in Russian. Consequently, from 1868 to 1918, civil vital records in Congress Poland were recorded in the Russian language. After World War I, with the re-birth of Poland as an independent state, the Polish language was restored for record-keeping.

Civil registration in Galicia began as early as 1787 and in Prussian Poland by 1812. These records were entered in a columnar format. Jewish records were maintained by the Jews in separate ledger books beginning in the early nineteenth century. In Galicia, the column headings were in German and/or Latin, and entries were made in German, Hebrew and/or Polish. Most of the ledgers from Galicia do not contain indexes. In addition to the information contained in the Russian records from Congress Poland, Galician birth records often contain the names of the grandparents (including both grandmothers' maiden names) and whether the child was legitimate or illegitimate. (As discussed above, Jewish children were usually registered as illegitimate, since their parents had not married in a civil ceremony.) Galician Jewish marriage records are sparse. Marriage records contain both the groom's and the bride's mothers' maiden names. Death records in Galicia often list the cause of death, with diphtheria and cholera being common causes of death during the nineteenth century.

Galicia was divided into 74 administrative divisions in 1875, after which civil registration of the entire administrative region was recorded in the chief town of the district. One ledger was maintained for the district, with records from all towns in the district recorded together chronologically. Thus, the vital records register for the Jarosław district includes records of the towns of Radymno, Sieniawa and Pruchnik. See Wynne, Suzan, "Demographic Records of Galicia 1772–1919," in *Avotaynu*, vol. 8, no. 2 (Summer 1992): 7.

In Prussia, the government's goal was to totally destroy the Polish language and culture. Therefore, the column headings were in German and/or Latin, while the actual documents were recorded in German and/or Hebrew.

After Poland was reborn in 1918, civil vital records throughout the country utilized the Napoleonic paragraph format in Polish. Separate ledger books were maintained for Jewish records. During World War II in German-occupied Poland, the Napoleonic format was continued, but the records were written in German.

For information on how to search metrical records that are *less* than 100 years old (by mail and in person in USC offices), see Chapter 4.

For information on how to search metrical records *more* than 100 years old (by mail and in person in the Polish State Archives), see Chapter 3.

LDS Collection of Polish Vital Records

The Family History Library of the Church of Jesus Christ of Latter-Day Saints (LDS Library) has microfilmed civil transcripts of church records and Jewish records from hundreds of Polish towns. These microfilms generally begin in 1808 and, in many cases, continue through the late 1800s. Consult a local Family History Center's Locality Catalogue to determine whether vital records for a specific town have been microfilmed. For those areas of present-day western Poland that were part of Germany before World War II, some of the LDS microfilming was done in Germany; therefore, these records are not contained in the Polish archival system.

The LDS Locality Catalogue lists the towns of Poland according to the province to which they were assigned during the period 1945–1975. For example, the town of Radomsko, which today is in Piotrków Trybunalski voivodship (province), is listed in the Locality Catalogue under its former location in Łódź province. The Locality Catalogue shows two listings for Radomsko. One, labeled "Church Records," includes the Catholic parish register transcripts of baptisms, births, marriages and deaths from 1816 to 1825. The second, labeled "Jewish Records," has the civil registration for the Jewish

Birth record of Abraham Ehrlich, 1812, Gliwice, son of Hirschel Ehrlich and Johanna Peretz

community from 1826 to 1888. The starting date of 1826 for Jewish records is a signal that registers for the years 1816–1825 for Congress Poland, listed as "Church Records," most likely include Jewish records.

Translating Vital Records

A good resource guide to the translation of Polish vital records is Frazin, Judith R., compiler and ed., *A Translation Guide to 19th-Century Polish-Language Civil-Registration Documents* (Chicago: Jewish Genealogical Society of Illinois, 1989, 2nd ed.). This book is extremely useful for translating nineteenth-century vital records from Congress Poland and includes numerous sample documents.

Consult also Shea, Jonathan D., *Russian Language Documents from Russian Poland: A Translation Manual for Genealogists* (Orem, UT: Genealogy Unlimited, 1989) and Shea, Jonathan D., and William F. Hoffman, *Following the Paper Trail: A Multilingual Translation Guide* (New Milford, CT: Language & Lineage Press, 1991; reprinted by Avotaynu, Inc., 1994). Both books include chapters on translating German, Polish, Ukrainian, Russian and Lithuanian vital records and other documents (*e.g.*, passports).

Also see Thode, Ernest, *German-English Genealogical Dictionary* (Baltimore: Genealogical Publishing Co., 1992) and Bents, Edna M., *If I Can, You Can Decipher Germanic Records* (Buffalo Grove: Genealogy Unlimited, Inc., 1996). Common terms listed as causes of death in Polish, German, Latin or Russian are translated in Chorzempa, Rosemary, *Morbus—Why and How Our Ancestors Died: A Genealogist's Dictionary of Terms Found in Vital Records with Descriptions of the Diseases as They Relate to the Health of Our Ancestors* (Chicago: Polish Genealogical Society of America, 1991).

LOCATING AN ANCESTRAL *SHTETL*

Gazetteers

To locate a Polish *shtetl* refer to Mokotoff, Gary, and Sallyann Amdur Sack, *Where Once We Walked: A Guide to the Jewish Communities Destroyed in the Holocaust* (Teaneck, NJ: Avotaynu, Inc., 1991). This comprehensive gazetteer includes a phonetic index. Thus, even though the current spelling of a town may not be known to the researcher, one should be able to find the town listed—for example, according to the name by which it was known to Jews before the war. For each town, the book specifies alternate names, latitude and longitude, distance and direction from a major city in the country, Jewish population before the Holocaust, and whether information about the town may be found in any one of more than 40 sources.

Prior to 1975, Poland was divided into 17 administrative provinces called voivodships (*województwa*). The voivodships were divided, in turn, into counties called powiats (*powiaty*). See *Spis Miejscowości Polskiej Rzeczypospolitej Ludowej* (A List of Place Names in the Polish People's Republic) (Warsaw: Wydawnictwo Komunikacji i Łączności, 1967), a gazetteer of modern-day Poland that lists the current vital records office (Urząd Stanu Cywilnego) for each locality listed. Since the publication of *Spis*, Poland's voivodship boundaries were redrawn; there are now 49 voivodships. *Nazwy Geograficzne Rzeczypospolitej Polskiej* (Geographical Names of the Republic of Poland) (Warszawa/Wrocław: Państwowe Przedsiębiorstwo Wydawnictw Kartograficznych, 1991) is the most current gazetteer of Poland listing town names in their present-day voivodships.

For a gazetteer of Poland between World Wars I and II, refer to Bystrzycki, Tadeusz, ed., *Skorowidz miejscowości Rzeczypos-politej Polskiej* (Index of Localities of the Polish Republic) (Przemyśl: Wydawnictwo Książnicy Naukowej, 1933).

For partitioned Poland before World War I, refer to Sulimierski, F., B. Chlebowski and W. Walewski, eds., *Słownik geograficzny Królestwa Polskiego i innych krajów słowiańskich* (Geographical Dictionary of the Kingdom of Poland and Other Slavic Countries) (Warsaw: Wieki, 1880–1902). This very detailed gazetteer covers not only Russian Poland, but also Prussian and Austrian Poland. Information about synagogues, town histories and the number of Jewish inhabitants is also included.

For Prussian Poland, refer to *Meyer's Orts-und Verkehrs-Lexikon des Deutschen Reichs* (Meyer's Gazetteer and Directory of the

Provincial Distribution of Polish Jewry in Towns and Villages, 1931   **Map 4**

German Empire) (Leipzig: Bibliographisches Institute, 1912). Mentions synagogue in town.

Gemeindlexikon für das Königreich Preussen (Gazetteer for the Kingdom of Prussia) (Berlin: Verlag des Königlichen statistischen Landesamts, 1907–1909). The gazetteer lists the town's Jewish population.

Kredel, Otto, and Franz Thierfelder, *German–Polish Place Name Changes*—Volume 2 of *Deutch–fremdsprachiges Ortnamen-verzeichnis* (German-Foreign Gazetteer) (Berlin: Deutsche Verlags-gesellschaft, 1931). The gazetteer includes place-name changes from German to Polish after World War I.

Kaemmerer, M., *Müllers Verzeichnis der jenseits der Oder-Neisse gelegenen unter fremder Verwaltung stehenden Ortschaftern* (Muller's Gazetteer of Localities Across the Oder-Neisse under Foreign Administration) (Wuppertal: Post-und Ortsbuchverlag, 1958). The gazetteer includes place-name changes from German to Polish after World War II.

For Galicia, refer to *Gemeindelexikon der im Reichsrathe vertretenen Königreiche und Länder* (Gazetteer of the Crown Lands and Territories Represented in the Imperial Council) (Vienna: K.K. Statistisches Zentral Commission, 1903–1908).

Maps

The map divisions of many major public libraries and universities as well as the Library of Congress have extensive map collections on Poland—both present-day and historical. The U.S. Army Map Service issued a very detailed 1:100,000 scale map of Poland in 1944. Town plans of many Polish cities may be obtained by writing to the Library of Congress, Geography and Map Division, Washington, D.C. 20540. Appendices F and G to Kurzweil, Arthur, and Miriam Weiner, eds., *The Encyclopedia of Jewish Genealogy—Vol. 1: Sources in the United States and Canada* (Northvale, NJ: Jason Aronson, Inc., 1991) have a partial listing of Library of Congress town plans. For a detailed description of the Library of Congress's map holdings, see Luft, Edward D., "Map Resources for the Genealogist at the U.S. Library of Congress," in *Avotaynu*, vol. 8, no. 4 (Winter 1991): 43–46.

Aerial photos of many Polish towns taken by German reconnaissance pilots during World War II at scales of 1:15,840 to 1:31,380 may be obtained by writing to the National Archives, Cartographic & Architectural Branch, 8601 Adelphi Road, College Park, MD 20740–6001. Appendix E to *The Encyclopedia of Jewish Genealogy* has a partial listing of the National Archives' aerial photos.

Copies of detailed maps of Poland made by the U.S. Defense Mapping Agency at a scale of 1:250,000 may be ordered from the Department of State, Map Release Officer, Defense Mapping Agency, Washington, D.C. 20315. Ask for map Series M501.

SYNAGOGUE RECORDS AND PINKASSIM

Many Jewish communities in Poland kept internal records that may supply considerable genealogical information. The communities usually created *pinkassim* (register books) or *księgi duchowne* (community books) to record births, marriages, deaths, community tax rolls, synagogue seat ownership, community charitable contributions and other information. Although the majority of these invaluable books were either destroyed in the Holocaust or ritually buried by the community to preserve them from profanation after becoming unusable, many miraculously have survived. The Central Archives for the History of the Jewish People in Jerusalem has one of the largest collections of extant *pinkassim*. For a partial listing of the *pinkassim* available at the Central Archives, see Teller, A., H. Volovici and H. Assouline, eds., *Guide to the Sources for the History of the Jews in Poland in the Central Archives* (Jerusalem: Central Archives for the History of the Jewish People, 1988). The Jewish Theological Seminary Library in New York and the Jewish National Library in Jerusalem also have collections.

YIZKOR BOOKS (MEMORIAL BOOKS)

Yizkor books were published after World War II by groups of *landsmanshaftn* (Jews from the same town or region) societies to commemorate the history and destruction of their towns. These books, hundreds of which have been published, are generally in Hebrew and Yiddish. They contain many photos, maps, memoirs, testimonies, town histories and lists of Jews who perished in the Holocaust. Many are indexed. Often a yizkor book for one town will include information about smaller nearby towns and villages.

A number of lists of such books exist, but since new memorial books are still being published, even the most current listing is already out of date. Consult the "Bibliography of Eastern European Memorial (Yizkor) Books," in Kurzweil, Arthur, *From Generation to Generation* (New York: Harper Collins, 1994), pp. 136–200, for the most recent version of this bibliography. The largest collection of yizkor books can be found in the Yad Vashem Library in Jerusalem. In the United States, the Library of Congress, the New York Public Library, YIVO Institute and the United States Holocaust Memorial Museum have the largest collections of yizkor books.

See also: Kugelmass, Jack, and Jonathan Boyarin, eds., *From a Ruined Garden: The Memorial Books of Polish Jewry* (New York: Schocken, 1983). This is an English-language anthology of articles from more than 60 yizkor books.

Excerpt from *Wolkovisker Yizkor Book* (vol. II) by Moses Einhorn

I do not doubt that others cherish the memories of their own native town as I do the memories of Wolkovisk. I do not compare it with other towns. I know only that there I spent my childhood; and that, thanks to my immediate family, relatives and friends, my childhood there was rich and happy; that the men and women I knew were simple, kind and good; and that through the long generations, the Jews of Wolkovisk created traditions of which not only its own inhabitants were proud, but all Israel. Now [Jewish] Wolkovisk is gone. Let one of her sons give expression to his love for her.

Of Wolkovisk now nothing remains. Like so many other Jewish towns and villages of Poland, it has been erased from the map of the world. Very little more than the old cemetery with its silent tombs is left to bear testimony to what once existed—a *zecher l'churban* (memorial of destruction).

—Einhorn, Moses, ed. *Wolkovisker yisker-bukh* (Wolkovisker Yizkor Book). New York: Wolkovisker Yizkor Book, 1949, p. 990

BUSINESS AND TELEPHONE DIRECTORIES

Prior to World War I, business directories for the areas that once comprised Poland were published in each of the three empires that ruled portions of Poland. In the Russian Empire at the end of the nineteenth century, business directories entitled *Vsia Rossiia* (All of Russia) were published. These directories, which are generally arranged by *guberniya*, town and then by business, include the 19 Polish *guberniyas* of the Russian Empire. For a description of these directories, see Boonin, Harry D., "Russian Business Directories," in *Avotaynu*, vol. 6, no. 4 (Winter 1990): 23–31; and Rhode, James, "Russian Business Directories as Aids in Genealogical Research," in *Avotaynu*, vol. 4, no. 2 (Spring 1988): 3–8. Copies of these directories may be found in the Microform Division of the Library of Congress, the Slavic and Baltic Division of the New York Public Library, and Widener Library at Harvard University.

In the Austro-Hungarian Empire, business directories covering Galicia were published as early as the 1850s. Some of these directories are arranged by town, while others are arranged by business or occupation. Generally, these directories include full names of proprietors and full street addresses. The Slavic and Baltic Division of the New York Public Library and the Library of Congress have copies of some of the following directories: *Handels-und Gewerbe-Adressenbuch der österreichischen Kaiserstaates* (Commercial and Business Directory of the Austrian Imperial State); *Adressenbuch für Handel, Gewerbe und Actien-Gesellschaften der Oesterreichisch-Ungarischen Monarchie* (Directory of Trade, Business and Stock Companies for the Austro-Hungarian Monarchy); *Kaufmännisches Adressbuch für Industrie, Handel und Gewerbe der Osterreichisch-Ungarischen Monarchie* (Commercial Directory for Industry, Trade and Business for the Austro-Hungarian Monarchy); and *Księga Adresowa Przemysłu Galicyjskiego* (Directory of Galician Industry).

The Family History Library has a series of microfilms of business directories of the German Empire, including western parts of Poland from the year 1898 and up to World War II. These directories are entitled *Deutsches Reichs-Adressbuch für Industrie Gewerbe und Handel* (German Empire Directories for Industry, Business and Trade).

Entry from 1936 PKO Bank records in Poland (list of depositors by town and country, worldwide)   2

170 Ędusz WOJEWÓDZTWO KIELECKIE Będzin

Kowale (*forgerons*): Krzewczyk B.
Spożywcze art. (*comestibles*): Balcerowska R. — Baras A. — Ludwik F. — Szopańska H.

BEDZIN.

Miasto pow. z przedmieściami: Gzichów, Koszelew, Ksawera, Małobądz i Warpie, 254 m n. poz. morza, siedziba sądu pok., sąd okr. Sosnowiec, 40 027 mieszk. linja kol. Sosnowiec-Ząbkowice (dworce kol.: Będzin i Będzin-Miasto). Władze i urzędy państwowe i samorządowe: Starostwo, Komenda powiatowa p. p., Komisarjat p. p., Urząd skarbowy podat., Kasa skarbowa, Magistrat, Wydział powiatowy. Kościoły i szkoły: 1 kat., 1 synag. 4 gimnazja, szkoła realna, liceum handlowe, 7 szkół powszechnych. Instytucje: Szpital powszechny, zakład położniczy, ambulatorjum miejskie, ambulatorjum kasy chorych, miejska przychodnia przeciwgruźlicza, 2 przytułki dla sierot, 2 przytułki dla starców. Związki zawodowe i stowarzyszenia: związek zawod. pracownik. handlowych, zw. zawod. pracown. igły, zw. majstrów krawieckich, cechy: ciesielski, murarski, stolarski, szewcki, zw. pracowników miejskich, zw. lekarzy, zw. kupców, zw. drobnych kupców. Targi: w każdą środę. Przemysł: Będzin stanowi jeden z najwybitniejszych osrodków Zagłębia Dąbrowskiego. Górnictwo jest tu reprezentowane przez szereg kopalń węgla kamiennego. Bliskość tych kopalń stwarza niezmiernie dogodne warunki dla rozwoju przemysłu; silnie rozwinięty przemysł metalurgiczny (fabryki: bieli cynk., blachy cynk., śrub, łańcuchów, wyr. metalowych), spożywczy (młynarstwo, browary, fabryki wódek, fabryka czekolady), ceramiczny (fabryka kafli, cegielnie) i chemiczny. Tartaki, kamieniołomy.

Chef-lieu de distr. y compris les faubourgs de Gzichów, Koszelew, Ksawera, Małobądź et Warpie, 254 m. d'altit., siège de la just. de paix, trib. d'arr-t Sosnowiec, 40 027 habit. ligne de Sosnowiec-Ząbkowice (gares de ch. de fer: Będzin et Będzin-Miasto). Autorités et services de l'Et. et autonomes: Starostie, Command-t de la police de distr., Commiss-t de police, Bureau des impôts et contrib., Caisse du trésor, Municipalité, Office de district. Eglises et écoles: 1 cath., 1 synag., 4 gymnases, école réale, lycée commercial, 7 écoles primaires. Institutions: Hôpital général, clinique d'accouchements, ambulance municip., ambulance de la Caisse des malades, dispensaire de tuberculeux, 2 orphelinats, 2 asiles de vieillards. Assoc. profess. et corporations: Assoc. profess. des employés du commerce, assoc. profess. des travaill. à l'aiguille, assoc. des tailleurs, corpor.: des charpentiers, maçons, menuisiers, cordonniers, assoc. des employés municip., assoc. des médecins, assoc. des commerç., assoc. de petits commerç. Marchés: mercredi. Industrie: Będzin est un des centres les plus industriels du Bassin de Dąbrowa. L'industrie minière y est représentée par de nombreuses mines de houille, dont la proximité favorise particulièrement le développement de l'industrie métallurgique (fabriques de blanc de zinc, de tôles de zinc, de boulonnerie, de chaînes et d'articles métalliques), de l'industrie alimentaire (minoteries, brasseries, fabr. d'eaux-de-vie et de chocolat), de l'industrie céramique (fabr. de carreaux, briqueteries) et de l'industrie chimique. Scieries, carrières de pierres.

Starosta (*Starostie*): Józef Boksa.
Prezydent miasta (*Président de la ville*): Artur Michael.
Prezes Rady Miejskiej (*Présid. du Conseil Municip.*): Franciszek Żebrowski.

Lekarze (*médecins*): Barylski Tad. dr. (wener), Małachowskiego 7 — Dunaj Julj. dr. (wewn), Kołłątaja 33 — Ferber Józ. dr., Małachowskiego 16 — Hałacz Józ. dr., (wen), Kołłątaja 29 — Kosibowicz Tad. dr. (chir), pl. 3 Maja 12 — Penski Józ. dr. (wewn), Sienkiewicza — Rechtszaft Ozj. dr. (dziec), Kołłątaja 33 — Walewski L. dr. (wewn), Kołłątaja 27 — Wassercwajg Maks. dr. (wewn), Sączewska 27 — Weinzieher Sal. dr. (wewn), ulica Kołłątaja nr. 31.
Broen A. dr., Kościuszki 22 — Jarzębowski Br. dr. (chir), Potockiego 2 — Teichner M. dr. (gin), Małachowskiego 25.
Lekarze dentyści (*médecins dentistes*): Erlich Blumenfrucht Rach., Sączewska 15 — Felzensztajn L., Kołłątaja 45 — Goldsztaub R. — Lebenbaum E., Kościuszki — Malewa Zofja, Kołłątaja 34 — Sztokhand Daw., Kołłątaja 28 — Weinzieher Ch., Kołłątaja 31.
Lekarze weterynarji (*médecins vétérinaires*): Raczyński Ant., Jasna 10.
Adwokaci (*avocats*): Agapow Jan, Kołłątaja 23 — Ferelle Bened., Sączewska 12 — Paradistal A., Kościuszki 30 — Rodzyn Leon, Małachowskiego 24 — Szeniec J., Małachowskiego 16.
Notarjusze (*notaires*): Szretter T., Modrzejowska 44.
Komornicy (*huissiers*): Koślacz Edmund, Małachowskiego 24.
Agentury (*commiss. en marchandises*): Gertner A., Małachowskiego 3 — Hercygier A., Sączewska 21 — Zaurompf L., Sączewska 2.
Cukierman J., Kościuszki — Feder J., Małachowskiego 14 — Fogelowicz G., Kołłątaja 24 — Kulawik J., Kołłątaja 3 — Numberg H., Kołłątaja 29 — Rottner D., Kołłątaa 39 — Szajn M., Sączewska 15 — Ullert N., Kołłątaja.
Akuszerki (*sages-femmes*): Nowak E. — Bluszcz A. — Bulina M. — Całka K. — Cheba E. — Cudak J. — Derlatko B. — Djament P. — Jagielska S. — Lech M. Lewi F. — Malczewska J. — Meljoch F. — Mühlsztajn M. — Szercz F. — Szerling M.
Apteczne artykuły — hurt (*prod. pharmaceutiques en gros*): Ordon J., oddz, Bocz. J. Cukiermana.
Apteczne składy (*drogueries*): Ejbuszyc J., Rynek 14 — ×Misiorski B. J., Kołłątaja 27 — ×Regirer I., Kołłątaja 13 — ×Wekselman T., Małachowskiego 14.
×Barcik i Ska. Kołłątaja.
Apteki (*pharmacies*): ×Baer S., Kołłątaja 2 — Chojłowicz W., Kołłątaja 19 — ×Gold Dawid, Kołłątaja 44 — ×Machajski A., 3 Maja 1.
Asenizacyjne przedsiębiorstwa (*assainissement*): Kłapcia A., Wiejska 35.
Banki (*banques*): ×Bank Dyskontowy Sp. z o. o., Sączowskiego 19 — ×Bank Handlowy w Warszawie, S. A., oddz., Sączewskiego 23 — Bank Kupiecki, Sp. z o. o., Kołłątaja 33

BANK KUPIECKI
Spółdz. z ogr. odp.
BĘDZIN, tel. 5-49. Dyr. 6-86
Adr. telegr.: „Bankup"
Rachunki: Bank Polski, oddział w Sosnowcu
P. K. O. Katowice 304.849.

×Bank Kredytowy, Sp. z o.o., Sączewska 13 — ×Bank Ludowy, Sp. z o. o., Małachowskiego 6 — ×Bank Spółdzielczy, Sp. z o. o., Sączewska 13.
Bednarze (*tonneliers*): Erbiński R., Zamek 5 — Lejtman I., Mostowa 17.
Betonowe wyroby — fabr. (*fabr. de produits en béton*): Woliński I., Sączewska 9.
Biel cynkowa (*blanc de zinc*): ×Huta Feniks, S. A., Kościuszki 40.
Biel cynkowa — fabryki (*fabr. de blanc de zinc*): ×„Huta Feniks", S. A., Mostowa 16 — ×Inwald B. i J., Kościuszki 42.
Bielizna (*lingerie*) Feldberg Ch., Rynek 18 — Manela F., Rynek 20.
Blacharskie zakłady (*fabr. de ferblanterie*): Liwer Ch., Podzamcze 63 — Sztybel M., Czeladzka 5.
Blacharze (*ferblantiers*): Birman S., Kołłątaja 15 — Brama L., Małachow. 16 — Erlich M., Świętojańska 5 — Golenzer, Modrzejewska 51 — Podoler M., St. Rynek 11.
Bławaty (*tissus*): ×Altman L., St. Rynek 9 — Blacharz, Plebańska 6 — Blajfer A., św. Jańska 8 — ×Blechman F., Rynek 22 — ×Blum B., Małachowskiego 52 — Blum M., Plebańska 13 — Blum S., Zawodzie 4 — Bosek B., Góra Zamkowa — Bratman J., Podz. 12 — Chachulska Kośc. 10 — Cymerman Ch., Modrzejowska 53 — Cymerman L., St. Rynek 27 — Cynamon I., Modrzejowska 55 — Cytron J., Zamkowa 12 — Czarnocha, Czeladzka 7 — Dancygier, Browarna 9 — ×Dancygier J. N., Modrzejowska 11 — Dreksler Ch., Plebańska 2 — Epsztajn N., Rynek 25 — ×Ehrlich H., Rynek 13 — Erlich. I., Modrzejowska 31 — ×Erlichman J. i Landau J., Rynek 11 — ×Ernst M., Rynek 19 — ×Fajgenbaum K., Zamkowa 18 — Fajner N., Zamkowa 27 — Faska H., Plebańska 13 — Faska I., Plebańska 16 — Feder F., Czeladzka 23 — Feldberg I., St. Rynek 9 — Feldman A. i Oksyński I., 3 Maja 10 — Ferszenfeld I., Boczna 6 — Ferszt J., St. Rynek 19 — Ferszt J., Kościelna 2 — Fiszel B., Małachowskiego 52 — Fiszel J., Plebańska 3 — Fiszel S., St. Rynek 25 — Fraind I., Modrzejowska 95 — Frajberg Z., St. Rynek 28 — Frenk D., Modrzejowska 85 — ×Frochtcwajg M., Rynek 4 — Frochtcwajg S., Sączewska 29 — Frydman E., Plac 3 Maja 7 — Fuks D., St. Rynek 4 — ×Fuks M., Zawale 36 — Garfinkiel W., St. Rynek 26 — Gertner I., Kołłątaja 2 — Ginsberg I., Małachowskiego 15 — Glenberg M., St. Rynek 20 — Goldberg K., Modrzejowska 42 — Hajdoch T., Targowa 24 — Joskowicz B., Potockiego 5 — Lewenzon I., Rynek 4 — ×Lewin S., Kołłątaja 20 — Lipner Ch., Kołłątaja 29 — Makowicz, Kośc. 2 — ×Przyrowski, Kołłątaja 22 — Rozen J., Zamkowa 3 — Salamson J., plac 3 Maja — ×Skoczylas E., św. Jańska 4 — Skóra Ch., Kołłątaja 24 — Sztrochlic J., Kołłątaja 22 — Szwajcer J. i Meryn T. Kołłątaja 8 — ×Ungier P., Kołłątaja 3 — ×Wajnsztajn I., Rynek 12 — Zaks M., Zamkowa 19 — Zylberberg Ch., Małachowskiego 6.
Browary (*brasseries*): „Grodziec", Modrzejowska 2 — ×„Korona", wł. Rozenblum S., Małachowskiego 13 — ×Browar T. A., dawn. Sercarz D., Czeladzka 14.
Budowlane przedsięb. (*entrepr. de constructions*): Kozioł St., Piaski 17 — ×Szperling S. i Olszenko P., Sp. z o. o., Kościuszki 30 — ×Weinzieher G., Sączewska 29.
Cegielnie (*briqueteries*) ×Cegielnia Sejmiku Będzińskiego, Okrzei 15 — „Dzwon", wł. Erlich M., Mostowa — Landau E., Koszelów 13 — Siwek F., Furmańska 21 — Waldman J., Szosowa 2.
×„Ceramika", Sp. z o. o., Mostowa — Polsko-Amerykańska Kompanja Węglowa, Mostowa 8.
Chemiczne produkty (*produits chimiques*): Ordon J., Bocznica J. Cukiermana.
Cieśle (*charpentiers*): Olszenko P., Modrzejowska 53.
Cukiernicze wyroby (*confiserie*): ×Gertner M., św. Jańska 4 — „Zgoda", wł. Frydman M. i Rotszajn M., Sączewska 21.
Cukiernie (*confiseurs*): ×Cukierman H., Kołłątaja 18 — Gold J. I., Kołłątaja 44 — ×Gold M., Kołłątaja 42 — Kowalski S., Małachowskiego 21 — Londner L., Małachowskiego 24 — Pilc Ch., Małachowskiego 46 — Rottsztajn M., Małachowskiego 13 — ×Wodzisław i Ska, wł. Wodzisław Hersz Lajb i Merin Chaim Dawid, Modrzejowska 48.
Czerwińska, Sączewska 29.
Cukry (*bonbons*): ×Cukierman Ch., ski M., Małachowskiego 26 — Szajer D., Czeladzka 5 — Szpiro Ch. M., Sączewska 11 — Śliwka J., Modrzejowska 58.
Ajzenberg E., Modrzejowska 70 — Majtlis N., Zamkowa 2 — Pilcer J., Małachowskiego 37 — Skoczylas H., Modrzejowska 64 — Waga N., Zawale 5.
Cynk — huty (*usines à zinc*): Bursztyn J., Mostowa 13 — „Leontyna", wł. Inwald B. i J., Kościuszki 42.
Cynk — walcownie (*laminoirs de zinc*): ×Polskie Zakłady Przemysłu Cynkowego, S. A., Sielecka 63.
Czapki (*casquettes*): Adlerfligiel I. Boczna 5 — Bergman H., Sączewska 19 — Braum S., Kołłątaja 16 — Czereśnia D., Rynek 28 — Fersztenfeld T., Małachowskiego 24 — ×Fiszer S., Czeladzka 2 — Frechtcwajg B., Rynek — Frydman H., Kołłątaja 19 — Gitler B., Kołłątaja 18 — Kisner H., Kołłątaja 17 — Kiśner J., Rynek 16 — Półtorak I., Zawale 38 — Sztajnic, Rynek 5. — Szwimer A., Małachowskiego 10 — Wieliński A., Małachowskiego 8 — Zajdeman J., Małachowskiego 8.
Czasopisma (*publications périod.*): ×Das Judisze Wochenblat, Kołłątaja.
Czekolada — fabryki (*fabr. de chocolat*): „Zgoda", Sączewskiego 7.
Domy handlowe (*maisons de commerce*): Salski Z., Małachowskiego 38 — Tow. Francusko-Włoskie, Koszelew.
Drób (*volailles*): Sztrubel M., Modrzejowska 53.
Druciane wyroby (*objets en fil de fer*): Grünwald A., Kołłątaja 45 — ×Szajn Bcia, Małachowskiego 29.
Drukarnie (*imprimeries*): Blumenfrucht B., Kościelna 2 — Blumenfrucht H., Modrzejowska 19 — ×Blumenfrucht M., Kołłątaja 29 — Drukarnia Pow. Zw. Komunalnego, Sączewska 12 — Golenzer I., Modrzejowska 17 — ×Monsiorski R., plac 3 Maja 4 — ×Szpiegelman L., Kołłątaja 34 — Zajdner M., plac 3 Maja 2.
Drzewo (*bois*): ×Brauner D., Sączewska 19 — Ferens M., Małachowskiego 5 — Gelbhard B., Czeladzka 25 — ×Gold M., 3 Maja 6 — Hampel M. i Glauzer Z., Czeladzka 33 — Kanał M., Gzichów 60 — Lichtensztajn N. i Erlich J., Modrzejowska 86 — Olmer J., Kołłątaja 16 — Pański A., Małachowskiego 26 — Podliński Sz. i Glik Wl. Kościuszki 20.
Cederbaum G. i Zysser L., Gzichowska 2 — Siegreich M., Gzichowska 4 — Wajnsztajn I. M., Małachowskiego..
Drzewo kopalniane (*bois de construction p. mines*): ×Borzykowski L., Kołłątaja 38 — ×Nunberg H., Kołłątaja 29 — ×Potok J. D., Modrzejewska 44.
Gelbard J., Małachowskiego 2.
Dywany (*tapis*): Wonn M. i W.
Dzienników biura (*journaux*): Kokotek I., Małachowskiego 39.
Ekspedycyjne biura (*expéditeurs*): Rozenberg M., Modrzejowska 89 — ×Zelingier F., Małachowskiego 4.
Cukierman J., Kościuszki.
Elektrotechnicy (*électriciens*): Rozenwald W., Małachowskiego 36.
Berkowicz G., Kołłątaja 25 — Retman H., Małachowskiego 6.
Elektrotechniczne artykuły (*appareillage électr.*): Bergier Sz. i Katz D., Kołłątaja 50.
Goldfeld J., Kołłątaja 39 — Retman i Berkowicz, Małachowskiego 1.
Farby (*couleurs*): ×Bryner J., Małachowskiego 14 — ×Fischel I., Rynek 13 — Fiszel W., Czeladzka 5 — Grynszpan M., Kołłątaja 29 — ×Najmark A., Małachowskiego 1 — Silberfreund M., Targowa 9 — Szterner M., Czeladzka 4.
Branicki I., Sielecka 15.
Farby — fabryki (*fabr. de couleurs*). ×„Reden", Sp. z o. o., Sielecka 55.
Farby miner. — fabryki (*fabr. de couleurs minérales*): ×Inwald Bcia i Sercarz A., Kościuszki 32.
Felczerzy (*barbiers-chirurg.*): Hartman A., Kołłątaja 24 — Krzymowski J., Kołłątaja 21 — Lewi G., Modrzejowska 57 — Słomicki I., Modrzejowska 93 — Szer H., Koł-

Entry from 1930 *Księga Adresowa Polska* (Polish Business Directory) for the town of Będzin 3

Kraków Brat—Cham

181 90 **Bratnia Pomoc Studentów Uniwersytetu Jagiellońskiego** (Prezydjum), Jabłonowskich 10/12.

105 57 **Bratnia Pomoc Studentów Uniw. Jagiellońskiego**, I. Dom Akademicki im. K. Wołodkowicza, Jabłonowskich 10/12. (dod.) Zarząd.

163 13 **Bratnia Pomoc Studentów Uniw. Jagiell.**, II. Dom Akademicki im. Prez. Ign. Mościckiego, Al. 3 Maja 5.

168 67 **Bratnia Pomoc Studentów U. J.**, (Hurtownia Tytoniowa), Jabłonowskich 10.

177 55 **Bratnia Pomoc Studentów W. S. H.**, Sienkiewicza 4.

177 55 **Bratnia Pomoc Studentów Wyż. Studjum Handlowego w Krakowie**, Stowarzyszenie zarejestrowane, Sienkiewicza 4.

166 66 **Braun Bronisław**, dr., asystent oddz. wewn., Szpitala św. Łazarza, specjalista chorób wewnętrznych, ul. Bracka 10, I. p.

105 55 **Braun Włodzimierz**, inżynier, Powroźnicza 6 (p. Kamieniołomy).

168 52 **Braw Moses**, krawiec damski, Florjańska 30.

126 09 **Breit Samuel**, towary żelazne, naczynia kuchenne i skł. metali półszlachetn., Sienna 1.

177 87 **Brem Zenon**, dr., adwokat, Basztowa 10.

166 68 **Brenner Artur**, architekt, Grodzka 36.

165 32 **Brenner L.**, zakład uniformowy, Florjańska 36.

143 09 **Brenner Leon**, sprzedaż węgla, Celna 12.

172 08 **Bribram Róża**, Krupnicza 14.

181 08 **Briefer Norbert**, kuśnierstwo, Grodzka 21.

137 63 **„Bristol"**, kawiarnia i restauracja, właśc. Natan Malter, św. Gertrudy 26 (p. Malter).

132 12 **Broder Ignacy**, Wrzesińska 4.

127 15 **Broder Jan**, inż., dr. oraz **Allerhand Zygmunt**, inż., radca kolei, Basztowa 23.

107 94 **Brodinger Ignacy**, dyrektor Tow. Ubezpieczeń, Kremerowska 3.

166 78 **Brodkiewicz Wacław**, dr., adwokat, Wielopole 6.

157 12 **Broni myśliwskiej pracownia**, Józef Splichal Syn, P. K. O. Kraków 410.303, Sławkowska 5.

148 60 **Bronner Dawid**, Długa 6.

182 94 **Bronowski Henryk**, dyr. oddziału krak. „Expressu Ilustrowanego", Syrokomli 17

132 69 **Bross A.**, właśc. firmy Łazarz Bross, Florjańska 44, płaszcze damskie i męskie, okrycia sportowe i skórzane, rękawiczki, mieszkanie telef. 128-41 (p. Bross Łazarz). Sklep Florjańska 44.

170 80 **Bross A.**, właśc. firmy Łazarz Bross, Rynek 12, damskie płaszcze, kostjumy, męskie płaszcze, okrycia sportowe i skórzane, rękawiczki, mieszkanie telef. 128-41 (p. Bross Łazarz). Rynek Gł. 12.

124 89 **Bross Ignacy**, Al. Krasińskiego 20.

134 82 **Bross Ignacy**, zastępstwo hut i fabryk wyrobów żelazn., Potockiego 4.

123 09 **Bross B.**, dr., adwokat i obrońca wojskowy, Grodzka 3.

170 80 **Bross Łazarz**, właśc. firmy „A. Bross", Rynek 12, mieszkanie telef. 128-41 (p. Bross A.), Rynek Gł. 12.

128 41 **Bross Łazarz**, właśc. firmy A. Bross, Rynek 12, tel. 170-80 i Florjańskiej 44, tel. 132-69, mieszkanie A. Potockiego 1.

132 69 **Bross Łazarz**, właśc. firmy „A. Bross", sklep Florjańska 44, mieszkanie telef. 128-41 (p. Bross A.), Florjańska 44.

100 53 **Browar Krakowski i Fabryka Przetworów Słodowych Jana Götza w Krakowie**, Lubicz 17

110 03 **Brown Tebezyński Repr.**, Kraków, Mostowa 12.

112 06 **Brown-Boveri. S. A.**, Polskie Zakłady Elektryczne, Reprezentacja w Krakowie, Akc. Tow. Elektr. przedtem Sokolnicki i Wiśniewski, Dominikańska 3 (p. Sokolnicki i Wiśniewski)

131 69 **Brozdowski Leopold**, dr., właśc. firmy „Kobierzec", Podwale 3 (p. Kobierzec).

121 14 **Brudzewski Karol**, dr., docent Uniw. Jagiel., okulista, Florjańska 40

149 55 **Bruyn J. L. de**, wicekonsul holenderski, Al. Grottgera 12.

165 86 **Brückner Józef**, dr., adwokat, Grodzka 15.

106 69 **Brüll Maurycy**, przemysł drzewny, Bracka 4.

177 87 **Bryliński Jerzy**, dr., adwokat, Basztowa 10.

131 81 **Bryndza Adolf**, dyrektor, Rynek Kleparski 4.

106 58 **„Brzeszcze"**, skład węgla Państw. Kopalni, Pawia 16, Kurniki 9 (p. Skład).

116 28 **Brzezicki Eugenjusz**, dr., docent Uniw., specjalista chorób nerwowych, Batorego 7.

125 08 **Brzeziński Kazimierz**, architekt budowniczy, Filarecka 10.

175 62 **Brzozowski Jan**, inż., Studencka 23.

134 84 **Brzozowski Z.**, Szewska 4 (p. Mydlarski).

142 49 **Buchelster I. i M. S.**, kupcy, Strardom 25.

180 77 **Buchheister Józef Leib**, Gertrudy 29.

176 10 **Buchner A.**, dypl. inż. chem., urządzenia laboratoryjne i chemikalja. Zaprzysiężony rzeczoznawca Sądu Apel. w zakresie aparatów dla fizyki i chemji i chemikalji, Dolnych Młynów 9.

141 83 **Buchweitz Jakób**, agencja handlowa, Nadwiślańska 1

131 57 **Budkiewicz Jan**, Czysta 10.

182 30 **Budowa Nowoczesnych Dróg, S. A.**, Syrokomli 23

106 06 **Budowlane Materjały i Betonowe Wyroby**, Silberbacha Emila, biuro i mieszkanie Wielopole 15 (p. Fabryka).

168 38 **Budryk Witold**, dr., inż., prof. Akademji Górniczej, Gramatyki 10.

155 11 **Budzłaszek Feliks**, maszynowa i ręczna cownia stolarska, Przemysłowa 7.

176 61 **Bufet Automat**, Dydaś Władysław, Florjańska 55.

170 58 **Bufet Śniadankowy i Sprzedaż Trunków**, Płoszaj Kaz., Prądnicka 2 (p. Płoszaj).

123 96 **Bujak Władysław**, dr., lekarz chorób dziecięcych, Długa 58.

140 60 **Bujański Eugenjusz**, dyrektor biura koncertowego, Dunajewskiego 2.

100 19 **Bujański W. Nast.**, biuro spedycyjne, Rynek Gł. 47.

100 19 **Bujański Władysław**, centralne biuro spedycyjne, Rynek Gł. 47 (A-B).

103 01 **Bujwid Odon**, dr., emer. prof. Uniw. Jag., zakłady dla wyrobu surowic i szczepionek, Lubicz 34.

106 98 **Bukowska Janina**, „Centra", Gołębia 5.

109 28 **Bukowska Janina**, Kielecka 22.

165 06 **Bukowski Marcin**, inż. - architekt, pl. Kossaka 2.

113 00 **Bulwa Dawid**, dr., adwokat, Grodzka 49.

134 59 **Bunsch Karol**, dr., adwokat, Retoryka 15.

139 46 **Burda Kazimierz**, współwł. f-my A. Łazar i Ska, Florjańska 37.

160 94 **Bursa Rękodzielnicza Sierot Żydów.**, Podbrzezie 6.

125 98 **Bursa Związku Młodzieży Przem. i Ręk.**, Skarbowa 2.

112 49 **Burtan Stanisław**, biuro, Basztowa 17.

134 71 **Burtan Stanisław**, mieszkanie prywatne Florjańska 18.

120 66 **Burtan Stanisław**, mieszk. prywatne Przegorzały.

126 33 **Burzyński Jan**, architekt, Krowoderska 69.

114 80 **Buszczyński Tadeusz**, mieszk. pryw. — (dod.) K. Buszczyński i S-wie, Hodowla nasion, inspekcja plantacji. Górka Narodowa.

145 69 **„Butonja"**, fabryka guzików perłowych i wyrobów galanteryjnych, Kącik 18.

138 49 **Buttner Izydor**, skład papieru, Krakowska 2.

178 50 **Büttner Andrzej**, inż., inżynier agrarny. Biegły sądowy w sprawach likwidacji szkód ogniowych, gradowych i kradzieżowych, Śląska 6.

163 67 **Bychunek S.**, wędliniarnia, Długa 29.

175 64 **Byłca Wacław**, fabryka gipsu „Łogo" i fabryka wyrobów betonowych, Łagiewniki p. Borek Fałęcki.

148 87 **Bystrzanowski Jan**, naczelnik wydz. drogow. P. K. P., mieszk. Lubicz 14.

181 62 **Bzowski Konstanty**, mieszk. Konfederacka 3.

C, Ć

140 90 **Caputa Michał**, inż., Szewska 22.

109 49 **„Caraco"**, Ska, fabryka chemiczna, Barska 87-89

115 25 **„Caro"**, Krakowska Kasa Targowa, Sp. z ogr. odp., Rzeźnicza 33.

109 34 **„Cartonlux"**, Leon Kluger, wyrób pudełek tekturowych, Tarnowskiego 4.

139 53 **Cebulski Józef**, wydawnictwo książek do nabożeństwa i skład dewocjonalij, Szewska 22.

163 61 **Cech Rzeźników i Masarzy gr. II**, B. Joselewicza 14.

128 55 **Cegielnia Emilewiczów**, Krasickiego 17.

116 25 **Cegielnia i Fabryka Dachówek w Jasieniu**, biuro szpitalna 38.

101 62 **Cegielnia Miejska**, Płaszów, Gromadzka 52

109 16 **Cegielnia Parowa Jakóba Grünberga**, spadkobiercy, dzierżawca Karol Ferber, Wodna 24.

104 10 **Cegielnia Parowa**, fabryka dachówek „Płaszowianka", tel. 142-45, biuro w Krakowie, Potockiego z (p. Fabryka)

103 00 **Cegielnia Parowa w Dąbiu**, M. Guttman, biuro, Zielona 18 (p. Guttman).

114 75 **Cegielnia Parowa**, właśc. S. Finkelstein, Kraków, ks. Józefa 32 (p. Finkelstein)

165 45 **Cegielnia, M. Wenzel**, Prądnik Czerwony (p. Wenzel).

111 18 **Cegielnia w Woli Duchackiej**.

121 05 **Cegielnia w Zielonkach**.

137 28 **Cegielski Wincenty i Ska**, zakład instalacyjny, Grodzka 31.

130 77 **Cellernowa Matylda**, Garbarska 6.

123 18 **Ceine Biuro Izby Handlowej i Przemysłowej**, Długa 1 (p. Izba Handlowa).

140 84 **Celnik Izrael**, kupiec, Warneńczyka 13

100 77 **Cementownia, Krakowska Fabryka Portland-Cementa, S. A.**, Kraków-Bonarka, (dawn. Dyrekcja Bernard Liban i Ska).

145 40 **Censor Ł.**, wyrób i sprzedaż przyborów wojskowych i urzędniczych, Szewska 18 (p. Wojskowe).

106 98 **„Centra"**, Bukowska Janina, Gołębia 5.

125 98 **Centrala Abstynencka Kół młodzieży**, Skarbowa 2

107 66 **Centrala Win Zagranicznych, Ska z o. o.**, św. Gertrudy 14, dyr. P. Rubinstein.

109 60 **Centralna Bibljoteka Nauczycielska O. S. K. w Krakowie**, Groble 9.

176 23 **Centralna Kasa Pożyczkowa i Oszczędnościowa, Spółdz. z o. o.**, Jagiellońska 5.

115 22 **Centralna Kasa Spółek Rolniczych**, oddział w Krakowie, biuro dyrektora pl. Szczepański 6

143 89 — biuro zastępcy i buchalterja.

109 23 — likwidatura i kasa

106 39 **Centralny Zarząd Wytwórni Wozów Taborowych**, Wielicka 2 (p. Wytwórnia).

144 41 **Centralny Związek Górników w Polsce**, Al. Z Krasińskiego 16.

138 27 **Centralny Związek Robotników Budowlanych w Polsce**, Zarząd główny, Dunajewskiego 5.

131 33 **Cenzorowska — Nieciowa Wiktorja**, sklep kolonjalno-spożywczy, Rakowicka 8.

157 24 **Cenzorowski Władysław**, zast. f-my Henryka Francka Syn. S. A., Pomorska 1.

114 72 **Ceramiczne Zakłady Miejskie**, centrala. Basztowa 14

173 73 **Ceruta**, św. Jana 18 (p. Eksploatacja fabryk ceraty).

103 37 **Cetnarowski Edward**, dr., położnik i lekarz chorób kobiecych, A. Potockiego 3.

142 38 **Chameides Marek**, dr., biuro adwokackie, Karmelicka 8.

162 12 **Chameides Marek**, dr., mieszkanie Siemiradzkiego 25.

For Poland between World Wars I and II, consult the various editions of *Księga Adresowa Polski* (Address Book of Poland). These business directories, which are in both Polish and French, have listings for even the smallest villages in Poland. They are available at the Slavic and Baltic Division of the New York Public Library.

For a detailed discussion of these directories, see Cymbler, Jeffrey K., "Nineteenth and Twentieth-Century Polish Directories as Resources for Genealogical Information," in *Avotaynu*, vol. 13, no. 1 (Spring 1997): 25–31.

CEMETERIES AND SYNAGOGUES

The existence and current status of Polish-Jewish cemeteries may be determined by contacting the Jewish Heritage Council of the World Monuments Fund. This organization has contracted with the U.S. Commission for the Preservation of America's Heritage Abroad to catalog, document and publish Jewish cemetery and synagogue information for several Eastern European countries, including Poland (Gruber, Samuel, and Phyllis Myers, eds., *Survey of Historic Jewish Monuments in Poland* [New York: Jewish Heritage Council, World Monuments Fund, 1996, 2nd ed.]). Also see the *Selected Reading* lists in Chapter 2 and Appendix 1 (*Selected Bibliography*) for an exhaustive listing of books and articles published on Polish-Jewish cemeteries and synagogues.

YIDDISH AND POLISH-LANGUAGE NEWSPAPERS

Prior to World War II, hundreds of Yiddish- and Polish-language Jewish newspapers flourished in Poland. They often included marriage and death notices as well as articles of interest to family historians. To determine whether your town had a Jewish newspaper, see Szeintuch, Yechiel, ed., *Preliminary Inventory of Yiddish Dailies and Periodicals Published in Poland Between the Two World Wars* (Jerusalem: Center for Research on the History and Culture of Polish Jews at Hebrew University, 1986) and Glikson, Paul, ed., *Preliminary Inventory of the Jewish Daily and Periodical Press Published in the Polish Language, 1823–1982* (Jerusalem: Hebrew University Institute of Jewish Studies, 1983).

For a detailed description of the Jewish press in Poland, see Flinkier, David, M. Canin, and S. Rozenfeld, eds., *Itonut Hayehudit Shehayta* (The Jewish Press That Once Was) (Tel Aviv: World Federation of Jewish Journalists, 1973), pp. 10–38; and Fuks, Marian, *Prasa żydowska w Warszawie 1823–1939* (The Jewish Press in Warsaw, 1823–1939) (Warsaw: Państwowe Wydawnictwo Naukowe, 1979).

Territories of Poland, 1921   **Map 5**

The Library of Congress, YIVO Institute, Jewish Theological Seminary Library, the New York Public Library–Jewish Division, the Jewish National Library in Jerusalem and the Jewish Historical Institute in Warsaw have large collections of these newspapers.

THE INTERNET

Until recently, genealogists were limited in their research by having to spend countless hours in libraries and dusty archives—many of which were hundreds, if not thousands, of miles away from home, had limited hours, and contained books and documents in foreign languages. With the advent of the Internet, there is now a wealth of information available that can be accessed from the comfort of one's home by computer through the World Wide Web, mailing lists, USENET newsgroups, Telnet, E-mail and a rapidly-expanding list of resources.

For example, rather than researching one of the many gazetteers listed above, anyone with Internet access can utilize the JewishGen ShtetlSeeker and locate a Polish town's latitude and longitude and a list of towns within a certain distance of such a town.

JewishGen is the official home of Jewish genealogy in cyberspace, which hosts a mailing list and web site. In addition to the ShtetlSeeker, JewishGen currently hosts the Jewish Records Indexing-Poland Project (JRI-PL) Special Interest Group, whose goal is to create a transliterated index in English of the Jewish vital records for all towns in Poland for which there are LDS microfilms.

Additional projects of JewishGen include the ShtetLinks project, which allows people with an interest in a particular *shtetl* to share information; and the JewishGen Family Finder (JGFF), which is a computer-indexed compilation of surnames and towns currently being researched by more than 8,000 genealogists worldwide and contains entries for almost every town in Poland where Jews once lived.

The advent of the Internet has provided a major tool whereby genealogists can tap into a wealth of resources and databases to share information around the globe. Ten years ago, it would have been difficult to fathom that there could be a communications explosion that would provide such access to the vast information and resources. Although cyberspace may never include the actual birth or death records of our ancestors or other genealogical documents listed in this book, who can predict what the future of the Internet holds in store for us?

Editor's Note: Portions of this chapter originally appeared in *Avotaynu*, vol. 9, no. 2 (Summer 1993): 4–12.

Jeffrey K. Cymbler, a professional genealogist and a practicing attorney in New York City, traces his roots in Poland back eight generations. Formerly a vice-president of the Board of the Jewish Genealogical Society of New York, he currently serves on its board.

USEFUL ADDRESSES

THE CENTRAL ARCHIVES FOR THE HISTORY OF THE JEWISH PEOPLE, P.O. Box 1149, Jerusalem 91010, Israel

DEPARTMENT OF STATE, Map Release Officer, Defense Mapping Agency, Washington, D.C. 20315

FAMILY HISTORY LIBRARY, 35 North West Temple Street, Salt Lake City, UT 84150 <http://www.lds.org>

JEWISH HERITAGE COUNCIL, World Monuments Fund, 949 Park Avenue, New York, NY 10028

JEWISH NATIONAL AND UNIVERSITY LIBRARY, Hebrew University, Givat Ram Campus, P.O. Box 503, Jerusalem 91004, Israel

JEWISH THEOLOGICAL SEMINARY, 3080 Broadway, New York, NY 10027

LIBRARY OF CONGRESS, Jefferson Building, Second Street SE, Washington, D.C. 20540 <http://lcweb.loc.gov/homepage>

UNITED STATES NATIONAL ARCHIVES, Cartographic & Architectural Branch, 8601 Adelphi Road, College Park, MD 20740-6001 <http://www.nara.gov>

NEW YORK PUBLIC LIBRARY, 42nd Street & Fifth Avenue, New York, NY 10018 <http://catnyp.nypl.org>

U.S. COMMISSION FOR PRESERVATION OF AMERICA'S HERITAGE ABROAD, 1101 15th Street NW #1040, Washington, D.C. 20005

UNITED STATES HOLOCAUST MEMORIAL MUSEUM, 100 Raoul Wallenberg Place SW, Washington, D.C. 20024 <http://www.ushmm.org>

YAD VASHEM, P.O. Box 3477, Jerusalem 91034 Israel <http://www.yad-vashem.org.il>

YIVO INSTITUTE FOR JEWISH RESEARCH, 555 West 57th St., 11th Floor, New York, NY 10019 <http://www.baruch.cuny.edu/yivo>

JewishGen Internet URLs

JewishGen <http://www.jewishgen.org>

JRI-PL <http://www.jewishgen.org/jri-pl>

ShtetLinks <http://www.jewishgen.org/ShtetLinks>

ShtetlSeeker <http://www.jewishgen.org/ShtetlSeeker>

JGFF <http://www.jewishgen.org/jgff>

JEWISH GENEALOGICAL SOCIETIES AND SPECIAL INTEREST GROUPS

There are more than 70 Jewish genealogical societies (JGSs) worldwide, with the number increasing at a rapid rate. For a complete and current list, contact:

ASSOCIATION OF JEWISH GENEALOGICAL SOCIETIES, 7604 Edenwood Court, Bethesda, MD 20817
<http://www.jewishgen.org/ajgs>

In addition to the JGSs, the following Special Interest Groups (SIGs) are composed of genealogists interested in a specific geographic region of Poland and those localities formerly within the Polish boundaries:

Galicia—c/o Shelly Kellerman Pollero, 549 Cypress Lane, Severna Park, MD 21146 <rpollero@umd5.umd.edu>
Kielce-Radom Gubernias—c/o Gene Starn, P.O. Box 520683, Longwood, FL 32752
   <http://www.jewishgen.org/krsig>
Suwałki & Łomża Gubernias—c/o Marlene Silverman, 3701 Connecticut Avenue NW, Apt. 228, Washington, D.C. 20008 <http://www.jewishgen.org/SuwalkLomza>

POLISH AND EASTERN EUROPEAN GENEALOGICAL SOCIETIES IN THE UNITED STATES

Networking with other Polish genealogists, even if not Jewish, may be helpful. You may find someone else researching the history of your town and other related documentation.

EAST EUROPEAN GENEALOGICAL SOCIETY, INC., P.O. Box 2536, Winnipeg, Manitoba, Canada R3C 4A7
FEDERATION OF EASTERN EUROPEAN GENEALOGICAL SOCIETIES, P.O. Box 510898, Salt Lake City, UT 84151-0898 <http://feefhs.org>

There are numerous active Polish genealogical societies throughout the United States, including the following:

POLISH GENEALOGICAL SOCIETY OF AMERICA, 984 North Milwaukee Avenue, Chicago, IL 60622
   <http://members.aol.com/pgsamerica>
POLISH GENEALOGICAL SOCIETY OF CALIFORNIA, P.O. Box 713, Midway City, CA 92655-0713
   <http://feefhs.org/pol/frgpgsca.html>
POLISH GENEALOGICAL SOCIETY OF CONNECTICUT AND THE NORTHEAST, 8 Lyle Road, New Britain, CT 06053-2104
   <http://feefhs.org/pol/frgpgsct.html>
POLISH GENEALOGICAL SOCIETY OF GREATER CLEVELAND, 906 College Avenue, Cleveland, OH 44113
   <http://feefhs.org/pol/frgpgsgc.html>
POLISH GENEALOGICAL SOCIETY OF MASSACHUSETTS, P.O. Box 381, Northampton, MA 01060-0381
   <http://feefhs.org/pol/frgpgsma.html>
POLISH GENEALOGICAL SOCIETY OF MICHIGAN, Detroit Public Library, 5201 Woodward Avenue, Detroit, MI 48202-4067
   <http://feefhs.org/pol/frgpgsmi.html>
POLISH GENEALOGICAL SOCIETY OF MINNESOTA, Branch of Minnesota Genealogical Society, P.O. Box 16069,
   St. Paul, MN 55116-0069 <http://feefhs.org/pol/frgpgsmn.html>
POLISH GENEALOGICAL SOCIETY OF TEXAS, 15917 Juneau Lane, Houston, TX 77040-2155
POLISH GENEALOGICAL SOCIETY OF WESTERN NEW YORK, 299 Barnard Street, Buffalo, NY 14206-3212
   <http://feefhs.org/pol/frgpgswn.html>
POLISH GENEALOGICAL SOCIETY OF WISCONSIN, P.O. Box 342341, Milwaukee, WI 53234-2341
   <http://feefhs.org/pol/frgpgswi.html>

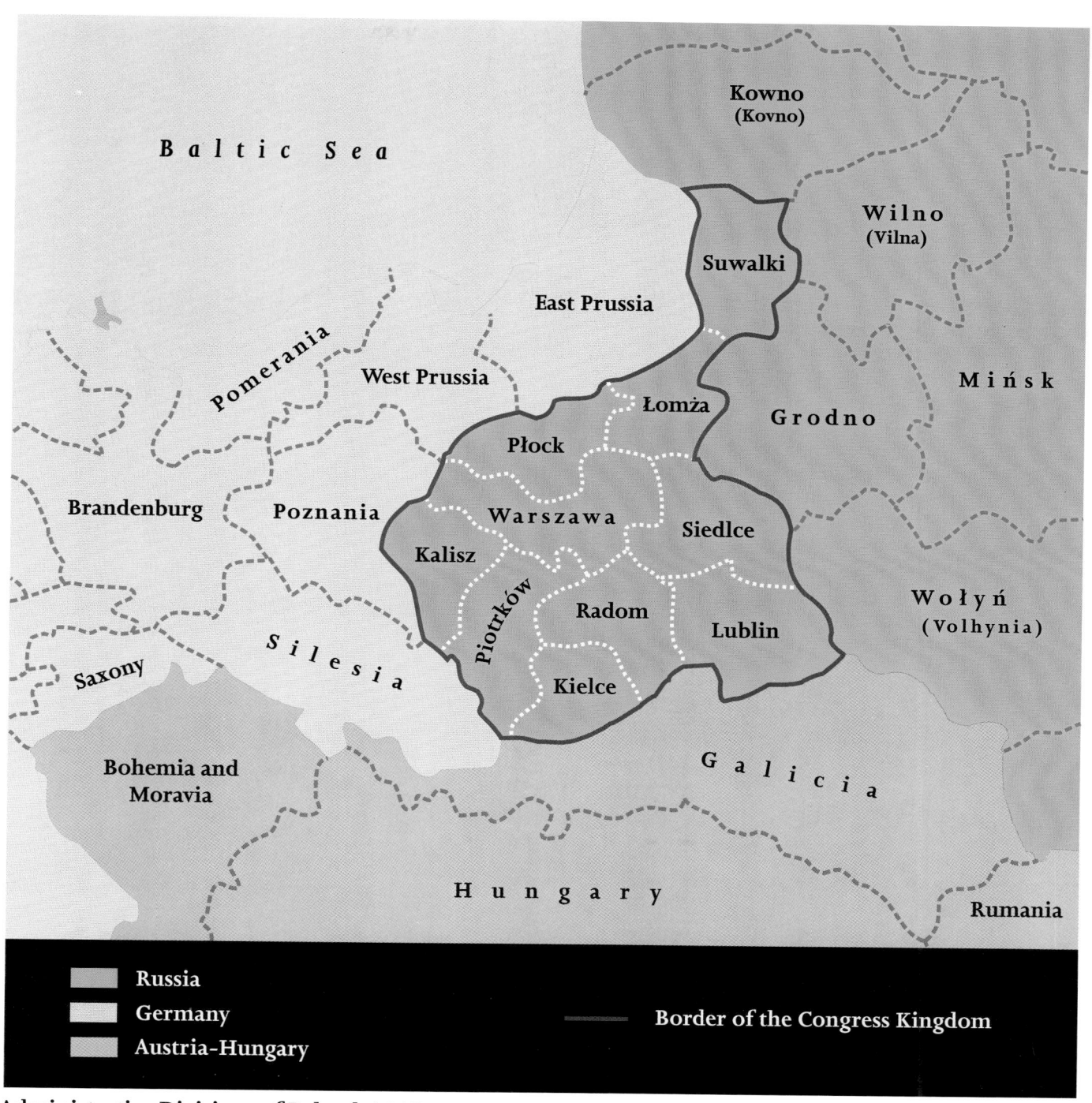

Administrative Divisions of Poland, 1917

Map 6

JAGIELLONIAN UNIVERSITY
The Research Center on Jewish History and Culture

by Joachim S. Russek
Assistant Director

THE RESEARCH CENTER ON
JEWISH HISTORY AND CULTURE
ul. Batory 12
31-135 Kraków

Tel: 48/12/337-058
Fax: 48/22/344-593

The Research Center on Jewish History and Culture was established on October 1, 1986, as an interfaculty and interdisciplinary unit of Jagiellonian University. For a number of years, there was both a growing awareness of the need to conduct research in this field and a growing interest in studying the Jewish past in Poland. Professor Józef Gierowski, a historian and rector (president, in U.S. terms) of the university, was one of the Center's strongest supporters. Eventually, he became its first director.

The Center is housed in a restored historic building in Kraków at 12 Batory Street. The Center has three basic goals: to conduct research on the history and culture of Jews in Poland and coordinate similar research at other Polish universities, with the participation of 70 researchers; on-going training of the academic staff; and to offer courses and disseminate knowledge on Jewish history and culture in Poland and on Polish-Jewish relations.

The development of the Center depends primarily on its contacts with foreign scholarly institutions and the ability to have access to relevant literature published abroad as well as technical assistance. The Center library currently has a collection of more than 1,000 books, many of which were donated by friends from abroad.

The Center has published inventories of Judaica and bibliographies of books and articles published in Poland during the years 1900–1939 and 1945–1985 as well as of the main collections of legal documents in Kraków.

The recently opened Center for Jewish Culture at Kazimierz, in the Jewish quarter of Kraków, culminates a lengthy project to provide a central gathering place for the increasing number of Jewish visitors to Kraków as well as the few remaining elderly Jews.

The Center offers a Yiddish-language course and a seminar entitled "Introduction to Jewish History and Culture in Poland." Once a month, the Center offers a lecture on Jewish topics which is open to the public. In addition, the Center organizes and participates in many international events.

The Center cooperates with numerous foreign institutions, including the Hebrew University in Jerusalem; the Institute on Polish-Jewish Relations at Oxford University; Oxford Center for Hebrew Studies; the University of Connecticut at Storrs; the Project Judaica Foundation in Washington, D.C.; and the United States Holocaust Memorial Museum in Washington, D.C.

Several Center projects are ongoing, including the following:

Bibliographical Projects
- A guide to bibliographies, inventories and catalogues of Polish Judaica
- Bibliography of Polish-language Judaica published between 1944 and 1989
- Bibliography of all Judaica published in Poland between 1901 and 1939
- Current bibliography of Judaica published in Poland
- Catalogue of Judaica in the Jagiellonian Library
- Bibliography of Polish Judaica from the sixteenth to the nineteenth centuries
- Bibliography of the contents of the Polish-language press published in Poland

Archival Inventories
- Inventory of Judaica in the Grodzki and Ziemski court registers, which are the main collections of legal documents in Kraków
- Inventory of Jewish archival materials at the State Archives in Rzeszów
- Archival survey related to the Holocaust period for the United States Holocaust Memorial Museum

Sociological Projects
- A sociological guide to Jewish landmarks in Galicia
- Attitude of Poles toward the Holocaust, based on research conducted in the town of Oświęcim (called "Auschwitz" by the Germans) and vicinity
- The State Museum of Auschwitz-Birkenau—its origin, present and future
- Psychiatric and psychosocial consequences of the persecutions experienced by Jews during World War II
- Stereotypes of Jews among Polish children and teenagers
- Oral history:
  a. Life stories of Polish Jews
  b. Life stories of those who saved Jews during the Holocaust and those awarded Righteous Among the Nations medal by Yad Vashem

Joachim S. Russek is president of the Center for Jewish Culture in Kraków and assistant director of The Research Center on Jewish History and Culture.

JUDAICA FOUNDATION OF POLAND

by Mark E. Talisman
Vice-Chairman

JUDAICA FOUNDATION OF POLAND
ul. Meiselsa 17
31-058 Kraków

Tel: 48/12/565-599
Fax: 48/12/255-034

The B'nai Emunah Prayer House on Meisels Street, in the famed Jewish quarter of Kraków known as Kazimierz, was in ruins when we first saw it in 1986. UNESCO had already designated this Jewish quarter as a world treasure in need of restoration and preservation, encouraging us to consider restoring this once active Jewish site to provide a critical cornerstone for the reconstruction of the entire area.

Preserving the memory of the once huge Jewish community in Poland, which flourished for nearly a thousand years, became an important priority in the restoration of this prayer house. Professor Józef Gierowski, then the distinguished rector (president) of Jagiellonian University, the oldest university in Poland, took the lead in this undertaking in 1986. He had been elected rector under the Communists, but he never lost his voice of truth, notwithstanding the personal risks he faced.

From the early planning stages in 1986, Professor Gierowski's very able executive assistant, Joachim Russek, shared his passion for learning and teaching the truth about the complicated history of the Jews in Poland and the interaction of the Jewish community with the larger Polish community.

In the ensuing years, the original Research Center on Jewish History and Culture at Jagiellonian University (see adjoining article, p. 22) has produced volumes of research on Jewish history in Poland, gathered extensive archival material, preserved priceless historical papers for future academic study and publication, and recently produced a valuable first volume on Jewish history. Leather-bound copies were formally presented to the U.S. Department of State, the United States Holocaust Memorial Museum, the U. S. Congress Law Library, the Library of Congress and the White House.

The Center has hosted a unique six-week, college-level educational program since 1990. This extensive and highly regarded college summer institute, in cooperation currently with Brandeis University, assists students in studying the rich Jewish history of Poland, as well as the Holocaust, with the finest faculty that can be assembled. Field visits to historical sites greatly enhance the experience of learning.

The Center offers public programs, readings, lectures, concerts and exhibitions. A recent annual listing of activities organized by Mr. Russek at the Center included the premiere of Gilbert Levine's music composed in the idiom of *klezmer*, which filled the byways of Kraków for centuries, and lectures by distinguished authors, historians, survivors, journalists and others from the faculty of Jagiellonian and other universities.

Numerous seminars on Jewish history have been presented at the Center in cooperation with other organizations from Europe, the United States and Israel. Newsmaking presentations by Jewish communal leaders from all parts of the world are frequently conducted at the Center. A major series of programs took place at the Center for the commemoration of the fiftieth anniversary of the liberation of Auschwitz-Birkenau.

There are important plans yet to be implemented in order to complete the effective utilization of this prime site. Two adjoining parcels of land expected to be developed as an integral part of the Center complex include an office facility for Jewish non-profit organizations working in Kraków and the construction and operation of a fully kosher hotel and restaurant (there are currently no other such facilities in Kraków) to serve the thousands of monthly visitors.

The Center has benefited extensively from foundation grants and from the Joint Commission for Humanitarian Assistance to Poland, which received its income from the sale of agricultural commodities to the Polish government. The Joint Commission is operated by the U.S. and Polish governments.

The interior of the Center for Jewish Culture in Kraków (renovated former B'nai Emunah synagogue)   5

Mark E. Talisman is president of the Project Judaica Foundation of Washington, D.C.; vice-chairman, Judaica Foundation, Kraków, Poland; and founding vice-chairman, United States Holocaust Memorial Council and Museum.

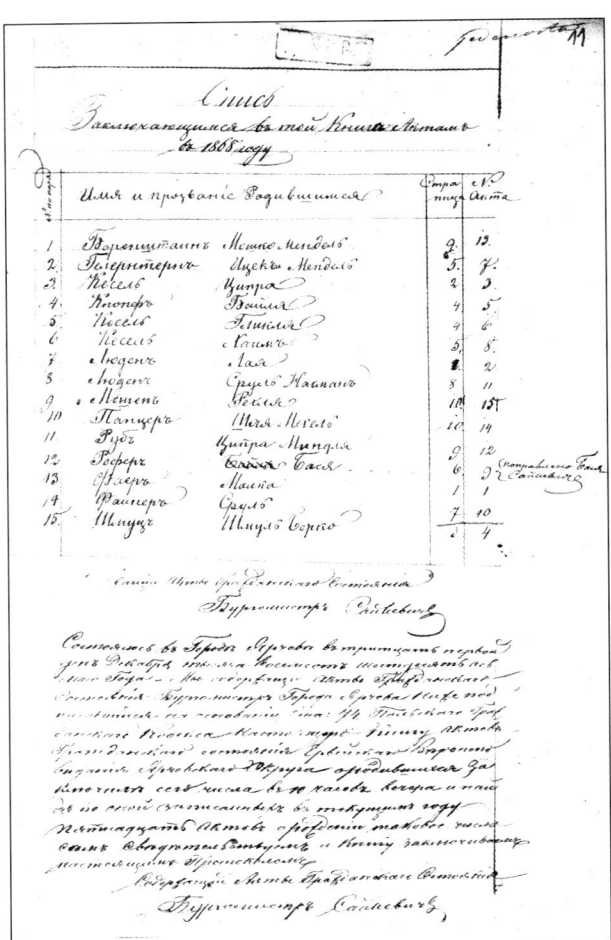

Index to Jewish birth records, Jarczów, 1868   6

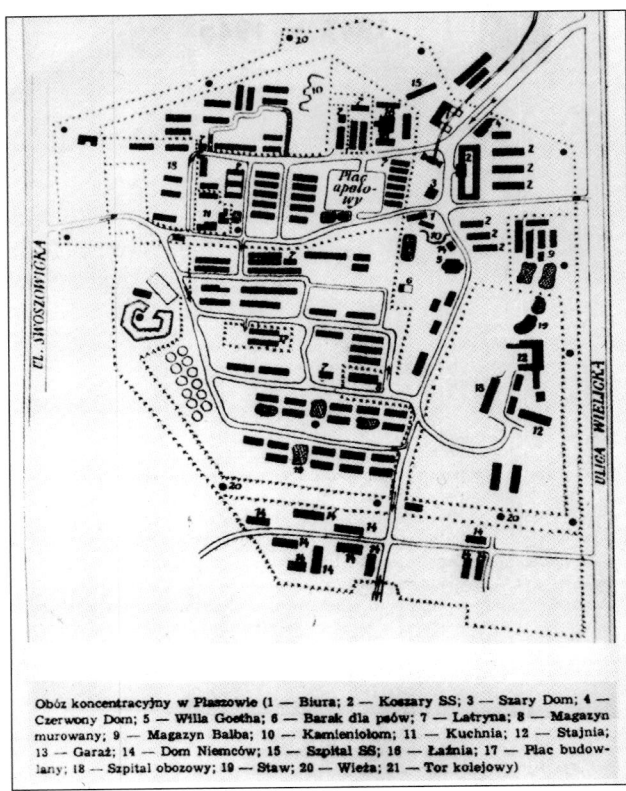

Obóz koncentracyjny w Płaszowie (1 — Biura; 2 — Koszary SS; 3 — Szary Dom; 4 — Czerwony Dom; 5 — Willa Goetha; 6 — Barak dla psów; 7 — Latryna; 8 — Magazyn murowany; 9 — Magazyn Balba; 10 — Kamieniołom; 11 — Kuchnia; 12 — Stajnia; 13 — Garaż; 14 — Dom Niemców; 15 — Szpital SS; 16 — Łaźnia; 17 — Plac budowlany; 18 — Szpital obozowy; 19 — Staw; 20 — Wieża; 21 — Tor kolejowy)

Plan of concentration camp in Płaszów, 1943–1945   8

Spis
zmarłych od dnia 20.4.1942 do dnia 1.10.1942 .

L.P.	Nazwisko i imię	Data zgonu	Nr. aktu	Uwagi
1.	Blufarb Menasza	20.4.1942	1461	z ul. Grodzkiej 23
2.	Gladsztein Sura	20.4. "	1147	
3.	Wajsman Jakub	20.4. "	1063	z ul. Lipowej 7
4.	Topas Moszek	20.4. "	1066	z ul. Zamkowej 9
5.	Przysucna Gitla	20.4. "	1261	Majdan-Tatarski
6.	Korn Judka	20.4. "	1062	z ul. Zamkowej 9
7.	Kataryniarz Hersz	20.4. "	1328	
8.	Sztejnberg Szyja	20.4. "	1338	z ul. Grodzkiej 20
9.	Goldman Josef	21.4. "	1068	z ul. Lipowej 7
10.	Erlich Majer	21.4. "	1067	z ul. Zamkowej 9
11.	Rozensztejn Mendel	21.4. "	1423	
12.	Grin Sura Szajndla	22.4. "	1390	
13.	Dorfgier Maszza Liba	22.4. "	1185	
14.	Herzberg Fajga	22.4. "	1186	z ul. Furmańskiej 2
15.	Hernhut Moszek	22.4. "	1187	
16.	Herzman Lewi Icek	22.4. "	1188	
17.	Tuchman Abuś David	22.4. "	1361	
18.	Edelsberg Fajga	22.4. "	1175	
19.	Pajczer Rubin	22.4. "	1515	
20.	Kaczkes	22.4. "	1085	z ul. Szerokiej 41
21.	Sieradzki Jakub	23.4. "	1069	z ul. Zamkowej 9
22.	Rubinzon Chana Gitla	24.4. "	1248	
23.	Blas Golda Cyrla	24.4. "	1517	
24.	Goldsobel Majer	25.4. "	1493	z ul. Zamkowej 9
25.	Kornsztejn Chaim	25.4. "	1070	z " " 9
26.	Rozen Szmul	26.4. "	1072	" " " 9
27.	Jachimowicz Moszek	27.4. "	1056	
28.	Ullman Ber	29.4. "	1520	z ul. Lipowej 7
29.	Holzneker Majer	29.4. "	1519	
30.	Szlakman Chana Elka	30.4. "	1522	
31.	Waserman Haszel	30.4. "	1521	z ul. Zamkowej 9
32.	Kerszenblut Jakub	1.5. "	1524	
33.	Rubinsztejn Chaja N.	2.5. "	1523	
34.	Ferdman Moszek	2.5. "	1525	
35.	Laciart Eliasz	2.5. "	1564	z ul. Zamkowej 9
36.	Zajdhaft Josef Hersz	2.5. "	1563	" " " 9
37.	Sroka Lejb	3.5. "	1555	" " " "
38.	Fruchtel Aba	3.5. "	1566	
39.	Rutman Chaja Ruchla	3.8. "	1526	z ul. Zamkowej 9
40.	Purzycki Mortek	4.5. "	1568	
41.	Bersztel Wolf	4.5. "	1527	z " " 9

A partial list of Jews in the Lublin ghetto who died between April 20 and October 1, 1942   7

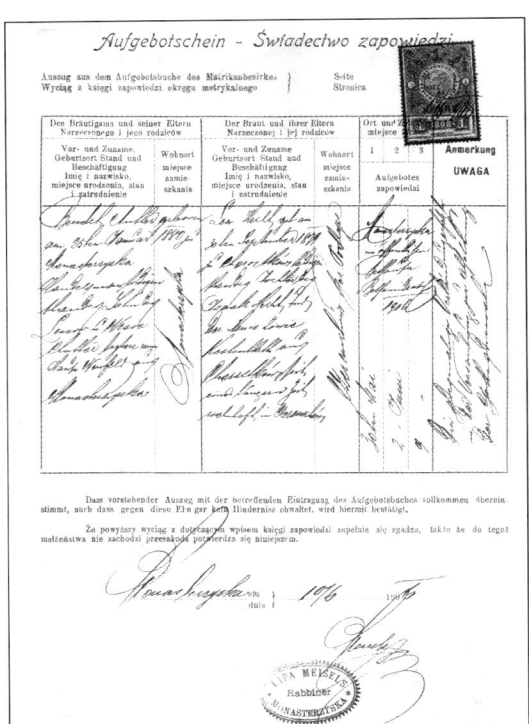

Marriage announcement (1906) of Bendet Antler, born   9
1880, son of Leiser and Nesie Antler from Monasterzyska,
to Lea Hecht, born 1879, daughter of Isaak Hecht and
Henia Ziwie Kestenblatt from Czortków

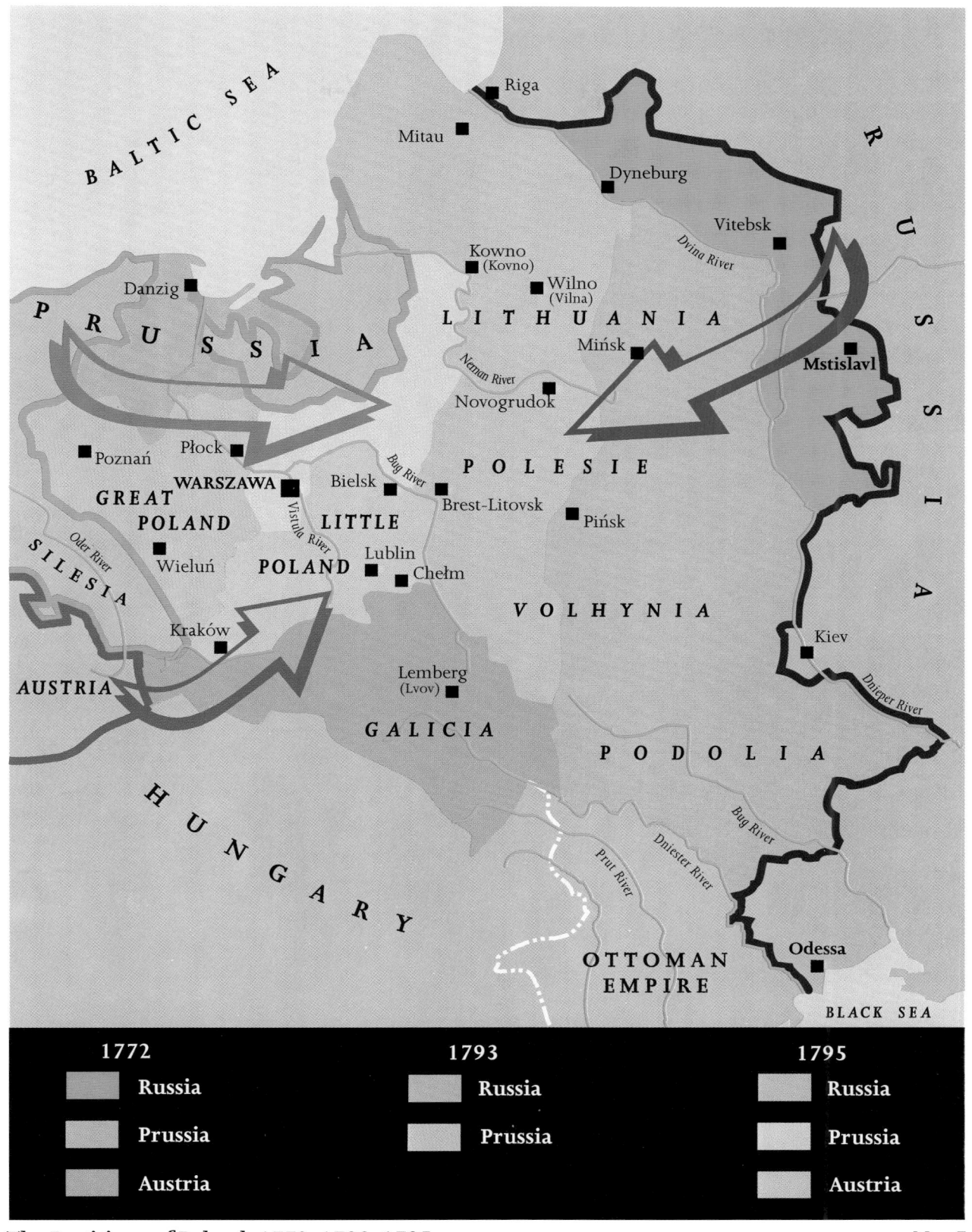

The Partitions of Poland: 1772, 1793, 1795

Map 7

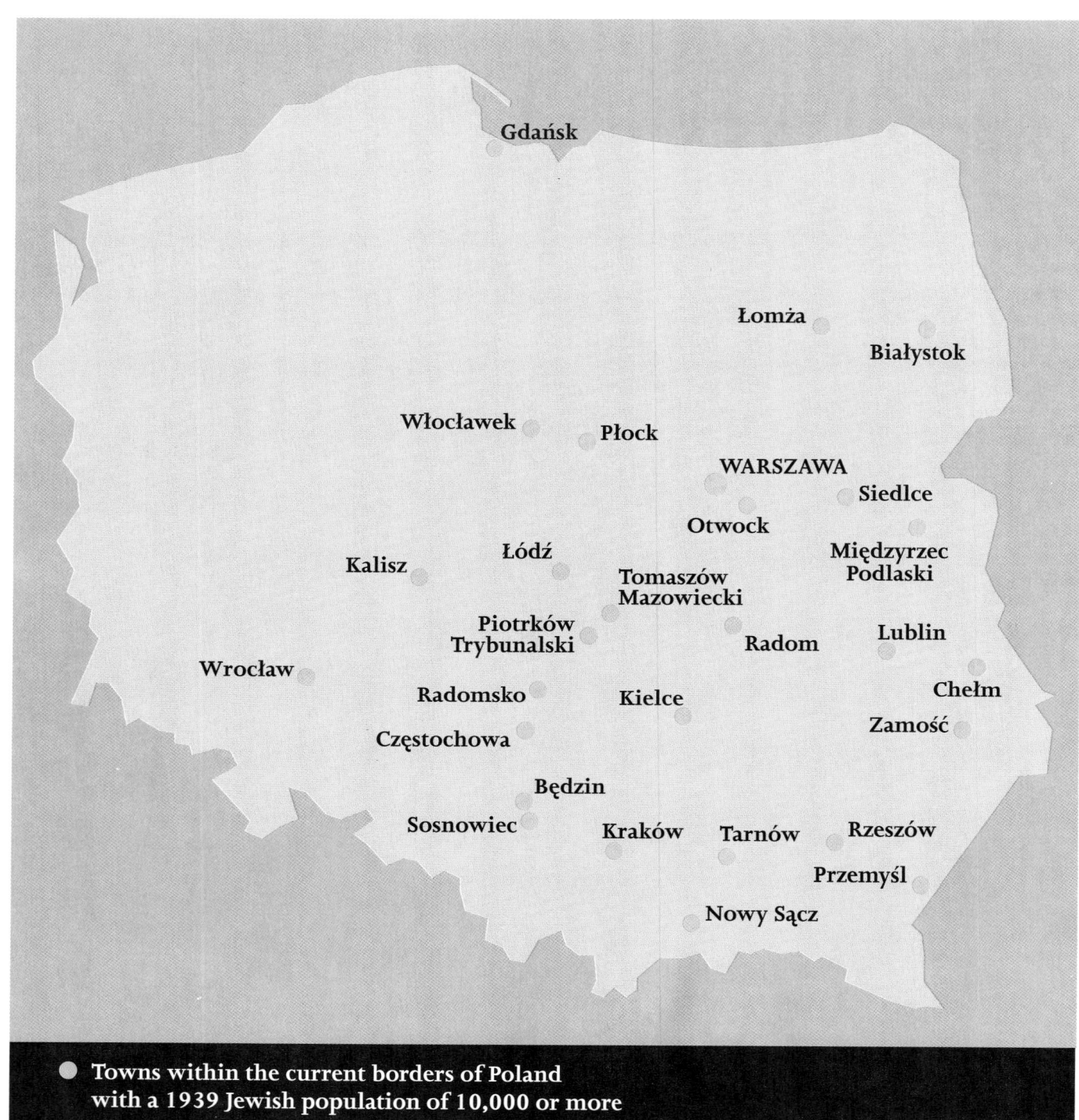

Gdańsk

Łomża

Białystok

Włocławek

Płock

WARSZAWA

Siedlce

Otwock

Międzyrzec
Podlaski

Kalisz

Łódź

Tomaszów
Mazowiecki

Piotrków
Trybunalski

Radom

Lublin

Wrocław

Radomsko

Kielce

Chełm

Zamość

Częstochowa

Będzin

Sosnowiec

Kraków

Tarnów

Rzeszów

Przemyśl

Nowy Sącz

● **Towns within the current borders of Poland
with a 1939 Jewish population of 10,000 or more**

Towns Included in Chapter 2

Map 8

CITIES AND TOWNS IN POLAND
PAGES FROM THE PAST AND PRESENT

by Miriam Weiner

INTRODUCTION

In the 1990s, increasing numbers of Jews from all over the world are traveling to their ancestral towns in Eastern Europe.

The travel agencies and organizations now offering Jewish "roots tours" provide a valuable option for those who feel the need to walk the streets of their ancestors. As an alternative to organized group tours, customized private family tours to Eastern Europe are becoming increasingly popular. Special planning and care (security), however, are necessary in the republics of the former Soviet Union.

Before the Holocaust, approximately 3.3 million Jews lived in Poland. An estimated 5,000 to 15,000 Jews now live in Poland, primarily in the larger cities of Warsaw, Łódź and Kraków. The uncertainty of the population range results from many factors, including the fact that some people are only now discovering their Jewish origins, while others have kept it hidden for many years from fear of repression and anti-Semitism. Almost daily, people come to the Jewish Historical Institute or Jewish organizations in Warsaw with stories about how they have discovered they may be Jewish and want to know more about their roots and their ancestors.

This chapter focuses on the 28 cities within the current borders of Poland that had a pre-Holocaust population of 10,000 or more Jewish inhabitants. The chapter is meant to provide an overall picture of what one may expect to find during a visit to these cities and towns or serve as a resource for those who are unable to make the trip.

There are many Jewish and historic sites remaining in numerous smaller towns throughout Poland. The following travel publications include maps, photographs and historical information:

Gruber, Ruth Ellen. *Jewish Heritage Travel: A Guide to Central and Eastern Europe.* New York: Wiley, 1994.

Kagan, Joram. *Hippocrene Insiders' Guide to Poland's Jewish Heritage.* New York: Hippocrene Books, 1992.

Stephenson, Jill, and Alfred Bloch. *Hippocrene Companion Guide to Poland.* New York: Hippocrene Books, 1991.

▌ *Poznań (Posen), Am Schloßplatz, 1916*   1

Other travel books on Poland that may be helpful include the following:

Dydyński, Krzysztof. *Poland: A Travel Survival Kit.* Hawthorn, Australia: Lonely Planet Publications, 1993.

Heine, Marc E. *Poland.* New York: Hippocrene Books, 1987.

Horn, Alfred, and Bożena Pietras, eds. *Insight Guides Poland.* Singapore: APA Publications (HK) Ltd., 1992.

Jordan, Alexander. *Hippocrene Insider's Guide to Poland.* New York: Hippocrene Books, 1990.

McLachlan, Gordon. *Off the Beaten Track Poland.* Derbyshire, England: Moorland Publishing, 1995.

Nagel's Encyclopedia Guide—Poland. Geneva: Nagel Publishers, 1986.

Przewodnik po Polsce (A Guide to Poland). Warsaw: Sport i Turystka, 1991.

Salter, Mark, and Gordon McLachlan. *The Real Guide—Poland.* New York: Prentice-Hall, 1991.

Salter, Mark, and Gordon McLachlan. *Poland: The Rough Guide.* London: Rough Guides Ltd., 1993.

Ward, Philip. *Polish Cities.* Gretna, LA: Pelican Publishing, 1989.

Jewish cemetery in Gorlice, pre-1939   2

CHAPTER RESOURCES

A typical town entry in this chapter includes a brief synopsis of the town history, pre- and post-Holocaust population figures, latitude/longitude and reference to a nearby larger town.

Spelling Variations

Alternative names and common spelling variations of town names are shown above the map in each town entry. The spelling of town names is a difficulty encountered by numerous researchers and family historians due to the many changes caused by shifting borders and alternative names. Alternative spellings of town names can also be found in publications listed in the sections within the town entry entitled *Selected Reading* and *Bibliographic Sources* as well as in other reference books.

Jarosław town hall, 1918   3

The source for the current spellings of the town names and the latitude/longitude is:

Nazwy Geograficzne Rzeczypospolitej Polskiej (Geographical Names of the Republic of Poland). Warszawa and Wrocław: Państwowe Przedsiębiorstw Wydawnictwo Kartograficznych, 1991.

The source for the map shown in each town entry is:

Polskie Przedsiębiorstwo Wydawnictw Kartograficznych, a publisher of maps and gazetteers in Warsaw.

Sources consulted for town histories:

Gutman, Israel, ed. *Encyclopedia of the Holocaust.* 4 vols. New York: Macmillan Publishing, 1990.

Pinkas Hakehillot: Poland. Vols. 1–4. Jerusalem: Yad Vashem, 1976–1984 (H).

Published local and regional histories

Roth, Cecil, editor-in-chief. *Encyclopaedia Judaica.* Jerusalem: Keter Publishing House, 1971–1972.

Yizkor books

Sources consulted for population figures:

Black Book of Localities Whose Jewish Population Was Exterminated by the Nazis. Jerusalem: Yad Vashem, 1965.

Encyclopedia of the Holocaust

Encyclopaedia Judaica

Klevan, Avraham, ed. *Jewish Communities Destroyed in the Holocaust.* Jerusalem: Yad Vashem, 1982.

Yizkor books

1994 statistics issued by the Republic of Poland

In a very few cases where the only available pre-Holocaust population figures were from the early 1920s, the 1939 Jewish population figures were estimated based upon previous growth figures. After the German invasion in September 1939, there was a significant influx of Jews to the larger cities from surrounding towns.

Sources consulted regarding data for synagogues, cemeteries and Holocaust memorials include:

Burchard, Przemysław. *Pamiątki i zabytki kultury żydowskiej w Polsce* (Landmarks and Monuments of Jewish Culture in Poland). Warszawa: P. Burchard, 1990.

Encyclopaedia Judaica

Gruber, Samuel, and Phyllis Myers. *Survey of Historic Jewish Monuments in Poland.* New York: Jewish Heritage Council, World Monuments Fund, 1995.

Hippocrene Insiders' Guide to Poland's Jewish Heritage

Jagielski, Jan. Director of Research and Documentation of Monuments at the Jewish Historical Institute in Warsaw.

Jewish Heritage Travel: A Guide to Central and Eastern Europe

Rosenstein, Neil. *Polish Jewish Cemeteries.* Elizabeth, NJ: Computer Center for Jewish Genealogy, 1983.

Data resulting from numerous onsite visits to towns in Poland by the author during the period 1989–1997.

Reports and photographs from travelers and researchers.

Yizkor books

Deportation sites refer to:

Forced labor camps

Concentration camps and ghettos

Deaths camps/extermination centers

Sources for Holocaust data include:

Encyclopaedia Judaica

Encyclopedia of the Holocaust

Mogilanski, Roman. *The Ghetto Anthology.* Los Angeles: American Congress of Jews from Poland and Survivors of Concentration Camps, 1985.

United States Holocaust Memorial Musem. *Historical Atlas of the Holocaust.* New York: Macmillan Publishing, 1996.

Yizkor books

Sources for historic and present–day photographs:

Most of the photographs included in this chapter and elsewhere in the book are reproductions of antique hand-tinted postcards from private collections (see Appendix 6). Some photographs were found in various archives and institutes throughout Poland. The present-day photographs were taken by both private individuals and professional photographers. In some instances, it was possible to show a contemporary photograph side-by-side with a pre-World War II view of the same site.

Author's Note: Due to space limitations within the town entries, synagogue references in this chapter are generally limited to the larger synagogues and those that survived the Holocaust.

▮ *Bobowa Jewish cemetery, 1976*   4

USEFUL ADDRESSES

FAMILY HISTORY LIBRARY, 35 North West Temple Street, Salt Lake City, UT 84150 <http://www.lds.org>

LIBRARY OF CONGRESS, Hebraic Section, African and Middle Eastern Division, Jefferson Building (First Floor), Second Street SE, Washington, D.C. 20540 <http://lcweb.loc.gov/homepage>

YAD VASHEM, P.O. Box 3477, Jerusalem 91034, Israel <http://www.yad-vashem.org.il>

YIVO INSTITUTE FOR JEWISH RESEARCH, 555 West 57th Street, 11th Floor, New York, NY 10019 <http://www.baruch.cuny.edu/yivo>

KEY TO SELECTED READING

The *Selected Reading* list within each town entry includes books and articles that were specifically written about the town. The list is not meant to represent a complete or exhaustive study, but will lead the reader to additional source material about the locality. References to books published outside the United States include the language of publication, while books published in the United States are assumed to be in the English language. Sources published outside the United States may be difficult to locate in American libraries. The researcher may wish to visit a local public or university library to consult the OCLC database to ascertain if a desired volume is available through interlibrary loan (ILL). Many of the books and periodicals published in Poland can be found in the library of the Jewish Historical Institute in Warsaw.

Within the *Selected Reading* list are many references to the *Bulletin of the Jewish Historical Institute in Poland* (Biuletyn Żydowskiego Instytutu Historyczynego w Polsce) which is shown hereafter by its standard abbreviation of BŻIH.

Selected Reading Lists

There are individual *Selected Reading* lists for each of the 28 towns described in Chapter 2. The language of publication is indicated in ( ) at the end of the bibliographic entry, as follows:

(F)	French	(P)	Polish
(G)	German	(R)	Russian
(H)	Hebrew	(Y)	Yiddish

KEY TO BIBLIOGRAPHIC SOURCES

The *Bibliographic Sources* list in the town entries of Chapter 2 consists of books that include information about the subject town and other localities.

Alphabetical codes within the source list (e.g., CTD) refer primarily to publications that include information about Jewish communities; the exceptions are the following organizations and institutions: CAHJP, LDS, LYV and RJHS.

CAHJP Central Archives for the History of the Jewish People

This facility contains both original source material and microfilms of documents from state (government) archives throughout the world. The material is often handwritten and generally in the language of the country in which the community was located. The CAHJP can supply information about available documents for the localities relevant to correspondents' queries, but does not generally engage in genealogical research. All town entries that include a CAHJP reference refer to source material from the following publication:

   📖 Teller, A., H. Volovici, and H. Assouline. *Guide to the Sources for the History of the Jews in Poland in the Central Archives.* Jerusalem: Central Archives for the History of the Jewish People, 1988.

CENTRAL ARCHIVES FOR THE HISTORY OF THE JEWISH PEOPLE, Sprinzak Building, Hebrew University Givat Ram Campus, Jerusalem, Israel (mailing address: P.O. Box 1149, Jerusalem 91010, Israel).

CTD Collection of Testimonies, Memoirs and Diaries

   📖 Klibanski, Bronia, ed. *Collection of Testimonies, Memoirs and Diaries.* Jerusalem: Yad Vashem Central Archives, 1990.

This work contains more than 1,500 testimonies, memoirs and diaries of the Holocaust period accumulated by Yad Vashem beginning in 1954.

EDRD Every Day Remembrance Day: A Chronicle of Jewish Martyrdom

   📖 Wiesenthal, Simon. *Every Day Remembrance Day: A Chronicle of Jewish Martyrdom.* New York: Henry Holt, 1986.

This book is a calendar of anti-Semitic events that have occurred every day of the year throughout history; primary emphasis is the Holocaust and the destruction of European Jewish communities.

EJ   **Encyclopaedia Judaica**

     📖 Roth, Cecil, ed. *Encyclopaedia Judaica*. 16 vols. Jerusalem: Keter Publishing House, 1971–1972. This work is considered by some as the definitive encyclopedia of Jewish history.

EOH   **Encyclopedia of the Holocaust**

     📖 Gutman, Israel, ed. *Encyclopedia of the Holocaust*. 4 vols. New York: Macmillan, 1990. There are almost 1,000 entries in EOH. Many focus on localities referenced in this book.

FRG   **From a Ruined Garden: The Memorial Book of Polish Jewry**

     📖 Kugelmass, Jack, and Jonathan Boyarin. *From a Ruined Garden: The Memorial Books of Polish Jewry*. New York: Schocken, 1983. This book is an anthology of accounts selected and translated from yizkor books.

GA   **The Ghetto Anthology**

     📖 Mogilanski, Roman. *The Ghetto Anthology*. Los Angeles: American Congress of Jews from Poland and Survivors of Concentration Camps, Inc., 1985. This book provides both statistical information and descriptions of ghettos, labor camps, concentration camps and annihilation centers in Poland.

GUM   **Guide to Unpublished Materials of the Holocaust Period**

     📖 Bauer, Yehuda, ed. *Guide to Unpublished Materials of the Holocaust Period*. Jerusalem: Hebrew University and Yad Vashem.

       GUM3 Yad Vashem Archival Material, Part 1, vol. III, 1975.
       GUM4 Yad Vashem Archival Material, Part 2, vol. IV, 1977.
       GUM5 Yad Vashem Archival Material, Part 3, vol. V, 1979.
       GUM6 Moreshet Archives in Giv'at Haviva, vol. VI, 1981.

Volumes III–VI provide an index to archival material at Yad Vashem and other Israeli archives about Jewish communities affected by the Holocaust.

YAD VASHEM, P.O. Box 3477, Jerusalem 91034, Israel.

GYLA   **A Guide to YIVO's Landsmanshaftn Archive**

     📖 Schwartz, Rosaline, and Susan Milamed. *A Guide to YIVO's Landsmanshaftn Archive*. New York: YIVO Institute for Jewish Research, 1986. The guide describes the archival collection at YIVO Institute for Jewish Research of material concerning *landsmanshaftn* located primarily in New York City. *Landsmanshaftn* are Jewish immigrant organizations, most established at the turn of the century, composed of individuals from the same locality or region in Eastern Europe.

YIVO INSTITUTE, 555 West 57th Street, 11th Floor, New York, NY 10019.

HSL   **Hebrew Subscription Lists**

     📖 Kagan, Berl. *Hebrew Subscription Lists*. New York: Ktav Publishing, 1975. Noted in this book are the Yiddish names of more than 8,700 towns whose residents subscribed to Yiddish- and Hebrew-language books published during the nineteenth and early twentieth centuries. An appendix lists the Roman-alphabet names of about 5,500 towns.

JE   **The Jewish Encyclopedia**

     📖 Singer, Isidore, ed. *The Jewish Encyclopedia*. 12 vols. New York/London: Funk and Wagnalls, 1901. The JE was the standard reference source on Jewish history for decades after its publication until the 1971–1972 publication of the *Encyclopaedia Judaica*.

JGFF   **JewishGen Family Finder**

     📖 *The JewishGen Family Finder*. Houston, JewishGen, Inc., 1996– (formerly Jewish Genealogical Family Finder, published by JGS, Inc., 1982–1996). This reference is an up-to-date, computerized database of towns and surnames being researched by more than 4,000 Jewish genealogists throughout the world.

JEWISHGEN, INC., 12 Greenway Plaza #1100, Houston, TX 77046.
<http://www1.jewishgen.org/jgff.html>

JHT　**Jewish Heritage Travel**

📖 Gruber, Ruth Ellen. *Jewish Heritage Travel: A Guide to Central and Eastern Europe*. New York: John Wiley, 1994.

The opening chapter of JHT includes a historical perspective and geographical listing of Jewish sites. Useful addresses, references to local publications and moving personal anecdotes are interspersed with photographs taken by the author. The practical travel information covers Poland, the Czech Republic, Slovakia, Hungary, Rumania, the former Yugoslavia and Bulgaria. Also included are comprehensive listings and descriptions of remaining synagogue buildings, cemeteries, Jewish quarters and other vestiges of once-thriving communities.

KH　**Kiddush Hashem**

📖 Huberband, Shimon. *Kiddush Hashem: Jewish Religious and Cultural Life in Poland During the Holocaust*. Hoboken, NJ/New York: Ktav/Yeshiva University Press, 1987.

Rabbi Shimon Huberband was a close associate of Dr. Emmanuel Ringelblum in his "Oneg Shabbos" project to record events and conditions in the Warsaw ghetto and in all German-occupied Poland. These secret archives were uncovered after the war in the ruins of the Warsaw ghetto. Rabbi Huberband's work focuses on the fate of Orthodox Jews during the Holocaust.

LDL　**Latter Day Leaders, Sages and Scholars**

📖 Rosenstein, Emanuel, and Neil Rosenstein, *Latter Day Leaders, Sages and Scholars*. Elizabeth, NJ: Computer Center for Jewish Genealogy, 1983.

This book lists the names of rabbis and scholars alphabetically by town name and surname.

LDS　**Latter-Day Saints Family History Library Locality Catalog**

The Family History Library of the Church of Jesus Christ of Latter-Day Saints (Mormons) has micro-filmed birth, marriage and death registers for towns throughout the world. These records are copies of documents kept at government archives in the countries of origin and are also accessible through these repositories. The LDS holdings are especially rich in Jewish vital statistics records from Germany, Hungary and Poland. Ongoing filming in the archives of Poland and the former Soviet Union is making it possible for researchers to access material not previously available to foreigners. The films may be consulted at the Family History Library in Salt Lake City, Utah, and at LDS Family History Centers all over the world. By policy of the church, these facilities are open to the public in a secular environment.

Family History Library, 35 North West Temple Street, Salt Lake City, UT 84150

LYV　*Landsmanshaftn* **Records on File at Yad Vashem**

Yad Vashem Martyrs' and Heroes' Remembrance Authority in Jerusalem maintains a list of *landsmanshaftn* located in Israel.

Yad Vashem, P.O. Box 3477, Jerusalem 91034 Israel.

PH　*Pinkas Ha-kehilot* **(Encyclopaedia of Jewish Communities)**

📖 Dąbrowska, Danuta, and Abraham Wein. *Pinkas Ha-kehilot: entsiklopediyah shel ha-yishuvim le-min hivasdam ve-ʿad le-aḥar shoat milḥemet ha-ʿolam ha-sheniyah-Polin (Pinkas Hakehillot: Encyclopaedia of Jewish Communities, Poland)*. Vols. 1–4. Jerusalem: Yad Vashem, 1976–1989. (H)

This continuing series will eventually document all the Eastern European towns where at least 100 Jews lived before the Holocaust. As of October 1997, some 16 volumes were completed, with more planned in the future. The relevant volumes for our purposes are:

　　PHP1　　*Pinkas Ha-kehilot: Poland—Vol. I, The Communities of Lodz and its Region, 1976.*
　　PHP2　　*Pinkas Ha-kehilot: Poland—Vol. II, Eastern Galicia, 1980.*
　　PHP3　　*Pinkas Ha-kehilot: Poland—Vol. III, Western Galicia and Silesia, 1984.*
　　PHP4　　*Pinkas Ha-kehilot: Poland—Vol. IV, Warsaw and Its Region, 1989.*

PJH   Poland's Jewish Heritage

📖 Kagan, Joram. *Poland's Jewish Heritage*. New York: Hippocrene Books, 1992.

The author, born in Lublin, has compiled a town-by-town guide, supplemented by close to 100 maps, biographies of prominent Jews from Poland, listings of congregations and synagogues, Jewish organizations and "practical information" based upon his early life and frequent trips back to Poland. The index of towns includes more than 250 communities of significant interest to Jews today. Along with the historical background in PJH, there are chronological tables showing the history of Polish Jewry throughout the years and its martyrdom during the Holocaust.

RJHS   Registry of Jewish Holocaust Survivors

📖 *Registry of Jewish Holocaust Survivors*. 2 vols. Washington, D.C.: United States Holocaust Memorial Museum/The American Gathering of Jewish Holocaust Survivors, 1996.

The American Gathering of Jewish Holocaust Survivors created a National Registry, now numbering more than 100,000 Holocaust survivors and their families living in the United States and Canada. The National Registry's database includes individuals' names before World War II (including maiden names of women), places of birth, towns of residence before the war and localities (including ghettos and camps) during the Holocaust. The Registry is now located at the United States Holocaust Memorial Museum, under the name *The Benjamin and Vladka Meed Registry of Jewish Holocaust Survivors*.

UNITED STATES HOLOCAUST MEMORIAL MUSEUM, 100 Raoul Wallenberg Place SW, Washington, D.C. 20024-2150.

AMERICAN GATHERING AND FEDERATION OF JEWISH HOLOCAUST SURVIVORS, 122 West 30th Street, New York, NY 10001.

SF   Shtetl Finder Gazetteer

📖 Cohen, Chester G. *Shtetl Finder Gazetteer*. Los Angeles: Periday Company, 1980/Bowie, MD: Heritage Books, 1989 (reprint).

For many years, *Shtetl Finder Gazetteer* was the only gazetteer of Eastern European Jewry. Town names are listed alphabetically by the Roman-alphabet version of the Yiddish name. Entries include names of prominent rabbis and local citizens along with subscribers to various rabbinical works.

▍ *Węgrów Jewish cemetery, 1976*   5

HISTORICAL BACKGROUND

by Michael C. Steinlauf

The cities and towns covered in this volume, currently all located within the Republic of Poland, were ruled until the end of the eighteenth century by the Polish nobility. The exceptions are Gdańsk (Danzig) and Wrocław (Breslau), which were populated and ruled primarily by Germans until World War II. Polish authority over the region was consolidated in the Middle Ages and reaffirmed under the Polish-Lithuanian Commonwealth (1569–1795), which at the peak of its expansion contained not only the area within today's Poland, but also the lands making up today's countries of Lithuania, Belarus, Ukraine and Slovakia as well as parts of Rumania and Hungary. It was in this vast territory, populated by a great variety of ethnic and religious groups, that Jews escaping persecution in Germany settled in the fourteenth and fifteenth centuries and then rooted themselves over the succeeding centuries.

In comparison to some Western European rulers, the Polish kings and landowners offered Jews favorable conditions under which to develop their lands. Within the relative tolerance and decentralization of the Polish Commonwealth, Jewish communities were able to rule themselves to a great extent. Jewish communities were run by elected councils, called *kehillas*, which were, in turn, subject to a kind of Jewish national council called the Council of the Four Lands. This high degree of political autonomy went hand in hand with religious and cultural autonomy. In other words, these Jewish communities were able to live according to their own traditions and lifestyles, with little outside interference, for many centuries. Within this vast area, which we call today Eastern Europe, they were able to establish a coherent Jewish civilization: the Yiddish-speaking world known as Eastern Ashkenaz.

In the late eighteenth century, foreign invasion and internal political turmoil led to the dissolution of the Polish Commonwealth. The cities and towns covered in this volume were then incorporated, depending on their location, either into the Austrian or the Russian Empire until the end of World War I. Both of these empires— the Austrian primarily with a carrot and the Russian primarily with a stick—tried to break down Jewish autonomy and turn the Jews into "loyal

subjects." During this period, two new movements divided these Jewish communities internally as well. The first was *Hasidism*, a mass religious movement, centered around charismatic leaders called *tsaddikim* or *rebbes*, that wanted to instill new life into Judaism. The second was *Haskalah*, a reform movement, at first involving only handfuls of Jews, which wanted Jews to model themselves after "progressive" Europeans. By the end of the nineteenth century, *Haskalah* had produced secular Jewish mass move-ments, including Zionism and Jewish socialism, which further divided the Jewish communities.

After World War I, the cities and towns in this volume were again under Polish rule, this time within a newly created Polish nation-state. In the new situation, the Jews encountered, on the one hand, comparative democracy to develop Jewish institutions and culture, both traditional and modern, but on the other hand, increasing anti-Semitism, fomented by Polish nationalists.

This was the situation when Germany invaded Poland and World War II began. Most of the cities and towns in this volume were immediately occupied by the Germans, several first by the Soviets and then by the Nazis. Soon after their entrance into a city, the Germans would select a Jewish Council,

❚ *Town square in Staszów, 1996*

6

Synagogue in Włodawa now houses a museum with a Jewish section, c. 1985   7

Synagogue in Włodawa, interior, 1991 (see fig. 7)   8

which they called a *Judenrat*, to do their bidding, and also established a "Jewish residential quarter," or ghetto within which Jews were required to live. Within the ghettos, which were soon sealed, hunger and disease took a terrible toll. Eventually, the Jews within the ghettos were either shot on the spot or shipped to camps, where most were immediately murdered and many of the remainder worked to death. Three million Jewish citizens of the pre-war Polish state were murdered; they accounted for half the Jewish victims of the Holocaust. The Germans also killed 2 million non-Jewish Poles.

The reconstituted Poland that arose after the war lost its eastern territories to the Soviet Union, but in return, acquired previously German lands in the west. During the first post-war years, some 50,000 Polish Jews who had survived the Holocaust in Poland, joined by 200,000 who had survived in the Soviet Union, attempted to reestablish lives in Poland. However, a ruined economy combined with near-civil war between Communists and nationalists, and above all, violent anti-Semitism that culminated in a pogrom in Kielce in 1946 in which 42 Jews were murdered, resulted in the departure, primarily for Israel and the United States, of most surviving Polish Jews. Of the handful who remained, some found positions in the government of the so-called Polish People's Republic, which remained within the Soviet bloc until 1989. In 1968–1970, a government-sponsored "anti-Zionist campaign," linked to an attack on attempted reforms of the Communist system, drove 20,000 Jews, primarily employed in the government, out of the country.

Beginning in 1980, with the rise of the Solidarity movement which eventually helped to overthrow communism in Poland, some Poles, especially in student and intellectual circles, began to express interest in Jews, Judaism and Poland's Jewish past. Such interest has deepened since the fall of communism and has taken many forms. Often with help from Jews abroad, Holocaust-related monuments have risen throughout Poland; there are festivals of Jewish music, art and film; in Warsaw and Kraków, there are research institutes for the study of Jewish history and culture; over the past seven years, more than 20 books by Isaac Bashevis Singer have been translated into Polish. At the same time, with censorship lifted, extreme nationalist and anti-Semitic rhetoric can be heard as well. But, particularly as compared to other post-Communist societies, such views have remained marginal and relatively inconsequential.

Today, there are an estimated 5,000–15,000 Jews in Poland, several Jewish periodicals, a Yiddish theater, a Jewish school, a pre-school, summer camp and functioning synagogues in a number of the larger cities of Poland.

Michael C. Steinlauf writes and teaches about Eastern European Jewish history and culture. He is the author of *Bondage to the Dead: Poland and the Memory of the Holocaust* (Syracuse: Syracuse University Press, 1997) as well as studies of Jewish theater in Poland and Polish–Jewish relations. He is Senior Research Fellow at the YIVO Institute for Jewish Research in New York.

BĘDZIN

Będzin existed as a Polish colony in Silesia long before King Casimir the Great granted it a municipal charter in 1358. On the site of a thirteenth-century wooden castle, he erected a stone fortress to guard the Polish border against Germanic invaders. In 1583, King Stefan Batory allowed Jews to live in the city and to enjoy full economic rights. A Jewish cemetery was established in 1592, another in response to a cholera epidemic in 1831, and two more at the end of the nineteenth century.

The Jewish population grew as Będzin became an industrial center in the latter half of the nineteenth century. Between the world wars, Jews were active as both entrepreneurs and workers in mining and related metallurgical industries as well as in the production of chemicals, paints, candles and bakelite. Local Jewish industrialists supported modern Jewish elementary and secondary schools. Nearly 1,000 Jews belonged to the network of Jewish credit cooperatives and free-loan societies. In 1931, there were more than 20,000 Jews in Będzin, comprising nearly half the town's population.

The Germans occupied Będzin on September 4, 1939, and renamed it Bendsburg. Five days later, they burned the Great Synagogue to the ground with some 200 Jews locked inside. At first, there was no ghetto in Będzin; as a result, many Jews fleeing or expelled from other towns sought refuge there. The absence of a ghetto did not prevent the Nazis from deporting Jews to Auschwitz—several thousand in May 1942 and 5,000 more in August. A ghetto was finally established in January 1943 in the suburb of Kamionka, but it was liquidated in August in the face of Jewish armed resistance; these Jews were also shipped to Auschwitz. Several Jewish men and women from Będzin played a major role in the uprising that destroyed one of the gas chamber–crematorium units at Auschwitz in October 1944. Some survivors returned to Będzin after the war and attempted to reestablish a Jewish community, but most of them left Poland after the Kielce pogrom of July 1946.

Location

19 km N of Katowice
50°19′/19°08′
Voivodship: Katowice

General Population, 1939

60,000 (45% Jewish)

General Population, 1994

63,599

BENDIN, BENDZIN

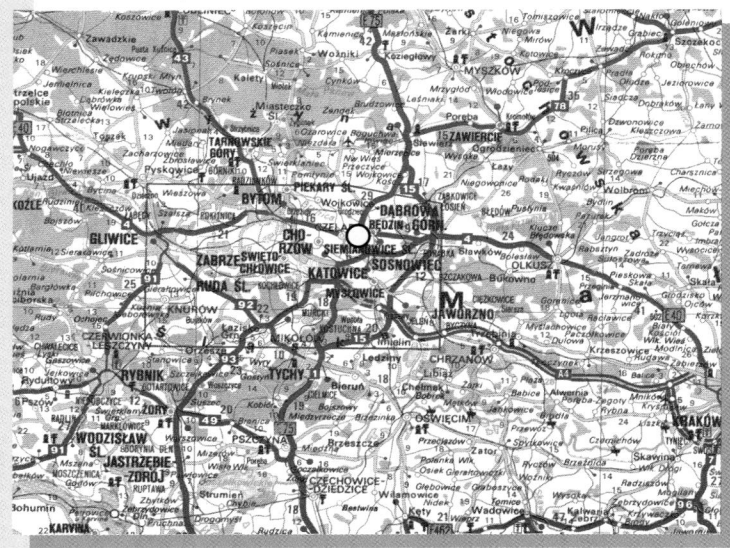

SYNAGOGUE

Great Synagogue, near Góra Zamkowa (Castle Mountain) Built in 1881 and burned by the Germans on September 9, 1939.

▌ *ul. Stanisława Małachowskiego, today* 1

■ Old cemetery, ul. Podzamcze, 1992   2

■ New cemetery, ul. Będzińska 64 in Czeladź, 1992   3

JEWISH CEMETERIES

ul. Podzamcze
300 tombstones dating from 1831.

ul. Zawale
Cemetery founded in 1592; destroyed by the Nazis. Current use: park.

ul. Będzińska 64 in town of Czeladź
Some restoration, with 5,000 tombstones dating from 1880s.

ul. Sielecka
Cemetery founded in 1900; completely destroyed.

■ *Synagogue (upper right), c. 1910*   4

Dedication of Holocaust memorial at site of former synagogue, 1993   5

HOLOCAUST MEMORIALS

Site of former synagogue (near castle)
Monument dedicated in 1993.

ul. 22 Lipca 23
Memorial plaque at courthouse for the 200 Jews who were burned alive by Nazis in the synagogue on September 9, 1939.

DEPORTATIONS

Auschwitz-Birkenau.

Jewish street, c. 1906   6

SELECTED READING

Akavia, Miriam. *Ha-derekh ha-aḥeret* (The Other Way: The Story of a Group [Nasza Grupa]). Tel Aviv: Yedioth Ahronoth Books, 1992. (H)

Będzin Chronicle. Tel Aviv, 1959.

Ben Tov, Arie. *Bedzin, 1938–1941*. Tel Aviv: Haemek, 1985. (H)

Brandes, Aaron. *Kets ha-yehudim be-ma'arav Polin* (The End of the Jews in Western Poland). Tel Aviv: Sifriat Ha-poalim, 1945. (H)

Brandes, Aharon, and Chaim Reshef. *Zvi Brandes: Me-rashe ha-maḥteret ha-ḥalutsit be-Zaglembiyah* (Zvi Brandes: A Leader of the Zagłębian Halutz Underground). Tel Aviv: Moreshet, 1978. (H)

Plac Wolności, today   7

Brownlow, Donald Grey, and John Eleuthere du Pont. *Hell Was My Home: The True Story of Arnold Shay, Survivor of the Holocaust.* West Hanover, MA: Christopher Publishing House, 1983.

Geshuri, Meir Shimon. *Sefer Sosnovits veha-sevivah be-Zaglembiyah* (Book of Sosnowiec and the Surrounding Region in Zagłębie). 2 vols. Tel Aviv: Sosnowiec Societies in Israel and the United States, France and other countries, 1973–1974. (H, Y)

Hampel, Mordecai. *Yediyot Bendin* (Bendin News). Tel Aviv: Association of Former Residents of Będzin in Israel, 1964. (H)

Jaworski, Wojciech. "Żydowskie gminy wyznaniowe w Zagłębiu Dąbrowskim" (The Jewish Communities in Zagłębie Dąbrowskie). BŻIH 1–2/145–146 (1988): 131–144. (P)

———. Żydzi Będzińscy (The Jews of Będzin). Będzin: Muzeum Zagłębia w Będzinie, 1993. (P)

Kantor, M., and N. Szternfinkiel. Żydzi w Zagłębiu (The Jews in Zagłębia). Sosnowiec: Sowa Press, 1993. (P)

■ Market square, c. 1917   8

Klinger, Haika. Mi-yoman ba-geto (From a Diary in the Ghetto). Merhavia, Israel: Hashomer Hatzair, 1959. (H)

Liwer, David. 'Ir ha-metim (City of the Dead). Tel Aviv: N. Twersky, 1946. (H)

Posmantier, Harry. The Last of the Numbered Men: A Memoir of the Holocaust. New York: Vantage Press, 1984.

Ranz, Jochanan. In Nazi Claws: Bendin, 1939–1944. New York: J. Ranz, 1956.

■ Old market square, today   9

Rapoport, J. Pinkas Zaglembie (Memorial Book, Zagłębie). Tel Aviv: Hamenorah, 1972. (H, Y, E)

Sack, John. An Eye for an Eye: The Untold Story of Jewish Revenge Against Germans in 1945. New York: Basic Books, 1993.

Bendzin.

■ Old views of Będzin, c.1917   10

Shpizman, L. "Yidn in Zaglembye beys der itstiker milkhome" (Jews in the Province of Zagłębie During the Present War). Yivo Bleter 19/2 (March–April 1942): 221–231. (Y)

■ Fortress, dating from c.1834   11

Stein, A. Sh. Pinkas Bendin (Pinkas Bendin: A Memorial to the Jewish Community of Bendin). Tel Aviv: Association of Former Residents of Będzin in Israel, 1959. (H, Y)

Zariz, Ruth. "Attempts at Rescue and Revolt—Attitude of Members of the Dror Youth Movement in Będzin to Foreign Passports as Means of Rescue." Yad Vashem Studies 20 (1990): 211–236.

FILMS

Diamonds in the Snow. Cinema Guild: Mira Reym Binford, 1994.

To the Smouldering Cities: Jews of Zagłembia. Tel Aviv: Beth Hatefutsoth, 1989.

BIBLIOGRAPHIC SOURCES

CAHJP; CTD; EDRD; EJ; EOH; FRG; GA; GUM3; GUM4; GUM5; GUM6; HSL; JE; JGFF; JHT; KH; LDL; LDS; LVY; PJH; RJHS; SF

BIAŁYSTOK

Białystok developed within a strongly multicultural setting. The land surrounding the city was owned by Polish gentry and was worked by Polish and White Russian peasants. The city itself was settled to a large extent by German traders and Jews. From the late eighteenth century until World War I, it was part of the Russian Empire; between the wars, it was Polish. By the twentieth century, Białystok was distinguished as one of the few cities in Eastern Europe whose population was primarily Jewish. Many large cities had populations that were one-third Jewish; Białystok's population was three-fifths Jewish.

Somewhat like Łódź, Białystok rose to prominence in the nineteenth century as a center of textile production. By the end of the century, Białystok was producing inexpensive cloth to meet the needs of the vast Russian Empire. Białystok was also a center of the tobacco industry. In the late nineteenth and early twentieth centuries, most of the textile mills and cigarette factories were in Jewish hands. Isaac Zabludovsky, a native son, was reputed to be the first Jewish millionaire in Russia. Białystok was also the birthplace of Ludwig Zamenhof, the creator of the "international" language Esperanto, and of Yitzhak Shamir, the Israeli prime minister. However, the overwhelming majority of Białystok Jews were neither rich nor famous; they were poor workers and small shopkeepers. Beginning in the 1880s, Białystok became a center of the Jewish labor movement; especially strong was the Jewish Socialist party known as the Bund.

In 1906, amidst the first Russian Revolution, Białystok was the site of a notorious pogrom. Violence on a vastly greater scale followed upon the German occupation of the city in June 1941. The Germans immediately burned down portions of the Jewish neighborhood, including the Great Synagogue, in which they had locked 1,500 Jews. In August, they established a ghetto. Two years later, the ghetto was liquidated and most of its 45,000 inmates were shipped to Treblinka. At that time, a revolt broke out that had been planned for months by the ghetto underground. Led by Mordechai Tenenbaum, it lasted only a few days, since the Germans, having just put down the Warsaw ghetto uprising, were better prepared to deal with resistance. A handful of Jews managed to reach the surrounding forests and link up with existing Jewish partisan units, most of which eventually joined the Soviet partisans.

Location

188 km NE of Warsaw
53° 08′/23° 10′
Voivodship: Białystok

General Population, 1939

100,000 (60% Jewish)

General Population, 1994

276,933

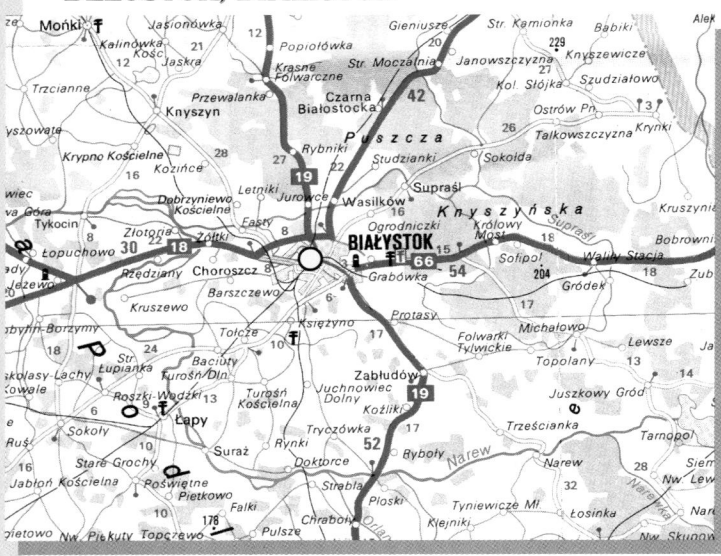

SYNAGOGUES

ul. Suraska 1
Site of Great Synagogue, built in 1909–1913.
Memorial plaque to the 1,500 Jews burned alive on June 27, 1941; reconstruction of the wrecked Great Synagogue's dome dedicated in August 1995.

ul. Branickiego 3
Shmuel Mogilewer Synagogue, built in 1902, was demolished by Nazis in 1941.
Plaque commemorates the site of the former synagogue.
Current site use: sports hall on synagogue foundation.

ul. Piękna 3
Piaskower Bet Midrash synagogue dating from 1890.
Plaque commemorates site of former synagogue.
Current use: office building.

ul. Waryńskiego 24A
Cytron synagogue dating from 1936–1937 and reconstructed in the 1970s.
Current use: art gallery.

■ Former Cytron Synagogue, ul. Waryńskiego 24A, 1994   1

Entrance to Jewish cemetery, ul. Wschodnia, 1994　　2

Jewish cemetery, today　　4

JEWISH CEMETERIES

ul. *Wschodnia*
Only one of six cemeteries to survive.
5,000+ tombstones dating from 1890.

ul. *Żabia*
Former ghetto cemetery dating from 1941
(3,500 Jews died here).
Current use: park (with remains of the wall that
surrounded the ghetto cemetery).

ul. *Bema*
Cemetery dating from 1840.
Completely destroyed.
Current use: market place.

ul. *Kalinowskiego (near ul. Grochowa)*
Cemetery founded in the 1760s.
Completely destroyed and now a park.

ul. *Sosnowa*
Cemetery completely destroyed.
Current use: park.

HOLOCAUST MEMORIALS

ul. *Żabia (former ghetto cemetery)*
Two monuments: one commemorates ghetto victims and
the second honors Jewish partisans.

ul. *Wschodnia (old Jewish cemetery)*
Tall granite monument commemorates site of mass grave
for 1906 pogrom victims.

Memorial to 1906 pogrom victims, 1994　　5

Highway 19 (en route to Augustów)
Las Pietrasze, a forest at the northern edge of Białystok.
About one-half mile into the forest is a cemetery park
where 5,000 Jews were shot and buried in a mass
grave on July 3 and 12, 1941. A memorial monument
is located at the site.

Jewish cemetery with pogrom monument in background, 1994　　3

Holocaust monument in Las Pietrasze Forest, 1993   6

OTHER JEWISH SITES AND MONUMENTS

ul. *Warszawska* 8
Plaque in Polish and Esperanto at site of school attended by Dr. Ludwik Zamenhof, creator of the Esperanto language, born in Białystok in 1859.

ul. *Lipowa* 41D
Former Jewish vocational school, *Wysocki*, founded by O.R.T.
Present use: trade school.

Entrance to monument in forest where Jews from the ghetto were   7
taken and killed, 1994 (see photo #6 above)

ul. *Kalinowskiego* 2
Former site of Jewish Community Center.

ul. *Malmeda* 10
Memorial plaque in honor of Itzhak Malmed, resistance fighter.

ul. *Malmeda* (public park)
Bust statue of Dr. Ludwik Zamenhof.

ul. *Zamenhofa* 26
Plaque (in Polish and Esperanto) indicating birthplace of Dr. Ludwik Zamenhof.

Former Jewish school, ul. Sienkiewicza 79, 1993   8

ul. *Sienkiewicza* 79 (north of ul. *Jagienki*)
Former Jewish school built in 1905 and attended by former Israeli Prime Minister Yitzhak Shamir.
Current use: hospital.

ul. *Warszawska* 15
Former Jewish hospital, constructed in 1840.
Oldest building now standing in Białystok.
Current use: hospital.

DEPORTATIONS

Treblinka, Biechów, Majdanek, Prużany, Theresienstadt, Auschwitz-Birkenau.

SELECTED READING

Bakhrakh, Yerukham. "Materyaln tsu der geshikhte fun di eltste yidishe yishuvim in Byalistoker gegnt in 17tn, 18tn un 19tn yorhundert" (Materials for the History of the Oldest Jewish Settlements in the Białystok Region in the Seventeenth, Eighteenth and Nineteenth Centuries). *Yivo Bleter* 28/2 (Winter 1946): 317–336. (Y)

Blumenthal, Nachman. *Darko shel yudenrat: te'udot mi-geto Byalistok* (The Workings of the Judenrat: Documents from the Białystok Ghetto). Jerusalem: Yad Vashem, 1962. (H)

Datner, Szymon. "Eksterminacja ludności żydowskiej w okręgu białostockim" (Extermination of Jews in the Białystok Region). *BŻIH* 60 (1966): 1–29. (P)

Eisenbach, Artur. "O sytuacji ludności żydowskiej w okręgu Białostockim w roku 1861" (On the Situation of the Jewish Population in Białystok District in 1861). *Rocznik Białostocki* 6 (1966): 459–471. (P)

▌ *ul. Lipowa, 1938*   10

Herschberg, Abraham, and Yudl Mark, eds. *Pinkes Byalistok; grunt-materyaln tsu der geshikhte fun di yidn in Byalistok biz nokh der ershter veltmilkhome* (Pinkes Białystok: The Chronicle of Białystok; Basic Material for the History of the Jews in Białystok Until the Period After the First World War). 2 vols. New York: Białystok Jewish Historical Association, 1949–1950. (Y)

Hindes, Leibl. *Mayne kinder-yorn oyf di Pyaskes: zikhroynes fun mayn heym-shtot Byalistok fun di yorn 1882–1905* (My Childhood on the Pyaskes: Memories of My Hometown Białystok from 1882 to 1905). Boston: L. Hindes bukh-komitet, 1963. (Y)

Kaplan, Pesach. "Eksterminacja Żydów w Białymstoku" (Extermination of Białystok Jews [Feb. 1943]). *BŻIH* 60 (1966): 121. (P)

Kaplan, Pesach, et al., eds. *Byalistoker leksikon: biografye fun Byalistoker yidishe perzenlekhkeytn* (Białystok Lexicon: Biographies of Białystok Jewish Personalities). Białystok, 1935. (Y)

Klementynowski, David. *Lebn un umkum in Byalistoker geto* (Life and Death in the Białystok Ghetto). New York, 1946. (Y)

▌ *Białystok, c. 1930*   9

Frank, Herman, ed. *Natsyonale un politishe bavegungen bay yidn in Byalistok* (National and Political Movements Among Jews in Białystok). New York: Gezelshaft far geshikhte fun Byalistok, 1951. (Y)

Fuks, Marian. "Prasa żydowska w Białymstoku: 1918–1939" (Jewish Press in Białystok: 1918–1939). *BŻIH* 1–2/145–146 (1988): 145–152. (P)

Goldstein, Z. *Di yidishe prese in Byalistok* (The Jewish Press in Białystok). Białystok, 1931. (Y)

Grossman, Chaika. *The Underground Army: Fighters of the Białystok Ghetto.* New York: Holocaust Library, 1987.

▌ *ul. Lipowa, today*   11

Klibański, Bronia. "The Underground Archives of the Białystok Ghetto Founded by Marsik and Tenenbaum," *Yad Vashem Studies* 2 (1958): 295–329.

Korzec, Paweł. "Rzemiosło żydowskie w Białymstoku na przełomie wieku XIX i XX" (Jewish Handicraft in Białystok at the Turn of the Nineteenth and Twentieth Centuries). BŻIH 50 (1964): 23–35. (P)

ul. Grochowa, Nowolipie Bet Midrash, c.1918, destroyed

12

Kot, Srolke. *Khurbn Byalistok* (The Destruction of Białystok). Buenos Aires, 1947 (Y)

Linder, Menakhem. "Der khurbn funem yidishn handl in Byalistoker rayon" (The Jewish Trade in Białystok Region). Yidishe Ekonomik 1/2-3 (1937): 13–33. (Y)

Maḥteret geto Byalistok u-mefakdah (The Underground of the Białystok Ghetto and Its Leader). Bet Lohame Ha-Getaot, 1985. (H)

Mark, Bernard. *Der oyfshtand in Byalistoker geto* (The Uprising in the Białystok Ghetto). Warsaw: Jewish Historical Institute, 1950. (Y)

————. *Megilat Byalistok; ha-mered ba-geto* (The Białystok Scroll: Rebellion in the Ghetto). Tel Aviv, 1945. (H)

Nof, Noomi. *Ha-etmol be-`afar* (Yesterday in Ashes).Haifa, 1979. (H)

ul. Nikolayska, c. 1917

13

Raizner, R. Umkum fun Byalistoker yidntum: 1939–1945 (The Destruction of Białystok Jewry: 1939–1945). Melbourne, Australia: Białystoker Centre, 1948. (Y)

Samid, Yaœeakov, ed. *Ha-Gimnasyah ha-`ivrit be-Byalistok (Polin) 1919–1939* (Białystok Hebrew Gymnasium). Haifa, 1991. (H)

Shmulewitz, I., ed. *Der Byalistoker yisker-bukh* (The Białystoker Memorial Book). New York: Białystoker Center, 1982. (Y, E)

Sohn, David, ed. *Byalistok bilder-album* (Białystok: Photo Album). New York: Białystoker Album Committee, 1951. (Y, E)

————. *Di tetigkeyt fun der Byalistoker landsmanshaft in Amerika* (The Activities of the Białystoker Landsmanshaft in America). New York, 1934. (Y)

Sokół, Zofia. "Publiczne bibliotekarstwo żydowskie w Białymstoku, 1918–1939" (Jewish Public Librarianship in Białystok, 1918–1939). BŻIH 3/103 (1977): 15–26. (P)

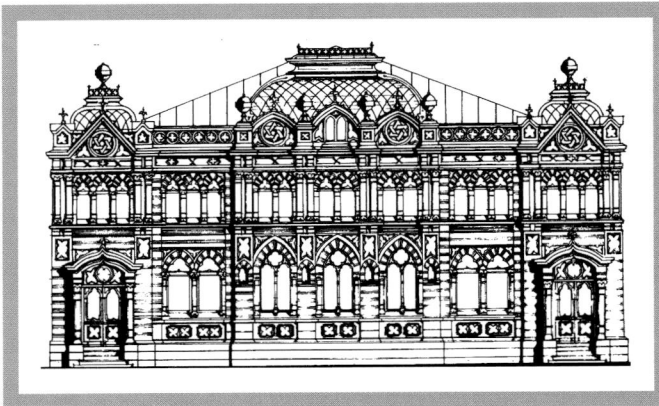

Sketch of Shmuel Mogilewer Synagogue, ul. Branickiego 3

14

Town hall and part of market square, today   15

Tennenbaum-Backer, Nina. *Ha-adam veha-loḥem: Mordekhai Tenenboim-Tamarof, gibor ha-getaot* (The Man and the Fighter: Mordekhai Tenenbaum-Tamarof, Hero of the Ghettos). Jerusalem: Yad Vashem, 1974. (H)

Wiśniewski, Tomasz. *Bóżnice Białostocczyzny: Żydzi w Europie wschodniej do roku 1939* (Synagogues in the Białystok Region: Jews in Eastern Europe Before 1939). Białystok: David, 1992. (P, E)

Zable, Arnold. *Jewels and Ashes.* New York: Harcourt Brace, 1991.

FILM

The Jews of Poland: Five Cities. Spielberg Jewish Film Archives, 1988.

Not Like Sheep to the Slaughter: The Story of the Białystok Ghetto. Jerusalem: Israel Film Service, 1990.

Market square, c. 1930   16

Zabłudowski synagogue dating from 1834, ul. Żydowska: 17
Burned in 1943 during liquidation of ghetto (photo c. 1925)

Holocaust memorial to Jewish partisans at former ghetto   18
cemetery, ul. Żabia, 1994

BIBLIOGRAPHIC SOURCES

CAHJP; CTD; EDRD; EJ; EOH; GA; GUM3; GUM4; GUM5; GUM6; GYLA; HSL; JE; JGFF; JHT; KH; LDL; LDS; LVY; PJH; RJHS; SF

CHEŁM

The town has a rich history dating back conclusively to 1442 and anecdotally to the twelfth century. The seventeenth century found Chełm deeply immersed in the trade and exporting of leather and textiles, especially wool and flax. In 1648, Chełm was particularly hard hit by the Cossack armies of Bogdan Chmielnicki, who slaughtered Jews and Polish gentry throughout the region. In the mid-nineteenth century, an important Hasidic community was founded here. In the 1920s, Chełm experienced an economic revival with the establishment of a railroad station.

The Soviets occupied Chełm briefly in September 1939; when they withdrew, several hundred young Jews also left the town before the arrival of the Germans. On December 1, 1939, the Germans deported 1,800 Jewish men toward the Soviet-held town of Sokal; *en route*, 1,400 of the men were shot. In May and November 1942, most of the remaining Chełm Jews were sent to the Sobibór death camp. When Soviet forces arrived in July 1944, they found only 15 Jews left.

Location

68 km E of Lublin
51°08′/23°29′
Voivodship: Chełm

General Population, 1939

31,000 (50% Jewish)

General Population, 1994

68,846

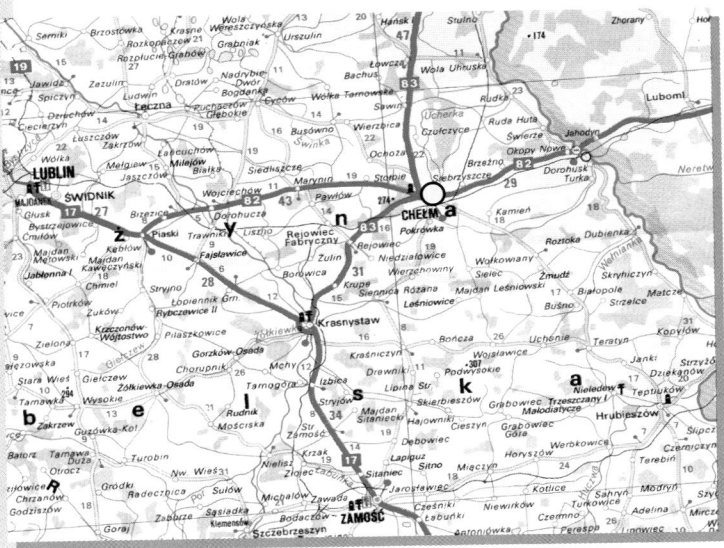

CHELEM, CHELEM, KHELM

SYNAGOGUES

ul. Jatkowa
Great Synagogue dating from fifteenth century.
Destroyed by Germans in 1940.

ul. Kopernika 8
Former synagogue dating from 1914.
Current use: technical club.

Great Synagogue, ul. Jatkowa, pre–1939

2

JEWISH CEMETERY

ul. Starościńska
Cemetery founded in sixteenth century.
100 tombstones dating from twentieth century.
Now part of a park.

DEPORTATIONS

Sobibór, Majdanek.

Chełm. Ul. Lubelska.

ul. Lubelska, c. 1917

1

Chełm, today   3

ul. Starościńska, Jewish cemetery tombstone   4
erected by U.S. relative

Chełm, Jewish cemetery, 1975   5

SELECTED READING

Bakalczuk-Felin, Meilech, ed. *Yisker-bukh Khelm* (Commemoration Book of Chełm). Johannesburg: Former Residents of Chełm, 1954. (Y)

Herzog, Paul. "Chełm: Heads of Skulls." *Partisan Review* (Nov.–Dec. 1946): 553.

Hyatt, Felicia B. *Close Calls: Memoirs of a Survivor*. New York: Holocaust Library, 1991.

Kanc, Shimon, ed. *Sefer ha-zikaron li-kehilat Ḥelm; 40 shanah le-ḥurbanah* (Yizkor Book in Memory of Chełm, 40 Years After Its Destruction). Tel Aviv: Chełm Society in Israel and the U.S., 1980–1981. (H, Y)

"The Nazis in Chełm" (a report received by the United Relief Committee for Polish Jews from Dr. J. L.). *Jewish Frontier* (Nov. 1942): 13–14.

Market square, c. 1921   6

Shalit, Levi. "The Chełm That Once Was." *Jewish Affairs* 10, no. 4 (April 1955): 19–21.

Simon, Solomon. *Di heldn fun Khelm* (The Heroes of Chełm). New York: Posy-Shoulson Press, 1942. (Y)

———. *The Wise Men of Helm and Their Merry Tales*. New York: Behrman House, 1945.

Tenenbaum, Samuel. *The Wise Men of Chełm*. New York: T. Yoseloff, 1945.

BIBLIOGRAPHIC SOURCES

CAHJP; EDRD; EJ; FRG; GA; GUM3; GUM4; GUM5; GUM6; HSL; JGFF; JHT; LDL; LDS; LVY; PJH; RJHS; SF

CZĘSTOCHOWA

The shrine of the Black Madonna of Jasna Góra in Częstochowa is the most sacred Catholic site in Poland, to which thousands of pilgrims have streamed annually since the seventeenth century. A Jewish community was not formally organized until 1808. Jews played important roles in the development of industry and commerce and were particularly active in mining, metallurgy and the production of Christian religious souvenirs. During the interwar period, the latter activity became the focus of intense protest and anti-Jewish legislation by the church and Polish nationalists, leading many Jews to convert their factories to toy production.

When the Germans entered Częstochowa on September 3, 1939, the Jews were immediately subjected to a reign of terror that took hundreds of lives within the first days of the occupation. Thousands of Jewish refugees poured into the city from other parts of western Poland. A ghetto was imposed in April 1941. Between September 23 and October 5, 1942, about 39,000 Jews were deported to Treblinka; 2,000 others were shot in the city. The *Żydowska Organizacja Bojowa* (a united Jewish Fighting Organization) led by Mendel Fiszlewicz was formed in December 1942 and made repeated efforts at armed resistance in the city and the formation of guerrilla units in the forests. In June 1943, the Częstochowa ghetto was liquidated; most of the surviving Jews were transferred to slave-labor factories. After the war, survivors returned to rebuild the Jewish community, but most eventually left Poland.

Location

114 km NW of Kraków
50°48´/19°07´
Voivodship: Częstochowa

General Population, 1939

129,486 (22% Jewish)

General Population, 1994

259,722

CHENSTOKHOV, TSHENSTOKHOV

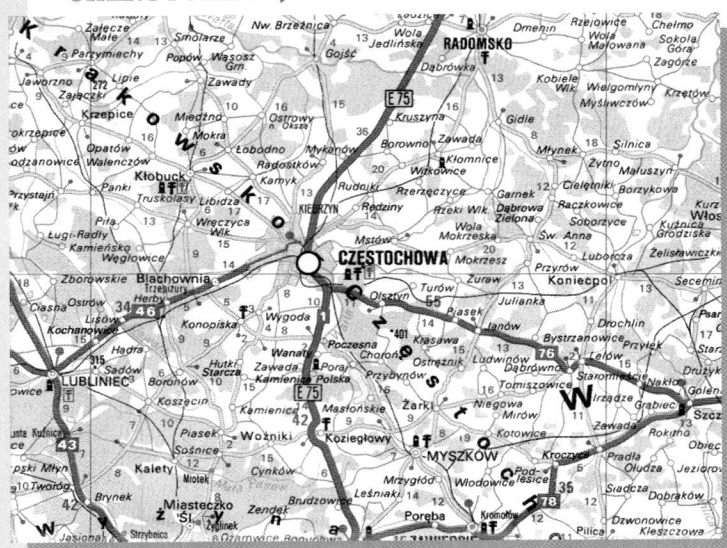

SYNAGOGUE

ul. *Wilsona* 16
Great Synagogue constructed in 1899.
Burned by Germans on December 25, 1939
(only synagogue foundation remains).
Current site use: Częstochowa Philharmonic Orchestra.

JEWISH CEMETERY

ul. *Złota*
Cemetery founded in eighteenth century.
1,000 tombstones remain.
Cemetery is now within the premises of the steelworks.

Great Synagogue, ul. *Wilsona* 16, c. 1919

1

Jewish cemetery, ul. Złota, 1983   2

HOLOCAUST MEMORIALS

ul. Kawia 20–21
Monument and memorial plaque commemorating Jews
shot during liquidation of ghetto on September 24, 1942.

ul. Złota
Monument and mass grave in Jewish cemetery where
Jews from the ghetto were killed.
Second monument to Jewish resistance fighters.

Monument at *Plac Bohaterów Getta* (*Ghetto Heroes Square*).

Monument and mass grave, ul. Złota, 1983   3

DEPORTATIONS

Treblinka, Cieszanów, Buchenwald, Gross-Rosen,
Ravensbrück.

SELECTED READING

Brener, Liber. "O pracy przymusowej ludności żydowskiej w
Częstochowie w okresie okupacji hitlerowskiej" (The
Forced Labor of the Jewish Population in Częstochowa
During the German Nazi Occupation of Poland). BŻIH 22
(1957): 45–60. (P, E)

—————. *Vidershtand un umkum in Tshenstokhover geto* (The
Uprising and Destruction of the Częstochowa Ghetto).
Wrocław: Yidisher Historisher Institute in Poyln, 1950. (Y)

Glicksman, William. "Daily Record Sheet of the Jewish Police
(District I) in the Częstochowa Ghetto (1941–1942)." *Yad
Vashem Studies* 6 (1967): 331–358.

—————. *A Kehillah in Poland During the Inter-War Years.*
Philadelphia: M.E. Kalish Folkshul, 1969.

Częstochowa, c. 1915   4

Glicksman, Wolf (William). "Silent Night, Holy Night (A
Temple Burns)." *Jewish Forum* 30/1 (Jan. 1947): 15–16.

Jakubowski, Zbigniew. *Żydzi w dziejach Częstochowy* (Jews in
the History of Częstochowa). Częstochowa: Wyższa Szkoła
Pedagogiczna w Częstochowie, 1991. (P)

Kaufman, Abe, ed. *Tshenstokhov, mayn geboyrnshtot*
(Częstochowa, My Hometown). New York, 1950. (Y)

Klein, Harry, ed. *Czenstochow: Our Legacy.* Montreal: Harry Klein,
1993. (Y, E)

Landau, Yeshaiahu. *Lizkor ha-kol ve-davar lo lishkoaḥ*
(Remembering Everything and Forgetting Nothing). Ramat
Gan, 1965. (H)

Mahler, Raphael, ed. *Tshenstokhover yidn* (The Jews of
Częstochowa). New York: United Czestochower Relief
Committee and Ladies Auxiliary, 1947. (Y)

Orenstein, Benjamin. *Churban Czenstochow* (The Destruction of Czenstokov). Western Germany: Central Farwaltung fun der Czenstochower Landsmanszaft in der Amerikaner Zone in Dajczland, 1948. (Y, in Latin characters)

————. *Der umkum un vidershtand fun a yidisher shtot* (The Destruction and Resistance of a Jewish City). Montreal, 1949. (Y)

Orenstein, Benjamin, ed. *Tshenstokhover landsmanshaft in Montreal* (Czenstochover Landsmanshaft in Montreal). Montreal: The Czenstochover Society in Montreal, 1966. (Y)

Schutzman, M., ed. *Sefer Tshenstokhov* (Memorial Book of Czestochow). 2 vols. Jerusalem: Encyclopedia of the Jewish Diaspora, 1967–1968. (H, Y)

▌ *I. L. Peretz House, ul. Krótka, pre–Holocaust* 5

Silberstein, Adam. *Be-getaot Varsha; Tshenstokhov* (In the Ghettoes of Warsaw and Częstochowa). Merhavya, Israel: Sifriat Ha-poalim, 1945. (H)

Singer, S. D., ed. *Tshenstokhov; naye tsugob-material tsum bukh "Tshenstokhover yidn"* (Czenstochov; a new supplement to the book "Czenstochover Yidn"). New York: United Relief Committee in New York, 1958. (Y)

Surviving Jews in Czestochowa. New York: World Jewish Congress, c. 1945.

▌ *ul. Aleja II, c. 1917* 6

Szymański, Stanisław. "Do dziejów Żydów w Częstochowie w Okresie Konstytucyjnym Królestwa, 1815–1830" (To the History of the Jews in Częstochowa During the Constitutional Era of the Polish Kingdom, 1815–1830). BŻIH 39 (1961): 17–38. (P)

Tenenbaum, J. *Underground: The Story of a People.* New York: Philosophical Library, 1952.

Waga, Solomon. *Khurbn Tshenstokhov* (The Destruction of Częstochowa). Buenos Aires: Tsentral-farband fun Poylishe Yidn in Argentine, 1949. (Y)

Żmigrodzki, Z., and K. Nabidlek. "O Żydach częstochowskich w piśmiennictwie" (Częstochowa Jews in Literature). BŻIH 2/58 (1991): 99–103. (P)

▌ *ul. Warszawska, c. 1917* 7

BIBLIOGRAPHIC SOURCES

CAHJP; CTD; EDRD; EJ; EOH; GA; GUM3; GUM4; GUM5; GUM6; HSL; JE; JGFF; LDL; LDS; LVY; PJH; RJHS; SF

■ *Aleja 1, c. 1917*

8

■ *Aleja NMP, 1994*

11

■ Monastery and fortress at Jasna Góra, c. 1990

9

■ Housing development at Bleszno, today

12

■ Market square, 1916

10

■ *Warsaw-Vienna railroad terminal, c. 1917*

13

51

GDAŃSK

For most of its history, this was the Baltic port city of Danzig. Populated primarily by Germans, for centuries it was a center of trade between Eastern and Western Europe. During the interwar period, it was located in the so-called Polish Corridor, a strip of land that gave the new Polish state access to the sea; Danzig itself was officially a Free City under the League of Nations, with special rights for Poland. With Hitler's rise to power, the Nazis became increasingly powerful in the city; on September 1, 1939, the same day he invaded Poland, Hitler annexed Danzig. After the war, as a result of territorial changes that shifted the boundaries of Poland considerably to the west, Danzig became the Polish city of Gdańsk. Accordingly, its remaining German population was expelled and replaced by Poles. In 1980, Gdańsk was the birthplace of the Solidarity movement, which, nine years later, helped to overthrow communism in Poland.

Until the mid-fifteenth century, Jews were not allowed to settle in Danzig, but they were granted the right to trade. This situation did not change significantly under Polish rule (1454-1793). Although Jews were permitted to enter the city during the semiannual fairs, those who tried to stay afterward were expelled by the city council. Under Prussian rule, after 1793, a Jewish community was established and was granted full legal equality in 1869.

In early 1939, the Jewish community of Danzig reached an agreement with local authorities whereby the Great Synagogue and the Jewish cemetery were sold for a fraction of their actual value in exchange for 2,800 passports that enabled Jews to travel to Palestine. Many ritual objects were shipped to the United States; most of these treasures are now at the Jewish Museum in New York. By the time the Germans annexed Danzig, only 1,600 Jews remained.

Location

181 km N of Toruń
54°22′/18°38′
Voivodship: Gdańsk

General Population, 1937

390,000 (3.2% Jewish)

General Population, 1994

463,644

DANZIG

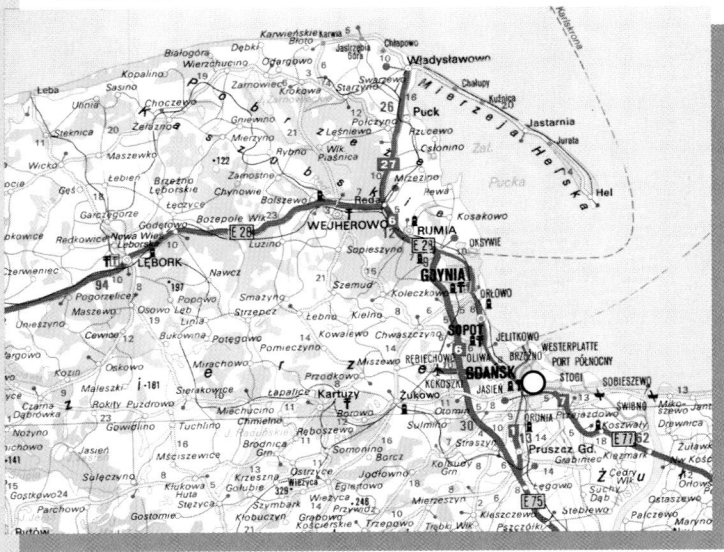

SYNAGOGUES

ul. Bogusławskiego (formerly ul. Ujeżdżalnia)
Great Synagogue built in 1887.
Dismantled in early 1939 (the last service was held on April 15).

ul. Partyzantów 7, Wrzeszcz
Former synagogue, constructed in 1927.
Current use: music school.

ul. Rycerska 2
Former Synagogue, built in 1849.
Current use: store.

Former synagogue, ul. Partyzantów 7, in Wrzeszcz   1

Jewish cemetery, ul. Cmentarna, 1991   2

JEWISH CEMETERIES

Wrzeszcz quarter of Gdańsk
Żydowska Górka (ul. Traugutta)
Cemetery was founded in 1823.
Fewer than ten tombstones remain.

ul. Cmentarna
Cemetery was founded in 1786; it still existed
immediately after the war and then was heavily damaged
by neglect and vandalism.
Remaining tombstones: 100.

DEPORTATIONS

Theresienstadt, Warsaw ghetto.

SELECTED READING

Andrzejewski, Marek. "Uwagi o dziejach Żydów w wolnym
mieście Gdańsku w okresie międzywojennym" (Obser-
vations About the History of the Jews in the Free City of
Gdańsk in the Inter-War Period). BŻIH 4/112 (1979):
67–98. (P)

Berendt, Grzegorz. Żydzi na terenie Wolnego Miasta Gdańska
1920–1945: działalność polityczna, kulturalna i socjalna (Jews
in the Free City of Danzig 1920–1945 and Their Political,
Cultural and Social Activities). Gdańsk: Gdańskie
Towarzystwo Naukowe, 1997. (P)

Domańska, Hanna. "Mój dom będzie zwany domem
modlitwy" (My House Will Be Called a House of Prayer).
Kalendarz Żydowski (1991–1992): 78–100. (P)

Echt, Samuel. Die Geschichte der Juden in Danzig (The History
of the Jews in Danzig). Rautenberg, Germany: Leer-
Osffriesland, 1972. (G)

Kirschbaum, J. Geshikhte fun di Yidn in Dantsig (History of the
Jews in Danzig). Danzig, 1926. (Y)

Lichtenstein, Erwin. Die Juden der freien Stadt Danzig unter der
Herrschaft des Nationalsozialismus (The Jews in the Free City
of Danzig Under National-Socialist Rule). Tubingen,
Germany: J.C.B. Mohr, 1973. (G)

Stein, Abraham. Die Geschichte der Juden zu Danzig (History of
the Danzig Jews). Danzig: Backer, 1933. (G)

Twersky, Isadore, ed. Danzig Between East and West: Aspects of Modern
Jewish History. Cambridge, MA: Harvard University Press, 1985.

FILM
Danzig 1939. National Center for Jewish Film, Brandeis University.

BIBLIOGRAPHIC SOURCES
CAHJP; CTD; EDRD; EJ; EOH; GUM3; GUM4; GUM5; GUM6;
HSL; JE; JGFF; LDS; PJH; RJHS

River view, c. 1919   3

River view, today   4

KALISZ

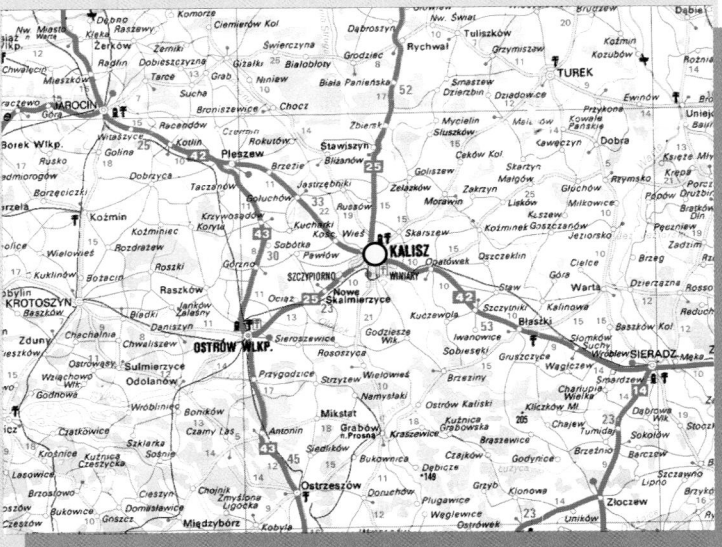

One of the oldest Polish cities, the town of Kalisz in western Poland was the home of one of the oldest Jewish communities in Poland. Minters to King Mieszko III, Jews lived in the city in the latter part of the twelfth century. A Jewish community was founded in the mid-thirteenth century. In 1264, Kalisz was granted a favorable charter of privileges, known as the Statute of Kalisz, which became a model for such documents for centuries to come. At first, the Jews engaged in moneylending, but increasingly they turned to trade with Kraków and Breslau and to crafts including goldsmithing, tailoring and butchering. In the fifteenth century, Kalisz Jews helped found new Jewish settlements throughout Poland. Subjected to occasional persecution, especially as a result of rivalry with Christian merchants and artisans, the Jewish community nevertheless flourished in the sixteenth century. The community was sorely afflicted by the wars of the mid-seventeenth century—in 1659, Russian troops razed the Jewish quarter—but Kalisz Jews quickly rebuilt their community. By the end of the century, Kalisz had become a center of Talmudic learning and the site of an important yeshiva.

Kalisz was briefly taken by Prussia, but then passed to the czars in the nineteenth century. Beginning in the 1840s, Jews became active in a variety of industrial enterprises, opening factories, producing soap, candles, liquor and lace. At the beginning of the twentieth century, Jews founded modern textile mills and knitting factories. By the interwar period, there was a sizable Jewish working class, including garment and leather workers and porters. Jewish institutions included a secondary school, three Yiddish elementary schools, three Yiddish weeklies, two synagogues and about 35 prayer houses. Polish nationalists, organized in the National Democratic Party, were increasingly strong in Kalisz in the interwar years, fomenting anti-Semitic propaganda and organizing an economic boycott of Jewish businesses. On the eve of the Holocaust, there were some 20,000 Jews in the city, making up nearly half the population.

The Germans occupied Kalisz on September 6, 1939; the city was incorporated into the Reich. Jews were seized for slave labor and made to wear the yellow badge. Thousands managed to escape to other parts of Poland; thousands more were forcibly evicted to make room for ethnic German settlers. Nearly 7,000 Kalisz Jews made their way to Warsaw. By January 1, 1940, only 612 Jews remained in the city. Of these, the chronically ill were murdered in October 1940; 200 Jews were sent to the Chełmno death camp at the end of 1941 and the remainder to the Łódź ghetto shortly thereafter.

Location

103 km W of Łódź
51° 46′/18° 06′
Voivodship: Kalisz

Population, 1939

45,000 (45% Jewish)

Population, 1994

106,763

Synagogue (in background), ul. Złota, 1914

1

SYNAGOGUE

ul. Złota

Synagogue dating to 1264; destroyed during the Holocaust.

Cemetery, ul. Nowy Swiat, pre-1939   2

Holocaust memorial, ul. Podmiejska 21, 1964   4

JEWISH CEMETERIES

ul. Nowy Świat (old cemetery)
Cemetery founded in c. 1287
Some tombstones were retrieved from the river and moved to the new cemetery when this cemetery was destroyed during the Holocaust.

ul. Podmiejska 21 (new cemetery)
Cemetery founded in 1867.
Tombstones remaining: 500+.

HOLOCAUST MEMORIAL

ul. Podmiejska 21 (new cemetery).

DEPORTATIONS

Chełmno, Łódź ghetto.

Cemetery, ul. Nowy Swiat, pre-1939   3

Cemetery, ul. Podmiejska, 1994   5

▌ *Market square, c. 1918*　　　　　　　　　　　　　　　　　　6

▌ *Local view, today*　　　　　　　　　　　　　　　　　　7

Town hall, today   8

Jewish cemetery, ul. Podmiejska, ruins of pre-burial building, 1990   9

SELECTED READING

Bet-Halevi, Ysrael David. *Toledot yehude Kalish* (History of the Jews of Kalisz). Tel Aviv, 1960–1961. (H)

Kalish she-hayeta; 'ir va-em be-Yisrael be-medinat "Polin-Gadol" (The Kalisz That Was: A Jewish Metropolis in Greater Poland). Haifa: Bet ha-sefer ha-reali ha-ivri and The Kalisz Society, 1979–1980. (H)

Klein, Jean. *Not Now, Not Ever*. Pittsburgh: Seven Seas Books, 1967.

Lask, Israel Meir, ed. *The Kalish Book*. Tel Aviv: The Societies of Former Residents of Kalish and the Vicinity in Israel and the United States, 1968. (E)

Pakentreger, Aleksander. "Prasa żydowska w Kaliszu, 1918–1939" (The Jewish Press in Kalisz, 1918–1939). BŻIH 1/89 (1974): 97–106. (P)

———. "Spółdzielczość żydowska w Kaliszu w latach międzywojennych, Część 1" (The Jewish Cooperative Movement in Kalisz in the Interwar Years, Part 1). BŻIH 1–2/145–146 (1988): 77–90. (P)

———. "Spółdzielczość żydowska w Kaliszu w latach międzywojennych, Część 2" (The Jewish Cooperative Movement in Kalisz in the Interwar Years, Part 2). BŻIH 3-4/147–148 (1988): 111–125. (P)

———. "Sytuacja ekonomiczna Żydów w Kaliszu po I wojnie światowej, 1918–1921" (The Economic Situation of the Jewish Population in Kalisz After World War I, 1918–1921). BŻIH 1–2/129–130 (1984): 25–37. (P)

Sefer Kalish (The Kalish Book). 2 vols. Tel Aviv: The Israel-American Book Committee, 1964–1968. (H, Y)

Szczepaniak, Marian. "Karczma wiejska w rejonie Kalisza w drugiej połowie XVII i XVIII wieku" (A Village Inn in the Kalisz District in the Second Half of the Seventeenth and in the Eighteenth Century). *Rocznik Kaliski* 5 (1972): 91–111. (P)

BIBLIOGRAPHIC SOURCES

CAHJP; CTD; EDRD; EJ; GA; GUM3; GUM4; GUM5; GUM6; HSL; JE; JGFF; LDL; LDS; LVY; PHP1,PJH; RJHS; SF

KIELCE

For seven centuries, until 1789, Kielce was the property of the bishops of Kraków and Jews were banned from the city. Jews were admitted in 1818, but it was not until 1868 that czarist authorities recognized an official Jewish community in the city. Jews established themselves in industries related to natural resources, as the city's economy was based primarily on metallurgy and mining. In the interwar period, Kielce was known for its strong Jewish educational system and its large library sponsored by the Zionist cultural organization, *Tarbut*.

In April 1941, the Nazis created a ghetto in Kielce into which Jews from neighboring small towns were also driven, along with 1,000 Viennese Jews. The 27,000 inmates were rapidly reduced through starvation, shootings and an epidemic of typhus. In August 1942, the ghetto was liquidated and its surviving inhabitants shipped to Treblinka. After the war, Kielce was the site of an infamous pogrom. On July 4, 1946, responding to a rumor that a missing Christian child had been murdered by Jews, a mob attacked a residence for Holocaust survivors, killing 42 Jews and wounding more than 100. This pogrom became an impetus for the mass migration of Jewish survivors out of Poland.

Location

114 km NNE of Kraków
50° 53´/20° 37´
Voivodship: Kielce

General Population, 1939

48,000 (50% Jewish)

General Population, 1994

214,484

KELTS, KELTZ, KILTS, KILTZ

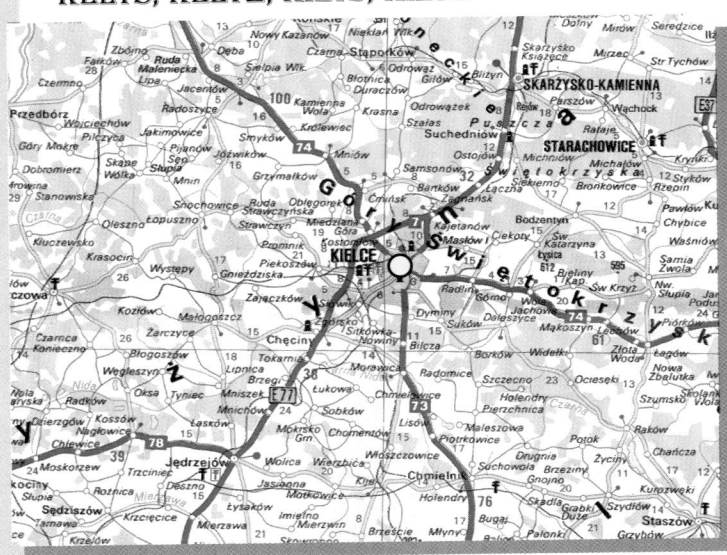

SYNAGOGUES

ul. *Warszawska 17*
Synagogue constructed in 1903.
Current use: State Archives.
Memorial commemorating Poles who helped Jews during the war (dedicated in 1996).
Monument in memory of 27,000 Jews of Kielce (dedicated in 1996).

ul. *Słowackiego 3*
Synagogue constructed in 1921.
Current use: warehouse.

DEPORTATIONS

Treblinka, Auschwitz-Birkenau, Buchenwald, Pionki, Skarżysko-Kamienna, Bliżyna.

■ Market square, c. 1918   1

■ Former synagogue, ul. *Warszawska 17*, 1995   2

58

Jewish Cemetery, 1915   3

JEWISH CEMETERY

ul. Pakosz Dolny
Cemetery founded in 1867.
Tombstones remaining: 150.

ul. Borzęcka, 1918   4

HOLOCAUST MEMORIAL

ul. Pakosz Dolny (cemetery)
Memorial to 45 children killed on May 23, 1943.

Holocaust memorial in Jewish cemetery to 45 children
killed on May 23, 1943 (photo, 1987)   5

Memorial to July 4, 1946, pogrom victims, ul. Pakosz Dolny, 1981   6

OTHER MEMORIALS

ul. Pakosz Dolny (cemetery)
Monument commemorating victims of 1946 pogrom.

ul. Planty 7
Memorial plaque on former Jewish communal building
(dedicated in 1990).
Memorial commemorating the 1946 pogrom erected
next to the former Jewish communal building
(dedicated in 1996).

Memorial plaque, ul. Planty 7, 1996   7

SELECTED READING

Chęciński, Michael. "The Kielce Pogrom: Some Unanswered Questions." *Soviet Jewish Affairs* 5, no. 1 (1975): 57–72.

Fuerst, Dorothy. "The Story of Kielce, a Cemetery and a Survivor." *Martyrdom and Resistance* 14/2 (Nov.–Dec. 1987): 5, 11.

Grzywna, Józef. "Żydowski robotniczy ruch oświatowo-kulturalny w województwie kieleckim w latach 1918–1939" (Educational and Cultural Activities of the Jewish Labor Movement in Kielce Voivodship in the Years 1918–1939). BŻIH 3/4 155–156 (1990): 121–140. (P)

ul. *Konstantynowska, 1917*   8

Meducka, Marta. "Żydowskie instytucje kulturalne w Kielcach" (Jewish Cultural Institutions in Kielce, 1918–1939). BŻIH 1/2 129–130 (1984): 61–73. (P)

———. "Żydowskie stowarzyszenia sportowe w województwie kieleckim w latach 1918–1939" (Jewish Athletic Groups in the Province of Kielce for the Period 1918–1939). BŻIH 3/4 155–156 (1990): 141–152. (P)

Bazaar, 1917   9

Meducki, Stanisław, and Zenon Wrona. *Antyżydowskie wydarzenie kieleckie 4 lipca 1946* (Anti-Semitic Events in the Kielce Region on July 4, 1946). Kielce: Urząd Miasta Kielce, 1992. (P)

Pawlina-Meducka, Marta. *Kultura Żydów województwa kieleckiego, 1918* (Jewish Culture in the Province of Kielce, 1918). Kielce: Kieleckie Towarzystwo Naukowe, 1993. (P)

Penkalla, Adam. *Żydowskie ślady w województwie kieleckim i radomskim* (Jewish Traces in Kielce and Radom Vovoidships). Radom: Tramp, 1992. (P)

Penkalla, Adam, and Jerzy Szczepański. "Synagoga w Kielcach" (The Synagogue in Kielce). BŻIH 4/120 (1981): 53–58. (P)

Renz, Regina. "Drobnomieszczaństwo żydowskie w województwie kieleckim w okresie międzywojennym" (Jewish Lower-Middle Class in Kielce Voivodship in the Inter-War Period). BŻIH 3/4 155–156 (1990): 101–120. (P)

Shtokfish, David, ed. `Al betenu she-ḥarav. Fun der khorever heym (About Our House Which Was Devastated). Tel Aviv: Kielce Societies in Israel and in the Diaspora, 1981. (H, Y, P, E)

ul. *Czarnowska, today*   10

ul. Sienkiewicza, today   11

ul. Sienkiewicza, c. 1918   12

Szaynok, Bożena. *Pogrom Żydów w Kielcach 4 Lipca 1946* (The Jewish Pogrom in Kielce on July 4, 1946). Warsaw: Bellona, 1992. (P)

Urbański, Krzysztof. "Czas pionierów czyli społeczność żydowska w Kielcach w latach 1863–1904" (The Time of the Pioneers in the Jewish Community of Kielce in the Years 1863–1904). BŻIH 1/2 145–146 (1988): 33–46. (P)

———. *Kieleccy Żydzi* (The Jews of Kielce). Kraków: Pracownia Konserwacji Zabytków w Kielcach, 1993. (P)

———. *Zagłada ludności żydowskiej Kielc 1939–1945* (Destruction of the Kielce Jewish Community, 1939–1945). Kielce: Kieleckie Towarzystwo Naukowe, 1994. (P)

Zitron, P. *Sefer Kielts; toledot kehilat Kielts* (The History of the Community of Kielce). Tel Aviv: Former Residents of Kielce in Israel, 1957. (H, Y, E)

Bazaar, 1916   13

BIBLIOGRAPHIC SOURCES

CTD; EDRD; EJ; EOH; GA; GUM3; GUM4; GUM5; GUM6; HSL; JGFF; JHT; LDL; LDS; LVY; PJH; RJHS; SF

Panoramic view of Kielce, c. 1918   14

KRAKÓW

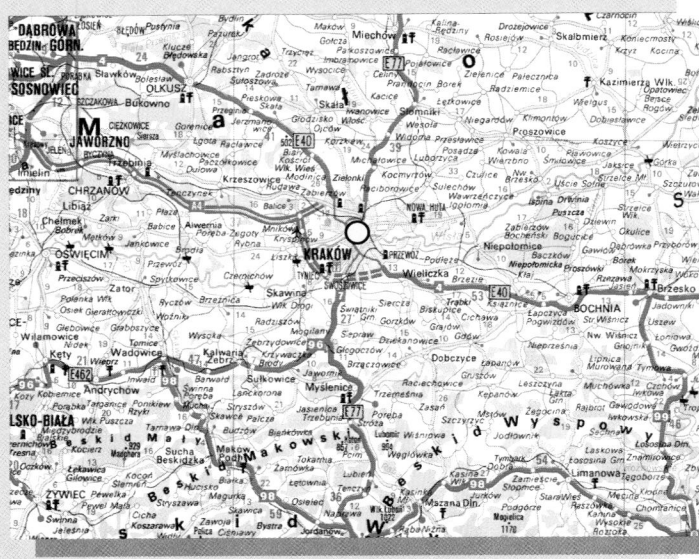

Kraków, a former capital of Poland, has had a Jewish presence since at least the early fourteenth century. Jews settled here probably because of the city's location on the Vistula River, central to European trade routes. A Jewish street is mentioned in documents from 1304, and the first of Kraków's famous synagogues dates from 1407.

The origins of Jewish settlement in Kraków are associated with the legend of a Jewish queen named Esterke, said to be the wife of King Casimir (Kazimierz) the Great, who admitted Jews into Poland in the fourteenth century and granted them a favorable charter of privileges. A similar legend exists among Poles, but in the Polish story, Esterke was Casimir's concubine. No historical evidence has been found to substantiate either story, but guides in Kraków continue to lead tourists to "Esterke's house."

In 1494, Jews were expelled from Kraków proper and required to live in the suburb of Kazimierz (Kuzmir). In later centuries, as Kraków grew, Kazimierz was incorporated into the city and became its Jewish quarter. In the sixteenth and seventeenth centuries, Kraków Jews were both merchants and artisans such as tailors, goldsmiths and butchers. One of the first Hebrew printers in Poland set up shop in the city in 1530. Kraków was the home of Rabbi Moses Isserles (c. 1530–1572), known as the *Remu*, whose annotated version of the *Shulkhan Aruk*, the handbook of religious law, defined Jewish life for centuries. In the mid-seventeenth century, along with other Polish cities, Kraków began to decline as a result of wars and political turmoil in the Polish Commonwealth.

For most of the nineteenth century, after the disintegration of the Commonwealth, Kraków was incorporated into the Austro-Hungarian Empire. Kraków's reputation as a center of Polish culture grew during this time, when, under the rule of the comparatively liberal Austrians, Polish literature and theater flourished.

By the twentieth century, Jews made up more than a quarter of the city's population and lived not only in the Kazimierz neighborhood, but throughout the city. Many Kraków Jews found the lure of Polish culture irresistible. Moreover, it was not only the assimilating middle-class Jews who spoke Polish in Kraków; by the interwar period, visitors to Kraków were often surprised to hear the children of Hasidim speaking Polish to each other in the street. By this time, Kraków boasted a strong Jewish culture in both Polish and Yiddish; of particular importance were the Polish-language Jewish press and a modern Yiddish theater.

The Germans occupied Kraków on September 6, 1939. The city became the capital of the so-called *General-gouvernement*, embracing the region of central and southern Poland not directly annexed to the Reich. Deportations began in 1940; a ghetto, established in March 1941, held from 15,000 to 18,000 people. Deportations resumed in June and October 1942, and the ghetto was liquidated on March 13–14, 1943. Beginning in 1940, two underground organizations commenced resistance activities. Kraków was the site of the famous factory of Oskar Schindler, whose enterprise enabled more than 1,000 Jews to survive the Holocaust.

Immediately after the war, returning Holocaust survivors brought the Jewish population of the city to 10,000, but amidst the turmoil of the postwar years, during which hostility to Jews was punctuated by physical attacks, most left, primarily for Palestine/Israel and the United States. Today, only about 200 Jews, mostly elderly, remain in Kraków. Beginning in the 1980s, Kraków became the center of a Polish revival of interest in Jews and Judaism. Today, there is a Research Center on Jewish History and Culture at Jagiellonian University, a Jewish cultural center in Kazimierz, and an annual festival of Jewish music in the streets of Kazimierz.

Location

295 km SW of Warsaw
50°03′/19°57′
Voivodship: Kraków

General Population, 1939

260,000 (25% Jewish)

General Population, 1994

745,799

The Temple (Reform Synagogue), ul. Miodowa 24, today   1

SYNAGOGUES

ul. *Miodowa 24*
The Temple (Reform Synagogue), erected between 1860–1862 by Progressive Israelites Society.
Current use: Synagogue.

ul. *Szeroka 40*
Remu Synagogue, founded in 1553 by Israel Isserles, father of the famous Rabbi Moses Isserles for whom the synagogue was named.
Current use: Synagogue.

Remu Synagogue, ul. Szeroka 40, today   2

SITES OF SOME FORMER SYNAGOGUES

ul. *Szeroka 16*
Bocian (Popper) Synagogue, founded in 1620 by Wolf Bocian and reconstructed in 1965 after Nazi devastation.
Current use: District Culture Club Studio.

ul. *Szeroka 24*
Old Synagogue, built in second half of fifteenth century, reconstructed in 1570 and again in 1904 and 1913. Destroyed during Nazi occupation and reconstructed by State Office for Preservation of Cultural Property in 1956–1958.
Current use: Jewish Historical Museum with permanent exhibition.

The Old Synagogue in Kazimierz, ul. Szeroka 24, today   3

ul. *Kupa 16*
Isaac Synagogue, constructed in 1638 by one of the most affluent Kraków Jews of the time, Isaak Jakubowicz; it was devastated during World War II. In the 1950s, the building was reconstructed by the Fine Arts Association in Kraków and underwent additional reconstruction in 1983. The stucco decorations on the ceiling and wall paintings in the gallery for women are the only preserved elements from the original building. Nearby is the reconstructed Mizrahi prayer house.

ul. *Jonatana Warschauera 8*
Kupa Synagogue, built in the first half of the seventeenth century by contributions from the Jewish goldsmith's guild. It was devastated during World War II.
Current use: under restoration.

ul. *Józefa 38*
Wysoka (High) Synagogue, erected from 1556 to 1563.
Current use: Historical Monuments Preservation Workshop.

Wysoka (High) Synagogue, ul. Józefa 38, today 4

JEWISH CEMETERIES

ul. Szeroka 40
The Remu Cemetery adjoins the synagogue on the north
and west sides and is one of the oldest cemeteries in
Europe. The Kraków *kehilla* purchased the land in 1533,
and the cemetery was founded in 1551. The cemetery was
almost totally devastated by the Nazis; however, in 1959,
during archaeological excavations, about 700 ancient
tombstones and fragments were found buried and later
re-erected in the sites where they now stand. The graves
of Rabbi Moses Isserles and his family members are in a
fenced plot. Other prominent Kraków rabbis buried there
include Rabbis Moses Isserles, Natan Nata Spira, Joel
Sirkes, Abraham Joshua Heszel and Yomtov Lipman Heller.

▌ *Remu Cemetery, ul. Szeroka 40, 1978* 5

ul. Miodowa 55
New Cemetery, founded in 1800 and damaged during the
Nazi occupation. It was reconstructed in 1957 and is still
active. The oldest preserved tombstones date back to the
1840s, with about 10,000 tombstones remaining.

▌ *New Cemetery, ul. Miodowa 55* 6
▌ *Memorial to Jews from Slomniki, 1993*

ul. Abrahama and Jerozolimska
The two cemeteries located between the above streets
were founded in 1932. One tombstone remains. The rest
were completely destroyed or used as foundations for
barracks or for other construction purposes at the Płaszów
concentration camp, built on this site.

▌ *Remu Synagogue, interior, 1977* 7

New Cemetery, ul. Miodowa 55, 1983   8

HOLOCAUST MEMORIALS

Plac Bohaterów Getta (pre-war: Plac Zgody)
From here, Jews from the ghetto were deported to
concentration and extermination camps in Bełżec and
Auschwitz-Birkenau.

Remu Cemetery, ul. Szeroka 40, today   9

Plac Bohaterów Getta 6 (Ghetto Heroes' Square)
Former headquarters of the Jewish Fighters Organization
(ŻOB) marked with a commemorative plaque.

Plac Bohaterów Getta 18
Museum of National Remembrance on the grounds of the
former Kraków ghetto. The *Pod Orłem* pharmacy, run by
Tadeusz Pankiewicz, served as a place of refuge and
exchange of information within the ghetto. A museum on
this site houses a permanent exhibition commemorating
life in the ghetto and the life of Pankiewicz.

ul. Lwowska 25
Fragments of the ghetto walls remain, with a
commemorative plaque erected on the fortieth anniversary
of the ghetto's liquidation.

ul. Miodowa 55 (New Jewish Cemetery)
Memorial "in commemoration of murdered Jews, victims
of Nazi genocide in the years 1939–1945," from Kraków.
Among the tablets is one dedicated to Dr. Rafał Landau,
the last chairman of the Kraków *kehilla* before the
outbreak of World War II. There are also monuments to
murdered Jews from Skawina and Limanowa.

New Cemetery, ul. Miodowa 55   10
Holocaust memorial to Jews of Kraków, 1993

ul. Kamieńskiego
Small monument commemorating Jewish victims of
Płaszów concentration camp, located near the larger
general monument.

Monument at site of Płaszów concentration camp, today   11

OTHER SITES

ul. Józefa 42
Former Bet Midrash Kovea Itim L'Torah, erected in 1810
and renovated in 1912.
Current use: private apartments.

ul. Szeroka 6
Former mikvah, constructed in the sixteenth century and
rebuilt in 1974.
Current use: small hotel.

ul. Bocheńska 7
Former Jewish Theatre (1927–1939).
Current use: Railroad Workers' Theatre.

ul. Skawińska 8
Israelite Hospital constructed in 1861.
Following World War II, it was remodeled again.
Current use: Kraków health service.

ul. Bocheńska 4
Former Bet Midrash Sheeirit B'nei Emunah.
Current use: House of Culture.

ul. Brzozowa 6
Former Bet Midrash of Salomon Deiches,
constructed in the early twentieth century.
Current use: office of a Kraków cooperative.

ul. Miodowa 24
Mikvah, attached to The Temple (Reform Synagogue).

ul. Lipowa
Former site of Oskar Schindler's factory, whose 1,100
Jewish workers survived the Holocaust. A monument was
erected in the factory courtyard.
Current use: electronics factory.

ul. Meiselsa 17
Former B'nei Emunah prayer house.
Current use: Center for Jewish Culture (see Chapter 1).

ul. Batorego 12 (part of Jagiellonian University)
Research Center on Jewish History and Culture in Poland
(see Chapter 1).

DEPORTATIONS

Auschwitz-Birkenau, Bełżec, Płaszów.

SELECTED READING

Bałaban, Majer. *Dzieje Żydów w Galicyi w Rzeczypospolitej Krakowskiej 1772–1868* (History of the Jews in Galicia and in the Commonwealth of Krakow in 1772–1868). Lwów: Księgarnia Polska, 1916. (P)

———. *Dzieje Żydów w Krakowie i na Kazimerzu: 1304–1868* (History of the Jews in Kraków and Kazimierz, 1304–1868). 2 vols. Kraków: "Nadzieja" Towarzystwo ku Wspieraniu Chorej Młodzieży Żydowskiej Szkół Średnich w Wyższych w Krakowie, 1931 and 1936. (P)

Cloth Hall, 1918   12

———. *Przewodnik po żydowskich zabytkach Krakowa* (Guide to Jewish Historic Landmarks in Kraków). Kraków: Stowarzyszenie Solidarność B'nai B'rith, 1935. (P)

Bauminger, Arieh L. *Loḥame geto Krakuv* (The Fighters of the Kraków Ghetto). Jerusalem: Keter, 1986. (H)

Bauminger, Arieh L., et al., eds. *Sefer Kroke, 'ir va-em be-Yisrael* (Memorial Book of Kraków: A Mother Community in Israel). Jerusalem: The Rav Kuk Institute and Former Residents of Kraków in Israel, 1959. (H)

Wawel Castle, c. 1917   13

Market square and town hall, 1918   14

Bieberstein, Aleksander. *Zagłada Żydow w Krakowie* (The Destruction of the Jews in Kraków). Kraków: Wydawnictwo Literackie, 1985. (P)

Duda, Eugeniusz. *A Guide to Jewish Cracow*. Warsaw: Jewish Information and Tourist Bureau, 1992. (E)

————. *Krakowskie Judaica* (Kraków's Judaica). Warsaw: Wydawnictwo PTTK "Kraj," 1991. (P, E, G)

Frejlichówna, J. "Problemy likwidacji długów społeczności Kazimierza po trzecim rozbiorze, 1795–1809" (The Problems of Liquidating the Debts of the Kazimierz [Kraków] Community After the Third Partition, 1795–1809). *Miesięcznik Żydowski* 3/5-6 (Warsaw, 1933): 467–478. (P)

Freudenheim, Mieczysław. "Wspomnienie o dwóch księgarniach krakowskich" (Recollection About Two Kraków Bookstores). *BŻIH* 1/117 (1981): 83–94. (P)

Friedberg, Bernhard. *Ha-defus ha-`ivri be-Kraka* . . . (Geschichte der Hebräischen Typographie in Krakau von 1530 bis auf die Gegenwart)(History of Hebrew Printing in Kraków from 1530 to the Present Time). Kraków: Verlag des Verfassers, 1900. (H)

Wawel Castle, today   15

Gelber, Nathan Michael. *Zapiski historyczne Żydów w Krakowie 1815–1846* (Notes on Jewish History in Kraków, 1815–1846). Kraków: Nowy Dziennik, 1924. (P)

Graf, Malvina. *The Kraków Ghetto and the Płaszów Camp Remembered*. Tallahassee: Florida State University Press, 1989.

Ludwikowski, Leszek. *Stara bóżnica na Kazimierzu w Krakowie* (The Old Synagogue in the Kazimierz District of Kraków). Kraków: Muzeum Historyczne m. Krakowa, 1981. (P)

Mahler, Ozjasz. *Przewodnik po żydowskich zabytkach Krakowa* (A Guidebook of Jewish Landmarks in Kraków). Kraków: Nakład Własny, 1936. (P)

Former Bet Midrash Kovea Itim La Torah, ul. Józefa 42,   16
now private apartments, c. 1989

Markowski, Stanisław. *Krakowski Kazimierz: Dzielnica żydowska, 1870–1988* (Kazimierz: The Jewish Quarter of Cracow, 1870–1988). Kraków: Wydziałowikultury i Sztuki Urzędu Miasta Krakowa, 1992. (P, E)

Pankiewicz, Tadeusz. *The Cracow Ghetto Pharmacy*. New York: Holocaust Library, 1987.

Peleg, M., and M. Benzvi. *Beḥuts ḥome ha-geto be-Krakuv* (Outside the Walls of the Ghetto in Occupied Kraków). Jerusalem, 1986. (H)

Peleg, Miryam. *Witnesses: Life in Occupied Kraków.* New York: Routledge, 1991.

Rączka, Jan Władysław. *Kazimierz Krakowa* (The Kazimierz District of Kraków). Krakow: Wydawnictwo Literackie, 1982. (P)

Swiszczowski, S. *Miasto Kazimierz pod Krakowem* (Kazimierz near Kraków). Kraków: Wydawnictwo Literackie, 1981. (P)

Weingarten, Roman, and Norbert Friedman, eds. *New Cracow Friendship Society Silver Anniversary: 1965–1990.* New York: The New Cracow Friendship Society, 1990.

Fortress and Florianska Gate, c. 1917   18

Bocian Synagogue, ul. Szeroka 16, c.1989   17

Wettstein, Feivel Hirsch. *Mi-pinkase ha-kahal bi-Kraka* (From the Record Books of the Kraków Community). Breslau: Shlezishe Bukhdrukeray, 1900. (H)

Wojak, Sławomir, ed. *Kraków, A Journey into the Past.* Warsaw: Państwowe Wydawnictiwo, 1987. (P, E)

Wroński, T. *Obóz w Płaszowie, miejsce masowej eksterminacji ludności żydowskiej, polskiej i innych narodowości w latach 1942–1945* (The Camp in Płaszów, the Place of the Mass Extermination of Jews, Poles and Other Nationalities in the Years 1942–1945). Warsaw: Sport i Turystyka, 1981. (P)

Wroński, Tadeusz. *Kronika okupowanego Krakowa* (Chronicle of Occupied Kraków). Kraków: Wydawnictwo Literackie, 1974. (P)

Żbikowski, Andrzej. *Żydzi krakowscy i ich gmina w latach 1869–1919* (The Jews of Kraków and Their Community: 1869–1919). Warsaw: Jewish Historical Institute, 1994. (P, E)

BIBLIOGRAPHIC SOURCES

CAHJP; CTD; EDRD; EJ; EOH; GA; GUM3; GUM4; GUM5; GUM6; HSL; JE; JGFF; JHT; LDL; LDS; LVY; PJH; RJHS; SF

Panoramic view, c. 1918   19

■ Former mikvah, ul. Szeroka 6, c. 1989　　　　20

■ Former prayer house, ul. Meiselsa 17, c. 1990 (see photo #21 below)　　23

■ Center for Jewish Culture (renovated B'nai Emunah prayer house), ul. Meiselsa 17, 1994　　21

■ Old synagogue, ul. Szeroka 24, 1977　　　22

■ Rynek Kleparski, 1905　　　24

ŁÓDŹ

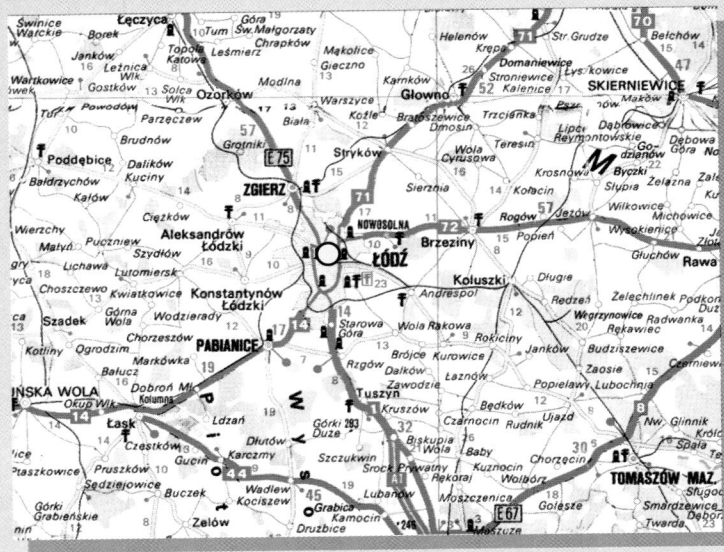

The history of Łódź, like the history of capitalism in Poland, is short, beginning only in the mid-nineteenth century, when the czar encouraged German weavers to settle in Poland. By the second half of the century, handweaving had been superseded by large textile mills established by German and Jewish entrepreneurs employing Polish laborers. Łódź, known as the "Polish Manchester," emerged as the center of textile production for the Russian Empire. By the beginning of the twentieth century, Jewish industrialists such as Israel Poznański and Asher Kon were among the wealthiest men in Poland. In proletarian Łódź, Jews also increasingly worked with their hands as manual weavers and in the needle trades; but they were largely excluded from employment in the largest, most modern, and best-paying textile mills. The northern neighborhood known as Bałuty became a synonym for poverty and a hotbed for the Jewish socialist Bund.

By 1939, the Jewish population of Łódź was second only to Warsaw's; there were nearly a quarter of a million Jews, constituting more than a third of the city's population. The grimy "city of labor" was the scene of a complex Jewish communal life that played itself out in hundreds of synagogues and prayer halls, an array of Jewish political parties and movements, scores of Jewish labor unions and charitable associations, along with a varied daily and periodical press in Yiddish, Hebrew and Polish. The "city without a past" developed a unique modern Jewish culture that was brash and creative; modernist painting and avant-garde Yiddish literature, theater and cabaret flourished.

The Łódź ghetto, established by the Germans in the spring of 1940, was the second to be set up in Poland and the last to be destroyed. Mordechai Chaim Rumkowski, named by the Nazis to be the "Elder of the Jews" in a city renamed Litzmannstadt, was a controversial figure who attempted to promote the survival of Jews by demonstrating the importance of Jewish factories to the German war effort. Rumkowski, who issued postage stamps and coins bearing his likeness, negotiated successive deportations of "unproductive" Jews, including virtually all children and the elderly, believing that a remnant of Jews could be saved. However, in August 1944, as the Soviet Army was approaching and the war was ending, the Łódź ghetto was liquidated. Rumkowski and nearly all the 70,000 remaining Jews were loaded into freight cars and sent to Auschwitz-Birkenau. When the Soviets entered Łódź in January 1945, they found only 877 Jews.

In the immediate postwar period, some 38,000 Jews settled in Łódź, making it Poland's most important Jewish community. However, confronted by economic hardship, political violence, repression and anti-Jewish hostility, most of this community emigrated. After the "anti-Zionist" campaign of 1968–1970, only several hundred Jews remained in Łódź, with a single synagogue and Jewish cultural club.

Location

134 km SW of Warsaw
51°47′/19°28′
Voivodship: Łódź

General Population, 1939

750,000 (34% Jewish)

General Population, 1994

831,272

Synagogue interior, ul. Południowa 28, c. 1993   1

SYNAGOGUE

ul. Południowa 28
Synagogue dates from 1885–1900 and was damaged by fire in 1987. The synagogue was built by Wolf Reichert, who died in the Łódź ghetto. It was rebuilt with financial assistance from the Ronald S. Lauder Foundation.

Synagogue, ul. Południowa 28, c. 1993   2

Synagogue, ul. Spacerowa, c. 1914   3

SITES OF SOME FORMER SYNAGOGUES

Aleje Kościuszki (formerly Spacerowa)
Reform Synagogue; burned by the Germans in November 1939.
Current use: parking lot.

ul. *Wólczańska 6*
Ohel Yaakov synagogue dating from 1899–1904; burned by the Germans in November 1939.

Ohel Yaakov Synagogue, ul. Wólczańska 6, 1939   4

ul. Zielona (near Zachodnia St.)
Great Synagogue dating from 1883 to 1887; burned by
Nazis in November 1939.

ul. Wolborska 20
Altschule Synagogue, dating from 1860 to 1871.

ul. Piotrkowska 114/116
Former prayer house.

Memorial wall at Jewish cemetery, ul. Bracka and Zmienna, 1994   5

JEWISH CEMETERIES

ul. Bracka and Zmienna
180,000 tombstones dating from 1892.
More than 40,000 ghetto victims buried in one section
on ul. Bracka. Key is available at the Jewish Community
Office, ul. Zachodnia 78.

ul. Wesoła
Old Cemetery dating from 1811.
Completely destroyed by Germans and paved over after
1945.

Jewish cemetery, ul. Bracka and Zmienna,   6
1994

Mausoleum of Israel and Eleonora Poznański;   7
Jewish cemetery, ul. Bracka and Zmienna, 1994

HOLOCAUST MEMORIALS

ul. Limanowskiego (corner of Zgierska)
Memorial plaque, at site of former Gestapo office in
ghetto, dedicated to the 210,000 local Jews and Romani
(Gypsies) who were victims of Nazi war crimes.

ul. Lutomierska
Memorial to murdered Jews from Hamburg.

ul. Bracka and Zmienna (Jewish cemetery)
Memorial in memory of 200,000 Jews from Łódź and
nearby towns.

Holocaust memorial in cemetery, ul. Bracka and Zmienna, 1994   8

Memorial to Jews from Hamburg who died in Łódź ghetto; ul. Lutomierska, 1994   9

OTHER SITES

ul. Sterlinga
Former Jewish Hospital.
Current use: general hospital.

ul. Więckowskiego 15
Former Yiddish State Theatre, after 1945.
Current use: general theater.

ul. Więckowskiego 32
Former Jewish Peoples' Library.
Current use: Jewish Social and Cultural Association.

ul. Zachodnia 78
Prayer house and Jewish community office (maintains a list of burials in the Jewish cemetery and information as to when the cemetery is open).

DEPORTATIONS

Chełmno, Auschwitz-Birkenau, Poznań.

Memorial plaque, ul. Limanowskiego, 1994;   10
former Gestapo office (in ghetto)

SELECTED READING

Aescoly, Aaron Zeev. Kehilat Lodz; 'ir va-em be-yisrael (The Community of Łódź; a Jewish Mother City). Jerusalem: Youth Section of the Zionist Organization, 1947–1948. (H)

Bałaban, Majer. Przedmowa dla A. Alperina "Żydzi w Łodzi: Początek gminy żydowskiej, 1780–1822" (Preface to A. Alperin, "Jews in Łódź: Beginnings of the Jewish Community, 1780–1822"). Rocznik Łódzki 1 (1928): 147–150. (P)

Diamant, Adolf, ed. Getto Litzmannstadt (Łódź Ghetto). Frankfurt: A. Diamant, 1986. (G)

Dobroszycki, Lucjan, ed. The Chronicle of the Łódź Ghetto, 1941–1944. New Haven: Yale University Press, 1984.

ul. Piotrkowska, c. 1918   11

Frank, Shlomo. Togbukh fun Lodzher Geto (Łódź Ghetto Diary). Tel Aviv: Hamenora, 1958. (Y)

Friedman, Philip. Dzieje Żydów w Łodzi od początków osadnictwa Żydów do r. 1863 (History of Jews in Łódź from the Beginning of Jewish Settlement Until 1863). Łódź: Łódzki Oddział Towarzystwa Krajoznawczego w Polsce, 1935. (P)

———. "Di industrializatsye un proletarizatsye fun di Lodzher yidn in di yorn 1860–1914" (Industrialization and Proletarization of Jews in Łódź in the Years 1860–1914). Lodzher Visnshaftlekhe Shriftn 1 (1938): 63–132. (Y)

———. "Łódzka Chewra Kadisza i jej dzieje" (History of the Burial Society in Łódź). Stary Cmentarz Żydowski (1938): 37–111. (P)

■ *Market square, 1920*

12

———. "Rola Żydów w rozwoju łódzkiego przemysłu włókienniczego" (Role of Jews in the Development of the Łódź Textile Industry). Miesięcznik Żydowski 1 (1930–1931): 431–450. (P)

Hertz, Jacob Sholem. *Di geshikhte fun Bund in Lodzh* (History of the Jewish Labor Bund in Łódź). New York: Ferlag Unser Tsayt, 1958. (Y)

Hirshkovitch, B. "The Ghetto in Litzmannstadt (Łódź)." *YIVO Annual* 5 (1950): 85–122.

Jasny, A. Wolf. *Di geshikhte fun yidn in Lodzh in di yorn fun der daytsher yidn-oysrotung* (History of the Jews in Łódź in the Years of the German Extermination of Jews). 2 vols. Tel Aviv: I. L. Peretz, 1960. (Y)

Kerz, Izaak. *Szkice z dziejów gminy żydowskiej oraz cmentarza w Łodzi* (Sketches from the Annals of the Jewish Community and the Cemeteries of Łódź). Łódź : Oficyna Bibliofilów, 1996. (P, H)

Lodhzer yisker-bukh (Łódź Yizkor Book). New York: United Emergency Relief Committee for the City of Łódź, 1943. (Y)

Lodz-Names. Tel Aviv: Organization of the Lodz Former Residents in Israel, 1989. (E)

Podgarbi, Bronisław. *Cmentarz żydowski w Łodzi* (The Jewish Cemetery in Łódź). Łódź: Wydawnictwo "Artus," 1990. (P,E)

POLIN: A Journal of Polish-Jewish Studies. Vol. 6. Oxford: Blackwell, 1991.

Pukaczewski, Andrzej. *Hortus Iudaeorum: Cmentarz żydowski w Łodzi* (Garden of the Jews: The Jewish Cemetery in Łódź). Łódź: Wydawnictwo Łódzkie, 1992. (P)

Singer, Israel Joshua. *The Brothers Ashkenazi*. Translated from Yiddish by Maurice Samuel. New York: Alfred A. Knopf, 1936.

Stary cmentarz żydowski w Łodzi: dzieje i zabytki (The Old Jewish Cemetery in Łódź). Łódź: Wydawnictwo Sport i Turystka, 1989. (P)

Trunk, I. *Lodzher geto: a historishe un sotsyologishe shtudye* (Ghetto Łódź: A Historical and Sociological Study). New York: YIVO, 1962. (Y, E)

Yiddish Lodz; A Yizkor Book. Melbourne: Lodzer Center, 1974. (Y, E)

FILM

Cohen, Peter. *The Story of Chaim Rumkowski and the Jews of Łódź*. New York: The Cinema Guild, 1982.

ADDITIONAL RESOURCES

Two valuable databases are maintained by the Organization of Former Residents of Łódź in Israel, 158 Dizengoff Street, Tel Aviv 63461, Israel. One list (200,000 names) includes residents of the Łódź ghetto from February 1940 to August 1944. The second list (160,000 names) is a compilation of cemetery records from 1895 through the final liquidation in August 1944.

BIBLIOGRAPHIC SOURCES

CAHJP; CTD; EDRD; EJ; EOH; GA; GUM3; GUM4; GUM5; GUM6; HSL; JGFF; JHT; LDL; LDS; LVY; PHP1; PJH; RJHS; SF

Grand Hotel, c. 1917

13

ul. Piotrkowska and Zielona, c.1917

15

Old market square, c. 1917

14

Fragment of old market square, today

16

ul. Zielona, 1917

17

Bazaar, c. 1916

18

Plac Wolności, today

19

ul. Piotrkowska, 1917

20

ul. Dzielna, c. 1918

21

ul. Piotrkowska and Przejazd, c. 1918

22

Edward Herbst's palace, today

23

ŁOMŻA

The history of Łomża dates back to the tenth century. It received a municipal charter in 1418, and from the mid-sixteenth century, because it was granted the status of a royal town, it became an important political, cultural, religious and economic center of the Eastern Mazovia region. Jews who previously lived in Łomża were expelled in 1556 when the town granted the privilege *de non tolerandis Judaeis* [of not tolerating Jews]. They were not allowed to return until 1815. In the latter part of the nineteenth century, many Jews were involved in the grain and timber trades. By the twentieth century, Łomża had developed a politically and culturally active Jewish community represented by such institutions as a yeshiva, several Jewish schools, newspapers and political parties, and a Jewish hospital. On the eve of the Holocaust, Jews made up slightly over half the population of the town.

Łomża was in the part of Poland seized by the Soviets in 1939. In June 1941, it was occupied by the Germans, who imposed a ghetto two months later. Jews were forced to make shoes for the Germans and to clean the streets. From June to September 1941, 3,500 Jews were murdered in the nearby woods. In November 1942, the ghetto was liquidated and the Jews shipped to a camp in Zambrów, where some were murdered on the spot and others were sent to Treblinka.

Location

79 km W of Białystok
53°11′/22°04′
Voivodship: Łomża

General Population, 1939

20,000 (55% Jewish)

General Population, 1994

54,800

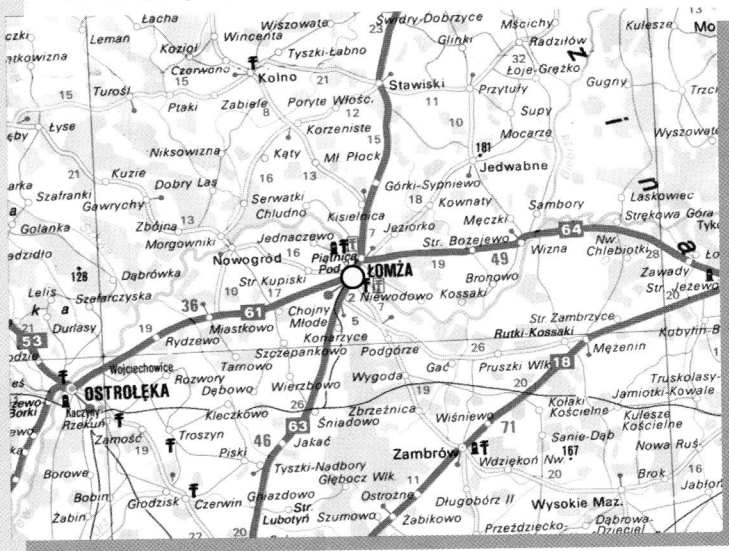

LOMZHA, LOMZHE

SYNAGOGUE

Corners of ul. *Senatorska* and *Gielczyńska*
Great Synagogue built in 1880.
Destroyed in September 1941.

Łomża today   1

Great Synagogue, c. 1917   2

Jewish cemetery, ul. Wąska 69   3

JEWISH CEMETERIES

ul. *Wąska 69*
New cemetery dates back to nineteenth century.
Remaining tombstones: 500+.

ul. *Rybki*
Old cemetery dates back to 1820.
Remaining tombstones: 200.

HOLOCAUST MEMORIALS

ul. *Senatorska 8*
Memorial plaque (site of former synagogue).

Village of Giełczyn
Memorial dedicated in 1989; commemorates place of
execution of several thousand Jews, including Jews from
Łomża.

ul. *Wąska 69 (Jewish cemetery)*
Monument.

DEPORTATIONS

Zambrów, Auschwitz-Birkenau, Treblinka.

SELECTED READING

Lewiński, Yom-Tov. *Sefer zikaron li-kehilat Lomza* (Łomża—In
Memory of the Jewish Community). Tel Aviv: Former
Residents of Łomża in Israel, 1952. (H)

Lomzhe: momentn un zikhroynes (Łomża: Moments and Memories).
New York: United Lomzer Relief Committee, 1946. (Y)

Sabotka, H., ed. *Lomzhe; ir oyfkum un untergang* (The Rise and
Fall of Łomża). New York: American Committee for the
Book of Łomża, 1957. (Y)

Shapiro, Chaim. "Lomza: A Yeshiva Grew in Poland." *The Jewish
Observer* 9/10 (1974): 13–16.

Silverman, Marlene, ed. *Landsmen*. Washington, D.C.: Suwalk-
Lomza Interest Group for Jewish Genealogists, 1990–
current (quarterly).

Holocaust memorial in nearby village of Giełczyn, 1989   4

BIBLIOGRAPHIC SOURCES

CAHJP; EDRD; EJ; GA; GUM3; GUM4; GUM5; GUM6; GYLA; HSL;
JE; JGFF; JHT; LDL; LDS; LVY; PHP4; PJH; RJHS; SF

Łomża in the distance, c. 1916   5

LUBLIN

The Jewish community of Lublin was celebrated for its commercial activity and venerable traditions of piety and scholarship. Jews lived adjacent to the city in the fourteenth century. In the sixteenth century, they acquired land within the city limits for Jewish institutions and a cemetery. Jewish merchants were active in the international Lublin trade fairs; though often opposed by Christian guilds, Jews also worked as tailors, furriers, brushmakers, brewers and bakers. Every spring at the time of the fair, the Council of the Four Lands, the supreme governing body of Polish Jews, convened in Lublin. Beginning in the sixteenth century, Lublin became a center of Hebrew printing. The city was also the site of the first great yeshiva in Poland, headed by Rabbi Shalom Shakhna (c. 1500–1558), which initiated the tradition of Talmudic scholarship for which Poland became celebrated.

Beginning in the nineteenth century, Hasidism acquired a large following in Lublin through such figures as Jacob Isaac, known as the Seer of Lublin, and the Eiger dynasty. In the second half of the century, Lublin expanded its economic importance through trade with the vast Russian market. One of the largest cigarette factories in Poland was founded by a Jew, and the tanning industry was also in Jewish hands. By the end of the century, Jewish workers in Lublin were organizing unions, and the Jewish socialist Bund became prominent. During the interwar period, in the face of mounting anti-Semitism, Lublin Jews, more than one-third of the city's population, developed a gamut of institutions and organizations: Jewish political parties, school systems, drama societies, libraries, orchestras and sports clubs. Yeshivat Hakhmei Lublin (Yeshiva of the Sages of Lublin), the most famous yeshiva in interwar Poland, founded by Rabbi Yehuda Meir Shapira, opened in an imposing new building in 1930. Although Lublin was occupied by the Germans in 1939, a ghetto was not formally imposed until March 1941. Only a year later, 30,000 Jews were deported to the death camp at Bełżec. A handful of Jews who were skilled craftsmen continued to work in Lublin; but in May 1943, the workshops were liquidated and the Jews shipped to Majdanek, the death camp that had been constructed on the outskirts of Lublin.

The Red Army liberated Lublin in July 1944, and it became the provisional capital of Poland until the liberation of Warsaw in January 1945. At first, Jewish survivors flocked to Lublin, and some Jewish cultural and social institutions were reestablished, but most of these Jews left Poland during the continuing turmoil and violence after the war.

LUBLIN

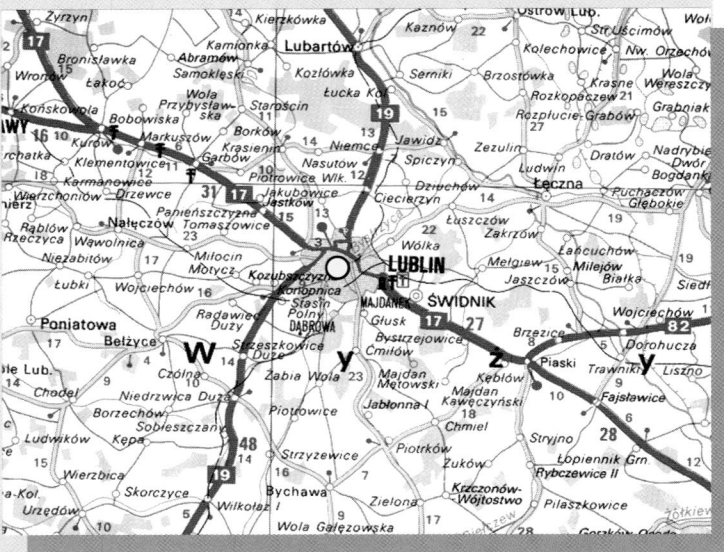

Location

161 km ESE of Warsaw
51°14´/22°34´
Voivodship: Lublin

General Population, 1939

122,000 (34% Jewish)

General Population, 1994

352,148

Exit from the Old Town to the castle and Podzamcze district; known as the Jewish Gate, pre-Holocaust

1

Interior of former Maharshal Synagogue, pre-1939   2

SYNAGOGUES

ul. Lubartowska 10
Active synagogue and museum.

Al. Tysiąclecia (formerly ul. Jałeczna)
Maharshal and Maharam Synagogues, dating from 1567, devastated in the Holocaust and subsequently destroyed by local authorities.
Memorial plaque below the castle.

Holocaust monument in new cemetery, 1991   3

JEWISH CEMETERIES

ul. Kalinowszczyzna and ul. Sienna
The old cemetery, dating from the early sixteenth century, is the oldest Jewish cemetery in Poland today. The cemetery was heavily damaged by the Nazis, but more than 100 tombstones remain, which have been partially preserved, particularly the tombstones of famous tsaddikim (rebbes or leaders). Some tombstones that had fallen were re-erected with the assistance of the Society for the Protection of Jewish Monuments.

Old Jewish cemetery, ul. Kalinowszczyzna, 1993;   4
tombstones date from the 16th century

ul. Wałęcznych
The new cemetery, founded in 1829, with several remaining tombstones, is used by the small surviving Jewish community. Restoration work financed by the Sara and Manfred Frankel Foundation of Antwerp resulted in a small modern synagogue being built and a new fence, made from symbolic tombstones, enclosing the cemetery. The new synagogue (Remembrance Chamber) was dedicated in a ceremony in 1991, attended by hundreds of people, including prominent Jews from Belgium, Israel and the United States.

ul. Leszczyńskiego (Wieniawa section of Lublin)
Site of former Jewish cemetery dating from 1828.
Current use: sports stadium.

HOLOCAUST MEMORIALS

ul. Grodzka 11
Plaque at site of Jewish orphanage records the murder of Jewish children.

ul. Rady Delegatów and ul. Hanki Sawickiej
A monument to 46,000 Holocaust victims from Lublin and environs can be found in the square between these two streets.

Remembrance Chamber, ul. *Walecznych*, 1991   6

Holocaust monument, ul. *Rady Delegatów*, 1991   5

OTHER SITES

ul. Lubartowska 85
Site of Yeshivat Hakhmei Lublin, built in 1930. Current use: Medical Academy of Lublin University.

ul. 19 Szeroka
Site of house where the Council of the Four Lands met during the sixteenth and seventeenth centuries.

ul. Lubartowska 10
Jewish community center.

ul. Lubartowska 10 (synagogue)
The Society for Care of Monuments of Jewish Culture in Lublin.

ul. Okopowa 12, apt. 3
The Social and Cultural Society of Jews in Poland.

Remembrance Chamber (rear view), 1991   7

DEPORTATIONS

Bełżec, Majdanek.

Yeshivat Hakhmei Lublin, ul. Lubartowska 85, c. 1990   8

Memorial wall at Jewish cemetery, ul. Walecznych, 1991   9

SELECTED READING

Adamczyk, Władysław. *Ceny w Lublinie od XVI do końca XVIII wieku* (Prices in Lublin from the Sixteenth to the End of the Eighteenth Centuries.). Lwów, 1935. (P)

Bałaban, Majer. "Getta miast polskich: Lublin" (The Ghettos in Polish Cities: Lublin). *Nowe Życie* 2 (1924): 61–67.

————. *Die Judenstadt von Lublin* (The Jewish Town of Lublin). Berlin: Jüdischer Verlag, 1919. (G)

Blumental, Nachman. *Te'udot mi-geto Lublin: ha mo'atsah ba-geto beli kivunim* (Documents from Lublin Ghetto: Judenrat Without Direction). Jerusalem: Yad Vashem, 1967 (H)

Blumental, Nachman, and M. Korzeń, eds. *Kerekh Lublin* (The Lublin Volume). Jerusalem: Encyclopaedia of the Jewish Diaspora, 1957. (H, Y)

ul. Namiestnikowska, c. 1917   10

Ćwik, Władysław. "Ludność żydowska w miastach królewskich Lubelszczyzny w drugiej polowie XVIII w." (Jewish Population of Royal Towns in the Lublin Region in the Second Half of the Eighteenth Century). *BŻIH* 59 (1966): 29–62. (P)

Friedberg, Bernhard. *Historiyah shel defuse Lublin* (History of Hebrew Typography in Lublin). Kraków: B. Friedberg, 1890. (H)

Friedman, Phillip. "The Lublin Reservation and the Madagascar Plan: Two Aspects of Nazi Jewish Policy During the Second World War." *YIVO Annual* 8 (1953): 151–177.

Fuks, M. "Prasa żydowska w Lublinie i na Lubelszczyźnie, 1918–1939" (The Jewish Press in Lublin and in the Lublin Region, 1918–1939). *BŻIH* 4/112 (1979): 49–65. (P)

Hotel Europejski, c. 1917   11

Kruk, Stefan. "Lubelskie występy Żydowskiego Teatru Narodowego z Odessy, 22 sierpień–17 wrzesień, 1863" (Lublin Performances of the Jewish National Theatre from Odessa, August 22–September 17, 1863). *BŻIH* 1/105 (1978): 69–81. (P)

————. "Teatr żydowski w Lublinie w latach 1916–1917" (The Jewish Theatre in Lublin in the Years 1916–1917). *BŻIH* 3–4 (1982): 123–124, 49–63. (P)

Lewin, Yitshak. "Yeshivat Ḥakheme Lublin" (Academy of the Lublin Sages). *Sefer ha-shanah/yorbukh* 2 (1967): 381–388. (H)

Mandelsberg-Szyldkraut, Bela. *Meḥkarim le-toledot yehude Lublin* (Studies in the History of Lublin Jewry). Tel Aviv: B. Mandelsberg-Szyldkraut, 1965. (H)

Marszałek, Józef. *Majdanek: The Concentration Camp in Lublin*. Warsaw: Interpress, 1986.

ul. Krakowskie Przedmieście, today   12

Moldawer, S. "The Road to Lublin." *Contemporary Jewish Record* (March–April 1940): 119–133.

Nissenbaum, Solomon Baruch. *Le-korot ha-yehudim be-Lublin* (History of the Jews in Lublin). Lublin: M. M. Shnaidmesser, 1920. (H)

Opas, Tomasz. "Sytuacja ludności żydowskiej w miastach szlacheckich województwa lubelskiego w XVIII wieku" (Jews in Towns Owned by Nobles in the Lublin Region in the Eighteenth Century). BŻIH 67 (1968): 3–37. (P)

Roszgold, Mosze, ed. *Dos bukh fun Lublin* (The Memorial Book of Lublin). Paris: Former Residents of Lublin in Paris, 1952. (Y)

Old view, c. 1917   13

Seidman, Hillel. *Szlakiem nauki Talmudycznej: wiedza judaistyczna i wyższa Uczelnia Talmudyczna w Lublinie* (On the Path of Talmudic Learning: Judaic Scholarship and the Higher Talmudic School in Lublin). Warsaw: F. Hoesick, 1934. (P)

Shapira, Meyer. "Dos toyre lernen: religyeze yeshives un Yeshives khokhmey Lublin" (The Teaching of Torah: Religious Academies and the Yeshivat Ḥakheme Lublin). *Der Yud* 38 (Nov. 2, 1928): 7–8. (Y)

Shemen, Nachman. *Lublin, Shtot fun toyre, rabones un khsidizm.* (Lublin: City of Torah, Rabbinics and Piety). Toronto: Pomer Publishing, 1951. (Y)

Plac Zebrań Ludowych, location of former Jewish quarter, 1976   14

ul. Krakowskie Przedmieście, 1916   15

BIBLIOGRAPHIC SOURCES

CAHJP; CTD; EDRD; EJ; EOH; GA; GUM3; GUM4; GUM5; GUM6; HSL; JE; JGFF; JHT; LDL; LDS; LVY; PJH; RJHS; SF

Lublin, c. 1917 (see photo #18 without Hertzman store) 16

Lublin, c. 1971 (see photo #16) 18

Majdanek Death Camp

Established in 1941, the Majdanek Death Camp was located on the outskirts of Lublin and is preserved by the Polish government as a monument. On November 3, 1943, about 19,000 Jews were shot and buried in an area that is visible to this day in the form of shallow ravines. It is estimated that more than 350,000 people were murdered here, including more than 100,000 Jews from the Warsaw and Lublin ghettos. When Red Army units arrived in July 1944, they found only a few hundred surviving prisoners, though the camp itself was largely intact. A memorial made from a huge mound of human ashes commemorates the victims, and near the camp entrance is a huge monument in the form of a menorah. There is also a museum and archives (see Chapter 6).

Grodzka gate (Jewish gate) to Old Town, c. 1990 19

Corner of ul. Mostowa and Jałeczna, c. 1905 17

Krakowska gate, c. 1917 20

Międzyrzec, the property of some of the most celebrated noble families in Poland, was incorporated as a town in the fifteenth century. There are records of Jews living in the town in the sixteenth century; an official Jewish community existed by the mid-seventeenth century. The town's owners, particularly the Czartoryskis in the eighteenth century, encouraged Jewish settlement. Międzyrzec developed as a commercial center and became known for its biannual fairs, in which local Jews played a prominent role. By the mid-nineteenth century, Hasidism had won many adherents in the town. In 1863, local Jewish craftsmen assisted Polish rebels in their doomed uprising against the Russians. By the end of the nineteenth century, Jewish workers employed in sawmills, tanneries, clothing manufacture and transport began to organize into unions. In the interwar period, most Jewish political parties were represented here; there was a range of educational institutions, including Orthodox, Hebrew and Yiddish schools; there was also a local Yiddish weekly. On the eve of the Holocaust, the 12,000 Jews in Międzyrzec comprised approximately 75 percent of the town's population.

During the first year of the German occupation, Jews from other cities and towns both near and far (including several thousand Czech and Slovak Jews) were forced to settle in Międzyrzec. During the second half of 1942, more than 11,000 Jews were deported to various camps, primarily Treblinka, where they were murdered. During this period, a ghetto was briefly established. A second ghetto was created at the end of 1942; it was liquidated in mid-1943, with the deportation of its inmates to Treblinka and Majdanek. After the war, about 100 Jewish survivors tried briefly to re-establish a Jewish community.

Location

99 km N of Lublin
51°59′/22°48′
Vovoidship: Biała Podlaska

General Population, 1939

16,000 (75% Jewish)

General Population, 1994

55,889

MEZERITZ

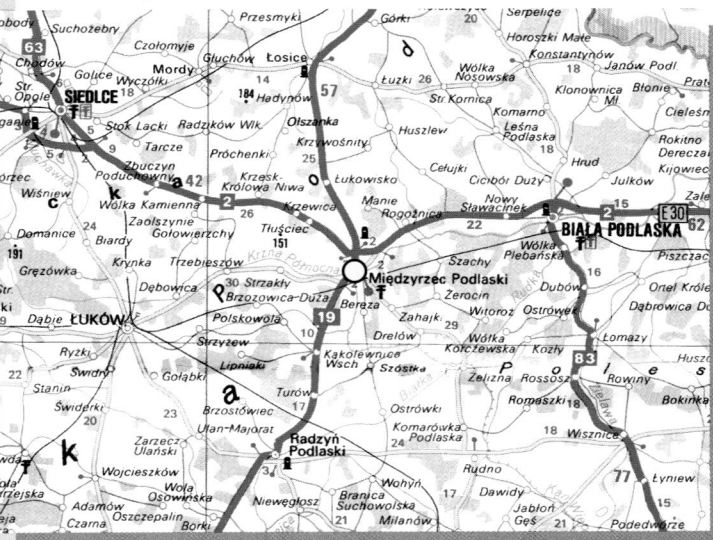

SYNAGOGUE

ul. Nassuta, Poprzeczna and Nadbrzezna
Synagogue destroyed during the Holocaust.
Current site use: apartment complex.

Synagogue, c. 1919   1

Former Jewish region, now part of town square, 1997   2

ul. *Brzeska 60, Jewish cemetery, 1997*   3

JEWISH CEMETERY

ul. *Brzeska 60*
Founded in the nineteenth century next to the old cemetery. Tombstones are from both the old and new cemeteries, with the oldest dating from 1708. Remaining tombstones: 200.

HOLOCAUST MEMORIAL

ul. *Brzeska 60 (Jewish cemetery)*
Monument to Jewish victims from Międzyrzec and surrounding towns.

ul. *Brzeska 60, Jewish cemetery, 1997;*   4
Holocaust monument

DEPORTATIONS

Treblinka, Trawniki, Majdanek.

SELECTED READING

Aryeh, Mendl. *Zikhroynes fun mayn alter heym, Mezritsh* (Memoirs of My Old Home, Miedzyrzec). Haifa: M. Aryeh, 1966. (Y)

Edelboim, Meir. *Di yidn-shtot Mezritsh; fun ir breyshis biz erev der velt-milkhome* (*Historia de Mezritch* [*Mezritch Podlasie*]; *su población judia* [History of the Jewish Population of Międzyrzec]). Buenos Aires: Sociedad de Residentes de Mezritch en la Argentina, 1957. (Y)

Heller, Binem, and Yitzhak Ronkin, eds. *Sefer Mezritsh; lezeykher di kdoyshim fun undzer shtot* (Mezritsh Book, in Memory of the Martyrs of Our City). Tel Aviv: Mezritsh Societies in Israel and the Diaspora, 1978. (H, Y)

ul. *Brzeska 60, Jewish cemetery, 1997;*   5
portion of wall made from tombstone fragments

Hendl, M. "Mezritsher pinkeysim" (Międzyrzec Record Books). *YIVO Bleter* 8, no. 1 (Jan. 1935): 61–67. (Y)

Horn, Jose. *Mayn Khoreve heym, a idish shtetl in Poyln tsvishn beyde velt-milkhome* (My Destroyed Home: A Jewish Town in Poland Between the World Wars). Buenos Aires: Cultura, 1946. (Y)

Horn, Y., ed. *Mezritsh; zamlbukh* (The Mezritsh Volume). Buenos Aires: Association of Former Residents of Mezritsh in Argentina, 1952. (Y)

Lazar, Mordechai. *Le-hisared ule-saper* (To Survive and to Tell). Tel Aviv: M. Lazar, 1990. (H)

Rylski, H. "Mezritsh in period fun der hitlerisher okupatsye" (Międzyrzec in the Period of Hitler's Occupation). *Bleter far geshikhte* 8, no. 3/4 (July–Dec. 1955): 34–50. (Y)

BIBLIOGRAPHIC SOURCES

CAHJP; CTD; EDRD; EJ; FRG; GA; GUM3; GUM4; GUM5; GUM6; GYLA; HSL; JGFF; JHT; KH; LDL; LDS; LYV; PJH; RJHS; SF

NOWY SĄCZ

Established in 1292 on a trade route between Poland and Hungary, Nowy Sącz became an important commercial center. By the fifteenth century, it was the fourth-largest city of Małopolska (Little Poland), after Kraków, Sandomierz and Lublin. The Jewish presence in Nowy Sącz is attested in a document from 1469, but it was not until 1676 that a royal privilege granted Jews the right to build houses and engage in commerce. Jews played an important role in trade, carpentry, tailoring and engraving.

Taking advantage of the political chaos in Poland, Austrian authorities took over Nowy Sącz in 1770, two years before the first partition of the Polish Commonwealth. Under Austrian rule, the once prosperous city declined, its population decreased significantly, and the Jews were compelled to live in a special quarter. In the early nineteenth century, the Zanzer (from Zanz, the Jewish name of the town) Hasidic dynasty was founded in Nowy Sącz by Rebbe Chaim Ben Arieh Leib Halberstam. During the interwar period, the community supported several Jewish schools, a yeshiva, a hospital, and various sports clubs.

Following the German occupation of Nowy Sącz, the Nazis established a ghetto in July 1941. In the following year, they created forced-labor camps in Ronów and Lipie. In the ghetto, Jews worked for the Germans as tailors, shoemakers, and carpenters, and they also loaded and unloaded trains. The ghetto was liquidated in August 1942. The Jews from Nowy Sącz were murdered in the Bełżec death camp.

Location

97 km ESE of Kraków
49°37´/20°42´
Vovoidship: Nowy Sącz

General Population, 1939

31,000 (34% Jewish)

General Population, 1994

62,568

SYNAGOGUES

ul. Bóżnicza 1 [Synagogue Street]
The Great Synagogue was constructed in 1746.
Current use: art museum (Muzeum Okręgowe).

ul. Jagiellońska 50
Current use: apartments.

Synagogue, ul. Bóżnicza 1, c. 1968   1

JEWISH CEMETERY

ul. Rybacka 12
From 25,000 burials, 200 tombstones remain.

DEPORTATIONS

Bełżec.

Jewish cemetery, ul. Rybacka 12, 1993 2

Holocaust memorial in Jewish cemetery, 1993 3

HOLOCAUST MEMORIAL

ul. Rybacka 12 (Jewish cemetery)
A monument commemorates the sites of mass executions of 25,000 Jews.

ul. Krakowska, c. 1915 4

SELECTED READING

Krupiński, Andrzej B. *Dawna synagoga nowosądecka* (The Old Synagogue in Nowy Sącz). Nowy Sącz: Muzeum Okręgowe w Nowym Sączu: 1985. (P)

Mahler, Raphael. *Mekorot le-toledot kehilat yehudit be-Polin (Tsants)* (Sources for the History of the Jewish Community in Poland [Santz]). Tel Aviv: Tel Aviv University, 1963. (H)

————. "Z dziejów Żydów w Nowym Sączu w XVII i XVIII wieku" (Chapters in the History of the Jews in Nowy Sącz in the Seventeenth and Eighteenth Centuries). BŻIH 55 (1965): 3–32; 56 (1965): 28–58. (P)

Nowy Sącz, today 5

Mahler, Raphael, ed. *Sefer Sants* (The Book of Sants). New York: Former Residents of Sants in New York, 1970. (H, Y)

Podhorizer-Sandel, E. "O zagładzie Żydów w dystrykcie krakowskim" (On the Extermination of the Jews in Kraków District). BŻIH 30 (1959): 87–109. (P)

Sygański, Jan. *Historia Nowego Sącza* (History of Nowy Sącz). 3 vols. Lwów: J. Sygański, 1901–1902. (P)

————. *Nowy Sącz, jego dzieje i pamiątki. Szkic historyczny* (Nowy Sącz, Its History and Monuments. A Historical Sketch). Nowy Sącz: Urzędu Miejskiego w Nowym Sączu, 1892. (P)

Tefuhah, Ya'akovi, ed. *Le-zekher kehilat Tsants* (In Memory of the Community of Tsants). Jerusalem: Bet ha-sefer hatikhon ha-dati la-banot Oylinah di Rotshild, 1967–1968. (H)

BIBLIOGRAPHIC SOURCES

CAHJP; CTD; EDRD; EJ; GA; GUM3; GUM4; GUM5; GUM6; GYLA; HSL; JGFF; JHT; LDL; LYV; PHP3; PJH; RJHS; SF

OTWOCK

OTVOSK, OTVOTSK, USHVOTSK, OSHVOTSK

Otwock, located just south of Warsaw, is mentioned in fifteenth-century sources, but a Jewish community there dates only from the late nineteenth century. When a Hasidic dynasty established itself in the town, a Jewish community formed around the rebbe's residence and study house, built in the middle of the surrounding forest. In 1893, Dr. J. Geisler opened a sanatorium for people suffering from tuberculosis, and Otwock soon developed into a fashionable health resort attracting particularly middle-class Jews from Warsaw and central Poland.

In the fall of 1940, the Germans imposed a ghetto in Otwock, through which passed more than 12,000 Jews from Otwock and the surrounding area. Some 2,000 Jews died of hunger and typhus, and another 2,000 were shot during the ghetto's liquidation in August 1942. The remaining Jews were deported to Treblinka. About 400 Jews settled in Otwock after the war; a home for Jewish children and a Jewish sanatorium functioned for several years.

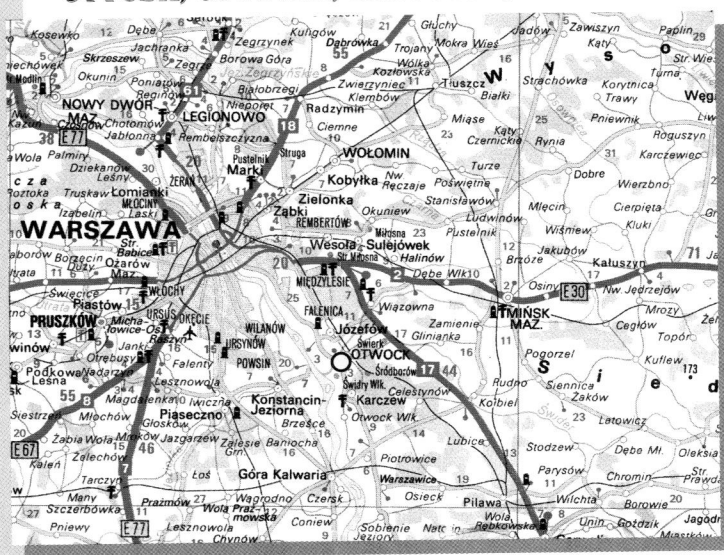

Location

27 km ESE of Warsaw
52°07′/21°15′
Voivodship: Warsaw

General Population, 1939

30,000 (45% Jewish)

General Population, 1994

43,719

SYNAGOGUES

All five synagogues burned in October 1939.

ul. *Górna* 6
Bet Midrash Reindorf (Mikvah was next door).

ul. *Warszawska* 41
Bet ha-Keneset Goldberg.

ul. *Kupiecka* (formerly *Aleksandrova*)
Bet Midrash Blas.

ul. *Reymonta* and *Zeromskiego*
Bet ha-Keneset Weinberg.

ul. *Zeromskiego* (continuation of ul. *Warszawska*)
Bet ha-Keneset Jablonski.

DEPORTATIONS

Tyszowce, Treblinka.

■ ul. *Kościelna*, 1929   1   ■ *Former synagogue, Bet Midrash Reindorf, ul. Górna 6*   2

Jewish cemetery in Anielin (includes Otwock burials), 1995　　3

JEWISH CEMETERIES

In nearby village of Anielin
The cemetery was established in the nineteenth century.
Remaining tombstones: 200, dating from 1915.

ul. Szkolna (in nearby Karczew)
Remaining tombstones: 50, dating from 1876.

Jewish cemetery in Karczew (includes Otwock burials), 1996　　4

HOLOCAUST MEMORIAL

Monument at ul. Reymonta, where more than 6,000 Jews in the Otwock ghetto were shot between August 19 and 30, 1942.

Holocaust memorial, ul. Reymonta, 1995　　5

SELECTED READING

Fox, Frank, ed. and trans. *Am I a Murderer? Testament of a Jewish Ghetto Policeman.* Boulder, CO: Westview Press, 1996. (Translation of Calel Perechodnik, *Czy ja jestem morderca?* [Am I a Murderer?]). Warsaw: Karta, 1993.) (P)

Kanc, Shimon, ed. *Yisker bukh: Otvotsk-Kartshev* (Memorial Book: Otwock-Karczew). Tel Aviv: Former Residents of Otvozk-Kartshev, 1968. (H,Y)

Sanatorium (resort), c. 1990　　6

Oliwa, Franciszek. "Dom Ocalonych Dzieci w Otwocku 1945–1949" (The Home of Saved Children in Otwock: 1945–1949). BŻIH 3–4/139–140 (1986): 89–105. (P)

Orenstein, Benjamin. *Khurbn Otvotsk, Falenits, Kartshev* (The Destruction of Otvotsk, Falenits, Kartshev). Bamberg, Germany: Former Residents of Otvotsk, Falenits and Kartshev in the American Zone in Germany, 1948. (Y)

Train station, c. 1985　　7

BIBLIOGRAPHIC SOURCES

CTD; EDRD; EJ; FRG; GA; GUM3; GUM4; GUM5; GUM6; HSL; JGFF; KH; PHP4; PJH; RJHS; SF

PIOTRKÓW TRYBUNALSKI

Jews were granted rights to settle in designated areas of Piotrków in the mid-sixteenth century, but were expelled following a blood libel (accusation of ritual murder) in 1590. In 1679, the Polish king Jan Sobieski granted permission for Jews to return, conduct trade, and build a synagogue. After the partitions of the Polish Commonwealth, Piotrków passed first to Prussia and then to the czars. The city profited from the opening of a railway line connecting Warsaw and Vienna, and from the development of industry in central Poland in the mid-nineteenth century. Jews founded textile mills in Piotrków; Jewish workers were employed in the timber and textile industries. In 1861, as part of a series of Russian reforms in central Poland, Jews obtained the right to vote and stand for election to the municipal council.

Piotrków became an important Jewish cultural and religious center, fueled by a thriving Hebrew press and other publishing activities. During the interwar period, most Jewish political parties were represented in Piotrków. There were three weekly Yiddish newspapers, a Jewish musical society and numerous other associations and institutions. Particularly well known was Rabbi Yehuda Meir Shapira, the community's chief rabbi from 1924 to 1931. Shapira was a member of the Polish Parliament from the religious Agudes Israel Party, and the founder and head of Yeshivat Hakhmei Lublin (Yeshiva of the Sages of Lublin), the modern religious seminary in Lublin that was celebrated in Poland and in Jewish communities throughout the world.

The ghetto in Piotrków Trybunalski was established by the Germans on October 8, 1939, making it the first in German-occupied Poland. The ghetto swelled with refugees from surrounding towns, and by October 1942, numbered about 25,000 Jews. At the end of that month, some 22,000 Jews were deported to the Treblinka death camp. The remainder worked at slave labor, but nearly all of them were murdered by 1944. Several hundred Jews managed to escape the ghetto and join partisans in the surrounding forests. A number of Piotrków's sons became prominent figures in Jewish political and religious affairs after the war. Among them were Israel Meir Lau, later the chief rabbi of Israel, and Naphtali Lau-Lavie, later the Israeli ambassador to the United States.

Location
    42 km SSE of Łódź
    51°24′/19°41′
    Voivodship: Piotrków Trybunalski
General Population, 1939
    54,000 (33% Jewish)
General Population, 1994
    81,479

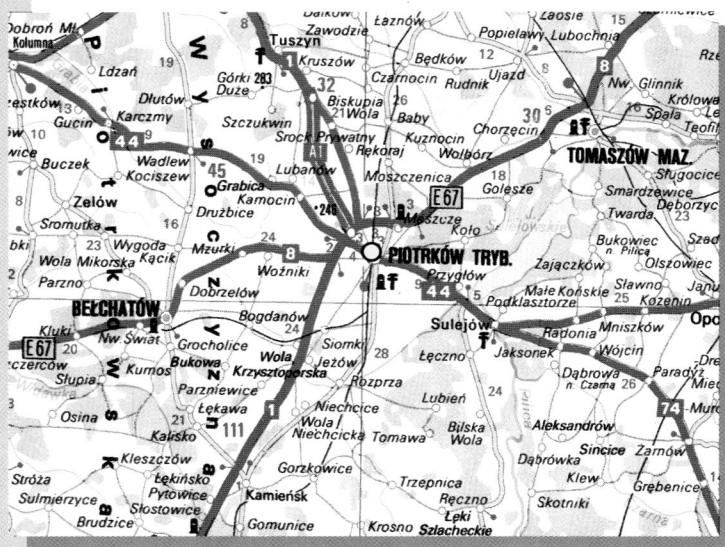

PETRIKAU, PETRIKAU, PETROKOW, PIOTRKOW

SYNAGOGUES

ul. Jerozolimska
Large synagogue dates from the nineteenth century.
Rebuilt in 1964.
Current use: public library.

ul. Jerozolimska (adjacent to Large Synagogue)
Small synagogue built in 1781.
Current use: children's library.
A large Hebrew mural is still visible behind the stacks.

DEPORTATIONS

Buchenwald, Bergen-Belsen, Treblinka, Mauthausen, Ravensbrück.

HOLOCAUST MEMORIAL

ul. Spacerowa (Jewish cemetery)
A symbolic grave where ghetto inhabitants were executed (1940–1943).

▌ Piotrków Synagogue, ul. Jerozolimska, 1995

Piotrków cemetery, 1995   2

JEWISH CEMETERIES

ul. Spacerowa 93
Tombstones date from 1795.
Remaining tombstones: 1,000+.

Staro-Warszawska and Zamurowa Streets, c. 1917   3

ul. Wojska Polskiego
Cemetery completely destroyed (dating from 1677).
Current use: grassy area directly behind
the large synagogue.

Segment of Plac Trybunalski, today   4

SELECTED READING

Baranowski, Jerzy, and Henryk Jaworowski. "Historia i rozwój przetrzenny synagogi w Piotrkowie Trybunalskim" (The History and Development of the Synagogue in Piotrków Trybunalski). BŻIH 57 (1966): 121–133. (P)

Birnbaum, Jacob. "Piotrków Trybunalski: The Last Chapter." In Roman Mogilanski, The Ghetto Anthology. Los Angeles: American Congress of Jews from Poland, 1985.

Eisenbach, A. "Materiały do struktury, działalności gospodarczej ludności żydowskiej w Królestwie Polskim w latach osiemdziesiątych XIX wieku" (Material About the Economic Structure and Activity of the Jewish Population in the Kingdom of Poland in the Eighties of the Nineteenth Century). BŻIH 29 (1959): 72–111. (P)

Feinkind, Mojżesz. Dzieje Żydów w Piotrkowie i okolicy (History of the Jews in Piotrków and Environs). Piotrków: Nakład własny, 1930. (P)

Fijałek, Jan. "Do zagadnienia szpitalnictwa żydowskiego w Piotrkowie Trybunalskim w połowie XIX w." (Concerning the Jewish Hospitals in Piotrków Trybunalski in the Mid-Nineteenth Century). BŻIH 31 (July–Sept. 1959): 38–56. (P)

Giladi, Ben, ed. A Tale of One City: Piotrków Trybunalski. New York: Shengold Publishers, 1991.

Lubliner, Michael. "The Purim Massacre in Piotrków." In Roman Mogilanski, The Ghetto Anthology. Los Angeles: American Congress of Jews from Poland, 1985.

Melz, Yaakov, and N. (Lavy) Lau, eds. Piotrkov-Tribunalski vehasevivah: sefer zikaron (Piotrków Trybunalski and Vicinity: A Memorial Book). Tel Aviv: Former Residents of Piotrków Trybunalski in Israel, 1965. (H, Y, E)

Sanik, Leibel. Someday We'll Be Free. New York: C.I.S. Publishers, 1994.

Socken, Rochele: "Reflection: Piotrków Revisited." New Bulletin 13 (Jan.–Feb. 1986): 14–17.

BIBLIOGRAPHIC SOURCES

CAHJP; CTD; EDRD; EJ; EOH; GA; GUM3; GUM4; GUM5; GUM6; GYLA; HSL; JE; JGFF; JHT; KH; LDL; LDS; LVY; PHP1; PJH; RJHS; SF

PŁOCK

The history of Płock goes back to the eleventh century, when its location on the crossroads of two major trade routes determined its strategic, political and economic importance. In 1237, Płock was the first town in the Mazovia region to receive a municipal charter. The Płock Jewish community, dating to the early thirteenth century, was one of the oldest in Poland. The Jews were initially engaged in money-lending; but, after King Zygmunt August granted them economic rights in 1555 equal to those of other citizens, they became involved in trade and crafts.

The first synagogue was established in 1534 and served a community of 600 strong. After the partitions of the Polish Commonwealth, Płock passed first under Prussian and then Russian rule. By the beginning of the twentieth century, Jews were employed in commerce, clothing and metal industries, food processing and printing. Płock was a stronghold of the Jewish socialist Bund, the Zionist Socialists and the Po'alei Zion (workers of Zion) movements. Płock's prominent Jewish citizens included the Yiddish writer Sholem Asch and two important Zionist leaders, Nahum Sokolow and Yitzhak Gruenbaum; the latter, who served in the Polish Parliament, was the most popular Jewish political leader in interwar Poland.

Soon after the Germans occupied the city on September 9, 1939, they imposed a ghetto. Two major deportations, on February 20 and February 28, 1941, nearly wiped out the Jewish community. Only some 100 Jews survived. A handful of Jews settled briefly in Płock after the war.

Location

104 km N of Łódź
52°33′/19°42′
Voivodship: Płock

General Population, 1939

30,000 (33% Jewish)

General Population, 1994

126,325

PLOTSK, PLOTZK

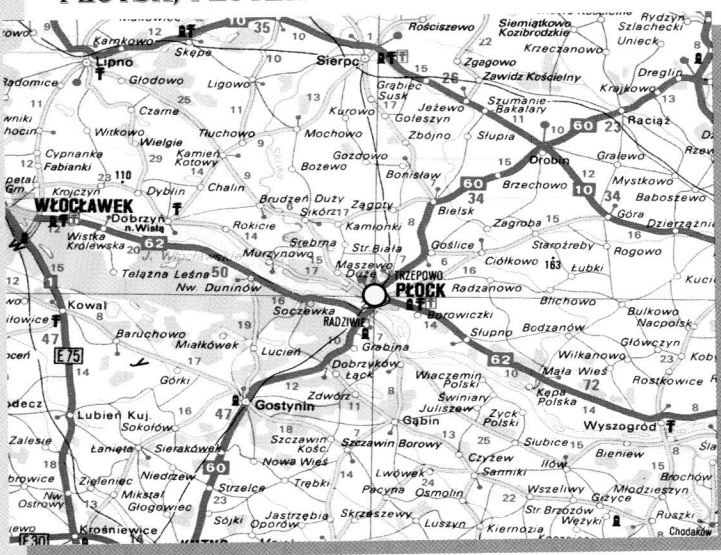

SYNAGOGUE

ul. Kwiatka 7
Synagogue dates from 1810.
Current use: abandoned factory.

▌ Synagogue, ul. Kwiatka 7   1

▌ Płock, c. 1917   2

Remnants of Jewish cemetery, ul. Mickiewicza, 1994   3

JEWISH CEMETERIES

ul. 3 Maja 3
Cemetery, dating from the 1700s.
Completely destroyed.
Current site use: high school.

ul. Mickiewicza (formerly ul. Sportowa)
Cemetery (dating from 1845) was heavily damaged;
several tombstones remain, and additional fragments are
encased in a memorial wall.

HOLOCAUST MEMORIAL

ul. Mickiewicza (Jewish cemetery)
Memorial to Holocaust victims from Płock who were
killed in the camps.

DEPORTATIONS

Działdowo, Treblinka, Sobibór, Auschwitz-Birkenau,
Bełżec.

Płock today   4

SELECTED READING

Benoit-Lapierre, Nicole. *Le Silence de la memoire: A la recherche des juifs de Płock* (The Silence of Memory: In Search of the Jews of Płock). Paris: Plon, 1989. (F)

Eisenberg, Eliyahu, ed. *Plotsk; toledot kehilah `atikat yomin, be-Polin* (Płock; A History of an Ancient Jewish Community in Poland). Tel Aviv: World Committee for the Plotzk Memorial Book, 1967. (H, Y, E)

Greenspan, S. *Yidn in Plotsk* (Jews in Płock). New York, 1960. (Y)

Horn, Yosef, ed. *Plotsk; bletlekh geshikhte fun idishn lebn in der alter heym* (Płock; Pages of History of Jewish Life in the Old Hometown of Płock). Buenos Aires: Sociedad de Residentes de Płock en la Argentina, 1945. (Y)

Entrance to Jewish cemetery, ul. Mickiewicza, 1994   5

ul. Grodzka, c. 1917   6

Przedpełski, Jan. *Żydzi płoccy, dzieje; martyrologia 1939–1945* (The Jews of Płock: History, Martyrology, 1939–1945). Płock: Fraza, 1993. (P)

Trunk, Isaiah. *Di geshikhte fun di yidn in Plotsk, 1237–1657* (The History of Jews in Płock, 1237–1657). Warsaw: Yidisher Visnshafrlekher Institut, 1939. (Y)

BIBLIOGRAPHIC SOURCES

CAHJP; EDRD; EJ; GA; GUM3; GUM4; GUM5; GUM6; GYLA; HSL; JE; JGFF; JHT; LDL; LDS; LVY; PHP4; PJH; RJHS; SF

PRZEMYŚL

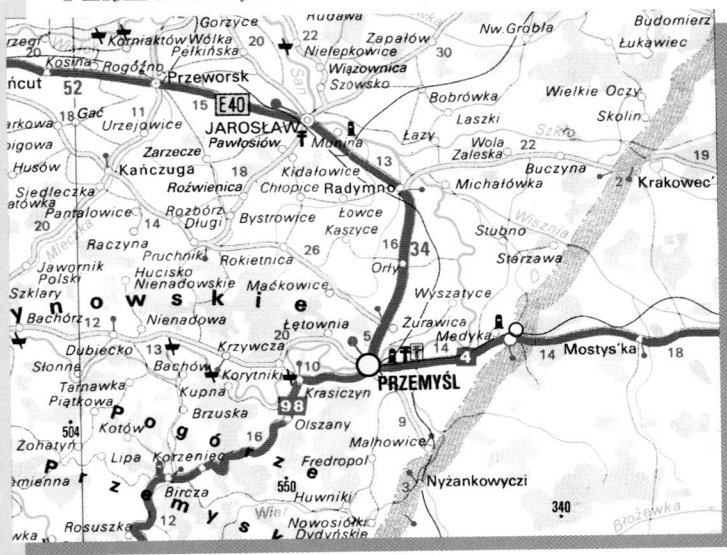

Przemyśl, located on important medieval trade routes, is one of the oldest towns in Poland. According to a Hebrew source, in the eleventh century the city had a significant colony of Khazar Jewish merchants (Khazars were a Central Asian tribe said to have converted to Judaism). In the fourteenth century, the city and its region became part of Poland; Polish kings granted the Jewish community charters of rights in the sixteenth century, and the city experienced growing prosperity as trading links developed with the port city of Gdańsk (Danzig) and later with Silesia and Hamburg. Przemyśl became an important center of trade in salt, freshwater fish and livestock.

The city and its Jews suffered greatly during the economic and political decline of the Polish Commonwealth in the eighteenth century. Under the Austrians, who ruled from 1772 to 1919, there were at first new restrictions on Jews, but also new educational and political opportunities; in the nineteenth century, half the members of the Przemyśl city council were Jews. By the interwar period in independent Poland, most Jewish political parties, including various Zionist parties, the Jewish socialist Bund, the orthodox Agudas Israel and the Folkist Party, were active in Przemyśl. The city was the home of Mojżesz Schorr, an outstanding Assyriologist and historian of the Przemyśl Jewish community.

In September 1939, Przemyśl was briefly, but brutally, occupied by the Germans, who then turned it over to the Soviets. In June 1941, the city fell to the Germans, who immediately deported 12,500 Jews to the Bełżec death camp. They established a ghetto for the remainder, who were also subjected to periodic deportations until the ghetto was liquidated in September 1943 with the deportation of 3,500 Jews to Auschwitz-Birkenau. In April 1943, a group of young Jews fled the ghetto hoping to join partisans in the nearby woods, but they were all killed. Under the auspices of the Red Army, which liberated the city in July 1944, some Jewish communal activity resumed and continued for several years under the postwar Polish government.

Location

185 km S of Lublin
49°48´/22°47´
Voivodship: Przemyśl

General Population, 1939

80,000 (33% Jewish)

General Population, 1994

71,000

SYNAGOGUES

ul. Słowackiego 15
Steinbach Synagogue, constructed in 1910.
Current use: library.

ul. Unii Brzeskiej 6, Zasanie Quarter
Synagogue constructed in 1890.
Current use: office.

JEWISH CEMETERIES

ul. Słowackiego
Cemetery founded in 1822.
Remaining tombstones: 1,000.
Holocaust memorial in cemetery.

ul. Rakoczego
Former cemetery, completely destroyed.
Current use: vegetable garden.

Former Steinbach Synagogue (right) in Przemyśl, now a library, 1976

1

HOLOCAUST MEMORIALS

ul. *Kopernika 14*
Memorial tablet erected in 1956 at place where 2,000 Jews died in the ghetto.

▌ *Holocaust memorial,*   2
▌ *ul. Kopernika 14, 1956*

Near Fort Kunkowce
Monument to Jews who died in small ghetto.

DEPORTATIONS

Bełżec, Auschwitz-Birkenau, Janowska camp in Lwów.

▌ *Market square, c. 1915*   3

▌ *Market square, today*   4

SELECTED READING

Bałaban, Majer. "Z historii Żydow w Polsce: szkice i studia" (Essays and Studies on the History of the Jews in Poland). *Warsaw* (1920): 147–154. (P)

Menczer, Arie, ed. *Sefer Pshemishel* (Przemyśl Memorial Book). Tel Aviv: Former Residents of Przemyśl in Israel, 1964. (H, Y)

Schorr, Moses. *Aus der Geschichte der Juden in Przemysl, Eine Skitze* (Jewish History in Przemyśl: A Sketch). Vienna: R. Lowitt, 1915. (G)

▌ *Jewish cemetery, ul. Słowackiego, 1994*   5

Schorr, Mojżesz. *Żydzi w Przemyślu do końca XVIII wieku, wyjaśnienie i publikacja materiału archiwalnego* (Jews in Przemyśl Until the End of the Eighteenth Century: Elaboration and Publication of Archival Material). Lwów: Nakładem Funduszu Konkursowego, 1903. (P, H)

Warschauer, Adolf. "Żydzi" (The Jews). In *Catalogue of the Archives of Old Documents of the Town of Przemyśl.* Przemyśl, 1927, pp. 190–198; 591–594. (P)

Wierzbieniec, Wacław. *Społeczność żydowska Przemyśla w latach 1918–1939* (The Jewish People of Przemyśl in the Years 1918–1939). Rzeszów: Wydawnictwo Wyższej Szkoły Pedagogicznej, 1996. (P, E)

BIBLIOGRAPHIC SOURCES

CAHJP; COH; CTD; EDRD; EJ; EOH; ER; FRG; GA; GUM3; GUM4; GUM5; GUM6; GYLA; HSL; JE; JGFF; LDL; LYV; PHP2; PJH; RJHS; SF

RADOM

The Jewish community of Radom was relatively young. Although Jews first appeared in the city in the seventeenth century—primarily to attend sessions of the Polish Parliament or negotiate with the tribunal of the treasury—they were not permitted to settle in Radom until late in the eighteenth century. An organized community was formed only in the early nineteenth century; a cemetery was established in 1831, and the first synagogue was built in 1884. By the end of the century, there were 11,000 Jews in Radom, active in commerce and as entrepreneurs and workers in leather, iron and ceramics production. Many Radom Jews were Hasidim, but by the interwar period, there were increasing numbers of acculturating secular Jews. A daily Yiddish newspaper was published in the city as well as a number of Yiddish weeklies and a Polish-language weekly for Jews.

The Germans occupied Radom in September 1939 and in April 1941 established two separate ghettos. In August 1942, both ghettos were liquidated and most of their 30,000 inhabitants shipped to Treblinka and other death camps. Several thousand were spared to perform forced labor for the Germans, but they also were gradually murdered. Hundreds of Jews fled to the woods during the deportations to fight with partisan units; they were all killed in battle. Soviet troops found 300 surviving Jews in Radom when they liberated the city in January 1945. Several hundred Jews settled in the city after the war, but, faced with political turmoil and hostility, they soon left.

Location

103 km S of Warsaw
51°24′/21°10′
Voivodship: Radom

General Population, 1939

90,000 (33% Jewish)

General Population, 1994

232,135

RODEM

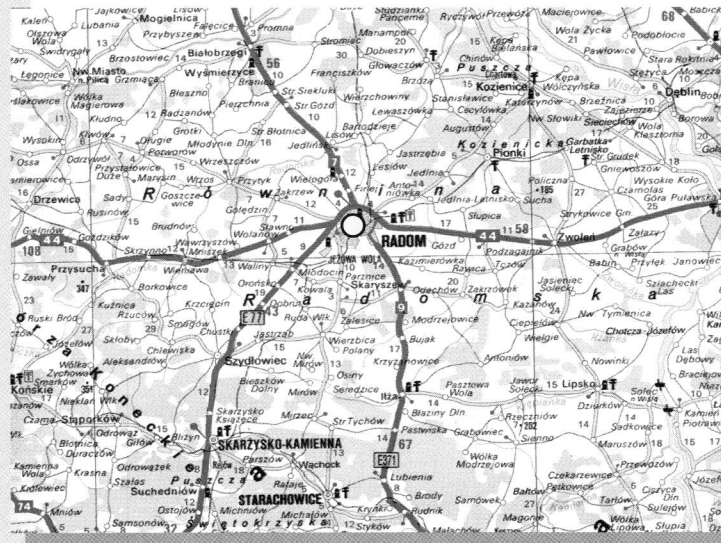

SYNAGOGUES

ul. Bóżnicza (Synagogue Street)
Great Synagogue was destroyed by the Nazis, along with all other synagogues.

■ *Aged Home Synagogue, interior, pre-1939*　　　　1

DEPORTATIONS

Auschwitz-Birkenau, Treblinka.

Plaque at base of Holocaust memorial, 1990   2

Holocaust memorial at site of former synagogue, 1995   5

JEWISH CEMETERY

ul. Towarowa
Cemetery was founded in 1831 and devastated during the
Holocaust.
Remaining tombstones: 500.
In 1984, Radom survivors in Israel built a new gate and
wrought-iron fence around the cemetery.

HOLOCAUST MEMORIAL

ul. Bóżnicza (Synagogue Street)
Memorial to 33,000 Jews killed from Radom ghetto.

Entrance to Jewish cemetery, ul. Towarowa, 1994   3

Plac 800-lecia, 1992   6

Jewish cemetery, ul. Towarowa, 1994   4

ul. Rwańska, c. 1917   7

SELECTED READING

Dos yidishe Radom in khurves; ondenkbukh (The Havoc of Jewish Radom; Memorial Book). Stuttgart: The Committee of Radom Jews in Stuttgart, 1948. (Y)

Friedman, Towiah. *Toldot kehilat yehude Radom bi-tekufat ha-shoah 1939–1945* (The History of the Jews of Radom During the Holocaust 1939–1945). 3 vols. Jerusalem: Hebrew University, 1974. (H)

Habas, Bracha. "How the Jewish Community of Radom Was Exterminated." *Jewish Frontier* (May 1943): 7–12.

Lipson, Alfred, ed. *The Book of Radom: The Story of a Jewish Community in Poland Destroyed by the Nazis.* New York: United Radomer Relief of the United States and Canada, 1963.

Street scene, 1990   8

Luboński, Jan. *Monografja historyczna miasta Radomia* (A Historical Monograph on the City of Radom). Radom: Gebethner and Wolff, 1907. (P)

Penkalla, Adam. *Żydowskie ślady w województwie kieleckim i radomskim* (Traces of Jews in Kielce and Radom Voivodships). Radom: Tramp, 1992. (P)

Penkalla, Adam, and Jerzy Szczepański. "Żydowskie budowie instytutowe w miastach guberni radomskiej w połowie XIX w" (Jewish Public Buildings in the Towns of Radom Province in the Mid-Nineteenth Century). BŻIH 1/101 (1977): 77–83. (P)

Perlov, Isaac, and Alfred Lipson, eds. *Sefer Radom* (Memorial Book of Radom). Tel Aviv: Former Residents of Radom in Israel and the USA, 1961. (Y, E)

Government district offices, c. 1917   9

Rothenberg, Moshe. "Jews in the Leather Industry." *Voice of Radom* 32, no. 1 (Sept. 1987); 8, no. 2 (Dec. 1987): 18.

———. "Some Pages from Our Recent History." *Voice of Radom* 30, no. 4 (June/July 1986): 8–9.

Rutkowski, A. "Hitlerowskie obozy pracy dla Żydów w dystrykcie radomskim" (Nazi Forced Labor Camps for Jews in the Radom District). BŻIH 17–18 (1956): 106–170. (P, E)

———. "Martyrologia, walka i zagłada ludności żydowskiej w dystrykcie radomskim podczas okupacji hitlerowskiej " (Martyrdom, Resistance and Destruction of the Jewish Community in the Radom District During the German Occupation). BŻIH 15–16 (1955): 75–182. (P)

Stein, Abram Shmuel, ed. *Radom: A Memorial to the Jewish Community of Radom.* Tel Aviv: Former Residents of Radom in Israel and in the Diaspora, 1961. (H)

Waks, Szymon. "Leder fabrykatsye in Radom" (The Tanning Industry in Radom). *Yidishe ekonomik* 2/3–4 (1938): 151. (Y)

Former Jewish street, today   10

■ *Aerial view, c. 1917* 11

■ *Town hall, c. 1917* 14

■ *Gimnazjum (school) for boys, c. 1917* 12

■ *ul. Kościelna, c. 1917* 15

■ *Market square, c. 1917* 13

■ *ul. Lubelska, c. 1917* 16

BIBLIOGRAPHIC SOURCES

CAHJP; CTD; EDRD; EJ; EOH; GA; GUM3; GUM4; GUM5; GUM6; GYLA; HSL; JE; JGFF; LDL; LDS; LVY; RJHS; SF

RADOMSKO

Radomsko's location on the trade routes between Poznań and Wrocław in the west and Lublin and Lwów in the east contributed to its economic development in the fifteenth century. In 1643, the city was granted the royal privilege *de non tolerandis Judaeis* (of not tolerating Jews), and it was not until the nineteenth century that Jews were permitted to settle within the city limits. A Jewish cemetery was established in 1816, and in 1843, the Radomsker Hasidic dynasty was founded by Solomon ha-Kohen Rabinowich.

With the opening of the Vienna–Warsaw railway in 1846, the town developed rapidly. By the end of the nineteenth century, Jews were involved in the timber and grain trades and worked in carpentry and weaving. The Jewish community expanded throughout the interwar years; the number of Jews employed in large factories doubled. The Jews of Radomsko supported, among other institutions, a range of Jewish schools—both religious and secular—a new library and several sports clubs. On the eve of the Holocaust, Jews made up more than half the population of the town.

Following the German occupation of the town, a ghetto was established in the spring of 1940. It was liquidated in October 1942, and most of the Jews were deported to Treblinka. Hundreds of Jews from Radomsko escaped to the surrounding forests and joined the Jewish partisan groups. However, conditions were so difficult for these groups in the winter of 1942 that 4,500 Jews were lured back to Radomsko by German propaganda and placed in a new ghetto. In January 1943, this ghetto was liquidated as well. Jews who resisted were shot on the spot, and the rest were deported to Treblinka. A number of Jews from Radomsko survived to become active in partisan groups and resistance organizations.

Location

56 km NNE of Częstochowa
51° 04´/19°27´
Voivodship: Piotrków Trybunalski

General Population, 1935

23,000 (55% Jewish)

General Population, 1994

50,998

NOVO RADOMSK, RADOMSK

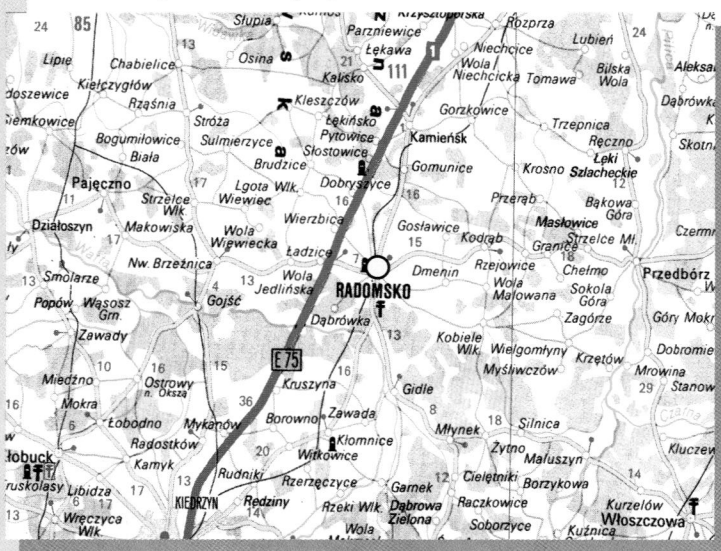

SYNAGOGUE

ul. *Berka Joselewicza*
Great Synagogue constructed in 1899; destroyed during the Holocaust.

▌ Great Synagogue, ul. Berka Joselewicza, pre-1939   1

▌ Town hall, today   2

Jewish cemetery, today 3

JEWISH CEMETERY

ul. Świerczewskiego 196
1,000+ tombstones dating from 1816.
Radomsker Rebbes' *ohel* (tomb) is still a frequent
pilgrimage site.

Jewish cemetery, 1995 4

HOLOCAUST MEMORIAL PLAQUE

ul. Świerczewskiego 196 (Jewish cemetery)
Memorial plaque commemorates mass executions in
1940–1943 and the deaths of 1,500 Jews from the
ghetto in 1943.

DEPORTATIONS

Treblinka, Skarżysko.

SELECTED READING

Fishman, Paul S., ed. *Nowo-Radomsker Society Golden Jubilee Souvenir Journal: 1899–1949*. New York: Novo-Radomsker Society, 1949.

Fishman, Paul S., and Morris Schwartz, eds. *Nowo-Radomsker Almanakh* (New Radomsko Calendar). Vol. 1, 1899–1939. New York: Novo-Radomsker Society, 1939. (Y, E)

Market square, c. 1917 5

Losh, L. *Sefer yizkor li-kehilat Radomsk veha-sevivah* (Memorial Book of the Community of Radomsk and Vicinity). Tel Aviv: Former Residents of Radomsk, 1967. (H, Y)

ul. Władysława Reymonta, today 6

BIBLIOGRAPHIC SOURCES

CAHJP; CTD; EJ; GA; GUM3; GUM4; GUM5; GUM6; HSL; JGFF; JHT; KH; LDL; LDS; LVY; PHP1; RJHS; SF

RZESZÓW

Rzeszów received a municipal charter in 1354, but remained a private town, owned by Polish nobility, until the partitions of the Polish Commonwealth. There was a Jewish presence in the town from the fourteenth century onward. By the eighteenth century, the Jewish community was a large and important one. The Jewish goldsmiths, seal engravers and cloth merchants of Rzeszów were renowned throughout Europe. A non-Jewish traveler in the mid-nineteenth century called Rzeszów "Little Jerusalem." After the partitions, this Galician town passed under Austrian rule. Hasidism gained adherents, but the town also became a center of the Haskalah. By the end of the nineteenth century, the Jews of Rzeszów had civil rights, including voting privileges in local and parliamentary elections. In the twentieth century, the Zionist movement became particularly influential in Rzeszów. The town's last chief rabbi, Aaron Lewin, was repeatedly elected to the Polish Parliament.

The Germans entered Rzeszów on September 10, 1939; a ghetto was imposed in January 1942 and liquidated six months later, when more than 20,000 Jews were shipped to the Bełżec death camp. Another ghetto, established in November, became a forced-labor camp for 3,000 remaining Jews. The workers' families were deported to Auschwitz-Birkenau in September 1943 and most of the workers to a labor camp at Szebnia. About 600 Jews remained slave laborers near Rzeszów until July 1944, when the Germans began to retreat. Some Jews then escaped to the surrounding woods, while others were deported to Germany.

Location

165 km E of Kraków
50°03′/22°01′
Voivodship: Rzeszów

General Population, 1939

42,000 (33% Jewish)

General Population, 1994

159,372

SYNAGOGUES

ul. Bóżnicza 4
Old Town Synagogue dating from seventeenth century.
Current use: State Archives.

ul. Sobieskiego 18
New Town Synagogue dating from 1686.
Current use: art gallery.

JEWISH CEMETERIES

ul. Rejtana
300 tombstones dating from the nineteenth century.

ul. Zwycięstwa (now Plac Ofiar Getta [Ghetto Victim's Square])
Cemetery was founded in the seventeenth century.
Current use: town square and park.
Several tombstones were moved to ul. Rejtana cemetery.

Synagogue (now the State Archives), ul. Bóżnicza 4, 1967

Jewish cemetery, ul. Rejtana, 1993 2

HOLOCAUST MEMORIALS

Monument in Jewish cemetery, ul. Rejtana.

ul. *Sobieskiego 18*
Memorial plaque on former New Town Synagogue.

Town square, 1912 3

DEPORTATIONS

Bełżec, Auschwitz-Birkenau, Pełkinie, Szebnia.

Rzeszów today 4

SELECTED READING

Leder, Herman. *Reysher yidn* (The Jews of Rzeszów). Washington, D.C., 1953. (Y)

Poradowski, Stanisław. "Zagłada Żydów rzeszowskich" (The Extermination of the Jews of Rzeszów). Part 1. BŻIH 2–3 (1983): 126–127, 37–49; Part 2. BŻIH 1–2 (1984): 129–130, 89–108; Part 3. BŻIH 3–4 (1985): 135–136, 77–101; Part 4. BŻIH 1–2 (1988): 145–146, 97–113. (P)

Yaari-Wold, Moshe, ed. *Kehilat Raysha; sefer zikaron* (Rzeszów Jews: Memorial Book). Tel Aviv: Former Residents of Rzeszów in Israel and the USA, 1967. (H, Y, E).

Holocaust memorial, Jewish cemetery, 1993 5

ADDITIONAL RESOURCE

The Jewish History Research Center in Rzeszów was established in 1989 by order of the director of the Polish State Archives. The Research Center is housed in the Archives (ul. Bóźnicza 4) and has produced exhibitions from materials in the Archives, including architectural plans of the synagogues, photographs of tombstones, documents, passports from 1920 to 1930 and old Jewish books.

BIBLIOGRAPHIC SOURCES

CTD; EDRD; EJ; EOH; GA; GUM3; GUM4; GUM5; GUM6; HSL; JGFF; JHT; LDL; LVY; PHP3; PJH; RJHS; SF

SIEDLCE

The first mention of Siedlce dates from the mid-fifteenth century. Later, in 1532, the Polish king Zygmunt August granted Siedlce a municipal charter, whereby the town was permitted to organize weekly markets as well as three fairs a year. Around the mid-sixteenth century, Jews settled in Siedlce, where they were innkeepers at first, then also craftsmen and merchants. Despite the fires that devastated the city in the second half of the seventeenth century, Siedlce was an important artisan, commercial and cultural center by the beginning of the eighteenth century.

During the second half of the eighteenth century, Siedlce's rabbis frequently visited Warsaw to serve Jews who were living there illegally. After the third partition of the Polish Commonwealth, the city briefly fell under Austrian rule, but then passed to the Russians. By the end of the nineteenth century, various Socialist parties, including the Bund, were active in Siedlce; Zionists became the dominating political force during the interwar period. A Jewish high school was opened during World War I; after the interwar period, several local Yiddish weeklies, a Jewish hospital and a range of Jewish organizations—both traditional and secular—flourished.

The German occupation of Siedlce began on September 11, 1939. The Germans repeatedly extorted large sums of money from the Jewish community, and on December 24, 1939, the synagogue was burned down. In August 1941, the Jews were forced into a ghetto that was sealed on October 1. In August 1942, some 10,000 Jews were deported to Treblinka; several thousand more were shot in the forced labor camp established in Siedlce by the end of the year. Hundreds of Jews succeeded in escaping to the forests and organizing partisan groups, some of which continued to fight until the autumn of 1943.

Location

89 km E of Warsaw
52°11′/22°17′
Voivodship: Siedlce

General Population, 1939

35,000 (45% Jewish)

General Population, 1994

73,847

SHEDLETS, SHEDLITZ

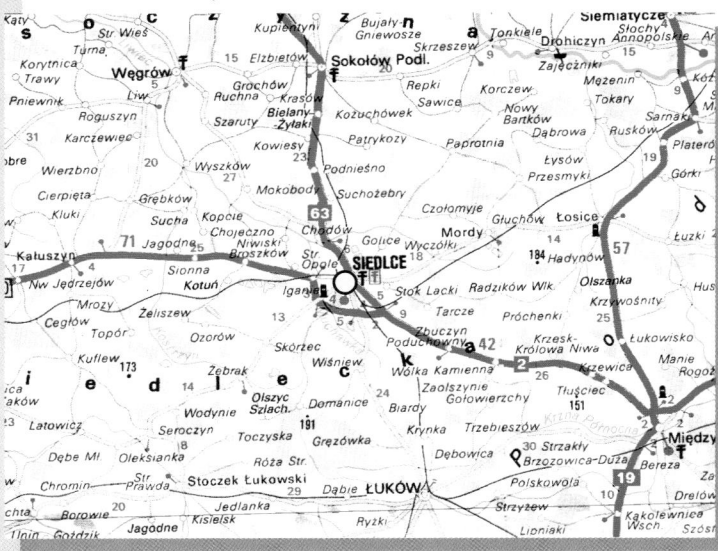

SYNAGOGUES

ul. *Bohaterów Getta*
Great Synagogue, destroyed December 24, 1939.

ul. *Czerwonego Krzyża 13*
Bet Midrash, dating from nineteenth century.
Current use: warehouse.

▌ *Great Synagogue, pre-1939*   1

▌ *Bet Midrash, ul. Czerwonego Krzyża 13, 1994*   2

JEWISH CEMETERY

ul. Szkolna
Cemetery founded in 1807.
About 1,000 tombstones remain, dating from the nineteenth century.

◾ *Holocaust monument, ul. Bohaterów Getta, 1994*   3

HOLOCAUST MEMORIALS

ul. Bohaterów Getta (*site of former synagogue*)
Monument in memory of 17,000 Jews deported to Treblinka.

ul. Szkolna (*Jewish cemetery*)
Holocaust monument formed from 100 tombstones.

◾ *ul. Ogrodowa, c. 1917*   4

DEPORTATIONS

Treblinka.

SELECTED READING

Fainzilber, M. *Oyf di khurves fun mayn heym:khurbn Shedlets* (On the Ruins of My Home: The Destruction of Siedlce). Tel Aviv: Committee of Townspeople, 1952. (Y).

Kaspi, Isaac. *Megilat pera'ot Shedlets bi-shenat 1906* (Chronicle of the Siedlce Pogrom in 1906). Tel Aviv: I. Kaspi, 1947. (H).

◾ *Jewish cemetery, ul. Szkolna, 1994*   5

————. "Yidishe prese in Shedlets: 1894–1939" (The Jewish Press in Siedlce: 1894–1939). *YIVO Bleter* 36 (1952): 361–362. (Y)

Śmieciuch, Paweł. "Społeczność żydowska w Siedlcach w latach 1919–1938 w świetle sprawozdań sytuacyjnych starosty powiatu siedleckiego" (Jewish Community of Siedlce in the Years 1919–1938 in Light of the County Administration: Reports of the Siedlce County Administration). *BŻIH* 1/161 (1992): 79–84. (P)

Yassni, A. Wolf, ed. *Sefer yizkor li-kehilat Shedlets* (Memorial Book of the Community of Siedlce). Buenos Aires: Former Residents of Siedlce in Israel and Argentina, 1956. (H, Y)

◾ *Siedlce, today*   6

BIBLIOGRAPHIC SOURCES

CAHJP; CTD; EDRD; EJ; GA; GUM3; GUM4; GUM5; GUM6; HSL; JGFF; LDL; LDS; LVY; PHP1; PJH; RJHS; SF

SOSNOWIEC

Sosnowiec, in the Upper Silesia region, owed its rapid development to the Industrial Revolution: the opening of the first coal mines at the beginning of the nineteenth century and the subsequent establishment of metal and chemical factories. The city was not granted municipal status until 1902. The first Jews who settled in Sosnowiec came from nearby Będzin and Olkusz; until 1899, communal matters were handled through the Będzin kehillah (Jewish community). Jews were primarily employed in commerce and crafts, but there were also Jewish coal-mine operators and industrialists as well as many Jewish workers and professionals. A Jewish labor movement began early in the twentieth century organized by the Jewish socialist Bund and Poalei Zion (Workers of Zion). By the interwar period, the Jewish community had developed a range of Jewish institutions, including a hospital, secondary schools and associations of Jewish artists, merchants and industrialists.

The Germans entered Sosnowiec on September 4, 1939. Jews were immediately attacked, and on September 9, the Great Synagogue was set on fire. From May to August 1942, more than 10,000 Jews were deported to nearby Auschwitz-Birkenau. Two ghettos were then established: one in the suburb of Środula, the other in Stary Sosnowiec. From May to August 1943, most of the Jews were shipped to Auschwitz-Birkenau. Several hundred Jews continued to work in slave-labor factories until January 1944. In the ghettos, there was considerable underground activity organized by Jewish youth organizations. Several hundred Jews settled briefly in Sosnowiec after the war.

Location

58 km S of Częstochowa
50°17′/19°03′
Voivodship: Katowice

General Population, 1939

130,000 (22% Jewish)

General Population, 1994

250,000

SYNAGOGUES

ul. Dekerta
Great Synagogue, built in 1894.
Burned by the Nazis on September 9, 1939.

ul. Floriańska
Synagogue no longer exists.

▌ ul. Targowa 12, Bet Midrash, pre-1939   2

▌ ul. Kolejowa, c. 1917   1

▌ ul. Modrzejowska, c. 1917   3

■ *Cemetery, ul. Gospodarcza 1, 1984*   4

JEWISH CEMETERIES

ul. Gospodarcza 1
Remaining tombstones: 300+ dating from 1896.

Niwka Pasterna (region of Sosnowiec)
Cemetery founded in the nineteenth century.
A few dozen tombstones remain.

HOLOCAUST MEMORIALS

Memorial plaque in Gospodarcza cemetery
In memory of Jews killed from Sosnowiec and
surrounding towns.

Środula quarter of Sosnowiec
Memorial plaque dedicated in 1985 to Jews killed in the
ghetto.

DEPORTATIONS

Auschwitz-Birkenau, Tyszowce.

■ *ul. Modrzejowska, today*   5

SELECTED READING

Friedman, Philip. "The Messianic Complex of a Nazi
Collaborator in a Ghetto: Moses Merin of Sosnowiec." In
Roads to Extinction: Essays on the Holocaust. Philadelphia:
Jewish Publication Society, 1980, pp. 353–364.

———. "Two 'Saviors' Who Failed: Moses Merin of
Sosnowiec and Jacob Gens of Vilna." *Commentary* 26
(1958): 479–491.

Geshuri, Meier Shimon. *Sefer Sosnovits veha-sevivah be-
Zaglembyah* (Book of Sosnowiec and the Surrounding
Region in Zagłębie). 2 vols. Tel Aviv: Sosnowiec Societies
in Israel, the United States, France and other Countries,
1973–1974. (H, Y)

Jaros, J. "Wiadomości o Żydach czynnych w polskim przemyśle
węglowym" (Notes on Jews Active in the Polish Coal
Industry). *BŻIH* 35 (1960): 87–99. (P)

Kantor, M., and N. Szternfinkiel. *Żydzi w Zagłębiu* (The Jews in
Zagłębie). Sosnowiec: Sowa Press, 1993. (P)

Klajner, A. "Di kleyn-industrye in Sosnovtse" (Small Industry
in Sosnowiec). *Yidishe ekonomik* 2/5–6 (1938): 266. (Y)

Rappaport, J., ed. *Pinkas Zaglembie* (Memorial Book Zagłębie).
Tel Aviv: Hamenorah, 1972. (H, Y, E)

Shapell, Nathan. *Witness to the Truth*. New York: David McKay
Company, Inc., 1974.

Szternfinkiel, Nathan E. *Zagłada Żydów Sosnowca* (Destruction
of the Jews of Sosnowiec). Katowice, 1946. (P)

FILM

To the Smouldering Cities: Jews of Zaglembia. Tel Aviv: Beth
Hatefutsoth, 1989.

BIBLIOGRAPHIC SOURCES

CAHJP; CTD; EDRD; EJ; EOH; GA; GUM3; GUM4; GUM5; GUM6;
HSL; JGFF; KH; LDL; LVY; PJH; RJHS; SF

TARNÓW

Located on the crossroads of trade routes leading to both Hungary and Russia, this Galician town emerged as a significant commerical center between the fourteenth and sixteenth centuries. Jews are mentioned in records dating from the fifteenth century. Beginning in 1581, the Polish nobles who owned the town offered Jews attractive charters of privileges to settle there. Wars, fires and epidemics caused Tarnów's decline in the second half of the seventeenth century.

After Poland's first partition, Tarnów began to recover under Austrian rule; Jews came to play an important role in its revival, establishing factories that produced agricultural equipment and glass. While most Tarnów Jews were Hasidim, Haskalah became increasingly influential in the nineteenth century, as did Zionism by the end of the century. Expanding cloth and hat industries employed many Jews, and concurrently a strong workers' movement also developed. The greatest Jewish historian of the twentieth century, Salo Wittmayer Baron, was a native of Tarnów.

Shortly after the Germans occupied Tarnów on September 8, 1939, they began to deport Jewish leaders to Auschwitz. In March 1941, a ghetto was imposed. During the summer and fall of 1942, some 23,000 Jews were deported to the Bełżec death camp; most of the remaining Jews were sent to Auschwitz and Płaszów in September 1943. In December, the town was declared *Judenrein* (free of Jews). After the war, over 700 Jews settled in Tarnów, but most soon left.

Location

86 km E of Kraków
50°02´/21°00´
Voivodship: Tarnów

General Population, 1939

55,000 (40% Jewish)

General Population, 1994

122,211

TARNA, TARNOV, TARNUV, TORNE

SYNAGOGUES

ul. Żydowska (Jewish Street)
Old Synagogue dating from 1630, situated in a park.
All that remains is the Bimah and a segment of iron fence surrounding the Old Synagogue.

ul. *Goldhammera 1*
Formerly a prayer house, now a private apartment.

ul. *Nowa*
Site of New Synagogue dating from 1908.
Destroyed by Nazis in 1939.
There is a memorial plaque on the building occupying the site today.

Synagogue, ul. Nowa, destroyed in 1939

Plaque at synagogue ruins (inside Bimah), ul. Żydowska, 1992   2

JEWISH CEMETERY

ul. Szpitalna (between ul. Słoneczna and ul. Nowodąbrowska)
Cemetery dates from 1734.
Remaining tombstones: 3,000.

Jewish cemetery, 1993   3

OTHER JEWISH SITES

ul. Goldhammera 5
Former home of local Jewish Credit Company.
Memorial tablets commemorating Herman Merz, former head of the Jewish community, and Eliasz Goldhammer, deputy mayor.

ul. Kołłątaja 14
Former Jewish orphanage from 1913.
Current use: preschool.

Rynek 20
Regional Museum with Judaica exhibition.

Pl. Więźniow Oświęcimia (formerly ul. Bóżnicza)
Mikvah, constructed in 1904.
Current use: under renovation.

ul. Szpitalna
Jewish hospital, founded in 1842.
Current use: hospital.

ul. Nowodąbrowska 25
Jewish Home for the Aged, founded in 1913.
Current use: hospital.

ul. Baluta 6 (formerly ul. Topolowa)
Hebrew High School, founded in 1899.
Current use: boarding house for students.

ul. Św. Anny 1
Hebrew School, founded in 1923.
Current use: boarding house.

ul. Sienna 5
Talmud Tora for poor families, constructed prior to World War I.
Current use: medical school.

Surviving Bimah from old synagogue at ul. Żydowska, 1992   4

DEPORTATIONS

Auschwitz-Birkenau, Bełżec, Płaszów, Szebnia.

▌ *Plac. Więźniów Oświęcimia (Auschwitz Prisoners' Square), 1993*　　5

HOLOCAUST MEMORIALS

ul. Szpitalna (Jewish cemetery)
Memorial to 20,000 Jewish victims incorporating column from devastated New Synagogue.

Plac Więźniów Oświęcimia
Memorial to local residents of Tarnów, including Jews, transported to Auschwitz-Birkenau, June 14, 1940.

Zbylitowska Góra (forest near Tarnów)
A memorial commemorating 800 Jewish children from Tarnów murdered in June 1942.
A second memorial commemorating 10,000 victims of Nazi terror erected by Tarnów government officials.

▌ *City hall, c. 1917*　　6

SELECTED READING

Bartosz, Adam. *In the Footsteps of the Jews of Tarnów.* Tarnów: Regional Museum in Tarnów, 1993. (E)

———. "Synagoga Nowa w Tarnowie" (New Synagogue in Tarnów). BŻIH 3–4/147–148 (1988): 185–196. (P)

———. *Żydowskie zabytki województwa tarnowskiego* (Jewish Monuments in Tarnów Province). Tarnów: Muzeum Okręgowe w Tarnowie, 1989. (P)

Chomet, A., ed. *Tarnov; kiyuma ve-ḥurbanah shel ʿir yehudit* (Tarnów: The Existence and Destruction of a Jewish City). 2 vols. Tel Aviv: Association of Former Residents of Tarnów, 1954–1968. (H, Y)

▌ *Holocaust memorial, Jewish cemetery,*　　7
ul. Szpitalna, 1995

Cienciała, Teodor. "Szpital Żydowski w Tarnowie" (Jewish Hospital in Tarnów. BŻIH 50 (1964): 83–90. (P)

Katalog Biblioteki Żydowskiej w Tarnowie (Catalogue of the Jewish Library in Tarnów). Tarnów, 1924. (P)

Piszowa, Aniela. *600-lecie Tarnowa, 1330–1930* (The 600th Anniversary of Tarnów, 1330–1930). Tarnów, 1930. (P)

Ruta, Zygmunt. "Z dziejów żydowskiego szkolnictwa średniego w Tarnowie" (From the History of Jewish High-School Education in Tarnów). BŻIH 3/103 (1977): 27–34. (P)

Simche, Zdzisław. *Tarnów i jego okolice* (Tarnów and Vicinity). Tarnów: Municipality of Tarnów, 1930. (P)

▌ *ul. Krakowska, c. 1917*   8

▌ *ul. Krakowska, c. 1994*   11

▌ Interior of New Synagogue, 1916   9

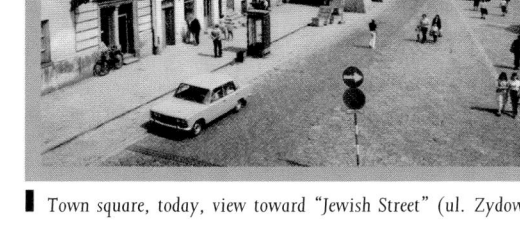

▌ *Town square, today, view toward "Jewish Street" (ul. Zydowska)*   12

▌ *Plaque at base of Holocaust memorial in cemetery (see fig. 7), 1993*   13

▌ *Tarnów railway station, 1914*   10

BIBLIOGRAPHIC SOURCES

CAHJP; CTD; EDRD; EJ; EOH; GA; GUM3; GUM4; GUM5; GYLA; HSL; JE; JGFF; JHT; LDL; LDS; LVY; PHP3; PJH; RJHS; SF

TOMASZÓW MAZOWIECKI

Tomaszów Mazowiecki emerged with the Polish textile industry during the second quarter of the nineteenth century. The Polish owner of the town, Count Antoni Ostrowski, invited Jewish weavers and entrepreneurs to settle there in the 1820s, and a Jewish community was officially organized in 1831. However, the czar exiled Ostrowski for participating in the 1831 Polish uprising and confiscated his estates. The Jewish community continued to grow in the second half of the century, as Jews set up textile mills and were active in other industries, including carpentry, cloth-dyeing and construction. The Great Synagogue was completed in 1878, and in 1889, a kosher kitchen was established to cater to Jewish soldiers serving in the Russian Army who were stationed in Tomaszów. In the early twentieth century, a strong workers' movement emerged. By the interwar period, all the Jewish political parties were represented in the town. A weekly Yiddish newspaper was established, and there was a Hebrew high school. Leon Pinsker, a pioneer of political Zionism, was a native of Tomaszów.

After the Germans occupied Tomaszów, they imposed a ghetto in December 1940 for the Jews of Tomaszów and surrounding towns. In March 1941, several thousand Jews from Płock were also forced to settle there. In November 1942, the Germans liquidated the ghetto and some 15,000 Jews were deported and murdered in Treblinka. The ghetto became a forced-labor camp for the remaining Jews until May 1943, when they were transferred to camps at Bliżyn and Starachowice, where most of them died.

Location

48 km ESE of Łódź
51°32′/20°02′
Voivodship: Piotrków Trybunalski

General Population, 1938

45,000 (26% Jewish)

General Population, 1994

69,811

TOMASHOV MAZOVYETSK, TOMASZÓW RAWSKI

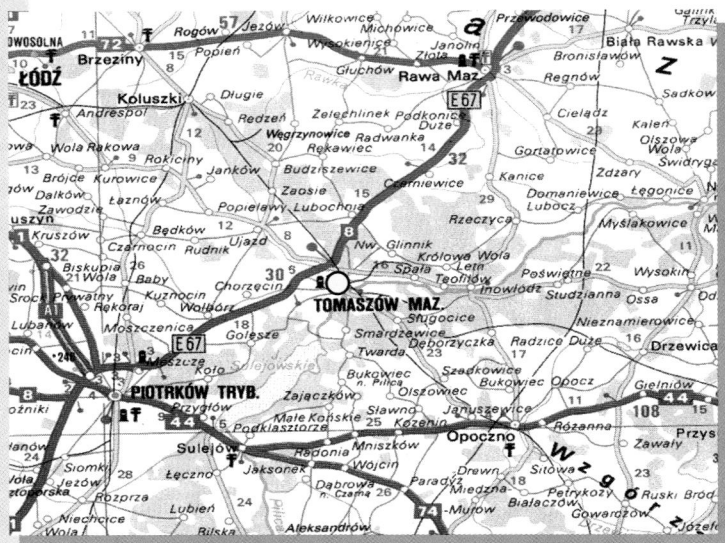

SYNAGOGUE

Great Synagogue constructed in 1864–1878.
Destroyed by the Germans in 1939.

Great Synagogue being dismantled in 1940, after it was virtually destroyed by the Germans.   1

Town square, 1952   2

Jewish cemetery, ul. Smutna 12   3

JEWISH CEMETERY

ul. Smutna 12
Cemetery was founded in 1831.
There is a Holocaust monument in the cemetery.
Remaining tombstones: 2,000.

Jewish cemetery, ul. Smutna 12   4

DEPORTATIONS

Treblinka, Bliżyn, Starachowice.

Plac Tadeusza Kościuszki, today   5

SELECTED READING

Wajsberg, Moshe, ed. *Sefer zikaron li-kehilat Tomashov Mazovyetski*
    (Tomaszów-Mazowiecki: A Memorial to the Jewish
    Community of Tomaszów-Mazowiecki). Tel Aviv:
    Tomaszov Organization in Israel, 1969. (H, Y, E, F)

ul. Warszawska, c. 1912   6

Plac Tadeusza Kościuszki, today   7

BIBLIOGRAPHIC SOURCES

CTD; CAHJP; EDRD; EJ; GA; GUM3; GUM4; GUM5; GUM6; HSL;
JGFF; JHT; LDL; LDS; LVY; PHP1; PJH; RJHS; SF

WARSZAWA

In the Middle Ages, Warsaw was only a regional center; it grew to greater importance after it replaced Kraków in 1611 as the capital of the vast Polish-Lithuanian Commonwealth. Warsaw experienced strong growth in the eighteenth century, precisely at a time when other Polish cities were declining. After the partitions of the Commonwealth, Warsaw was given to Prussia; then briefly occupied by Napoleon; and finally, along with the surrounding provinces, incorporated into the Russian Empire. Warsaw became a cradle of Polish nationalism, as two doomed uprisings against the Russians were centered here. Beginning in the 1860s, Warsaw began a rapid rise to prominence, with booming commerce and industry, along with a soaring population—from 230,000 in 1861 to 844,000 in 1914. During the interwar period, as capital of the new Polish nation, its population was more than 1 million.

For centuries, Warsaw was a multiethnic city. Jews, whose presence is documented in the city as early as 1414, became the second-largest group, after Poles. By 1861, Jews comprised one-third of the population, a proportion they maintained until the Holocaust. In 1939, there were about 350,000 Jews in Warsaw, making it the largest Jewish community in Europe, and second only to New York in the world.

During the first half of the nineteenth century, Warsaw Jews were still encumbered by numerous residential and employment restrictions as well as special taxes. But in the 1860s, in an effort to win the support of Jews against the Poles, the czar lifted many of the restrictions against the Jews in Warsaw and the surrounding provinces. Economic activity surged as Warsaw was flooded with new residents—small-town Jews and peasants fleeing the overpopulated countryside. By the end of the nineteenth century, Warsaw had become the economic, political and cultural capital of the Jews of Poland.

Hasidism sank deep roots in Warsaw in the nineteenth century. At the same time, a group of upper-class, Polish-speaking Jews began to advocate the integration of Jews into Polish society. Beginning in the late nineteenth century, Warsaw became the headquarters for a large number of Jewish political parties that advanced a variety of ideologies based on different combinations of socialism and nationalism. By the interwar period, even Orthodox Jews had organized themselves into a powerful political party.

Under the influence of I. L. Peretz, who lived in Warsaw from 1890 to 1915, Warsaw became the center of a rapidly growing modern culture based in the Yiddish language; the city was a magnet for Yiddish novelists, poets, journalists and theater people. At the same time, some Jews began to use the Polish language as a way of meeting Jewish needs, and in some circles, modern Hebrew began to develop as well. Nor did traditional life languish. In Warsaw in the 1920s, according to incomplete statistics, there were 442 synagogues and prayer houses for a population of 350,000 Jews. Jewish cooperatives, credit unions, orphanages, hospitals, newspapers, publishing houses, theater companies, orchestras, choirs, sports clubs and cultural societies were the links in a far-flung network whose center was Jewish Warsaw.

The Germans occupied Warsaw in September 1939. In October 1940, a ghetto was established; it was sealed the following month. Half a million Jews were packed into the ghetto, making it the largest in German-occupied Europe. Over the next two years, the death rate in the ghetto from starvation and disease was 10 percent annually. Nevertheless, a multitude of organizations, from soup kitchens to schools to theaters, continued to function, and a resistance movement began to form.

From July to September 1942, the Nazis shipped 250,000 Jews from the infamous *Umschlagplatz* (transfer point) in Warsaw to the death camp at Treblinka. During the following months, the Jewish resistance movement came into its own. It repelled an attempt to deport more Jews in January 1943, then organized the final defense of the ghetto. The Warsaw Ghetto Uprising, which began on April 19, 1943, pitted about 750 barely armed youngsters and some 40,000 unarmed Jews who had dug into underground bunkers against 2,000 superbly armed German troops. The uprising lasted nearly a month; its defeat required the incineration of nearly every building in the ghetto. The old Jewish quarter of Warsaw was completely destroyed. Mordechai Anielewicz, the leader of the uprising, and his general staff committed suicide in their bunker at Miła 18 to avoid capture. To celebrate his victory, General Jurgen Stroop, the German commander, ordered the dynamiting of Warsaw's Great Synagogue.

Several thousand Jews returned to Warsaw after the war. Most of those who remained after the first postwar years assimilated into Polish society. Most of these Jews, however, were driven from Poland in the years 1968 to 1970 during an official "anti-Zionist" campaign; nevertheless, a small organized Jewish community has managed to survive until the present. Today, with substantial aid from Jewish groups abroad such as the Ronald S. Lauder Foundation, and some Polish government support, this community supports a Jewish elementary school, a preschool, summer camp Yiddish theater, a newspaper, and two rabbis. Other groups, such as a society of child survivors of the Holocaust, function as well. Warsaw is also the site of the Jewish Historical Institute, which houses invaluable Jewish archival documents and objects.

Location

134 km NE of Łódź
52°12´/21°02´
Voivodship: Warsaw

General Population, 1939

1,181,850 (33% Jewish)

General Population, 1994

1,641,941

▌ *Nożyk Synagogue, ul. Twarda 6, today*   1

SYNAGOGUE

ul. Twarda 6
Nożyk Synagogue, the only synagogue not destroyed by the Nazis and today Warsaw's only Jewish place of worship, was founded in 1902 by Zalman Nożyk, a Warsaw merchant. Services are held daily and led by Rabbi Menachem Joskowicz, who has served as chief rabbi of Warsaw since 1989. During the war, the Germans used the synagogue as a stable and barn. It was rebuilt after the war and renovated in 1983.

▌ *Nożyk Synagogue, ul. Twarda 6, today*   2

Nożyk Synagogue interior, ul. Twarda 6, today   3

SITES OF SOME FORMER SYNAGOGUES

ul. Tłomackie
(directly opposite the Jewish Historical Institute)
Great Synagogue, completed in 1878 and blown up by Nazis on May 16, 1943, after the Warsaw Ghetto Uprising. The modern blue glass skyscraper now occupying this site encountered extensive delays (30 years) and problems during construction. Local legend interprets the long delay as a form of retribution for rebuilding on the site of the destroyed synagogue.

ul. Szeroka and Petersburska
(now Wójcika and Jagiellońska)
Synagogue built in 1840, devastated during the Holocaust and destroyed in the 1950s.

Great Synagogue interior, ul. Tłomackie, pre-Holocaust   5

FORMER PRAYER HOUSES

ul. Twarda 4; ul. Bródnowska 8; ul. Gęsia 5; ul. Wspólna 20; ul. Nalewki 27

Pre-1939, Warsaw had more than 450 Jewish houses of prayer, ranging from great synagogues to hundreds of Shtiblekh.

Great Synagogue, ul. Tłomackie, built in 1878, destroyed by Nazis in 1943   4

Jewish Historical Institute (former Library of Great Synagogue and Institute for Judaic Studies), 1994   6

JEWISH CEMETERIES

ul. Okopowa (entrance on Gęsia Street)
The old cemetery, established in 1806, functions to this day and is surrounded by a brick wall. There are approximately 250,000 tombstones, including those of many well-known figures in Polish-Jewish culture. Among them are Szymon Anski (1863–1920), ethnographer and author of the celebrated Yiddish play *The Dybbuk*; historian and diplomat Szymon Askenazy (1866–1935); Jewish historian Majer Bałaban (1877–1942); banker and art collector Mathias Bersohn (1824–1908); Adam Czerniaków (1880–1942), head of the Warsaw *Judenrat* (Jewish Council) under the Germans; Ester Rachel Kamińska (1870–1925), known as the mother of Yiddish theater; Ludwik Natanson (1822–1896), physician and communal leader; Samuel Orgelbrand (1810–1868), publisher; I. L. Peretz (1852–1915), known as the father of modern Yiddish literature; Ber Sonnenberg (1764–1822), merchant; and Ludwik Zamenhof (1859–1917), creator of the "international language" Esperanto. Much of the cemetery is overgrown with shrubs, weeds and trees, which often makes it impossible to search for individual tombstones. The cemetery caretaker, Bolesław Szenicer, has numerous handwritten notebooks documenting thousands of tombstones. Within the last few years, he has entered about 42,000 names and tombstone locations into a computer database, and he can be very helpful in locating individual tombstones. There is a small bookshop in the cemetery office.

ul. Św. Wincentego and ul. Odrowąża
(Bródno quarter of Warsaw)
Cemetery established in 1780 and devastated by Nazis in 1941. About 1,000 tombstones are preserved.

▮ *Jewish cemetery, ul. Okopowa, today*   8

HOLOCAUST MEMORIALS AND MONUMENTS

Monuments and markers are part of the "Memorial Route of Jewish Martyrdom and Struggle," designed by architects Z. Gąsior and S. Jankowski.

ul. Anielewicza
Named for Mordechai Anielewicz, commander of the Jewish Fighters Organization (ŻOB) during the Warsaw Ghetto Uprising in 1943.

▮ *Institute for Judaic Studies and the Great Synagogue, pre-Holocaust*   7

▮ *Monument to Janusz Korczak at Jewish cemetery,*   9
ul. Okopowa, c. 1990

ul. Miła 18
Site of Jewish resistance bunker where Mordechai Anielewicz and others committed suicide.

ul. Długa 29
Former site of Hotel Polski, from which hundreds of Jews with Latin American passports were deported on July 15, 1943, to death camps after being promised a safe exit to neutral countries.

ul. Dzielna 24/26
Former Nazi Pawiak Prison, now a museum.

ul. Jaktorowska 8 (formerly ul. Krochmalna 92)
Monument to Dr. Janusz Korczak (Henryk Goldszmit), director of a Jewish orphanage in the Warsaw Ghetto. Korczak went to his death at Treblinka along with the children he refused to abandon.

ul. Zamenhofa
The 36-foot bronze sculpture by Natan Rapaport, built in 1948, is inscribed in Yiddish, Hebrew and Polish: "From the Jewish People to Its Fighters and Martyrs."

■ *The Umschlagplatz Monument, ul. Stawki, c. 1988*   14

ul. Stawki (Umschlagplatz)
Monument at site of transfer point (*Umschlagplatz*) from which 300,000 Jews from the Warsaw ghetto were deported to Treblinka in 1942–1943.

ul. Stawki 5/7
Former SS building where deportations from the *Umschlagplatz* were ordered.
Current use: University faculty building.

ul. Stawki 6/8
Building where Jews were held prior to deportation to Treblinka.

ul. Złota 60 and Sienna 55
Fragments of the Warsaw ghetto walls.

■ *Fragment of Warsaw ghetto wall, ul. Sienna 55, today*   15

DEPORTATIONS

Treblinka, Auschwitz-Birkenau, Ravensbrück, Gross-Rosen, Majdanek, Sachsenhausen; concentration camps, prisons or slave labor sites in Germany.

ul. Twarda 6
Jewish community complex, including:
Building 1: Synagogue, kosher kitchen, *mikvah*, Jewish community office.
Building 2: The Ronald S. Lauder Foundation, Assocation of Child Survivors of the Holocaust, Polish Union of Jewish Students, Association of Jewish War Veterans, Jewish kindergarten, Kosher kitchen, "Our Roots," Joint Distribution Committee, periodicals *Midrash* and *Jidełe*.

Plac Grzybowski 12/16 (near synagogue)
Jewish Cultural House, consisting of Yiddish State Theater and Social and Cultural Society of Jews in Poland. The theater presents regular performances of Yiddish plays. Until 1968, the theater's director and star performer was Ida Kamińska, daughter of the legendary Yiddish actress Ester Rachel Kamińska, for whom the theater was named. In the same building are editorial offices of *Słowo Żydowskie*, the only Jewish newspaper in Poland published in both Yiddish and Polish.

■ *The Yiddish State Theater, Plac Grzybowski 12/16, today*   16

ul. Sienna 60
Bersohn's and Bauman's Children's Hospital.
Current use: hospital.

ul. Jagiellońska 88 (Praga section of Warsaw)
Building of Michał Bersohn Jewish Educational Center (1911–1914).
Current use: Baj Theater for children.

ul. Zamenhofa 5
Plaque on building in honor of Dr. Ludwik Zamenhof, the Białystok physician who invented the international language, Esperanto, in 1887.

ul. Sierakowskiego 7 (Praga Section of Warsaw)
Building of Jewish Academic House.
Current use: police department.

Old Town square, View 1, c. 1917   17

Old Town square, View 2, c. 1917   19

INSTITUTIONS AND ORGANIZATIONS

The Ronald S. Lauder Foundation (RSLF)

ul. Twarda 6
00-104 Warszawa
Tel: 620-3496; 652-2150

Since 1988, the RSLF has organized summer (three two-week sessions) and winter (two one-week sessions) programs for young and old alike. In 1989, the RSLF opened the first Jewish kindergarten (with 34 children today) and, in 1994, a Jewish primary school (with 67 children today). In 1993, the RSLF opened the first Jewish Educational Center/Young Club in Warsaw. Today, there are also clubs in Kraków, Wrocław, Łódź and Gdańsk. The main weekly event is a Friday night Shabbat dinner, open to both local residents and visitors. The RSLF also supports the Makabi Sports Club; Bejtejnu (the Holocaust Survivor Center); the Polish Union for Jewish Students; the Association of Children of the Holocaust; Jewish War Veterans; and two Jewish periodicals in Polish: *Jidełe*, a student magazine, and *Midrash*, a monthly.

American-Polish-Israeli Shalom Foundation

Pl. Grzybowski 12/16
00-104 Warszawa
Tel: 620-0559

Established in 1988 in Warsaw by Golda Tencer, director general, the foundation promotes Polish and Jewish culture and supports Jewish artistic culture in Poland.

Social and Cultural Society of Jews in Poland

Pl. Grzybowski 12/16
00-104 Warszawa
Tel: 620-0554

The Society has branches throughout Poland and is a lay organization engaged in the promotion of Jewish culture through lectures and meetings. The Society cooperates with the Jewish Historical Institute, the Yiddish Theatre and the Jewish Religious Union in Poland.

Town hall, c. 1917   18

Old Town in distance, today   20

Old Town square, View 3, c. 1917   21

Old Town square (rebuilt), today   23

Jewish Information and Tourist Bureau (Our Roots)
ul. Twarda 6
00-105 Warszawa
Tel/fax: 620-0556

Travel agency specializing in Jewish sites. Local guidebooks to Jewish sites are available in this office for Warsaw, Kraków, Lublin and Łódź. Arrangements can also be made for out-of-town excursions with car, driver and translator. The staff is very knowledgeable and helpful.

Remembrance Foundation
Aleje Ujazdowskie 9
00-583 Warszawa
Tel: 625-5339; fax: 694-7345

Upkeep and repair of Jewish cemeteries; renovation and commemoration of synagogues and other Jewish monuments; cultural and educational activities concerning Polish-Jewish relations.

JEWISH HISTORICAL INSTITUTE
(ŻYDOWSKI INSTYTUT HISTORYCZNY)

Before the war, this building housed the Main Judaic Library and Institute for Judaic Studies. Now, the Jewish Historical Institute occupies the building and includes a museum, library and archives (see Chapter 5).

Monument to Warsaw Jews, raised on April 19, 1946, on the ghetto ruins, ul. Anielewicza, 1977   24

Local view, c. 1917   22

Ajnenkiel, Andrzej. "Społeczność żydowska w Warszawie międzywojennej" (Jewish Community in Interwar Warsaw). BŻIH 3/4 107–108 (1978): 65–71. (P)

Bałaban, Majer. "Varshe, di greste yidishe gemaynde in Eyrope" (Warsaw, the Greatest Jewish Community in Europe). *Haynt Jubilee Book* (1928): 117–120. (Y)

Bartoszewski, Władysław. *Warszawski pierścień śmierci, 1939–1944* (Warsaw Death Ring, 1939–1944). Warsaw: Interpress Publishers, 1968. (P)

Bartoszewski, Władysław T., and Antony Polonsky, eds. *The Jews in Warsaw.* Oxford: Blackwell, 1991.

ul. *Marszałkowska, c. 1918*   25

Baumgarten, Leon. "Pierwsze kółko żydowskiej młodzieży rewolucyjnej w Warszawie" (The First Circle of Jewish Revolutionary Youth in Warsaw). BŻIH 63 (1967): 65–88. (P)

Borzymińska, Zofia. *Szkolnictwo żydowskie w Warszawie 1831–1870* (Jewish Schools in Warsaw, 1831–1870). Warsaw: Jewish Historical Institute, 1984. (P)

Corrsin, Stephen D. *Warsaw Before the First World War: Poles and Jews in the Third City of the Russian Empire, 1880–1914.* New York: Columbia University Press, 1989.

Czerniaków, Adam. *The Warsaw Diary of Adam Czerniaków: Prelude to Doom.* New York: Stein and Day, 1979.

Datner, Szymon. "Działalność warszawskiej Gminy Wyznaniowej Żydowskiej w dokumentach podziemnego archiwum getta warszawskiego" (Activities of the Warsaw Jewish Consistory as Reflected in the Documents of the Underground Archive of the Warsaw Ghetto). BŻIH 73 (1970): 101–132. (P)

ul. *Aleje Jerozolimskie, c. 1918*   26

Eisenbach, Artur. "Status prawny ludności żydowskiej w. Warszawie w końcu XVIII i na początku XIX wieku" (Legal Status of the Jewish Population in Warsaw at the End of Eighteenth and Beginning of Nineteenth Century). BZIH 39 (1961): 3–16. (P)

———. "Struktura ludności żydowskiej w. Warszawie w. świetle spisu 1810 r" (The Structure of the Jewish Population of Warsaw on the Basis of the Census of 1810). BŻIH 13–14 (1950): 73–121. (P)

———. *Żydzi w Warszawie i sprawa żydowska w XVIII w.* (The Jews in Warsaw and the Jewish Question in the Eighteenth Century). 1975. (P)

Fuks, Marian. *Prasa żydowska w Warszawie 1823–1939* (The Jewish Press in Warsaw, 1823–1939). Warsaw: Państwowe Wydawnictwo Naukowe, 1979. (P)

Gruenbaum, Yitzhak. *Varsha* (Warsaw). 3 vols. Jerusalem: The Encyclopaedia of the Jewish Diaspora, 1953–1973. (H, Y)

Aleje Jerozolimskie and ul. Marszałkowska, today   27

Palace in Wilanów, today 28

Grynberg, Michał, ed. *Pamiętniki z getta warszawskiego* (Memoirs from the Warsaw Ghetto). Warsaw: Państwowe Wydawnictwo Naukowe, 1988, 1993.

Gutman, Israel. *The Jews of Warsaw, 1939–1943: Ghetto, Underground, Revolt*. Bloomington: Indiana University Press, 1982.

———. *Resistance: The Warsaw Ghetto Uprising*. Boston: Houghton Mifflin, 1994.

Hirshaut, Julien. *Jewish Martyrs of Pawiak*. New York: Holocaust Library, 1982.

Jagielski, Jan, and Robert Pasieczny. *A Guide to Jewish Warsaw*. Warsaw: Jewish Information and Tourist Bureau, 1990. (E)

Katsh, Abraham I., ed. *Scroll of Agony: The Warsaw Diary of Chaim A. Kaplan*. New York: Collier Books, 1973.

Katz, P., et al., eds. *Pinkes Varshe* (Book of Warsaw). Buenos Aires: Former Residents of Warsaw and Surroundings in Argentina, 1955. (Y)

Palace in Wilanów, c. 1918 29

Kermish, Joseph, ed. *To Live with Honor and Die with Honor: Selected Documents from the Warsaw Ghetto Underground Archives "O.S." (Oneg Shabbath)*. Jerusalem: Yad Vashem, 1986. (E)

Kowalska-Glikman, Stefania. "Ludność żydowska Warszawy w połowie XIX w. w świetle akt stanu cywilnego" (The Jewish Population of Warsaw in Light of Vital Records). BŻIH 2/118 (1981): 37–49. (P)

Kroszczor, Henryk. "Główna biblioteka żydowskich dokumentów historycznych w Warszawie" (The Main Library of Jewish Historical Documents in Warsaw). BŻIH 2/78 (1971): 3–10. (P)

Hotel Bristol, 1909 30

Hotel Bristol, today 31

———. "Wielka synagoga na Placu Tłomackiem" (The Great Synagogue at Tłomacki Square). BŻIH 3/95 (1975): 3–16. (P)

Kroszczor, Henryk, and Ryszard Zabłotniak. "Żydowska komisja do spraw pomocy sanitarnej w Warszawie, 1914–1915" (Jewish Commission for Sanitary Aid in Warsaw, 1914–1915). BŻIH 1/81 (1972): 91–97. (P)

View of the Barbican, c. 1991   32

Kroszczor, Henryk, and Henryk Zimler. *Cmentarz żydowski w Warszawie* (The Jewish Cemetery in Warsaw). Warsaw: Państwowe Wydawnictwo Naukowe, 1983. (P)

Levinson, Abraham. *Toledot yehude Varsha* (History of the Warsaw Jews). Tel Aviv: 'Am 'oved, 1952–1953. (H)

Lewin, Sabina. "Warszawski dom sierot w XIX w." (The Warsaw Orphanage in the Nineteenth Century). BŻIH 3/ 4 123–124 (1982): 31–47. (P)

Mark, Ber. *Uprising in the Warsaw Ghetto*. New York: Schocken Books, 1976.

Meed, Vladka. *On Both Sides of the Wall*. New York: Holocaust Library, 1989.

Podhorizer-Sandel, Erna. "Żydowskie dokumenty historyczne w Muzeum Narodowym w Warszawie" (Jewish Historical Documents in the National Museum in Warsaw). BŻIH 2/ 78 (1971): 55–60. (P)

Park Ujazdowski, pre-1918   33

Ravitch, Melech, ed. *Dos amolike yidishe Varshe, biz der shvel fun dritn khurbn; yisker-bletlekh nokh tayere noente umgekumene* (Jewish Warsaw That Was; a Yiddish Literary Anthology; Yizkor Pages for the Dearly Beloved Victims). Montreal: Farband of Warsaw Jews in Montreal, 1967. (Y)

Ringelblum, Emmanuel. *Notes from the Warsaw Ghetto: The Journal of Emmanuel Ringelblum*. Ed. and trans. by Jacob Sloan. New York: McGraw-Hill, 1958.

―――. *Żydzi w Warszawie* (The Jews in Warsaw). Warsaw: Towarzystwo Miłośników Historji, 1932. (P)

Roland, Charles G. *Courage Under Siege: Starvation, Disease and Death in the Warsaw Ghetto*. Oxford: Oxford University Press, 1992.

Shatzky, Jacob. *Di geshikhte fun Yidn in Varshe* (History of Jews in Warsaw). 3 vols. New York: YIVO, 1947–1953. (Y)

ul. Krakowskie Przedmieście, c. 1917   34

―――. "Warsaw Jews in Polish Cultural Life of the Early 19th Century." *YIVO Annual* 5 (1950): 41–54.

Shulman, Abraham. *The Case of Hotel Polski*. New York: Holocaust Library, 1982.

Trunk, Isaiah. "Biblioteka Żydowskiego Instytutu Historycznego" (The Library of the Jewish Historical Institute). BŻIH 2 (1950): 24ff. (P)

Vaykhert, Mikhl. *Zikhroynes fun Varshe* (Memoirs from Warsaw). Vol. 2 of 4 volumes. Tel Aviv: Hamenora, 1961. (Y)

Wein, Adam. "Organiczenie napływu Żydów do Warszawy: 1815–1862" (Restrictions on Influx of Jews to Warsaw: 1815–1862). BŻIH 49 (1964): 3–34. (P)

―――. "Żydzi poza rewirem żydowskim w Warszawie, 1809–1862" (Jews Outside the Jewish District in Warsaw, 1809–1862). BŻIH 41 (1962): 45–70. (P)

1982   35

Jewish Cemetery, ul. Okopowa
(figs. 35 and 37 are details of fig. 36)

Upper left (fig. 35): Bas-relief illustrating Psalm 137: "By the rivers of Babylon we sat down, there we wept, when we remembered Zion. On the willows nearby, we hung up our harps."

Center left (fig. 36): Monument of banker Berek Sonnenberg (1764–1822), son of wealthy merchant, Samuel Zbytkower. The two elaborate sculptured panels on the monument are described in figs. 35 and 37. Sculpture is attributed to David Friedlander.

Lower left (fig. 37): Bas-relief depicts view of Praga, a Warsaw suburb across the Vistula River, including the Jewish cemetery, at ul. Wincentego.

1982   36

Monument to Bund members who perished during the Warsaw Ghetto Uprising (sculpture by Natan Rapaport), 1982   38

1990   37

BIBLIOGRAPHIC SOURCES

CAHJP; CTD; EDRD; EJ; EOH; FRG; GA; GUM3; GUM4; GUM5; GUM6; HSL; JE; JGFF; JHT; LDL; LDS; LVY; PHP4; PJH; RJHS; SF

WŁOCŁAWEK

Włocławek, located in central Poland, is one of the oldest Polish towns, but it was not until the beginning of the nineteenth century that Jews were permitted to settle there in designated areas. When restrictions on settlement were lifted in 1862, the community rapidly grew in size; by 1909, Jews constituted 21 percent of the town's population. The first synagogue was erected in 1854. In the interwar period, there was a Jewish high school in Włocławek, and two Yiddish weeklies were published there. Zionists, especially followers of the religious Mizrahi movement and right-wing Zionist Revisionists, were particularly influential.

Włocławek was occupied by the Germans on September 14, 1939, renamed Leslau, and, like Łódź, incorporated into the German Reich. All the synagogues were burned down; thousands of Jews were deported to eastern Poland or fled on their own to other cities, especially Warsaw. A ghetto was established in November 1940 for the 3,000 remaining Jews. In October of the following year, some of its inmates were transferred to the Łódź ghetto; the remaining Jews were deported to the Chełmno death camp in April–May 1942, and the ghetto was burned down.

After the war, survivors from Włocławek, along with Jews returning from the Soviet Union, settled in the town and, aided by the American Joint Distribution Committee, began to rebuild a Jewish community. However, the community gradually dwindled. Finally, it dissolved during the so-called anti-Zionist campaign of 1968–1970.

Location

103 km NNW of Łódź
52°39′/19°03′
Voivodship: Włocławek

General Population, 1939

59,000 (23% Jewish)

General Population, 1994

123,135

VLATZLAVEK, VLOTSLAVSK, ALT LESLE, LESLAU

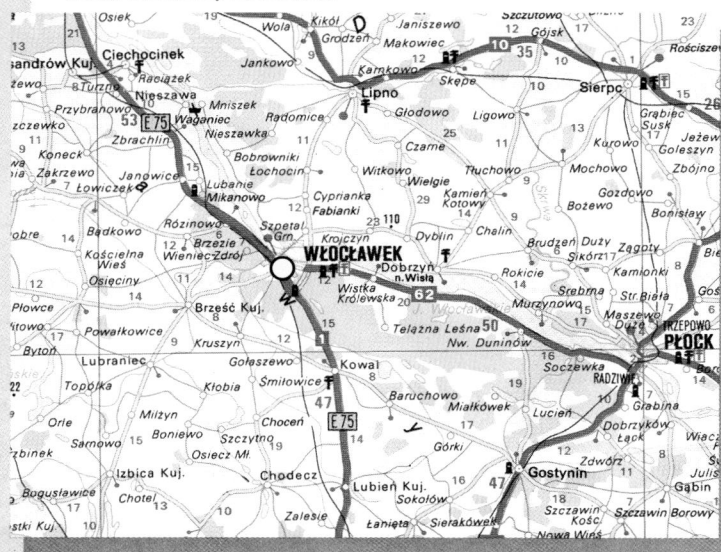

SYNAGOGUES

Among the synagogues destroyed during the Holocaust were the Great Synagogue, constructed in 1854, and a second synagogue dating from 1908.

▌ Great Synagogue, pre-1918   1

JEWISH CEMETERIES

ul. Chopina (Jewish section in communal cemetery)
About two dozen tombstones remain from the nineteenth century, including a few tombstones from the Żałobna cemetery.

ul. Nowomiejska (formerly ul. Żałobna)
Cemetery completely destroyed.
Current site use: vocational school.

Holocaust monument, ul. Chopina, 1992

2

HOLOCAUST MEMORIAL

ul. Chopina (communal cemetery)
Monument in Jewish quarter.

Town square today

3

DEPORTATIONS

Łódź ghetto, Chełmno.

View of Vistula River, today

4

SELECTED READING

Miasto Włocławek. Krótki rys jego rozwoju (The City of Włocławek and Its Growth. A Brief Sketch). Warsaw, 1933. (P)

Morawski, Marian. Monografja Włocławka (A Monograph on Włocławek). Włocławek: M. Morawski, 1933. (P)

ul. Szeroka, c. 1916

5

Thursh, Katriel Fishel, and Meir Korzen, eds. Vlotslavek veha-sevivah; sefer zikaron (Włocławek and Vicinity: Memorial Book). Tel Aviv: Association of Former Residents of Włocławek in Israel and the USA, 1967. (H, Y).

Market square, 1915

6

BIBLIOGRAPHIC SOURCES

CTD; EDRD; EJ; GA; GUM3; GUM4; GUM5; GUM6; HSL; JGFF; LDL; LDS; LVY; PHP4; PJH; RJHS; SF

BRESLAU

Wrocław, the chief town of Lower Silesia in what is today southwestern Poland, known for centuries as Breslau, was ruled by Poland from the end of the tenth century, passed to the Austrian Empire in 1526, and then to Prussia in 1742. During the Middle Ages, Poles as well as Germans lived in Breslau, but by the end of the nineteenth century, it had become an entirely German city. After World War II, it was included in the lands returned by Germany to Poland. Now called Wrocław, its German population was voluntarily repatriated or expelled and replaced by Poles, many from the region of the prewar Polish city of Lwów, which passed to the Soviet Union after the war.

The history of the town is rooted in trade between Germany and Poland; the international fairs of Breslau were famous for centuries. A tombstone attests to the presence of Jews in the town as early as 1203; the medieval Jewish community owned synagogues, a bathhouse and cemeteries; however, beginning in the fourteenth century, Jews were persecuted and expelled from the town. In 1455, the town was awarded the privilege *de non tolerandis Judaeis* (of not tolerating Jews) except for those attending the fair. Small numbers of Jews received privileges to live in Breslau over the succeeding centuries; when the Prussians took the town, an official Jewish community was recognized.

Breslau became a center of Hebrew printing and talmudic scholarship. The first modern Jewish theological seminary was founded by Zachariah Frankel in 1854 and functioned as a legendary center of Jewish learning until 1938. Breslau also became a center of conflict between followers of Reform and Orthodox Judaism; the preeminent Reform leader Abraham Geiger was rabbi in the city from 1840 to 1863. Other Jewish natives of Breslau were Henrich Graetz, the first modern Jewish historian, and Ferdinand Lassalle, a founder of the German workers' movement.

After World War I, there was a renewal of Jewish communal life; several Jewish schools were founded, as were a youth institute and a home for the aged. On the eve of Hitler's ascension to power in 1933, there were some 20,000 Jews in Breslau; six years later, half had fled. In November 1938, all Jewish institutions, including schools and synagogues (with one exception, the Storch Synagogue), were destroyed. Beginning in September 1941, Breslau Jews were deported to camps in Silesia and from there to Auschwitz-Birkenau. The following spring, the remaining Jews were shipped directly to Auschwitz-Birkenau, Sobibór, Riga (ghetto) and Theresienstadt. The archives of the Breslau Jewish community survived and are located today in the Jewish Historical Institute in Warsaw.

After the war, Polish authorities encouraged Jewish survivors from all over Poland to resettle in Wrocław; a Yiddish school and a Yiddish theater were established. In 1960, there were some 1,200 Jewish families living in the city, but few remained after the anti-Zionist campaign of 1968–1970.

Location

176 km WNW of Częstochowa
51°07´/17°02´
Voivodship: Wrocław

General Population, 1939

630,000 (1.5% Jewish)

General Population, 1994

643,106

Storch Synagogue, ul. Włodkowica 7, 1976

1

SYNAGOGUES

ul. Łąkowa
Great Synagogue dating from 1872, destroyed in 1938.

ul. Włodkowica 7
Storch Synagogue dating from 1829. Now under renovation.

ul. Złote Koło 2
Sklowar Synagogue dating from 1790; partially destroyed by Germans in 1938 and later used by them as a wine cellar and warehouse.

Storch Synagogue interior, ul. Włodkowica 7, 1976

2

Jewish cemetery, ul. Ślężna   3

JEWISH CEMETERIES

ul. *Gwarna*
Oldest Jewish cemetery, dating from 1761, destroyed.

ul. *Ślężna (part of City's Architectural Museum)*
Remaining tombstones: 6,000, dating from 1856.

ul. *Lotnicza 51*
Remaining tombstones: 8,000, dating from 1900.

OTHER SITES

ul. *Wiśniowa*
Former Jewish Hospital dating from 1726.
Current use: railroad hospital.

ul. *Włodkowica 9*
Jewish Community Office and prayer house.

Wrocław (Breslau), c. 1916   5

Market square, today   6

HOLOCAUST MEMORIAL

Plac *Bohaterów Ghetta*
Memorial to ghetto heroes.

DEPORTATIONS

Auschwitz-Birkenau, Theresienstadt, Riga ghetto, Sobibór.

Great Synagogue, burned by Nazis in 1938   4

SELECT READING

Brilling, Bernhard. "Das Archiv der Breslauer Jüdischen Gemeinde " (Archives of the Jewish Breslau Community). *Jahrbuch der Schlesischen Friedrich-Wilhelms Universitat zu Breslau* 18 (1973): 258–284. (G)

———. *Geschichte der Jüden in Breslau von 1454–1702* (History of the Jews in Breslau from 1454–1702). Stuttgart: W. Kohlhammer, 1960. (G)

Bronsztejn, Szyja. "A Questionnaire Inquiry into the Jewish Population of Wrocław." *Jewish Social Studies* (Dec. 1965): 246–275.

Hoffman, Zygmunt. "Noc Kryształowa na obszarze wrocławskiego nadodcinka SS" (Crystal Night in the Area of the Wrocław Supersect [SS Ober abschitt sudost] of Wrocław District of SS). BŻIH 2/98 (1976): 75–96. (P)

Łagiewski, Maciej. *Macewy mówią* (Tombstones Speak). Warsaw: Państwowe Wydawnictwo Naukowe, 1983. (P)

Na starym cmentarzu żydowskim Wrocławia (In the Old Jewish Cemetery of Wrocław). Wrocław: Architectural Museum, 1986. (P).

Poloński, F. "Holocaust we Wrocławiu i na Dolnym Śląsku (1941–1944) w świetle dokumentów administracji skarbowej" (The Holocaust in Wrocław and in Lower Silesia in Light of the Documents of the Finance Administration). *Dzieje Najnowsze* 18/3–4 (1986): 235–248. (P)

Tausk, W. *Breslauer Tagebuch 1933–1940* (Breslau Diary, 1933–1940). Berlin: Rütten & Loening, 1975. (G)

Walk, J., ed. *Als Jude in Breslau: Aus den tagebuchern von Studienrat a. D. Dr. Willy Israel Cohn* (As a Jew in Breslau: From the Diaries of Retired Teacher Dr. Willy Israel Cohn). Gerlingen, West Germany: Bleicher, 1984. (G).

BIBLIOGRAPHIC SOURCES

CAHJP; CTD; EDRD; EJ; GUM3; GUM4; GUM5; GUM6; HSL; JE; JGFF; JHT; LDL; LDS; PJH; RJHS

▌ Town view, pre-1939

7

ZAMOŚĆ

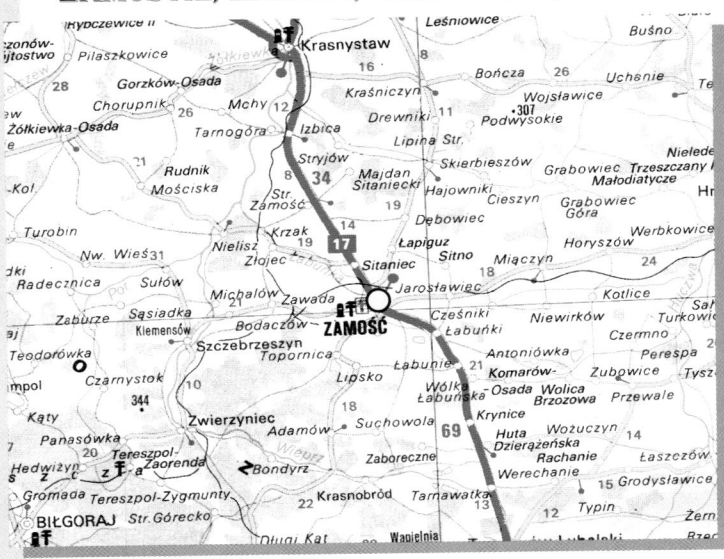

The town of Zamość dates back to the late sixteenth century, when Prince Jan Zamoyski imported Italian architects to build a town in the Renaissance style. Even in a world of shifting borders, the fate of Zamość was particularly complex. In the nineteenth century, it belonged first to Austria and then to Russia. Sephardic Jews were the first Jews to settle in Zamość at the end of the sixteenth century; they were followed by a larger decisive settlement of Ashkenazic Jews. Haskalah, the Jewish Enlightenment movement, flourished in Zamość in the nineteenth century. It was the birthplace of both Róża Luxemburg, a fiery radical active in the founding of the Communist parties of Russia, Germany and Poland, and of I. L. Peretz, known as the father of modern Yiddish literature. Peretz modeled the setting of his famous play, *Night at the Old Marketplace*, after the magnificent Zamość marketplace. World War I devastated Zamość, but by 1939, Jewish life had revived and about 12,000 Jews were living there.

When the Germans invaded Poland, Zamość came under Soviet occupation; about 5,000 Jews retreated with the Red Army. In the spring of 1942, the Germans established a ghetto in Zamość to which they shipped Jews from other cities in occupied Poland as well as from Germany and Czechoslovakia; about 9,000 Jews passed through the ghetto. Successive deportations, primarily to the Bełżec death camp, emptied the ghetto; it was liquidated in October 1942.

Location

89 km SE of Lublin
50°43´/23°16´
Voivodship: Zamość

General Population, 1939

24,000 (50% Jewish)

General Population, 1994

65,955

SYNAGOGUES

ul. Gminna 32
Constructed in 1872; destroyed in 1939; reconstructed after the Holocaust.
Current use: nursery school.

Dawna Synagogue, ul. Zamenhofa 9, 1916   2

ul. Zamenhofa 9
Constructed 1620, extensively damaged during the Holocaust; rebuilt in 1950s.
Current use: library.

OTHER SITES

ul. Zamenhofa 5
Mikvah constructed in 1877.
Current use: jazz club.

Dawna Synagogue, ul. Zamenhofa 9, today a library   1

Holocaust Memorial, ul. Prosta, 1996   3

JEWISH CEMETERIES

ul. Partyzantów
Old cemetery destroyed during Holocaust.
Current use: cultural center.

ul. Prosta
New cemetery founded in 1906.
About 50 tombstones remain.
Current use: lapidarium.

Dawna synagogue interior, pre-Holocaust   4

The town hall on the Great Market Square, 1995   5

HOLOCAUST MEMORIALS

ul. Prosta (former Jewish cemetery)
Monument (obelisk) constructed in 1950 from
tombstone fragments.

ul. Męczenników Rotundy
The Museum of Martyrology (in Rotunda)
Constructed on the site of mass executions.

DEPORTATIONS

Izbica, Bełżec.

ul. Ormiańska, c. 1933   6

135

Dawna Synagogue (cross section), pre-1939   7

Portal and vestibule, Dawna Synagogue, pre-1939   8

Portal of Dawna Synagogue (elevation), pre-1939   9

SELECTED READING

Baranowski, Zofia, and Jerzy Baranowski. "Dzielnica żydowska i synagoga w Zamościu" (The Jewish Quarter and Synagogue in Zamość). BŻIH 63 (1967): 39–56. (P)

Bernstein, Maroqued, ed. Pinkes Zamoshtsh; yisker-bukh (Zamość Chronicle: Memorial Book). Buenos Aires: Tsentral-Komitet far Pinkes Zamoshtsh, 1957. (Y)

Klausner, I. A. "Zamoshtsh—ha-'ir shel Y. L. Perets" (Zamość—City of I. L. Peretz). He-Avar 13 (1966): 98–117. (H)

Morgensztern, Janina. "Nieznany list Seymu Czterech ziem z 1605 r. w sprawie sefardyjskiego Żyda w Zamościu" (An Unknown Letter of the Council of Four Lands in the Matter of a Sephardic Jew in Zamość). BŻIH 43/44 (1962): 110–112. (P)

———. "O działalności gospodarczej Żydów w Zamościu w XVI i XVII w. (handel)" (On the Economic Activities of the Jews in Zamość in the Sixteenth and Seventeenth Centuries: Merchandise and Handicrafts). BŻIH 53 (1965): 3–32; 56 (1965): 3–28. (P)

———. "Operacje kredytowe Żydów w Zamościu w XVII w." (Credit Operations of Zamość Jews in the Seventeenth Century). BŻIH 64 (1967): 3–32. (P)

———. "Uwagi o Żydach sefardyjskich w Zamościu w latach 1588–1650" (Notes on the Sephardim in Zamość, 1588–1650). BŻIH 38 (1961): 69–82. (P)

———. "Zadłużenie gmin żydowskich w ordynacji zamojskiej w II połowie XVII w." (Indebtedness of the Jewish Community in Zamość in the Second Half of the Seventeenth Century). BŻIH 73 (1970): 47–65. (P)

Sawa, Bogumiła. "Przyczynek do sytuacji prawnej Żydów zamojskich od II połowy XVI do XIII w." (A Contribution to the Legal Status of Zamość Jews from the Mid-Sixteenth and Seventeenth Centuries). BŻIH 3/99 (1976): 27–40. (P)

Tamari, Moshe, ed. Zamoshtsh bi-genonah uve-shivrah (Zamość at Its Height and Its Destruction). Tel Aviv: Former Residents of Zamość in Israel, 1953. (H, P)

BIBLIOGRAPHIC SOURCES

CTD; EDRD; EJ; EOH; GA; GUM3; GUM4; GUM5; GUM6; GYLA; HSL; JGFF; JHT; KH; LDL; LDS; LYV; PJH; RJHS; SF

JEWISH GENEALOGICAL RESEARCH IN THE POLISH STATE ARCHIVES

by Professor
Jerzy Skowronek

INTRODUCTION

Jews have lived in the territories of the Polish Republic for almost 1,000 years.

Rich archival materials document the existence and creativity of many generations, although a large percentage of these materials were tragically destroyed in the horrors of the Holocaust. The surviving archival materials have been carefully protected in Poland and are well preserved and saved as an integral, extremely valuable part of our national archival holdings.

The totality of Judaica in Polish archival collections probably measures several running kilometers of files. Although the largest and most significant collections are stored at the Jewish Historical Institute (*Żydowski Instytut Historyczny*) in Warsaw, documents and materials concerning Polish Jews are found in state archives all over the country. They consist of approximately 100 units and are more or less basic parts of several hundred archival fonds.

In addition, archival materials concerning Jewish communities or their individual representatives are found in at least several hundred archival fonds and manuscript collections of such well-known academic libraries as the National Library in Warsaw, the Jagiellonian University Library and Polish Academy of Sciences in Kraków, Ossoliński Library in Wrocław, Łopaciński Library in Lublin, Działyński Library in Kórnik (near Poznań), and the Archives of the Ministries of Interior, National Defense and Foreign Affairs. Records pertaining to conversions to Christianity (Catholic or Protestant) may be found in church archives. (Addresses for these libraries and archives are listed at the end of this chapter.)

The Archives of the Central Commission on the Crimes Against the Polish Nation (*Główna Komisja do Badania Zbrodni Przeciwko Narodowi Polskiemu*) include material on the Holocaust and on crimes against the population of the former Second Republic of Poland committed by the Soviet Union (and the Polish secret police after 1945), collected for specific cases (trials, investigation of Nazi war criminals and those responsible for the Kielce pogrom, etc.). The Archives of the Polish Academy of Sciences are useful for their (mostly posthumous) works of individual Jewish scientists.

Professor Jerzy Skowronek and Miriam Weiner sign contract for book publication, 1993

1

DOCUMENTS DATING FROM THE FOURTEENTH CENTURY

Documents and manuscripts in Polish archives concerning the Jews reach back to the fourteenth century. The materials refer to various areas of life and activities of the Jewish population in Poland, primarily in the areas of economics and culture and, to a lesser degree, in politics.

With minor exceptions, documents and materials held in Polish archives originated only in the territories within the present boundaries of Poland. Documents of offices (and institutions from the regions of modern-day Lithuania, Belarus and Ukraine) remain in the archives of those countries (or in Russian archives). At the end of World War II, as a result of extensive wartime transfers, some Polish archival collections remained in Germany or the Soviet Union; their repatriation still poses problems that are difficult to overcome.

❚ *Sign at entrance to AGAD Archives, Warsaw* 2

Most valuable for genealogical studies are priceless archives of Jewish communities going back to the Middle Ages. According to Polish archival law, such archives are taken over when a specific Jewish community ceases to exist. Unfortunately, the Holocaust and military actions taken during World War II caused great losses in these materials. Very little remained in some archives, such as that in Białystok. In other archives, such as those in Kielce, Poznań, Rzeszów, Sandomierz and Wrocław, a large proportion of the Jewish communal archives has been preserved.

GENEALOGICAL DATA IN ARCHIVES, MUSEUMS AND LIBRARIES

Documents and material concerning the Polish-Jewish population can be found in many other archival collections. Even though no clearly marked connection with Judaica is evident in the names or character of the collections, they often include single documents (or whole groups of documents) of great value to a historian dealing with genealogical research.

Periods of violence and the partitions of Poland also affected the fate of archival collections, since less differentiation was made between documents gathered into archives, on the one hand, and those preserved in central libraries and museums, on the other hand. In fact, all three types of institutions—archives, libraries and museums—hold fonds of family documents. In some rare cases, parts of state archive holdings (such as those of a local administration or even of various ministries) were included in a library or museum collection as a result of either donation or purchase. For this reason, collections in museums and libraries should also be investigated as a part of any thorough genealogical query.

Other genealogical documents and materials may be found in the fonds of different municipal councils and other authorities or among well-preserved notary public and mortgage documents. Documents of some public institutions are of significant value. Files concerning population statistics and migrations; those of educational, cultural, economic, and political institutions and activities; censuses; archives of authorities dealing with religious affiliations and national minorities; and police documents all belong to that large group.

ON-GOING ACQUISITION OF JEWISH DOCUMENTS

Almost every month brings further enrichment of documentary sources. For example, the State Archives in Szczecin, Gorzów Division, recently has acquired court files comprised of (among other registry files) birth, marriage and death certificates of the Jewish population of Barlinek and other districts for the years 1847–1874. Similar files have also been acquired by many other local state archives within the past few years. A full-scale inventory of Jewish cemeteries and graves is becoming a new, valuable source of genealogical information (see Gruber, Samuel, and Phyllis Myers, *Survey of Historic Jewish Monuments in Poland*. New York: Jewish Heritage Council, World Monuments Fund, November 1995).

With reference to the most stable, systematically gathered documents of registry, notary public and mortgage offices, one should remember that books and other materials from these offices are usually transferred to the State Archives 100 years after the documents are created (see Chapters 1 and 4). In some regions of the country, however, mortgage files from the period up to World War II have already been transferred to archives, because the proprietary issues are considered to have been closed.

STARTING PLACES FOR GENEALOGICAL INQUIRIES

In the beginning of the research process, as with historical studies in other areas, all genealogical queries to the Polish State Archives should consider the following:

- A detailed definition of the subject (or the objective) of the research.
- The acquisition of precise information on archival resources concerning the given subject.

When beginning genealogical studies concerning specific persons or families, information must be made available on where (i.e., in which place) and when (i.e., in which years or period of time) a given person or family lived or, preferably, when (exact date specifying a day or a year) and where (name of a place) they were born, married or died. If the information requested by a person or an institution conducting the genealogical research is not specific enough, the actual performance of the research may be assigned to staff archivists in the State Archives in order to get the appropriate information. Currently, this research is done on a commercial basis for a fee of $15 per hour.

The Polish State Archives does have centralized information on the holdings of its archives throughout Poland regarding the list of fonds in every archive and expects to have the information computerized by the end of 1997. The Center of Archival Information (*Centralny Ośrodek Informacji Archiwalnej*) at the Chief Administrative Offices of the State Archives (*Naczelna Dyrekcja Archiwów Państwowych, ul. Długa 6, 00-950 Warszawa*), supervised by Dr. Andrzej Biernat, was established long ago. Its

activities are limited, however, to gathering and verifying information on the collections of documents of different archives. The data was collected in the form of a list of fonds of archive files (i.e., documents and materials created by a given office or institution, and collections of documents). In the best cases, we have detailed inventories of files referring to individual fonds.

Of course, the foregoing lists and inventories did not include the great collections of documents and manuscripts held in central libraries and museums. Only now are libraries beginning the difficult job of organizing computerized databases. In a few years, we anticipate the creation of very detailed and precise series of catalogs of the manuscripts for (among others) the Ossolineum Library in Wrocław, the libraries of the Polish Academy of Sciences, the Jagiellonian and Czartoryski Libraries in Kraków, the libraries of the Polish Academy of Sciences in Kórnik near Poznań, the Raczyński Library in Poznań, the National Library in Warsaw, and the libraries of Warsaw University and the Central School of Commerce in Warsaw. Most of these libraries have published catalogs of their manuscript collections, but they are usually summarized into single-sheet catalogs preserved in a given library and available only on site. A printed guide to state and church museums was created by Danuta Kamolowa and

House plans for Abram and Ester Odnoposow, Piotrków Trybunalski, 1912

3

Krystyna Maszyńska. (See Zbiory rękopisów w bibliotekach i muzeach w Polsce [Collections of Manuscripts in Libraries and Museums in Poland]. Warsaw: Biblioteka Narodowa, 1988.)

Each archive has unpublished inventories on site that can be consulted by researchers. Many of the State Archives have published guides to their holdings, including the State Archives in Gdańsk, Kalisz, Kielce, Poznań, Radom, Wrocław and Łódź; the Central Archives of Historical Records; and the Archives of Contemporary Records in Warsaw. Guides to the holdings of other state archives are in progress. Some archives develop and publish inventories of their most valuable fonds, while some others have produced detailed subject directories. Note, for example, Krochmal, Anna, Akta wyznaniowe w zasobie archiwum Państwowego w przemyślu (Religious Records in the Holdings of the State Archives in Przemyśl) (Przemyśl: Archiwum Państowe w Przemyślu, 1993). The Judaica holdings are noted on pages 180–190.

Material in the State Archives at Rzeszów has been the subject of research conducted on the history of the Polish Jewish population. The Center on Archival Information in Warsaw has also gathered information about Judaica holdings in our archives. Both are valuable in the initial determination of the range of sources for specific archival queries. Individual, specific studies on the history of the Polish-Jewish population as reflected in archival materials have been conducted by a number of archivists in different regions of our country. Among

them have been archivists in Białystok, Lublin and Suwałki. In Pułtusk, Dr. Janusz Szczepański wrote Dzieje społeczności żydowskiej powiatów Pułtusk i Maków Mazowiecki (The History of the Jewish Population from the Districts of Pułtusk and Maków Mazowiecki) (Warsaw: Pułtuskie Towarzystwo Społeczno-Kulturalne and Towarzystwo Miłośników Makowa Mazowieckiego, 1993).

From all of the necessarily general information above, it is obvious that the Polish State Archives are a very rich and important source of data for Jewish genealogical research. As such, we do try to ensure the best possible working conditions for each researcher, within the limitations of our imperfect technical facilities.

ACCESS TO POLISH STATE ARCHIVES

Access to the Polish State Archives is regulated by a law enacted on July 14, 1983, which provides that individuals seeking admission to archives for academic research may be permitted to work at the discretion of each individual archive director. For those individuals seeking admission to the archives for the purpose of researching genealogy, property ownership, citizenship changes (by the German government during World War II), permission must first be obtained from the main director in Warsaw. This permission may be requested prior to arrival in Warsaw by letter or fax or by applying in person at ul. Długa 6 in Warsaw (tel: 831-9584; fax: 831-7563).

Will of Nuta Maizels (first page), Nowy Korczyn, 1905   4A

Last page of Nuta Maizels' will, dividing 400 rubles among his children   4B

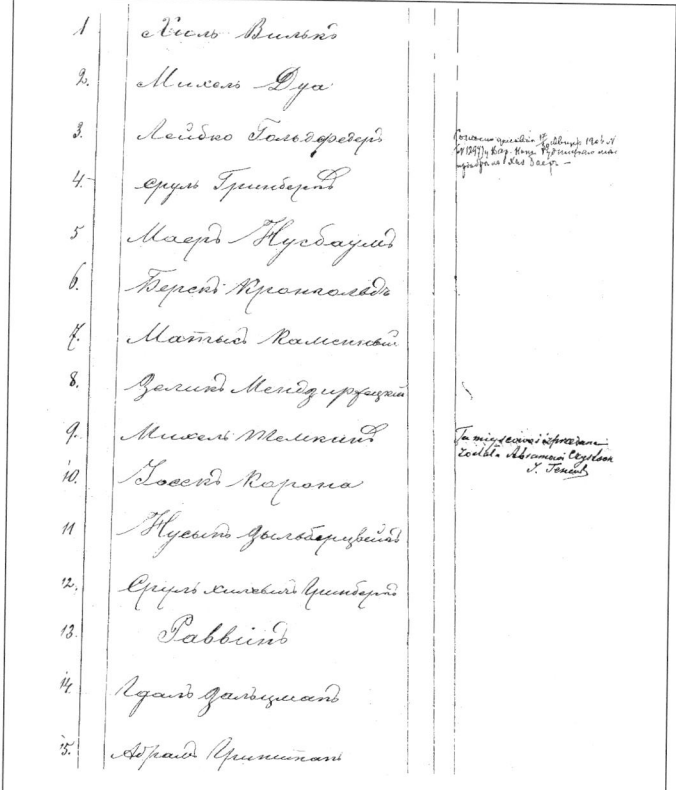

List of purchasers of seats in Siedlce Synagogue, 1906   5A

Siedlce Synagogue tax list in Hebrew, with a total of 401 names   5B

All existing directories, guides and inventories are accessible to researchers. If necessary, initial assistance (*i.e.*, information) is given by archivists in the form of advice about fonds related to a given subject that should be examined. After the initial recommendations from the archivists, the remaining (substantial) work should be done by the researchers themselves. Both an individual and an institution conducting research are obliged to substantiate *in writing* the grounds for conducting a particular genealogical query. This might be a proven family relationship with a given person or family, or a written assignment to conduct genealogical queries given by any of the living descendants of a specific person or family. It is possible that large-scale studies of demographic and social, or social and genetic, relations may constitute such grounds. We make this requirement because the very personal nature of genealogical queries imposes an obligation on the archives to see that personal properties or rights are not infringed upon.

HIRING PRIVATE RESEARCHERS AND RESEARCH FIRMS

The execution of some, or even all, specific tasks connected with genealogical research may be assigned to special genealogical associations or professional research firms. Some associations are not always reliable and may not complete their research work or do it well. The same is true of some individual "freelancers" who assume such assignments. That said,

however, it should be noted, that there are reliable and responsible professional research firms which work regularly in our archives and are familiar with our holdings.

Thorough genealogical studies require extensive knowledge of the holdings of different archives with respect to their collections of documents and, above all, knowledge of the differentiation of fonds of records in different archives. This explains why the results of genealogical research carried out by associations or by researchers taking individual assignments who are not experienced genealogical researchers or familiar with our holdings could produce less than satisfactory results. Assignments executed as a result of individual agreements between an individual and any person or research entity other than the State Archives are not subject to any control or evaluation by the State Archives.

The State Archives is able to carry out all (or selected) stages of tasks connected with the examination of genealogical materials. Because the budgets of our archives do not finance such work, the cost must be assumed by the person or institution requesting the work. The fact that the work is done by an archivist well acquainted with the document collections in our archives ensures the reliability and thoroughness of such research. Currently, the fee for this service is $15 per hour. All preserved vital register documents are consulted. Any extension of the research into different types of documents involves much more time and work and, thus, increases the cost. There is an additional charge for copies.

STEPS TO INITIATE A GENEALOGICAL SEARCH

To initiate a search by the Polish State Archives, one must:

- Define in the most precise possible manner the range of a search—that is, a date and place of birth, marriage or death.
- Send an advance payment equal to a one-hour fee for a qualified archivist.

The second condition results from the necessity to cover the cost of a preliminary search for specific documents concerning an individual person or family. Polish archives do not have access to specific information indicating in which fond the data on a given person can be found. Such data can be acquired only by actually going through the records manually.

In the case of completed studies with a positive result, the advance payment is applied to the total costs. For a variety of reasons, however, such work often is not successful. Sometimes gaps exist in the registry books; at other times, the date and place of birth or death provided by the person initiating the research is incorrect. In any event, as is customary with professional genealogists, time spent doing research must be paid for whether or not the search is successful.

Since prices do change from time to time, it is best to write and request a current price list, which will include charges for duplicates, photocopies, microfilms or certified copies of documents ordered by a person requesting genealogical research. The fees of the Polish State Archives are lower than those charged by the archives of some of our neighboring countries, such as Latvia, Lithuania and Russia. Charges for photocopies are deliberately high so as to minimize the number of such requests. Exposure to the strong light of photocopying has a destructive effect on archival documents and, thus, should be done as rarely as possible. Unfortunately, we do not have equipment to scan or copy microfilms, nor does our budget include money to purchase modern technical equipment. In the future, however, we will endeavor not to make photocopies of archival documents at all— a limitation that already exists in many archives in Western Europe.

FEES FOR GENEALOGICAL RESEARCH

Charges for our services, calculated according to the price list, are to be paid after completion of the research—that is, when the results actually are sent to the person ordering the search. Fees are updated only every few years, despite the relatively high yearly inflation rate in Poland these days. The Chief Administrative Office of the State Archives, acting as an intermediary, guarantees that the research is reliable and has been properly evaluated. Since the fee structure changes periodically, please write and request a current fee schedule to be sent to you.

Address requests to: ARCHIWUM PAŃSTWOWE
skr. poczt. 1005, ul. Długa 6
00-950 Warszawa, Poland

Editor's Note: An earlier version of this material appeared in *Avotaynu*, vol. 10, no. 2 (Summer 1994): 5–8.

Professor Jerzy Skowronek was born in Radom, Poland. He earned his Ph.D. in history at Warsaw University. In 1984, he was named an Extraordinary Professor of that university. His specialty was Polish history of the nineteenth century. In his 32 years in the History Department of Warsaw University, he held numerous organizational and administrative positions. On January 1, 1993, he was appointed the general director of the State Archives of Poland.

Professor Skowronek published 12 books and approximately 100 papers, articles and research notes. He conducted research in France, Italy, Yugoslavia, Bulgaria, Great Britain and the republics of the former Soviet Union. He lectured at several European universities and participated in more than 50 congresses and international seminars.

Professor Skowronek was the recipient of six awards from the president of Warsaw University, two first prizes from the Minister of Science and the award of the Scientific Secretary of the Polish Academy of Sciences. Among his many distinctions was a medal from the National Education Commission and the French Palmes Academiques for his scientific and civic activities.

Editor's Note: Professor Skowronek died in an automobile accident in France in July 1996.

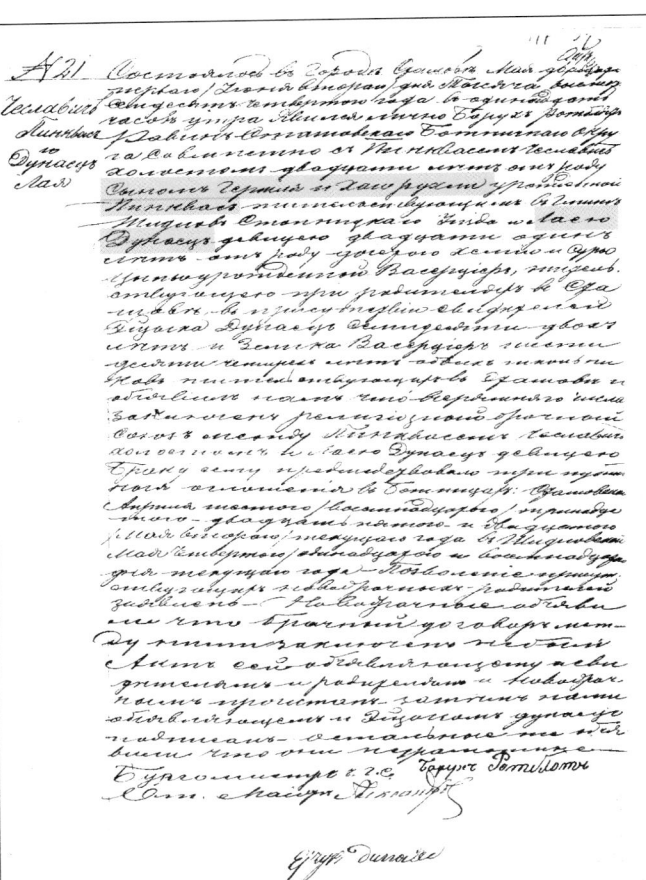

Marriage, 1874, Staszów: Pinkas Czeslowicz, age 20 (son of Hersh and Chaya Ruchla) and Leah Dunajec, age 21 (daughter of Chaim and Sura Cipa Wasercycer)

6

Death record of Moses Spielholz, Tarnów, House #70   7
(died in 1848 at age 17)

Family list entry for Szlomo-Ber and Sura Rywka Ciesla, 1940, Lubartów;   8
their sons: Srul-Dawid and Nuchim
Szlomo-Ber's parents: Pinkas and Sima Leja

Book of residents, 1902–1931, Nowy Korczyn: Family of Shaya Gancwaig (1871–1916, son of Israel Leib   9
Gancwaig and Zlata Berger) and his wife Dina Brandla Maizels (born 1870, daughter of Nutka Maizels and
Pesla Hendler) and their children: Israel (born 1892); Perla (1896–1912); Curtla (born 1898); Nutka (born
1901); and Hersch Mendel (born 1911)

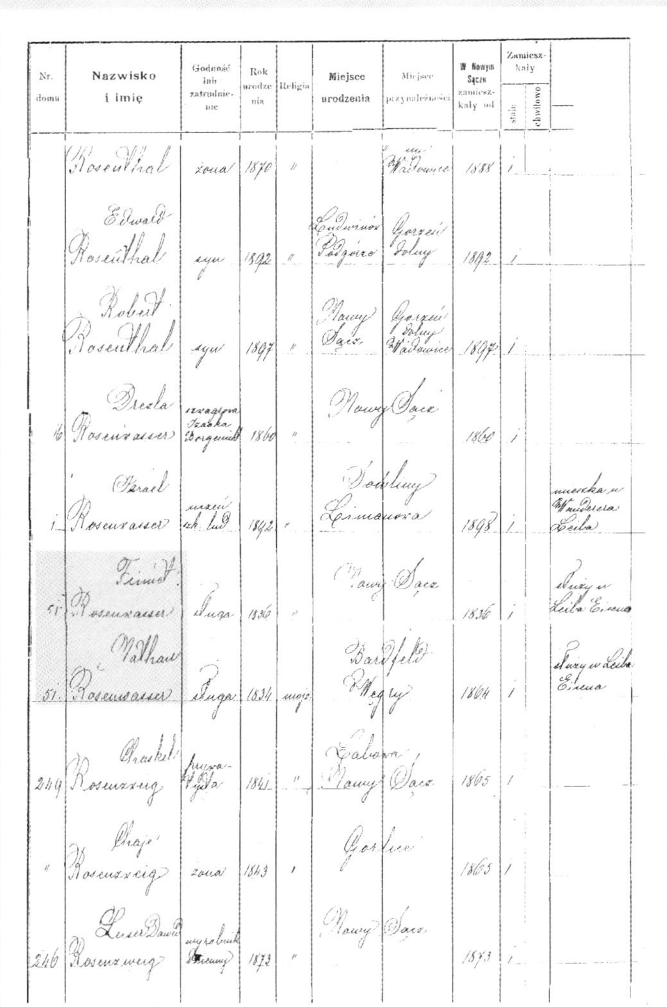

List of residents, Nowy Sącz, 1870:
Nathan and Frimet Rosenwasser, from Bardfeld, Hungary

10

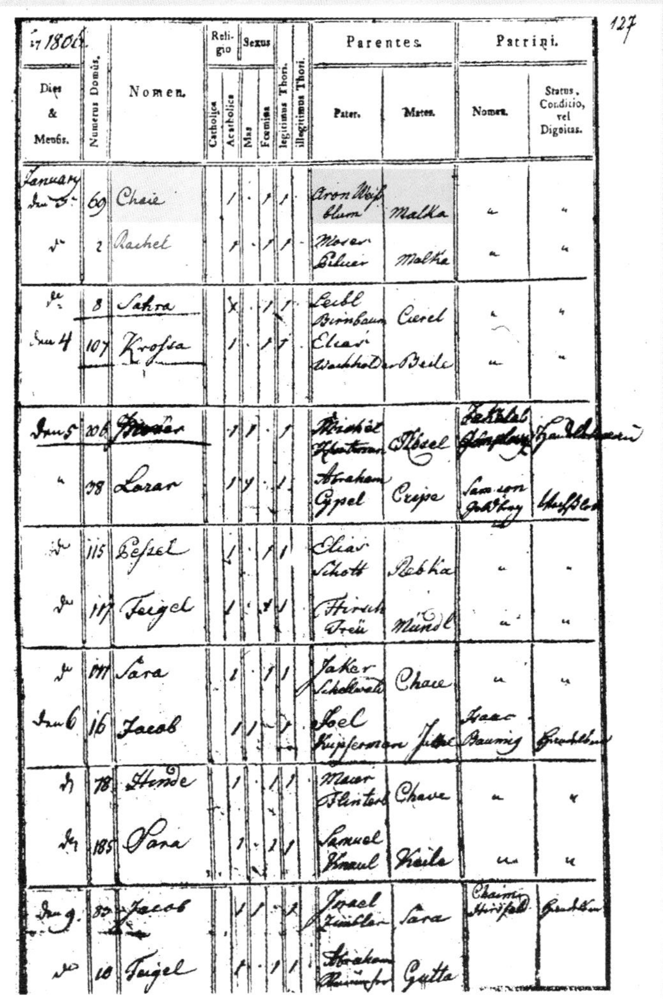

Birth record, 1806, Kraków:
Chaya Weisblum, daughter of Aron and Malka Weisblum

11

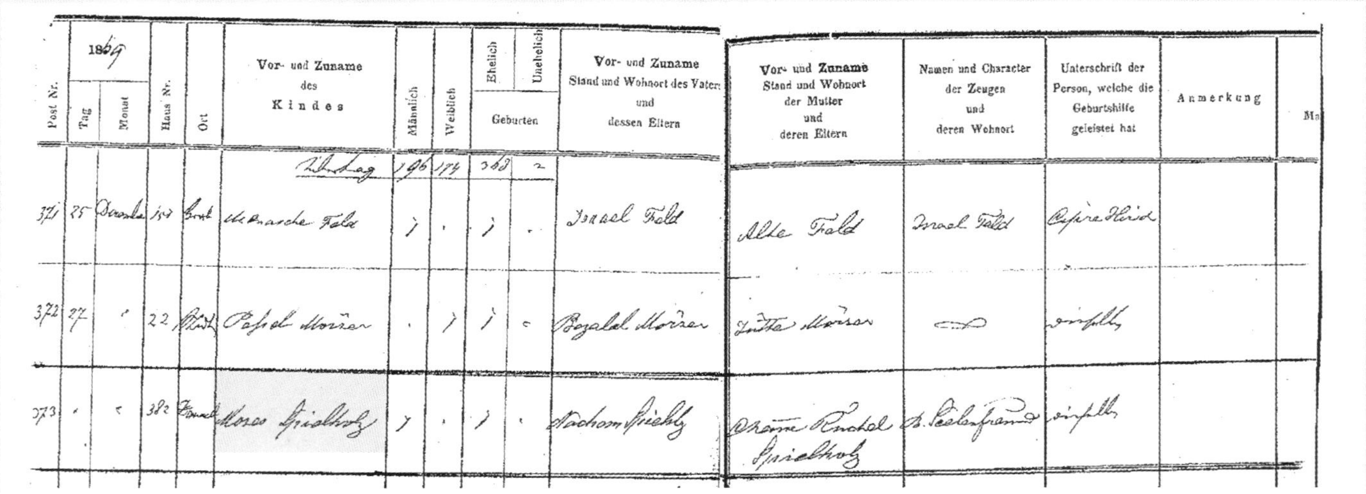

Birth record of Moses Spielholz, born 1869 in Tarnów, son of Nachum and Chana Ruchel Spielholz

12

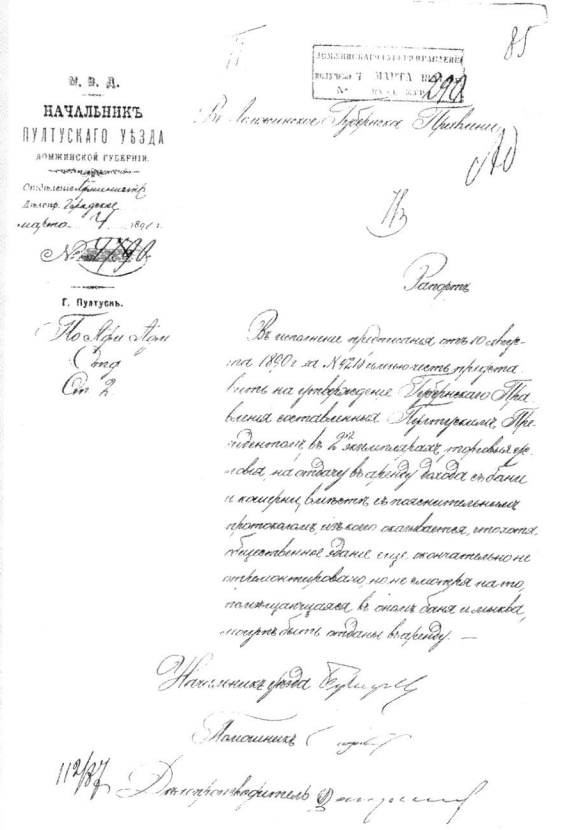

Land office in Pułtusk gives permission to Jewish community for reconstruction of mikvah, 1891 — 13

Notary documents, Frysztak, 1920:
Transfer of property by Hersch and Chana Englehardt — 14

Death record of Berek Radzinski, died April 24, 1880 in Pińczów, at age four (son of Chaim Fishel Radzinski and Frimet Waisgorberg) — 15

Imię, mianowicie nazwisko familii (nazwisko), imię chrzestne, przydomek szlachecki i stopień szlachecki. Имя, т. е. имя родины (прозвище), имя крестное, придомокъ шляхотскій и степень шляхотства.	Płeć — Родъ (полъ)		Rok urodzenia — Рокъ рожденія	Religia — Религія (вѣра)	Stan familii — Станъ родины	
a	b	c		d	e	f
1 Kepper Mojzesz Ekiwe	1		1826	Mojzeszow	żonaty	Sa
2 dtto Hene żona		1	1834	"	"	
3 dtto Samuel Mendl syn	1		1862	"	wolny	—
4 dtto Hirsch syn	1		1866	"	"	—
5 dtto Matke Feigel córka		1	1868	"	"	—

Census, 1870, Kraków: Family of Mojzesz Kepper (born 1826); his wife, Hene (born 1834); a son, Samuel Mendl (born 1862); a son, Hirsch (born 1866); and a daughter, Malke Feigel (born 1868)

lub zatrudnienie / или занятіе		Miejsce urodzenia / Мѣсто рожденія	Przynależ- ność / Принадлеж- ность	Obecny / Присут- ствующій	Nieobecny / Отсутству- ющій	Uwaga / Примѣчаніе
zatrudnienie.	Stosunek służby lub pracy.	Kraj / Powiat / Miejscowose. — Край / Повѣтъ / Мѣстце.	To w odpowiedni rubryce cyfrą 1 oznaczyć należy...	Obecność i nieobecność każdej wpisanej osoby uwidocznić trzeba cyfrą 1 w odnośnej rubryce.		Jeśli osoba jest całkiem ciemną lub głuchoniemą to należy tutaj nadmienić...
				Przynależ- ny do gminy / Obcy		
				Ts- jemny / Чужин- нада		
h		i	k	l	m	n
	Kraków	1		1		
—	do	1		1		
—	do	1		1		
—	do	1		1		
—	do	1		1		

16

№ дома. № по поряд-ку.	ИМЯ И ФАМИЛІЯ.		Имена родителей и родовая фамилія матери.	Время рожденія.			Мѣсто рожден
	Мужчинъ.	Женщинъ, фамилія до вступленія въ бракъ и по мужу.		День.	Мѣсяцъ.	Годъ.	
1.		*Хая Лерманъ, рожденная Цынге*	*Аронъ и Марія рожденная Конъ*	*Августа*		*1839*	*Горо Веделга*
2.	*Шляма Лерманъ*		*Разведенная Хая Лерманъ, рожденная Цынге*	*Въ 1907 г. Плоцкаго при по Заваду пив. прибут Августа*		*1886 1886*	*Горо Пло*
3.	*Мойсей Лерманъ*		*Шляма Лерманъ и незамужняя Марьемъ Дайч*	*23 6*	*Ноября Декабря*	*1908*	*г. Пло*
4.	*Давидъ-Лейбъ Лерманъ*		*Шляма Лерманъ и Дзвица Марьемъ Дайчъ*	*2/ 15*	*Іюня*	*1913*	*гор Плоц*
		Шлама Lerman	*Шлама, Марьем рожд. Дайез*	*акт знания*		*1902*	*Плос*
7.							

Book of residents, 1830–1930, Płock: Family of Chaja Lerman (born 1839); a son, Szlama (born 1886); and all family members

нать, ужняя, нѣтъ.	Происхожденіе.	Вѣроисповѣданіе.	Средства къ содержанію.	Мѣсто прежняго жительства.	Примѣчаніе. 16 (Здѣсь отмѣчаются всѣ перемѣны, происшедшія въ положеніи лицъ, записанныхъ въ книгу народонаселенія, какъ то: смерть, переселеніе, переходъ въ другой номеръ дома и проч., согласно § 15 инструкціи.)
бедем-	Мѣщан-ское	Худей-ское	Зара-ботки	Ст. кни. Широкая № 30 стр. 91	П. 8068 _____
_____	Мѣщан-ское	Худей-ское	При матери	Изъ акта знанія	П. 8037 _____ Паш. № 14944/1902 _____
сть	мѣщан-ское	Гудейское	приходи-телято	акта ро Дсіи.	
ств	мѣщан-ское	Гудей-ское	при родите-лямъ	Уч Акта о рожденіи	
на	miejscowy	Мир	_____	z akt. stanu	_____ на dk. 56-tej _____
	_____ 57 Raport _Ministra Spraw Wewn._ z dnia _____ о _____ i księgach ludności _____ _____ z dnia 31. XII. 1930 roku. _____				

17

Birth record of Bendet Antler, born 1880, Monastyriska: son of Leisor Antler (merchant) and Nesi Antler   18

Tax list of Kromołów Jewish community, 1864   20

List of prisoners, Lublin ghetto, 1941   19

Birth record of Litman Brawerman, born 1856 in Terespol   21

Death record of Izrael Monszayin, died 1838 in Pilica (age nine), son of Jakub and Rochli   22

Death record of Helena Markus, died in 1878 in Janowitz, daughter of Edward Markus and Hanna Stremchewska   24

Tax list of Krasnystaw Jewish community, 1928   23

	Nazwisko i imię	Zawód	Miejsce zamieszkania		Uwagi
1	Apgsdamer Majer	rzeźnik	Krasnystaw	20	
2	Ajzen Chaim	Kupiec		30	
3	Ajzenberg Debe	Kupcowa		8	
4	Akierman Abraham	Kupiec		2	
5	Adelsberg Dawid	"		5	
6	" Hersz	"		15	
7	Ajnwejner Cyrla	Kupcowa	"	20	
8	" Jankiel	Rzeźnik	"	5	
9	" Chaim	Rzeźnik		10	
10	" Froim F.	Krawiec		2	
11	" Menachim	Stolarz		10	
12	Ajzensztajn Szymon Lejb wł. Młyna		"	250	
13	Ajchenblat Benjamin	Szewc		2	
14	Akierman Icek	Stolarz		2	
15	" Symcha			2	
16	Abensztajn Mojżesz	Handlarz		2	
17	" Huta			10	
18	Adelsberg Hejnoch	Kupiec		10	
19	Brenkmajn Aron	"		10	
20	Bergierman Icchek	"		10	
21	Blat Icek			10	
22	Birman Grul Icek	Krawiec		20	
23	Borensztajn Hersz	Rymarz		5	
24	Baum Dawid	Mełamed		2	
25	" Nusen	Kupiec		25	
26	" Symcha			5	
27	Baumfeld Izjer			30	
28	" Dawid			30	
29	Belik Całka			5	
30	" Abraham	Krawiec		5	
31	" Abraham	Kupiec		2	
32	Binder Mendel			10	
	Do przeniesienia			581	

Transport list of Jews to Majdanek, 1942–1943   25

Nr.	Vorname	Name	Geburtstag	Geburtsort	Bar.
		Judentransport nach Lublin			
112.	Mendl	Sznajder	13.9.18.	Knyszyn	46
113.	Beniamin	G lisztajn	7.2.21.	Sarny	46
114.	Chaim	Irycanewicz	1.1.19.	Nowogred	46
115.	Beniamin	Negiensky	6.51.21.	Rutki	46
116.	Szeja	Rapaport	19.13.88.	Rutki	46
117.	Motel	Tuchweber	14.4.94.	Wengrow	46
118.	Z	Amrafel	15.5.93.	Szczucin	46
119.	Hersz	Kohn	1.12.97.	"	46
120.	Lejba	Rozensztajn	2.2.20.	"	46
121.	Abram	Du inski	15.7.08.	"	46
122.	Eljasz	Sokulski	13.4.92.	"	46
123.	Dawid	Grzesztejn	3.5.94.	"	46
124.	Baruch	Skubelski	26.10.90.	"	46
125.	Jankiel	Zanelson	15.3.17.	Lomza	46
126.	..	"	15.3.89.	Sokorow	46
127.	S.	Zalinski	3.8.12.	Bialystok	46
128.	Josef	Dik	26.8.09.	Wilna	46
129.	H.	Fribal	10.4.09.	Laremby	46
130.	Jstan	Rezentak	27.11.20.	Knyszyn	46
131.	Z.	Sosnowski	17.9.98.	Szczucin	46
132.	Chaim	Dorf	6.5.25.	"	46
133.	Judel	Halpern	17.11.16.	"	46
134.	Joszek	Sacharewicz	18.11.96.	"	46
135.	Chaim	Gewen	1.2...	"	46
136.	Lejba	Monk	15.5.93.	"	46
137.	Alter	Lichtensztajn	10.3.23.	"	46
138.	Lejber	Rotsztajn	20.5.94.	"	46

ARCHIVES AND LIBRARIES IN POLAND
(Outside of the Polish State Archives System)

The following archives and libraries in Poland have many important documents and manuscripts that would be of interest to researchers of Jewish family history. There are many other smaller repositories with equally interesting material.

PLACE/Address	T(elephone)/F(ax)	
NATIONAL LIBRARY		
(BIBLIOTEKA NARODOWA)	25-92-71	T
Warszawa 02-973	25-92-72	T
Al. Niepodległości 213	25-91-73	T
JAGIELLONIAN LIBRARY		
(BIBLIOTEKA JAGIELLOŃSKA)	33-63-77	T
30-059 Kraków	33-09-03	T
Al. A. Mickiewicza 22	33-19-71	T
POLISH ACADEMY OF SCIENCES LIBRARY		
(BIBLIOTEKA PAN)	22-29-15	T
31-016 Kraków	22-73-04	T
ul. Sławkowska 17	22-27-91	F
OSSOLIŃSKI LIBRARY		
(BIBLIOTEKA PAN ZAKŁADU NARODOWEGO IM. OSSOLIŃSKICH)		
50-139 Wrocław		
ul. Szewska 37	44-44-71	T
ŁOPACIŃSKI LIBRARY		
(BIBLIOTEKA ŁOPACIŃSKICH)		
20-950 Lublin		
ul. Staszica 16	250-41	T
and		
ul. Narutowicza 4	209-31	T
DZIALYŃSKI LIBRARY		
(BIBLIOTEKA KÓRNICKA PAN)		
(branch of Poznań library)		
63-120 Kórnik Zamek		
Palac Działyńskich		
61-772 Poznań	44-44-71	T
Stary Rynek 78/79	44-44-71	T

PLACE/Address	T(elephone)/F(ax)	
ARCHIVES OF THE MINISTRY OF INTERIOR		
(ARCHIWUM MSW)	52-89-29	T
02-517 Warszawa	21-02-51	T
ul. Rakowiecka 2A	49-78-08	F
ARCHIVES OF NATIONAL DEFENSE		
(ARCHIWUM MINISTERSTWA OBRONY NARODOWEJ)		
00-904 Warszawa		
ul. Rakowiecka 4A	21-02-61	T
ARCHIVES OF FOREIGN AFFAIRS		
(ARCHIWUM MSZ)		
00-580 Warszawa	49-78-08	F
Al. Szucha 23	623-9380	T
LIBRARY OF THE POLISH ACADEMY OF SCIENCE		
(BIBLIOTEKA PAN WARSZAWA)		
00-901 Warszawa	620-3302	T
Pałac Kultury i Nauki	620-0211	T
CZARTORYSKI LIBRARY		
(BIBLIOTEKA KSIĄŻĄT CZARTORYSKICH)		
31-018 Kraków	22-11-72	T
ul. św. Marka 17		
ARCHIVES OF THE CENTRAL COMMISSION ON THE CRIMES AGAINST THE POLISH NATION		
(GŁÓWNA KOMISJA BADANIA ZBRODNI PRZECIWKO NARODOWI POLSKIEMU)	226-2441	T
ul. Krakowskie Przedmieście	26-21-39	T/F
Correspondence:		
00-898 Warszawa		
Al. Solidarności 127		

Source: The above list was provided by Professor Jerzy Skowronek to be included in this chapter.

Author's note: Jewish vital records are also interspersed with the Roman Catholic vital records for the period of 1810–1825 (separate records by religious community began in 1826). Therefore, the archives of the local Catholic Archdiocese (in Poland) should also be researched in addition to the Polish State Archives and local USC offices.

URZĄD STANU CYWILNEGO OFFICES

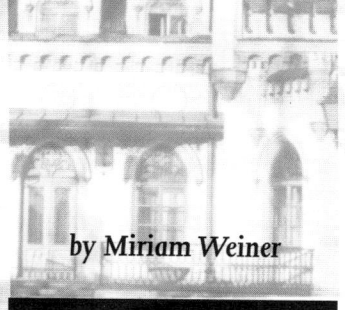

by Miriam Weiner

INTRODUCTION

In Poland, it is the responsibility of the local Urząd Stanu Cywilnego (USC) office to record births, deaths, marriages and divorces in books known as "księgi metrykalne."

Each city and town in Poland has a USC office (generally located in the town hall) that performs these duties as prescribed by law. Very small villages will record these events in a nearby larger town designated as the *gmina* (local administrative district) for the small villages.

Among the 2,500 existing USC offices in Poland, the largest (based upon the number of registered records and the number of books) are located in a few of the larger voivodship towns, including Warsaw, Wrocław, Łódź, Kraków, Gdańsk and Poznań. Depending upon the administrative structure of the region, there can be one main office with branches in particular districts of the city (as in Warsaw, Kraków and Łódź); or, what was common in the beginning of the 1890s, a few separate offices that are man-aged by the administration of certain local district authorities. There are also some cases in which offices for certain districts are located in the same building to facilitate registration.

In various Slavic and other languages, the term *metryka* refers to, among other things, registers of vital statistics. However, in many transliterated English-language versions of material referring to these registers, the registers are commonly referred to as *metrical books*. That terminology is used in this book.

According to Polish law, the metrical books are retained in the local USC offices for a period of 100 years. Books older than 100 years are to be transferred to the Polish State Archives. When the record books include multiple years, the books are retained in the local USC office until all documents in the book are more than 100 years old. This regulation often causes confusion as to where documents are actually kept.

Public access to USC documents is regulated by law, described more fully later in this chapter.

Janet Greenberg (above left) discovers the birth certificate for her father in the Rejowiec USC office as her translator (center) and the USC director (right) assist her, 1990

Although Polish law prohibits on-site access and research by individuals looking for multiple records for genealogical purposes, it is not uncommon to find a sympathetic clerk in a local USC office who will cooperate to varying degrees in order to accommodate the visitor to the repository. However, this is a courtesy response and not available upon demand.

It is possible to write to the local USC office for your ancestral town, preferably a brief factual letter in Polish. See letter-writing guide and helpful instructions in Frazin, Judith R., comp. and ed., *A Translation Guide to 19th-Century Polish-Language Civil-Registration Documents* (2nd ed. Chicago: Jewish Genealogical Society of Illinois, 1989). Again, local USC offices may not respond to general genealogical search requests (for example, everyone with the same last name), but you may receive a response to requests for one or two documents in the form of a certified extract on a typed form. Sometimes these are mailed directly from the USC office. It is also possible that you will receive a letter from the Polish Consulate advising that it is holding the certified copies of the documents and will send them upon receipt of a fee.

The Jewish documents were recorded in separate books from 1826 to 1943. While many documents were destroyed, it is not uncommon to find an almost complete set of metrical books for the period 1826–1943 (except for a few years during World War I). It is also not uncommon to find the books for one town in several different repositories in different towns.

Town Hall and USC Offices in Nowy Sącz, 1993   2

Prior to 1826, the documents from all religions were recorded together in the same volumes.

In western Poland (formerly Prussia), separate Jewish metrical books were not maintained, and the registrations are mixed with the general populace for towns in the following voivodships: Bydgoszcz, Elbląg, Gdańsk, Gorzów Wielkopolski, Jelenia Góra, Koszalin, Legnica, Leszno, Olsztyn, Opole, Piła, Poznań, Słupsk, Szczecin, Toruń, Wałbrzych, Wrocław and Zielona Góra.

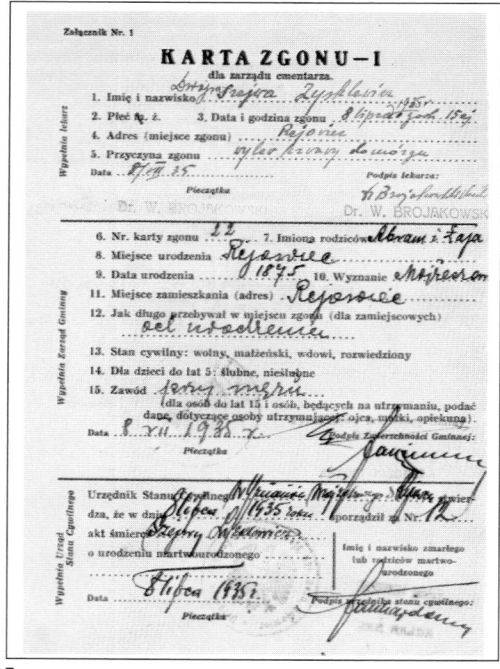

Death record of Dwojra Szejwa Zysklewicz in Rejowiec   3
(born 1895, died 1935), daughter of Abram and Laja

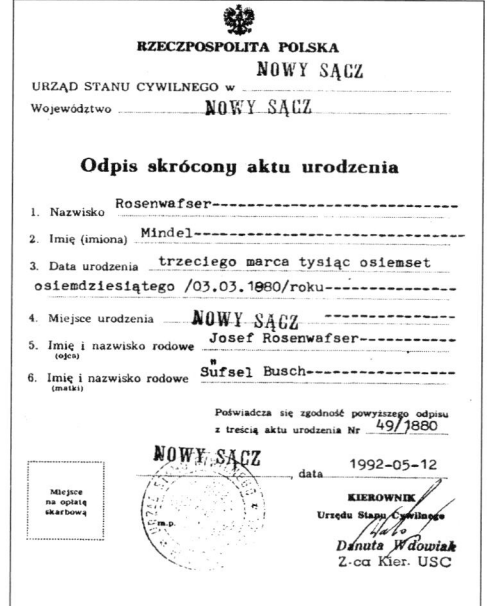

Birth record (extract) of Mindel Rosenwafser,   4
born 1880 in Nowy Sącz; daughter of
Josef Rosenwasser and Süfsel Busch

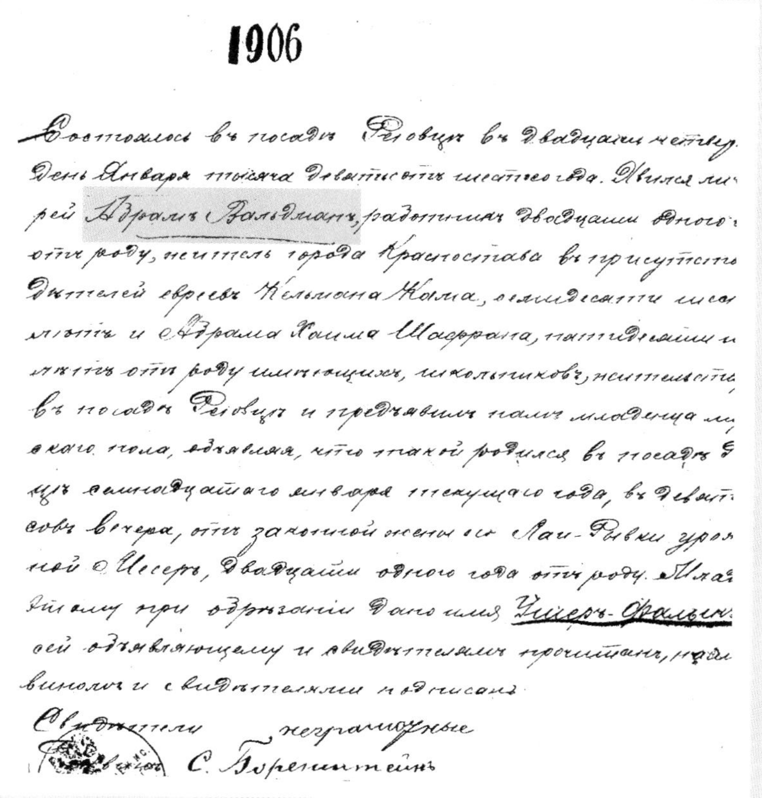

1906

[Handwritten Russian birth record in cursive]

Состоялся въ посадѣ Рейовцѣ въ двадцать четвер-
тый день Января тысяча девятьсотъ шестаго. Явился Ев-
рей Авраамъ Вальдманъ, работникъ двадцати одного
отъ роду, житель города Красностава въ присутствіи
жителей евреевъ Кельмана Камъ, семидесяти шес-
ти лѣтъ и Аврама Хаима Шафрана, пятидесяти ше-
сти отъ роду имѣющихъ, учителей, жительствѣ
въ посадѣ Рейовцѣ и предъявили намъ младенца му-
жескаго пола, объявляя, что такой родился въ посадѣ Рейовцѣ семнадцатаго января текущаго года, въ девять
часовъ вечера, отъ законной жены его Лаи-Ривки урож-
денной Месеръ, двадцати одного года отъ роду. Мла-
денцу сему при обрѣзаніи дано имя Ушеръ-Фалекъ.
Сей объявляющему и свидѣтелямъ прочитанъ, нами
и свидѣтелями подписанъ.

Свидѣтели неграмотные

С. Беренштейнъ

Birth record of Usher Falek Valdman, born 1906 in Rejowiec;
son of *Abram Valdman* and *Lea Rivka Meser*

5

SUMMARY TRANSLATION OF DOCUMENT #5 (see left)

In Rejowiec, on January 24, 1906, appeared Abram Valdman, a Jew, age 21, living in Krasnystaw.

In the presence of Kelman Kam, age 76, and Abram Chaim Shafran, 56 years, a teacher, both residents of Rejowiec, Abram Valdman testified to the birth on January 17, 1906, in Rejowiec, at 9:00 PM, of a child born to him and his wife, Lea Rivka (née Meser), age 21.

During the circumcision, the name Usher Falek was given.

This document was read to those present and to the witnesses and it was signed by the father and the witnesses.

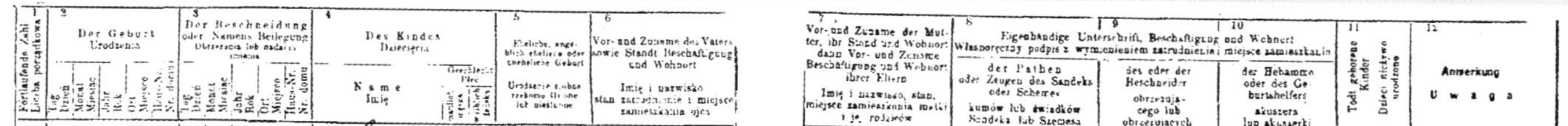

[Handwritten German/Polish columnar birth register table with entries 161, 162, 163 — names include Ester, Leine, Osias, Salomon Wolf, Salomon Fall, Jaroslau, etc.]

Birth record of Osias Fall, born 1905 in Jarosław, son of *Salman Fall*, and *Chana Sima Nadel* (daughter of *Leiser* and *Elka Nadel*)

6

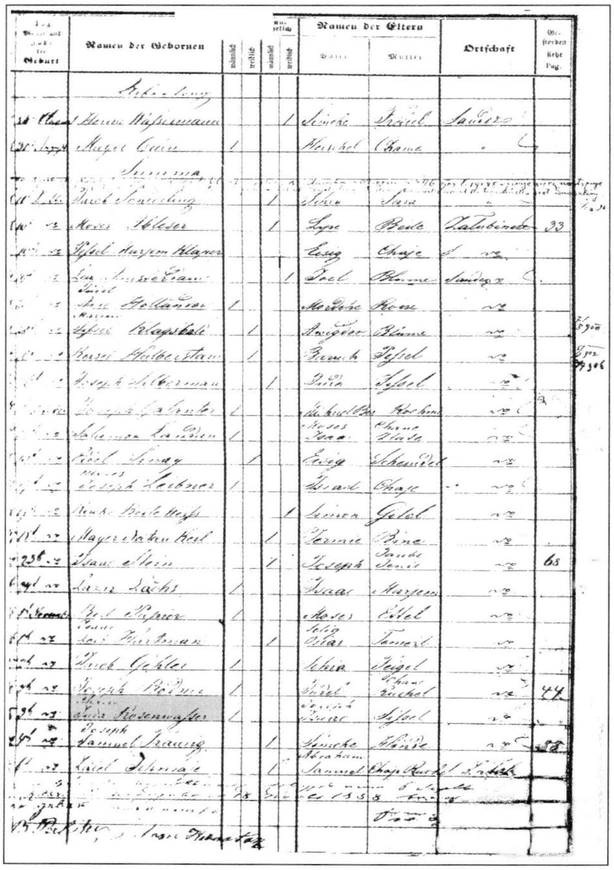

Birth record of Chaim Juda Rosenwafser, born in 1858, son of Josef Isaac and Sifsel Rosenwafser, from Świniarsko

7

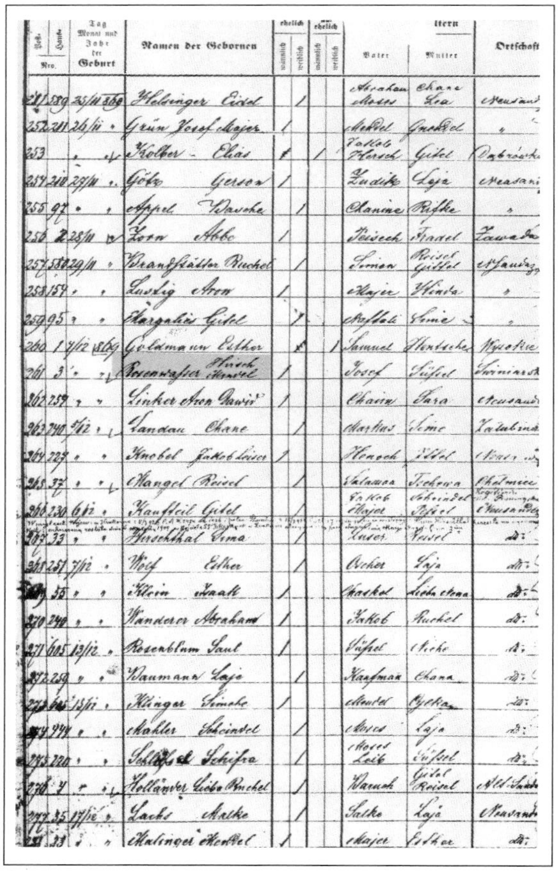

Birth record of Hirsch Mendel Rosenwafser, born in 1869, son of Josef and Süfsel Rosenwafser from Świniarsko

8

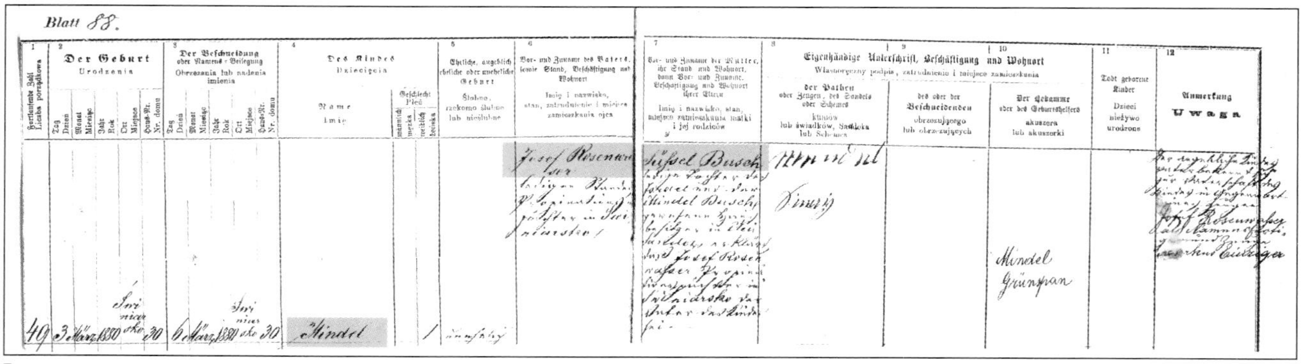

Birth record of Mindel Rosenwafser, born in 1880, daughter of Josef Rosenwafser from Świniarsko and Süfsel Busch (daughter of Israel and Mindel Busch) from Neü Sandez (now Nowy Sącz)

9

Marriage record (extract), 1923, Rejowiec;
Chaim Mordko Waldman, age 28 (son of
Gierszon Waldman and Golda Glachman)
and Fajga-Maria Zysklewicz, age 21 (daughter of
Zolman Zysklewicz and Dwojra-Szaja Szafran)

10

Birth records of Blume and Malke Rosenwafser, twins born
in 1868; daughters of Josef and Süfsel Rosenwafser from
Świniarsko

11

TRANSFER OF THE JEWISH CEMETERY
IN REJOWIEC

PROTOCOL

A protocol written on 24 May 1933 in the office of the Rejowiec municipal council (*gmina*) in the county (*district*) of Chełm in the presence of the town's administrator (*wójt*), Stanisław Majewski; secretary, Jan Wajda; representatives of the Rejowiec Jewish community council (*kehilla*): Gotlib Pinkwas, chairman; Zysla Biderman, Matys Szczupak, Chaim Urman and Nachman Goldsztajn, and delegates of the Religious Society "Chewra Kedysza" (burial society), Mordke Perelmuter and Towie Ajzenberg.

In compliance with regulation number LAZ 4/23/33 issued by the provincial administration (*starost*) in Chełm on 6 May 1933, the above-mentioned delegates of the religious society "Chewra Kedysza" today transferred the ownership and administration of the Jewish cemetery in Rejowiec together with all the rights and obligations resulting from this transfer to the Rejowiec Jewish community council. The transfer of the cemetery took place in the presence of representatives of the Rejowiec municipal council, Jan Wajda (secretary); Rejowiec Jewish community council and of the above-mentioned religious society. The watchman of the cemetery, Jan Szyszka, as well as the grave-digger, Hersz Akselrod, were informed that as of this date, the cemetery would be adminsitered only by the Jewish community council and therefore, they are expected to comply with the regulations issued by this council and they should not allow any people and corpses to be brought there without the council's approval.

(signatures of all parties present)

Rejowiec town records for the transfer of ownership of the Jewish cemetery, 1933

12

URZĄD STANU CYWILNEGO WARSAW ŚRÓDMIEŚCIE
(With Jewish Documents from Galicia)

by Kazimierz Kotlarski
Director, USC Offices in Warsaw

Urząd Stanu Cywilnego
Warszawa Śródmieście
00-950 Warszawa
skr. poczt. 18, ul. Jezuicka 1/3

Monday: 8:00 AM–6:00 PM
Tues-Fri: 8:00 AM–4:00 PM

Tel: 31-71-81
        31-28-32

BACKGROUND

The archives were formed in 1949 as part of the USC Warsaw Śródmieście (district) when an agreement between Poland and the Ukrainian Soviet Socialist Republic (then part of the Soviet Union) was signed. It was agreed that the metrical books from voivodships that belonged to Poland prior to 1939 would be transferred to Poland. These voivodships included Tarnopol, Stanisławów, Lwów, Wołyń and parts of Polesie.

The books were transferred in stages beginning with the larger towns of Lwów, Stanislawów and Tarnopol voivodships, which were the main economic, social and cultural centers in the region before World War II.

The prewar registration system of civil records was based to a large extent upon religious registrations. The records for the Christians (Roman Catholics, Greek Catholics, Russian Orthodox, Protestants) were prepared by priests or ministers. The documents for non-Christians (including Jews) were prepared by clerks of the public administration assigned to this specific task.

The records were written and stored in Jewish vital registration offices, which had their seats in the local town administration building. The first postwar regulations about civil records from 1946 state that one universal (secular) method of civil vital record registration would be introduced, which is why the records that were previously "scattered around" were transferred to this specially created archive.

JEWISH METRICAL BOOKS

This archive is the repository for Jewish metrical books from the area of the former Lwów, Stanisławów and Tarnopol voivodships (now Lviv, Ivano Frankivsk and Ternopil oblasts in Ukraine). The record books are held in a collection known as the Zabużańskie ("East of Bug River") archives. The contents of these records are generally written in Polish. In the areas formerly known as Galicia (included in the Austro-Hungarian Empire), the Polish language was accorded equal status with the German language, *e.g.*, vital statistic registrations. However, some books between October 1939 and mid-1941 are written in German or Ukrainian.

The composition of a metrical book is very clear and easy to understand, with a few records per page. There are separate books for births, marriages and deaths.

Generally, the books are in fairly good physical condition, which facilitates their use. It should be noted that the books brought to Poland after the war had traces of neglect and poor storage conditions (some were stored in dirty, wet cellars or attics). However, due to extensive and expensive preservation efforts, many books were saved from destruction.

The typical birth record consists of:
- Sequential order number
- Day, month, year and place (street, house number) of circumcision or naming of the child
- Name of child
- Sex
- Status (legitimate or not) (ritual/religious marriage not recognized)
- Name, profession and place of residence of father
- Name, profession and place of residence of mother, mother's parents' names
- Signature, profession, place of residence of:
  a. witnesses
  b. person who performed circumcision
  c. midwife

Archivist Grzegorz Mucha shows Gloria Resin examples of Jewish metrical books

13

- If the child was stillborn:
  a. note about death
  b. date and place of child's parents' civil marriage
  c. note if child was identified as legitimate
  d. note that father recognized child as his

RESEARCH POLICIES AND ACCESS TO ZABUŻAŃSKIE ARCHIVES

The metrical books in these archives generally date from 1896. Older books are transferred to Archiwum Główne Akt Dawnych (AGAD) in Warsaw at ul. Długa 7 (see Chapter 3).

This USC office is not open to the public for research. Requests for specific documents can be submitted in person at the counter or by correspondence sent through the Polish Consulate or Embassy in the requestor's country.

According to the law concerning civil records in USC offices, certified copies (typed on a form) may be issued, but xerox copies are not generally permitted because of the fragile condition of the books and the need to safeguard the documents for future generations. This same regulation prohibits genealogical searches.

There is a card catalog for birth and marriage records that facilitates the search for these documents, but the index cards do not include all the data from the actual document.

For marriage records, the index card lists only the groom's name. If the last name of the male is unknown, a search cannot be performed through the index cards, as regulations prohibit general genealogical searches in the books without specific data.

Written requests should include the following information:

- Name of person requesting the search and his/her relationship to individual(s) whose documents are requested
- First and last names (also include maiden names)
- Date/place where the event occurred. If exact date is unknown, provide a two-to three-year span.
- Parents' first and last names (also include maiden names)

Author's Note: Jewish metrical books for the former Polish voivodships of Lwów, Stanislawów and Tarnopol (now in Ukraine) can be found in at least four separate archives. The earliest records are housed in the Lviv Historical Archives in Ukraine; the next group of records are in the AGAD Archives (Polish State Archives) in Warsaw (p. 364); twentieth century records are in the USC Warsaw Śródmieście (p. 384) and some twentieth century metrical books are kept in the local archives (ZAGS Offiices) of the above three cities.

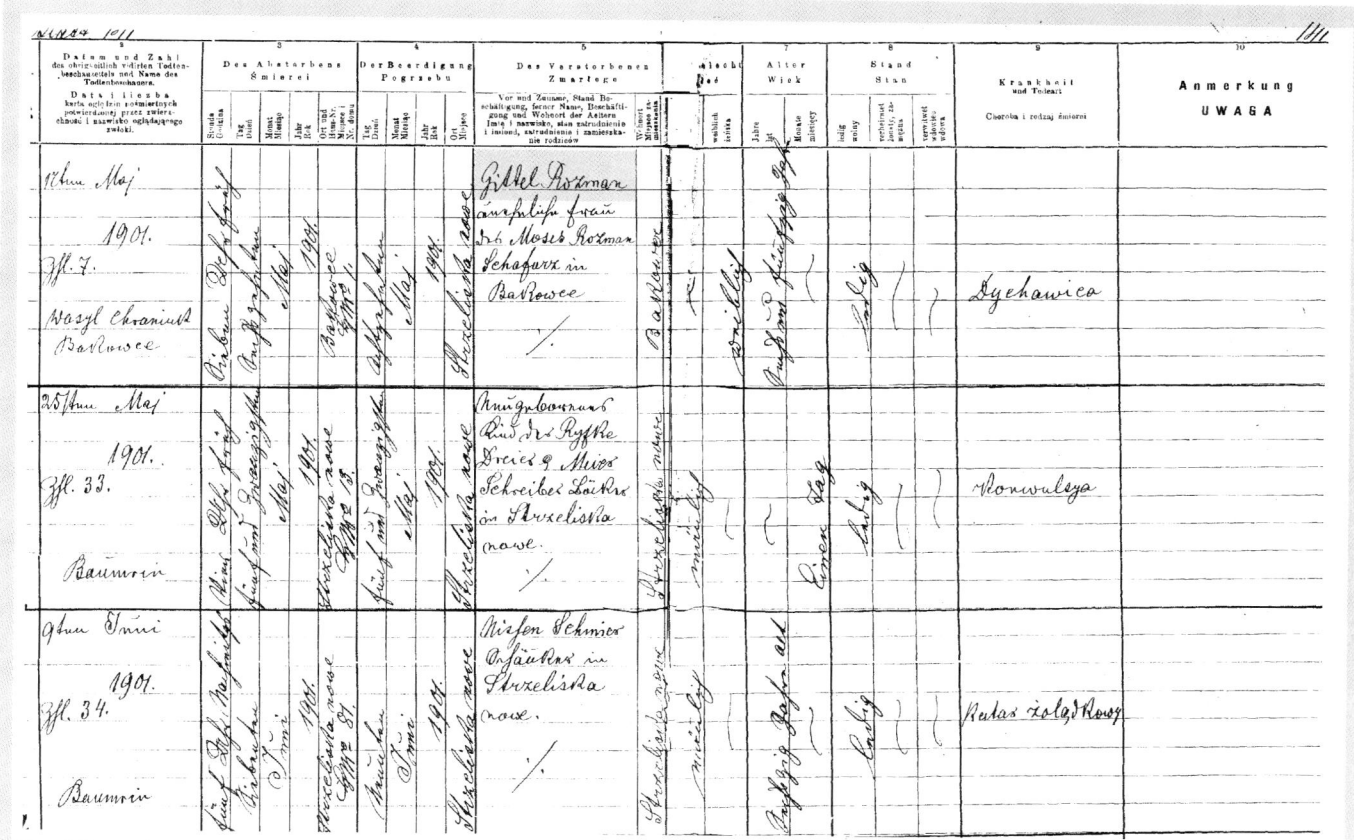

Death record for Gittel Rozman, died in 1901, wife of Moses Rozman, living in Bakowce, house #1

14

CONCLUSION

It is not an exaggeration to describe the Zabużańskie Archives as one of the most well-known archives in Poland because of its unique holdings, as evidenced by the 2,000 to 3,000 requests per year both from within Poland and abroad.

Recently, it has become popular to look for "roots," particularly in the United States, which has resulted in increasing visits by those who wish to explore their ancestry. Many ethnic groups, including Jews, trace their roots to Eastern Europe, especially to Poland in its pre-1939 borders.

The workers in our archives derive great satisfaction when they locate records for a person who visits the USC office. Often, the person's reaction is spontaneously accompanied by memories from the town of their childhood. The people who visit us often had a very difficult and complicated life in Poland, where they, in many cases, lost their entire families during the tragic years of the war.

Also, the USC office and the Zabużańskie Archives have unique metrical books for parishes in the central part of Warsaw (called Śródmieście), including those for the Jewish religion, where the books (until 1939) were kept by officers of the State Police.

The vast damage to Warsaw during World War II devastated and destroyed a major part of our archival material, including many Jewish metrical books. The liquidation of the Warsaw ghetto resulted in the worst destruction. The remnants that survived are missing large fragments, and often there are gaps between the years.

We have recently begun computerizing the metrical books (current registrations), which will ultimately make it easier and quicker to find records.

Birth record of Zygmunt Nadel (son of Efraim Nadel) and Freide Streisand (daughter of Hersch and Jútty Streisand), born 1896 in Lwów (first page of document)

NARZECZONEGO		Wiek		Stan		3	NARZECZONEJ		Wiek		Stan		4	Zaślubin		5	Własnoręczny podpis		6	7	
Imię i nazwisko, miejsce urodzenia, zatrudnienie, miejsce zamieszkania i Nr. domu, niemniej imiona, zatrudnienie i miejsce zamieszkania jego rodziców		Rok	Miesiąc	Wolny	Wdowiec		Imię i nazwisko, miejsce urodzenia, niemniej imiona, zatrudnienie, miejsce zamieszkania i Nr. domu jej rodziców		Rok	Miesiąc	Wolna	Wdowa		Dzień	Miesiąc	Rok	Miejsce	funkcjonującego przy zaślubinach rabina (szkolnika)	świadków i ich zatrudnienie z wymienieniem miejsca zamieszkania		UWAGA	

Leib Blank urodzony i zamieszkały w Czortkowie, fryzjer, syn Sary Blank z Czortkowa		1	Pepi Antler urodzona i zamieszkała w Monasterzyskach, krawczyni, córka Salomona Antlera i Chai Chany z domu Blech w Monasterzyskach				16	Styczeń	1938	Monasterzyska	Lipe Meisels rabin w Monasterzyskach	Henryk Hachel i Osias Ferber obaj krojczy w Monasterzyskach		

Marriage record (1938) of Leib Blank, born 1906 in Czortków (son of Sara Blank) and Pepi Antler, born 1909 in Monasterzyska (daughter of Salomon Antler and Chaya Chana Blech)

15

Księga urodzin izraelickiego okręgu metrykalnego **Lwów** na rok 1896.

Geburtsbuch des israelitischen Matrikenbezirkes **Lemberg** Jahrgang 1896.

136

7	8	9	10	11	12
Imię i nazwisko matki, stan i zamieszkanie, jako też imię nazwisko, zatrudnienie i miejsce zamieszkania jej rodziców / r- und Zuname der Mutter, Stand und Wohnort, dann Vor- und -name, Beschäftigung und Wohnort ihrer Eltern	Własnoręczny podpis z wymienieniem zatrudnienia i miejsca zamieszkania / Eigenhändige Unterschrift mit Angabe der Beschäftigung und des Wohnortes — kumów lub świadków Sandeka lub Szamesa / der Pathen oder Zeugen, des Sandek oder Schames	obrzezującego lub obrzezujących / des oder der Beschneider	akuszerki lub akuszera / der Hebamme oder des Geburtshelfers	Dzieci nieżywo urodzone / Todtgeborene Kinder	UWAGA / Anmerkung
...aje Lemel, zamężna we Lwowie, ...ka nauczyciela Judy Halpern i Drezli Halpern we Lwowie.	Chaim Juda Halpern, nauczyciel dzieci we Lwowie, sandek, podpisani na karcie meldunkowej	Samuel Belf	Regina Halpern, Hladik	~ ~	Rodzice ślub w Kleparowie obok Lwowa dnia 20 lipca 1894 roku, wedle okazanej metryki ślubu wystawionej d. 29 lipca 1894 przez M. Weissa, prowadzącego metryki izr. w Zniesieniu (z tamt. Księgi Zaślubin na rok 1894 stron 17 poz. 51)
...eide Streisand (Streisand) ...na, we Lwowie wspólnie z grajkiem ...rimem Nadel zamieszkała, ...ka rzekomych małżonków ...edytora w Przemyślu Her... ...a Streusand (Streisand) i ...p. Jütty.	Dawid Reich, właściciel realności we Lwowie, sandek, podpisani na karcie meldunkowej	R.F. Bodek	Julia Hecher	~ ~	Podpisany Efraim Nadel przyznaje się do ojcostwa i prosi o wpisanie go jako ojca tego dziecka (Zygmunta) Efraim Nadel ... Salomon Albert ... Bernard ... świadek ... Zgadza się jako ... Znak ręczny Freidy Streisand jako ... położnicy i świadek Salomon Albert ... #

(second page of document, see left)

16

▌ *Klimontów, Jewish cemetery, 1952*   17

▌ *Synagogue in Końskie, early 20th century*   18

▌ *Synagogue in Końskie, 1995 sketch from 1907 photograph*   19

JEWISH HISTORICAL INSTITUTE
(ŻYDOWSKI INSTYTUT HISTORYCZNY)

by Miriam Weiner

The Jewish Historical Institute, located in the building of the Main Judaic Library, is one of the very few Jewish research centers in post-Communist Europe and the only one whose activities have continued uninterrupted throughout the postwar years.

The Jewish Historical Institute (JHI) consists of five divisions: Archives, Library, Museum, Research, and Documentation of Monuments. The Jewish Historical Association of Poland is the legal owner of the Institute's holdings.

ARCHIVES

The Archives contain collections spanning the seventeenth to twentieth centuries, including one of the most important collections of Holocaust documentation in the world: materials from the ghettoes of Będzin, Białystok, Częstochowa, Kraków, Lwów, Łódź and Warsaw (the Ringelblum Archive); the testimonies and memoirs of 7,000 Holocaust survivors collected immediately after the war; more than 10,000 photographs; and a major collection of underground publications. The Archives also document centuries of Jewish life in communities such as Kraków and Wrocław (formerly Breslau), as well as the postwar years in Poland.

LIBRARY

The Library, containing 60,000 volumes, includes significant collections of medieval Hebrew manuscripts and early books. The periodicals division, specializing in the Yiddish press published in Poland, has assembled one of the largest such collections in Poland, including the German-Jewish press of the nineteenth century. The Library also possesses a complete collection of postwar Polish Judaica and many anti-Semitic publications.

MUSEUM

The Museum houses 11,000 objects: traditional ritual art, oil paintings and graphics by famous Polish-Jewish painters of the nineteenth and twentieth centuries, and objects connected to the Holocaust. The collection of ritual objects is as important as more well-known Judaica collections in Western Europe and the United States. The collections of Jewish art and Holocaust material are unique on a world scale.

RESEARCH DIVISION

The Research Division employs 14 historians engaged in the study of Jewish history in Poland from its beginnings to the present. Over the years, such research has resulted in numerous important historical works. The Institute publishes the *Biuletyn*

Left: Jewish Historical Institute; right: "Blue skyscraper" on site of the Great Synagogue   1

Żydowskiego Instytutu Historyczynego w Polsce (Bulletin of the Jewish Historical Institute in Poland) in Polish. Between 1948 and 1993, the Institute also published *Bleter far geshikhte* (Pages of History: Quarterly Bulletin of the Jewish Historical Institute in Poland), in Yiddish.

ARCHIVAL HOLDINGS

Most of the archival collections of the Jewish Historical Institute were gathered in the 1940s–1950s. More than 1,950 running feet of records were divided chronologically into three main departments, based upon historical periods containing 84 groups. Documents consist of:

- Old records of Jewish communities (1672–1939)
- Records from the period of World War II
- Modern records produced after 1945

In the first group are documents preserved almost in their entirety from:

- The Jewish community of Wrocław (from the end of the eighteenth century until 1938)
- Jewish communities of the Province of Silesia [Śląsk] (1742–1942)
- Jewish community of Kraków (1701–1939)

One of the highlights of this group is the *"Varia"* collection. It contains 718 pieces from the eighteenth and nineteenth centuries, primarily publications by students of academic and rabbinical schools consisting of texts on the Bible, religion, religious literature (Hebrew and Yiddish), history, Jewish philosophy and law.

Other documents of unique value are the copies of masters theses written under the academic supervision of Professor Majer Bałaban and Dr. Ignacy Schiper before 1939. These theses were based to a great degree on source material that was later destroyed during World War II.

The second group of documents forms the main body of the Archives: Sixty percent of all the records are documents connected with the Holocaust. First, there is the *Underground Archive of the Warsaw Ghetto*, founded and managed by Dr. Emmanuel Ringelblum. These records were discovered after the war under the rubble at 68 Nowolipki Street. They still are of primary importance when researching the history of the Warsaw ghetto and the Holocaust.

Also of great importance are the *Testimonies of Surviving Jews* in the form of eyewitness accounts given mainly between 1945 and 1948 to the Historical Commission of the Central Committee of Jews in Poland.

Similar to the above are *Memoirs of Jews*, seven of which are memoirs of children, written by Jews in ghettoes, labor camps or in hiding (see Umińska, Apolonia, and Natalia Aleksiun-Mądrzak, *Inwentarz zbioru 'Pamiętniki Żydów' 1939–1945, Archiwum Żydowskiego Instytutu Historycznego* [Inventory of the Collection "Memoirs of Jews" 1939–1945, Archives of the Jewish Historical Institute]. Warszawa: Żydowski Instytut Historyczny, 1994).

This group also contains documents of the Jewish Councils (*Judenrate*) from the towns of Będzin, Częstochowa, Falenica,

1945 registration of Olek Aronowicz, born 1938 in Warsaw

Jasło, Jędrzejów, Kamieńsk, Kraków, Lublin, Lwów, Radom, Staszów and Włoszczowa. Among them are almost entirely preserved records produced by the Directorate of Representatives of the Jewish Population of Będzin in 1941–1942. Similar records were preserved at the Council of Elders in Częstochowa. From the Kraków *Judenrat* are personal records with photographs attached to applications for an identity card (*Ausweis*) from 1940. There are also documents of the Jewish Council of Lwów from 1941.

The original documents from POW camps are unique personal records with photographs of Jewish inmates (Jewish soldiers serving in the Polish Army) selected by the Germans from the POW camps after the September 1939 campaign. These Jews were imprisoned in Lublin at 7 Lipowa Street and then exterminated.

The *Underground* file contains fragmentary materials of the resistance press of the Jewish National Committee (ŻKN), the Jewish Coordination Commission of the ŻKN and the Bund, and of the Jewish Fighters Organization (ŻOB). Some of the documents (created by Mordechai Anielewicz) are appeals for weapons and help in organizing the Warsaw ghetto uprising.

The Archives also have records of the Jewish Social Mutual Aid from 1940 to 1941 and records of the American Jewish

Joint Distribution Committee from 1939 to 1941. The Archives of the Central Committee of Jews in Poland consist of documents for its 18 departments and independent bodies: Social Courts; the Organization for the Development of Creativity (1946–1950); the Society for Health Protection, known as TOZ (Towarzystwo Ochrony Zdrowia) (1945–1949); and Zionist Organizations (1945–1950). This group also contains a wide array of works from the Institute's employees and contributors.

The Archives own a rich and important collection of more than 10,000 photographs from World War I, the 1920s–1930s, World War II (covering Poland in its pre-1939 borders) and the postwar period, along with another 7,000 photographs of monuments of Jewish culture.

The Archives have a separate Cartographic Collection covering the period of World War II, including posters, bills and ghetto maps.

The Institute continues to receive objects and documents from the local population as they are discovered throughout the countryside—sometimes buried behind a house, thrown into a trash receptacle, or retained in an attic for years, only to be found by new generations of family members.

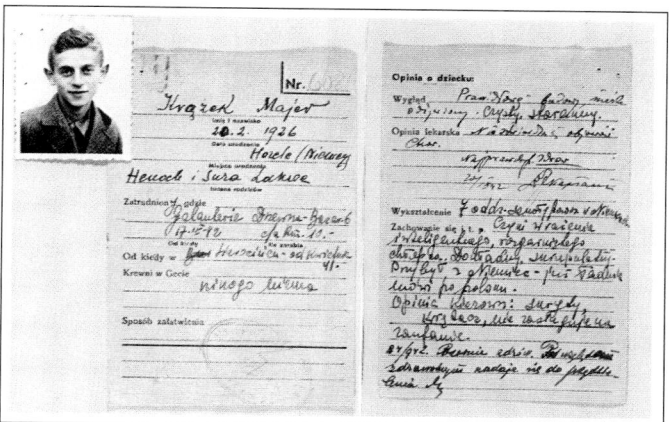

Registration (1942) of Majer Krążek, born 1926, son of Henoch and Sura 4

ON-SITE RESEARCH

On-site research is available, but staff assistance with language and translations is limited due to time constraints. During on-site research, if photocopies of a few pages are desired, the copies may be made quickly. If it is a large copy order, the copying is done later and mailed to the address provided. Copy costs vary according to the number and purpose (scholarly research/institutional affiliation receive a discount).

WRITTEN REQUESTS FOR RESEARCH

Research requests should be brief and provide as much specific data as possible. Research requests sent by mail may be written in any language and should include the following specific information:

- Town(s) to be researched
- Family names and first names with spelling variations
- Time period of interest
- Types of documents to be searched

While the archivists are skilled researchers, they can accept official assignments to research material only within the Institute.

While there is no set fee schedule for research requests to the Institute, contributions are welcome. The funds are used for restoration and preservation of material.

THE RONALD S. LAUDER FOUNDATION GENEALOGY PROJECT

The Ronald S. Lauder Foundation Genealogy Project, established in 1994, is the genealogical research arm of the Jewish Historical Institute. The Project seeks to help Jews with Polish roots (and Poles with Jewish roots) explore and document their family histories. The Project has been instrumental in reuniting Holocaust survivors, helping child survivors learn their true identities and the fates of their relatives, locating new sources of genealogical information and creating finding aids to previously uncatalogued materials.

The Project does not charge for its services. However, it does encourage voluntary contributions, to be used exclusively for the physical conservation of Polish Jewish archives and the creation of finding aids to those materials.

Ghetto registration, Chaim Brenner, born 1901, 3
living in Kraków in 1939–1940

Eleonora Bergman is vice-director of the Jewish Historical Institute. Since the early 1980s, she has published many articles on the subject of synagogue architecture in Poland. While working in the state-owned Workshops for Conservation of Monuments, she has authored and co-authored numerous documentation works on urban history. Ms. Bergman is currently working with Jan Jagielski in the Jewish Historical Institute on a catalogue of the extant synagogues in Poland.

Eleonora Bergman, vice-director of the Jewish Historical Institute, 1996   5

The Jewish Historical Institute in Poland

ul. Tłomackie 3/5	HOURS: 9:00 AM–3:00 PM
00-090 Warsaw	Archives & Museum: 11:00 AM–6:00 PM (Thursday only)
Tel: 22/827-9221	Library: 8:00 AM–3:00 PM (Monday–Thursday)
Fax: 22/827-8372	9:00 AM–Noon (Friday)
e-mail: zihinb@ikp.atm.com.pl	

The Institute's building is currently undergoing extensive renovation. As a result, there will be limited access to the Library and Museum through 1997.

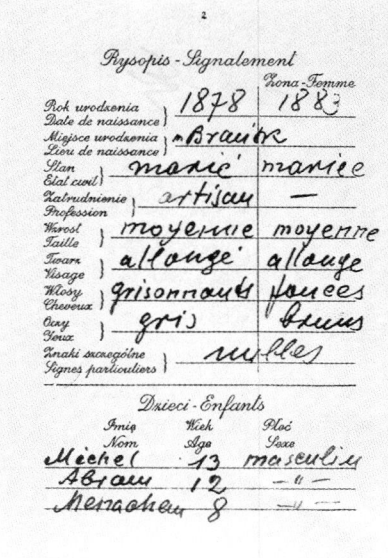

Passport for Jankiel Zylbersztajn and his family, c. 1935   6

Record of the Joint Distribution Committee with lists of names of those who received assistance, 1941   7

L. №	Zu- u. Nazwisko i imię	Vorname	Adresse Adres		Geburtsdatum Data urodzenia	Beruf Zawód	Bemerkungen Uwagi
2363	Cymberg	Lipa	Zawale	28	1909	Schneider	
04	"	Ita	Modrzejowska	88	1914	Arbeiterin	
5	"	Frajda	"	"	1937	b.Eltern	
6	"	Mala	"	"	1938	"	
7	Cymbler	Chaja Rajzla	Zawale	30	1885	b.Kindern	
8	"	Dawid	Grobla	3	15.IV. 1903	Gumaschenmacher	
9	"	Fajwel	"	"	30.12. 1924	b.Eltern	
2370	"	Izrael Lojzze	"	"	3.XII. 1928	" "	
1	"	Icie	"	"	25.I. 1930	" "	
2	"	Rywka	"	"	6.VII. 1933	" "	
3	"	Hersz	"	"	30.XII. 1866	Hausbesitz.	
4	"	Rozalia	"	"	27.II. 1875	b.Mann	
5	"	Ruchla	"	"	13.VI. 1906	" Eltern	
6	"	Dwojra	"	"	26.VI. 1924	" "	
7	"	Josl Wolf	"	"	12.VIII. 1928	" "	
8	"	Chaja Ita	"	"	20.II. 1923	" "	
9	"	Icek	Reuthenerstr. 31 /Kożżataju/		1899	Schuhmacher	
2380	"	Szlama			1913	b.Pater	
1	"	Szewija			1919	"	
2	"	Josek	Czichowska	66	13.X. 1904	Schneider	
3	"	Chaja Maria	"	"	10.V. 1901	b.Mann	
4	"	Robert	"	"	5.VIII. 1926	" Eltern	
5	"	Dawid Izydor	"	"	23.VI. 1936	" "	
6	"	Mendel	Podzamcze	11	14.III. 1904	Träger	
7	"	Zurech	Podwale	30	1906	Arbeiter	
8	"	Gela	"		1913	b.Mann	
9	"	Jehuda	"		1936	" Eltern	
2390	Cymbler	Ruchla Laja	Podzamcze	46	20.IV. 1906	Arbeiterin	
1	"	Rywka	"	"	1938	b.Mutter	
2	"	Frajda			1935	"	
3	Cymerman	Abram	Modrzejowska	53	1895	Kaufmann	
4	"	Chaja	"		1895	b.Mann	
5	"	Derek	"		1924	b.Eltern	
6	"	Josek	"		1926	" "	
7	"	Ita	"		1927	" "	
8	"	Chaja	Ozeladzka	11	1884	Händlerin	
9	"	Szyl	"		15.IV. 1917	b.Mutter	
2400	"	Doba	Kattowitzerstr. 19		18.V. 1911	Näherin	

List of Jews (prepared by the Judenrat in 1943) from Będzin, including 20 members of the Cymbler family, with occupations, addresses and years of birth   8

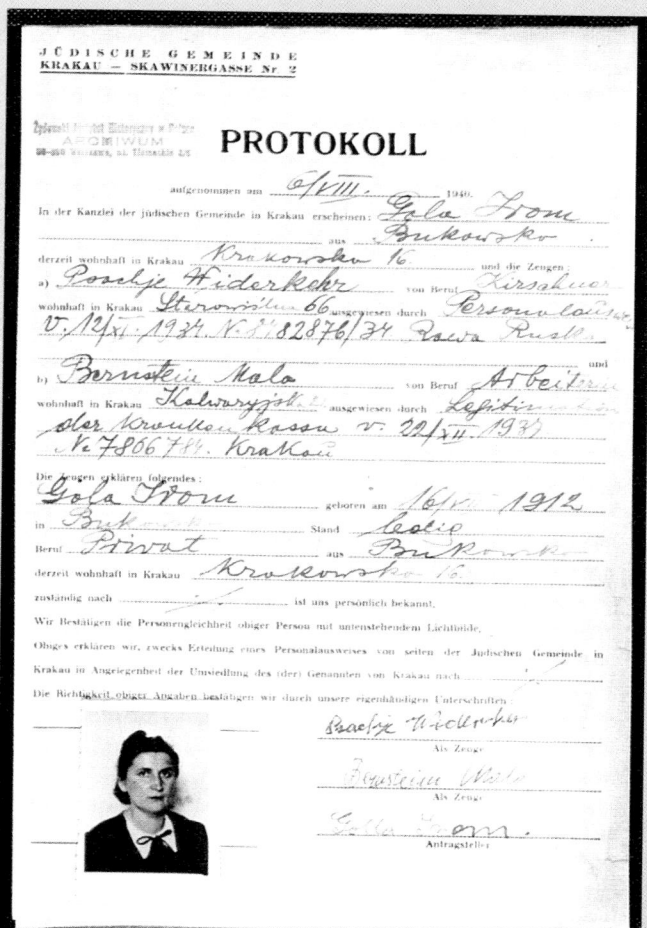

Protokoll of Golla From, Kraków, 1940   9

Title page of journal "Ilustrite Vokh," published in *Warsaw*, 1928   10

–376–				
Nazwisko i imię	Data ur.	Imiona rodziców	Adres 1939r.	Adres obecny
107225				
Krieger Heresz 1918		Jojne, Gitla	Łódz	Łódz
Krieger Idesa 1898		Fajwel, Racha	"	Kraków
Krieger Irena 1936		Zygmunt, Fela	"	
Krieger Izak 1903		Jakób, Roza	Lwów	Szczecin-Zelechowo,Szcz panowskiego 44
Krieger Izak 1910		Nusyn, Dwojra	Jarosław	Łódz, Jakuba 16
Krygier Izak 1911		Abram, Chaja	Łaszczów	
Krieger Izrael 1915			Kozienice	Gliwice,Okrywalcze
Krieger Izrael 1914		Salomon, Chaja	Mława	Szczecin, Heleny 15/5
Krygier Jakub 1909		Eliasz, Mariem	Łódz	Łódz, Jakuba 16
Krygier Jakub 1920		Josek, Nechuma		
Krugier Jakób 1928				Szwajcaria
Krygier Janina 1895			Kraków	Ząbkowice D/S
Krigier Jarosłan 1888			Jarosław	Bytom,Chrobrego 2
Krygier Jojne 1884		Dawid, Rywa	Łódz	Łódz,Sródmiejska 30
Kriger Judel 1884				Nowa Ruda D/S
Kriger Julek 1934				Zatrzebie D.Dziecka
Kriger Julian 1930		Herman, Estera		Przemysl
Kriger Józef 1946		Eliasz, Pora		Sobiecin, Zechodnia 5
Krygier Józef Mordka 1893			Stryjów	Łódz
Krygier Józef 1912			w-wa	" Piotrkowska 104 a
Krieger Karol 1919				Marktretwits, Blandl.67
Krieger Karol 1910			Skole	Kraków,Konarskie 25
Krygier Karola 1908		Chaim,Noma	Łódz	Łódz,Jakuba 16
Krygier Łaja 1931		Jojne,Gitla		" Sródmiejska 30
Kriegler Leib 1891		Salomon,Maria	N.Sącz	Nowy Sącz
Krygier Lejb 1930		Jojne,Gitla	Łódz	Łódz,Sródmiejska 30
Krigger Lejb 1907			Jasło	Kraków
Krygier Lajzer 1904		wolf,Brajndla	Łódz	Łódz
Krygier Lejzor 1930			w-wa	Warszawa,st. u..eta
Krygier Lea 1923		Mendel,Chawa	Łódz	Łódz
Krieger Linka 1930			Lwów	Kraków,Karmelicka 62
Krieger Lisa 1926		Isydor,Lili	Kraków	Sarego 15
Krygier Lola 1927		Mendel,Lola		Ozorków
Krygier Lola 1925				Frydland D/S
Krieger Lusia 1919			Jarosław	Kraków,Długa 38
Krygier Maks 1936				Łódz,Jakuba 16
Krieger Maks 1936				Przemysl
Krieger Małka 1943		Simcha,Rajsla		Łódz,Kosciuszki 32
Krieger Marek 1936		Maurycy,Helena		Tarnów
Krieger Maria 1901		Karol,Ernestine	Berlin	Bytom,Kopalniana 6a
Krygier Maryla 1927		Jakub,Tauba	Ozorków	Ozirków,Joselewicza 1.
Krygier Maurice 1932				Paris
Krieger Mechel 1912		Baruch,Sura	Krosno	Bytom,Krakowska 6
Krieger Mela 1927				Sosnowiec Giesscze Puste D/S
Krieger Wendel 1929		Szloma	Leszczów	Swidnica D/S
Krieger Meta 1927				Wałbrzych,Auenstr.32
Krygier Mieczysław 1917			Lachowicze	poczta polowa 66843
Krügier Mina 1910			Jarosław	Kraków
Krygier Wojtecz 1907		Abraham,Leja	Lwów	Stołoszyn,Nad Odrą 26
Krygier Mojżecz 1916		Jojne,Gitla	Łódz	Łódz,Zgierska 25

Post-Holocaust survivor list showing multiple entries for Krieger families   11

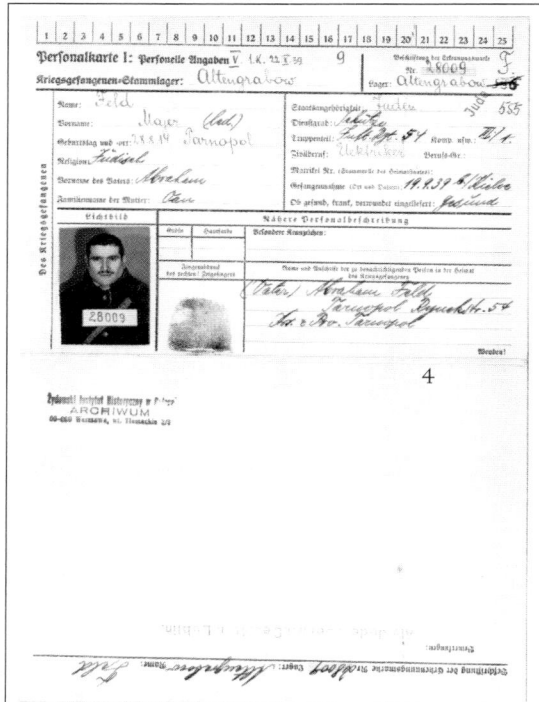
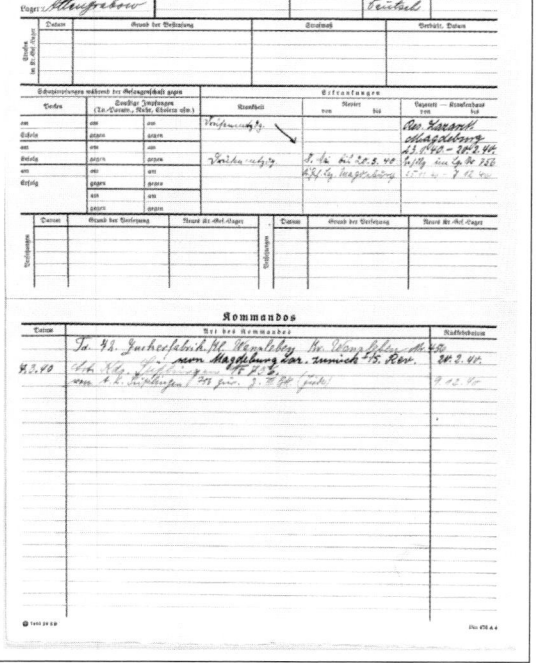

File of Majer Feld, Jewish POW soldier in the Polish Army, born in 1914 in Tarnopol; son of *Abraham Feld*, living at 54 Rynek Street, Tarnopol, 1939   12

CONCENTRATION CAMP ARCHIVES

by Miriam Weiner

INTRODUCTION

Virtually all the State Archives throughout Poland include documents from the Holocaust period. Many different kinds of documents exist, including transport lists, lists of confiscated property, ghetto registrations, tax lists, general lists of inhabitants and many other documents that tell the tragic story of Polish Jewry.

In addition to those documents that can be found in the Polish State Archives and the Jewish Historical Institute in Warsaw, many documents, maps and photographs are located in the archives of the State Museum of Auschwitz-Birkenau in Oświęcim and the Majdanek Museum Archives in Lublin, described in this chapter.

There are also university libraries, regional museums, local archives, collections of private individuals and various other sources for Holocaust-related documents in Poland. Many documents from the Holocaust period have been microfilmed in Poland and can be found in the United States Holocaust Memorial Museum Archives in Washington, D.C., and at the Yad Vashem Archives in Jerusalem.

In addition, many Holocaust-related documents pertaining to events in Poland can be found in archives of neighboring countries, including Germany, Austria, Ukraine, Lithuania, Russia and Belarus, as well as in archives in Canada and the United States. While some of these are original documents, many are microfilms of documents stored in Polish archives, *e.g.* microfilms by the Family History Library.

The documents from archives of the former Soviet Union that have become accessible in the past few years include many transport and victim lists, providing documentation of hundreds of thousands of Jews who perished during the Holocaust. See also Chapters 3 and 5.

The "Auschwitz Complex" (also referred to as KL [*Konzentrationslager*] Auschwitz) included Auschwitz I, Auschwitz II–Birkenau and Auschwitz III–Monowitz. Within this book, the terms Auschwitz, KL Auschwitz and Auschwitz–Birkenau are used interchangeably.

∎ *Sign on the grounds of the State Museum of Auschwitz-Birkenau, 1990* 1

USEFUL ADDRESSES FOR THIS SECTION

UNITED STATES HOLOCAUST MEMORIAL MUSEUM, 100 Raoul Wallenberg Place SW, Washington, D.C. 20024-2150 <http://www.ushmmp.org>
UNITED STATES NATIONAL ARCHIVES, Pennsylvania Avenue at 8th Street NW, Washington, D.C. 20408 <http://www.nara.gov>
YAD VASHEM, P.O. Box 3477, Jerusalem 91034, Israel <http://www.yad-vashem.org.il>

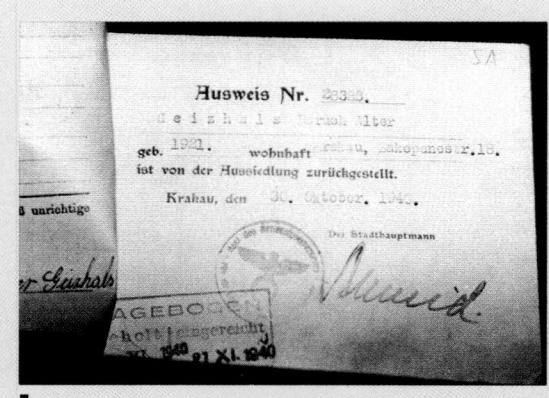

Kraków ghetto registration, 1940, for Baruch (Benek) Alter Geizhals (two-page registration) 2

KRAKOW GHETTO DOCUMENTS
RELATING TO BENJAMIN GEIZHALS

In 1940 and 1941, in cities and ghettos throughout Poland, the Germans organized deportations, forcibly transferring the Jewish population to various concentration camps and extermination centers, where most were murdered.

Within the context of the above situation, the document dated October 30, 1940 (fig. 3), spared Benjamin (formerly Baruch Alter) Geizhals from being deported to a death camp and allowed him to remain in Kraków.

The document dated February 4, 1941 (fig. 4), also served to prolong Geizhals' life by allowing him again to evade deportation. The German authorities issued the document, known as a *Kennkarten*, to Geizhals. It prevented him from being sent to Bełżec, the notorious death camp. The document allowed Geizhals to remain in the Kraków ghetto until its liquidation by the Germans in March 1943, at which time Geizhals was deported to the Plaszów concentration camp.

Author's note: Benjamin Geizhals survived the Holocaust and is a printing consultant for this book.

Resident permit dated October 30, 1940, Kraków 3

Permit to remain in the ghetto, dated February 4, 1941, Kraków 4

MAJDANEK MUSEUM ARCHIVES

by Janina Kiełboń
Archives Director

ARCHIWUM PAŃSTWOWEGO
MUZEUM NA MAJDANKU
ul. Droga Męczenników
Majdanka 67
20-325 Lublin
Hours: 8:00 AM–3:00 PM

Tel: 81/744-2647
Fax: 81/744-0526

BACKGROUND

The Majdanek Museum was established in October 1944. It covers one-third of the area of the former death camp and is located in a suburb of Lublin. Its purpose is the preservation of camp objects, the collection of documents and accounts of the World War II period and the exhibition of the Nazi genocide apparatus.

From the very beginning, the Majdanek Museum has made intensive efforts to collect as many documents as possible, but the majority of files were destroyed by the staff during the evacuation of the camp in 1944. The surviving files, consisting of three groups of documents, were placed in the Archives. The most important of these were the files created by the camp offices in the years 1941–1944. The second group consists of documents created outside the camp, but directly connected to it. The third group of documents includes files concerning various aspects of the occupation of the Lublin area indirectly connected with the Majdanek camp. The camp documents were divided into six file sections according to the camp's organizational structure:

- Camp commandant's office
- Political department
- Prisoners' camp
- Administration
- Camp doctor
- Camp guards

HOLDINGS

The smallest number of preserved documents were from the camp commandant's office, political department and prisoners' camp management. Documents that also partially survived were orders, instructions and announcements from the commandant's office for the years 1943–1944, fragmentary reports about the number of prisoners, and announcements sent to the families about the deaths of prisoners and about inmates released from the camp. However, a small number of instructions from the political department to the effects department (*Effektenkammer*) concerned the ownership of property of those who died in the camp and of the prisoner interrogations. Also surviving, though incomplete, are records of the announcements

of new arrivals, listing the total number of men, women and children brought to the camp.

Of the records of those who died in the camp, only one book survived, kept during the period May–September 1942, along with daily reports of prisoners' deaths in the second half of 1942, and the register of those who died in October and November 1943, men from Field IV.

Documents from the camp employment office are fairly well represented, consisting of detailed daily reports concerning the work of prisoners; work brigades; summary reports; cards from work files; and permanent permits, which enabled specialists to pass from one Field to another.

The greatest number of documents survived from the administration department responsible for provisions: files for clothing and other articles taken from prisoners after admission to the camp (5,000 items); cash files (2,000 items); a register of names of arrivals, transfers and deaths, with the money and valuables owned by them shown; and lists of cash and valuables taken from prisoners in 1944. Included in this section of documents are the accounting and financial records.

A separate group consists of files concerning the dispatch of hair from the camp in 1942–1944. From this correspondence, we learn that, from September 1942 to the first quarter of 1944, 730 kilograms of human hair were sent from Majdanek.

■ *View of the mausoleum at Majdanek*   5

Documents concerning the transportation of Zyklon B gas were also preserved. The orders, urgent reminders, delivery notes and explanations for the years 1941–1944 allow us to estimate that, from July 1942 to July 1944, some 7,711 kilograms of Zyklon B were delivered to the Majdanek camp.

Only a small number of documents survived from the office of the camp doctor: questionnaires and fragments of patients' cards, temperature charts and several dozen doctors' reports of prisoners' deaths in 1944. From Department VI, to which belonged the guards and the security of the camp, most of the documents preserved are concerned with the guard service. These are the name records of particular guard companies for the years 1942–1944, records of the guards of the Women's Field, a few personnel files, daily strength reports of the guard company, service orders, code words, orders and regulations for the guard shifts and the commandant's office orders.

Also important are files created by other institutions, but directly connected with Majdanek, relating to general camp plans as well as particular fields and buildings. In addition, there are bills and correspondence of the Central Construction Office of the SS occupied with the building of the camp, of which the majority of the documentation (280 files) is kept in the State Archives in Lublin. The announcements concerning the deaths of prisoners directed to the Roman Catholic parishes of Saint Paul and Saint John in Lublin were sent to the museum.

Very precious is the collection of documents described as "Archives of the Prisoners' Organization," concerning the resistance movement in the camp, self-help and aid given to the prisoners from outside. This material consists mostly of illegal correspondence: notes smuggled out and sent to the prisoners' families, to acquaintances and to people who organized aid with the help of free workers or inmates working outside the camp.

Of extreme interest are personal documents of prisoners of various nationalities, collected after their arrival and found after the liberation of the camp. These consist of passports, identity cards, employment cards, certificates, diplomas, etc. This is a very valuable source of material for research into the international composition of the inmates, their professional structure and social backgrounds.

In 1958, the Museum took possession of the files of the Polish Red Cross, Lublin region, concerning mostly the aid given in 1943–1944 to Majdanek prisoners. Among others, there are files containing more than 10,000 cards with the names of inmates who, with the intervention of the Polish Red Cross, received parcels. In 1971, the Museum received the files of the AK (Home Army) cell, which was called the *Centralna Opieka Podziemia* (OPUS)—Central Underground Welfare—which rendered aid to the persecuted members of the AK and their families. These files contain lists of inmates and reports on the situation in the camp.

The Museum at Majdanek also possesses a very interesting photographic collection. These are private photographs brought into the camp by prisoners and found after the liberation in one of the barracks: photographs of the camp in the years 1941–1944 (30 items), camp buildings after the liberation in 1944 and in later years, photographs of former prisoners and people who rendered aid to them, photographs of the camp personnel and photographs of important observances and events in the State Museum at Majdanek.

The Museum continues to collect diaries, recollections and accounts by prisoners. At present, the number of written recollections amounts to 1,200 items, to which have been added 480 tape recordings and about 100 video recordings. The forms filled in by the former witnesses are also a rich source of information; more than 2,000 of them have been collected.

Most of the files dealing with prisoners of Jewish descent originate from the years 1942 to 1943. These consist of announcements of the sending of group transports to the camp from Slovakia, Germany and Poland as well as information about the settlement of individual people, fragmentary remains of records, name indices and examples of clothing and money indices. The Jews are mentioned as a separate group in the numerical records of prisoners and also in the summary lists of those directed to work. Much data about the Jews brought

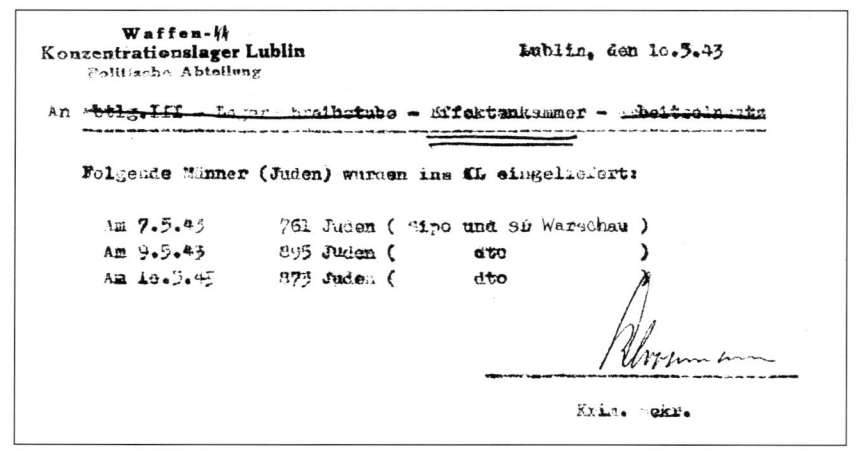

Notification of deportation of a transport of Jews from Warsaw to KL Lublin   6

from various countries are to be found in the collection of prisoners' documents. These are the personal documents certifying the education, professions, businesses and family situations of Jewish prisoners. Among them, correspondence can be found dating from before the outbreak of war and detailing the attempts to obtain permission to leave for the United States or Australia from countries endangered by Hitler's aggression—for example, Slovakia and Austria. In addition to these documents, partial records of Jews who died in the camp have survived. Also, there is a small collection of documents from *Aktion Reinhard*. These materials pertain to the warehouse on Chopin Street in Lublin in which items taken from the murdered Jews were stored. They consist mainly of lists of plunder and requisitions for these items, not only from various institutions, but also from private individuals.

A part of the files concerned with the Majdanek camp are located outside the museum in other Polish archives, such as the State Archives in Lublin and archives in Warsaw: the Archives of Contemporary Documents, the General Administration of the Polish Red Cross and the Main Commission for the Investigation of Crimes Against the Polish Nation/Institute of National Memory. Some of the documents created in the camp are to be found in archives in Russia and Germany. The museum possesses microfilms, photographs and photocopies of the most well-known files kept in other archives.

ACCESS TO ARCHIVAL MATERIAL

Information about former prisoners of the camp can be obtained through an on-site visit or by written request. There is no fee involved.

The following information should be provided:
- First/last name of person being sought
- Date/place of birth
- Names of parents
- Address before arrest/deportation
- Date of arrival to Majdanek

Partial report of prisoners who died in Majdanek, 1942   7

Majdanek memorial to 18,000 Jews killed on November 3, 1943   8

List of money and valuables taken from prisoners at Majdanek extermination camp and its branches 9

Clothing index, Majdanek camp, 1942 10

MAIN HOLDINGS RELATING TO JEWISH VICTIMS

- Death record books from 1942 (sygn. 1d.19). May 18–September 28, 1942 (with gaps in May–June). Includes 6,716 names including 2,849 Jews from Slovakia; 1,155 from Poland; 1,060 from Czechoslovakia; and 772 from Germany. Further information can be found in the article by Dr. Janina Kiełboń published in *Zeszyty Majdanka* XV, 1993.
- Remnants of death book from 1942–1943 (Fot. 407). Specifically, November 20, 1942–January 20, 1943. Includes 1,650 names (many Jewish names) and a summary of those who died in November (2,999 persons, including 2,190 Jews) and December 1942 (2,983 persons, including 2,505 Jews).
- Reports about deaths of prisoners (sygn. 1d.18, vols. 1–4) from April 3 to September 29, 1942 (many gaps).
- A list of prisoners by name (the majority are Jewish). The documents were found in the territory of the camp during destruction. Only some pages are in one piece; the majority of them are in fragments.
- A file about prisoners' clothes (sygn. 1d.6).
- Fragments of transport lists, some single reports concerning people who were arrested and lists of employed workers.

According to the most recent calculations of Dr. Czesław Rajca, published in *Zeszyty Majdanka* XIV, 1992, Majdanek had approximately 300,000 prisoners (including 120,000 Jews, or 40 percent). Of this number, 110,000 Jews perished, representing 47 percent of the total number of the victims of Majdanek.

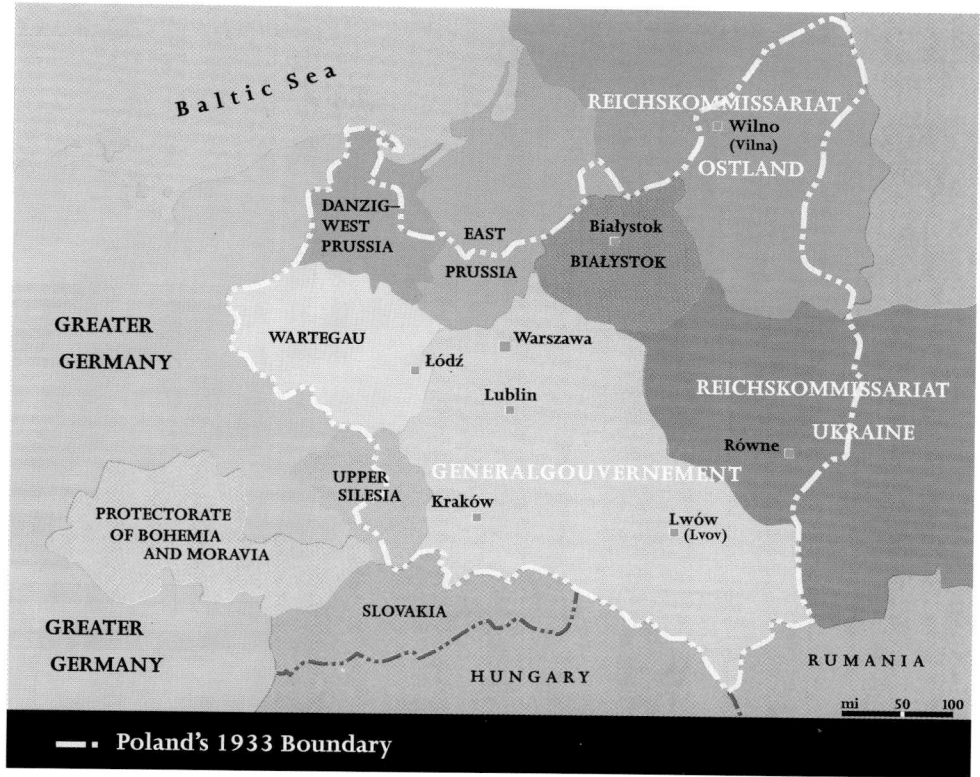

German Administration of Poland, 1942

Map 9

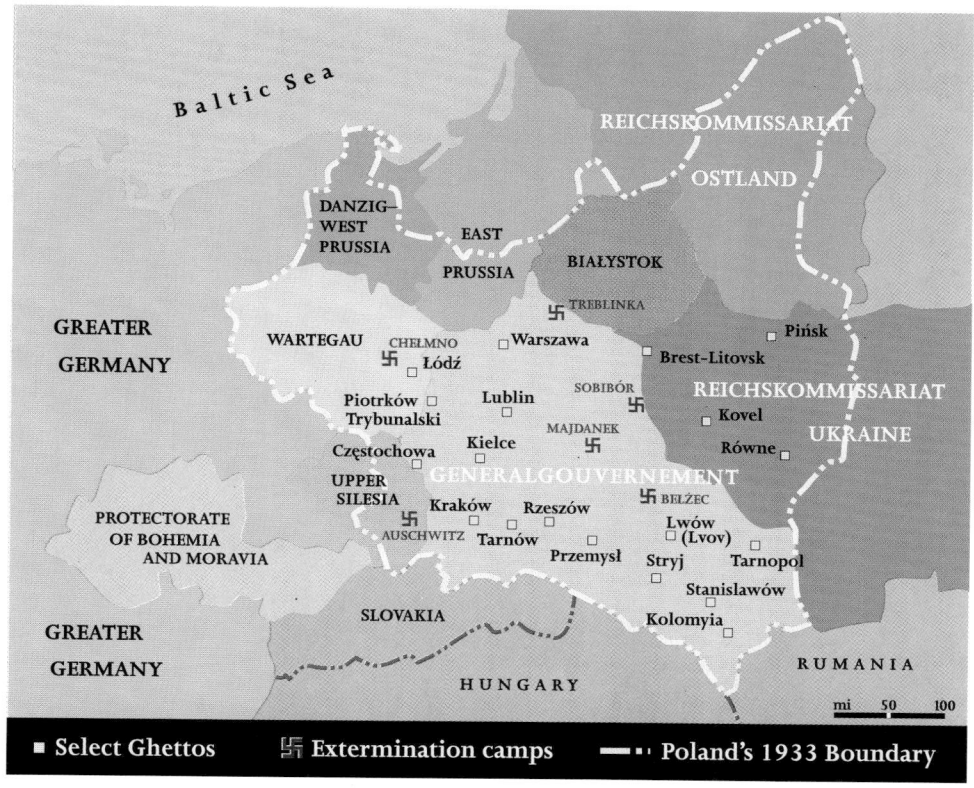

Extermination Camps, 1942

Map 10

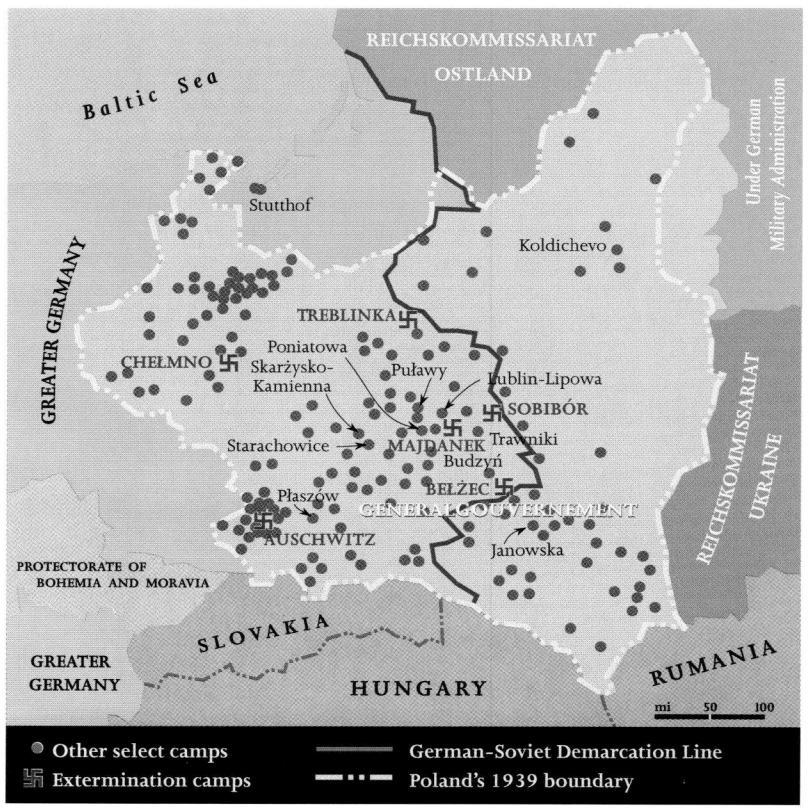

Nazi Camps in Occupied Poland, 1939–1945 Map 11

Ghettos in Occupied Poland, 1939–1941 Map 12

STATE MUSEUM OF AUSCHWITZ-BIRKENAU
THE ARCHIVES

by Barbara Jarosz and Helena Śliż
Archivists

ARCHIWUM PAŃSTWOWEGO
MUZEUM W OŚWIĘCIMIU-
BRZEZINCE
ul. Więźniów
32-603 Oświęcim

Tel: 33/43-20-22 ext. 245-245
Fax: 33/43-19-34
and 43-22-27

BACKGROUND

The Archives were created as a separate section of the State Museum of Auschwitz-Birkenau in 1957 by Tadeusz Iwaszko, who also served as director. Before the Archives were organized, the section of documentation (which functioned through the Committee to Search for Nazi Crimes in Kraków) had functioned for this purpose, and in 1950, it was transferred to Auschwitz-Birkenau.

The purpose of the Archives is to maintain and provide access to their holdings. The Archives of the State Museum of Auschwitz-Birkenau have a specific character: they collect various materials connected with the history of KL Auschwitz and, in some instances, other camps. Their holdings consist of original German documents, copies of documents, testimonials and memories of former inmates and postwar documents.

HOLDINGS

The original documents form a small percentage of what was generated in the camp offices. During the liquidation and evacuation of the camp, SS authorities gave an order to destroy or remove all documentation in order to erase traces of the crime. The majority of the original documents that are in the Museum were found on the grounds of the liberated camp and in places where the documents were secretly sent during the operation of the camp. In addition, the Museum received documents from former inmates, their families and various industrial factories where subcamps of KL Auschwitz were set up.

Documents were created according to the structure of SS camp authorities. The following documents are connected with the commandant's office: *Kommandant-urbefehle, Standortbefehle* and *Sturmbannbefehle.* A large group of documents consist of records about SS officers and members of the Auschwitz-Birkenau camp staff. There is a large collection of camp letters written by prisoners (both original letters and copies), consisting of more than 8,000 letters and postcards.

The following documents remained from the political department of the camp:

- Transport lists of prisoners brought to KL Auschwitz in 1941
- Transport lists of Jews from 1942
- Personal records of prisoners
- Reports about punishments of prisoners

There are also 46 volumes of original death records of those who perished in KL Auschwitz. The death records were finally returned to the Museum in 1991–1992 by the Center for the Preservation and Storage of Historical Documents in Moscow, after years of effort. In the volumes that cover the period from August 1941 to December 1943, there are 69,000 death records.

The documents about the management of the camp and the employment department consist of:

- A book with the prisoners' numbers
- Books (incomplete) of daily status reports saved from January to August 1942
- Record books of the Romani (Gypsy) camp (men and women)
- A bunker book
- A book from the punishment unit
- Record books from Block No. 4 and 16A in KL Auschwitz I; Block 22B in KL Auschwitz II (Birkenau)
- Index card file of the Soviet prisoners of war
- Index card file of Block No. 11
- Telegrams and letters about prisoner employment
- Index card file of locksmiths, electricians and installers
- Lists of employed prisoners (men and women)

Gloria Resin looks for information about her family in the Auschwitz Archives, 1991 11

Evidence of the administrative work performed in the Auschwitz-Birkenau camp may be found in the following documents:

- The personnel changes of the SS
- Orders of SS officers to tailor and shoemaker workshops
- Food coupons for the SS
- Receipts for belongings of deceased persons
- Documents regarding vehicular use
- Orders of material to crematoria to burn bodies

There is a significant collection of camp hospital documents. Most important are the documents from hospital barracks No. 20, 21, and 28: x-ray records; the dental station records; ambulance records; Buna hospital records; registration records of medicines given to prisoners; fever records; lists of prisoners who died in the camp between October 7, 1941, and August 31, 1943 (morgue registry); death books of Soviet prisoners of war; and reports about removing gold teeth and other reports/orders.

A separate group of documents are *Zentral bauleitung der Waffen SS und Polizei Auschwitz* I, II, III and documents of different German companies working for the needs of the camp. Among these documents are correspondence, expense lists, maps, and drawings of camp and subcamp objects. The documents of the SS–Hygiene Institute contain the referral slips to the laboratory for urine testing, blood, etc., for both prisoners and SS men (and their families).

There are remnants of subcamp documents of KL Auschwitz I, for example, correspondence and plans (drawings). There are also a large number of court (trial) documents of the commandant of the camp, Rudolf Höss and SS staff (78 volumes), and the court documents of Gerhard Maurer, Adolf Eichmann and Oswald Pohl. This file is augmented continually by new trial documents coming into the Archives.

Another archival collection consists of a group of documents from other Nazi camps, including Buchenwald, Dachau, Flossenburg, Mauthausen and Ravensbrück. These documents consist of copies of transport lists received from different institutions or death records received from former prisoners or their families. The original index card file of Mauthausen prisoners (who had previously been in KL Auschwitz) was brought to Auschwitz by former Mauthausen prisoners. It consists of 30,000 files from the employment division and 62,000 files from the registration department.

Another group of documents consists of testimonials and memories of the former prisoners, mainly from KL Auschwitz. More than 3,000 reports are included in 128 volumes, and more than 1,000 memoirs in 185 volumes. The reports and memoirs were written or recorded by workers of the Museum. The memoirs were sent to competitions organized in recent years by the Museum and different institutions or were given spontaneously by former prisoners. The Archives still receive this kind of documentation, which, in many cases, is the only source of information for those who research and document the history of Auschwitz-Birkenau.

List of new arrivals, 1941, Auschwitz, Bohdan Weber   12

In the years 1945–1980, in the area of Birkenau, the diaries of *Sonderkommando* prisoners were found buried in the ground. These prisoners were employed in the crematoria and burning areas, and their testimonials are a very valuable source of information.

Documents about the resistance movement are unique. Among them are secret messages sent from the camp by the members of the movement to organizations acting in Kraków or near the camp, reports written by prisoners who escaped from the camp (Tabeau, Wetzler, Vrba, Stanisław Chybinski, Rosin-Mordowicz), illegal photographs and copies of documents. This material is gathered in 40 volumes and, because of it, the world learned (during the war) the truth about Auschwitz-Birkenau.

Also in the archive collection are approximately 39,000 original negatives of photographs of camp prisoners and 30,000 different photographs. The most valuable are photographs taken by SS officers Ernst Hofman and Bernhard Walter during the selection of Hungarian Jews that took place in 1944 on the railway ramp at Birkenau. There are also photographs of the Central Construction Headquarters that include photo documentation of the construction of the camp buildings (crematoria and gas chambers), private photographs brought to the camp by prisoners and found after the war (about 2,500 photos) and aerial photographs taken by Allied air forces in 1944–1945.

Audio-visual material consists of documentary and feature films connected with the camp and World War II, records, tapes and videocassettes with recorded memories and reports of the prisoners. In the last few years, the Archives have received 1,562 tapes with recorded memories of former prisoners from Polish Radio in Katowice.

The Archives also collect materials created after World War II connected with the occupation and the camp. Among them are press articles, reports, scripts, reviews and academic publications. The majority of this material was created on the basis of material in the Archives, and access is given to those who are interested. Many university theses and articles are based upon archival material, and dozens of films were made utilizing this data.

Researchers from many countries (in 1995, *e.g.*, from the Czech Republic, Israel, Japan, Germany and Poland), along with historians, sociologists, students, journalists, and filmmakers, use our material. Archivists provide written and oral information about collections, conduct research, make photocopies of photographs and documents, and give lectures in Polish and German to groups of young people and teachers who visit the Archives.

There is an Information Office in the Archives that provides former prisoners with written statements confirming their stay in the camp. Written and oral information is also given to relatives of prisoners as well as to different institutions in Poland and abroad that want to know about prisoners in KL Auschwitz.

The Photo Laboratory does work requested by the Archives (microfilms, negatives, xerox copies, photographs), museums, private individuals, institutions in Poland and abroad, publications and various exhibitions.

In Moscow, in the Center for Preservation of Historical Documentary Collections, there is a rich collection of original documentation connected with the Central Construction Headquarters, *Waffen* SS and SS Police in Auschwitz-Birkenau. This collection includes the construction plans of the camp as well as projects for enlarging it, a list of SS men from *Zentralbauleitung der Waffen* SS and Auschwitz Police, lists of chief workers and 125,000 files of civil workers employed by different German companies.

A part of the KL Auschwitz documentation was taken after the war to the Military-Medical Museum in Leningrad. This includes:

- A list of female prisoners who died or were murdered in KL Auschwitz in December 1943 (836 names)

- A list of prisoners who died in January 1944 (921 names)

- The camp hospital surgical registry

- Camp statistics about illnesses among prisoners

Auschwitz I.D. (1942) for Berek Cymbler, born 1879 in Olkusz   13

- Correspondence with the Topf und Sohne Company in the years 1941–1943 about building crematoria
- Correspondence of the administration of the camp for the years 1941–1943 with WVHA (Main Administration and Economic Office of SS) about enlarging the camp
- A list of employed prisoners from 1944
- The diary of the *Sonderkommando* prisoner Zalmen Gradowski, which was found in March 1945 in the area of the crematorium in Birkenau

In 1992, an agreement between the Polish State Archives and the Committee for Archives of the Federal Government of Russia was signed in Moscow about returning archival records of Polish origin, including documentation of KL Auschwitz. The Archives have already received some of those documents. The Polish Military Archival Committee xeroxed about 5,000 selected documents for the State Museum of Auschwitz-Birkenau. Among them are documents concerning *Zentralbauleitung* and other branches: *Kommandanturbefehle* (1940–1944), *Standortbefehle* and *Sturmbannbefehle*. Further efforts are proceeding through government and diplomatic channels. The cooperation that began in 1992 with the Military-Medical Museum in St. Petersburg is also very fruitful. On the basis of a bilateral agreement, part of the documents and exhibits were given to Auschwitz-Birkenau in the form of yearly transfers.

The Archives cooperate with different institutions of similar character in Poland and abroad, such as the Main Committee to Search Crimes Against the Polish Nation and Regional Committees, Internationaler Suchdienst from Arolsen in the Federal Republic of Germany, Yad Vashem in Israel, the United States Holocaust Memorial Museum in Washington, D.C., and the Russian Archives. The Archives also have contact with former prisoners and their families. Through this cooperation, many copies of documents about KL Auschwitz have been retrieved.

In 1991, a computer section was established in the Archives to computerize the data from the KL Auschwitz prisoners' documents. The next step will be the input of data from other archival documents. In addition to microfilming, and as another method of protection and preservation, the documents will be scanned using optical discs, which will make academic research easier.

On the basis of this data, *Memorial Book: The Gypsies at Auschwitz-Birkenau* was published. Additionally, the Auschwitz Archives published *Death Books from Auschwitz* (three volumes), including 69,000 prisoners' names who perished in KL Auschwitz in the period between August 1941 and December 1943.

To accommodate the Archives' needs, a list of original preserved negatives of photographs of camp prisoners was prepared in the order of camp numbers (five volumes).

Barbara Jarosz is a historian and graduate of Jagiellonian University in Kraków. Jarosz is director of the Archives at the State Museum of Auschwitz-Birkenau and is the author of a publication about the camp resistance movement.

Helena Śliż was born in 1953 in Sokołów Mazowiecki. In 1975, Śliż graduated from Śląski Unviersity in Katowice. She currently works in the Archives of the State Museum of Auschwitz-Birkenau.

List of illnesses to be used as "causes of death"   14

Town square, Oświęcim (near Auschwitz-Birkenau camp), 1916   15

Bohdan Weber, born March 28, 1908 in Budweis, Bohemia, clerk. Transported to KL Auschwitz from Brno on October 24, 1941. Registered as a Polish Jew, he was a political prisoner, placed in Block 11 and shot on November 6, 1941, "while fleeing" with his brother, Jarosław Weber.

18

Death record for Bohdan Israel Weber, who died November 6, 1941

16

Report on the extraction of gold teeth from the corpse of Richard Israel Lanyi before cremation

17

Registration of Bohdan Weber, Block 11, Auschwitz

19

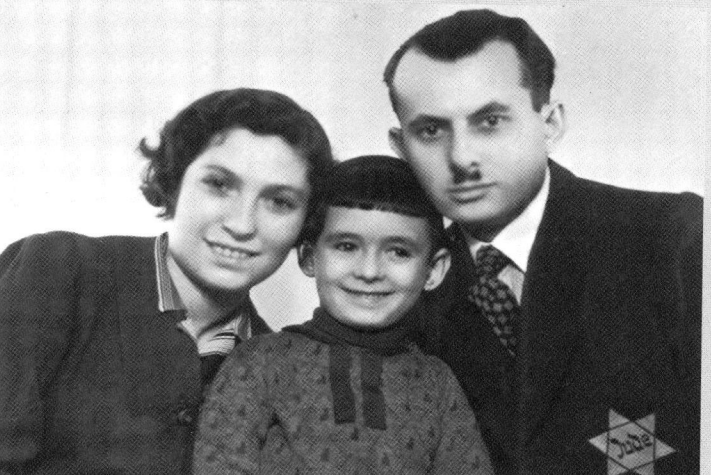

These five photographs from the archives of the State Museum of Auschwitz-Birkenau are among thousands confiscated from deportees upon their arrival in the camps.

20

STATE MUSEUM OF AUSCHWITZ-BIRKENAU
Regulations for Access to Archival Documents

Jerzy Wróblewski, *Director*

1. Visitors (users) can access archival documents in the reading room of the Archives every day between 8:00 AM and 2:00 PM, except holidays and other stated days for closing.
2. Prior to archival research, permission must be obtained by the director or the vice-director of the Archives. Those individuals wishing permission to research archival documents must complete an application card, listing the purpose of their research, or the title of their proposed publication, and then register in a book for users of the archives.
3. Users may be given material in the form of copies and microfilms. In exceptional cases, original documents for academic research purposes and publication purposes are also provided. Access to archival material of a personal nature (family correspondence of living individuals and other documents relating to living people) can be obtained only with written permission from the person or institution that deposited the material in the Archives or after the stated release date, named by the individual or institution.

The director of the Archives or his deputy has the right to:
- Withhold permission to access documents if they are in poor condition or because of other reasonable reasons.
- Withdraw access permission in the event the user does not observe the regulations or does not follow conditions of the access permission. An individual who is denied access to archival documents by the Archives director or vice-director may appeal to the director of the museum.

The user is permitted to:
- Use inventories, lists and other helpful sources for the work.
- Order copies of documents, photocopies, and negatives in a quantity that the archive director considers possible for the photo lab to process. The user pays the costs of the service according to the price list. The completion date of the processing is determined by the Archives director.

The user is obligated to:
- Inform the Archives in advance regarding the date of arrival and subject of research, so as to allow the Archives to prepare the requested material.
- Provide an introduction/recommendation letter if a student or a representative of institutions, associations or state administrative institutions. Without this letter, permission to research documents may be denied.
- Be familiar with the regulations and obey them.
- Return material every day to the person who is in charge of the reading room.
- Provide the Archives with one copy of the published work that was based upon the archival material.

The user is not permitted to:
- Personally make reproductions of any archival material.
- Make any markings or notes on archival material.
- Change the order of the archival material.
- Give access to material to other users in the reading room.
- Bring briefcases or bags into the reading room.
- Do anything that negatively affects the archival material.

Only specific institutions (television, film studios, press, etc.) may be given permission to photograph archival material.

The Archives do not lend material to individuals, but do lend material to museums. If there is a need, a microfilm can be loaned to academic institutions.

Museum workers may use original documents and other files only in the reading room. They may take copies to their offices only for a certain time designated by the director of the Archives. If it is necessary, the director can request that the material be returned earlier. In the event that Museum workers are absent for an extended period of time, they are obliged to return the borrowed material.

Original documents may be loaned for exhibitions only in exceptional cases after obtaining permission from the Main State Archives.

Permission to microfilm archival materials for other institutions in Poland and abroad cooperating with the Museum is given by the director of the Museum.

Regulations dated as of January 1, 1993.
STATE MUSEUM OF AUSCHWITZ-BIRKENAU

Former yeshiva building in Oświęcim; now houses offices of the Polish-Israeli Friendship Society
21

Plaque at site of Bet Midrash in Oświęcim, in memory of the owner of the textile factory in Kęty, Shlomo Zalman Felczman, born 1906.
22

THE PEOPLE WERE SELECTED ON THE RAILWAY PLATFORM. THOSE TO BE GASSED WERE ASSURED THAT THEY WERE GOING TO TAKE A BATH. DUMMY SHOWERS WERE FIXED TO THE CEILING. CUDGELLED AND HALLOOED WITH DOGS 2000 VICTIMS WERE CRAMMED IN THE CHAMBER 210 SQUARE METERS / APPROX. 235 SQ. YARDS / IN AREA. THE CHAMBER DOOR WAS LOCKED. AND CYCLON B WAS POURED. AFTER 15-20 MINUTES THE CHAMBER WAS OPENED. CORPSES WERE STRIPPED OF GOLD TEETH HAIR EARRINGS, RINGS. AND THEN TRANSPORTED TO A CREMATORY. VICTIMS PERSONEL DOCUMENTS WERE DESTROYED.

▌ Caption beneath *Auschwitz model of the crematoria, 1991*　23

IN 20.01.1942 - AFTER CONFERENCE IN WANNSEE AUSCHWITZ WAS DESIGNED AS CENTER FOR JEWS EXTERMINATION FROM THE COUNTRIES OCCUPIED BY NAZI GERMANY.
AMONG FOUR CREMATORIES WHICH WERE BUILT IN BIRKENAU, CREMATORY NUMBER 2 WAS ACTIVE FROM SPRING 1943. THERE WERE A GAS CHAMBER AND STOVES FOR CORPS BURNING. TA MASK THE CRIMES, NAZISTS PLANTED POPLARS ON THE TERRAIN AROUND THE CREMATORY.
DESIGNATION OF SELECTED PARTS OF THE CREMATORY WAS AS FOLLOWS :
1. UNDRESSING ROOM.
2. GAS CHAMBER - THERE WERE KILLED TWO THOUSAND PEOPLE IN THE SINGLE CHARGE.
3. ELECTRICAL CRANE FOR CORPS TRANSPORTATION TO THE STOVES.
4. THE CHAMBER, WHERE WAS CARRIED HAIR-CUT FOR KILLED WOMEN.
5. CREMATORIES STOVE HALL, WHERE GOLD TEETH WERE PULLED OFF. AND LATER CORPS WERE BURNED.
6. STOVE FOR PERSONAL DOCUMENTS BURNING AND OTHERS USELESS PROPERTIES CAPTURED FROM KILLED.
ON OCTOBER 7TH 1944 JEWISH PRISONERS EMPLOYED WITH CORPS BURNING STARTED UPRISING IN THE CREMATORY NUMBER FOUR, THEY KILLED TWO SS-MEN AND KAPO, AND THEN CUT OFF BARBED WIRE AND RUN AWAY TO THE VILLAGE RAJSKO. ALL OF THEM WERE SURRAAUNDERED BY SS-MEN AND IN THE FIGHTING WERE KILLED.

▌ Caption beneath *Auschwitz model of the crematoria, 1991*　24

▌ *Shelves of record books in the Auschwitz-Birkenau Archives, 1990*　25

▌ *Remaining barracks at Auschwitz, 1991*　26

▌ *View through chain-link fence at Auschwitz, 1990*　27

▌ *Remains of gas chambers at Birkenau, 1990*　28

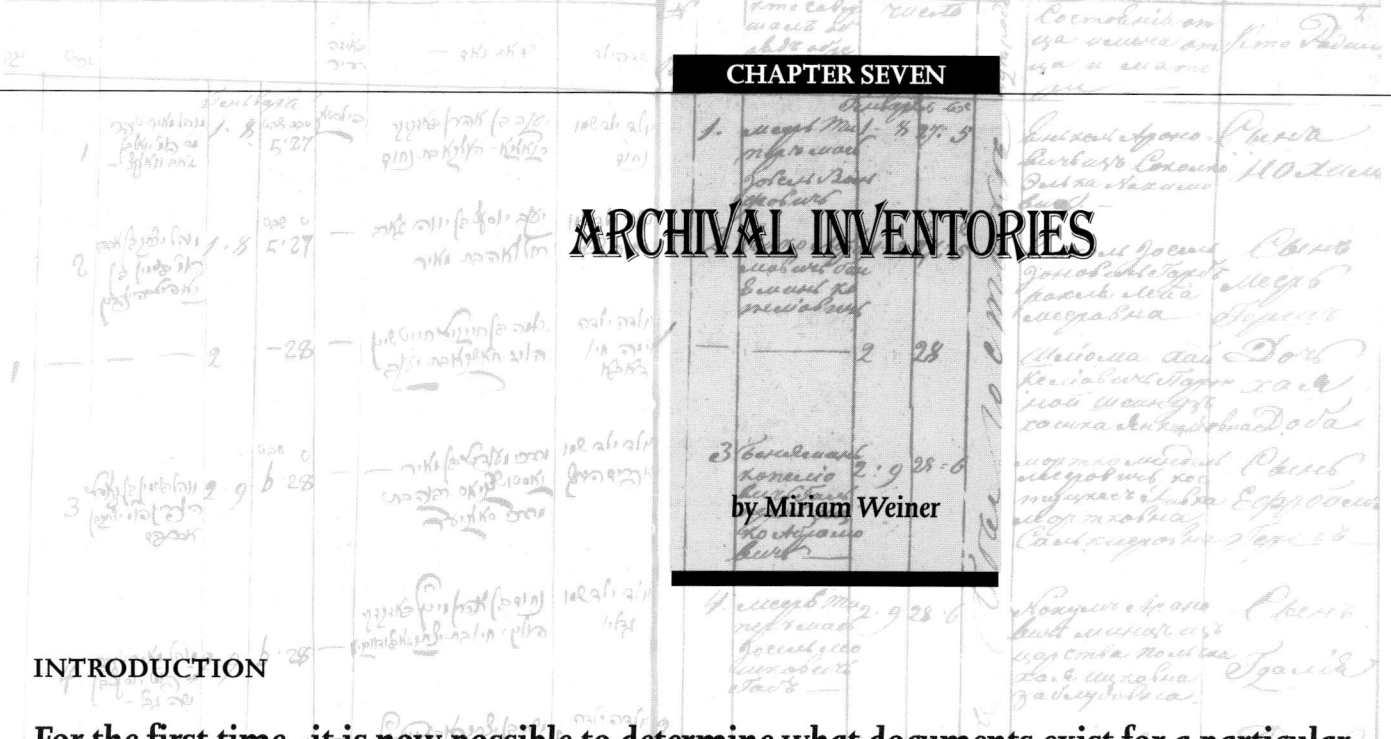

ARCHIVAL INVENTORIES

by Miriam Weiner

INTRODUCTION

For the first time, it is now possible to determine what documents exist for a particular town among the major archival repositories in Poland.

Those of us interested in tracing our family history back to the "Old Country" have long been frustrated by the inability to determine what documents exist, where they are and what years are available. The situation is further complicated by the fact that documents for a particular ancestral town could be in several different archives in different cities, and in more than one country. Furthermore, depending upon the time period of the documents' creation, the documents could be written in more than one language or in difficult-to-read handwriting. The realities of research in the archives of Eastern Europe and particularly Poland and the republics of the former Soviet Union have discouraged many people. Even today, working conditions in archives in this area are not what one encounters here in North America and elsewhere.

Working with documents in the various archives in Poland requires knowledge of Polish, German and Russian (see Appendix 4). Some documents are written in both Yiddish and Russian. In the smaller archives of Poland, it is more the exception than the rule to find archivists who speak English. Therefore, in order to work with these documents, one must plan on bringing a translator. Of course, it is helpful if the translator has some prior experience working with archival documents.

The following inventory lists provide a poignant trail of the devastation of Jewish life and documentation of the Jewish presence in Poland. The recording of Jewish vital records began in 1826 and virtually stopped by 1943. For hundreds of localities,

there are no surviving records at all, but for hundreds of other towns, many thousands of documents survived.

Author's note: Jewish vital records were also interspersed with the Roman Catholic vital records for the years 1810–1825 (separate records by religious community began in 1826). Therefore, the archives of the local Catholic Archdiocese should also be researched in addition to the Polish State Archives and local USC offices.

Archivist Hubert Wajs in AGAD Archives in Warsaw, with display of Jewish books for Jewish genealogy tour group in 1990

1

SPELLING OF TOWN NAMES
IN UKRAINE AND BELARUS

The archival inventories include towns now in western Ukraine that formerly were part of Poland (and at one time identified as being in Galicia and the Austro-Hungarian Empire). After its independence, Ukraine reclaimed its national language. Although one will hear Polish and Russian spoken amongst the citizens of this region, the official language is Ukrainian.

The Jewish metrical books for western Ukraine (eastern Galicia) include the oblasts (districts) of Lvov, Ivano Frankovsk and Tarnopol. In Galicia, the column headings of the metrical books were in German and/or Latin, and entries were made in German, Yiddish and/or Polish. The book cover, title pages and archival finding aids for these metrical books are primarily in Russian, since Ukrainian was not the official language at the time the finding aids were created and was not used in record-keeping. Therefore, for clarity and consistency purposes, the transliteration of the town names in the aforementioned oblasts are from the Russian spellings rather than the current-day Ukrainian spellings (see Appendix 3 for place-name variants of the above localities included in the archival inventories).

In the repository inventories, towns in Belarus and Lithuania today are also transliterated from the Russian spelling since the entries are in the Russian language.

SOURCES FOR ARCHIVAL INVENTORIES

The following sources were consulted as part of the survey of archives and in the preparation of this inventory:
- Published archival inventories in Poland
- Teller, A., ed., *Guide to the Sources for the History of the Jews in Poland in the Central Archives.* Jerusalem: Central Archives for the History of the Jewish People, Jerusalem, 1988.
- *Miasta polskie: Dokumentacja archiwalna.* Warsaw-Łódź: Państwowe Wydawnictwo Naukowe, 1981.
- Inventories compiled by researchers and archivists on assignment for this book
- "Polish-Jewish Records in the Genealogical Society of Utah." *Avotaynu,* vol. 2, no. 2 (January 1986): 5–17.
- Gostin, Ted, "Polish-Jewish Records at the Family History Library, an Update." *Roots-Key* (Summer 1995): 8–10.
- *Urzędy Stanu Cywilnego, Informator, Część I.* Ministerstwo Spraw Wewnętrznych: Departament Społeczno-Administracyjny [Ministry of Internal Affairs], 1984. This book is based on a national survey of metrical books in more than 2,000 USC offices (the Ministry has not done a subsequent survey and, thus, this inventory is based upon the 1984 data with updating as documents were transferred from USC offices to the State Archives.).
- Polish archivists who added material during the verification process and American researchers who submitted data based upon onsite archival research.

GEOGRAPHIC COMPOSITION
OF THE INVENTORIES

The inventory of archival documents is presented in two separate lists of archival holdings, described as follows:
- **Towns in Poland.** Includes documents for towns within the current borders of Poland and also entries for Polish towns that are in archives in neighboring countries. For example, the town entry for Białystok (now in Poland) includes Białystok documents that are in the Grodno Oblast Archives and Grodno Historical Archives in Belarus.
- **Repositories in Poland.** Includes documents for towns now in Poland and towns formerly in Poland (but now in Ukraine, Belarus and Lithuania).

Therefore, the repository inventory includes documents in the Polish State Archives for the former Polish cities of Grodno (Hrodna, now in Belarus), Wilno (Vilnius, now in Lithuania) and Lwów (Lviv, now in Ukraine).

REPOSITORY INVENTORIES

The repository inventories represent the following collections:
- Jewish Historical Institute (in Warsaw)
- Urząd Stanu Cywilnego (USC) Warsaw Śródmieście. Only those documents (less than 100 years old) relating to the registration of Jewish birth, marriage and death records in the former Polish provinces of Stanisławów, Lwów and Tarnopol. The towns represented in these provinces are now within the current borders of Ukraine (see Chapter 4).
- Polish State Archives

The archival inventories for the Polish State Archives include all district archives (*Archiwum Państwowe*) along with most of their branch (*oddział*) archives. A few small branch archives are omitted because either they did not reply to requests for inventory data or they indicated that they did not have material relevant to this survey.

DUPLICATION AND OVERLAPPING
OF ARCHIVAL DATA

In a few instances, there is overlapping and/or duplication of data in the archival inventories for a specific town. Generally, this refers to duplicate copies of record books or situations where one book stops in the middle of a year and the next book begins with the completion of that year.

NAMES OF ARCHIVAL COLLECTIONS
IN USC OFFICES

Sygnatura/Zespół numbers (archival file numbers) are provided for metrical books in the Polish State Archives. The individual USC offices (local town halls) throughout Poland do not use the same system of numbering; thus, the metrical books in the USC offices are accessible by town name rather than by numbers.

LUBLIN ARCHIVES—KEY TO ARCHIVAL COLLECTIONS

Some branches of the Polish State Archives use abbreviations in describing their holdings. The branch archives in Lublin very kindly supplied a key to the abbreviations of its archival collections.

RGL IV ADM.	Russian Lublin's Governor's Office, IV Section—Administration, 1867–1918	**ZPŁUK**	Russian Prefect of Łuków County, 1866–1915
POLISH RGL	Governor's Office in Lublin, 1832–1866	**ZPZ**	Russian Prefect of Zamość County, 1866–1915
RGCH	Russian Chełm's Governor's Office, 1911–1915	**ZPB**	Russian Prefect of Biała Podlaska County, 1866–1915
UWL WSP	Office of Lublin's Voivodship, Social-Political Section, 1918–1939	**ZPK**	Russian Prefect of Krasnystaw County, 1866–1915
SPL	Prefect of Lublin County, 1919–1939	**NPK**	Polish Prefect of Krasnystaw County, 1831–1866
SPH	Prefect of Hrubieszów County, 1919–1939		
SPB	Prefect of Biała Podlaska County, 1919–1939	**AMO**	Acts of *miasta* (town records), Ostrów Lubelski, 1890–1955
SPŁUK	Prefect of Łuków County, 1919–1939	**AMLUB**	Acts of *miasta* (town records), Lubartów, 1570–1950
SPJ	Prefect of Janów Lubelski County, 1921–1935	**AML**	Acts of *miasta* (town records), Lublin, 1809–1915
ZPCH	Russian Prefect of Chełm County, 1866–1915		
ZPG	Russian Prefect of Garwolin County, 1866–1915 (now in Siedlce Archives)		

JEWISH HISTORICAL INSTITUTE—KEY TO ARCHIVAL COLLECTIONS

"Silesian Province" (Prowincja Śląska) is a designation in the JHI Archives for records of the Jewish communities under German Imperial Rule before the dissolution of the German Empire in 1918. The Silesian Province covered roughly the territory of today's provinces of Lower Silesia, parts of Upper Silesia and Great Poland.

ADDRESSES OF ARCHIVES OUTSIDE OF POLAND
WITH POLISH DOCUMENTS INCLUDED IN TOWN INVENTORY

The following archives include among their holdings documents for towns now in Poland (see also Introduction, page 2–3, regarding German-held microfilms of Polish Jewish records).

GRODNO HISTORICAL ARCHIVE
ul. Lenina 2
230023 Grodno
Belarus
375/152/44-94-66 **T**

GRODNO OBLAST ARCHIVES
ul. Dzerzhenskogo 84
230005 Grodno
Belarus
375/152/72-24-43 **T**

LVIV HISTORICAL ARCHIVES
ul. Sobornaya 3a
290008 Lviv
Ukraine
380/322/72-30-63 **T**
380/322/72-35-08 **F**

LVIV OBLAST ARCHIVES
ul. Pidvalna 13
290006 Lviv
Ukraine
380/322/72-00-30 **T**

LITHUANIAN STATE HISTORICAL ARCHIVES
Gerosios Vilties 10
2009 Vilnius
Lithuania
370/2/23-74-82 **T**
370/2/23-76-12 **F**

DOCUMENT TYPES INCLUDED IN INVENTORIES

During the survey for this inventory, every effort was made to include material that included family names rather than general correspondence, regulations, decrees or other documents of a historical nature. However, it was not possible to review the vast majority of the material included in the inventories. Therefore, it is possible that the documents listed in the inventory may be of a general nature in some instances. For example, *kahal* material may relate to a dispute between members of the synagogue board of directors, correspondence with the local authorities about the cemetery, or a multitude of other matters that could be of historical interest, but not relating to specific individuals.

There are three types of documents of a more general nature. In a few instances, where the specific document description was stated, there are some descriptive words about the documents. For example:

H Holocaust (*i.e.*, lists of confiscated property, transport lists)
K *Kahal* (*i.e.*, lists of burials, synagogue membership lists)
Z Local government records (*i.e.*, court documents, wills)

The archival inventory **by town** includes documents pertaining to the listed town and surrounding villages (in smaller villages, vital record registrations were recorded in the nearby regional vital statistics center). In addition, many documents were recorded on a higher district level. Therefore, it is possible that some archival collections referred to in these inventories include more than one city; every effort was made to list each town separately in the inventory. Locality entries which include surrounding villages are followed by the word "region," *e.g.*, Lublin region, which would include surrounding villages.

The following letter codes are used to designate the general nature of the documents:

A Army and draft registrations (do not include actual military records).

B Birth registrations in separate Jewish metrical books (in Polish, German and Russian, with Yiddish translations in some cases).

C Lists of inhabitants, family lists and books of residents. Generally, all members of the household are listed, with ages and relationships to the head of household. Some document formats include occupations, date/place where the family lived before or where they moved to. In some parts of Poland, these records were recorded on a regular basis (every ten years), while in other localities, the timing of registrations was influenced by events and the political situation. The books of residents include entire pages for one family and the registration of births, deaths, marriages and migrations that were recorded through the generations for the family members. Some family pages cover more than 50 years of recorded events.

D Death registrations in separate Jewish metrical books (in Polish, German and Russian, with Yiddish translations in some cases).

E Election and voters lists.

F Letter not used.

G Migration and immigration documents, including registrations as individuals moved from one town or district to another within Poland, as well as documents relating to those people who emigrated from the country.

H Holocaust material, including lists of confiscated property, deportation lists, lists of those killed, transport and inmate lists of concentration camps and ghettos.

I Letter not used.

J Judaica (includes Torah collections and other Judaic items).

K *Kahal* or Jewish community records (includes documents and correspondence relating to synagogues, Jewish cemeteries, correspondence with local government officials, membership and tax lists of Jewish societies and organizations, and other materials).

L Land and property records (includes correspondence and documents relating to private residences and businesses).

M Marriage registrations in separate Jewish metrical books (in Polish, German and Russian with Yiddish translations in some cases).

N Name changes.

O Police and KGB files relating to many civil matters in addition to criminal files (including membership in Jewish organizations, residence registrations, possession of "inflammatory literature" and other "so-called" crimes).

P Pogrom files.

Q Letter not used.

R Reference books, including address directories, business/ professional directories and telephone books.

S School records, including correspondence, lists and documents containing many names of students and teachers in both Jewish and public schools

T Tax lists, correspondence and documents, including many Jewish names.

U Letter not used.

V Divorce registrations in separate Jewish metrical books (in Polish, German and Russian, with Yiddish translations in some cases).

W Lists of Jewish workers by profession and business; business license applications.

X Hospital records, including material for primarily Jewish hospitals, *e.g.*., correspondence and name lists.

Y Notary records relating to transactions involving the purchase/sale of property and businesses, wills, military draft notices, school records, copies of birth, marriage and death records, and court records.

Z Local government records (correspondence and documents including many Jewish names).

ARCHIVAL LIST CODES

Since some archives in neighboring countries (Lithuania, Belarus and Ukraine) have documents for towns now in Poland, the following list codes and archive references include the appropriate descriptions used in the neighboring countries (see also page 188).

Repository Location   *Town/city where material is located*

Repository locations outside of Poland (see page 189):

Grodno	Grodno (now Hrodna) Historical Archives (Belarus)
Grodno2	Grodno (now Hrodna) Oblast Archives (Belarus)
Vilnius	Lithuanian State Historical Archives (Lithuania)
Lvov	Lvov (now Lviv) Historical Archives (Ukraine)
Lvov2	Lvov (now Lviv) Oblast Archives (Ukraine)

Repository locations within Poland (when more than one in the same city):

Warsaw	AGAD (Archives of Ancient Acts)
Warsaw2	Archiwum Państwówe m. Warszawy (Warsaw Municipal District Archives)

Country   *The current location of the town/city*
Voivodship/Oblast   *Current administrative district where town is located*
Town Name   *Poland (current spelling); Ukraine and Belarus (transliterated from Russian)*
Years Available   *Year span of archival material*

Example: 1892–1939 (material from 1892 to 1939, with no known gaps)

1892/1939 (material within these years, but with gaps)

Zespół/Sygnatura or Fond/Opis/Delo Numbers (not applicable in USC offices)

In Poland

Zespół name or number is used to describe a group of archival documents.

Sygnatura (Sygn) refers to the file numbers within the *Zespół*.

Some archives in Poland identify the archival group with the town name in addition to the archive numbers.

In Ukraine, Belarus and Lithuania

Fond describes a group of documents (material generated by a single entity), *i.e.*, record group.

Opis designates the list number within the *Fond*.

Delo signifies the file within the *Fond* and *Opis*.

Example: 227/5/43,17;226/42

Fond 227/Opis 5/Files 43 and 17; Fond 226/Opis 42

Archival numbers are assigned to each document or group of documents .

Zespół/Fond numbers are separated by ";"

Fond/Opis/Delo numbers are separated by "/"

Repository Type

A   Archive
G   LDS Microfilms of German-Held Documents (for towns within the current borders of Poland)
J   Jewish Historical Institute (in Warsaw)
U   Urząd Stanu Cywilnego (local town halls in Poland generally holding documents less than 100 years old)

Important Note to Remember

The inventory lists provided by the Polish State Archives and Jewish Historical Institute listed the year span of documents followed by the archival numbers. Thus, it is not always possible to identify which archival number corresponds to a particular year or year span.

Example: 1842–1844; 1857; 1859–1861; 1873
270/2/4,7,9,12;273/1/3–4;279/1/78

Therefore, the archival inventories in this book should be used **in conjunction with** the *zespół/signatura* numbers (or names) held in the Polish State Archives and the Jewish Historical Institute in Warsaw.

ARCHIVAL HOLDINGS INDEXED BY TOWN

by Miriam Weiner

TOWN NAME	VOIVODSHIP (Province)			Zespoł / Sygnatura (Poland)
Repository Location	Repository Type	Document Code	Years	Fond/Opis/Delo (Belarus, Ukraine,Lithuania)
ADAMÓW	**SIEDLCE**			
ADAMÓW	U	B	1928–1937	
ADAMÓW	U	D	1928–1930; 1932–1934	
LUBLIN	A	K	1925–1935	SPŁUK/627
ADAMÓW	U	M	1929–1930; 1932–1934	
LUBLIN	A	T	1925–1935	SPŁUK/627
ALEKSANDRÓW KUJAWSKI	**WŁOCŁAWEK**			
WARSZAWA	J	C	1919/1939	105
WARSZAWA	J	E	1919/1939	105
WARSZAWA	J	K	1919/1939	105
ALEKSANDRÓW ŁÓDZKI	**ŁÓDŹ**			
ŁÓDŹ	A	B	1826–1892	270
ALEKSANDRÓW ŁÓDZKI	U	B	1893–1939	
ŁÓDŹ	A	D	1826–1892	270
ALEKSANDRÓW ŁÓDZKI	U	D	1893–1939	
ŁÓDŹ	A	K	1822–1865; 1871–1914	1
PABIANICE	A	L	1918–1939	147
ŁÓDŹ	A	M	1826–1892	270
ALEKSANDRÓW ŁÓDZKI	U	M	1893–1939	
PABIANICE	A	T	1914–1939	147
ALLENSTEIN	**SEE OLSZTYN**			
ANDRZEJEWO	**ŁOMŻA**			
PUŁTUSK	A	B	1826–1859	252
ANDRZEJEWO	U	B	1882–1935	
PUŁTUSK	A	D	1826–1859	252
ANDRZEJEWO	U	D	1882–1935	
PUŁTUSK	A	M	1826–1859	252
ANDRZEJEWO	U	M	1882–1935	
ANGERSBURG	**SEE WĘGORZEWO**			
ANIN STARY	**WARSZAWA**			
WARSZAWA	U	D	INCLUDED IN WARSZAWA/PRAGA POLUDNIE REGION	
ANNOPOL	**TARNOBRZEG**			
LUBLIN	A	B	1826–1855	113
SANDOMIERZ	A	B	1856–1883	487
ANNOPOL	U	B	1918–1924; 1931–1940	
LUBLIN	A	D	1826–1855	113
SANDOMIERZ	A	D	1856–1865	487
ANNOPOL	U	D	1918–1933	
LUBLIN	A	K	1867–1912; 1922–1935	RGL IV ADM; UWL WSP/783
LUBLIN	A	M	1826–1855	113
SANDOMIERZ	A	M	1856–1865	487
ANNOPOL	U	M	1882–1895; 1915–1918; 1934–1940	
LUBLIN	A	T	1867–1912; 1922–1935	RGL IV ADM; UWL WSP/783
ARNSWALDE	**SEE CHOSZCZNO**			
AUGUSTÓW	**SUWAŁKI**			
SUWAŁKI	A	B	1850–1870 (INDEX ONLY); 1906–1907; 1903–1904 (INDEX ONLY)	12/295, 308, 322
AUGUSTÓW	U	B	1926–1931; 1935	
SUWAŁKI	A	C	MID–19TH CENT./EARLY 20TH CENT.	
SUWAŁKI	A	D	1850–1870; 1880–1892; 1896–1897; 1903–1904; 1906–1907	12/295, 300, 307–308, 322
AUGUSTÓW	U	D	1926–1935	

Repository type: **A** = Archive **G** = LDS Films of German-held Records **J** = Jewish Historical Institute **U** = Urząd Stanu Cywilnego

TOWN NAME	VOIVODSHIP (Province)			Zespół/Sygnatura (Poland) Fond/Opis/Delo (Belarus, Ukraine, Lithuania)
Repository Location	Repository Document Type	Code	Years	
VILNIUS	A	G	1885–1917	1010
SUWAŁKI	A	K	1809; 1890; 1897	12/92, 100, 102–103, 108–109
SUWAŁKI	A	L	1945–1949	313/146–147, 179–180
SUWAŁKI	A	M	1850–1870 (INDEX ONLY); 1903–1904 (INDEX ONLY)	12/295, 308, 322
AUGUSTÓW	U	M	1926–1930; 1935	
SUWAŁKI	A	S	1870; 1873; 1882; 1891–1892; 1897; 1902–1904	12/104–107, 133–136
WARSZAWA	A	T	1820–1832	KRSW 4795–4797
SUWAŁKI	A	X	1907–1909	12/243
SUWAŁKI	A	Y	1808–1835	220–226
SUWAŁKI	A	Z	1863–1870; 1903–1907	12
AUGUSTÓW REGION	**SUWAŁKI**			
SUWAŁKI	A	T	1900–1911; 1913–1914	12/94–96; 23/1–15
BABIAK	**KONIN**			
POZNAŃ	A	B	1826–1859; 1882–1893	3741/1–34
BABIAK	U	B	1894–1939	
POZNAŃ	A	D	1826–1859; 1882–1893	3741/1–34
BABIAK	U	D	1894–1939	
POZNAŃ	A	M	1826–1859; 1882–1893	3741/1–34
BABIAK	U	M	1894–1939	
BABIMOST	**ZIELONA GÓRA**			
BERLIN	G	B	1817–1847	
POZNAŃ	A	C	1916–1920	314/313–315, 329, 1027–1029, 3227
POZNAŃ	A	K	1835–1912	314/1049, 1051–1052
BERLIN	G	N	1847–1916	
POZNAŃ	A	X	1858–1897	314/1053
BACHÓW	**PRZEMYŚL**			
PRZEMYŚL	A	C	1931/1945	203/17, 27, 38–40
BAHN	**SEE BANIE**			
BAKAŁARZEWO	**SUWAŁKI**			
SUWAŁKI	A	B	1809–1813; 1815–1818; 1820–1822; 1826–1833; 1839–1843; 1852–1864; 1866–1867; 1870–1875; 1877–1879; 1883–1885; 1887; 1889	149/197
BAKAŁARZEWO	U	B	1893; 1897–1899; 1903–1906; 1921–1923	
SUWAŁKI	A	D	1808–1813; 1815–1821; 1823–1833; 1839–1843; 1852–1864; 1866–1867; 1870–1875; 1877–1879; 1883–1885; 1887; 1889	149; 197
BAKAŁARZEWO	U	D	1893; 1897–1899; 1903–1906; 1921–1923	
SUWAŁKI	A	M	1808–1813; 1815–1818; 1820; 1822–1823; 1826–1837; 1839–1843; 1852–1864; 1866–1867; 1870–1875; 1877–1879; 1883–1885; 1887; 1889	149; 197
BAKAŁARZEWO	U	M	1893; 1897–1899; 1903–1906; 1921–1923	
WARSZAWA	A	T	1811–1865	KRSW 4818–4821
BALIGRÓD	**KROSNO**			
SANOK	A	C	1929–1946	30/26–28
SANOK	A	H	1944–1947	80/106
LVOV	A	L	1785–1788; 1819–1820	19/XV/156; 20/XV/2
BANIE	**SZCZECIN**			
BERLIN	G	B	1848–1874	
BERLIN	G	D	1848–1874	
SZCZECIN	A	K	1839–1846	REGIERUNG STETTIN, I/10732
BERLIN	G	M	1848–1874	
SZCZECIN	A	S	1822–1873	MAGISTRAT BAHN 168
SZCZECIN	A	Z	1871–1906	MAGISTRAT BAHN 170
BARANÓW	**KALISZ**			
POZNAŃ	A	B	1835–1846	3573/1–13
POZNAŃ	A	D	1835–1846	3573/1–13
POZNAŃ	A	M	1835–1846	3573/1–13
LUBLIN	A	B	1826–1851; 1853–1855; 1859; 1862; 1864; 1868; 1872–1889; 1891–1893	113
BARANÓW	U	B	1894–1907	
LUBLIN	A	D	1826–1851; 1853–1860; 1862; 1864; 1868; 1871–1889; 1891–1893	113
BARANÓW	U	D	1894–1907	
PRZEMYŚL	A	K	1890–1897	74/29, 32
LUBLIN	A	M	1826–1851; 1853–1855; 1857; 1859; 1862; 1864; 1868; 1872–1889; 1891–1893	113
BARANÓW	U	M	1894–1907	

A Army/recruit lists; **B** Birth; **C** Census; **D** Death; **E** Voter lists; **G** Immigration; **H** Holocaust; **J** Judaica; **K** Kahal; **L** Land; **M** Marriage; **N** Name changes; **O** Police files; **P** Pogroms; **R** Reference; **S** School records; **T** Tax lists; **V** Divorce; **W** Occupation lists; **X** Jewish hospital; **Y** Notary records; **Z** Local government records

TOWN NAME Repository Location	VOIVODSHIP (Province) Repository Document Type Code		Years	Zespół/Sygnatura (Poland) Fond/Opis/Delo (Belarus, Ukraine, Lithuania)
BARANOWICE	**KATOWICE**			
RACIBÓRZ	A	B	1846–1859	118/1
RACIBÓRZ	A	D	1846–1859	118/1
RACIBÓRZ	A	M	1846–1859	118/1
BARANOWO	**OSTROŁĘKA**			
BARANOWO	U	B	1927–1934	
BARANOWO	U	D	1927–1934	
BARANOWO	U	M	1927–1934	
BARCIANY	**OLSZTYN**			
BERLIN	G	B	1848–1874	
BERLIN	G	D	1848–1874	
BERLIN	G	M	1848–1874	
BARCZEWO	**OLSZTYN**			
OLSZTYN	A	B	1874–1894	699/I
OLSZTYN	A	C	1874; 1881/1897; 1900; 1903; 1906; 1935–1939	247/I
OLSZTYN	A	D	1874–1894	699/I
OLSZTYN	A	M	1874–1894	699/I
BARGŁOW DWORNY	**SUWAŁKI**			
SUWAŁKI	A	B	1869–1882	
SUWAŁKI	A	D	1869/1873; 1874–1881	
SUWAŁKI	A	M	1869/1882	
BARLINEK	**GORZÓW WIELKOPOLSKI**			
SZCZECIN	A	B	1847–1874	AMTSGERICHT
SZCZECIN	A	D	1847–1874	AMTSGERICHT
SZCZECIN	A	M	1847–1873	AMSTGERICHT
BARTEN	**SEE BARCIANY**			
BARTENSTEIN	**SEE BARTOSZYCE**			
BARTOSZYCE	**OLSZTYN**			
KOBLENZ	G	B	1848–1938	
KOBLENZ	G	D	1848–1938	
KOBLENZ	G	M	1848–1938	
BARWALDE	**SEE BARWICE**			
BARWICE	**KOSZALIN**			
LEIPZIG	G	B	1848–1874	
LEIPZIG	G	D	1848–1874	
LEIPZIG	G	M	1848–1874	
BAŻANÓWKA	**KROSNO**			
SANOK	A	C	1931–1949	21/56–58
BĘDKÓW	**PIOTRKOW**			
ŁÓDŹ	A	B	1826–1846	270
TOMASZÓW MAZOWIECKI	A	B	1826–1846	244
ŁÓDŹ	A	D	1826–1846	270
ŁÓDŹ	A	M	1826–1846	270
TOMASZÓW MAZOWIECKI	A	M	1826–1845	244
ŁÓDŹ	A	Z	1849–1864; 1901; 1906	1
BĘDZIN	**KATOWICE**			
ŁÓDŹ	A	A	1891–1904	17
KATOWICE	A	B	1826–1883; 1909–1911	788/1–35; 773/334
BĘDZIN	U	B	1895–1926; 1928–1942	
KATOWICE	A	C	1826–1865; 1931	773/965
WARSZAWA	J	C	1939	212–213
KATOWICE	A	D	1826–1883	788/1–35
BĘDZIN	U	D	1895–1926; 1928–1942	
KATOWICE	A	E	1916–1919; 1925; 1928	773/731–741
KATOWICE	A	G	1920–1921	773/959
WARSZAWA	J	H	1939–1943	212–213
KATOWICE	A	H	1943–1944	773/1194
ŁÓDŹ	A	K	1841–1866; 1885–1915	1
KATOWICE	A	K	1844–1873; 1881; 1892–1903; 1909; 1919–1923	773/33–35, 169, 235, 307, 339–384; 770/508–509
KATOWICE	A	L	1892–1912; 1914; 1942	773/239–240, 249–250, 255, 261, 279, 295,310, 312, 333, 337–338, 344–345, 350–351, 356, 359–361, 370, 1206
KATOWICE	A	M	1826–1883	788/1–35
BĘDZIN	U	M	1895–1926; 1928–1942	
ŁÓDŹ	A	O	1898–1914	42

Repository type: **A** = Archive   **G** = LDS Films of German-Held Records   **J** = Jewish Historical Institute   **U** = Urząd Stanu Cywilnego

TOWN NAME	VOIVODSHIP (Province)			Zespół/Sygnatura (Poland)
Repository Location	Repository Type	Document Code	Years	Fond/Opis/Delo (Belarus, Ukraine, Lithuania)
ŁÓDŹ	A	X	1899–1912	15
ŁÓDŹ	A	S	1871–1914	83
KATOWICE	A	Y	1870–1938	811/1–278; 812/1–19; 813/1–10; 814/1–2; 815/1–35; 816/1–20; 817/1–32; 818/1–16; 819/1–11; 820/1–84; 821/1–6; 822/1–72
ŁÓDŹ	A	Z	1908–1913	1
BEŁCHATÓW	**PIOTRKOW**			
ŁÓDŹ	A	B	1824–1872	270
PIOTRKÓW TRYBUNALSKI	A	B	1873–1895	330
BEŁCHATÓW	U	B	1896–1914; 1920–1941	
PIOTRKÓW TRYBUNALSKI	A	C	1906–1931	8/1–12
ŁÓDŹ	A	D	1824–1872	270
PIOTRKÓW TRYBUNALSKI	A	D	1873–1895	330/4–26
BEŁCHATÓW	U	D	1896–1913; 1921–1941	
ŁÓDŹ	A	K	1890–1911	1
PIOTRKÓW TRYBUNALSKI	A	L	1796–1946	377
ŁÓDŹ	A	M	1824–1854	270
PIOTRKÓW TRYBUNALSKI	A	M	1855–1895	330/1–2, 5–22, 24–27
BEŁCHATÓW	U	M	1896–1915; 1920–1940	
ŁÓDŹ	A	T	1843–1866	23
PIOTRKÓW TRYBUNALSKI	A	Y	1919–1952	167–175; 376
PIOTRKÓW TRYBUNALSKI	A	Z	1906–1944	8
BELGARD	**SEE BIAŁOGARD**			
BELGRAD	**SEE BIAŁOGARD**			
BEŁŻCE	**LUBLIN**			
LUBLIN	A	B	1826–1868	113
BEŁŻCE	U	B	1894–1938	
LUBLIN	A	D	1826–1868	113
BEŁŻCE	U	D	1882–1938	
LUBLIN	A	E	1869–1914	RGL IV ADM.
LUBLIN	A	H	1939–1944	KREISHAUPTMANSCHAFT LUBLIN
LUBLIN	A	K	1811–1856 (CEMETERY RECORDS); 1869–1914; 1919–1938	27/18; RGL IV; SPL/645; UWL WSP/801
LUBLIN	A	M	1826–1868	113
BEŁŻCE	U	M	1882–1938	
LUBLIN	A	N	1821–1847	27/28
BERENT	**SEE KOŚCIERZYNA**			
BERGSTADT	**SEE LEŚNICA**			
BERLINCHEN	**SEE BARLINEK**			
BERNSTADT IN SCHLESIEN	**SEE BIERUTÓW**			
BERNSTEIN	**SEE PEŁCZYCE**			
BERŹNIKI	**INCLUDED IN SEJNY**			
BESKO	**KROSNO**			
SANOK	A	C	1931–1950	21/59–68
BETSCHE	**SEE PSZCZEW**			
BEUTHEN	**SEE BYTOM**			
BIAŁA	**OPOLE**			
LEIPZIG	G	B	1847/1874	
LEIPZIG	G	D	1847/1874	
LEIPZIG	G	M	1847/1874	
BIAŁA	U	B	1890–1945	
BIAŁA	U	D	1890–1945	
LVIV	A	L	1785–1788; 1819–1820	186/1
BIAŁA	U	M	1890–1945	
BIAŁA PODLASKA	**BIAŁA PODLASKA**			
LUBLIN	A	B	1826–1894	113
BIAŁA PODLASKA	U	B	1895–1914; 1919–1942	
LUBLIN	A	C	1833/1950	20
LUBLIN	A	D	1826–1894	113
BIAŁA PODLASKA	U	D	1895–1914; 1919–1942	
LUBLIN	A	E	1913–1915	RGCH/458
WARSZAWA	J	H	1941–1942 (RESIDENT BOOKS OF 3, 000 JEWS SENT TO GHETTO IN MIĘDZYRZECZ)	
LUBLIN	A	K	1913–1915; 1924–1937	RGCH/458; 403/754–759; 404/203–208; 49
LUBLIN	A	M	1826–1894	113

A Army/recruit lists; **B** Birth; **C** Census; **D** Death; **E** Voter lists; **G** Immigration; **H** Holocaust; **J** Judaica; **K** Kahal; **L** Land; **M** Marriage; **N** Name changes; **O** Police files; **P** Pogroms; **R** Reference; **S** School records; **T** Tax lists; **V** Divorce; **W** Occupation lists; **X** Jewish hospital; **Y** Notary records; **Z** Local government records

TOWN NAME	VOIVODSHIP (Province)			Zespół/Sygnatura (Poland)
Repository Location	Repository Type	Document Code	Years	Fond/Opis/Delo (Belarus, Ukraine, Lithuania)
BIAŁA PODLASKA				
BIAŁA PODLASKA	U	M	1895–1914; 1919–1942	
KRAKÓW	A	W	1936–1938	536/IT–2034
LUBLIN	A	T	1913–1915; 1927–1936	RGCH/458; UWL WSP/754
BIAŁA RAWSKA	**SKIERNIEWICE**			
ŁÓDŹ	A	A	1898–1901	131
ŁÓDŹ	A	B	1826–1874	270
RAWA MAZOWIECKA	A	B	1853; 1856–1857; 1862–1868; 1871–1892	272
RAWA MAZOWIECKA	A	C	1835/1944	157/342, 355, 371–372, 389–390, 420, 427, 463, 476
ŁÓDŹ	A	D	1826–1874	270
RAWA MAZOWIECKA	A	D	1853; 1856–1857; 1862–1890	272
ŁÓDŹ	A	K	1899–1913	1
ŁÓDŹ	A	M	1826–1868	270
RAWA MAZOWIECKA	A	M	1853; 1856–1857; 1862–1890	272
BIAŁOBOKI	**PRZEMYŚL**			
PRZEWORSK	A	S	1888–1946	56/1–15, 17–44
BIAŁOBRZEGI	**RADOM**			
RADOM	A	B	1862–1893; 1904–1939	183
BIAŁOBRZEGI	U	B	1894–1908; 1916–1923; 1930–1937; 1940–1941	
RADOM	A	D	1862–1893; 1904–1939	183
BIAŁOBRZEGI	U	D	1894–1908; 1916–1923; 1930–1937; 1940–1941	
RADOM	A	M	1862–1893; 1904–1939	183
BIAŁOBRZEGI	U	M	1894–1908; 1916–1923; 1930–1937; 1940–1941	
BIAŁOGARD	**KOSZALIN**			
KOSZALIN	A	B	1813–1847	52/I/48; 142/I/1680
KOSZALIN	A	D	1813–1847	52/I/48; 142/I/1680
KOSZALIN	A	M	1813–1847	52/I/48; 142/I/1680
BIAŁY BÓR	**KOSZALIN**			
LEIPZIG	G	B	1812–1874	
LEIPZIG	G	D	1812–1874	
SZCZECIN	A	K	1843–1938	GMINY ZYDOWSKIE Z POMORZA ZACHODNIEGO 1/4
LEIPZIG	G	M	1812–1874	
SZCZECIN	A	S	1820–1888	MAGISTRAT BIAŁY BÓR (BALDENBURG) /71
BIAŁYSTOK	**BIAŁYSTOK**			
BIAŁYSTOK	A	A	1903–1917	42
BIAŁYSTOK	A	B	1835; 1839; 1846; 1848; 1855–1866; 1869; 1871–1872; 1874–1875; 1877–1884; 1886; 1888–1894	264
BIAŁYSTOK	U	B	1895–1912; 1914–1915; 1917–1936; 1938; 1941–1942	
GRODNO	A	C	1795/1882	2/2/69; 24/7/152–227
BIAŁYSTOK	A	C	1847–1850	64/24
BIAŁYSTOK	A	D	1846; 1852; 1854–1877; 1879–1882; 1884–1886; 1888–1890; 1892–1894	264
BIAŁYSTOK	U	D	1897–1900; 1902–1939; 1942	
WARSZAWA	J	H	1939–1942	204
GRODNO2	A	H	1941–1943	1/150; 1/271; 1/346
BIAŁYSTOK	A	K	1913	447/1–2
BIAŁYSTOK	A	L	1853; 1910	733/2; 30/3
BIAŁYSTOK	A	M	1854; 1856–1894	264
BIAŁYSTOK	U	M	1895–1942	
WARSZAWA	A	T	1806	2/1717B/110–144
BIAŁYSTOK	A	V	1858–1862; 1864–1873; 1875–1876; 1878–1882; 1884–1894	264
GRODNO	A	X	1832/1913	321; 9/1/1770
BIAŁYSTOK	A	X	1913	441
BIAŁYSTOK	A	Y	1882–1914; 1919–1939	280–298
BIAŁYSTOK	A	Z	1941–1944 (MORTGAGE REGISTRATIONS)	561/338
BICZYCE DOLNE	**INCLUDED IN NOWY SĄCZ**			
BIECZ	**KROSNO**			
PRZEMYŚL	A	B	1850/1937	154/1
BIECZ	U	B	1898–1907	
SKOŁYSZYN	A	C	1930	1/27
PRZEMYŚL	A	D	1851/1874	154/2
BIECZ	U	D	1882–1915	
SKOŁYSZYN	A	G	1926	1/28

Repository type: **A** = Archive **G** = LDS Films of German-Held Records **J** = Jewish Historical Institute **U** = Urząd Stanu Cywilnego

TOWN NAME	VOIVODSHIP (Province)				
Repository Location	Repository Document Type	Code	Years		Zespół/Sygnatura (Poland) Fond/Opis/Delo (Belarus, Ukraine, Lithuania)
SKOŁYSZYN	A	H	1940–1942; 1945–1946		1/40–42, 90–91
PRZEMYŚL	A	K	1914–1916; 1922		680/20; 791/17
SKOŁYSZYN	A	L	1930		1/14
BIECZ	U	M	1918–1942		
BIELAWY	**SKIERNIEWICE**				
ŁOWICZ	A	B	1820–1821; 1856–1884; 1896–1912; 1935		234
ŁÓDŹ	A	B	1826–1855		270
BIELAWY	U	B	1894–1939		
ŁOWICZ	A	D	1820–1821; 1856–1884; 1896–1912; 1935		234
ŁÓDŹ	A	D	1826–1855		270
BIELAWY	U	D	1894–1939		
ŁOWICZ	A	M	1820–1821; 1856–1884; 1896–1912; 1935		234
ŁÓDŹ	A	M	1826–1855		270
BIELAWY	U	M	1894–1939		
BIELSK	**PŁOCK**				
PŁOCK	A	B	1826–1870		172
PŁOCK	A	D	1826–1839; 1841; 1843–1870		172
PŁOCK	A	M	1826–1870		172
BIELSK PODLASKI	**BIAŁYSTOK**				
BIAŁYSTOK	A	B	1835; 1842; 1871		545
MINSK	A	C	1795/1882		
GRODNO	A	C	1855		24/7/243
BIAŁYSTOK	A	D	1835		545
GRODNO	A	G	1912–1915		
GRODNO	A	K	1835–1846		1165
BIAŁYSTOK	A	M	1835; 1868		545
BIAŁYSTOK	A	Y	1883–1909		553–560
BIELSKO	**BIELSKO**				
BIELSKO	U	B	1882–1938		
BIELSKO	U	D	1882–1925		
BIELSKO	U	M	1900–1922; 1924–1926; 1928–1929; 1936; 1938		
BIERUŃ NOWY	**KATOWICE**				
PSZCZYNA	A	B	1847–1874		67/I/1–2
PSZCZYNA	A	D	1848–1874		67/I/4–5
PSZCZYNA	A	M	1848–1873		67/I/3
BIERUŃ STARY	**KATOWICE**				
PSZCZYNA	A	H	1939–1942		55/I/717
PSZCZYNA	A	T	1899–1924		55/I/48
KATOWICE	A	K	1922–1924		27/I–VI/1990
BIERUTÓW	**WROCŁAW**				
KOBLENZ	G	B	1847–1887		
WARSZAWA	J	C	1810/1908		PROVINCE: ŚLĄSK
KOBLENZ	G	D	1847–1887		
WARSZAWA	J	D	1851–1908		
WARSZAWA	J	K	1810/1908		PROVINCE: ŚLĄSK
KOBLENZ	G	M	1847–1887		
WARSZAWA	J	Z	1810/1908		PROVINCE: ŚLĄSK
BIEŻUŃ	**CIECHANÓW**				
PŁOCK	A	B	1826–1856		201
DZIAŁDOWO	A	B	1857–1858; 1877–1884		77
PŁOCK	A	D	1826–1856		201
DZIAŁDOWO	A	D	1857–1858; 1878–1884		77
PŁOCK	A	M	1826–1856		201
DZIAŁDOWO	A	M	1857–1858		77
BIŁGORAJ	**ZAMOŚĆ**				
LUBLIN	A	B	1870–1875		113
ZAMOŚĆ	A	B	1876–1893		209/1–18
BIŁGORAJ	U	B	1894–1914; 1917–1937		
LUBLIN	A	D	1870–1875		113
ZAMOŚĆ	A	D	1876–1893		209/1–18
BIŁGORAJ	U	D	1894–1913; 1920–1921; 1923; 1927; 1929–1930; 1934; 1936–1937		
LUBLIN	A	E	1870–1909; 1911–1915		RGL ADM; RGCH/484
LUBLIN	A	H	1942		DIST.LUBLIN/749
LUBLIN	A	K	1870–1909; 1911–1915; 1922–1937		RGL ADM; RGCH/484; 403/760–766
LUBLIN	A	M	1869–1875		113
ZAMOŚĆ	A	M	1876–1893		209/1–18
BIŁGORAJ	U	M	1894–1913; 1920–1937		

A Army/recruit lists; **B** Birth; **C** Census; **D** Death; **E** Voter lists; **G** Immigration; **H** Holocaust; **J** Judaica; **K** Kahal; **L** Land; **M** Marriage; **N** Name changes; **O** Police files; **P** Pogroms; **R** Reference; **S** School records; **T** Tax lists; **V** Divorce; **W** Occupation lists; **X** Jewish hospital; **Y** Notary records; **Z** Local government records

TOWN NAME	VOIVODSHIP (Province)			Zespół/Sygnatura (Poland)
Repository Location	Repository Document Type	Code	Years	Fond/Opis/Delo (Belarus, Ukraine, Lithuania)
LUBLIN	A	T	1870–1909; 1911–1915; 1927	RGL ADM; RGCH/484; UWL WSP/760
BIRCZA	**PRZEMYŚL**			
PRZEMYŚL	A	Y	1909–1911; 1934–1944	728; 1075–1080
BIRNBAUM	**SEE MIĘDZYCHÓD**			
BISCHOFSBURG	**SEE BISKUPIEC**			
BISKUPICE	**LUBLIN**			
LUBLIN	A	B	1826–1888	113
LUBLIN	A	D	1826–1888	113
LUBLIN	A	G	1940–1941	2–6; 140
LUBLIN	A	H	1939–1942 (JUDENRAT)	618/2–6; 501/140
LUBLIN	A	K	1869–1914; 1919–1936	RGL IV ADM; SPL/646
LUBLIN	A	M	1826–1888	113
LUBLIN	A	W	1940–1941	2–6
BISKUPIEC	**OLSZTYN**			
LEIPZIG	G	B	1847–1874	
OLSZTYN	A	B	1878; 1880–1882; 1886; 1888; 1890–1891	854/I
LEIPZIG	G	D	1847–1874	
OLSZTYN	A	D	1876; 1878–1880; 1882; 1886; 1888–1889; 1892	854/I
LEIPZIG	G	M	1847–1874	
OLSZTYN	A	M	1876; 1878–1882; 1884–1885; 1889–1891	854/I
BISKUPIEC POMORSKI	**TORUŃ**			
OLSZTYN	A	C	1812–1892	248/I
BŁASZKI	**SIERADZ**			
POZNAŃ	A	B	1826–1855; 1861–1893	3742/1–3, 7–8, 10
BŁASZKI	U	B	1899–1904; 1911; 1913; 1915–1939	
KALISZ	A	C	1872; 1917–1951	1/900–918; 53/1–56
POZNAŃ	A	D	1855–1872	3742/6, 9
BŁASZKI	U	D	1899–1911; 1915–1939	
KALISZ	A	E	1907; 1909	1/18–19
KALISZ	A	L	1848–1861	1/650
POZNAŃ	A	M	1850–1857; 1866–1867	3742/4–5
BŁASZKI	U	M	1892–1911; 1915–1939	
ŁÓDŹ	A	O	1904–1912	117
POZNAŃ	A	S	1861–1893; 1937–1939	805/143
KALISZ	A	W	1831–1846	1/84
BŁAŻOWA	**RZESZÓW**			
RZESZÓW	A	G	1939–1941	71/38
RZESZÓW	A	H	1940–1944	71/38, 49
RZESZÓW	A	L	1943–1944	71/49
LVOV	A	L	1785–1788; 1819–1820	19/II/113; 20/II/11
BŁĘDÓW	**RADOM**			
BŁĘDÓW	U	B	1917–1941	
BŁĘDÓW	U	D	1917–1941	
BŁĘDÓW	U	M	1917–1941	
BLEDZEW	**GORZÓW WIELKOPOLSKI**			
BERLIN	G	N	1839–1888	
BLESEN	**SEE BLEDZEW**			
BŁONIE	**WARSZAWA**			
BŁONIE	U	B	1899–1940	
BŁONIE	U	D	1899–1940	
BŁONIE	U	M	1899–1940	
BOBOLICE	**KOSZALIN**			
KOBLENZ	G	B	1812–1874	
KOBLENZ	G	D	1812–1874	
SZCZECIN	A	K	1893–1938	GMINY ZYDOWSKIE Z POMORZA ZACHODNIEGO 5/7
KOBLENZ	G	M	1812–1874	
BOBOWA	**NOWY SĄCZ**			
BOBOWA	U	B	1882–1895; 1903–1909; 1911–1912	
BOBOWA	U	D	1882–1904; 1939–1942	
LVOV	A	L	1785–1788; 1819–1820	19/IV/168; 20/IV/8
BOBOWA	U	M	1882–1910; 1929–1942	
BOBROWNIKI	**LUBLIN**			
OTWOCK	A	B	1826–1858	167
LUBLIN	A	B	1892–1893	113
OTWOCK	A	D	1826–1858	167

Repository type: **A** = Archive   **G** = LDS Films of German-Held Records   **J** = Jewish Historical Institute   **U** = Urząd Stanu Cywilnego

TOWN NAME	VOIVODSHIP (Province)			Zespół/Sygnatura (Poland) Fond/Opis/Delo (Belarus, Ukraine, Lithuania)
Repository Location	Repository Type	Document Code	Years	
LUBLIN	A	D	1892–1893	113
LUBLIN	A	K	1867–1893 (AFTER 1893, INCLUDED IN IRENA)	RGL IV ADM.
OTWOCK	A	M	1826–1858	167
LUBLIN	A	M	1892–1893	113
LUBLIN	A	T	1867–1893 (AFTER 1893, INCLUDED IN IRENA)	RGL IV ADM.
BOCHNIA	**TARNÓW**			
BOCHNIA	A	A	1937 (ALPHA INDEX)	1 ZMB/501
KRAKÓW	A	B	1825–1869	526/MIB–O/1
BOCHNIA	U	B	1894–1910; 1919–1943	
BOCHNIA	A	C	1830/1952	1 ZMB/141, 144, 499–499A; 1/535
BOCHNIA	U	D	1901–1943	
BOCHNIA	A	G	1922–1943	1 ZMB/496, 500
BOCHNIA	A	H	1940; 1943	1/ZMB/766
BOCHNIA	A	L	1926	1/ZMB/503
LVIV	A	L	1785–1788; 1819–1820	186/1/1,7,19–20, 24
BOCHNIA	U	M	1894–1910; 1919–1943	
BOCHNIA	A	T	1941–1945	1/824, 835
BOCHNIA	A	W	1830/1952	1/ZMB 499
BOCHNIA	A	Z	1924–1933 (LIST OF BUSINESSES)	ZMB/535
BODZANÓW	**PŁOCK**			
PŁOCK	A	B	1826–1832; 1834–1836; 1838–1883; 1886–1894	173
BODZANÓW	U	B	1895–1941	
PŁOCK	A	D	1826–1832; 1834–1836; 1838–1883; 1886–1894	173
BODZANÓW	U	D	1895–1941	
PŁOCK	A	M	1826–1832; 1834–1836; 1838–1883; 1886–1894	173
BODZANÓW	U	M	1895–1941	
BODZENTYN	**KIELCE**			
KIELCE	A	B	1869–1895	421
BODZENTYN	U	B	1896–1941	
KIELCE	A	D	1869–1895	421
BODZENTYN	U	D	1896–1941	
KIELCE	A	M	1869–1895	421
BODZENTYN	U	M	1896–1941	
BOGORIA	**TARNOBRZEG**			
SANDOMIERZ	A	B	1826–1894	251
BOGORIA	U	B	1895–1942	
SANDOMIERZ	A	D	1826–1894	251
BOGORIA	U	D	1895–1942	
SANDOMIERZ	A	M	1826–1894	251
BOGORIA	U	M	1895–1942	
BOJANÓW	**TARNOBRZEG**			
PRZEWORSK	A	C	1949	13/45–47
PRZEWORSK	A	E	1949	13/22
PRZEWORSK	A	T	1948; 1951	13/38–44
BOLESŁAWIEC	**KALISZ**			
ŁÓDŹ	A	B	1826–1838	270
ŁÓDŹ	A	D	1826–1838	270
ŁÓDŹ	A	M	1826–1838	270
BOLESTRASZYCE	**PRZEMYŚL**			
PRZEMYŚL	A	C	1935–1939; 1948	212/21–24
BOLIMÓW	**SKIERNIEWICE**			
ŁÓDŹ	A	B	1826–1858; 1882–1884; 1886–1890	270
ŁOWICZ	A	B	1889–1937	295
ŁÓDŹ	A	D	1826–1858; 1882–1884; 1886–1890	270
ŁOWICZ	A	D	1889–1937	295
ŁOWICZ	A	L	1940	14/119–120
ŁÓDŹ	A	M	1826–1858; 1882–1884; 1886–1890	270
ŁOWICZ	A	M	1889–1937	295
ŁOWICZ	A	W	1940	14/119–120
BOMST	**SEE BABIMOST**			
BOREK WIELKOPOLSKI	**LESZNO**			
BERLIN	G	B	1833–1837	
BERLIN	G	D	1833–1837	
BERLIN	G	M	1833–1837	
BRANIEWO	**ELBLĄG**			
OLSZTYN	A	C	1904–1905; 1908; 1910–1912; 1914; 1916; 1922; 1938–1939	10/1

A Army/recruit lists; **B** Birth; **C** Census; **D** Death; **E** Voter lists; **G** Immigration; **H** Holocaust; **J** Judaica; **K** Kahal; **L** Land; **M** Marriage; **N** Name changes; **O** Police files; **P** Pogroms; **R** Reference; **S** School records; **T** Tax lists; **V** Divorce; **W** Occupation lists; **X** Jewish hospital; **Y** Notary records; **Z** Local government records

TOWN NAME	VOIVODSHIP (Province)			Zespół/Sygnatura (Poland)
Repository Location	Repository Type	Document Code	Years	Fond/Opis/Delo (Belarus, Ukraine, Lithuania)

BRAŃSK	**BIAŁYSTOK**			
BIAŁYSTOK	A	T	1946–1950	566
BIAŁYSTOK	A	Y	1924–1932	862
BRATZ	**SEE BRÓJCE**			
BRAUNSBERG	**SEE BRANIEWO**			
BRDÓW	**KONIN**			
ŁÓDŹ	A	K	1891	92
BRESLAU	**SEE WROCŁAW**			
BRIEG	**SEE BRZEG**			
BRODNICA	**TORUŃ**			
TORUŃ	A	B	1840–1870	616/1
TORUŃ	A	D	1840–1847	616/1
TORUŃ	A	M	1840–1847; 1850–1874	616/1
BRÓJCE	**GORZÓW WIELKOPOLSKI**			
GORZÓW WIELKOPOLSKI	A	B	1817–1823; 1825–1831; 1833–1835; 1841; 1845–1847	AMTSGERICHT MESERITZ 247/5593
POZNAŃ	A	B	1847	3754/1
GORZÓW WIELKOPOLSKI	A	D	1817–1823; 1825–1831; 1833–1835; 1841; 1845–1847	AMTSGERICHT MESERITZ 247/5595
POZNAŃ	A	D	1847	3754/1
GORZÓW WIELKOPOLSKI	A	M	1817–1823; 1825–1831; 1833–1835; 1841; 1845–1847	AMTSGERICHT MESERITZ 247/5594
POZNAŃ	A	M	1847	3754/1
BROK	**OSTROŁĘKA**			
PUŁTUSK	A	B	1826–1892	135
BROK	U	B	1893–1918; 1921–1937	
PUŁTUSK	A	D	1826–1892	135
BROK	U	D	1893–1918; 1921–1937	
PUŁTUSK	A	M	1826–1892	135
BROK	U	M	1893–1918; 1921–1937	
BRUDZEW	**KALISZ**			
KALISZ	A	C	1872; 1917–1951	1/919–935; 53/57–121
KALISZ	A	E	1907; 1909	1/18–19, 21
BRUŻYCA	**INCLUDED IN ALEKSANDRÓW ŁÓDZKI**			
BRZEG	**OPOLE**			
OPOLE	A	B	1778–1847	4
KOBLENZ	G	B	1794/1874	
OPOLE	A	D	1810–1812; 1829–1868	4
KOBLENZ	G	D	1810–1874	
WARSZAWA	J	D	1937	
WARSZAWA	J	E	1742/1937	PROVINCE: ŚLĄSK
WARSZAWA	J	K	1742/1937	PROVINCE: ŚLĄSK
OPOLE	A	M	1809–1811	4
KOBLENZ	G	M	1847–1874	
WARSZAWA	J	S	1742/1937	PROVINCE: ŚLĄSK
WARSZAWA	J	T	1742/1937	PROVINCE: ŚLĄSK
OPOLE	A	T	1786–1842	4
WARSZAWA	J	Y	1742/1937	PROVINCE: ŚLĄSK
WARSZAWA	J	Z	1742/1937	PROVINCE: ŚLĄSK
BRZEŚĆ KUJAWSKI	**WŁOCŁAWEK**			
WARSZAWA	J	C	1909–1939	105
WARSZAWA	J	E	1909–1939	105
WARSZAWA	J	K	1909–1939	105
WŁOCŁAWEK	A	M	1829–1833 (MARRIAGE APPLICATIONS)	
WARSZAWA	J	T	1909–1939	105
BRZESKO	**TARNÓW**			
BRZESKO	U	B	1894–1942	
BRZESKO	U	D	1894–1941	
BRZESKO	U	M	1894–1942	
BRZEZINY	**SKIERNIEWICE**			
ŁÓDŹ	A	A	1891–1901	17
TOMASZÓW MAZOWIECKI	A	B	1808–1809; 1826–1832; 1841–1860; 1866–1886	244
ŁÓDŹ	A	B	1826–1876	270
BRZEZINY	U	B	1893–1938	
ŁÓDŹ	A	D	1826–1876	270
TOMASZÓW MAZOWIECKI	A	D	1826–1832; 1845–1861; 1877–1886	244

Repository type: **A** = Archive   **G** = LDS Films of German-Held Records   **J** = Jewish Historical Institute   **U** = Urząd Stanu Cywilnego

TOWN NAME			VOIVODSHIP (Province)	
Repository Location	Repository Type	Document Code	Years	Zespół/Sygnatura (Poland) Fond/Opis/Delo (Belarus, Ukraine, Lithuania)
RAWA MAZOWIECKA	A	D	1877–1892	
BRZEZINY	U	D	1893–1938	
PIOTRKÓW TRYBUNALSKI	A	G	1920–1950	115
ŁÓDŹ	A	K	1885–1915	1
ŁÓDŹ	A	M	1826–1876	270
TOMASZÓW MAZOWIECKI	A	M	1826–1858; 1876–1885	244
RAWA MAZOWIECKA	A	M	1877–1892	
BRZEZINY	U	M	1893–1938	
ŁÓDŹ	A	S	1889–1898; 1912–1913	83
TOMASZÓW MAZOWIECKI	A	T	1865/1942	108/17, 192–378, 382, 389–399
PIOTRKÓW TRYBUNALSKI	A	Y	1808–1949	30–31; 33–40; 116; 120–121; 128–129; 258–261
PIOTRKÓW TRYBUNALSKI	A	Z	1843–1950	108
BRZEŹNICA			**ŁÓDŹ**	
ŁÓDŹ	A	B	1826–1864	270
ŁÓDŹ	A	D	1826–1864	270
ŁÓDŹ	A	M	1826–1864	270
BRZOSTEK			**TARNÓW**	
BRZOSTEK	U	B	1882–1936	
BRZOSTEK	U	D	1894–1939	
BRZOSTEK	U	M	1894–1936	
BRZOZÓW			**KROSNO**	
SANOK	A	A	1849–1866; 1884–1918	16/81, 83
SANOK	A	E	1873; 1876; 1878; 1907; 1912; 1914; 1919; 1922; 1927–1928; 1930; 1934–1935; 1938–1939	16/18–19, 378–379
SANOK	A	S	1913	16/50
SANOK	A	T	1778–1779	16/38
PRZEMYŚL	A	Y	1903–1904; 1934–1935	730; 996
BUETOW			**SEE BYTÓW**	
BUK			**POZNAŃ**	
POZNAŃ	A	C	1933–1938	4377/42
BUKOWSKO			**KROSNO**	
PRZEMYŚL	A	K	1897; 1932–1944	154/1; 174/158
LVOV	A	L	1785–1788; 1819–1820	19/XV/105; 20/XV/188
PRZEMYŚL	A	Y	1910–1919; 1929–1937	729; 955–956
BURZENIN			**SIERADZ**	
ŁÓDŹ	A	B	1826–1864; 1883–1885; 1888–1894; 1896	270
BURZENIN	U	B	1897–1939	
ŁÓDŹ	A	D	1826–1864; 1883–1885; 1888–1894	270
BURZENIN	U	D	1897–1939	
ŁÓDŹ	A	M	1826–1864; 1883–1885; 1888–1894	270
BURZENIN	U	M	1897–1939	
BUSKO–ZDRÓJ			**KIELCE**	
BUSKO–ZDRÓJ	A	B	1875–1896	
BUSKO–ZDRÓJ	U	B	1897–1906; 1908–1912; 1915–1937; 1939–1942	
PIŃCZÓW	A	C	1876–1922	11
BUSKO–ZDRÓJ	A	D	1875–1896	
BUSKO–ZDRÓJ	U	D	1897–1906; 1908–1912; 1915–1937; 1939–1942	
BUSKO–ZDRÓJ	U	M	1897–1906; 1908–1912; 1916–1937; 1939–1940; 1942	
BUSKO–ZDRÓJ	A	M	1875–1896	
BUSZKOWICE			**PRZEMYŚL**	
PRZEMYŚL	A	C	1932; 1948	212/25–28
BUTOW			**SEE BYTÓW**	
BYCHAWA			**LUBLIN**	
LUBLIN	A	B	1826–1893	113
BYCHAWA	U	B	1894–1942	
LUBLIN	A	D	1826–1893	113
BYCHAWA	U	D	1894–1942	
LUBLIN	A	H	1940–1942	KREISHAUPTMANSCHAFT LUBLIN
LUBLIN	A	K	1797–1808; 1871–1914; 1919–1936	RGL IV ADM; SPL/647
LUBLIN	A	M	1826–1893	113
BYCHAWA	U	M	1894–1942	
BYDGOSZCZ			**BYDGOSZCZ**	
BYDGOSZCZ	A	B	1823–1894	378; 1663
WARSZAWA	J	C	1838/1939	104; 224
BYDGOSZCZ	A	D	1823–1894	378; 1663

A Army/recruit lists; **B** Birth; **C** Census; **D** Death; **E** Voter lists; **G** Immigration; **H** Holocaust; **J** Judaica; **K** Kahal; **L** Land; **M** Marriage; **N** Name changes; **O** Police files; **P** Pogroms; **R** Reference; **S** School records; **T** Tax lists; **V** Divorce; **W** Occupation lists; **X** Jewish hospital; **Y** Notary records; **Z** Local government records

TOWN NAME Repository Location	VOIVODSHIP (Province) Repository Document Type	 Code	 Years	Zespół/Sygnatura (Poland) Fond/Opis/Delo (Belarus, Ukraine, Lithuania)
BYDGOSZCZ	A	K	1874–1939	224
BYDGOSZCZ	A	M	1823–1894	378; 1663
BYDGOSZCZ	A	S	1826–1921	2
WARSZAWA	J	T	1838/1939	104; 224
WARSZAWA	J	Y	1838–1939	104; 224
BYDGOSZCZ	A	Z	1773–1919	189
BYTOM	**KATOWICE**			
KATOWICE	A	B	1847–1849; 1861–1885	674/I/362–364, 374–397; 749/I/1–96
KATOWICE	A	C	1792–1804; 1820–1864; 1908–1915; 1938	645/I/3123, 3126–3128; 164
KATOWICE	A	D	1847–1885	674/I/592–594; 604–615; 749/I/1–96
KATOWICE	A	M	1847–1885	674/I/443–514; 749/I/1–96
KATOWICE	A	T	1850; 1861–1863; 1867; 1879–1881; 1884–1895; 1899; 1903; 1907; 1910	645/1/82–98; 3126
WARSZAWA	J	Z	1814; 1835; 1855	PROVINCE: ŚLĄSK
BYTOM ODRZAŃSKI	**ZIELONA GÓRA**			
LEIPZIG	G	B	1847–1874	
LEIPZIG	G	D	1847–1874	
LEIPZIG	G	M	1847–1874	
BYTOM REGION	**KATOWICE**			
KATOWICE	A	B	1847–1849; 1861–1885	674/I/362–364, 374–397; 750/I/1–39; 753/I/1–36; 754/I/1–6
KATOWICE	A	D	1874–1885	750/I; 753–754/I
BYTÓW	**SŁUPSK**			
LEIPZIG	G	B	1812–1874	
LEIPZIG	G	D	1812–1874	
LEIPZIG	G	M	1812–1874	
CAMMIN	**SEE KAMIEŃ POMORSKI**			
CEGŁÓW	**SIEDLCE**			
SIEDLCE	A	B	1826; 1828; 1833–1836	204/1–11
SIEDLCE	A	D	1827; 1829; 1833–1835	204/1–11
SIEDLCE	A	M	1832–1834; 1836	204/1–11
CHARSZNICA	**KIELCE**			
CHARSZNICA	U	B	1886–1942	
CHARSZNICA	U	D	1886–1942	
CHARSZNICA	U	M	1886–1942	
CHĘCINY	**KIELCE**			
KIELCE	A	B	1826–1894	79
CHĘCINY	U	B	1895–1907; 1910–1941	
KIELCE	A	D	1826–1894	79
CHĘCINY	U	D	1895–1907; 1910–1941	
KIELCE	A	M	1826–1894	79
CHĘCINY	U	M	1895–1907; 1910–1941	
KIELCE	A	Z	1787–1791; 1824–1915	121
CHEŁM	**CHEŁM**			
LUBLIN	A	B	1826–1890; 1892	113
CHEŁM	U	B	1893–1915; 1922–1939	
LUBLIN	A	D	1823–1894	113
CHEŁM	U	D	1895–1897; 1899–1920; 1922–1939	
LUBLIN	A	E	1870–1915	RGL ADM; RGCH/480
LUBLIN	A	G	1919/1950	117–118
LUBLIN	A	K	1842; 1870–1915; 1922; 1927–1936	RGL ADM; RGCH/480; UWL WSP/766; 416
LUBLIN	A	M	1826–1890; 1892	113
CHEŁM	U	M	1893–1898; 1900–1914; 1922–1923; 1925; 1927–1935; 1937–1939	
LUBLIN	A	T	1744–1786; 1870–1915; 1927–1936	RGL ADM; RGCH/480; UWL WSP/766
CHEŁM WIELKI	**KATOWICE**			
KATOWICE	A	S	1908–1928	9/I/5–6
CHEŁMIEC	**INCLUDED IN NOWY SĄCZ**			
CHEŁMNO	**TORUŃ**			
TORUŃ	A	B	1847–1874	616/1
TORUŃ	A	C	1832–1844; 1853; 1921–1939	93/1
TORUŃ	A	M	1847–1874	616/1
TORUŃ	A	N	1801/1812; 1845	93/1
TORUŃ	A	T	1773–1920	93/1
TORUŃ	A	V	1829–1830	616/1

Repository type: **A** = Archive **G** = LDS Films of German-Held Records **J** = Jewish Historical Institute **U** = Urząd Stanu Cywilnego

TOWN NAME	VOIVODSHIP (Province)			Zespół/Sygnatura (Poland)
Repository Location	Repository Type	Document Code	Years	Fond/Opis/Delo (Belarus, Ukraine, Lithuania)
CHMIELNIK	**KIELCE**			
PIŃCZÓW	A	B	1876–1896	371
CHMIELNIK	U	B	1897–1939; 1941	
PIŃCZÓW	A	D	1876–1896	371
CHMIELNIK	U	D	1897–1939; 1941	
PIŃCZÓW	A	M	1876–1896	371
CHMIELNIK	U	M	1897–1939; 1941	
PIŃCZÓW	A	Y	1863	121
CHOCISZEWO	**WARSZAWA**			
NOWY DWÓR MAZOWIECKI	A	B	1809–1812	287
NOWY DWÓR MAZOWIECKI	A	D	1809–1812	287
NOWY DWÓR MAZOWIECKI	A	M	1809–1812	287
CHOCZ	**KALISZ**			
KALISZ	A	C	1872	1/936–941
KALISZ	A	E	1907; 1909	321/18–19, 21
KALISZ	A	W	1834–1848	1/90
CHODECZ	**WŁOCŁAWEK**			
WŁOCŁAWEK	A	C	1850–1931	22
WARSZAWA	J	C	1919/1939	105
WARSZAWA	J	E	1919/1939	105
WARSZAWA	J	K	1919/1939	105
WARSZAWA	J	T	1919/1939	105
CHODEL	**LUBLIN**			
LUBLIN	A	B	1870–1888	113
CHODEL	U	B	1895–1945	
LUBLIN	A	D	1870–1888	113
CHODEL	U	D	1895–1945	
LUBLIN	A	E	1869–1912	RGL IV ADM.
LUBLIN	A	H	1941	498
LUBLIN	A	K	1869–1912; 1919–1938	RGL IV ADM; SPL/648
LUBLIN	A	M	1870–1888	113
CHODEL	U	M	1895–1945	
LUBLIN	A	T	1869–1912; 1919–1938	RGL IV ADM; SPL/648
CHODZIEŻ	**PIŁA**			
POZNAŃ	A	K	1833–1865	906
POZNAŃ	A	S	1837–1907	1029/41–46
CHOJNA	**SZCZECIN**			
BERLIN	G	B	1799/1874	
BERLIN	G	D	1799/1874	
BERLIN	G	M	1799/1874	
CHOJNÓW	**LEGNICA**			
LEGNICA	A	H	1945–1949	488/99
WARSZAWA	J	K	1846/1922	PROVINCE: ŚLĄSK
WARSZAWA	J	Z	1846/1922	PROVINCE: ŚLĄSK
CHOROSZCZ	**BIAŁYSTOK**			
BIAŁYSTOK	A	A	1903–1914	42
BIAŁYSTOK	A	B	1882–1888; 1890–1892	935
CHOROSZCZ	U	B	1897–1903	
CHOROSZCZ	U	V	1883–1888; 1892–1913	
CHORZELE	**OSTROŁĘKA**			
PUŁTUSK	A	B	1826/1893	229
CHORZELE	U	B	1894–1912; 1919–1939	
PUŁTUSK	A	D	1826/1893	229
CHORZELE	U	D	1894–1912; 1919–1939	
PUŁTUSK	A	M	1826–1893	229
CHORZELE	U	M	1894–1912; 1920–1939	
CHORZÓW	**KATOWICE**			
KATOWICE	A	B	1847–1849; 1872	674/I/365, 368A, 685
KATOWICE	A	C	1938	646/I/2109
KATOWICE	A	D	1847–1849; 1872–1885	674/I/595A, 596, 598A, 709
KATOWICE	A	K	1871–1879; 1886; 1911–1933	27/VOL.I–VI/1994–1995; 61/I/85; 646/I/1581, 1583
KATOWICE	A	M	1847–1849	647/1/434, 439A
CHOSZCZNO	**GORZÓW WIELKOPOLSKI**			
BERLIN	G	B	1779–1812; 1847–1853	
BERLIN	G	D	1791–1812; 1847–1853	
BERLIN	G	M	1847–1853	

A Army/recruit lists; **B** Birth; **C** Census; **D** Death; **E** Voter lists; **G** Immigration; **H** Holocaust; **J** Judaica; **K** Kahal; **L** Land; **M** Marriage; **N** Name changes; **O** Police files; **P** Pogroms; **R** Reference; **S** School records; **T** Tax lists; **V** Divorce; **W** Occupation lists; **X** Jewish hospital; **Y** Notary records; **Z** Local government records

TOWN NAME		VOIVODSHIP (Province)			Zespół/Sygnatura (Poland)
Repository Location	Repository Type	Document Code	Years		Fond/Opis/Delo (Belarus, Ukraine, Lithuania)

CHRISTBURG		**SEE DZIERZGOŃ**		
CHRUŚLIN		**SKIERNIEWICE**		
ŁOWICZ	A	B	1870	235
ŁOWICZ	A	D	1870	235
ŁOWICZ	A	M	1870	235
CHRUSZCZEWKA		**SIEDLCE**		
SIEDLCE	A	C	1931	74/35
CHRZANÓW		**KATOWICE**		
CHRZANÓW	U	B	1941–1942	
CHRZANÓW	U	D	1898; 1939–1942	
KRAKÓW	A	K	1787–1815	526/IT 222A–C
CHRZANÓW	U	M	1920–1921; 1939; 1942–1943	
CHYRZYNA		**PRZEMYŚL**		
PRZEMYŚL	A	C	1931/1943	203/18, 28
CIECHANÓW		**CIECHANÓW**		
MŁAWA	A	B	1826–1876; 1878–1895	572
CIECHANÓW	U	B	1896–1913; 1917–1918; 1920–1938	
MŁAWA	A	D	1826–1876; 1878–1895	572
CIECHANÓW	U	D	1896–1913; 1917–1918; 1920–1938	
MŁAWA	A	M	1826–1876; 1878–1895	572
CIECHANÓW	U	M	1896–1913; 1917–1918; 1920–1938	
MŁAWA	A	Y	1849–1939	192–195; 197; 202–203; 206; 209–212; 214; 243
CIECHANOWIEC		**ŁOMŻA**		
ŁOMŻA	A	B	1826–1829; 1833–1839 (& INCLUDED IN WYSOKIE MAZOWIECKI)	177
BIAŁYSTOK	A	B	1839; 1843–1847; 1849–1851; 1853–1859; 1865; 1867–1870	544
BIAŁYSTOK	A	D	1839; 1843–1847; 1849–1851; 1853–1859; 1865; 1867–1870	544
CIECHANOWIEC	U	D	1930	
BIAŁYSTOK	A	M	1839; 1843–1847; 1849–1851; 1853–1859; 1865; 1867; 1869–1870	544
CIECHANOWIEC	U	M	1899; 1901; 1925; 1930; 1934	
CIEPIELÓW		**RADOM**		
STARACHOWICE	A	B	1826–1873	162
RADOM	A	B	1874–1894	486/1
CIEPIELÓW	U	B	1895–1912; 1924–1941	
STARACHOWICE	A	D	1826–1873	162
RADOM	A	D	1874–1894	486/1
CIEPIELÓW	U	D	1895–1912; 1924–1940	
STARACHOWICE	A	M	1826–1873	162
RADOM	A	M	1852–1853; 1874–1894	486/1
CIEPIELÓW	U	M	1895–1911; 1924; 1926–1930; 1932–1934; 1936–1940	
CIESZYN		**BIELSKO BIAŁA**		
CIESZYN	A	A	1662/1945	13/I/214–219, 245–264
CIESZYN	A	B	1841–1849	13/I/470
CIESZYN	A	C	1851–1905; 1911–1931	13/I/476
CIESZYN	A	D	1838–1846	13/I
CIESZYN	A	E	1861–1902; 1922; 1935–1938	13/I/130–147, 154–179
CIESZYN	A	K	1839–1843	13/I/1155
KATOWICE	A	K	1929–1939	27/I/596
CIESZYN	A	L	1839–1843	13/I/1155
KATOWICE	A	L	1637/1784	
CIESZYN	A	Z	1919–1945	13/I
ĆMIELÓW		**TARNOBRZEG**		
SANDOMIERZ	A	C	1945	10/97
CMOLAS		**RZESZÓW**		
RZESZÓW	A	C	1931	90/1–5
COSEL		**SEE KOŹLE**		
CULM		**SEE CHEŁMNO**		
CZAJKI		**INCLUDED IN KRASNYSTAW**		
CZAPLINEK		**KOSZALIN**		
KOBLENZ	G	B	1829–1852	
KOSZALIN	A	C	1840	117/I/11

Repository type: **A** = Archive   **G** = LDS Films of German-Held Records   **J** = Jewish Historical Institute   **U** = Urząd Stanu Cywilnego

TOWN NAME	VOIVODSHIP (Province)			Zespół/Sygnatura (Poland)
Repository Location	Repository Document Type	Code	Years	Fond/Opis/Delo (Belarus, Ukraine, Lithuania)
KOBLENZ	G	D	1829–1852	
KOSZALIN	A	T	1810–1934	117/I/22–40
CZARNA	**RZESZÓW**			
RZESZÓW	A	C	1937	246/186–191
CZARNIKAU	**SEE CZARNKÓW**			
CZARNKÓW	**PIŁA**			
POZNAŃ	A	B	1823–1840	3575/1
POZNAŃ	A	D	1823–1840	3575/1
POZNAŃ	A	M	1823–1840	3575/1
CZCHÓW	**TARNÓW**			
TARNÓW	A	B	1877–1893	
CZCHÓW	U	B	1894–1942	
TARNÓW	A	D	1877–1893	
CZCHÓW	U	D	1894–1896	
LVOV	A	L	1785–1788; 1819–1820	19/1/20; 20/1/297
TARNÓW	A	M	1877–1893	
CZCHÓW	U	M	1904–1939	
CZELADŹ	**KATOWICE**			
CZELADŹ	U	B	1929–1942	
CZELADŹ	U	D	1929–1942	
CZELADŹ	U	M	1929–1935; 1937–1942	
CZEMIERNIKI	**BIAŁA PODLASKA**			
LUBLIN	A	B	1828–1855; 1858–1874; 1877–1878; 1882	113
CZEMIERNIKI	U	B	1890–1893, 1896–1897; 1899; 1901; 1903–1904; 1906; 1908; 1917–1938	
LUBLIN	A	D	1828–1855; 1858–1874; 1877–1878; 1882	113
CZEMIERNIKI	U	D	1890–1892; 1896; 1899; 1901; 1904; 1924; 1928	
LUBLIN	A	K	1868–1912; 1921–1927	RGL IV ADM; UWL WSP/796
LUBLIN	A	M	1828–1855; 1858–1874; 1877–1878; 1882	113
CZEMIERNIKI	U	M	1890–1892; 1896–1897; 1899; 1901; 1904; 1908; 1928; 1935	
CZERSK	**WARSZAWA**			
GÓRA KALWARIA	A	B	1828–1836	128
GÓRA KALWARIA	A	D	1828–1836	128
GÓRA KALWARIA	A	M	1828–1836	128
CZERWIŃSK NAD WISŁA	**PŁOCK**			
NOWY DWÓR MAZOWIECKI	A	B	1826–1854; 1858–1865	117
NOWY DWÓR MAZOWIECKI	A	D	1826–1854; 1858–1865	117
NOWY DWÓR MAZOWIECKI	A	M	1826–1854; 1858–1865	117
CZĘSTOCHOWA	**CZĘSTOCHOWA**			
ŁÓDŹ	A	A	1891–1902	17
CZĘSTOCHOWA	A	B	1826–1895	58
CZĘSTOCHOWA	U	B	1896–1942; 1945	
CZĘSTOCHOWA	A	C	1915–1939	1
WARSZAWA	J	C	1930–1938	113
CZĘSTOCHOWA	A	D	1826–1895	58
CZĘSTOCHOWA	U	D	1896–1942; 1945	
WARSZAWA	J	H	1940–1943 (LIST OF 4, 700 CAMP WORKERS IN HASAG LABOR CAMP)	207, 212
CZĘSTOCHOWA	A	K	1933–1939	60
CZĘSTOCHOWA	A	L	1918–1939	1
CZĘSTOCHOWA	A	M	1826–1895	58
CZĘSTOCHOWA	U	M	1896–1942; 1945	
ŁÓDŹ	A	O	1905–1914	43
ŁÓDŹ	A	S	1843/1913	1; 83
CZĘSTOCHOWA	A	S	1915–1917	1
ŁÓDŹ	A	W	1864/1914	1/19
CZĘSTOCHOWA	A	W	1940–1941; 1945	1
ŁÓDŹ	A	X	1900–1913	15
CZĘSTOCHOWA	A	X	1915–1917	1
CZĘSTOCHOWA	A	Z	1835/1914	1
ŁÓDŹ	A	Z	1908–1912	1
CZŁUCHÓW	**SŁUPSK**			
SZCZECIN	A	K	1856–1938	GMINY ZYDOWSKIE Z POMORZA ZACHODNIEGO 8/53, 53A
CZUDEC	**RZESZÓW**			
RZESZÓW	A	B	1940–1942	736/16

A Army/recruit lists; **B** Birth; **C** Census; **D** Death; **E** Voter lists; **G** Immigration; **H** Holocaust; **J** Judaica; **K** Kahal; **L** Land; **M** Marriage; **N** Name changes; **O** Police files; **P** Pogroms; **R** Reference; **S** School records; **T** Tax lists; **V** Divorce; **W** Occupation lists; **X** Jewish hospital; **Y** Notary records; **Z** Local government records

TOWN NAME	VOIVODSHIP (Province)			Zespół/Sygnatura (Poland)
Repository Location	Repository Type	Document Code	Years	Fond/Opis/Delo (Belarus, Ukraine, Lithuania)
RZESZÓW	A	C	1935–1937; 1940–1942	736/17, 20, 59
RZESZÓW	A	D	1940–1942	736/16
RZESZÓW	A	H	1939–1942	736/18–20; 726/134
RZESZÓW	A	K	1922–1928; 1939–1942	716/1–12, 9–20; 736
RZESZÓW	A	L	1939–1942	725/134
LVOV	A	L	1785–1788; 1819–1820	19/II/159; 20/II/336
RZESZÓW	A	M	1940–1942	736/16
RZESZÓW	A	W	1940–1941	736/18–19
CZYŻEW–OSADA	**ŁOMŻA**			
PUŁTUSK	A	B	1826–1859	258
ŁOMŻA	A	B	1860–1893	175; 415
CZYŻEW–OSADA	U	B	1886–1915; 1923–1936	
PUŁTUSK	A	D	1826–1859	258
ŁOMŻA	A	D	1860–1893	175; 415
CZYŻEW–OSADA	U	D	1886–1915; 1923–1936	
PUŁTUSK	A	M	1826–1859	258
ŁOMŻA	A	M	1860–1893	175; 415
CZYŻEW–OSADA	U	M	1886–1915; 1923–1936	
ŁOMŻA	A	Y	1869–1939	409–413
DABER	**SEE DOBRA**			
DĄBIE	**KONIN**			
POZNAŃ	A	B	1826–1891	3743/1–67
DĄBIE	U	B	1892–1938	
POZNAŃ	A	D	1826–1891	3743/1–67
DĄBIE	U	D	1892–1938	
POZNAŃ	A	G	1918–1950	13/404–422
POZNAŃ	A	M	1826–1891	3743/1–67
DĄBIE	U	M	1892–1938	
DĄBROWA GÓRNICZA	**KATOWICE**			
DĄBROWA GÓRNICZA	U	B	1911–1939	
KATOWICE	A	C	1864–1935	775/40, 46–47, 54, 68, 76–, 81, 83, 91, 97 104, 118, 124, 132, 142–147, 160–162, 175–178, 205–207, 229
DĄBROWA GÓRNICZA	U	D	1911–1940	
KATOWICE	A	K	1883–1884; 1888–1900; 1911–1914	775/157, 171, 191
ŁÓDŹ	A	K	1907–1913	1
DĄBROWA GÓRNICZA	U	M	1911–1941	
ŁÓDŹ	A	O	1906	42
KATOWICE	A	S	1875–1880; 1908; 1912–1914	775/128, 174, 196, 220
KATOWICE	A	Y	1908–1938	824/1–107
KATOWICE	A	Z	1893–1894; 1898–1900; 1915	775/50–51, 66, 261
ŁÓDŹ	A	Z	1896–1898	1
DĄBROWA TARNOWSKA	**TARNÓW**			
TARNÓW	A	B	1882–1885	
DĄBROWA TARNOWSKA	U	B	1886–1892; 1900–1913; 1915–1920; 1922–1925; 1927–1938; 1940	
DĄBROWA TARNOWSKA	U	D	1915–1917; 1919–1920; 1922; 1925–1927; 1929–1932; 1935–1936; 1938; 1940–1941	
DĄBROWA TARNOWSKA	U	M	1915–1918; 1920–1939	
KRAKÓW	A	M	1919	526/MID/1
DĄBRÓWNO	**OLSZTYN**			
LEIPZIG	G	B	1847–1874	
LEIPZIG	G	D	1847–1874	
LEIPZIG	G	M	1847–1874	
DACHNÓW	**PRZEMYŚL**			
PRZEMYŚL	A	E	1938	637/4
DALESZYCE	**KIELCE**			
KIELCE	A	B	1826–1870	83
DALESZYCE	U	B	1894–1941	
KIELCE	A	D	1826–1893	83
DALESZYCE	U	D	1894–1941	
KIELCE	A	M	1826–1893	83
DALESZYCE	U	M	1894–1941	
DANZIG	**SEE GDAŃSK**			
DARŁOWO	**KOSZALIN**			
KOBLENZ	G	B	1846–1861	

Repository type: **A** = Archive **G** = LDS Films of German-Held Records **J** = Jewish Historical Institute **U** = Urząd Stanu Cywilnego

TOWN NAME	VOIVODSHIP (Province)				Zespół/Sygnatura (Poland)
Repository Location	Repository Document Type	Code	Years		Fond/Opis/Delo (Belarus, Ukraine, Lithuania)
DĘBICA	**TARNÓW**				
RZESZÓW	A	A	1919–1939		518/23
RZESZÓW	A	C	1945		69/28
RZESZÓW	A	D	1937–1939; 1942–1944; 1949		518/1, 28; 882/1
RZESZÓW	A	E	1927–1938		518/17
RZESZÓW	A	G	1927–1939		518/18
PRZEMYŚL	A	H	1939		682/2
RZESZÓW	A	H	1942–1944		882/1
PRZEMYŚL	A	Y	1864–1934		77; 949–954
DĘBLIN	**LUBLIN**				
DĘBLIN	U	B	1882–1913; 1921–1938		
DĘBLIN	U	D	1882–1913; 1921–1938		
DĘBLIN	U	M	1882–1913; 1921–1939		
DĘBÓW	**PRZEMYŚL**				
PRZEWORSK	A	S	1896–1948		57/1–10, 17–43
DEBRZNO	**SŁUPSK**				
SZCZECIN	A	K	20TH CENT.		GMINY ZYDOWSKIE Z POMORZA ZACHODNIEGO 54
DEUTSCH EYLAU	**SEE IŁAWA**				
DEUTSCH KRONE	**SEE WAŁCZ**				
DIRSCHAU	**SEE TCZEW**				
DŁUGIE	**KROSNO**				
SANOK	A	C	1931–1949		21/69–70
DŁUGOSIODŁO	**OSTROŁĘKA**				
DŁUGOSIODŁO	U	B	1910–1935		
DŁUGOSIODŁO	U	D	1910–1935		
DŁUGOSIODŁO	U	M	1910–1935		
DOBIEGNIEW	**ZIELONA GÓRA**				
KOBLENZ	G	B	1770/1854		
KOBLENZ	G	D	1770/1854		
KOBLENZ	G	M	1770/1854		
DOBRA	**SZCZECIN**				
SZCZECIN	A	B	1876–1891		STANDESAMIT DABER
SZCZECIN	A	D	1876–1891		STANDESAMIT DABER
SZCZECIN	A	K	1817–1846		MAGISTRAT DABER 371–374
SZCZECIN	A	M	1876–1885; 1887–1891		STANDESAMIT DABER
SZCZECIN	A	Z	1716–1843		MAGISTRAT DABER 361–370
DOBRE MIASTO	**OLSZTYN**				
KOBLENZ	G	D	1846–1937		
DOBRODZIEŃ	**CZĘSTOCHOWA**				
TARNOWSKIE GÓRY	A	E	1915–1923		19/173
TARNOWSKIE GÓRY	A	G	1842–1927		19/244
WARSZAWA	J	K	1825/1929		PROVINCE: ŚLĄSK
TARNOWSKIE GÓRY	A	K	1931–1932		19/311
WARSZAWA	J	S	1825/1929		PROVINCE: ŚLĄSK
WARSZAWA	J	Y	1825/1929		PROVINCE: ŚLĄSK
WARSZAWA	J	Z	1825/1929		PROVINCE: ŚLĄSK
DOBROSOLOWO	**KONIN**				
POZNAŃ	A	B	1826–1891		3621
POZNAŃ	A	D	1826–1891		3621
POZNAŃ	A	M	1826–1891		3621
DOBRZYCA	**KALISZ**				
BERLIN	G	B	1817–1864		
BERLIN	G	D	1817–1864		
BERLIN	G	M	1817–1864		
DOBRZYŃ NAD WISŁĄ	**WŁOCŁAWEK**				
WŁOCŁAWEK	A	B	1826–1908		563
DOBRZYŃ NAD WISŁĄ	U	B	1927–1938		
WŁOCŁAWEK	A	D	1899–1936		563
WŁOCŁAWEK	A	M	1826–1898		563
DOBRZYŃ NAD WISŁĄ	U	M	1928–1938		
DRAMBURG	**SEE DRAWSKO POMORSKIE**				
DRAWSKO POMORSKIE	**KOSZALIN**				
KOBLENZ	G	B	1779/1874		
KOBLENZ	G	D	1779/1874		

A Army/recruit lists; **B** Birth; **C** Census; **D** Death; **E** Voter lists; **G** Immigration; **H** Holocaust; **J** Judaica; **K** Kahal; **L** Land; **M** Marriage; **N** Name changes; **O** Police files; **P** Pogroms; **R** Reference; **S** School records; **T** Tax lists; **V** Divorce; **W** Occupation lists; **X** Jewish hospital; **Y** Notary records; **Z** Local government records

TOWN NAME Repository Location	VOIVODSHIP (Province) Repository Document Type Code		Years	Zespół/Sygnatura (Poland) Fond/Opis/Delo (Belarus, Ukraine, Lithuania)
KOBLENZ	G	M	1779/1874	
DROBIN	**PŁOCK**			
PŁOCK	A	B	1826–1894	174
DROBIN	U	B	1895–1912; 1916–1938	
PŁOCK	A	D	1826–1894	174
DROBIN	U	D	1895–1912; 1916–1938	
PŁOCK	A	M	1826–1894	174
DROBIN	U	M	1895–1912; 1916–1938	
DROHOBYCZKA	**PRZEMYŚL**			
PRZEMYŚL	A	C	1931–1950	200/19–24
DROSSEN	**SEE OŚNO**			
DRZEWICA	**RADOM**			
DRZEWICA	U	B	1904–1907; 1910–1911; 1920–1932; 1935–1941	
DRZEWICA	U	D	1895–1913; 1920; 1922–1924; 1926; 1941	
DRZEWICA	U	M	1895–1913; 1920; 1922–1924; 1926; 1941	
DUBECZNO	**CHEŁM**			
RZESZÓW	A	D	1889/1909	533/18–19
DUBIECKO	**PRZEMYŚL**			
PRZEMYŚL	A	C	1930–1940; 1946–1950	200/25–29
PRZEMYŚL	A	D	1939–1952	200/142
LVOV	A	L	1785–1788; 1819–1820	19/XV/306; 20/XV/112
PRZEMYŚL	A	Y	1874–1875; 1882–1892; 1924–1926; 1944–1949	79; 1069–1074
DUBIENKA	**CHEŁM**			
LUBLIN	A	B	1826–1853; 1857–1894	113
DUBIENKA	U	B	1895–1914; 1916–1925; 1927–1940	
LUBLIN	A	D	1826–1853; 1857–1894	113
DUBIENKA	U	D	1895–1914	
LUBLIN	A	M	1826–1853; 1857–1894	113
DUBIENKA	U	M	1895–1914	
LUBLIN	A	T	1795–1797; 1867–1907; 1927; 1929–1933	RGL IV; UWL WSP/779; SPH/509
LUBLIN	A	W	1785	30
DUKLA	**KROSNO**			
DUKLA	U	B	1916–1917; 1920; 1925–1926; 1930–1933; 1939–1941	
SKOLYSZYN	A	C	1906–1927	2/2
DUKLA	U	D	1914–1933; 1939–1941	
SKOLYSZYN	A	H	1944–1949	2/55
LVOV	A	L	1785–1788; 1819–1820	19/II/1; 20/II/90
DUKLA	U	M	1914–1916; 1939–1940	
PRZEMYŚL	A	Y	1924–1934	742; 1026–1027
DUŃKOWICZKI	**PRZEMYŚL**			
PRZEMYŚL	A	C	1930/1948	207/16–17
DURACZÓW	**KIELCE**			
KIELCE	A	C	1939	524
DYNÓW	**PRZEMYŚL**			
LVOV	A	L	1785–1788; 1819–1820	19/15/279; 20/15/80
PRZEMYŚL	A	Y	1934	772; 1064–1065
DZIAŁOSZYCE	**KIELCE**			
PIŃCZÓW	A	B	1826–1864; 1873–1894	143
WARSZAWA	J	B	1829/1846	
DZIAŁOSZYCE	U	B	1895–1898; 1903–1906; 1910–1942	
PIŃCZÓW	A	D	1826–1864; 1873–1894	143
WARSZAWA	J	D	1829/1846	
DZIAŁOSZYCE	U	D	1895; 1906; 1910–1915; 1924; 1927; 1930; 1932	
PIŃCZÓW	A	M	1826–1894	143
WARSZAWA	J	M	1829/1846	
DZIAŁOSZYCE	U	M	1896; 1917–1921; 1924; 1927; 1930; 1932–1941	
DZIAŁOSZYN	**SIERADZ**			
ŁÓDŹ	A	B	1828–1837	270
ŁÓDŹ	A	D	1828–1837	270
ŁÓDŹ	A	M	1828–1837	270
DZIEDZICE	**KATOWICE**			
KATOWICE	A	K	1925–1932	27/VOL.I–VI/1991
DZIERZGOŃ	**ELBLĄG**			
LEIPZIG	G	B	1847–1875	
LEIPZIG	G	D	1847–1875	

Repository type: **A** = Archive **G** = LDS Films of German-Held Records **J** = Jewish Historical Institute **U** = Urząd Stanu Cywilnego

TOWN NAME	VOIVODSHIP (Province)				
Repository Location	Repository Document Type	Code	Years		Zespół/Sygnatura (Poland) Fond/Opis/Delo (Belarus, Ukraine, Lithuania)
LEIPZIG	G	M	1847–1875		
DZIERŻONIÓW	**WAŁBRZYCH**				
WARSZAWA	J	G	1812/1912		PROVINCE: ŚLĄSK
WROCŁAW	A	K	1654/1945		27/I
WARSZAWA	J	T	1812/1912		PROVINCE: ŚLĄSK
ELBING	**SEE ELBLĄG**				
ELBLĄG	**ELBLĄG**				
GDAŃSK	A	B	1801–1808; 1812–1874		369/2/4899; 372/47, 50–51
GDAŃSK	A	C	1812/1900		369/2/4901
GDAŃSK	A	D	1812–1874		372/47–48, 50–51
GDAŃSK	A	K	1772/1912; 1939		373/72
GDAŃSK	A	M	1801–1808; 1812–1874		369/2/4899; 372/47; 49–51
EŁK	**SUWAŁKI**				
OLSZTYN	A	C	1838; 1864–1874; 1901–1906		4/I
FALENICA	**WARSZAWA**				
WARSZAWA	J	K	1940–1943		212
FALKENBERG	**SEE NIEMODLIN**				
FESTENBERG	**SEE TWARDOGÓRA**				
FIDDICHOW	**SEE WIDUCHOWA**				
FILIPÓW	**SUWAŁKI**				
SUWAŁKI	A	B	1808; 1821–1825; 1829–1879; 1884–1891; 1894		151; 198
FILIPÓW	U	B	1898–1899; 1903; 1906–1908; 1920–1929; 1931–1938		
SUWAŁKI	A	D	1808–1825; 1829–1879; 1884–1891; 1894		151; 198
FILIPÓW	U	D	1898; 1903; 1906–1908; 1920–1929; 1931–1938		
SUWAŁKI	A	K	1926–1938		31/132–138, 157
SUWAŁKI	A	M	1808–1825; 1829–1877; 1884–1891; 1894		151; 198
FILIPÓW	U	M	1898; 1906–1908; 1920–1929; 1931–1938		
WARSZAWA	A	T	1811–1865		KRSW 4834–4837
FIRLEJ	**LUBLIN**				
LUBLIN	A	B	1826–1831		113
LUBLIN	A	D	1826–1831		113
LUBLIN	A	M	1826–1831		113
FLATAU	**SEE ZLOTÓW**				
FLATOW	**SEE ZLOTÓW**				
FORDON	**BYDGOSZCZ**				
BYDGOSZCZ	A	B	1820–1892		380; 1685
BYDGOSZCZ	A	D	1820–1892		380; 1685
BYDGOSZCZ	A	M	1820–1892		380; 1685
FRAMPOL	**ZAMOŚĆ**				
LUBLIN	A	B	1871–1875		113
ZAMOŚĆ	A	B	1876–1893		209/1–18
FRAMPOL	U	B	1894–1913; 1915–1934		
LUBLIN	A	D	1871–1875		113
ZAMOŚĆ	A	D	1876–1893		209/1–18
FRAMPOL	U	D	1894–1913; 1915–1934		
LUBLIN	A	E	1878–1914		RGL IV ADM
LUBLIN	A	K	1878–1914; 1927		RGL IV ADM; UWL WSP/761
LUBLIN	A	M	1871–1875		113
ZAMOŚĆ	A	M	1876–1892		209/1–17
FRAMPOL	U	M	1893–1913; 1915–1934		
FRANKENSTEIN	**SEE ZĄBKOWICE**				
FRAUSTADT	**SEE WSCHOWA**				
FRIEDEBERG	**SEE MIRSK**				
FRIEDEBERG IN NEUMARK	**SEE STRZELCE KRAJEŃSKIE**				
FRIEDLAND	**SEE KORFANTÓW**				
FRYSZTAK	**RZESZÓW**				
RZESZÓW	A	H	1939–1944		731/54
LVOV	A	L	1785–1788; 1819–1820		19/II/150; 20/II/328
PRZEMYŚL	A	Y	1920–1928; 1934		727; 957–958
GĄBIN	**PŁOCK**				
PŁOCK	A	T	1820–1871		2
PŁOCK	A	Y	1868–1939		272–277; 472–473
GAĆ	**PRZEMYŚL**				
PRZEWORSK	A	S	1884/1952		58/1–2, 5–27

A Army/recruit lists; **B** Birth; **C** Census; **D** Death; **E** Voter lists; **G** Immigration; **H** Holocaust; **J** Judaica; **K** Kahal; **L** Land; **M** Marriage; **N** Name changes; **O** Police files; **P** Pogroms; **R** Reference; **S** School records; **T** Tax lists; **V** Divorce; **W** Occupation lists; **X** Jewish hospital; **Y** Notary records; **Z** Local government records

TOWN NAME	VOIVODSHIP (Province)			Zespół/Sygnatura (Poland)
Repository Location	Repository Document Type	Code	Years	Fond/Opis/Delo (Belarus, Ukraine, Lithuania)

GALICIA REGION	**RZESZÓW**			
RZESZÓW	A	B	1880/1927	533/19; 1/2738, 2741
RZESZÓW	A	D	1894/1909	533/19
RZESZÓW	A	M	1894/1909	533/19
GARWOLIN	**SIEDLCE**			
LUBLIN	A	E	1895; 1913–1915	RGL IV ADM
LUBLIN	A	K	1895; 1913–1915; 1921–1936	RGL IV ADM; 403/770
LUBLIN	A	T	1895; 1913–1915; 1927–1936	RGL IV ADM; UWL WSP/770
GAWRYCHY	**ŁOMŻA**			
ŁOMŻA	A	C	1933–1939	157
GDAŃSK	**GDAŃSK**			
GDAŃSK	A	G	1932–1939	260/2171–2177
GDAŃSK	A	H	1933–1941	96/85; 264/23, 27
GDAŃSK	A	K	1545/1793; 1807–1814	10; 98/276; 300
GDAŃSK	A	O	1922–1932	14/5945
GDAŃSK	A	P	1938	2384/50/VI/20
GDAŃSK	A	T	1377/1794; 1807–1814	300/12
GDAŃSK	A	W	1405/1814	300; 58/50, 78–79
GDAŃSK	A	Z	1559–1794; 1807–1814	300; 93/55E
GDAŃSK REGION	**GDAŃSK**			
GDAŃSK	A	B	1828/1846; 1847–1879; 1880/1934	1497/1–2, 5–16, 46, 48, 50, 56, 61–62, 65, 71–76
GDAŃSK	A	D	1828/1840; 1841–1879; 1880/1934	1497/1; 35–46; 53–54; 58; 60–61; 64–65; 71–76
GDAŃSK	A	H	1939–1941	263/2
GDAŃSK	A	L	1939–1941	264/23, 27
GDAŃSK	A	M	1828/1846; 1847–1879; 1880/1934	1497/1, 3–4, 17–34, 46–47, 49, 51–52, 57, 59, 61, 63, 65, 67–76
GDYNIA	**GDAŃSK**			
GDAŃSK	A	G	1925–1939	1036/42–44, 47, 78–79, 149–151, 1067, 1091–1093; 124/2299–2301
GDAŃSK	A	H	1939–1941	264/23, 27
GDAŃSK	A	L	1939–1941	264/23, 27
GĘBICE	**BYDGOSZCZ**			
INOWROCŁAW	A	B	1832–1845; 1847–1848	110/1–2
INOWROCŁAW	A	D	1832–1845; 1847–1848	110/1–2
INOWROCŁAW	A	M	1832–1845; 1847–1848	110/1–2
GIDLE	**CZĘSTOCHOWA**			
GIDLE	U	B	1882–1889; 1891–1912; 1919–1927; 1929–1940	
GIDLE	U	D	1882–1889; 1891–1912; 1919–1927; 1929–1940	
GIDLE	U	M	1882–1889; 1891–1912; 1919–1927; 1929–1940	
GILGENBURG	**SEE DĄBRÓWNO**			
GIŻYCKO	**SUWAŁKI**			
OLSZTYN	A	C	1812; 1904–1905	4/I; 11/I
GLATZ	**SEE KŁÓDŻKO**			
GLEIWITZ	**SEE GLIWICE**			
GLIWICE	**KATOWICE**			
GLIWICE	A	B	1812–1847	1/I/5852
WARSZAWA	J	B	1812–1847	107
GLIWICE	A	C	1812–1822; 1846–1874	1/I/5861–5863
GLIWICE	A	D	1812–1849	1/I/5855
WARSZAWA	J	D	1847–1870	107
GLIWICE	A	E	1811–1861	1/I/5840
WARSZAWA	J	E	1812/1939	107; 112
WARSZAWA	J	K	1812/1939	107; 112
WARSZAWA	J	L	1812/1939	107; 112
GLIWICE	A	M	1812–1847	1/I/5859
WARSZAWA	J	S	1812/1939	107; 112
WARSZAWA	J	Y	1812/1939	107; 112
WARSZAWA	J	Z	1812/1939	107; 112
GLIWICE REGION	**KATOWICE**			
GLIWICE	A	K	1812–1900	1/I/5813–5863
GLOGAU	**SEE GŁOGÓW**			
GŁOGÓW	**LEGNICA**			
KOBLENZ	G	B	1812/1938	
KOBLENZ	G	C	1812	

Repository type: **A** = Archive   **G** = LDS Films of German-Held Records   **J** = Jewish Historical Institute   **U** = Urząd Stanu Cywilnego

TOWN NAME	VOIVODSHIP (Province)			Zespół/Sygnatura (Poland)
Repository Location	Repository Document Type	Code	Years	Fond/Opis/Delo (Belarus, Ukraine, Lithuania)
WARSZAWA	J	D	1796; 1828/1850	PROVINCE: ŚLĄSK
KOBLENZ	G	D	1812/1938	
WARSZAWA	J	M	1796; 1828/1850	PROVINCE: ŚLĄSK
KOBLENZ	G	M	1812/1938	
STARY KISIELIN	A	Z	1582/1858	13
GŁOGÓW MALOPOLSKI	**RZESZÓW**			
RZESZÓW	A	C	1945–1947	335/96–97
LVOV	A	L	1785–1788; 1819–1820	19/V/33; 20/V/28
PRZEMYŚL	A	Y	1886–1939	80; 1128–1137
GŁOGÓWEK	**OPOLE**			
LEIPZIG	G	B	1847/1874	
LEIPZIG	G	D	1847/1874	
LEIPZIG	G	M	1847/1874	
GŁOGOWIEC	**PRZEMYŚL**			
PRZEWORSK	A	S	1885/1949	59/4–15, 19–39
GŁOWACZÓW	**RADOM**			
RADOM	A	B	1883–1894	433/1
GŁOWACZÓW	U	B	1895–1940	
RADOM	A	D	1883–1894	433/1
GŁOWACZÓW	U	D	1895–1940	
RADOM	A	M	1883–1894	433/1
GŁOWACZÓW	U	M	1895–1940	
GŁOWNO	**ŁÓDŹ**			
ŁÓDŹ	A	B	1812–1893	270
GŁOWNO	U	B	1894–1910; 1912–1913; 1915–1931; 1933–1938	
ŁÓDŹ	A	D	1812–1893	270
GŁOWNO	U	D	1894–1899; 1901–1910; 1912–1926; 1928; 1930–1931; 1933–1939	
ŁÓDŹ	A	K	1822–1866	1
ŁÓDŹ	A	M	1812–1893	270
GŁOWNO	U	M	1894–1899; 1901–1910; 1912–1913; 1916–1939	
ŁÓDŹ	A	O	1906	44
ŁÓDŹ	A	Z	1822/1866; 1897–1914	1
GŁUBCZYCE	**OPOLE**			
OPOLE	A	B	1830–1917	293
OPOLE	A	M	1870–1922	293
GŁUCHOŁAZY	**OPOLE**			
BERLIN	G	B	1851/1873	
BERLIN	G	D	1851/1873	
BERLIN	G	M	1851/1873	
GŁUSK	**LUBLIN**			
LUBLIN	A	B	1826–1886	113
GŁUSK	U	B	1887–1927	
LUBLIN	A	C	1854	6
LUBLIN	A	D	1826–1905	113
GŁUSK	U	D	1894–1927	
LUBLIN	A	E	1869–1914	RGL IV ADM.
LUBLIN	A	K	1845; 1869–1914; 1920–1928	22; RGL IV; SPL/649; UWL WSP/805
LUBLIN	A	M	1826–1886	113
GŁUSK	U	M	1887–1927	
LUBLIN	A	W	1819–1866	1
GNIEWCZYNA	**PRZEMYŚL**			
PRZEWORSK	A	S	1888–1951	60/3–24, 29–60
GNIEWKOWO	**BYDGOSZCZ**			
INOWROCŁAW	A	B	1815–1847	111
INOWROCŁAW	A	D	1816–1847	111
INOWROCŁAW	A	L	1836–1920	56/362–545, 907–912
INOWROCŁAW	A	M	1825–1847	111
INOWROCŁAW	A	S	1844/1907	56
INOWROCŁAW	A	T	1836–1920	56/787–788, 1161–1234
GNIEWOSZÓW	**RADOM**			
RADOM	A	B	1826–1894	184
GNIEWOSZÓW	U	B	1898–1913; 1920; 1922–1923; 1925; 1931–1935; 1938–1939	
RADOM	A	D	1826–1894	184
GNIEWOSZÓW	U	D	1898–1913; 1920; 1922–1923; 1925; 1931–1935; 1938–1939	

A Army/recruit lists; **B** Birth; **C** Census; **D** Death; **E** Voter lists; **G** Immigration; **H** Holocaust; **J** Judaica; **K** Kahal; **L** Land; **M** Marriage; **N** Name changes; **O** Police files; **P** Pogroms; **R** Reference; **S** School records; **T** Tax lists; **V** Divorce; **W** Occupation lists; **X** Jewish hospital; **Y** Notary records; **Z** Local government records

| TOWN NAME | VOIVODSHIP (Province) | | | Zespół/Sygnatura (Poland) |
Repository Location	Repository Type	Document Code	Years	Fond/Opis/Delo (Belarus, Ukraine, Lithuania)
RADOM	A	M	1826–1894	184
GNIEWOSZÓW	U	M	1898–1913; 1920; 1922–1923; 1925; 1931–1935; 1938–1939	
GNIEZNO	**POZNAŃ**			
POZNAŃ	A	B	1823–1848	3576/1, 3–11
POZNAŃ	A	D	1840–1848	3576/2–11
WARSZAWA	J	K	1917–1918	
POZNAŃ	A	K	1926–1938	4058/1170–1175
POZNAŃ	A	M	1840–1847	3576/3–11
POZNAŃ	A	S	1819–1918	4058/600–624, 1166–1168
GOŁAŃCZ	**PIŁA**			
POZNAŃ	A	K	1834–1912	338/263–266
POZNAŃ	A	S	1865–1870	338/586
GOLENIÓW	**SZCZECIN**			
SZCZECIN	A	B	1848–1874	AMTSGERICHT GOLLNOW 158
SZCZECIN	A	D	1847–1874	AMTSGERICHT GOLLNOW 160
SZCZECIN	A	M	1847–1874	AMTSGERICHT GOLLNOW 159
GOLINA	**KONIN**			
POZNAŃ	A	B	1826–1830; 1832–1836; 1838; 1840–1846; 1848–1862; 1864; 1867–1870	3744/1–34, 36–39
POZNAŃ	A	D	1826–1830; 1832–1836; 1838; 1840–1846; 1848–1862; 1864; 1866–1870	3744/1–33
POZNAŃ	A	M	1826–1830; 1832–1836; 1838; 1840–1846; 1848–1862; 1869	3744/1–39
GOLLNOW	**SEE GOLENIÓW**			
GOLUB–DOBRZYN	**TORUŃ**			
TORUŃ	A	B	1808–1856; 1858–1876; 1878; 1881; 1885–1886; 1888–1898; 1907–1909; 1911; 1917–1918; 1922–1928; 1933	672/1
TORUŃ	A	D	1808–1874; 1876; 1878; 1881; 1885–1886; 1888–1899; 1907–1909; 1911; 1916–1917; 1922–1928; 1933; 1935–1939	672/1
TORUŃ	A	G	1830/1927; 1939–1942	96/1
TORUŃ	A	M	1808–1876; 1878; 1881; 1885–1886; 1888–1899; 1907–1909; 1911; 1919; 1922–1928	672/1
TORUŃ	A	T	1793/1919	96/1
GÓRA KALWARIA	**WARSZAWA**			
GÓRA KALWARIA	A	B	1808–1810; 1813–1816; 1818; 1820–1893	171; 127
GÓRA KALWARIA	U	B	1894–1910; 1917–1938; 1945	
GÓRA KALWARIA	A	D	1806–1810; 1813–1816; 1818; 1820–1893	171; 127
GÓRA KALWARIA	U	D	1894–1910; 1917–1938; 1945	
GÓRA KALWARIA	A	M	1808–1810; 1813–1816; 1818; 1820–1893	171; 127
GÓRA KALWARIA	U	M	1894–1910; 1917–1938; 1945	
GÓRA KALWARIA	A	Y	1808–1834; 1876–1939	92–94; 101; 116–119
GORAJ LUBELSKI	**ZAMOŚĆ**			
LUBLIN	A	K	1875–1914; 1927–1928	RGL IV ADM; UWL WSP/762, 1556
LUBLIN	A	T	1875–1914; 1927–1928	RGL IV ADM; UWL WSP/762, 1556
GORLICE	**NOWY SĄCZ**			
SKOŁYSZYN	A	A	1889–1910	3/717
GORLICE	U	B	1904–1921 (INDEX ONLY)	
SKOŁYSZYN	A	C	1922	3/1003
GORLICE	U	D	1928–1942	
SKOŁYSZYN	A	E	1900; 1907; 1914; 1922; 1924; 1927	3/25, 50, 74, 110, 123, 143, 148
PRZEMYŚL	A	E	1935	791/17
SKOŁYSZYN	A	G	1885–1886; 1893; 1898; 1900; 1905–1906; 1910	3/715, 772
SKOŁYSZYN	A	K	1902–1919	945
SKOŁYSZYN	A	L	1915; 1926–1927; 1949	3/146, 617, 895; 6/28
PRZEMYŚL	A	L	1920–1925	791/11–14
LVOV	A	L	1785–1788; 1819–1820	19/II/326; 20/II/71
GORLICE	U	M	1928–1937	
SKOŁYSZYN	A	S	1899–1913	3/64, 328
SKOŁYSZYN	A	X	1907	3/296
GORLICZYNA	**PRZEMYŚL**			
PRZEWORSK	A	S	1929–1960	82/1–16
GÓROWO IŁAWIECKIE	**OLSZTYN**			
OLSZTYN	A	B	1874–1893	692/I

Repository type: **A** = Archive **G** = LDS Films of German-Held Records **J** = Jewish Historical Institute **U** = Urząd Stanu Cywilnego

TOWN NAME	VOIVODSHIP (Province)			Zespół/Sygnatura (Poland)
Repository Location	Repository Type	Document Code	Years	Fond/Opis/Delo (Belarus, Ukraine, Lithuania)
OLSZTYN	A	D	1874–1893	692/I
OLSZTYN	A	M	1874–1893	692/I
GORZKÓW	**ZAMOŚĆ**			
LUBLIN	A	B	1826–1843; 1845–1870; 1875	113
ZAMOŚĆ	A	B	1871–1874; 1876–1890; 1892–1893	209/1–21
GORZKÓW	U	B	1894–1938	
LUBLIN	A	C	1910	ZPK/123
LUBLIN	A	D	1826–1843; 1845–1870; 1875	113
ZAMOŚĆ	A	D	1871–1874; 1876–1890; 1892–1893	209/1–21
GORZKÓW	U	D	1894–1938	
LUBLIN	A	E	1873–1913	RGL IV ADM
LUBLIN	A	K	1873–1913; 1925–1927	RGL IV ADM; UWL WSP/1559
LUBLIN	A	M	1826–1843; 1845–1870; 1875	113
ZAMOŚĆ	A	M	1871–1874; 1876–1890; 1892–1893	209/1–21
GORZKÓW	U	M	1894–1938	
LUBLIN	A	T	1866; 1873–1913; 1925–1927 (AND ALSO INCLUDED IN: KRASNYSTAW)	NPK/16; RGL IV ADM; UWL WSP/1559
GORZÓW ŚLĄSKI	**CZĘSTOCHOWA**			
CZĘSTOCHOWA	A	B	1874–1884	226
WARSZAWA	J	C	1796/1934	PROVINCE: ŚLĄSK
KOBLENZ	G	D	1843–1844	
CZĘSTOCHOWA	A	D	1874–1884	226
WARSZAWA	J	D	1934	
WARSZAWA	J	K	1796/1934	PROVINCE: ŚLĄSK
WARSZAWA	J	M	1860–1863	
CZĘSTOCHOWA	A	M	1874–1884	226
WARSZAWA	J	S	1796/1934	PROVINCE: ŚLĄSK
WARSZAWA	J	T	1796/1934	PROVINCE: ŚLĄSK
WARSZAWA	J	Y	1796/1934	PROVINCE: ŚLĄSK
WARSZAWA	J	Z	1796/1934	PROVINCE: ŚLĄSK
GORZÓW WIELKOPOLSKI	**GORZÓW WIELKOPOLSKI**			
GORZÓW WIELKOPOLSKI	A	B	1837–1865; 1870–1872	AMTSGERICHT LANDSBERG/W.28/1338–1343
GORZÓW WIELKOPOLSKI	A	D	1847–1874	AMTSGERICHT LANDSBERG/W.28/1337A–1337F
GORZÓW WIELKOPOLSKI	A	E	1927; 1935	MAGISTRAT LANDSBERG/W.30/6637
GORZÓW WIELKOPOLSKI	A	K	1656/1842	MAGISTRAT LANDSBERG/W.30/1978–2016, 6636–6648
GORZÓW WIELKOPOLSKI	A	M	1847–1870; 1872–1874	AMTSGERICHT LANDSBERG/W.28/1346–1347B
GOSTYŃ	**LESZNO**			
LESZNO	A	C	1885–1900	16
PŁOCK	A	Y	1820–1857; 1876–1939	268–271; 278–279; 281; 469–470
GOSTYNIN	**PŁOCK**			
GOSTYNIN	U	B	1917–1935	
GOSTYNIN	U	D	1927–1935	
GOSTYNIN	U	M	1920–1926	
GOSZCZYN	**RADOM**			
GÓRA KALWARIA	A	B	1808–1837	150; 35
GÓRA KALWARIA	A	C	1885–1931	61
GÓRA KALWARIA	A	D	1808–1836	150; 35
GÓRA KALWARIA	A	M	1808–1836	150; 35
GOWARCZÓW	**RADOM**			
KIELCE	A	B	1826–1859	553
RADOM	A	B	1869–1939	449
KIELCE	A	D	1826–1859	553
RADOM	A	D	1867–1894; 1920–1940	449
KIELCE	A	M	1826–1859	553
RADOM	A	M	1847–1913; 1920–1934	449
GOWOROWO	**OSTROŁĘKA**			
GOWOROWO	U	B	1917; 1920; 1922; 1924–1929; 1931–1935	
GOWOROWO	U	D	1917; 1920; 1922; 1924–1929; 1931–1935	
GOWOROWO	U	M	1917; 1920; 1922; 1924–1929; 1931–1935	
GRABÓW	**KALISZ**			
KALISZ	A	C	1946	18/30
POZNAŃ	A	K	1841–1907	333/268–270
KALISZ	A	K	1886–1912	18/31

A Army/recruit lists; **B** Birth; **C** Census; **D** Death; **E** Voter lists; **G** Immigration; **H** Holocaust; **J** Judaica; **K** Kahal; **L** Land; **M** Marriage; **N** Name changes; **O** Police files; **P** Pogroms; **R** Reference; **S** School records; **T** Tax lists; **V** Divorce; **W** Occupation lists; **X** Jewish hospital; **Y** Notary records; **Z** Local government records

TOWN NAME Repository Location	VOIVODSHIP (Province) Repository Document Type	 Code	 Years	Zespół/Sygnatura (Poland) Fond/Opis/Delo (Belarus, Ukraine, Lithuania)
GRABOWIEC	**ZAMOŚĆ**			
LUBLIN	A	B	1826–1875	113
ZAMOŚĆ	A	B	1876–1893	209/1–18
GRABOWIEC	U	B	1894–1901; 1903–1904; 1906–1908; 1911–1914; 1919–1939	
LUBLIN	A	D	1826–1875	113
ZAMOŚĆ	A	D	1876–1893	209/1–18
GRABOWIEC	U	D	1894–1901; 1903–1904; 1906–1908; 1911–1914; 1917–1939	
LUBLIN	A	K	1867–1912; 1921–1935	RGL IV ADM.; UWL WSP/780
LUBLIN	A	M	1826–1875	113
ZAMOŚĆ	A	M	1876–1893	209/1–18
GRABOWIEC	U	M	1894–1901; 1903–1904; 1906–1908; 1911–1914; 1919–1939	
LUBLIN	A	T	1867–1912; 1921–1935	RGL IV ADM.; UWL WSP/780
GRAJEWO	**ŁOMŻA**			
ŁOMŻA	A	B	1832–1894	269
GRAJEWO	U	B	1895–1900; 1918–1923; 1925–1926; 1928–1931; 1933	
ŁOMŻA	A	D	1832–1894	269
GRAJEWO	U	D	1895–1900; 1918–1923; 1925; 1928–1931; 1933	
BIAŁYSTOK	A	K	1911	6/167
ŁOMŻA	A	M	1832–1894	269
GRAJEWO	U	M	1895–1900; 1918–1923; 1925–1926; 1928–1931; 1933	
WARSZAWA	A	T	1823–1833	KRSW 4842
EŁK	A	Y	1902–1914; 1919–1939	63–64, 140, 185
GRAUDENZ	**SEE GRUDZIĄDZ**			
GREIFENBERG	**SEE GRYFICE**			
GREIFENHAGEN	**SEE GRYFINO**			
GROCHOLICE	**PIOTRKÓW TRYBUNALSKI**			
ŁÓDŹ	A	B	1826–1869	270
ŁÓDŹ	A	D	1826–1869	270
ŁÓDŹ	A	M	1826–1869	270
GRODKÓW	**OPOLE**			
OPOLE	A	B	1797/1874	11
OPOLE	A	C	1759/1933	
OPOLE	A	D	1815–1874	11
WARSZAWA	J	E	1880/1936	PROVINCE: ŚLĄSK
OPOLE	A	G	1842/1938	2; 11
WARSZAWA	J	K	1880/1936	PROVINCE: ŚLĄSK
OPOLE	A	M	1815/1927	11
OPOLE	A	T	1778/1942	
GRODZISK MAZOWIECKI	**WARSZAWA**			
ŻYRARDÓW	A	B	1826–1882	280
GRODZISK MAZOWIECKI	U	B	1883–1940	
ŻYRARDÓW	A	D	1826–1882	280
GRODZISK MAZOWIECKI	U	D	1883–1940	
ŻYRARDÓW	A	M	1826–1882	280
GRODZISK MAZOWIECKI	U	M	1883–1939	
GRODZISK WIELKOPOLSKI	**POZNAŃ**			
POZNAŃ	A	C	1797/1939	63, 652
BERLIN	G	D	1817–1837	
GRODZISKO DOLNE	**RZESZÓW**			
RZESZÓW	A	C	1936	248/43–55, 58
LVOV	A	L	1785–1788; 1819–1820	19/V/27; 20/V/36
GROJEC	**RADOM**			
GÓRA KALWARIA	A	B	1808–1811; 1813–1875	151; 36
RADOM	A	B	1876–1941	510/1
GÓRA KALWARIA	A	C	1870–1931	87
GÓRA KALWARIA	A	D	1808–1811; 1813–1875	151; 36
RADOM	A	D	1876–1941	510/1
GÓRA KALWARIA	A	M	1808–1811; 1813–1875	151; 36
RADOM	A	M	1876–1941	510/1
GROSS STREHLITZ	**SEE STRZELCE OPOLSKIE**			
GROSS WARTENBERG	**SEE SYCÓW**			

Repository type: **A** = Archive   **G** = LDS Films of German-Held Records   **J** = Jewish Historical Institute   **U** = Urząd Stanu Cywilnego

TOWN NAME	VOIVODSHIP (Province)				Zespół/Sygnatura (Poland)
Repository Location	Repository Document Type	Code	Years		Fond/Opis/Delo (Belarus, Ukraine, Lithuania)
GROTTKAU	**SEE GRODKÓW**				
GRUDZIĄDZ	**TORUŃ**				
TORUŃ	A	B	1834–1874		616/1
TORUŃ	A	D	1837–1846; 1860–1874		616/1
WARSZAWA	J	K	1847		114
TORUŃ	A	M	1837–1874		616/1
GRUENBERG	**SEE ZIELONA GÓRA**				
GRYBÓW	**NOWY SĄCZ**				
GRYBÓW	U	B	1878–1881; 1883–1885; 1888–1889		
NOWY SĄCZ	A	C	1928–1936 (LISTING OF ORPHANS); 1884; 1891; 1897; 1910; 1922; 1927–1928; 1930; 1935; 1938–1939		158; 12–15; 17–18
GRYBÓW	U	D	1878–1881; 1883–1885; 1888–1889		
NOWY SĄCZ	A	E	1891–1939		17
NOWY SĄCZ	A	K	1901; 1906–1916		111; 154
LVOV	A	L	1785–1788; 1819–1820		19/IV/213; 20/IV/29
GRYBÓW	U	M	1878–1881; 1883–1885; 1888–1889		
NOWY SĄCZ	A	Z	1878–1931		169
GRYFICE	**SZCZECIN**				
LEIPZIG	G	B	1815–1874		
LEIPZIG	G	D	1815–1874		
SZCZECIN	A	K	1831–1852		REGIERUNG STETTIN I/10734
LEIPZIG	G	M	1815–1874		
GRYFINO	**SZCZECIN**				
SZCZECIN	A	K	1826–1854		REGIERUNG STETTIN I/10735
GRZEGÓRZKI	**KRAKÓW**				
KRAKÓW	U	B	1890–1942		
KRAKÓW	U	D	1890–1942; 1945		
KRAKÓW	U	M	1889–1945		
GUBIN	**ZIELONA GÓRA**				
WILKOWO	A	L	1828/1943		39
GUTTENTAG	**SEE DOBRODZIEŃ**				
GUTTSTADT	**SEE DOBRE MIASTO**				
HADLE KAŃCZUCKIE	**PRZEMYŚL**				
PRZEWORSK	A	S	1910–1957		79/2–10, 12–41
HADLE SZKLARSKIE	**PRZEMYŚL**				
PRZEWORSK	A	S	1916–1957		61/1, 3–19, 22–31
HAYNAU	**SEE CHOJNÓW**				
HEILSBERG	**SEE LIDZBARK WARMIŃSKI**				
HINDENBURG	**SEE ZABRZE**				
HIRSCHBERG	**SEE JELENIA GÓRA**				
HOHENSTEIN	**SEE OLSZTYNEK**				
HORODŁO	**ZAMOŚĆ**				
LUBLIN	A	B	1826–1854		113
ZAMOŚĆ	A	B	1880–1890		209/1–2; 2A–2C; 3–4; 4A; 5–7
HORODŁO	U	B	1891–1896; 1898–1908; 1910–1911; 1923–1936		
LUBLIN	A	D	1826–1854		113
ZAMOŚĆ	A	D	1880–1890		209/1–2; 2A–2C; 3–4; 4A; 5–7
HORODŁO	U	D	1891–1896; 1898–1908; 1910; 1923–1924; 1926; 1928; 1930–1932; 1936		
LUBLIN	A	K	1867–1912; 1916–1917; 1927		RGL IV; RGCH/654; UWL WSP/781
LUBLIN	A	L	1742; 1744		33
LUBLIN	A	M	1826–1854		113
ZAMOŚĆ	A	M	1880–1890		209/1–2; 2A–2C; 3–4; 4A; 5–7
HORODŁO	U	M	1891–1896; 1898–1908; 1910–1911; 1923–1928; 1930–1932; 1936		
LUBLIN	A	T	1867–1912; 1916–1917; 1927		RGL IV; RGCH/654; UWL WSP/781
LUBLIN	A	Z	1600/1809		33
HRUBIESZÓW	**ZAMOŚĆ**				
LUBLIN	A	B	1826–1875		113
ZAMOŚĆ	A	B	1870; 1875–1885; 1887–1893		209/00; 0; 0A; 1; 1A; 2–6; 6A; 7–20
HRUBIESZÓW	U	B	1894–1930; 1934–1942		
LUBLIN	A	D	1826–1875		113
ZAMOŚĆ	A	D	1870; 1875–1884; 1887–1893		209/00; 0; 0A; 1; 1A; 2–6; 6A; 7–20
HRUBIESZÓW	U	D	1894–1912; 1914–1918; 1920–1927; 1930–1942		

A Army/recruit lists; **B** Birth; **C** Census; **D** Death; **E** Voter lists; **G** Immigration; **H** Holocaust; **J** Judaica; **K** Kahal; **L** Land; **M** Marriage; **N** Name changes; **O** Police files; **P** Pogroms; **R** Reference; **S** School records; **T** Tax lists; **V** Divorce; **W** Occupation lists; **X** Jewish hospital; **Y** Notary records; **Z** Local government records

TOWN NAME	VOIVODSHIP (Province)			Zespół/Sygnatura (Poland)
Repository Location	Repository Type	Document Code	Years	Fond/Opis/Delo (Belarus, Ukraine, Lithuania)
LUBLIN	A	E	1870–1909	RGL IV ADM.
LUBLIN	A	K	1870–1909; 1921–1936	RGL IV; 403/778–782; 405/511
LUBLIN	A	M	1826–1875	113
ZAMOŚĆ	A	M	1870; 1875–1884; 1887–1893	209/00; 0; 0A; 1; 1A; 2–6; 6A; 7–20
HRUBIESZÓW	U	M	1894–1913; 1919–1927; 1930–1942; 1945	
LUBLIN	A	T	1870–1909; 1927–1936	RGL IV; UWL WSP/778; SPH/511
HUCISKO NIENADOWSKIE	**PRZEMYŚL**			
PRZEMYŚL	A	C	1931–1939	200/30–31
IŁAWA	**OLSZTYN**			
BERLIN	G	B	1847–1875	
OLSZTYN	A	B	1874–1894	311/I
BERLIN	G	D	1847–1875	
OLSZTYN	A	D	1874–1894	311/I
BERLIN	G	M	1847–1875	
OLSZTYN	A	M	1874–1894	311/I
IŁŻA	**RADOM**			
STARACHOWICE	A	B	1850–1875	48
RADOM	A	B	1876–1894	443/1
IŁŻA	U	B	1895–1942	
STARACHOWICE	A	D	1850–1875	48
RADOM	A	D	1876–1894	443/1
IŁŻA	U	D	1895–1942	
STARACHOWICE	A	M	1850–1875	48
RADOM	A	M	1876–1894	443/1
IŁŻA	U	M	1895–1942	
IMIELIN	**KATOWICE**			
PSZCZYNA	A	B	1847–1874	67/I/2
PSZCZYNA	A	D	1848–1874	67/I/5
PSZCZYNA	A	M	1848–1873	67/I/3
INOWŁÓDŻ	**PIOTRKÓW TRYBUNALSKI**			
TOMASZÓW MAZOWIECKI	A	B	1811; 1826; 1828; 1830; 1832–1838; 1841–1849; 1852; 1854–1857	244
TOMASZÓW MAZOWIECKI	A	D	1811; 1826; 1828; 1830; 1832–1838; 1841–1849; 1852; 1854–1857	244
TOMASZÓW MAZOWIECKI	A	M	1811; 1826; 1828; 1830; 1832–1838; 1842–1849; 1852; 1854–1857	244
ŁÓDŻ	A	Z	1825–1866; 1900–1913	1
INOWROCŁAW	**BYDGOSZCZ**			
INOWROCŁAW	A	C	19TH CENTURY–1950	57
INOWROCŁAW	A	K	1938	2
INOWROCŁAW	A	Y	1834–1868	1
IŃSKO	**SZCZECIN**			
SZCZECIN	A	K	1821–1852	REGIERUNG STETTIN I/10736
IRENA	**LUBLIN**			
LUBLIN	A	B	1869–1891	113
LUBLIN	A	D	1869–1891	113
LUBLIN	A	E	1860–1864; 1868–1911	POL. RGL/1716; RGL ADM.
LUBLIN	A	K	1860–1864; 1868–1911; 1922–1927	POL. RGL/1716; RGL IV; UWL WSP/812
LUBLIN	A	M	1869–1891	113
LUBLIN	A	T	1860–1864; 1868–1911; 1922–1927	POL. RGL/1716; RGL IV; UWL WSP/812
ISKAŃ	**PRZEMYŚL**			
PRZEMYŚL	A	C	1931–1939; 1947	200/33–36
IWANOWICE	**KALISZ**			
KALISZ	A	C	1872; 1874–1931	1/942–944; 53/241–244
KALISZ	A	E	1907; 1909	321/18–19, 21
KALISZ	A	W	1831–1865	1/92
IZBICA	**ZAMOŚĆ**			
LUBLIN	A	B	1826–1872; 1875	113
ZAMOŚĆ	A	B	1873–1874; 1876–1893	209/1–20
IZBICA	U	B	1894–1940	
LUBLIN	A	C	1910	ZPK/124
LUBLIN	A	D	1826–1861; 1863–1864	113
ZAMOŚĆ	A	D	1862; 1876–1893	209/1–20
IZBICA	U	D	1894–1940	
LUBLIN	A	E	1873–1915	RGL IV ADM.
LUBLIN	A	G	1859	22/51
LUBLIN	A	K	1873–1915; 1927	RGL IV ADM; UWL WSP/789

Repository type: **A** = Archive   **G** = LDS Films of German-Held Records   **J** = Jewish Historical Institute   **U** = Urząd Stanu Cywilnego

TOWN NAME	VOIVODSHIP (Province)			Zespół/Sygnatura (Poland) Fond/Opis/Delo (Belarus, Ukraine, Lithuania)
Repository Location	Repository Document Type	Code	Years	
LUBLIN	A	M	1826–1864	113
ZAMOŚĆ	A	M	1873–1874; 1876–1893	209/1–20
IZBICA	U	M	1894–1940	
IZBICA KUJAWSKA	**WŁOCŁAWEK**			
POZNAŃ	A	B	1810–1811; 1819–1821; 1860–1865; 1882–1883; 1914–1916; 1919	3745/1, 3, 5, 8, 11–54
WŁOCŁAWEK	A	B	1866–1881; 1884; 1886–1893	563
IZBICA KUJAWSKA	U	B	1894–1909; 1912–1913; 1920–1938	
WARSZAWA	J	C	1919/1939	105
POZNAŃ	A	D	1810–1811; 1817; 1819–1821; 1860–1861; 1882–1883; 1914–1916; 1919	3745/1, 4, 7, 10–54
WŁOCŁAWEK	A	D	1866–1881; 1884; 1886–1893	563
IZBICA KUJAWSKA	U	D	1894–1909; 1912–1913; 1920–1938	
WARSZAWA	J	E	1919/1939	105
WARSZAWA	J	K	1919/1939	105
POZNAŃ	A	M	1810–1811; 1819–1821; 1858; 1860–1865; 1882–1883; 1914–1916; 1919	3745/2, 6, 9, 11–54
WŁOCŁAWEK	A	M	1866–1881; 1884; 1886–1893	563
IZBICA KUJAWSKA	U	M	1894–1909; 1912–1913; 1920–1938	
JABŁONKA	**ŁOMŻA**			
ŁOMŻA	A	B	1827; 1834–1836; 1844; 1846–1849; 1852; 1857; 1859–1861; 1863–1866; 1869; 1871	176
JABŁONKA	U	B	1909–1910	
ŁOMŻA	A	D	1826–1857; 1859–1861; 1863–1866; 1869; 1871	176
JABŁONKA	U	D	1909–1910	
ŁOMŻA	A	M	1827; 1834–1836; 1844; 1846–1849; 1852; 1857; 1859–1861; 1863–1866; 1869; 1871	176
JABŁONKA	U	M	1909–1910	
JAĆMIERZ	**KROSNO**			
SANOK	A	C	1931–1945	21/71–73, 82–83
JAGIEŁŁA	**PRZEMYŚL**			
PRZEWORSK	A	S	1893–1935	62/2–3
JAMNICA KUNÓW	**INCLUDED IN NOWY SĄCZ**			
JANÓW	**CZĘSTOCHOWA**			
CZĘSTOCHOWA	A	B	1863–1895	309
JANÓW	U	B	1896–1908; 1910–1913; 1918–1941	
CZĘSTOCHOWA	A	C	1914	67
CZĘSTOCHOWA	A	D	1880–1895	309
JANÓW	U	D	1896–1908; 1910–1913; 1918–1941	
CZĘSTOCHOWA	A	M	1880–1895	309
JANÓW	U	M	1896–1908; 1910–1913; 1918–1941	
ŁÓDŹ	A	Z	1849–1866; 1893–1913	1
JANÓW LUBELSKI	**TARNOBRZEG**			
SANDOMIERZ	A	B	1883–1887	510
JANÓW LUBELSKI	U	B	1888–1941	
LUBLIN	A	C	1900–1942	TOWN ACTS (SEE KRAŚNIK)
JANÓW LUBELSKI	U	D	1892–1941	
LUBLIN	A	E	1870–1914	RGL IV ADM.
LUBLIN	A	K	1870–1914; 1924–1935	RGL IV ADM.; SPJ/13
JANÓW LUBELSKI	U	M	1885–1902; 1917–1934; 1937–1939; 1941	
JANÓW PODLASKI	**BIAŁA PODLASKA**			
LUBLIN	A	B	1826–1892	113
JANÓW PODLASKI	U	B	1893–1906; 1922–1941	
LUBLIN	A	D	1826–1892	113
JANÓW PODLASKI	U	D	1893–1906; 1922–1941	
LUBLIN	A	K	1927	UWL WSP/793
LUBLIN	A	M	1826–1892	113
JANÓW PODLASKI	U	M	1893–1906; 1922–1941	
JANOWIEC	**LUBLIN**			
LUBLIN	A	B	1817–1894	113
JANOWIEC	U	B	1895–1907; 1909–1911; 1923–1925; 1927–1933; 1935–1938	
LUBLIN	A	C	1774	22/299A
LUBLIN	A	D	1817–1894	113
JANOWIEC	U	D	1895–1907; 1909–1911; 1923–1925; 1927–1933; 1935–1938	
LUBLIN	A	M	1817–1894	113

A Army/recruit lists; **B** Birth; **C** Census; **D** Death; **E** Voter lists; **G** Immigration; **H** Holocaust; **J** Judaica; **K** Kahal; **L** Land; **M** Marriage; **N** Name changes; **O** Police files; **P** Pogroms; **R** Reference; **S** School records; **T** Tax lists; **V** Divorce; **W** Occupation lists; **X** Jewish hospital; **Y** Notary records; **Z** Local government records

| TOWN NAME | VOIVODSHIP (Province) | | | Zespół/Sygnatura (Poland) |
Repository Location	Repository Document Type Code		Years	Fond/Opis/Delo (Belarus, Ukraine, Lithuania)
JANOWIEC	U	M	1895–1907; 1909–1911; 1923–1925; 1927–1933; 1935–1938	
JANOWO	**OLSZTYN**			
OLSZTYN	A	B	1810/1912	635/I
OLSZTYN	A	D	1810/1912	635/I
OLSZTYN	A	M	1810/1912	635/I
JARCZÓW	**ZAMOŚĆ**			
LUBLIN	A	B	1826–1875	113
ZAMOŚĆ	A	B	1876–1892	209/1–17
JARCZÓW	U	B	1893–1913; 1926; 1929–1935; 1937–1939	
LUBLIN	A	D	1826–1875	113
ZAMOŚĆ	A	D	1876–1892	209/1–17
JARCZÓW	U	D	1893–1913; 1926; 1929–1935; 1937–1939	
LUBLIN	A	K	1892–1913	RGL IV ADM
LUBLIN	A	M	1826–1875	113
ZAMOŚĆ	A	M	1876–1892	209/1–17
JARCZÓW	U	M	1893–1913; 1926; 1929–1935; 1937–1939	
JAROCIN	**KALISZ**			
BERLIN	G	D	1810–1879	
BERLIN	G	M	1810–1879	
PRZEWORSK	A	G	1945	14/35–36, 39
PRZEWORSK	A	T	1943–1954	14/6–10, 54–75
JAROSŁAW	**PRZEMYŚL**			
PRZEMYŚL	A	B	1867–1918	154/1
JAROSŁAW	U	B	1879–1938 (INDEX ONLY: 1879; 1927)	
PRZEMYŚL	A	C	1939–1940	174/52
PRZEMYŚL	A	D	1865–1908	154/1–2
JAROSŁAW	U	D	1890–1938 (INDEX ONLY: 1904)	
JARCZÓW	U	M	1893–1913; 1926; 1929–1935; 1937–1939	
LUBLIN	A	T	1892–1913	RGL IV ADM
JAROCIN	**KALISZ**			
BERLIN	G	D	1810–1879	
BERLIN	G	M	1810–1879	
PRZEWORSK	A	G	1945	14/35–36, 39
PRZEWORSK	A	T	1943–1954	14/6–10, 54–75
JAROSŁAW	**PRZEMYŚL**			
PRZEMYŚL	A	B	1867–1918	154/1
JAROSŁAW	U	B	1879–1938 (INDEX ONLY: 1879; 1927)	
PRZEMYŚL	A	C	1939–1940	174/52
PRZEMYŚL	A	D	1865–1908	154/1–2
JAROSŁAW	U	D	1890–1938 (INDEX ONLY: 1904)	
PRZEMYŚL	A	G	1940–1941	174/150
PRZEMYŚL	A	H	1944–1945; 1947–1949	431/124; 29/147, 156
PRZEMYŚL	A	L	1944; 1946	431/107
LVOV	A	L	1785–1788; 1792–1793; 1819–1820	19/XIII/48; 166/1/2277–2327; 20/XIII/316
PRZEMYŚL	A	M	1877	154/1
JAROSŁAW	U	M	1878–1938 (INDEX ONLY: 1910)	
PRZEMYŚL	A	Y	1899; 1934–1950	81; 999–1007
JAROSŁAW REGION	**PRZEMYŚL**			
PRZEMYŚL	A	C	1932–1944	172–182/153–171
JAROSŁAWIEC	**ZAMOŚĆ**			
LUBLIN	A	B	1874–1875	113
ZAMOŚĆ	A	B	1881–1886; 1889; 1891–1893	209/1–10
LUBLIN	A	D	1874–1875	113
ZAMOŚĆ	A	D	1881–1886; 1889; 1891–1893	209/1–10
LUBLIN	A	M	1874–1875	113
ZAMOŚĆ	A	M	1881–1886; 1889; 1891–1893	209/1–10
JASIENICA ROSIELNA	**KROSNO**			
JASIENICA ROSIELNA	U	B	1939–1941	
JASIENICA ROSIELNA	U	D	1939–1941	
PRZEMYŚL	A	K	1872; 1901; 1913	843/5
LVOV	A	L	1785–1788; 1819–1820	19/15/242; 20/15/306
JASIENICA ROSIELNA	U	M	1939–1941	
JASIONÓWKA	**BIAŁYSTOK**			
JASIONÓWKA	U	B	1883–1884; 1886–1914	
JASIONÓWKA	U	D	1882–1883; 1885; 1887–1890; 1899; 1902; 1905–1914	

Repository type: **A** = Archive **G** = LDS Films of German-Held Records **J** = Jewish Historical Institute **U** = Urząd Stanu Cywilnego

TOWN NAME Repository Location	VOIVODSHIP (Province) Repository Document Type	Code	Years	Zespół/Sygnatura (Poland) Fond/Opis/Delo (Belarus, Ukraine, Lithuania)
JASIONÓWKA	U	M	1882–1884; 1888; 1890; 1892; 1894–1895; 1898–1905; 1907; 1909; 1912–1914	
JASŁO	**KROSNO**			
PRZEMYŚL	A	A	1915–1918	678/7–16
JASŁO	U	B	1890–1937	
SKOŁYSZYN	A	C	1946	7/103, 123
JASŁO	U	D	1890–1936	
PRZEMYŚL	A	E	1920/1927	790/15–17
SKOŁYSZYN	A	H	1945–1946; 1949	7/97
PRZEMYŚL	A	K	1915/1927	790/64–67
WARSZAWA	J	K	1940–1943	212
LVOV	A	L	1785–1788; 1819–1820	19/II/335; 20/II/342
JASŁO	U	M	1890–1937	
JASŁO REGION	**KROSNO**			
PRZEMYŚL	A	C	1926	790/69
JASTRÓW	**SEE JASTROWIE**			
JASTROWIE	**PIŁA**			
KOBLENZ	G	B	1816–1847	
KOBLENZ	G	D	1816–1847	
KOBLENZ	G	M	1816–1847	
JASTROWO	**SEE JASTROWIE**			
JAUER	**SEE JAWOR**			
JAWOR	**LEGNICA**			
KOBLENZ	G	B	1815–1863	
KOBLENZ	G	D	1815–1863	
LEGNICA	A	K	1752/1936	2/9–14
KOBLENZ	G	M	1815–1863	
KOBLENZ	G	N	1819	
JĘDRZEJÓW	**KIELCE**			
JĘDRZEJÓW	A	B	1875–1893	333
JĘDRZEJÓW	U	B	1894–1941	
JĘDRZEJÓW	A	C	1886–1943	6
JĘDRZEJÓW	A	D	1876–1892	333
JĘDRZEJÓW	U	D	1893–1928; 1931–1941	
WARSZAWA	J	K	1940–1943	212
JĘDRZEJÓW	A	L	1940–1941	6
JĘDRZEJÓW	A	M	1875–1893	333
JĘDRZEJÓW	U	M	1894–1928; 1931–1941	
JĘDRZEJÓW	A	T	1941–1944	6
JELENIA GÓRA	**JELENIA GÓRA**			
JELENIA GÓRA	A	B	1820–1831	3/I/3070
JELENIA GÓRA	A	C	1820–1869	3/I/228
JELENIA GÓRA	A	D	1820–1831	3/I/3070
JELENIA GÓRA	A	E	1869–1936	3/I/7745–7749
JELENIA GÓRA	A	K	1886–1909 (CEMETERY RECORDS)	3/I/7742
JELENIA GÓRA	A	M	1820–1831	3/I/3070
JELENIEWO	**SUWAŁKI**			
SUWAŁKI	A	B	1808–1893	152; 204
JELENIEWO	U	B	1922–1923	
SUWAŁKI	A	D	1808–1893	152; 204
JELENIEWO	U	D	1922–1923	
SUWAŁKI	A	K	1925–1926	31/144
SUWAŁKI	A	M	1808–1893	152; 204
JELENIEWO	U	M	1922–1923	
JEZIORZANY	**LUBLIN**			
JEZIORZANY	U	B	1882–1920; 1929–1936	
JEZIORZANY	U	D	1882–1906; 1919–1925; 1938	
JEZIORZANY	U	M	1882–1910; 1929–1938	
JEŻÓW	**SKIERNIEWICE**			
ŁÓDŹ	A	B	1826–1889	270
TOMASZÓW MAZOWIECKI	A	B	1826–1838; 1845–1865; 1888–1889	244
JEŻÓW	U	B	1890–1941	
ŁÓDŹ	A	D	1826–1889	270
TOMASZÓW MAZOWIECKI	A	D	1828–1837; 1839–1844; 1888–1889	244
JEŻÓW	U	D	1890–1939	
ŁÓDŹ	A	M	1826–1889	270

A Army/recruit lists; **B** Birth; **C** Census; **D** Death; **E** Voter lists; **G** Immigration; **H** Holocaust; **J** Judaica; **K** Kahal; **L** Land; **M** Marriage; **N** Name changes; **O** Police files; **P** Pogroms; **R** Reference; **S** School records; **T** Tax lists; **V** Divorce; **W** Occupation lists; **X** Jewish hospital; **Y** Notary records; **Z** Local government records

TOWN NAME	VOIVODSHIP (Province)			Zespół/Sygnatura (Poland)
Repository Location	Repository Type	Document Code	Years	Fond/Opis/Delo (Belarus, Ukraine, Lithuania)
TOMASZÓW MAZOWIECKI	A	M	1826–1836; 1845–1884; 1888–1889	244
JEŻÓW	U	M	1890–1941	
ŁÓDŹ	A	Z	1879–1912	1
JEŻOWE	**TARNOBRZEG**			
PRZEWORSK	A	C	1946–1947; 1950–1951	15/35–46
PRZEWORSK	A	G	1945–1948	15/34
PRZEWORSK	A	T	1935–1953	15/5–7, 71–123
JOHANNISBURG	**SEE PISZ**			
JORDANÓW	**NOWY SĄCZ**			
ŻYWIEC	A	G	1888–1896; 1934–1938	27/120–121
LVOV	L	A	1785–1788; 1819–1820; 1853–1896	12/VIII/183; 20/VIII/248; 186/1/4007–4010
ŻYWIEC	A	Z	1806; 1825; 1872–1876; 1939; 1942–1943; 1945–1946	27/10–11, 119–220, 226, 237, 262, 273
JÓZEFÓW	**ZAMOŚĆ**			
LUBLIN	A	B	1826–1875	113
ZAMOŚĆ	A	B	1876–1882; 1884–1885; 1887–1893	209/1–16
JÓZEFÓW	U	B	1894–1914; 1919–1925; 1927–1938	
LUBLIN	A	D	1826–1875	113
ZAMOŚĆ	A	D	1876–1877; 1879; 1881–1882; 1884–1885; 1887–1893	209/1–2, 4, 6–16
JÓZEFÓW	U	D	1894–1914; 1919–1925; 1927–1938	
LUBLIN	A	K	1867–1914; 1922–1927	RGL ADM; UWL WSP/763
LUBLIN	A	M	1826–1875	113
ZAMOŚĆ	A	M	1876; 1881–1882; 1884–1885; 1887–1890; 1892–1893	209/1, 6–13; 15–16
JÓZEFÓW	U	M	1894–1914; 1919–1925; 1927–1938	
JÓZEFÓW NAD WISLĄ	**LUBLIN**			
LUBLIN	A	B	1826–1895	113
LUBLIN	A	D	1826–1893	113
LUBLIN	A	K	1872–1914; 1927	RGL IV ADM; UWL WSP/813
LUBLIN	A	M	1826–1893	113
LUBLIN	A	T	1872–1914; 1927	RGL IV ADM; UWL WSP/813
JUTROSIN	**LESZNO**			
LESZNO	A	B	1820–1885	17
BERLIN	G	D	1817–1843	
LESZNO	A	D	1820–1885	17
POZNAŃ	A	K	1860–1917; 1929–1933; 1937	331/142–143; 4310/838–839
LESZNO	A	M	1820–1885	17
POZNAŃ	A	S	1889–1911	4310/240–244
KALISZ	**KALISZ**			
KALISZ	A	A	1836–1856	610/37–85
POZNAŃ	A	B	1809–1874	3746/1–3, 6, 8–21, 24, 27–36, 39–73
KALISZ	A	B	1875–1894; 1922–1923	693/74–93; 3/223
KALISZ	U	B	1895–1913; 1915–1940	
KALISZ	A	C	1872; 1919	1/945–948; 11/114
POZNAŃ	A	D	1809–1874	3746/2, 5, 7–20, 23, 26–35, 38–73
KALISZ	A	D	1875–1894; 1922–1923	693/74–93; 3/223
KALISZ	U	D	1895–1913; 1915–1940; 1945	
KALISZ	A	E	1907; 1909	321/18–19, 21
KALISZ	A	G	1836–1856; 1909; 1923–1951	610/37–85; 645/1/19
ŁÓDŹ	A	G	1881/1914; 1923–1957	19; 92
KALISZ	A	K	1843–1851 (CIRCUMCISIONS, MARRIAGES, FUNERALS)	1/457
KALISZ	A	L	1852–1863; 1886–1954	1/427, 433, 672, 866; 3/222; 203
POZNAŃ	A	M	1809–1874	3746/2, 4, 8–20, 22, 25, 27–35, 37, 39–73
KALISZ	A	M	1875–1894; 1922–1923	693/74–93; 3/223
KALISZ	U	M	1895–1913; 1916–1939; 1945	
KALISZ	A	N	1833–1846	1/74
ŁÓDŹ	A	O	1881/1914	114–115
KALISZ	A	S	1863–1864; 1934	1/473; 3/216
ŁÓDŹ	A	S	1894–1914	122
POZNAŃ	A	S	1937–1939	805/145–150
KALISZ	A	W	1846–1852; 1863–1866; 1892–1893	1/335, 428, 434, 605, 627, 647, 900
ŁÓDŹ	A	X	1822/1914	111
KALISZ	A	Y	1808–1951	94–139; 413–432
KALISZ	A	Z	1832–1862 (RELIGION CONVERSIONS); 1865 (LIST OF RABBIS)	1/125, 139, 214, 689, 821
ŁÓDŹ	A	Z	1871–1914	92

Repository type: **A** = Archive   **G** = LDS Films of German-Held Records   **J** = Jewish Historical Institute   **U** = Urząd Stanu Cywilnego

TOWN NAME Repository Location	VOIVODSHIP (Province) Repository Document Type Code		Years	Zespół/Sygnatura (Poland) Fond/Opis/Delo (Belarus, Ukraine, Lithuania)
KALISZ POMORSKI	**KOSZALIN**			
BERLIN	G	B	1778–1874	
BERLIN	G	D	1778–1874	
SZCZECIN	A	K	1856–1898	GMINY ZYDOWSKIE Z POMORZA ZACHODNIEGO 55–56
BERLIN	G	M	1778–1874	
KALISZ REGION	**KALISZ**			
KALISZ	A	W	1855–1865	1/901
KALLIES	**SEE KALISZ POMORSKI**			
KAŁUSZYN	**SIEDLCE**			
SIEDLCE	A	B	1826–1881; 1883; 1885–1888; 1890–1891	473/1–67
KAŁUSZYN	U	B	1892–1945	
SIEDLCE	A	D	1826–1881; 1883; 1885–1888; 1890–1891	473
KAŁUSZYN	U	D	1892–1945	
SIEDLCE	A	M	1826–1881; 1883; 1885–1888; 1890–1891	473
KAŁUSZYN	U	M	1892–1945	
KAMIEŃ	**RZESZÓW**			
PRZEWORSK	A	A	1944; 1947–1948	16/86
PRZEWORSK	A	C	1935–1948	16/1–9, 84
PRZEWORSK	A	E	1954	16/55, 83
PRZEWORSK	A	G	1944; 1953–1954	16/81
KAMIEŃ POMORSKI	**SZCZECIN**			
LEIPZIG	G	B	1778–1874	
LEIPZIG	G	D	1778–1874	
LEIPZIG	G	M	1778–1874	
KAMIENNA GORA	**JELENIA GÓRA**			
JELENIA GÓRA	A	B	1848–1888	94/I/193
KOBLENZ	G	C	1839–1842	
KOBLENZ	G	D	1881–1938	
KOBLENZ	G	G	1812–1848	
JELENIA GÓRA	A	K	1846–1887	7/I/1143
WARSZAWA	J	K	1908/1939	PROVINCE: ŚLĄSK
JELENIA GÓRA	A	M	1827–1874	7/I/1549
WARSZAWA	J	W	1908/1939	PROVINCE: ŚLĄSK
KAMIEŃSK	**PIOTRKÓW TRYBUNALSKI**			
ŁÓDŹ	A	B	1826–1830; 1832–1857	270
PIOTRKÓW TRYBUNALSKI	A	B	1849–1893	331/6–9, 11–43
ŁÓDŹ	A	D	1826–1830; 1832–1857	270
PIOTRKÓW TRYBUNALSKI	A	D	1832–1840; 1848–1893	331/1–5, 11–43
ŁÓDŹ	A	M	1826–1830; 1832–1857	270
PIOTRKÓW TRYBUNALSKI	A	M	1860–1893	331/10–43
ŁÓDŹ	A	Z	1821–1866; 1900–1912	1
KAMIONKA	**LUBLIN**			
LUBLIN	A	B	1826–1894	113
KAMIONKA	U	B	1895–1934	
LUBLIN	A	D	1826–1894	113
KAMIONKA	U	D	1895–1934	
LUBLIN	A	E	1867–1914	RGL IV ADM.
LUBLIN	A	K	1867–1914; 1922–1927	RGL IV ADM; UWL WSP/797
LUBLIN	A	M	1826–1894	113
KAMIONKA	U	M	1895–1934	
KAŃCZUGA	**PRZEMYŚL**			
KAŃCZUGA	U	B	1937–1941	
PRZEMYŚL	A	C	1931–1944	133/23–24
KAŃCZUGA	U	D	1937–1940	
LVOV	A	L	1785–1788; 1819–1820	19/V/127; 20/V/61
KAŃCZUGA	U	M	1937–1939	
KRAKÓW	A	Z	1874–1936	526/UMI KM1; IT 2149
KANTH	**SEE KĄTY WROCŁAWSKIE**			
KARCZEW	**WARSZAWA**			
OTWOCK	A	B	1826–1892	42
KARCZEW	U	B	1893–1935	
OTWOCK	A	D	1826–1892	42
KARCZEW	U	D	1893–1911	
OTWOCK	A	M	1826–1892	42
KARCZEW	U	M	1893–1939	

A Army/recruit lists; **B** Birth; **C** Census; **D** Death; **E** Voter lists; **G** Immigration; **H** Holocaust; **J** Judaica; **K** Kahal; **L** Land; **M** Marriage; **N** Name changes;
O Police files; **P** Pogroms; **R** Reference; **S** School records; **T** Tax lists; **V** Divorce; **W** Occupation lists; **X** Jewish hospital; **Y** Notary records; **Z** Local government records

TOWN NAME	VOIVODSHIP (Province)			Zespół/Sygnatura (Poland)
Repository Location	Repository Type	Document Code	Years	Fond/Opis/Delo (Belarus, Ukraine, Lithuania)
KARGE	**SEE KARGOWA**			
KARGOWA	**ZIELONA GÓRA**			
KOBLENZ	G	B	1817–1874	
KOBLENZ	G	C	1824/1945	
KOBLENZ	G	D	1840–1848	134
WARSZAWA	J	K	1834/1891	PROVINCE: POZNAŃ
POZNAŃ	A	K	1857–1907	314/1048, 1058, 1060
WILKOWO	A	L	1847–1943	185
BERLIN	G	M	1817–1874	
WARSZAWA	J	T	1834/1891	PROVINCE: POZNAŃ
STARY KISIELIN	A	Z	1824/1945	356
KARTHAUS	**SEE KARTUZY**			
KARTUZY	**GDAŃSK**			
GDAŃSK	A	O	1921–1923	44/21, 28, 32
KATOWICE	**KATOWICE**			
KATOWICE	A	B	1848–1899	674/I/368, 372–373
KATOWICE	A	K	1922–1931, 1935–1939	27/I–VI/1992–1993; 40/I/180
KATOWICE	A	M	1860	1/I/101
KATOWICE	A	N	1921; 1930–1931	27/I–VI/1440–1442, 1477–1503
KATOWICE	A	S	1843–1909; 1922–1939	27/I/1; 64/I/1–169
KATOWICE REGION	**KATOWICE**			
KATOWICE	A	D	1844–1849	674/I/370–371
KATOWICE	A	E	1922–1935	18/I/1–24
KATSCHER	**SEE KIETRZ**			
KĄTY WROCŁAWSKIE	**WROCŁAW**			
WROCŁAW	A	B	1874–1877; 1886; 1888–1889; 1892–1893	556/II
WROCŁAW	A	D	1874–1882; 1888; 1890–1893	556/II
BERLIN	G	G	1823–1869	
WROCŁAW	A	M	1874–1880; 1890–1893	556/II
KAZANÓW	**RADOM**			
RADOM	A	B	1828–1864; 1866–1868; 1870–1892	185
KAZANÓW	U	B	1893–1914; 1919–1921; 1923–1942	
RADOM	A	D	1828–1864; 1866–1868; 1870–1892	185
KAZANÓW	U	D	1893–1914; 1919–1921; 1923–1942	
RADOM	A	M	1828–1858; 1878–1892	185
KAZANÓW	U	M	1893–1914; 1919–1921; 1923–1942	
KAZIMIERZ	**KRAKÓW**			
KRAKÓW	U	B	1890–1942	
LUBLIN	A	C	1865	37/114
KRAKÓW	U	D	1890–1942; 1945	
KRAKÓW	U	M	1889–1945	
KRAKÓW	A	Z	1335–1860	34; 35/IUD/CAS.III/11 1–13
KAZIMIERZ DOLNY	**LUBLIN**			
LUBLIN	A	B	1826–1842; 1848; 1859; 1863	91; 113
KAZIMIERZ DOLNY	U	B	1882–1939	
LUBLIN	A	C	1864–1865	93, 114
LUBLIN	A	D	1826–1842; 1848; 1859; 1863	92; 113
KAZIMIERZ DOLNY	U	D	1882–1939	
LUBLIN	A	E	1867–1914	RGL IV ADM.
LUBLIN	A	K	1849–1850; 1858–1914; 1922–1927	160–169; RGL IV; UWL WSP/812
LUBLIN	A	M	1826–1842; 1848; 1863	113
KAZIMIERZ DOLNY	U	M	1882–1939	
LUBLIN	A	T	1858–1914	RGL IV ADM.; 176
LUBLIN	A	Z	1799–1809	44–45; 47; 63–64
KĘPNO	**KALISZ**			
POZNAŃ	A	B	1825; 1827; 1830–1847	3577/1, 4, 7, 10, 13, 15, 18, 21, 24, 27, 30, 33, 36, 39, 43, 47, 51, 55, 59, 63
KALISZ	A	C	1910; 1916; 1918; 1921; 1927–1930	20/65, 237
POZNAŃ	A	D	1825; 1827; 1830–1847	3577/2, 6, 9, 12, 14, 17, 20, 23, 26, 29, 32, 35, 38, 42, 46, 50, 54, 58, 62, 66
KĘPNO	U	D	1897	
POZNAŃ	A	M	1826–1827; 1830–1831	3577/3, 5, 8, 11, 16, 19, 22, 25, 28, 31, 34, 37, 40, 44, 48, 52, 56, 60, 64
KĘTRZYN	**OLSZTYN**			
KOBLENZ	G	B	1813–1874	
OLSZTYN	A	B	1881–1882; 1890–1891	735/I
OLSZTYN	A	C	1825; 1833; 1864; 1932–1933; 1939	12/I; 254/I

Repository type: **A** = Archive **G** = LDS Films of German-Held Records **J** = Jewish Historical Institute **U** = Urząd Stanu Cywilnego

TOWN NAME	VOIVODSHIP (Province)			
Repository Location	Repository Document Type	Code	Years	Zespół/Sygnatura (Poland) Fond/Opis/Delo (Belarus, Ukraine, Lithuania)
KOBLENZ	G	D	1813–1874	
OLSZTYN	A	D	1878–1879; 1886–1887; 1891	735/I
KOBLENZ	G	M	1813–1874	
OLSZTYN	A	M	1877–1881; 1884–1886; 1890–1891	735/I
KIELCE	**KIELCE**			
KIELCE	A	B	1868–1896	422
KIELCE	U	B	1897–1941	
KIELCE	A	C	1868–1939	122
KIELCE	A	D	1868–1896	422
KIELCE	U	D	1897–1941	
KIELCE	A	M	1868–1896	422
KIELCE	U	M	1897–1941	
KIETRZ	**OPOLE**			
LEIPZIG	G	B	1812–1874	
LEIPZIG	G	D	1812–1874	
LEIPZIG	G	M	1812–1874	
KISIELICE	**ELBLĄG**			
KOBLENZ	G	D	1893–1930	
KLECKO	**POZNAŃ**			
POZNAŃ	A	K	1854–1911	4061/223–227
KLECZEW	**KONIN**			
POZNAŃ	A	B	1808–1815; 1817; 1820–1824; 1826–1827; 1829–1881; 1883; 1886–1887; 1889; 1891–1892; 1898	3747/1–6, 10–11, 13, 15–18, 20–23, 25, 27, 29, 31, 33–34, 36, 38, 40, 42, 44, 46, 48, 50, 52, 55, 57–102; 3650/4, 7, 10
KLECZEW	U	B	1899; 1902; 1904–1905; 1908; 1911; 1913; 1917–1918; 1922–1923	
POZNAŃ	A	D	1809–1815; 1817; 1820–1823; 1825–1827; 1829–1831; 1866; 1883; 1887; 1889; 1891–1892; 1898	3747/2–5, 8–11, 13, 15–18, 20–23, 25, 27, 29, 31–34, 36, 38, 40, 42, 44, 46, 48, 50, 53, 55, 57, 59, 61, 63–102; 3650/6, 9
KLECZEW	U	D	1896–1899; 1902; 1904–1905; 1908; 1911; 1913; 1917–1918; 1922–1923	
POZNAŃ	A	G	1940	4299/526
POZNAŃ	A	M	1809–1815; 1817; 1820–1823; 1826–1827; 1829–1831; 1866–1870; 1883; 1886–1887; 1889; 1891–1892; 1898	3747/2–5, 7, 10–102; 3650/5, 8
KLECZEW	U	M	1896–1899; 1902; 1904–1905; 1908; 1911; 1913; 1917–1918; 1922–1923	
POZNAŃ	A	T	1921–1922	4299/375–376
KLEPARZ	**KRAKÓW**			
KRAKÓW	U	B	1890/1942	
KRAKÓW	U	D	1890/1942; 1945	
KRAKÓW	U	M	1889/1945	
KLIMONTÓW	**TARNOBRZEG**			
SANDOMIERZ	A	B	1826–1893	171
KLIMONTÓW	U	B	1894–1912; 1922–1942	
SANDOMIERZ	A	D	1826–1877; 1880–1893	171
KLIMONTÓW	U	D	1894–1912; 1922–1942	
SANDOMIERZ	A	M	1826–1877; 1880–1893	171
KLIMONTÓW	U	M	1894–1912; 1922–1942	
KŁOBUCK	**CZĘSTOCHOWA**			
CZĘSTOCHOWA	A	B	1826–1895	107
KŁOBUCK	U	B	1896–1902; 1909; 1913–1930; 1932–1941; 1945	
CZĘSTOCHOWA	A	D	1826–1895	107
KŁOBUCK	U	D	1896–1907; 1909; 1913–1945	
CZĘSTOCHOWA	A	M	1826–1895	107
KŁOBUCK	U	M	1896–1941	
ŁÓDŹ	A	O	1897–1899	113
ŁÓDŹ	A	Z	1835–1866; 1899–1912	1
KŁODAWA	**KONIN**			
POZNAŃ	A	B	1826–1863; 1865–1894	3748/1–15, 17, 19, 21–24, 26, 28, 30, 32, 34, 36, 38, 40, 42, 44–45, 47, 49, 52–55, 57, 59, 61–62, 64, 66, 68–103
KŁODAWA	U	B	1895–1938	
POZNAŃ	A	C	1933–1939; 1942	18/37
POZNAŃ	A	D	1826–1863; 1865–1894	3748/1–15, 17, 19, 21–24, 26, 28, 30, 32, 34, 36, 38, 40, 42, 44–45, 47, 49, 52–55, 57, 59, 61–62, 64, 66, 68–103
KŁODAWA	U	D	1895–1938	

A Army/recruit lists; **B** Birth; **C** Census; **D** Death; **E** Voter lists; **G** Immigration; **H** Holocaust; **J** Judaica; **K** Kahal; **L** Land; **M** Marriage; **N** Name changes; **O** Police files; **P** Pogroms; **R** Reference; **S** School records; **T** Tax lists; **V** Divorce; **W** Occupation lists; **X** Jewish hospital; **Y** Notary records; **Z** Local government records

TOWN NAME		VOIVODSHIP (Province)		Zespół/Sygnatura (Poland)
Repository Location	Repository Type	Document Code	Years	Fond/Opis/Delo (Belarus, Ukraine, Lithuania)
POZNAŃ	A	E	1931–1939	18/1–3, 7, 9, 11–13
POZNAŃ	A	M	1826–1863; 1865–1894	3748/1–103
KŁODAWA	U	M	1895–1938	
KŁÓDŻKO		**WAŁBRZYCH**		
WROCŁAW	A	D	1817–1820; 1828–1836; 1838; 1843–1844; 1847; 1875–1892	557/II
WARSZAWA	J	K	1805/1916	PROVINCE: ŚLĄSK
WARSZAWA	J	T	1805/1916	PROVINCE: ŚLĄSK
KLONOWA		**SIERADZ**		
KLONOWA	U	B	1940–1944	
KLONOWA	U	D	1940–1944	
KLONOWA	U	M	1940–1943	
KLUCZBORK		**OPOLE**		
OPOLE	A	B	1814–1924	13
OPOLE	A	C	1845; 1927; 1947	13; 68
OPOLE	A	D	1814–1924	13
WARSZAWA	J	E	1840/1918	PROVINCE: ŚLĄSK
OPOLE	A	K	1818–1944	13
WARSZAWA	J	K	1840/1918	PROVINCE: ŚLĄSK
OPOLE	A	M	1814–1924	13
OPOLE	A	S	1818–1857	13
WARSZAWA	J	S	1840/1918	PROVINCE: ŚLĄSK
OPOLE	A	T	1802–1933	
OPOLE	A	W	1824–1927	13
WARSZAWA	J	Y	1840/1918	PROVINCE: ŚLĄSK
WARSZAWA	J	Z	1840/1918	PROVINCE: ŚLĄSK
KLUKOWO		**ŁOMŻA**		
KLUKOWA	U	B	1933–1934	
KLUKOWA	U	M	1926–1938	
KLWÓW		**RADOM**		
KIELCE	A	B	1851–1860	594
RADOM	A	B	1875–1894	76/1
KLWÓW	U	B	1895–1902; 1904–1910; 1920–1923; 1925–1929; 1932–1934	
KIELCE	A	D	1851–1860	594
RADOM	A	D	1875–1894	76/1
KLWÓW	U	D	1895–1902; 1904–1910; 1920–1923; 1925–1929; 1932–1934	
KIELCE	A	M	1851–1860	594
RADOM	A	M	1875–1894	76/1
KLWÓW	U	M	1895–1902; 1904–1910; 1920–1923; 1925–1929; 1932–1934	
KNYSZYN		**BIAŁYSTOK**		
KNYSZYN	U	D	1882–1884; 1891–1893; 1895; 1897–1898; 1900–1901; 1906–1909; 1911; 1914	
VILNIUS	A	M	1871	728/1/1124
KNYSZYN	U	M	1889; 1894; 1897; 1899–1900; 1905; 1907–1909; 1913–1914, 1931–1932; 1937	
KOCK		**LUBLIN**		
LUBLIN	A	B	1826–1894	113
KOCK	U	B	1895–1909; 1914; 1918–1938; 1941–1942	
LUBLIN	A	C	1877/1915	
LUBLIN	A	D	1826–1894	113
KOCK	U	D	1895–1896; 1899; 1903–1909; 1918–1937; 1939; 1941–1942	
LUBLIN	A	E	1913	RGL IV ADM.
LUBLIN	A	K	1913; 1927	RGL IV; UWL WSP/808
LUBLIN	A	M	1826–1894	113
KOCK	U	M	1895–1897; 1899; 1903–1909; 1918–1925; 1927; 1931–1932; 1937	
LUBLIN	A	T	1913; 1924–1935	RGL IV; UWL WSP/808; SPŁUK/628
KODEŃ		**BIAŁA PODLASKA**		
LUBLIN	A	B	1826–1893	113
KODEŃ	U	B	1894–1912; 1923–1936	
LUBLIN	A	D	1826–1893	113
KODEŃ	U	D	1894–1912; 1923–1936	
LUBLIN	A	K	1924; 1927	SPB/204; UWL WSP/755
LUBLIN	A	M	1826–1893	113

Repository type: **A** = Archive   **G** = LDS Films of German-Held Records   **J** = Jewish Historical Institute   **U** = Urząd Stanu Cywilnego

TOWN NAME	VOIVODSHIP (Province)			
Repository Location	Repository Document Type	Code	Years	Zespół/Sygnatura (Poland) Fond/Opis/Delo (Belarus, Ukraine, Lithuania)
KODEŃ	U	M	1894–1912; 1923–1936	
LUBLIN	A	T	1924; 1927	SPB/204; UWL WSP/755
KOLBERG	**SEE KOŁOBRZEG**			
KOŁBIEL	**SIEDLCE**			
SIEDLCE	A	B	1826–1837; 1854–1892	509
KOŁBIEL	U	B	1893–1929	
SIEDLCE	A	D	1826–1838; 1854–1892	509
KOŁBIEL	U	D	1893–1929	
SIEDLCE	A	M	1826–1836; 1854–1892	509
KOŁBIEL	U	M	1893–1929	
KOLBUSZOWA	**RZESZÓW**			
RZESZÓW	A	C	1945–1946	332/97
LVOV	A	L	1785–1788; 1819–1820	19/VII/336; 20/VII/162
RZESZÓW	A	L	1870–1873	416/16–17
KOBLUSZOWA GÓRNA	**RZESZÓW**			
RZESZÓW	A	A	1933–1939	390/10–11
RZESZÓW	A	C	1932–1949	390/1–9, 13, 26–49
KOLECHOWICE	**BIAŁA PODLASKA**			
KOLECHOWICE	U	B	1928–1938	
KOLECHOWICE	U	D	1930–1944	
KOLECHOWICE	U	M	1928–1941	
KOLMAR	**SEE CHODZIEŻ**			
KOLNO	**ŁOMŻA**			
ŁOMŻA	A	A	1872; 1898; 1915	25
ŁOMŻA	A	Y	1892–1932	206–209
KOŁO	**KONIN**			
POZNAŃ	A	B	1826–1893	3749/2, 5, 8–30, 53–61, 63–65, 67, 69, 71–73, 75–83, 85, 87–90, 92–99
KOŁO	U	B	1894–1940	
POZNAŃ	A	D	1825–1893	3749/1, 4, 7–30, 53–66, 68, 70–73, 75–77, 79–81, 83–85, 87–93, 95–99
KOŁO	U	D	1894–1940; 1945	
POZNAŃ	A	M	1826–1893	3749/3, 6, 8–61, 63–65, 68, 70–77, 79–81, 83, 85–90, 92–93, 95–99
KOŁO	U	M	1894–1940; 1945	
ŁÓDŹ	A	S	1893–1909	92; 122
POZNAŃ	A	S	1937–1939	805/157–158
ŁÓDŹ	A	Z	1893–1914	92, 96
KOŁOBRZEG	**KOSZALIN**			
SZCZECIN	A	K	1803–1806	GMINY ZYDOWSKIE Z POMORZA ZACHODNIEGO 57
KOLUSZKI	**PIOTRKÓW TRYBUNALSKI**			
KOLUSZKI	U	B	1882–1894	
PIOTRKÓW TRYBUNALSKI	A	C	1940–1950	126
KOLUSZKI	U	D	1882–1894	
KOLUSZKI	U	M	1882–1894	
PIOTRKÓW TRYBUNALSKI	A	Z	1940–1950	126
KOMARÓW	**ZAMOŚĆ**			
LUBLIN	A	B	1826–1872	113
ZAMOŚĆ	A	B	1873–1891	209/; OA; OB; 1–16
KOMARÓW	U	B	1892–1903; 1905–1911; 1921–1925; 1928–1930; 1932–1939	6–38
LUBLIN	A	D	1826–1872	113
ZAMOŚĆ	A	D	1873–1891	209/O; OA; OB; 1–16
KOMARÓW	U	D	1892–1903; 1905–1911; 1921–1925; 1928–1930; 1932–1939	6–38
LUBLIN	A	K	1872–1899; 1902; 1905; 1910; 1912–1913; 1927	RGL IV ADM; UWL WSP/836
LUBLIN	A	M	1826–1872	113
ZAMOŚĆ	A	M	1873–1891	209/O; OA; OB; 1–16
KOMARÓW	U	M	1892–1903; 1905–1911; 1921–1925; 1928–1930; 1932–1939	6–38
KOMORÓW	**TARNOBRZEG**			
RZESZÓW	A	C	1933–1939	220/1
KONIECPOL	**CZĘSTOCHOWA**			
ŁÓDŹ	A	B	1826–1842; 1844–1855; 1890	270
KONIECPOL	U	B	1900; 1903–1942	

A Army/recruit lists; **B** Birth; **C** Census; **D** Death; **E** Voter lists; **G** Immigration; **H** Holocaust; **J** Judaica; **K** Kahal; **L** Land; **M** Marriage; **N** Name changes; **O** Police files; **P** Pogroms; **R** Reference; **S** School records; **T** Tax lists; **V** Divorce; **W** Occupation lists; **X** Jewish hospital; **Y** Notary records; **Z** Local government records

TOWN NAME		VOIVODSHIP (Province)			Zespół/Sygnatura (Poland)
Repository Location	Repository Type	Document Code		Years	Fond/Opis/Delo (Belarus, Ukraine, Lithuania)
ŁÓDŹ	A	D		1826–1842; 1844–1855; 1890	270
KONIECPOL	U	D		1900; 1903–1913; 1915–1941	
ŁÓDŹ	A	K		1899–1913	1
ŁÓDŹ	A	M		1826–1842; 1844–1855; 1890	270
KONIECPOL	U	M		1900; 1903–1913; 1915–1941	
ŁÓDŹ	A	Z		1841–1866; 1891–1901	1
KONIN		**KONIN**			
POZNAŃ	A	B		1826–1853; 1855–1856; 1858–1860; 1862–1863; 1865–1866; 1869–1874; 1882–1889; 1891–1894	3750/2–57
KONIN	U	B		1895–1925; 1927–1933; 1935–1937	
POZNAŃ	A	C		1807/1914; 1920–1923; 1932–1940	4301/244–247, 395–396, 430–447, 510–513; 20/564–588
POZNAŃ	A	D		1826–1853; 1855–1856; 1858–1860; 1862–1863; 1865–1866; 1869–1874; 1882–1889; 1891–1894	3750/2–57
KONIN	U	D		1895–1925; 1927–1933; 1935–1937	
ŁÓDŹ	A	K		1893–1913	92, 96
POZNAŃ	A	M		1815; 1826–1853; 1855–1856; 1858–1860; 1862–1863; 1865–1866; 1869–1874; 1882–1889; 1891–1894	3750/1–57
KONIN	U	M		1895–1925; 1927–1933; 1935–1937	
POZNAŃ	A	S		1936–1939	805/159–160
ŁÓDŹ	A	Z		1895–1914	92, 96
KOŃSKIE		**KIELCE**			
KIELCE	A	B		1826–1894	555
KOŃSKIE	U	B		1895–1941	
KIELCE	A	C		1945–1950	519
KIELCE	A	D		1826–1894	555
KOŃSKIE	U	D		1895–1941	
KIELCE	A	G		1915–1940	447
WARSZAWA	J	K		1940–1943	212
KIELCE	A	M		1826–1894	555
KOŃSKIE	U	M		1895–1941	
KOŃSKOWOLA		**LUBLIN**			
LUBLIN	A	B		1826–1893	113
KOŃSKOWOLA	U	B		1894–1913; 1916–1939	
LUBLIN	A	D		1826–1893	113
KOŃSKOWOLA	U	D		1894–1913; 1916–1939	
LUBLIN	A	E		1873–1913	RGL IV ADM.
LUBLIN	A	K		1873–1913; 1923–1927	RGL IV ADM.; UWL WSP/815
LUBLIN	A	M		1826–1893	113
KOŃSKOWOLA	U	M		1894–1913; 1916–1939	
LUBLIN	A	T		1873–1913; 1923–1927	RGL IV ADM.; UWL WSP/815
KONSTADT		**SEE WOŁCZYN**			
KONSTANTYNÓW		**BIAŁA PODLASKA**			
LUBLIN	A	B		1826–1888	113
KONSTANTYNÓW	U	B		1889–1914; 1923–1937	
LUBLIN	A	D		1826–1888	113
KONSTANTYNÓW	U	D		1889–1914; 1923–1937	
LUBLIN	A	K		1922–1927	UWL WSP/794
LUBLIN	A	M		1826–1888	113
KONSTANTYNÓW	U	M		1889–1914; 1923–1937	
LUBLIN	A	T		1922–1927	UWL WSP/794
KONSTANTYNÓW ŁÓDŹKI		**ŁÓDŹ**			
ŁÓDŹ	A	B		1832–1889; 1891–1893	270
KONSTANTYNÓW ŁÓDŹKI	U	B		1895–1906; 1908; 1911–1920	
ŁÓDŹ	A	D		1832–1889; 1891–1893	270
KONSTANTYNÓW ŁÓDŹKI	U	D		1895–1906; 1908; 1911–1920	
ŁÓDŹ	A	K		1825–1860; 1895–1914	1
ŁÓDŹ	A	M		1832–1889; 1891–1893	270
KONSTANTYNÓW ŁÓDŹKI	U	M		1895–1906; 1908; 1911–1920	
ŁÓDŹ	A	Z		1895–1896	1, 5
KOPCIEWICE		**KATOWICE**			
PSZCZYNA	A	B		1847–1849	67/I/1
PSZCZYNA	A	D		1848	67/I/4
KOPRZYWNICA		**TARNOBRZEG**			
SANDOMIERZ	A	B		1857–1858; 1882–1893	172
KOPRZYWNICA	U	B		1894–1912; 1916–1918; 1920–1921; 1924–1941	
SANDOMIERZ	A	D		1857–1858; 1882–1893	172

Repository type: **A** = Archive **G** = LDS Films of German-Held Records **J** = Jewish Historical Institute **U** = Urząd Stanu Cywilnego

TOWN NAME	VOIVODSHIP (Province)			Zespół/Sygnatura (Poland)
Repository Location	Repository Document Type	Code	Years	Fond/Opis/Delo (Belarus, Ukraine, Lithuania)
KOPRZYWNICA				
SANDOMIERZ	U	D	1894–1899; 1904–1912; 1915–1917; 1921–1941	
KOPRZYWNICA	A	M	1857–1858; 1882–1893	172
	U	M	1894–1912; 1916–1917; 1921; 1924–1941	
KORCZYNA	**KROSNO**			
KORCZYNA	U	B	1899–1942	
KORCZYNA	U	D	1882–1942	
LVOV	A	L	1785–1788; 1819–1820	19/II/90, 228; 20/II/165,258
KORCZYNA	U	M	1894–1942	
KORFANTÓW	**OPOLE**			
BERLIN	G	B	1812–1874	
OPOLE	A	B	1863–1865; 1868–1869; 1872; 1875	14/49
BERLIN	G	D	1812–1874	
BERLIN	G	M	1812–1874	
KÓRNIK	**POZNAŃ**			
POZNAŃ	A	B	1811–1812	3579/1, 4, 6–18
POZNAŃ	A	D	1811–1812	3579/3, 5, 6–18
POZNAŃ	A	K	1842–1914; 1917–1934	4381/121–123, 398
POZNAŃ	A	M	1811–1812	3579/2, 6–18
POZNAŃ	A	S	1897–1913	4381/139, 141–143
KORONOWO	**BYDGOSZCZ**			
BYDGOSZCZ	A	B	1847–1894	381; 1713
BYDGOSZCZ	A	G	1920–1935	192
KOŚCIAN	**LESZNO**			
BERLIN	G	B	1827–1874	
LESZNO	A	C	1842–1881; 1939–1944	18
BERLIN	G	D	1827–1874	
BERLIN	G	M	1827–1874	
KOŚCIERZYNA	**GDAŃSK**			
GDAŃSK	A	B	1847–1884	1497/56
GDAŃSK	A	D	1847–1874	1497/58
GDAŃSK	A	M	1848–1874	1497/57
KOSIENICE	**PRZEMYŚL**			
PRZEMYŚL	A	C	1930/1948	207/20–21
KOSÓW LACKI	**SIEDLCE**			
SIEDLCE	A	B	1827–1828; 1832–1894	185/1–91
KOSÓW LACKI	U	B	1895–1936	
SIEDLCE	A	D	1827–1828; 1832–1894	185/1–91
KOSÓW LACKI	U	D	1895–1936	
LUBLIN	A	K	1913–1914; 1922–1936	RGL IV ADM; UWL WSP/826
SIEDLCE	A	M	1827–1828; 1832–1894	185/1–95
KOSÓW LACKI	U	M	1895–1936	
LUBLIN	A	T	1913–1914; 1922–1936	RGL IV ADM; UWL WSP/826
KOSTEN	**SEE KOŚCIAN**			
KOSTRZYN	**POZNAŃ**			
POZNAŃ	A	K	1835–1905	336/507–508
KOSZALIN	**KOSZALIN**			
KOSZALIN	A	B	1812–1874	52/I/10; 73/I/141
KOSZALIN	A	D	1812–1874	52/I/10; 73/I/143
SZCZECIN	A	K	1801–1894	GMINY ZYDOWSKIE Z POMORZA ZACHODNIEGO 58–78
KOSZALIN	A	M	1812–1874	52/I/10; 73/I/142
KOSZALIN	A	Z	1738–1816	33/I/446–450
KOSZAZOWO	**SEE KOSZALIN**			
KOSZTOWO	**PRZEMYŚL**			
PRZEMYŚL	A	C	1931–1939	200/37–39
KOSZYCE	**KIELCE**			
KOSZYCE	U	B	1894–1901; 1923–1942	
KOSZYCE	U	D	1925–1942	
KOSZYCE	U	M	1894–1901; 1923–1931	
KOWAL	**WŁOCŁAWEK**			
WŁOCŁAWEK	A	B	1839–1883 (ALPHA INDEX); 1879–1886	563
WARSZAWA	J	C	1919/1939	105
WŁOCŁAWEK	A	D	1883–1886	563
WARSZAWA	J	E	1919/1939	105
WARSZAWA	J	K	1919/1939	105

A Army/recruit lists; **B** Birth; **C** Census; **D** Death; **E** Voter lists; **G** Immigration; **H** Holocaust; **J** Judaica; **K** Kahal; **L** Land; **M** Marriage; **N** Name changes; **O** Police files; **P** Pogroms; **R** Reference; **S** School records; **T** Tax lists; **V** Divorce; **W** Occupation lists; **X** Jewish hospital; **Y** Notary records; **Z** Local government records

TOWN NAME	VOIVODSHIP (Province)			Zespół/Sygnatura (Poland)
Repository Location	Repository Document Type	Code	Years	Fond/Opis/Delo (Belarus, Ukraine, Lithuania)
WŁOCŁAWEK	A	M	1885–1886; 1821; 1863 (MARRIAGE APPLICATIONS)	563
WARSZAWA	J	T	1919/1939	105
KOZIENICE	**RADOM**			
RADOM	A	B	1826–1894; 1925–1939	186
KOZIENICE	U	B	1895–1942	
RADOM	A	D	1826–1894; 1925–1939	186
KOZIENICE	U	D	1895–1942	
RADOM	A	M	1826–1894; 1925–1937	186
KOZIENICE	U	M	1895–1942	
KOŹLE	**OPOLE**			
WARSZAWA	J	A	1908/1938	PROVINCE: ŚLĄSK
OPOLE	A	D	1826–1861	504
OPOLE	A	M	1812–1847	504
WARSZAWA	J	X	1908/1938	PROVINCE: ŚLĄSK
KOŹMIN	**KALISZ**			
POZNAŃ	A	B	1811–1812	3578/1
WARSZAWA	J	B	1821	
WARSZAWA	J	C	1801/1872	PROVINCE: POZNAŃ
POZNAŃ	A	D	1811–1812	3578/3
KALISZ	A	K	1810–1839	22/373–374
KALISZ	A	L	1861–1943	91/130–173
POZNAŃ	A	M	1811–1812	3578/2
WARSZAWA	J	S	1801/1872	PROVINCE: POZNAŃ
KALISZ	A	S	1826–1872	22/219, 332
KALISZ	A	T	1800–1918	
WARSZAWA	J	T	1801/1872	PROVINCE: POZNAŃ
POZNAŃ	A	Z	1760–1793	4331/I/21
KOŹMINEK	**KALISZ**			
KOŹMINEK	U	B	1882–1941	
KALISZ	A	C	1872–1948	1/957–964; 53/303–365
KOŹMINEK	U	D	1898–1940	
KALISZ	A	E	1907; 1909	321/18–19, 21
KOŹMINEK	U	M	1885–1897; 1919–1931	
KALISZ	A	W	1831–1866	1/98, 436
KOŻUCHÓW	**ZIELONA GÓRA**			
STARY KISIELIN	A	B	1847–1875	138/288–290
STARY KISIELIN	A	D	1847–1875	138/288–290
WARSZAWA	J	K	1883–1884	PROVINCE: ŚLĄSK
STARY KISIELIN	A	L	1864–1945	185
STARY KISIELIN	A	M	1847–1875	138/288–290
KRAJENKA	**PIŁA**			
KOBLENZ	G	B	1800–1863	
KOBLENZ	G	D	1800–1863	
KOBLENZ	G	M	1800–1863	
KRAKÓW	**KRAKÓW**			
KRAKÓW	A	A	1795	
KRAKÓW	A	B	1798–1854; 1869–1895	526/MIK 1–12; 335/M 1920–2102
WARSZAWA	J	C	1701/1939	101
KRAKÓW	A	C	1795–1853; 1857; 1870; 1880; 1890; 1900; 1910; 1921; 1939–1942	84–93; 684/TSCHN 1866; 33–VII/SMK 450–681
WARSZAWA	A	C	1811–1812; 1866–1888 1931–1932	194/903
KRAKÓW	A	D	1798–1854; 1871–1889	335/M 1920–2102; 526/MIK 1–12
WARSZAWA	J	D	1903–1929 (REQUESTS FOR PERMISSION TO BURY)	101
WARSZAWA	J	E	1701/1939	101
KRAKÓW	A	E	1865–1933	IT/1028, 1060, 1081–1082, 1310, 1936
KRAKÓW	A	H	1939–1945	33 VII/SMK 211, 772–774; 655/IT 1395
WARSZAWA	J	H	1940–1941 (INCLUDES APPLICATIONS FOR RESIDENCY: 19, 500 DOCUMENTS WITH PHOTOS)	206
WARSZAWA	J	K	1701/1939	101; 107; 109; 212
KRAKÓW	A	K	1939–1940	IT 1815
KRAKÓW	A	L	1790–1794	
WARSZAWA	J	M	1897–1929	101
KRAKÓW	A	R	1892; 1905; 1908; 1909; 1926; 1929–1930; 1932–1934	

Repository type: **A** = Archive   **G** = LDS Films of German-Held Records   **J** = Jewish Historical Institute   **U** = Urząd Stanu Cywilnego

TOWN NAME	VOIVODSHIP (Province)				
Repository Location	Repository Document Type	Code	Years		Zespół/Sygnatura (Poland) Fond/Opis/Delo (Belarus, Ukraine, Lithuania)
WARSZAWA	J	S	1701/1939		101
KRAKÓW	A	S	1801–1933		482–493
WARSZAWA	J	T	1701/1939		101
KRAKÓW	A	T	1796–1809; 1815–1853		33–II; 33–III; WMK, V–59, 102–105
KRAKÓW	A	V	1811–1853		335
KRAKÓW	A	W	1550–1860 (LIST OF JEWISH DOORKEEPERS)		35/III/11/9–12; 77/IT 638–640, 649–650
WARSZAWA	J	X	1701/1939		101
KRAKÓW	A	Z	1300–1945		1343/PMI/1–219; 33–I/33–VII, 34, 36, 53
WARSZAWA	J	Z	1701/1939		101
KRAKÓW	A	M	1798–1852; 1878–1895		335/M 1920–2102; 526/MIK 1–12
KRAKÓW PODGÓRZE	**KRAKÓW**				
KRAKÓW	U	B	1896–1899; 1902–1940		
KRAKÓW	U	D	1890–1942		
KRAKÓW	U	M	1896–1941		
KRAKÓW REGION	**KRAKÓW**				
KRAKÓW	A	C	1790–1792; 1795–1796		30/191A
KRAKÓW SRODMIESCIE	**KRAKÓW**				
KRAKÓW	U	B	1896–1942		
KRAKÓW	U	D	1890–1942; 1945		
KRAKÓW	U	M	1896–1940; 1945		
KRAPKOWICE	**OPOLE**				
OPOLE	A	B	1820–1873		58
OPOLE	A	C	1855–1857; 1860–1861; 1863–1864; 1870; 1872; 1876–1878; 1890–1894; 1908; 1910–1912		16/2348–2375
OPOLE	A	D	1820–1873		58
OPOLE	A	M	1827–1873		58
OPOLE	A	O	1938		16/1841
OPOLE	A	T	1894–1903; 1905–1914; 1916–1918		16/739–762
OPOLE	A	W	1937–1944		16/1792, 1819
KRAPPITZ	**SEE KRAPKOWICE**				
KRAŚNICZYN	**CHEŁM**				
LUBLIN	A	B	1826–1836		113
LUBLIN	A	C	1910 (INCLUDED IN KRASNYSTAW)		ZPK/125
LUBLIN	A	D	1826–1836		113
LUBLIN	A	E	1910–1914 (ALSO INCLUDED IN KRASNYSTAW)		RGL IV ADM
LUBLIN	A	K	1910–1914 (ALSO INCLUDED IN KRASNYSTAW)		RGL IV ADM
LUBLIN	A	M	1826–1836		113
LUBLIN	A	T	1910–1914 (ALSO INCLUDED IN KRASNYSTAW)		RGL IV ADM
KRAŚNIK	**LUBLIN**				
LUBLIN	A	B	1826–1855; 1866–1875; 1882–1884		113
KRAŚNIK	U	B	1885–1889; 1896–1908; 1913–1921; 1923–1929; 1931–1934; 1937–1942		
LUBLIN	A	D	1826–1886		113
KRAŚNIK	U	D	1887–1922; 1924–1942		
LUBLIN	A	K	1869–1914; 1922–1935		RGL IV ADM; UWL WSP/785
LUBLIN	A	M	1826–1886		113
KRAŚNIK	U	M	1887–1893; 1924–1927; 1935–1942		
LUBLIN	A	T	1869–1914; 1922–1935		RGL IV ADM; UWL WSP/785
KRASNOBRÓD	**ZAMOŚĆ**				
LUBLIN	A	B	1827–1873		113
ZAMOŚĆ	A	B	1874; 1876–1878; 1881–1893		209/1–16
KRASNOBRÓD	U	B	1894–1898; 1900–1904; 1906; 1911–1913; 1920–1921; 1923–1925; 1928–1939		
LUBLIN	A	D	1827–1873		113
ZAMOŚĆ	A	D	1874; 1876–1878; 1881–1893		209/1–16
KRASNOBRÓD	U	D	1894–1898; 1900–1904; 1906; 1911–1913; 1920–1921; 1923–1925; 1928–1939		
LUBLIN	A	K	1867–1910; 1922–1926		RGL IV ADM; UWL WSP/839
LUBLIN	A	M	1827–1873		113
ZAMOŚĆ	A	M	1874; 1876–1878; 1881–1893		209/1–16
KRASNOBRÓD	U	M	1894–1898; 1900–1904; 1906; 1911–1913; 1920–1921; 1923–1925; 1928–1939		
ZAMOŚĆ	A	S	1926–1927; 1934–1935		12/404–406
LUBLIN	A	T	1867–1910; 1922–1926		RGL IV ADM; UWL WSP/839

A Army/recruit lists; **B** Birth; **C** Census; **D** Death; **E** Voter lists; **G** Immigration; **H** Holocaust; **J** Judaica; **K** Kahal; **L** Land; **M** Marriage; **N** Name changes; **O** Police files; **P** Pogroms; **R** Reference; **S** School records; **T** Tax lists; **V** Divorce; **W** Occupation lists; **X** Jewish hospital; **Y** Notary records; **Z** Local government records

TOWN NAME	VOIVODSHIP (Province)			Zespół/Sygnatura (Poland)
Repository Location	Repository Type	Document Code	Years	Fond/Opis/Delo (Belarus, Ukraine, Lithuania)

KRASNOPOL	**SUWAŁKI**			
SUWAŁKI	A	B	1808–1826; 1828–1829; 1836/1862; 1866/1875; 1882–1885; 1894 (ALSO INCLUDED IN SEJNY)	155; 199; 207
KRASNOPOL	U	B	1897; 1901	
SUWAŁKI	A	D	1808–1826; 1828–1829; 1836/1862; 1866/1875; 1882; 1884–1885; 1894	155; 199; 207
KRASNOPOL	U	D	1897; 1901	
SUWAŁKI	A	M	1808–1826; 1828–1829; 1836/1862; 1866/1875; 1882; 1884–1885; 1894	155; 199; 207
KRASNOPOL	U	M	1897; 1901	
KRASNOSIELC	**OSTROŁĘKA**			
KRASNOSIELC	U	B	1897–1913; 1920–1935; 1937	
KRASNOSIELC	U	D	1897–1913; 1920–1935; 1937	
KRASNOSIELC	U	M	1897–1913; 1920–1935; 1937	
KRASNYSTAW	**CHEŁM**			
LUBLIN	A	B	1826–1833; 1835–1893	113
ZAMOŚĆ	A	B	1871–1872	209/1–2
KRASNYSTAW	U	B	1894–1933; 1937	
ZAMOŚĆ	A	C	1907–1951	22
LUBLIN	A	C	1910	ZPK/125
LUBLIN	A	D	1826–1833; 1835–1893	113
ZAMOŚĆ	A	D	1871–1872	209/1–2
KRASNYSTAW	U	D	1894–1931; 1933; 1937–1941	
LUBLIN	A	M	1826–1833; 1835–1893	113
ZAMOŚĆ	A	M	1871–1872	209/1–2
KRASNYSTAW	U	M	1894–1918; 1920–1939	
LUBLIN	A	T	1710; 1868–1914; 1922–1927; 1936	RGL IV ADM; UWL WSP 403/788
ZAMOŚĆ	A	Y	1876–1924	103–106/171
ZAMOŚĆ	A	Z	1916–1944	22
KREUZBURG	**SEE KREUZBURG**			
KRIEWIN	**SEE KRZYWIN**			
KROJANKE	**SEE KRAJENKA**			
KRÓLEWSKA HUTA	**KATOWICE**			
KATOWICE	A	K	1922–1932	27/I–VI/1994–1995
KROMOŁÓW	**KATOWICE**			
KATOWICE	A	B	1826–1854; 1909	887/196; 898/1–29
KATOWICE	A	D	1826–1854	898/1–29
ŁÓDŹ	A	K	1860–1913	1
KATOWICE	A	K	1908–1913	887/176, 225–227
KATOWICE	A	M	1826–1854	898/1–29
KATOWICE	A	S	1912	887/266
ŁÓDŹ	A	T	1860–1913	23
KROSNO	**KROSNO**			
KROSNO	U	B	1900–1910; 1912; 1915–1935; 1938; 1940–1942	
SKOŁYSZYN	A	C	1910–1941	5/131–132
KROSNO	U	D	1900–1905; 1907–1912; 1915–1933; 1937–1938; 1940–1941	
SKOŁYSZYN	A	E	1927–1939	5/47
SKOŁYSZYN	A	G	1900	5/129
SKOŁYSZYN	A	K	1927–1936	5/84
SKOŁYSZYN	A	L	1851	5/128
LVOV	A	L	1785–1788	19/IV/63
KROSNO	U	M	1900–1910; 1912; 1915–1935; 1938; 1940–1942	
PRZEMYŚL	A	Y	1928–1934	741; 1044
KROTOSZYN	**KALISZ**			
POZNAŃ	A	B	1817–1847	3580/1, 4, 7, 11, 14, 18, 22, 26, 30, 33, 36, 40, 43, 47
KALISZ	A	C	1823–1950	14/128–129, 171–172, 489; 23
POZNAŃ	A	D	1817–1847	3580/3, 6, 10, 13, 17, 21, 25, 29, 32, 35, 39, 46, 50
WARSZAWA	J	D	1846/1938	PROVINCE: POZNAŃ
KALISZ	A	L	1885–1944	91/174–175
POZNAŃ	A	M	1817–1847	3580/2, 5, 8, 12, 15, 19, 23, 27, 31, 34, 37, 41, 44, 48
KALISZ	A	Y	1830–1951	151–166; 778–788
KALISZ	A	Z	1884–1943	91/128–129

Repository type: **A** = Archive **G** = LDS Films of German-Held Records **J** = Jewish Historical Institute **U** = Urząd Stanu Cywilnego

TOWN NAME	VOIVODSHIP (Province)			Zespół/Sygnatura (Poland)
Repository Location	Repository Document Type	Document Code	Years	Fond/Opis/Delo (Belarus, Ukraine, Lithuania)
KRUSZWICA	**BYDGOSZCZ**			
INOWROCŁAW	A	B	1847–1854	59
INOWROCŁAW	A	D	1847–1854	59
KRUSZYNIANY	**BIAŁYSTOK**			
KRUSZYNIANY	U	B	1882–1939	
KRUSZYNIANY	U	D	1882–1914; 1922–1939	
KRUSZYNIANY	U	M	1882–1915; 1922–1939	
KRYŁÓW	**ZAMOŚĆ**			
LUBLIN	A	B	1826–1874	113
ZAMOŚĆ	A	B	1876–1880; 1882–1883; 1885–1890; 1892	209/1–14
KRYŁÓW	U	B	1893–1894; 1896–1898; 1900; 1903–1909; 1911–1912; 1924–1925; 1927–1938	
LUBLIN	A	D	1826–1874	113
ZAMOŚĆ	A	D	1876–1880; 1882–1883; 1885–1890; 1892	209/1–14
KRYŁÓW	U	D	1893–1894; 1896–1898; 1900; 1903–1909; 1911–1912; 1924–1925; 1927–1938	
LUBLIN	A	K	1867–1906	RGL IV ADM.
LUBLIN	A	M	1826–1874	113
ZAMOŚĆ	A	M	1876–1880; 1882–1883; 1885–1890; 1892	209/1–14
KRYŁÓW	U	M	1893–1894; 1896–1898; 1900; 1903–1909; 1911–1912; 1924–1925; 1927–1938	
LUBLIN	A	T	1867–1906	RGL IV ADM.
KRYNICA ZDRÓJ	**NOWY SĄCZ**			
NOWY SĄCZ	A	A	1867–1890; 1918–1939	AMK 36; 247
NOWY SĄCZ	A	D	1934–1938	AMK 233
NOWY SĄCZ	A	L	1918–1939	18
NOWY SĄCZ	A	T	1912–1917	18
KRYSK	**CIECHANÓW**			
NOWY DWÓR MAZOWIECKI	A	B	1826–1876	81
NOWY DWÓR MAZOWIECKI	A	D	1826–1876	81
NOWY DWÓR MAZOWIECKI	A	M	1826–1876	81
KRZECZOWICE	**PRZEMYŚL**			
LVOV	A	L	1785–1788; 1819–1820	19/5/164; 20/5/72
PRZEWORSK	A	S	1885–1951	63/2–15, 23–46, 50–57
KRZEPICE	**CZĘSTOCHOWA**			
CZĘSTOCHOWA	A	B	1830–1895	113
CZĘSTOCHOWA	A	D	1830–1895	113
ŁÓDŹ	A	K	1822–1866	1
CZĘSTOCHOWA	A	M	1830–1895	113
CZĘSTOCHOWA	A	S	1924	97
ŁÓDŹ	A	Z	1822–1866; 1888–1912	1
KRZESZÓW	**TARNOBRZEG**			
LUBLIN	A	B	1826–1832	113
SANDOMIERZ	A	B	1854–1875; 1877–1893	378
KRZESZÓW	U	B	1894–1911; 1926; 1928; 1936–1942	
LUBLIN	A	C	1786; 1795	71/1604–1605
SANDOMIERZ	A	D	1854–1874; 1877–1888	378
KRZESZÓW	U	D	1894–1911; 1926; 1928; 1936–1942	
LUBLIN	A	E	1872–1909	RGL IV ADM.
LUBLIN	A	K	1872–1909; 1924–1934	RGL IV ADM.; UWL WSP/764
LUBLIN	A	M	1826–1834	113
SANDOMIERZ	A	M	1854–1874; 1877–1893	378
KRZESZÓW	U	M	1894–1911; 1926; 1928; 1936–1942	
KRZYWCZA	**PRZEMYŚL**			
PRZEMYŚL	A	C	1931–1945	203/20, 44–46
LVOV	A	L	1785–1788; 1819–1820	19/XIII/120; 20/XIII/129
KRZYWIN	**LESZNO**			
POZNAŃ	A	B	1825–1847	3581/1, 4, 6, 9, 12, 15, 18, 21, 24, 27, 30, 33, 36
LESZNO	A	C	1926–1932	20
POZNAŃ	A	D	1825–1847	3581/3, 8, 11, 14, 17, 20, 23, 26, 29, 32, 35, 38
POZNAŃ	A	M	1825–1847	3581/2, 5, 7, 10, 13, 16, 19, 22, 25, 28, 31, 34, 37
KSIĄŻ WIELKI	**KIELCE**			
KSIĄŻ WIELKI	U	B	1892–1914; 1931–1939	
KSIĄŻ WIELKI	U	D	1916–1919	

A Army/recruit lists; **B** Birth; **C** Census; **D** Death; **E** Voter lists; **G** Immigration; **H** Holocaust; **J** Judaica; **K** Kahal; **L** Land; **M** Marriage; **N** Name changes; **O** Police files; **P** Pogroms; **R** Reference; **S** School records; **T** Tax lists; **V** Divorce; **W** Occupation lists; **X** Jewish hospital; **Y** Notary records; **Z** Local government records

TOWN NAME Repository Location	VOIVODSHIP (Province) Repository Type	Document Code	Years	Zespół/Sygnatura (Poland) Fond/Opis/Delo (Belarus, Ukraine, Lithuania)
KSIĄŻ WIELKI	U	M	1882–1914; 1920–1940	
KSIĄŻ WIELKI REGION	**KIELCE**			
KRAKÓW	A	C	1790–1792	30/191A
KUCZBORK	**CIECHANÓW**			
DZIAŁDOWO	A	B	1826–1863; 1865–1892; 1894–1907	151
DZIAŁDOWO	A	D	1826–1832; 1839–1846; 1848–1852;	151
			1854–1863; 1865–1892; 1894–1907	
DZIAŁDOWO	A	M	1826–1832; 1839–1846; 1848–1852;	56
			1854–1863; 1865–1892; 1894–1907	
KURÓW	**LUBLIN**			
LUBLIN	A	B	1828–1894	113
KURÓW	U	B	1895–1939	
LUBLIN	A	D	1828–1894	113
KURÓW	U	D	1895–1939	
LUBLIN	A	K	1873–1915; 1922–1935	RGL IV ADM; UWL WSP/816
LUBLIN	A	M	1828–1894	113
KURÓW	U	M	1895–1939	
LUBLIN	A	T	1873–1915; 1922–1935	RGL IV ADM; UWL WSP/816
KUROZWĘKI	**TARNOBRZEG**			
SANDOMIERZ	A	B	1875–1894	379
SANDOMIERZ	A	D	1875–1893	379
SANDOMIERZ	A	M	1875–1887; 1889; 1892–1894	379
KUTNO	**PŁOCK**			
ŁÓDŹ	A	B	1808–1833	270
ŁÓDŹ	A	D	1808–1833	270
ŁÓDŹ	A	M	1808–1833	270
KWIDZYN	**ELBLĄG**			
BERLIN	G	B	1847–1874	
BERLIN	G	D	1847–1874	
BERLIN	G	M	1847–1874	
BERLIN	G	S	1812–1862	
KWIECISZEWO	**BYDGOSZCZ**			
INOWROCŁAW	A	B	1832–1848; 1873	112/1–2
INOWROCŁAW	A	D	1832–1848; 1873	112/1–2
INOWROCŁAW	A	M	1832–1848; 1873	112/1–2
ŁABOWA	**SEE MACIEJOWA**			
LĄDEK	**KALISZ**			
ŁÓDŹ	A	G	1903–1904	92
ŁAGIEWNIKI	**KATOWICE**			
KATOWICE	A	B	1874–1885	751/I
KATOWICE	A	M	1874–1885	751/I
KATOWICE	A	S	1932	65/I/4–5; 81/I/134–137
ŁAŃCUT	**RZESZÓW**			
RZESZÓW	A	A	1919–1936	29/87–95A, 96
RZESZÓW	A	B	1883–1889	29/15–16
RZESZÓW	A	C	1883–1915	29/83
RZESZÓW	A	E	1927–1939	29/77
RZESZÓW	A	L	1921; 1932; 1937; 1941–1945	29/97–100, 192–195
LVOV	A	L	1785–1788; 1819–1820	19/V/52; 20/V/73
PRZEMYŚL	A	Y	1861–1934	86; 1109–1114
LANDEK IM SCHLESIEN	**SEE LĄDEK ZDROJ**			
LANDESHUT	**SEE KAMIENNA GORA**			
LANDSBERG AN DER WARTHE	**SEE GORZÓW WIELKOPOLSKI**			
LANDSBERG OST PREUSSEN	**SEE GÓROWO IŁAWIECKIE**			
ŁAPY	**BIAŁYSTOK**			
ŁAPY	U	B	1925; 1927; 1934; 1937	
ŁAPY	U	D	1925; 1927; 1934; 1937	
ŁAPY	U	M	1925; 1927; 1934; 1937	
ŁASIN	**TORUŃ**			
TORUŃ	A	B	1838–1859	616/1
TORUŃ	A	D	1824–1885	616/1
TORUŃ	A	M	1824–1885	616/1
ŁASK	**SIERADZ**			
ŁÓDŹ	A	B	1827–1893	270
ŁASK	U	B	1894–1939	

Repository type: **A** = Archive **G** = LDS Films of German-Held Records **J** = Jewish Historical Institute **U** = Urząd Stanu Cywilnego

TOWN NAME	VOIVODSHIP (Province)				Zespół/Sygnatura (Poland)
Repository Location	Repository Type	Document Code	Years		Fond/Opis/Delo (Belarus, Ukraine, Lithuania)
PABIANICE	A	C	1879–1939		7
ŁÓDŹ	A	D	1827–1893		270
ŁASK	U	D	1894–1927; 1932–1940		
ŁÓDŹ	A	K	1899–1913		1
ŁÓDŹ	A	L	1816–1866		1
ŁÓDŹ	A	M	1827–1893		270
ŁASK	U	M	1894–1939		
ŁÓDŹ	A	S	1889–1898		83
PABIANICE	A	T	1925/1940		7, 14
PABIANICE	A	Z	1892–1902; 1908–1909; 1904–1913		7
ŁASKARZEW	**SIEDLCE**				
LUBLIN	A	K	1927		UWL WSP/771
LUBLIN	A	T	1927		UWL WSP/771
ŁASZCZÓW	**ZAMOŚĆ**				
LUBLIN	A	B	1826–1875		113
ZAMOŚĆ	A	B	1876–1877; 1879–1882; 1884–1889; 1891–1893	209/1–15
ŁASZCZÓW	U	B	1901–1910; 1922–1937		
LUBLIN	A	D	1826–1875		113
ZAMOŚĆ	A	D	1876–1877; 1879–1882; 1884–1889; 1891–1893	209/1–15
ŁASZCZÓW	U	D	1901–1910; 1922–1937		
LUBLIN	A	K	1868–1903; 1906–1916; 1923–1929		RGL IV; RGCH/489; UWL WSP/837
LUBLIN	A	M	1826–1875		113
ZAMOŚĆ	A	M	1876–1877; 1879–1882; 1884–1889; 1891–1893	209/1–15
ŁASZCZÓW	U	M	1901–1910; 1922–1937		
LUBLIN	A	T	1868–1903; 1906–1916; 1923–1929		RGL IV; RGCH/489; UWL WSP/837
LATOWICZ	**SIEDLCE**				
SIEDLCE	A	B	1827–1836		202/1–10
LATOWICZ	U	B	1900–1911; 1916–1929		
SIEDLCE	A	D	1827–1836		202/1–10
LATOWICZ	U	D	1900–1911; 1928–1929		
SIEDLCE	A	M	1827–1836		202/1–10
LATOWICZ	U	M	1900–1911; 1916–1929		
LAUENBURG	**SEE LĘBORK**				
ŁAZY	**KATOWICE**				
KATOWICE	A	K	1930–1938		880/140
ŁEBA	**SŁUPSK**				
SZCZECIN	A	G	1818; 1850–1874		MAGISTRAT ŁEBA 45–46
LĘBORK	**SŁUPSK**				
GDAŃSK	A	K	1886–1940		1953/592
ŁĘCZNA	**LUBLIN**				
LUBLIN	A	B	1826–1894		113
ŁĘCZNA	U	B	1895–1937		
LUBLIN	A	C	1812–1856		44
LUBLIN	A	D	1826–1894		113
ŁĘCZNA	U	D	1895–1937		
LUBLIN	A	E	1872–1914		RGL IV ADM.
LUBLIN	A	K	1872–1914; 1922–1937		RGL IV ADM; UWL WSP/798
LUBLIN	A	M	1826–1894		113
ŁĘCZNA	U	M	1895–1937		
LUBLIN	A	T	1816–1827; 1872–1914; 1922–1937		RGL IV ADM; UWL WSP/798
ŁĘCZYCA	**PŁOCK**				
ŁÓDŹ	A	K	1878–1912		92
ŁĘCZYCA	A	Z	1806–1950		10
ŁÓDŹ	A	Z	1887–1912		92
LEGNICA	**LEGNICA**				
LEGNICA	A	B	1875; 1881–1884; 1886–1892		300
LEGNICA	A	D	1874–1884; 1886–1892		300
LEGNICA	A	K	1742–1774; 1776–1844		3
LEGNICA	A	M	1874–1875; 1877; 1885; 1887–1891		300
KOBLENZ	G	N	1812–1850		
LEGNISZEWO	**SEE LEGNICA**				
LELÓW	**CZĘSTOCHOWA**				
CZĘSTOCHOWA	A	B	1873–1895		246
LELÓW	U	B	1896–1913; 1915–1938; 1940		
CZĘSTOCHOWA	A	D	1873–1895		246
LELÓW	U	D	1896–1913; 1915–1938; 1940		
CZĘSTOCHOWA	A	M	1873–1895		246

A Army/recruit lists; **B** Birth; **C** Census; **D** Death; **E** Voter lists; **G** Immigration; **H** Holocaust; **J** Judaica; **K** Kahal; **L** Land; **M** Marriage; **N** Name changes;
O Police files; **P** Pogroms; **R** Reference; **S** School records; **T** Tax lists; **V** Divorce; **W** Occupation lists; **X** Jewish hospital; **Y** Notary records; **Z** Local government records

TOWN NAME Repository Location	VOIVODSHIP (Province) Repository Type	Document Code	Years	Zespół/Sygnatura (Poland) Fond/Opis/Delo (Belarus, Ukraine, Lithuania)
LELÓW	U	M	1896–1913; 1915–1938; 1940	
LELÓW REGION	**CZĘSTOCHOWA**			
KRAKÓW	A	C	1790–1792	30/191A
LEOBSCHUETZ	**SEE GŁUBCZYCE**			
LESCHNITZ	**SEE LEŚNICA**			
LESKO	**KROSNO**			
PRZEMYŚL	A	B	1882–1884	154/1
LESKO	U	B	1927–1940	
LESKO	U	D	1888–1900; 1907–1921	
LESKO	U	M	1910–1937	
LEŚNICA	**OPOLE**			
OPOLE	A	B	1818–1844	17
OPOLE	A	D	1818–1864	17
OPOLE	A	G	1870–1874	17
OPOLE	A	K	1837–1902 (CEMETERY RECORDS)	17
OPOLE	A	M	1818–1864	17
OPOLE	A	W	1834–1861	17
LESZNO	**LESZNO**			
LESZNO	A	B	1808–1809; 1847–1874	83; 403
LESZNO	A	C	1795–1915; 1921	21
LESZNO	A	D	1812–1874	83; 403
LESZNO	A	J	1808–1939	403
POZNAŃ	A	L	18TH CENT.	4314/I/512
LESZNO	A	M	1847–1874	83
POZNAŃ	A	T	1689; 1704–1705; 1711/1837	4314/I/512; I/596
POZNAŃ	A	Z	1711–1732; 1751; 1812–1821	4314/I/507; I/594
WARSZAWA	J	Z	1807/1936	PROVINCE: POZNAŃ
LEWIN BRZESKI	**OPOLE**			
KOBLENZ	G	B	1815–1836	
OPOLE	A	C	1934–1940	5
KOBLENZ	G	D	1815–1836	
OPOLE	A	J	1901; 1938–1941	5
KOBLENZ	G	K	1882–1934 (CEMETERY RECORDS)	
WARSZAWA	J	K	1902/1939	PROVINCE: ŚLĄSK
OPOLE	A	L	1938–1939	5
KOBLENZ	G	M	1815–1836	
KOBLENZ	G	N	1836–1850	
WARSZAWA	J	T	1902/1939	PROVINCE: ŚLĄSK
LEŻAJSK	**RZESZÓW**			
LEŻAJSK	U	B	1902–1906	
PRZEMYŚL	A	C	1927; 1942–1943	135/61, 156
PRZEMYŚL	A	D	1826–1866	154/1
LEŻAJSK	U	D	1898–1901	
PRZEMYŚL	A	E	1938–1939	135/17
PRZEMYŚL	A	G	1940–1944	135/156
PRZEMYŚL	A	H	1940–1944	135/89
PRZEMYŚL	A	L	1909–1918; 1936–1937	135/60, 62
LVOV	A	L	1785–1788; 1819–1820	19/V/286; 20/V/95
LEŻAJSK	U	M	1898–1901	
LIBRANTOWA	**INCLUDED IN NOWY SĄCZ**			
LIDZBARK WARMIŃSKI	**OLSZTYN**			
OLSZTYN	A	D	1877–1878; 1887–1891	634/I
OLSZTYN	A	M	1875; 1877–1883; 1890–1891	634/I
LIEBAU	**SEE LUBAWKA**			
LIEBENTHAL	**SEE LUBOMIERZ**			
LIEGNITZ	**SEE LEGNICA**			
LIPSKO	**RADOM**			
STARACHOWICE	A	B	1826–1874	165
RADOM	A	B	1837; 1875–1894	187/1
LIPSKO	U	B	1895–1908; 1910–1912; 1922–1924; 1927–1942	
STARACHOWICE	A	D	1826–1874	165
RADOM	A	D	1837; 1875–1894	187/1
LIPSKO	U	D	1895–1908; 1910–1912; 1922–1924; 1927–1942	
STARACHOWICE	A	M	1826–1874	165
RADOM	A	M	1837; 1875–1894	187/1
LIPSKO	U	M	1895–1908; 1910–1912; 1922–1924; 1927–1939	

Repository type: **A** = Archive   **G** = LDS Films of German-Held Records   **J** = Jewish Historical Institute   **U** = Urząd Stanu Cywilnego

TOWN NAME	VOIVODSHIP (Province)			Zespół/Sygnatura (Poland)
Repository Location	Repository Type	Document Code	Years	Fond/Opis/Delo (Belarus, Ukraine, Lithuania)
LISSA	**SEE LESZNO**			
LOBEN	**SEE LUBLINIEC**			
LOBSENS	**SEE ŁOBŻENICA**			
ŁOBŻENICA	**PIŁA**			
BYDGOSZCZ	A	G	1885–1912	194
BYDGOSZCZ	A	K	1837–1915; 1923–1930	194
BYDGOSZCZ	A	S	1857–1911	194
ŁÓDŹ	**ŁÓDŹ**			
ŁÓDŹ	A	A	1885/1935	221/11471–11482
ŁÓDŹ	A	B	1826–1893	221/270
ŁÓDŹ	U	B	1894–1939	
ŁÓDŹ	A	C	1809–1822; 1827–1939	221/101; 374; 629–633; 8709–8748, 9873
ŁÓDŹ	A	D	1826–1893	221/270
ŁÓDŹ	U	D	1894–1939	
ŁÓDŹ	A	G	1885/1935	221/8903–8904, 8915–8916, 8923–8999
WARSZAWA	J	H	1939–1945 (INCLUDES LIST OF 8, 000 SURVIVORS)	205
ŁÓDŹ	A	H	1939–1944	221/278
ŁÓDŹ	A	J	1884–1888 (CLOTHING)	221/7174–7178
ŁÓDŹ	A	K	1806–1807; 1818–1872; 1885–1939	221/1561, 1565–1572, 1598, 2931, 6790; 228
ŁÓDŹ	A	L	1836–1866; 1881; 1884–1913; 1915–1939	221/6021–6049, 6827, 7123
ŁÓDŹ	A	M	1826–1893	270
ŁÓDŹ	U	M	1894–1939	
ŁÓDŹ	A	N	1844–1845	221/588
ŁÓDŹ	A	O	1903–1912	221/38, 41
ŁÓDŹ	A	S	1818/1935	221/4630–4687, 7167–7173, 11949
ŁÓDŹ	A	T	1884/1935	221/5916–5948, 11804, 11806
ŁÓDŹ	A	X	1818/1914	221/7174–7178; 15
ŁÓDŹ	A	Z	1818/1914	1; 5; 221
ŁOMAZY	**BIAŁA PODLASKA**			
LUBLIN	A	B	1826–1854; 1856–1872	113
ŁOMAZY	U	B	1882–1939	
LUBLIN	A	D	1826–1854; 1856–1872	113
ŁOMAZY	U	D	1882–1939	
LUBLIN	A	E	1913–1915	RGCH/490
LUBLIN	A	K	1913–1915; 1923–1928	RGCH/490; SPB/205
LUBLIN	A	M	1826–1854; 1856–1872	113
ŁOMAZY	U	M	1882–1939	
LUBLIN	A	T	1913–1915; 1923–1928	RGCH/490; SPB/205
ŁOMŻA	**ŁOMŻA**			
ŁOMŻA	A	A	1867–1918	12
ŁOMŻA	A	B	1827–1867; 1869–1890	169
ŁOMŻA	U	B	1894–1911; 1916–1937; 1939–1940	
ŁOMŻA	A	C	1896–1897	19
ŁOMŻA	A	D	1827–1891	169
ŁOMŻA	U	D	1892–1919; 1921–1940	
BIAŁYSTOK	A	K	1868–1883; 1887–1889; 1893–1906	6/120; 15/92, 129
ŁOMŻA	A	L	1896–1897; 1935–1939	19; 64
ŁOMŻA	A	M	1827–1893	169
ŁOMŻA	U	M	1901–1906; 1916; 1918–1931; 1936–1937; 1939–1940	
ŁOMŻA	A	S	1825–1839	257–259; 261–262; 267
ŁOMŻA	A	W	1867–1918	7; 21
ŁOMŻA	A	X	1850–1868	275
BIAŁYSTOK	A	X	1902–1909	15/311
ŁOMŻA	A	Y	1903; 1938	210–211
ŁOMŻA	A	Z	1935–1939	64
ŁOMŻA REGION	**ŁOMŻA**			
BIAŁYSTOK	A	K	1910–1912; 1914–1915	6/143, 195
ŁOPIENNIK	**INCLUDED IN KRASNYSTAW**			
ŁOPUSZKA MAŁA	**PRZEMYŚL**			
PRZEWORSK	A	S	1893–1924; 1940–1958	64/3–28
ŁOPUSZNO	**KIELCE**			
KIELCE	A	B	1874–1894	810

A Army/recruit lists; **B** Birth; **C** Census; **D** Death; **E** Voter lists; **G** Immigration; **H** Holocaust; **J** Judaica; **K** Kahal; **L** Land; **M** Marriage; **N** Name changes; **O** Police files; **P** Pogroms; **R** Reference; **S** School records; **T** Tax lists; **V** Divorce; **W** Occupation lists; **X** Jewish hospital; **Y** Notary records; **Z** Local government records

TOWN NAME Repository Location	VOIVODSHIP (Province) Repository Type	Document Code	Years	Zespół/Sygnatura (Poland) Fond/Opis/Delo (Belarus, Ukraine, Lithuania)
ŁOPUSZNO	U	B	1895–1911; 1920–1938	
KIELCE	A	D	1874–1894	810
ŁOPUSZNO	U	D	1895–1911; 1920–1938	
KIELCE	A	M	1874–1894	810
ŁOPUSZNO	U	M	1895–1911; 1920–1938	
ŁOSICE	**BIAŁA PODLASKA**			
SIEDLCE	A	B	1829–1835; 1837–1841; 1844–1848; 1850–1860	190/1–27
LUBLIN	A	B	1864–1869; 1871–1875; 1887; 1891–1894	113
ŁOSICE	U	B	1895–1896; 1898–1900; 1902–1910; 1922–1928; 1930; 1932; 1934; 1936–1938	
SIEDLCE	A	D	1829–1835; 1837–1841; 1844–1848; 1850–1860	190/1–27
LUBLIN	A	D	1864–1869; 1871–1875; 1887; 1891–1894	113
ŁOSICE	U	D	1895–1896; 1898–1900; 1902–1910; 1922–1928; 1930; 1932; 1934; 1936–1938	
LUBLIN	A	K	1927	UWL WSP/756
SIEDLCE	A	M	1829–1830; 1834–1841; 1844–1848; 1850–1860	190/1–27
LUBLIN	A	M	1864–1869; 1871–1875; 1887; 1891–1894	113
ŁOSICE	U	M	1895–1896; 1898–1900; 1902–1910; 1922–1928; 1930; 1932; 1934; 1936–1938	
LUBLIN	A	T	1927	UWL WSP/756
LOTZEN	**SEE GIŻYCKO**			
LOWEN	**SEE LEWIN BRZESKI**			
LOWENBERG	**SEE LWÓWEK SLASKI**			
ŁOWICZ	**SKIERNIEWICE**			
ŁOWICZ	A	A	1873–1874	224/1–2
ŁOWICZ	A	B	1826–1832; 1835–1893	296
ŁOWICZ	U	B	1894–1930	
ŁOWICZ	A	D	1873–1893	
ŁOWICZ	U	D	1894–1930	
ŁOWICZ	A	G	1918–1947	
ŁOWICZ	A	L	1812–1861	276
ŁOWICZ	A	M	1873–1893	
ŁOWICZ	U	M	1894–1930	
ŁOWICZ	A	Z	1915–1916; 1918–1920; 1940–1941	7/52, 90, 105, 108, 144, 254, 358–359, 3045–3046
LUBACZÓW	**PRZEMYŚL**			
LUBACZÓW	U	B	1914–1938	
LUBACZÓW	U	D	1915–1932	
LUBACZÓW	U	M	1915–1924	
LUBARTÓW	**LUBLIN**			
LUBLIN	A	A	1919–1939	570–592
LUBLIN	A	B	1826–1939	113
LUBARTÓW	U	B	1894–1945	
LUBLIN	A	C	1823–1827; 1917–1940	AMLUB/12; 11; 505–519
LUBLIN	A	D	1826–1939	113
LUBARTÓW	U	D	1894–1938; 1945	
LUBLIN	A	E	1873–1914; 1919–1939	RGL IV ADM; 445–460
LUBLIN	A	G	1940–1943	833–834
LUBLIN	A	H	1940–1944	AM LUB/833
LUBLIN	A	K	1766; 1873–1914; 1919–1937	RGL IV ADM; 403/795–799; 476–486
LUBLIN	A	M	1826–1939	113
LUBARTÓW	U	M	1894–1926; 1928–1939	
LUBLIN	A	T	1873–1914; 1922–1935	RGL IV ADM; UWL WSP/795
LUBLIN	A	Z	1545–1570; 1714–1827	43
LUBAWA	**OLSZTYN**			
OLSZTYN	A	B	1874–1893	796/I
OLSZTYN	A	D	1874–1893	796/I
OLSZTYN	A	M	1874–1893	796/I
LUBAWKA	**JELENIA GÓRA**			
JELENIA GÓRA	A	C	1856	9/I/623
LUBIEŃ KUJAWSKI	**WŁOCŁAWEK**			
LUBIEŃ KUJAWSKI	U	B	1876–1939	
WARSZAWA	J	C	1919/1939	105
LUBIEŃ KUJAWSKI	U	D	1877–1940	
WARSZAWA	J	E	1919/1939	105
WARSZAWA	J	K	1919/1939	105
LUBIEŃ KUJAWSKI	U	M	1881–1939	

Repository type: **A** = Archive   **G** = LDS Films of German-Held Records   **J** = Jewish Historical Institute   **U** = Urząd Stanu Cywilnego

TOWN NAME		VOIVODSHIP (Province)			
Repository Location	Repository Document Type	Code	Years		Zespół/Sygnatura (Poland) Fond/Opis/Delo (Belarus, Ukraine, Lithuania)
LUBLIN		**LUBLIN**			
LUBLIN	A	A	1886–1915		22/983–1010
LUBLIN	A	B	1826–1894; 1941		113; 22/746
LUBLIN	U	B	1895–1945		
LUBLIN	A	C	1774; 1819; 1849; 1852–1853; 1858–1871; 1876–1915; 1920–1921; 1940–1950		22/71, 749, 1155, 1172–1174, 1176–1177, 1179, 1186–1187, 1199, 1222–1734, 3430, 3486; 20; 299A
LUBLIN	A	D	1826–1894; 1907–1942		113; 22/746
LUBLIN	U	D	1895–1942		
LUBLIN	A	E	1849; 1894–1918; 1924		AML/2415; 22/545–550; SPL/650
LUBLIN	A	G	1876–1895; 1940–1942		22/1735–5237; 43–49; 170–172
LUBLIN	A	H	1939–1943		20–21; 43-49; 131; 150–172; 301–304; 333; 498/891–898
WARSZAWA	J	H	1939–1945 (INCLUDES LIST OF 3, 000 JEWS IN CONCENTRATION CAMP IN LUBLIN WITH PHOTOS)		208
LUBLIN	A	K	1775–1782; 1812–1915; 1919–1939		289; 22/536–539, 551–630, 8271; 403/800–806; 410; 645–651; 411/49
WARSZAWA	J	K	1940–1943		212
LUBLIN	A	L	1940		300
WARSZAWA	J	L	1940–1941 (3, 000 NAMES OF PROPERTY OWNERS)		
LUBLIN	A	M	1826–1894; 1941		113
LUBLIN	U	M	1895–1942; 1944–1945		
LUBLIN	A	S	1861; 1869; 1871–1913		22/418–516, 540, 2415, 5869–5895
LUBLIN	A	T	1716; 1790; 1831; 1854; 1862–1915; 1924–1936		AML/2415; UWL WSP/800
LUBLIN	A	W	1735; 1752; 1812–1869		22/262–263, 265, 1083–1386
LUBLIN	A	X	1837–1880		22/1105–1106, 2219–2222, 2231
LUBLIN	A	Z	1736; 1765; 1791; 1844–1868		488; 1533–1737
LUBLIN REGION		**LUBLIN**			
WARSZAWA	J	L	1940 (CONFISCATION OF PROPERTY)		
LUBLINIEC		**CZĘSTOCHOWA**			
KOBLENZ	G	D	1820–1900		
TARNOWSKIE GÓRY	A	K	1858–1907; 1918–1921; 1926–1930; 1936		3/901–904; 20/1224; 5/394, 399
TARNOWSKIE GÓRY	A	L	1939		5/612
TARNOWSKIE GÓRY	A	S	1918–1921		20/1224
LUBLINIEC REGION		**CZĘSTOCHOWA**			
TARNOWSKIE GÓRY	A	C	1922–1939		5/278–285, 401–404
TARNOWSKIE GÓRY	A	E	1929–1930; 1935; 1937–1938		5/47–65
TARNOWSKIE GÓRY	A	G	1922–1939		5/401–404
TARNOWSKIE GÓRY	A	Z	1936		5/399
LUBOMIERZ		**JELENIA GÓRA**			
JELENIA GÓRA	A	L	1813–1884; 1888–1944		13/I/42–52
LUBRANIEC		**WŁOCŁAWEK**			
TORUŃ	A	C	1850–1932		30
WARSZAWA	J	C	1919/1939		105
WARSZAWA	J	E	1919/1939		105
WARSZAWA	J	K	1919/1939		105
WARSZAWA	J	T	1919/1939		105
LUBYCZA KRÓLEWSKA		**ZAMOŚĆ**			
LVOV	A	M	1880–1931		701/1/97
ŁUKÓW		**SIEDLCE**			
LUBLIN	A	B	1826–1872		113
SIEDLCE	A	B	1869–1891; 1894		602/1–9
ŁUKÓW	U	B	1895–1926; 1934–1939		
LUBLIN	A	C	1869–1877; 1944–1950		ZPLUG/164
LUBLIN	A	D	1826–1872		113
SIEDLCE	A	D	1871–1883; 1885–1894		602/1–9
ŁUKÓW	U	D	1895–1940		
LUBLIN	A	E	1913–1914		RGL IV ADM.
LUBLIN	A	K	1913–1914; 1923–1936		RGL IV ADM; UWL WSP/807–810; SPŁUK/629; 413/637–641
LUBLIN	A	M	1826–1872		113
SIEDLCE	A	M	1871–1883; 1885–1894		602/1–9
ŁUKÓW	U	M	1895–1940		
LUBLIN	A	T	1913–1914; 1925–1936		RGL IV; UWL WSP/807; SPŁUK/629
ŁUKOWE		**KROSNO**			
SANOK	A	C	1921–1953		27/21–28; 30–34

A Army/recruit lists; **B** Birth; **C** Census; **D** Death; **E** Voter lists; **G** Immigration; **H** Holocaust; **J** Judaica; **K** Kahal; **L** Land; **M** Marriage; **N** Name changes; **O** Police files; **P** Pogroms; **R** Reference; **S** School records; **T** Tax lists; **V** Divorce; **W** Occupation lists; **X** Jewish hospital; **Y** Notary records; **Z** Local government records

TOWN NAME	VOIVODSHIP (Province)			Zespół/Sygnatura (Poland)
Repository Location	Repository Document Type	Code	Years	Fond/Opis/Delo (Belarus, Ukraine, Lithuania)
ŁUPKÓW	**KROSNO**			
SANOK	A	C	1931–1945	31/2–8(5)
LUTOMIERSK	**SIERADZ**			
ŁÓDŹ	A	B	1826–1876	270
LUTOMIERSK	U	B	1940–1944	
ŁÓDŹ	A	D	1826–1876	270
LUTOMIERSK	U	D	1940–1944	
ŁÓDŹ	A	M	1826–1876	270
LUTOMIERSK	U	M	1940–1944	
PABIANICE	A	Z	1821–1866; 1894–1913	148
LUTOTÓW	**SIERADZ**			
LUTOTÓW	U	B	1882–1907; 1913; 1918; 1923–1939	
LUTOTÓW	U	D	1882–1926; 1928–1939	
LUTOTÓW	U	M	1882–1920; 1922–1939	
ŁÓDŹ	A	Z	1913–1914	92
LUTOWISKA	**KROSNO**			
PRZEMYŚL	A	Y	1916–1917	731
LVOV	A	L	1785–1788; 1819–1820; 1855; 1883; 1895	19/XV/183; 20/XV/165; 186/2/494; 186/1/4990; 186/10/2209
LVOV	A	S	1874-1911	178/2/797
LWÓWEK	**POZNAŃ**			
POZNAŃ	A	K	1919–1933	4383/318
POZNAŃ	A	S	1836–1919	4383/84–87
LWÓWEK SLASKI	**JELENIA GÓRA**			
JELENIA GÓRA	A	C	1742–1816; 1849–1889	10/I/120–123
KOBLENZ	G	K	1815–1932 (CEMETERY RECORDS)	
LYCK	**SEE EŁK**			
ŁYSOBYKI	**LUBLIN**			
LUBLIN	A	B	1826–1876; 1881	113
LUBLIN	A	D	1826–1876; 1881	113
LUBLIN	A	K	1913–1914; 1927; 1931–1935	RGL IV; UWL WSP/809; SPŁUK/630
LUBLIN	A	M	1826–1876; 1881	113
ŁYSZKOWICE	**SKIERNIEWICE**			
ŁOWICZ	A	B	1918–1939	305
ŁOWICZ	A	D	1918–1939	305
ŁOWICZ	A	M	1918–1939	305
MACIEJOWA	**INCLUDED IN NOWY SĄCZ**			
MACIEJOWICE	**SIEDLCE**			
LUBLIN	A	E	1914	RGL IV ADM
LUBLIN	A	K	1914; 1921–1936	RGL IV ADM; UWL WSP/772
LUBLIN	A	T	1914; 1921–1936	RGL IV ADM; UWL WSP/772
MAĆKOWICE	**PRZEMYŚL**			
PRZEMYŚL	A	C	1930–1941	207/22–23, 41, 56–57, 154, 164
MAERKISCH FRIEDLAND	**SEE MIROSŁAWIEC**			
MAGNUSZEW	**RADOM**			
RADOM	A	B	1826–1839; 1842–1866; 1868–1869; 1876; 1883; 1889; 1893–1894; 1901–1902; 1905–1913; 1919–1922; 1924–1932; 1934; 1938–1939	186
RADOM	A	D	1826–1839; 1842–1866; 1868–1869; 1876; 1883; 1889; 1893–1894; 1901–1902; 1905–1913; 1919–1922; 1924–1932; 1934; 1938–1939	188
RADOM	A	M	1826–1839; 1842–1866; 1868–1869; 1876; 1883; 1889; 1893–1894; 1901–1902; 1905–1913; 1919–1922; 1924–1932; 1934; 1938–1939	188
MAJDAN KRÓLEWSKI	**TARNOBRZEG**			
RZESZÓW	A	A	1918–1938	392/105–106, 117–118
RZESZÓW	A	L	1927	392/98
LVOV	A	L	1785–1788; 1819–1820	19/V/262; 20/V/136
MAKÓW MAZOWIECKI	**OSTROŁĘKA**			
MAKÓW MAZOWIECKI	U	B	1897–1915; 1917–1921; 1923–1939	
MAKÓW MAZOWIECKI	U	D	1897–1915; 1917–1921; 1923–1939	
BIAŁYSTOK	A	K	1914–1915	6/200, 203, 208
MAKÓW MAZOWIECKI	U	M	1897–1915; 1917–1921; 1923–1939	
MALBORK	**ELBLĄG**			
GDAŃSK	A	B	1847–1934	1497/46, 48, 50
MALBORK	A	C	1855/1940	60; 91/1–107

Repository type: **A** = Archive **G** = LDS Films of German-Held Records **J** = Jewish Historical Institute **U** = Urząd Stanu Cywilnego

TOWN NAME Repository Location	VOIVODSHIP (Province) Repository Document Type	Code	Years	Zespół/Sygnatura (Poland) Fond/Opis/Delo (Belarus, Ukraine, Lithuania)
GDAŃSK		A	D	1847/1906	
MALBORK		A	E	1885; 1896; 1908	1497/46, 53–54
MALBORK		A	J	1856–1937	60; 91/109–115
MALBORK		A	K	1818–1897	60/63–64
GDAŃSK		A	K	1906–1940	90/23–24, 45, 60; 92/1–61
GDAŃSK		A	M	1847–1916	508/2533–2534, 2536
MAŁKINIA GÓRNA	**OSTROŁĘKA**				1497/46–47, 49, 51–52
MAŁKINIA GÓRNA		U	B	1923–1925; 1927–1929; 1932–1936	
MAŁKINIA GÓRNA		U	D	1907; 1925; 1927–1928; 1933–1936	
MAŁKINIA GÓRNA		U	M	1923; 1925; 1927–1928; 1935–1936	
MAŁKOWICE	**PRZEMYŚL**				
PRZEMYŚL		A	C	1932	207/24–25, 42, 58, 59, 164
MAŁOGOSZCZ	**KIELCE**				
JĘDRZEJÓW		A	B	1826–1827; 1829; 1832–1855; 1857–1860; 1863–1867; 1885–1889	59
MAŁOGOSZCZ		U	B	1907; 1912; 1925–1928; 1934	
JĘDRZEJÓW		A	D	1826–1855; 1857–1860; 1863–1867; 1886–1889	59
MAŁOGOSZCZ		U	D	1907; 1910; 1912; 1926–1928; 1934	
JĘDRZEJÓW		A	M	1826–1827; 1829; 1832–1855; 1857–1860; 1863–1867; 1886–1889	59
MAŁOGOSZCZ		U	M	1907; 1912; 1916–1919; 1926–1928; 1934–1939	
MAŁY PŁOCK	**ŁOMŻA**				
ŁOMŻA		A	C	1899–1939	158
MANASTERZ	**PRZEMYŚL**				
PRZEWORSK		A	S	1896–1950	65/1–19, 23–40, 43–50
MARCINKOWICE	**NOWY SĄCZ**				
NOWY SĄCZ		U	B	INCLUDED IN NOWY SĄCZ	
NOWY SĄCZ		U	D	INCLUDED IN NOWY SĄCZ	
NOWY SĄCZ		U	M	INCLUDED IN NOWY SĄCZ	
MARGONIN	**PIŁA**				
POZNAŃ		A	S	1824–1912	1029/66
MARIENBURG	**SEE MALBORK**				
MARIENWERDER	**SEE KWIDZYN**				
MARKI	**WARSZAWA**				
WARSZAWA/PRAGA POLNOC		U	B	1920–1939	
WARSZAWA/PRAGA POLNOC		U	D	1928–1939	
WARSZAWA/PRAGA POLNOC		U	M	1920–1939	
MARKOWA	**RZESZÓW**				
PRZEMYŚL		A	C	1931–1952	196/13, 15, 19–20
MARKUSZÓW	**LUBLIN**				
LUBLIN		A	B	1826–1894	113
MARKUSZÓW		U	B	1895–1941	
LUBLIN		A	D	1826–1894	113
MARKUSZÓW		U	D	1895–1941	
LUBLIN		A	E	1868–1912	RGL IV ADM
LUBLIN		A	K	1868–1912; 1927–1929	RGL IV ADM; UWL WSP/817
LUBLIN		A	M	1826–1894	113
MARKUSZÓW		U	M	1895–1941	
LUBLIN		A	T	1868–1912; 1927–1929	RGL IV ADM; UWL WSP/817
MASSOW	**SEE MASZEWO**				
MASZEWO	**SZCZECIN**				
SZCZECIN		A	B	1847–1888	AMTSGERICHT MASSOW 153
SZCZECIN		A	D	1848–1874	AMTSGERICHT MASSOW 155
SZCZECIN		A	M	1849–1874	AMTSGERICHT MASSOW 154
MESERITZ	**SEE MIĘDZYRZEC**				
MIASTKO	**SŁUPSK**				
SŁUPSK		A	B	1813–1847	70/11
SŁUPSK		A	D	1813–1847	70/11
SŁUPSK		A	M	1813–1847	70/11
MICHALCZOWA	**INCLUDED IN NOWY SĄCZ**				
MICHAŁKOWICE	**OPOLE**				
KATOWICE		A	B	1844–1847	674/I/368C, 368D
KATOWICE		A	D	1844–1847	674/I/368C, 599
MICHÓW	**LUBLIN**				
LUBLIN		A	B	1826–1894	113

A Army/recruit lists; **B** Birth; **C** Census; **D** Death; **E** Voter lists; **G** Immigration; **H** Holocaust; **J** Judaica; **K** Kahal; **L** Land; **M** Marriage; **N** Name changes; **O** Police files; **P** Pogroms; **R** Reference; **S** School records; **T** Tax lists; **V** Divorce; **W** Occupation lists; **X** Jewish hospital; **Y** Notary records; **Z** Local government records

TOWN NAME	VOIVODSHIP (Province)			Zespół/Sygnatura (Poland)
Repository Location	Repository Type	Document Code	Years	Fond/Opis/Delo (Belarus, Ukraine, Lithuania)
MICHÓW	U	B	1895–1914; 1919–1925; 1927–1937	
LUBLIN	A	D	1826–1894	113
MICHÓW	U	D	1895–1914; 1919–1925; 1927–1937	
LUBLIN	A	E	1873–1914	RGL IV ADM.
LUBLIN	A	K	1873–1914; 1927–1936	RGL IV ADM; UWL WSP/799
LUBLIN	A	M	1826–1894	113
MICHÓW	U	M	1895–1914; 1919–1925; 1927–1937	113
MIECHÓW	**KIELCE**			397
JĘDRZEJÓW	A	B	1870–1880; 1888–1890	
MIECHÓW	U	B	1891–1895; 1897; 1900–1904; 1909–1918; 1921–1942	
JĘDRZEJÓW	A	D	1870–1880; 1888–1891	397
MIECHÓW	U	D	1892–1896; 1905–1914; 1918–1925; 1928; 1939	
JĘDRZEJÓW	A	M	1870–1880; 1888–1891	397
MIECHÓW	U	M	1892–1903; 1908–1942	
MIECHOWICE	**KATOWICE**			
KATOWICE	A	B	1848; 1874–1885	674/I/368E; 752/1
KATOWICE	A	D	1848; 1874–1885	674/I/368E; 752/1
KATOWICE	A	M	1848; 1874–1885	674/I/368E; 752/1
MIĘDZYBÓRZ	**KALISZ**			
KOBLENZ	G	B	1868–1883	
KOBLENZ	G	K	1870–1906 (CEMETERY RECORDS)	
WARSZAWA	J	T	1877–1878	PROVINCE: ŚLĄSK
MIĘDZYCHÓD	**GORZÓW WIELKOPOLSKI**			
LEIPZIG	G	B	1816	
POZNAŃ	A	C	1840–1858; 1870–1875; 1897–1913	313/141–143, 1131–1139,1149–1150,2124
LEIPZIG	G	D	1816	
POZNAŃ	A	K	1834–1914	313/459–464, 2117–2120, 2128–2130, 2133, 2135–2136
LEIPZIG	G	M	1816	
POZNAŃ	A	S	1853–1873	313/3126
MIĘDZYRZEC PODLASKI	**BIAŁA PODLASKA**			
LUBLIN	A	B	1826–1893	113
MIĘDZYRZEC PODLASKI	U	B	1894–1914; 1916–1938	
RADZYŃ PODLASKI	A	C	1924; 1934	24/225–227
LUBLIN	A	D	1826–1893	113
MIĘDZYRZEC PODLASKI	U	D	1894–1914; 1916–1938	
LUBLIN	A	E	1872; 1913–1914	RGL IV ADM
LUBLIN	A	K	1863–1866; 1872; 1913–1914; 1927–1936	RGL IV ADM; NPRADZYN/12; UWL WSP/821
LUBLIN	A	M	1826–1893	113
MIĘDZYRZEC PODLASKI	U	M	1894–1914; 1916–1938	
LUBLIN	A	T	1872; 1913–1914; 1920–1943	RGL IV; UWL WSP/821
MIĘDZYRZECZ	**GORZÓW WIELKOPOLSKI**			
GORZÓW WIELKOPOLSKI	A	B	1817–1825; 1828; 1835; 1837; 1839–1841; 1843–1844; 1846–1864	AMTSGERICHT MESERITZ 247/5590
GORZÓW WIELKOPOLSKI	A	D	1817–1825; 1828; 1835; 1837; 1839–1841; 1843–1844; 1846–1864	AMTSGERICHT MESERITZ 247/5592
GORZÓW WIELKOPOLSKI	A	M	1817–1825; 1828; 1835; 1837; 1839–1841; 1843–1844; 1846–1864	AMTSGERICHT MESERITZ 247/5591
BERLIN	G	N	1846–1903	
MIELCIESKO	**SEE MIEŚCISKO**			
MIELEC	**RZESZÓW**			
RZESZÓW	A	A	1847–1913; 1929–1932	752/36, 90–914
RZESZÓW	A	B	1920–1935	752/89
RZESZÓW	A	C	1940–1943	752/117
RZESZÓW	A	D	1920–1935	752/89
RZESZÓW	A	E	1914–1930	752/88
RZESZÓW	A	H	1940–1943	752/117
PRZEMYŚL	A	Y	1860–1873; 1875–1905; 1907–1936	87/1240–1245
MIELEC REGION	**RZESZÓW**			
RZESZÓW	A	C	1921–1944	765/2–3A
MIELĘCIN	**PIŁA**			
POZNAŃ	A	B	1840–1846	3582/1–7
POZNAŃ	A	D	1840–1846	3582/1–7
POZNAŃ	A	M	1840–1846	3582/1–7

Repository type: **A** = Archive   **G** = LDS Films of German-Held Records   **J** = Jewish Historical Institute   **U** = Urząd Stanu Cywilnego

TOWN NAME	VOIVODSHIP (Province)				
Repository Location	Repository Document Type	Document Code	Years		Zespół/Sygnatura (Poland) Fond/Opis/Delo (Belarus, Ukraine, Lithuania)
MIEŚCISKO	**PIŁA**				
POZNAŃ	A	K	1823–1913		338/267–271
MIESZKOWICE	**SZCZECIN**				
BERLIN	G	B	1847–1874		
BERLIN	G	D	1847–1874		
BERLIN	G	M	1847–1874		
MIKOŁÓW	**KATOWICE**				
KATOWICE	A	B	1849–1874		113/I/62
PSZCZYNA	A	C	1812–1847; 1863–1865; 1885–1886; 1901–1918; 1923–1938		56/I/71–73, 1412, 1415–1416, 1422
PSZCZYNA	A	G	1823–1847; 1862–1887; 1890–1917; 1921–1942		56/I/1416, 1421, 1423–1441
PSZCZYNA	A	H	1939–1941		56/I/2041–2042
KATOWICE	A	K	1921		27/I–VI/1996
KATOWICE	A	S	1938–1939		27/I–XIII/847
MIKSTAT	**KALISZ**				
POZNAŃ	A	B	1835–1846		3583/1–10
POZNAŃ	A	D	1835–1846		3583/1–10
POZNAŃ	A	M	1835–1846		3583/1–10
MIŁAKOWO	**OLSZTYN**				
OLSZTYN	A	B	1875–1880; 1882–1887; 1889–1894		746/I
OLSZTYN	A	D	1875–1878; 1880–1882; 1884–1889; 1892; 1894		746/I
OLSZTYN	A	M	1875–1876; 1878–1880; 1883–1889; 1891–1894		746/I
MIŁOMŁYN	**OLSZTYN**				
OLSZTYN	A	B	1874–1894		890/I
MIŁOSŁAW	**POZNAŃ**				
POZNAŃ	A	S	1833–1919		339/69–72
MIŃSK MAZOWIECKI	**SIEDLCE**				
SIEDLCE	A	B	1826–1829; 1832–1894		201/1–65
MIŃSK MAZOWIECKI	U	B	1895–1939		
OTWOCK	A	C	1890–1930; 1935–1939		35
SIEDLCE	A	D	1826–1829; 1832–1894		201/1–65
MIŃSK MAZOWIECKI	U	D	1895–1937		
OTWOCK	A	E	1922–1923; 1927; 1930–1935; 1939		35
OTWOCK	A	H	1937–1939; 1942–1944; 1949		35; 40
SIEDLCE	A	L	1821–1926		759/1–2448
SIEDLCE	A	M	1826–1829; 1832–1894		201/1–65
MIŃSK MAZOWIECKI	U	M	1895–1939		
MIROSŁAWIEC	**PIŁA**				
KOBLENZ	G	B	1815–1847		
KOBLENZ	G	C	1799–1810		
KOBLENZ	G	D	1815–1847		
KOBLENZ	G	M	1815–1847		
MIRSK	**JELENIA GÓRA**				
JELENIA GÓRA	A	C	1833–1902		12/2166
JELENIA GÓRA	A	T	1860–1931; 1933–1935; 1937–1938; 1941–1942		12/I/1522–1758
MŁAWA	**CIECHANÓW**				
MŁAWA	A	B	1829–1830; 1832; 1834–1836; 1838–1841; 1843–1852; 1854; 1856–1874; 1876–1879; 1881–1883; 1885–1887; 1889–1891; 1893–1895		56
MŁAWA	U	B	1896–1905; 1907–1909; 1911–1914; 1916–1919; 1921–1923; 1925–1931; 1934–1938		
MŁAWA	A	D	1829–1830; 1832; 1834–1836; 1838–1841; 1843–1852; 1854; 1856–1874; 1876–1879; 1881–1883; 1885–1887; 1889–1891; 1893–1895		56
MŁAWA	U	D	1896–1905; 1907–1909; 1911–1914; 1916–1919; 1921–1923; 1925–1931; 1934–1938		
MŁAWA	A	M	1829–1830; 1832; 1834–1836; 1838–1841; 1843–1852; 1854; 1856–1874; 1876–1879; 1881–1883; 1885–1887; 1889–1891; 1893–1895		56
MŁAWA	U	M	1896–1905; 1907–1909; 1911–1914; 1916–1919; 1921–1923; 1925–1931; 1934–1938		
MŁAWA	A	Y	1809–1952		191; 193; 196; 198–201; 204–205; 207–208; 213; 216–217; 227; 238–242; 300
MŁYNARY	**ELBLĄG**				
KOBLENZ	G	K	1873–1938 (CEMETERY RECORDS)		

A Army/recruit lists; **B** Birth; **C** Census; **D** Death; **E** Voter lists; **G** Immigration; **H** Holocaust; **J** Judaica; **K** Kahal; **L** Land; **M** Marriage; **N** Name changes; **O** Police files; **P** Pogroms; **R** Reference; **S** School records; **T** Tax lists; **V** Divorce; **W** Occupation lists; **X** Jewish hospital; **Y** Notary records; **Z** Local government records

TOWN NAME Repository Location		VOIVODSHIP (Province)			Zespół/Sygnatura (Poland) Fond/Opis/Delo (Belarus, Ukraine, Lithuania)
	Repository Document	Type	Code	Years	
MODLIBORZYCE		**TARNOBRZEG**			
LUBLIN	A	E	1868–1911		RGL IV ADM
LUBLIN	A	K	1868–1911; 1922–1935		RGL IV ADM; UWL WSP/786
LUBLIN	A	T	1790–1808; 1868–1911; 1922–1935		RGL IV ADM; UWL WSP/786
LUBLIN	A	Z	1641–1809		47
MOGIELNICA		**RADOM**			
GÓRA KALWARIA	A	B	1808–1813; 1815; 1818–1873		159; 37
RADOM	A	B	1872–1878; 1881–1894		472
MOGILENICA	U	B	1895–1941		
GÓRA KALWARIA	A	C	1885–1931		130
GÓRA KALWARIA	A	D	1808–1813; 1815; 1818–1873		159; 37
RADOM	A	D	1874–1878; 1881–1894		472
MOGILENICA	U	D	1895–1941		
GÓRA KALWARIA	A	M	1808–1813; 1815; 1818–1873		159; 37
RADOM	A	M	1871–1878; 1881–1894		472
MOGILENICA	U	M	1895–1941		
MOGILNO		**BYDGOSZCZ**			
INOWROCŁAW	A	B	1823–1874; 1875/1907		61/854
INOWROCŁAW	A	C	1834/1909; 1920–1939		61
INOWROCŁAW	A	D	1829–1846		61
INOWROCŁAW	A	E	1919–1935		61
INOWROCŁAW	A	K	1879/1919		5
INOWROCŁAW	A	M	1829–1846		61
INOWROCŁAW	A	T	1810–1939		61/110–174, 1124–1169
MOHRUNGEN		**SEE MORĄG**			
MOKOBODY		**SIEDLCE**			
SIEDLCE	A	B	1826–1841; 1843–1851; 1853–1860; 1862–1869		194/1–42
MOKOBODY	U	B	1902; 1906; 1908; 1914; 1917–1918; 1921–1924; 1926; 1929–1930; 1934–1938		
SIEDLCE	A	D	1827–1841; 1843–1851; 1853–1860; 1862; 1864–1869		194/1–42
MOKOBODY	U	D	1902; 1906; 1908; 1914; 1917–1918; 1921–1922; 1926; 1929–1930; 1934–1938		
LUBLIN	A	E	1913–1915		RGL IV ADM
LUBLIN	A	K	1913–1915; 1926–1927		RGL IV ADM; UWL WSP/1564
SIEDLCE	A	M	1827–1836; 1838–1840; 1843–1851; 1853; 1855; 1857–1860; 1862; 1864–1868		194/1–42
MOKOBODY	U	M	1902; 1906; 1908; 1914; 1917–1918; 1926; 1929–1930; 1934–1938		
LUBLIN	A	T	1913–1915; 1926–1927		RGL IV ADM; UWL WSP/1564
MOKRE		**KROSNO**			
SANOK	A	C	1937–1939		23/32
MORĄG		**OLSZTYN**			
OLSZTYN	A	B	1874–1894		744/I
OLSZTYN	A	D	1874–1894		744/I
OLSZTYN	A	M	1874–1894		744/I
MORDY		**SIEDLCE**			
SIEDLCE	A	B	1826–1833; 1835–1842; 1844–1850; 1852; 1856–1858; 1862–1863; 1867; 1870–1872; 1874; 1876–1889; 1894		196/1–46
MORDY	U	B	1896–1906; 1908; 1910–1912; 1917–1918; 1921–1922; 1929–1937		
SIEDLCE	A	D	1826–1833; 1835–1842; 1844–1850; 1852; 1856–1858; 1862–1863; 1867; 1870–1889; 1893–1894		196/1–46
MORDY	U	D	1896–1906; 1908; 1910–1912; 1917–1918; 1921–1922; 1929–1937		
LUBLIN	A	E	1913–1914		RGL IV ADM
LUBLIN	A	K	1913–1914; 1922–1929		RGL IV ADM; UWL WSP/824
SIEDLCE	A	M	1826–1830; 1832–1833; 1835–1850; 1852; 1856–1863; 1867; 1870–1872; 1874; 1876; 1878–1879; 1882; 1884–1885; 1889; 1894		196/1–46
MORDY	U	M	1896–1906; 1908; 1910–1912; 1917–1918; 1921–1922; 1929–1937		
LUBLIN	A	T	1913–1914; 1922–1929		RGL IV ADM; UWL WSP/824
MOSINA		**POZNAŃ**			
POZNAŃ	A	B	1835–1836		3584/1–2
POZNAŃ	A	D	1835–1836		3584/1–2

Repository type: **A** = Archive **G** = LDS Films of German-Held Records **J** = Jewish Historical Institute **U** = Urząd Stanu Cywilnego

TOWN NAME	VOIVODSHIP (Province)			Zespół/Sygnatura (Poland)
Repository Location	Repository Document Type	Code	Years	Fond/Opis/Delo (Belarus, Ukraine, Lithuania)
POZNAŃ	A	M	1835–1836	3584/1–2
MOSZCZENICA	**NOWY SĄCZ**			
ŻYWIEC	A	C	1934–1939	9/8
MRĄGOWO	**OLSZTYN**			
OLSZTYN	A	B	1874–1893	869/I
OLSZTYN	A	C	1840; 1842–1843; 1847; 1849; 1884/1936	16/I
OLSZTYN	A	D	1874–1893	869/I
OLSZTYN	A	M	1874–1893	869/I
MSTÓW	**CZĘSTOCHOWA**			
CZĘSTOCHOWA	A	B	1826–1895	92
MSTÓW	U	B	1896–1901; 1904; 1907–1941	
CZĘSTOCHOWA	A	D	1826–1895	92
MSTÓW	U	D	1896–1897; 1899–1902; 1904; 1907–1909; 1911–1941	
ŁÓDŹ	A	K	1887–1892	1
CZĘSTOCHOWA	A	M	1826–1895	92
MSTÓW	U	M	1896–1905; 1907–1909; 1911–1919; 1921; 1923–1926	
MSZCZONÓW	**SKIERNIEWICE**			
ŻYRARDÓW	A	B	1826–1869; 1872; 1875–1877	25
MSZCZONÓW	U	B	1882–1911; 1913–1914; 1916–1923; 1937–1938	
ŻYRARDÓW	A	D	1826–1869; 1872; 1875–1877	25
MSZCZONÓW	U	D	1882–1911; 1913–1914; 1916–1923; 1937–1938	
ŻYRARDÓW	A	M	1826–1869; 1872; 1875–1877	25
MSZCZONÓW	U	M	1882–1911; 1913–1914; 1916–1923; 1937–1938	
MUHLHAUSEN	**SEE MŁYNARY**			
MUNINA	**PRZEMYŚL**			
PRZEMYŚL	A	C	1937/1946	177/5, 58, 65, 69
PRZEMYŚL	A	E	1938	177/9
MUSZYNA	**NOWY SĄCZ**			
NOWY SĄCZ	A	C	1937	84
MYŚLIBÓRZ	**GORZÓW WIELKOPOLSKI**			
SZCZECIN	A	C	1934–1943	MAGISTRAT SOLDIN 28
KOBLENZ	G	D	1833–1847	
SZCZECIN	A	E	1871–1899	MAGISTRAT SOLDIN 32
KOBLENZ	G	M	1833–1847	
MYSŁOWICE	**KATOWICE**			
KATOWICE	A	B	1847–1874	82/I/416; 5/I/269–274
MYSŁOWICE	U	B	1875–1892	
KATOWICE	A	C	1785–1834	82/I/72
KATOWICE	A	D	1847–1874	82/I/416; 5/I/290–291
MYSŁOWICE	U	D	1875–1892	
KATOWICE	A	E	1930; 1935	82/I/759–761, 766–768
KATOWICE	A	G	1925–1933	82/I/742
KATOWICE	A	H	1940–1943	82/I/682–683
KATOWICE	A	K	1853; 1922–1932	27/I–VI/1997; 82/I/15
KATOWICE	A	L	1845	82/I/127
KATOWICE	A	M	1847–1874	82/I/416; 5/I/276–289
MYSŁOWICE	U	M	1875–1892	
KATOWICE	A	S	1908–1917	9/I/7
MYSZKÓW	**CZĘSTOCHOWA**			
MYSZKÓW	U	B	1930–1940	
MYSZKÓW	U	D	1940–1941	
MYSZKÓW	U	M	1930–1934	
NADARZYN	**WARSZAWA**			
ŻYRARDÓW	A	B	1826–1874	180
NADARZYN	U	B	1882–1914; 1917; 1919–1936	
ŻYRARDÓW	A	D	1826–1874	180
NADARZYN	U	D	1882–1914; 1917; 1919–1936	
ŻYRARDÓW	A	M	1826–1874	180
NADARZYN	U	M	1882–1914; 1917; 1919–1936	
NAKŁO NAD NOTECIĄ	**BYDGOSZCZ**			
BYDGOSZCZ	A	B	1823–1889	383; 1741
BYDGOSZCZ	A	C	1857–1945	195
BYDGOSZCZ	A	D	1823–1887	383; 1741
BYDGOSZCZ	A	M	1823–1887	383; 1741
NAMSLAU	**SEE NAMYSŁÓW**			

A Army/recruit lists; **B** Birth; **C** Census; **D** Death; **E** Voter lists; **G** Immigration; **H** Holocaust; **J** Judaica; **K** Kahal; **L** Land; **M** Marriage; **N** Name changes; **O** Police files; **P** Pogroms; **R** Reference; **S** School records; **T** Tax lists; **V** Divorce; **W** Occupation lists; **X** Jewish hospital; **Y** Notary records; **Z** Local government records

TOWN NAME	VOIVODSHIP (Province)			Zespół/Sygnatura (Poland)
Repository Location	Repository Type	Document Code	Years	Fond/Opis/Delo (Belarus, Ukraine, Lithuania)
NAMYSŁÓW	**OPOLE**			
OPOLE	A	B	1834–1868	18
OPOLE	A	C	1799–1885	18
KOBLENZ	G	D	1812–1847	
OPOLE	A	E	1888–1910	18
WARSZAWA	J	K	1851/1889	PROVINCE: ŚLĄSK
KOBLENZ	G	K	1914–1918 (CEMETERY RECORDS)	
OPOLE	A	M	1834–1868; 18	
OPOLE	A	S	1820	18
NAROL	**PRZEMYŚL**			
PRZEMYŚL	A	E	1934–1938	189/1–2
NASIELSK	**CIECHANÓW**			
PUŁTUSK	A	B	1875–1893; 1937	116
NASIELSK	U	B	1894–1913; 1917–1920; 1922–1935	
PUŁTUSK	A	D	1875–1893	116
NASIELSK	U	D	1894–1913; 1917–1920; 1922–1935	
PUŁTUSK	A	M	1875–1893	116
NASIELSK	U	M	1894–1913; 1917–1920; 1922–1935	
NAUGARD	**SEE NOWOGARD**			
NAWOJOWA	**INCLUDED IN NOWY SĄCZ**			
NEIDENBURG	**SEE NIDZICA**			
NEISSE	**SEE NYSA**			
NEU BENTSCHEN	**SEE ZBĄSZYNEK**			
NEUMARKT	**SEE ŚRODA ŚLĄSKA**			
NEUSALZ	**SEE NOWA SÓL**			
NEUSTADT	**SEE WEJHEROWO**			
NEUSTADT IN OBERSCHLESIEN	**SEE PRUDNIK**			
NEUSTETTIN	**SEE SZCZECINEK**			
NEUTEICH	**SEE NOWY STAW**			
NIDZICA	**OLSZTYN**			
OLSZTYN	A	B	1874–1881; 1883–1893	893/I
OLSZTYN	A	D	1874–1893	893/I
OLSZTYN	A	M	1874–1893	893/I
NIEBYLEC REGION	**RZESZÓW**			
RZESZÓW	A	B	1877; 1879–1885; 1887–1890; 1892; 1895; 1898; 1900–1904	907/3–26
RZESZÓW	A	D	1905–1906; 1912–1913	907/1–2
LVOV	A	L	1785–1788; 1819–1820	19/II/108; 20/II/200
NIEMODLIN	**OPOLE**			
OPOLE	A	B	1804–1823	1
BERLIN	G	B	1812–1874	
OPOLE	A	D	1804–1824	1
BERLIN	G	D	1812–1874	
BERLIN	G	M	1812–1874	
NIENADOWA	**PRZEMYŚL**			
PRZEMYŚL	A	C	1931–1939	200/42
NIESZAWA	**WŁOCŁAWEK**			
WŁOCŁAWEK	A	B	1826–1903	563
NIESZAWA	U	B	1904–1939	
WŁOCŁAWEK	A	D	1826–1836; 1865–1879	563
NIESZAWA	U	D	1882–1938	
WŁOCŁAWEK	A	M	1826–1894	563
NIESZAWA	U	M	1895–1939	
NISKO	**TARNOBRZEG**			
SANDOMIERZ	A	G	1918–1939	592
SANDOMIERZ	A	H	1943–1944	522
PRZEWORSK	A	T	1936/1951	17/25–33, 109–122
PRZEMYŚL	A	Y	1873–1934	88; 1100–1108
NISKO REGION	**TARNOBRZEG**			
PRZEWORSK	A	C	1931–1947	17/4–15, 80–82
PRZEWORSK	A	E	1939	17/2–3
PRZEWORSK	A	G	1932–1941; 1948–1951	17/16–18, 77–79
NIWISKA	**RZESZÓW**			
RZESZÓW	A	C	1931–1939	393/1–3

Repository type: **A** = Archive   **G** = LDS Films of German-Held Records   **J** = Jewish Historical Institute   **U** = Urząd Stanu Cywilnego

TOWN NAME	VOIVODSHIP (Province)				
Repository Location	Repository Document Type	Code	Years		Zespół/Sygnatura (Poland) Fond/Opis/Delo (Belarus, Ukraine, Lithuania)
NORENBERG	**SEE IŃSKO**				
NOWA BRZEŹNICA	**CZĘSTOCHOWA**				
NOWA BRZEŹNICA	U	B	1882–1938		
NOWA BRZEŹNICA	U	D	1883–1940		
NOWA BRZEŹNICA	U	M	1882–1928; 1930–1938		
NOWA SŁUPIA	**KIELCE**				
NOWA SŁUPIA	U	B	1890–1913; 1916; 1918–1920; 1922–1940		
NOWA SŁUPIA	U	D	1890–1913; 1916; 1918–1920; 1922–1940		
NOWA SŁUPIA	U	M	1890–1913; 1916; 1918–1920; 1922–1940		
NOWA SÓL	**ZIELONA GÓRA**				
WARSZAWA	J	D	1878–1927		PROVINCE: ŚLĄSK
WARSZAWA	J	K	1877/1937		PROVINCE: ŚLĄSK
NOWA WIEŚ	**KATOWICE**				
KATOWICE	A	B	1911–1920		107/I
NOWE MIASTO	**CIECHANÓW**				
NOWE MIASTO	U	B	1882–1885; 1887–1893; 1895–1916; 1918; 1920; 1934–1936		
NOWE MIASTO	U	D	1882–1885; 1887–1893; 1895–1916; 1918; 1920; 1934–1936		
NOWE MIASTO	U	M	1882–1885; 1887–1893; 1895–1916; 1918; 1920; 1934–1936		
NOWE MIASTO NAD WARTĄ	**POZNAŃ**				
BERLIN	G	B	1817–1836		
BERLIN	G	D	1817–1836		
POZNAŃ	A	K	1894–1918		4063/145
BERLIN	G	M	1817–1836		
NOWE MIASTO NAD PILICĄ	**RADOM**				
ŁÓDŹ	A	B	1826–1868		270
RADOM	A	B	1874–1877; 1880–1882; 1887–1891		450/1
NOWE MIASTO NAD PILICĄ	U	B	1893–1895; 1899–1901; 1908–1913; 1919; 1923; 1926–1927; 1933; 1936–1939		
PIOTRKÓW TRYBUNALSKI	A	C	1817–1950		117
ŁÓDŹ	A	D	1826–1868		270
RADOM	A	D	1874–1877; 1880–1882; 1887–1891		450/1
NOWE MIASTO NAD PILICĄ	U	D	1893–1895; 1899–1901; 1908–1910; 1912–1913; 1923–1924; 1927; 1937		
PIOTRKÓW TRYBUNALSKI	A	G	1817–1950		117
ŁÓDŹ	A	K	1820–1861; 1893–1912		1
ŁÓDŹ	A	M	1826–1868		270
RADOM	A	M	1874–1877; 1880–1882; 1887–1891		450/1
NOWE MIASTO NAD PILICĄ	U	M	1893–1901; 1898–1911; 1913; 1922–1923; 1927; 1929; 1939		
PIOTRKÓW TRYBUNALSKI	A	Y	1929–1947		130, 257
PIOTRKÓW TRYBUNALSKI	A	Z	1817–1953		117
NOWOGARD	**SZCZECIN**				
LEIPZIG	G	B	1800/1851		
LEIPZIG	G	D	1800/1851		
LEIPZIG	G	M	1800/1851		
NOWOGRÓD	**ŁOMŻA**				
ŁOMŻA	A	B	1826–1843; 1845–1864; 1866–1894		170
NOWOGRÓD	U	B	1895–1904; 1906–1909; 1912; 1916–1937		
ŁOMŻA	A	D	1826–1856; 1859–1860; 1862–1864; 1866–1891; 1894		170
NOWOGRÓD	U	D	1895–1914; 1916–1931; 1935; 1937		
ŁOMŻA	A	M	1826–1831; 1835–1837; 1839–1840; 1843–1894		170
NOWOGRÓD	U	M	1895–1896; 1898–1903; 1906–1912; 1920–1931; 1935; 1937		
NOWOSIELCE	**PRZEMYŚL**				
PRZEWORSK	A	S	1894–1953		66/2–32, 34–66
SANOK	A	C	1931–1949		21/74–75
NOWY BYTOM	**KATOWICE**				
KATOWICE	A	S	1933		65/I/9–10
NOWY DWÓR GDAŃSKI	**ELBLĄG**				
LEIPZIG	G	B	1855–1889		

A Army/recruit lists; **B** Birth; **C** Census; **D** Death; **E** Voter lists; **G** Immigration; **H** Holocaust; **J** Judaica; **K** Kahal; **L** Land; **M** Marriage; **N** Name changes; **O** Police files; **P** Pogroms; **R** Reference; **S** School records; **T** Tax lists; **V** Divorce; **W** Occupation lists; **X** Jewish hospital; **Y** Notary records; **Z** Local government records

TOWN NAME	VOIVODSHIP (Province)			Zespół/Sygnatura (Poland) Fond/Opis/Delo (Belarus, Ukraine, Lithuania)
Repository Location	Repository Document Type	Code	Years	
NOWY DWÓR MAZOWIECKI	**WARSZAWA**			
NOWY DWÓR MAZOWIECKI	A	B	1824; 1826–1828; 1830–1835; 1837; 1842–1846; 1850–1851; 1859; 1863–1865; 1872–1874; 1876–1877; 1880–1882; 1884; 1890; 1897; 1900; 1906; 1918; 1933; 1935	383
NOWY DWÓR MAZOWIECKI	U	B	1916–1918; 1920–1939	
NOWY DWÓR MAZOWIECKI	A	C	1938–1939	124
NOWY DWÓR MAZOWIECKI	A	D	1824; 1826–1828; 1830–1835; 1837; 1842–1846; 1850–1851; 1859; 1863–1865; 1871–1874; 1876–1877; 1880–1882; 1884; 1890; 1897; 1900; 1906; 1918; 1920–1921; 1933; 1935	383
NOWY DWÓR MAZOWIECKI	U	D	1917–1918; 1928–1936	
NOWY DWÓR MAZOWIECKI	A	M	1822; 1824; 1826–1828; 1830–1835; 1837; 1842–1846; 1850–1851; 1859; 1863–1865; 1871–1874; 1876–1877; 1880–1882; 1884; 1890; 1897; 1900; 1906; 1920; 1933; 1935	383
NOWY DWÓR MAZOWIECKI	U	M	1931–1938	
NOWY KORCZYN	**KIELCE**			
PIŃCZÓW	A	B	1826–1839; 1849; 1862; 1875–1884; 1886–1889; 1891–1895	372
NOWY KORCZYN	U	B	1896–1941	
PIŃCZÓW	A	C	1902–1931	398
PIŃCZÓW	A	D	1826–1839; 1849; 1862; 1875–1884; 1886–1889; 1891–1895	372
NOWY KORCZYN	U	D	1896–1941	
PIŃCZÓW	A	M	1826–1839; 1849; 1862; 1875–1884; 1886–1889; 1891–1895	372
NOWY KORCZYN	U	M	1894–1941	
PIŃCZÓW	A	Z	1876–1922 (COURT RECORDS)	1062
NOWY SĄCZ	**NOWY SĄCZ**			
NOWY SĄCZ	U	B	1853–1871; 1877–1942	
NOWY SĄCZ	U	B	1880; 1882; 1885–1886; 1900; 1918–1920; 1924–1926; 1928–1933; 1935 (INDEX ONLY)	
NOWY SĄCZ	A	C	1870; 1900; 1910–1927; 1932–1939	183/13, 15–17, 204, 232
NOWY SĄCZ	U	D	1882–1886; 1888; 1890–1891; 1893–1895; 1897–1898; 1905–1919; 1926; 1928–1941	
NOWY SĄCZ	U	D	1885–1942	
NOWY SĄCZ	A	E	1907; 1911	AMNS-I/259
NOWY SĄCZ	A	H	1939–1944 (DEPORTATION LISTS)	
NOWY SĄCZ	U	M	1876/1937	
NOWY SĄCZ	U	M	1882; 1886; 1891–1892; 1895–1898; 1904–1906; 1911–1912; 1914–1915; 1917–1918; 1930–1935; 1937 (INDEX ONLY)	
NOWY SĄCZ	A	T	1842–1843	15–16
NOWY STAW	**ELBLĄG**			
GDAŃSK	A	C	1900–1929	518/9
NOWY TARG	**NOWY SĄCZ**			
NOWY TARG	U	B	1890–1938	
KRAKÓW	A	C	1870; 1880; 1940–1942	208/GDK 42–53
NOWY TARG	U	D	1890–1938	
KRAKÓW	A	H	1940–1942	208/GDK 4
NOWY TARG	U	M	1890–1938	
NOWY TARG REGION	**NOWY SĄCZ**			
KRAKÓW	A	C	1940	208/GDK 54
NOWY TOMYŚL	**POZNAŃ**			
POZNAŃ	A	K	1847–1913	315/212
NOWY ŻMIGRÓD	**KROSNO**			
NOWY ŻMIGRÓD	U	B	1898–1936	
NOWY ŻMIGRÓD	U	D	1905–1909; 1919–1920; 1933–1936	
LVOV	A	L	1785–1788; 1819–1820	19/II/15; 20/II/111
NOWY ŻMIGRÓD	U	M	1891–1933	
NUR	**ŁOMŻA**			
PUŁTUSK	A	B	1826/1876	264
PUŁTUSK	A	D	1826/1876	264
PUŁTUSK	A	M	1826/1876	264
NYSA	**OPOLE**			
KOBLENZ	G	B	1809–1928	

Repository type: **A** = Archive **G** = LDS Films of German-Held Records **J** = Jewish Historical Institute **U** = Urząd Stanu Cywilnego

TOWN NAME	VOIVODSHIP (Province)				
Repository Location	Repository Document Type	Code	Years		Zespół/Sygnatura (Poland) Fond/Opis/Delo (Belarus, Ukraine, Lithuania)
OPOLE	A	B	1874–1894		964
KOBLENZ	G	D	1809–1930		
OPOLE	A	D	1874–1894		964
WARSZAWA	J	K	1816/1856		PROVINCE: ŚLĄSK
KOBLENZ	G	M	1809–1930		
OPOLE	A	M	1874–1894		964
OBERGLOGAU	**SEE GŁOGÓWEK**				
OBORNIKI	**POZNAŃ**				
LEIPZIG	G	B	1835–1839		
LEIPZIG	G	D	1835–1839		
LEIPZIG	G	M	1835–1839		
ODRZECHOWA	**KROSNO**				
SANOK	A	C	1931–1949		21/76–77
ODRZYWÓŁ	**RADOM**				
ODRZYWÓŁ	U	B	1935–1939		
ODRZYWÓŁ	U	D	1935–1936; 1938; 1941		
ODRZYWÓŁ	U	M	1935–1936; 1938		
OELS	**SEE OLEŚNICA**				
OHLAU	**SEE OŁAWA**				
OKUNIEW	**WARSZAWA**				
NOWY DWÓR MAZOWIECKI	A	B	1826–1829; 1833–1837		110
NOWY DWÓR MAZOWIECKI	A	D	1827–1829		110
NOWY DWÓR MAZOWIECKI	A	M	1827		110
OŁAWA	**WROCŁAW**				
WROCŁAW	A	B	1874–1892		556/II
WROCŁAW	A	D	1874–1892		556/II
WROCŁAW	A	K	1809–1945		172/II
WROCŁAW	A	M	1874–1892		556/II
OLCHOWA	**RZESZÓW**				
RZESZÓW	A	E	1938		11/1
OLEŚNICA	**WROCŁAW**				
KOBLENZ	G	B	1812–1859		
WROCŁAW	A	B	1875		556/II
WARSZAWA	J	D	1812		PROVINCE: ŚLĄSK
KOBLENZ	G	D	1812–1859		
WROCŁAW	A	D	1874–1877		556/II
WARSZAWA	J	K	1812/1920		PROVINCE: ŚLĄSK
WARSZAWA	J	M	1812		PROVINCE: ŚLĄSK
KOBLENZ	G	M	1812–1859		
WROCŁAW	A	M	1875–1877		556/II
WARSZAWA	J	Y	1812/1920		PROVINCE: ŚLĄSK
OLESNO	**CZĘSTOCHOWA**				
KOBLENZ	G	B	1812–1847		
CZĘSTOCHOWA	A	B	1874–1884		258
KOBLENZ	G	D	1812–1847; 1891–1938		
CZĘSTOCHOWA	A	D	1874–1884		258
WARSZAWA	J	E	1854/1897		PROVINCE: ŚLĄSK
WARSZAWA	J	K	1854/1897		PROVINCE: ŚLĄSK
KOBLENZ	G	M	1812–1847		
CZĘSTOCHOWA	A	M	1874–1884		258
WARSZAWA	J	S	1854/1897		PROVINCE: ŚLĄSK
WARSZAWA	J	Y	1854/1897		PROVINCE: ŚLĄSK
OLESZYCE	**PRZEMYŚL**				
PRZEMYŚL	A	B	1814–1876		154/1, 4
OLESZYCE	U	B	1886–1895; 1904–1933		
PRZEMYŚL	A	D	1814–1869		154/2
OLESZYCE	U	D	1891–1924		
PRZEMYŚL	A	M	1860–1876		154/3
OLKUSZ	**KATOWICE**				
KATOWICE	A	B	1827–1870; 1882–1893		27
OLKUSZ	U	B	1894–1943		
KATOWICE	A	D	1827–1870; 1882–1893		27
OLKUSZ	U	D	1894–1943		
KATOWICE	A	M	1827–1870; 1882–1893		27
OLKUSZ	U	M	1894–1943		

A Army/recruit lists; **B** Birth; **C** Census; **D** Death; **E** Voter lists; **G** Immigration; **H** Holocaust; **J** Judaica; **K** Kahal; **L** Land; **M** Marriage; **N** Name changes; **O** Police files; **P** Pogroms; **R** Reference; **S** School records; **T** Tax lists; **V** Divorce; **W** Occupation lists; **X** Jewish hospital; **Y** Notary records; **Z** Local government records

TOWN NAME	VOIVODSHIP (Province)			Zespół/Sygnatura (Poland)
Repository Location	Repository Type	Document Code	Years	Fond/Opis/Delo (Belarus, Ukraine, Lithuania)
OLKUSZ REGION	**KATOWICE**			
KIELCE	A	C	1843–1860	4
OŁPINY	**TARNÓW**			
OŁPINY	U	B	1889–1941	
OŁPINY	U	D	1918–1942	
LVOV	A	L	1785–1788; 1819–1820	19/II/322; 20/II/206
OŁPINY	U	M	1918–1941	
OLSZTYN	**OLSZTYN**			
BERLIN	G	B	1847–1874	
OLSZTYN	A	B	1874–1884; 1886–1894	705/I
OLSZTYN	A	C	1825; 1885–1886; 1890; 1893–1895; 1897; 1900; 1946–1947	19/I; 487/II
BERLIN	G	D	1847–1874	
OLSZTYN	A	D	1874–1889; 1893–1894	705/I
BERLIN	G	M	1847–1874	
OLSZTYN	A	M	1882; 1885; 1893–1894	705/I
OLSZTYNEK	**OLSZTYN**			
OLSZTYN	A	B	1874–1894	351/I
OLSZTYN	A	D	1874–1894	351/I
OLSZTYN	A	M	1874–1894	351/I
OPATÓW	**KALISZ**			
POZNAŃ	A	B	1835–1846	3585/1–11
POZNAŃ	A	D	1835–1846	3585/1–11
POZNAŃ	A	M	1835–1846	3585/1–11
SANDOMIERZ	A	B	1831–1884; 1889–1893	44
OPATÓW	U	B	1894–1909; 1914–1942	
SANDOMIERZ	A	C	1890–1941 (ALPHA INDEX: 1890–1930)	6/2
SANDOMIERZ	A	D	1831–1832; 1835–1893	44
OPATÓW	U	D	1894–1913; 1917–1942	
SANDOMIERZ	A	H	1940	6/57
SANDOMIERZ	A	M	1836–1893	44
OPATÓW	U	M	1894–1913; 1921–1942	
KRAKÓW	A	W	1720–1729	637/A SANG. RKPS 428
OPATÓWEK	**KALISZ**			
KALISZ	A	C	1872–1951	1/965–966; 53/394–457
KALISZ	A	E	1907; 1909	321/18–19, 21
KALISZ	A	W	1831–1856	1/103, 105
OPOCZNO	**PIOTRKÓW TRYBUNALSKI**			
KIELCE	A	B	1826–1874	582
PIOTRKÓW TRYBUNALSKI	A	B	1875; 1877–1894	332/23–38, 40, 42, 44, 46–47
OPOCZNO	U	B	1895–1945	
KIELCE	A	D	1826–1874	582
PIOTRKÓW TRYBUNALSKI	A	D	1875–1887; 1889–1894	332/10–22, 25–36, 39, 41, 43, 45–47
OPOCZNO	U	D	1895–1945	
PIOTRKÓW TRYBUNALSKI	A	L	1820–1972	351
KIELCE	A	M	1826–1874	582
PIOTRKÓW TRYBUNALSKI	A	M	1875–1887; 1893–1894	332/1–9, 25–36, 46–47
OPOCZNO	U	M	1895–1945	
PIOTRKÓW TRYBUNALSKI	A	Y	1810–1951	230–239
OPOLE	**OPOLE**			
OPOLE	A	B	1756–1781; 1847	60
OPOLE	A	E	1815–1860	22
OPOLE	A	K	1843–1940 (CEMETERY RECORDS)	22; 47
OPOLE	A	M	1933–1937	1
WARSZAWA	J	P	1846/1905	PROVINCE: ŚLĄSK
OPOLE	A	S	1820–1889	22
OPOLE LUBELSKIE	**LUBLIN**			
LUBLIN	A	B	1826–1879	113
OPOLE LUBELSKIE	U	B	1901–1914; 1917–1920	
LUBLIN	A	D	1826–1850; 1855–1873	113
OPOLE LUBELSKIE	U	D	1917–1940	
LUBLIN	A	K	1870–1914; 1926–1929	RGL IV ADM; UWL WSP/818
LUBLIN	A	M	1826–1875	113
OPOLE LUBELSKIE	U	M	1917–1940	
LUBLIN	A	Z	1510/1811	48
OPPELN	**SEE OPOLE**			

Repository type: **A** = Archive **G** = LDS Films of German-Held Records **J** = Jewish Historical Institute **U** = Urząd Stanu Cywilnego

TOWN NAME	VOIVODSHIP (Province)			Zespół/Sygnatura (Poland) Fond/Opis/Delo (Belarus, Ukraine, Lithuania)
Repository Location	Repository Document Type	Code	Years	
ORŁA	**BIAŁYSTOK**			
BIAŁYSTOK	A	B	1836; 1846	545
BIAŁYSTOK	A	D	1836	545
GRODNO	A	K	1897–1900	271
BIAŁYSTOK	A	M	1836; 1860	545
ORŁY	**PRZEMYŚL**			
PRZEMYŚL	A	C	1930/1941	207/26–27, 43, 60, 61
ORTELSBURG	**SEE SZCZYTNO**			
ORZECHOWCE	**PRZEMYŚL**			
PRZEMYŚL	A	C	1930–1948	207/28–29, 62–63
PRZEMYŚL	A	G	1931–1944	207/155, 159
OSIĘCINY	**WŁOCŁAWEK**			
AUGSBURG	G	B	1826–1934	
AUGSBURG	G	D	1826–1892; 1917–1938	
AUGSBURG	G	M	1826–1931	
WŁOCŁAWEK	A	M	1867–1871; 1885–1889 (MARRIAGE APPLICATIONS)	
OSIECK	**SIEDLCE**			
LUBLIN	A	K	1923–1936	UWL WSP/773
LUBLIN	A	T	1923–1936	UWL WSP/773
OSIECZNA	**LESZNO**			
LESZNO	A	B	1817–1847	23
LESZNO	A	D	1817–1847	23
LESZNO	A	M	1817–1847	23
OSIEK	**TARNOBRZEG**			
SANDOMIERZ	A	B	1888–1941	385
SANDOMIERZ	A	D	1888–1941	385
SANDOMIERZ	A	M	1888–1941	385
OSJAKÓW	**SIERADZ**			
OSJAKÓW	U	B	1913–1935	
OSJAKÓW	U	D	1913–1935	
OSJAKÓW	U	M	1913–1935	
OŚNO	**GORZÓW WIELKOPOLSKI**			
KOBLENZ	G	B	1813–1899	
KOBLENZ	G	D	1813–1899	
KOBLENZ	G	M	1813–1899	
OSTROŁĘKA	**OSTROŁĘKA**			
OSTROŁĘKA	U	B	1917–1927; 1930; 1933; 1936	
OSTROŁĘKA	U	D	1917–1927; 1930; 1933; 1936	
GRODNO	A	K	1828–1867	1534
BIAŁYSTOK	A	K	1910	6/148
OSTROŁĘKA	U	M	1917–1927; 1930; 1933; 1936	
OSTRÓW LUBELSKI	**LUBLIN**			
OSTRÓW LUBELSKI	U	B	1920–1940	
LUBLIN	A	B	1941	AMO/135
LUBLIN	A	C	1890; 1919; 1921; 1927	AMO/166–167, 169–170; 901/136
OSTRÓW LUBELSKI	U	D	1920–1926; 1928–1930; 1932–1933; 1937–1940	
LUBLIN	A	D	1941	AMO/135
LUBLIN	A	E	1912–1915; 1919; 1922; 1927–1928; 1934–1935; 1939	30–44; RGCH/657
LUBLIN	A	G	1922–1929	72–76
LUBLIN	A	H	1940–1942	901/134
LUBLIN	A	K	1912–1915; 1922–1935	RGCH/657;UWL WSP/831;AMO 128–133
OSTRÓW LUBELSKI	U	M	1920; 1923–1931; 1933–1935; 1937–1940	
LUBLIN	A	M	1941	AMO/135
OSTRÓW MAZOWIECKA	**OSTROŁĘKA**			
PUŁTUSK	A	B	1826–1892	94
OSTRÓW MAZOWIECKA	U	B	1893–1915; 1919–1939	
PUŁTUSK	A	D	1826–1892	94
OSTRÓW MAZOWIECKA	U	D	1893–1915; 1919–1939	
PUŁTUSK	A	M	1821–1829; 1831–1892	94
OSTRÓW MAZOWIECKA	U	M	1893–1915; 1919–1939	
OSTRÓW WIELKOPOLSKI	**KALISZ**			
KALISZ	A	C	1875–1945	8/61–64; 72/1–34
KALISZ	A	E	1907; 1909	321/18–19, 21
POZNAŃ	A	K	1834–1914	327/284, 287
BERLIN	G	N	1836–1838	

A Army/recruit lists; **B** Birth; **C** Census; **D** Death; **E** Voter lists; **G** Immigration; **H** Holocaust; **J** Judaica; **K** Kahal; **L** Land; **M** Marriage; **N** Name changes; **O** Police files; **P** Pogroms; **R** Reference; **S** School records; **T** Tax lists; **V** Divorce; **W** Occupation lists; **X** Jewish hospital; **Y** Notary records; **Z** Local government records

TOWN NAME	VOIVODSHIP (Province)			Zespół/Sygnatura (Poland)
Repository Location	Repository Document Type	Code	Years	Fond/Opis/Delo (Belarus, Ukraine, Lithuania)
KALISZ	A	P	1920–1921	3/1
OSTROWIEC ŚWIĘTOKRZYSKI	**KIELCE**			
STARACHOWICE	A	B	1826–1893	216
OSTROWIEC ŚWIĘTOKRZYSKI	U	B	1894–1901; 1907–1915; 1920–1940	
KIELCE	A	C	1887–1930	214
STARACHOWICE	A	D	1826–1893	216
OSTROWIEC ŚWIĘTOKRZYSKI	U	D	1894–1909; 1919–1946	
KIELCE	A	E	1939	214
STARACHOWICE	A	M	1826–1893	216
OSTROWIEC ŚWIĘTOKRZYSKI	U	M	1894–1928	
STARACHOWICE	A	Z	1923	214
OSTRZESZÓW	**KALISZ**			
POZNAŃ	A	B	1835–1846	3586/1–7
KALISZ	A	C	1919–1930	9/155; 27/304
POZNAŃ	A	D	1835–1846	3586/1–7
KALISZ	A	E	1923–1930	27/166–167
KALISZ	A	K	1927	27/247
POZNAŃ	A	M	1835–1846	3586/1–7
KALISZ	A	Y	1882–1915	176–182
OTWOCK	**WARSZAWA**			
OTWOCK	U	B	1916–1941	
OTWOCK	A	C	1940–1941	1
OTWOCK	U	D	1917–1941	
OTWOCK	A	G	1939	1
OTWOCK	A	H	1939	1
OTWOCK	A	L	1916/1950	1
OTWOCK	U	M	1917–1941	
OŻARÓW	**TARNOBRZEG**			
SANDOMIERZ	A	B	1826–1893	45
OŻARÓW	U	B	1894–1939	
SANDOMIERZ	A	D	1826–1893	45
OŻARÓW	U	D	1894–1940	
SANDOMIERZ	A	M	1827–1884; 1886–1893	45
OŻARÓW	U	M	1896–1938	
OZORKÓW	**ŁÓDŹ**			
ŁÓDŹ	A	M	1844/1902	270
ŁÓDŹ	A	S	1906–1909	83
PABIANICE	**ŁÓDŹ**			
ŁÓDŹ	A	B	1831–1874; 1887–1893	270
PABIANICE	U	B	1894–1942	
PABIANICE	A	C	1836–1862	8
ŁÓDŹ	A	D	1831–1874; 1884–1893	270
PABIANICE	U	D	1894–1942	
PABIANICE	A	G	1867/1914	8
PABIANICE	A	K	1901–1914	8
ŁÓDŹ	A	M	1831–1874; 1882–1893	270
PABIANICE	U	M	1894–1940	
ŁÓDŹ	A	O	1886–1914	39
ŁÓDŹ	A	S	1889–1909	83
PABIANICE	A	T	1867/1914	8
PACANÓW	**KIELCE**			
PIŃCZÓW	A	B	1826/1874; 1875–1884; 1886–1896	373
PACANÓW	U	B	1897–1902; 1905–1924; 1926–1941	
PIŃCZÓW	A	D	1826/1874; 1875–1884; 1886–1896	373
PACANÓW	U	D	1897–1902; 1905–1924; 1926–1941	
PIŃCZÓW	A	M	1826/1874; 1875–1884; 1886–1896	373
PACANÓW	U	M	1897–1902; 1905–1924; 1926–1941	
PAJĘCZNO	**CZĘSTOCHOWA**			
ŁÓDŹ	A	B	1826–1893	270
PAJĘCZNO	U	B	1894–1940	
ŁÓDŹ	A	D	1826–1893	270
PAJĘCZNO	U	D	1894–1940	
ŁÓDŹ	A	K	1822–1862; 1903–1913	1
ŁÓDŹ	A	M	1826–1893	270
PAJĘCZNO	U	M	1894–1940	
PAKOŚĆ	**BYDGOSZCZ**			
INOWROCŁAW	A	B	1825–1847	196
INOWROCŁAW	A	D	1825–1847	196

Repository type: **A** = Archive **G** = LDS Films of German-Held Records **J** = Jewish Historical Institute **U** = Urząd Stanu Cywilnego

TOWN NAME		VOIVODSHIP (Province)		
Repository Location	Repository Document Type / Code	Years		Zespół/Sygnatura (Poland) Fond/Opis/Delo (Belarus, Ukraine, Lithuania)

Repository Location	Type	Code	Years	Zespół/Sygnatura
INOWROCŁAW	A	E	1903–1914; 1933–1935	60
INOWROCŁAW	A	G	1847/1906	60
INOWROCŁAW	A	K	1854–1893	128
INOWROCŁAW	A	M	1823–1847	196
PANTALOWICE		**PRZEMYŚL**		
PRZEWORSK	A	S	1886–1944	67/1–53
PARCZEW		**BIAŁA PODLASKA**		
LUBLIN	A	B	1826–1832; 1846–1855	113
PARCZEW	U	B	1882–1883; 1887–1889; 1891–1898; 1901–1911; 1913–1928; 1933–1938	
LUBLIN	A	D	1825–1853	113
PARCZEW	U	D	1885–1898; 1908–1915; 1919–1939	
LUBLIN	A	E	1906; 1913–1915	RGL IV ADM
LUBLIN	A	K	1906; 1913–1915; 1927–1929	RGL IV ADM; UWL WSP/832
PARCZEW	U	M	1882–1915; 1919–1939	
LUBLIN	A	S	1630	25
LUBLIN	A	T	1906; 1913–1915; 1927–1929	RGL IV ADM; UWL WSP/832
LUBLIN	A	Z	1570–1629	63
PARYSÓW		**SIEDLCE**		
LUBLIN	A	E	1913–1915	RGL IV ADM
LUBLIN	A	K	1913–1915; 1922–1936	RGL IV ADM; UWL WSP/772
LUBLIN	A	T	1913–1915; 1922–1936	RGL IV ADM; UWL WSP/772
PASŁĘK		**ELBLĄG**		
KOBLENZ	G	K	1825–1907 (CEMETERY RECORDS)	
PASSENHEIM		**SEE PASYM**		
PASYM		**OLSZTYN**		
OLSZTYN	A	B	1874–1894	718/I
OLSZTYN	A	D	1874–1880; 1882–1894	718/I
OLSZTYN	A	M	1874–1894	718/I
PEŁCZYCE		**GORZÓW WIELKOPOLSKI**		
KOBLENZ	G	B	1825–1874	
KOBLENZ	G	D	1825–1874	
KOBLENZ	G	M	1825–1874	
PIASECZNO		**WARSZAWA**		
GÓRA KALWARIA	A	B	1808–1825; 1829; 1833–1836; 1869–1894; 1910	173; 123
PIASECZNO	U	B	1893–1909; 1911–1939	
GÓRA KALWARIA	A	C	1842–1852; 1889–1933	129
GÓRA KALWARIA	A	D	1808–1825; 1829; 1833–1836; 1869–1882; 1884; 1886–1887; 1889–1893; 1910	173; 123
PIASECZNO	U	D	1896–1935; 1938	
GÓRA KALWARIA	A	M	1808–1825; 1829; 1833–1836; 1869–1882; 1884; 1886–1887; 1889–1893; 1910	173; 123
PIASECZNO	U	M	1893–1935; 1938	
PIASKI		**LUBLIN**		
LUBLIN	A	B	1826–1893	113
PIASKI	U	B	1894–1940	
LUBLIN	A	D	1826–1893	113
PIASKI	U	D	1894–1940	
LUBLIN	A	H	1940–1942	KREISHAUPTMANSCHAFT LUBLIN
LUBLIN	A	K	1869–1915; 1919–1939	RGL IV ADM; SPL/651
LUBLIN	A	M	1826–1893	113
PIASKI	U	M	1894–1940	
PIĄTKOWA		**INCLUDED IN NOWY SĄCZ**		
PIĄTNICA		**INCLUDED IN ŁOMŻA**		
PIŁA		**PIŁA**		
POZNAŃ	A	S	1836–1891	1029/97–100
PILICA		**KATOWICE**		
KATOWICE	A	B	1826–1870; 1889; 1892	29
PILICA	U	B	1903–1911; 1913–1916; 1922–1942	
KATOWICE	A	D	1826–1870; 1889; 1892	29
PILICA	U	D	1903–1911; 1913–1916; 1922–1942	
KATOWICE	A	M	1826–1870; 1889; 1892	29
PILICA	U	M	1903–1911; 1913–1916; 1922–1942	
PILZNO		**TARNÓW**		
LVOV	A	L	1785–1788; 1819–1820	19/VII/145; 20/VII/251

A Army/recruit lists; **B** Birth; **C** Census; **D** Death; **E** Voter lists; **G** Immigration; **H** Holocaust; **J** Judaica; **K** Kahal; **L** Land; **M** Marriage; **N** Name changes; **O** Police files; **P** Pogroms; **R** Reference; **S** School records; **T** Tax lists; **V** Divorce; **W** Occupation lists; **X** Jewish hospital; **Y** Notary records; **Z** Local government records

TOWN NAME	VOIVODSHIP (Province)			Zespół/Sygnatura (Poland)
Repository Location	Repository Type	Document Code	Years	Fond/Opis/Delo (Belarus, Ukraine, Lithuania)
PRZEMYŚL	A	Y	1861–1934	90; 1250–1262
PIŃCZÓW	**KIELCE**			
PIŃCZÓW	A	B	1826–1865; 1867–1875; 1878–1886; 1888–1890; 1892–1894	233
PIŃCZÓW	U	B	1895–1898; 1900–1914; 1916–1921; 1923–1928; 1930–1940	
PIŃCZÓW	A	D	1826–1865; 1867–1875; 1878–1886; 1888–1890; 1892–1894	233
PIŃCZÓW	U	D	1895–1898; 1900–1914; 1916–1921; 1923–1928; 1930–1940	
PIŃCZÓW	A	M	1826–1865; 1867–1875; 1878–1886; 1888–1890; 1892–1894	233
PIŃCZÓW	U	M	1895–1898; 1900–1914; 1916–1921; 1923–1928; 1930–1940	
PIOTRKÓW KUJAWSKI	**TORUŃ**			
PIOTRKÓW KUJAWSKI	U	B	1921–1923; 1933–1938	
PIOTRKÓW KUJAWSKI	U	D	1908–1915; 1933–1938	
PIOTRKÓW KUJAWSKI	U	M	1933–1939	
WŁOCŁAWEK	A	B	1839–1852; 1859–1894	563
WŁOCŁAWEK	A	D	1838–1852; 1859–1896	563
WŁOCŁAWEK	A	M	1838–1857; 1859–1896	563
PIOTRKÓW TRYBUNALSKI	**PIOTRKÓW TRYBUNALSKI**			
ŁÓDŹ	A	A	1867–1917	17
PIOTRKÓW TRYBUNALSKI	A	A	1919–1939	1/1269–1845
ŁÓDŹ	A	B	1826–1873	270
PIOTRKÓW TRYBUNALSKI	A	B	1856–1894; 1938–1942	333/1–11, 25–61, 63, 65–66
PIOTRKÓW TRYBUNALSKI	U	B	1895–1942	
PIOTRKÓW TRYBUNALSKI	A	C	1865–1939	9/1671–1737; 1/1269–1845
ŁÓDŹ	A	D	1826–1873	270
PIOTRKÓW TRYBUNALSKI	A	D	1856–1889; 1891–1893; 1939; 1942	333/20–59, 64, 67–68
PIOTRKÓW TRYBUNALSKI	U	D	1894–1942	
ŁÓDŹ	A	G	1903–1911	1
PIOTRKÓW TRYBUNALSKI	A	G	1919–1939	1
PIOTRKÓW TRYBUNALSKI	A	H	1939–1944	9
ŁÓDŹ	A	K	1868/1914	1
PIOTRKÓW TRYBUNALSKI	A	L	1800–1876; 1919–1939	381; 400; BIBL.2251
PIOTRKÓW TRYBUNALSKI	A	M	1856–1889; 1891–1893; 1938–1942	333/12–19, 25–59, 62
PIOTRKÓW TRYBUNALSKI	U	M	1894–1942	
ŁÓDŹ	A	O	1903–1911	41
PIOTRKÓW TRYBUNALSKI	A	O	1915–1939	1; 352
PIOTRKÓW TRYBUNALSKI	A	R	1913; 1927; 1929; 1942	BIBL.3191
PIOTRKÓW TRYBUNALSKI	A	S	1858–1869	9/243
ŁÓDŹ	A	S	1859/1914	83
ŁÓDŹ	A	T	1816–1866; 1869–1918	23
PIOTRKÓW TRYBUNALSKI	A	T	1868–1944	699
ŁÓDŹ	A	W	1871/1914	19
ŁÓDŹ	A	X	1822/1913	15
PIOTRKÓW TRYBUNALSKI	A	X	1875/1940	89
PIOTRKÓW TRYBUNALSKI	A	Y	1807–1951	47–70, 150–166, 361–366
PIOTRKÓW TRYBUNALSKI	A	Z	1803–1945	9
PISZ	**OLSZTYN**			
OLSZTYN	A	C	1938	264/I
PISZCZAC	**BIAŁA PODLASKA**			
LUBLIN	A	B	1815; 1820; 1823; 1825–1871; 1874–1892	113
PISZCZAC	U	B	1893–1911; 1923–1937	
LUBLIN	A	D	1815; 1820; 1823; 1825–1871; 1874–1892	113
PISZCZAC	U	D	1893–1911; 1923–1937	
LUBLIN	A	K	1912–1914; 1923–1926	RGCH/444; UWL WSP/757
LUBLIN	A	M	1815; 1820; 1823; 1825–1871; 1874–1892	113
PISZCZAC	U	M	1893–1911; 1923–1937	
PŁAWNO	**CZĘSTOCHOWA**			
ŁÓDŹ	A	A	1897–1899	17
ŁÓDŹ	A	B	1826–1889; 1891–1893	270
PŁAWNO	U	B	1894–1912; 1919–1927; 1929–1940	
ŁÓDŹ	A	D	1826–1889; 1891–1893	270
PŁAWNO	U	D	1894–1912; 1919–1927; 1929–1940	
ŁÓDŹ	A	K	1822–1866; 1899–1914	1

Repository type: **A** = Archive **G** = LDS Films of German-Held Records **J** = Jewish Historical Institute **U** = Urząd Stanu Cywilnego

TOWN NAME	VOIVODSHIP (Province)			Zespół/Sygnatura (Poland)
Repository Location	Repository Document Type	Code	Years	Fond/Opis/Delo (Belarus, Ukraine, Lithuania)
ŁÓDŹ	A	M	1826–1889; 1891–1893	270
PŁAWNO	U	M	1894–1912; 1919–1927; 1929–1940	
PLESZEW	**KALISZ**			
POZNAŃ	A	B	1835–1847	3587/1–8
WARSZAWA	J	C	1785/1846	PROVINCE: POZNAŃ
KALISZ	A	C	1834–1903	28/1775, 1808–1809
POZNAŃ	A	D	1835–1847	3587/11
POZNAŃ	A	M	1835–1847	3587/9
BERLIN	G	N	1834–1839	
WARSZAWA	J	S	1785/1846	PROVINCE: POZNAŃ
KALISZ	A	S	1855–1906	28/352
KALISZ	A	Y	1835–1919	183–194
KALISZ	A	Z	1821–1920 (COURT RECORDS)	92
PŁOCK	**PŁOCK**			
PŁOCK	A	B	1808–1887	175; 373
PŁOCK	U	B	1888–1939	
PŁOCK	A	C	1830–1930; 1937–1949	90/133
WARSAW2	A	C	1939–1942	1362/II
PŁOCK	A	D	1811–1894	175; 373
PŁOCK	U	D	1895–1935; 1939	
PŁOCK	A	M	1811–1863; 1865–1871; 1873–1890	175; 373
PŁOCK	U	M	1891–1939	
PŁOCK	A	Y	1808–1946	225–262; 265–267; 437–440; 447
PŁOCK	A	Z	1808–1939; 1945–1950	1
WARSZAWA	A	Z	1939–1944	1362/II
PŁONNA	**KROSNO**			
SANOK	A	C	1937–1939	23/32
PŁOŃSK	**CIECHANÓW**			
NOWY DWÓR MAZOWIECKI	A	B	1826–1872; 1876	96
MŁAWA	A	B	1877–1895	474
PŁOŃSK	U	B	1896–1940	
NOWY DWÓR MAZOWIECKI	A	D	1826–1872; 1876; 1906	96
MŁAWA	A	D	1877–1895	474
PŁOŃSK	U	D	1896–1940	
NOWY DWÓR MAZOWIECKI	A	M	1826–1872; 1876; 1906	96
MŁAWA	A	M	1877–1895	474
PŁOŃSK	U	M	1896–1940	
NOWY DWÓR MAZOWIECKI	A	R	1931; 1940	62
POBIEDZISKA	**POZNAŃ**			
POZNAŃ	A	K	1880–1914	329/1223–1228
POZNAŃ	A	S	1893–1907	4387/188–189
PODDĘBICE	**SIERADZ**			
ŁÓDŹ	A	B	1817–1870	270
ŁÓDŹ	A	D	1817–1870	270
ŁÓDŹ	A	M	1817–1870	270
PODGÓRZE	**KRAKÓW**			
WARSZAWA	J	A	1893/1936	102
KRAKÓW	A	B	1804–1893	526/MIK–P1
KRAKÓW	A	C	1857; 1870; 1880; 1890; 1900; 1910	93
WARSZAWA	J	C	1893/1936	102
KRAKÓW	A	D	1804–1894	526/MIK–P1
WARSZAWA	J	K	1893/1936	102; 108
KRAKÓW	A	L	1838–1873	53
KRAKÓW	A	M	1804–1894	526/MIK–P1
KRAKÓW	A	R	1892; 1905; 1908; 1909	
WARSZAWA	J	T	1893/1936	102
WARSZAWA	J	Y	1893/1936	102
WARSZAWA	J	Z	1893/1936	102
PODZAMCZE	**KALISZ**			
POZNAŃ	A	B	1835–1846	3588/1–9
POZNAŃ	A	D	1835–1846	3588/1–9
POZNAŃ	A	M	1835–1846	3588/1–9
POGORZELA	**LESZNO**			
KALISZ	A	C	1921–1935	29/361–364, 366, 368–369
KALISZ	A	E	1918–1930	29/363–369
KALISZ	A	L	1834–1943	91/201–221
KALISZ	A	T	1883–1921	29/189–190

A Army/recruit lists; **B** Birth; **C** Census; **D** Death; **E** Voter lists; **G** Immigration; **H** Holocaust; **J** Judaica; **K** Kahal; **L** Land; **M** Marriage; **N** Name changes; **O** Police files; **P** Pogroms; **R** Reference; **S** School records; **T** Tax lists; **V** Divorce; **W** Occupation lists; **X** Jewish hospital; **Y** Notary records; **Z** Local government records

TOWN NAME	VOIVODSHIP (Province)			Zespół/Sygnatura (Poland)
Repository Location	Repository Document Type	Code	Years	Fond/Opis/Delo (Belarus, Ukraine, Lithuania)
POLAND / COUNTRY	**WARSZAWA**			
WARSZAWA	J	G	1935–1937 (IMMIGRATION TO PALESTINE)	115
WARSZAWA	J	H	1945–1946 (ALPHA LIST OF 250, 000 SURVIVORS)	
POŁANIEC	**TARNOBRZEG**			
SANDOMIERZ	A	B	1826–1893	252
POŁANIEC	U	B	1894–1913; 1915–1941	
SANDOMIERZ	A	D	1826–1893	252
POŁANIEC	U	D	1894–1913; 1915–1941	
SANDOMIERZ	A	M	1826–1893	252
POŁANIEC	U	M	1894–1913; 1915–1941	
PORĘBA	**KATOWICE**			
PORĘBA	U	B	1937–1940	
PORĘBA	U	D	1937–1940	
PORĘBA	U	M	1937–1940	
POSADA ZARSZYŃSKA	**KROSNO**			
SANOK	A	C	1931–1949	21/84
POTOK GÓRNY	**ZAMOŚĆ**			
KRAŚNIK	A	C	1882–1954	26
POZNAŃ	**POZNAŃ**			
POZNAŃ	A	C	1830–1940	474/12001–14226; 963–12000, 14227–15752, 15754–16000
LEIPZIG	G	D	1820–1850	
WARSZAWA	J	K	1700–1938	116
POZNAŃ	A	K	1845–1903	330/823
POZNAŃ	A	X	1929–1939	474/1898
PRABUTY	**ELBLĄG**			
OLSZTYN	A	B	1812–1874	319/I
OLSZTYN	A	D	1812–1874	319/I
OLSZTYN	A	M	1847–1874	319/I
PRASZKA	**CZĘSTOCHOWA**			
ŁÓDŹ	A	B	1826–1868	270
CZĘSTOCHOWA	A	B	1869–1895	267
PRASZKA	U	B	1899–1901; 1905–1906; 1909; 1912; 1915; 1917–1919; 1921–1927; 1933–1934; 1936	
ŁÓDŹ	A	D	1826–1868	270
CZĘSTOCHOWA	A	D	1869–1895	267
PRASZKA	U	D	1902; 1905–1906; 1909; 1912; 1915; 1917–1919; 1921–1927; 1933–1934; 1936	
ŁÓDŹ	A	K	1870–1875	1
ŁÓDŹ	A	M	1826–1868	270
CZĘSTOCHOWA	A	M	1869–1895	267
PRASZKA	U	M	1899; 1901–1902; 1906; 1909; 1912; 1915; 1917–1919; 1921–1924; 1927; 1933–1934	
PRAWDA	**INCLUDED IN GARWOLIN**			
PREUSSISCH FRIEDLAND	**SEE DEBRZNO**			
PREUSSISCH HOLLAND	**SEE PASŁĘK**			
PREUSSISCH STARGARD	**SEE STAROGARD**			
PRIEMHAUSEN	**SEE PROSZOWICE**			
PROSZOWICE	**KRAKÓW**			
KRAKÓW	A	Z	1474–1734	120
PROSZOWICE REGION	**KRAKÓW**			
KRAKÓW	A	C	1790–1792	30/191A
PRUCHNIK	**PRZEMYŚL**			
PRZEMYŚL	A	B	1834–1876	154/1
PRUCHNIK	U	B	1882–1942	
PRUCHNIK	U	D	1882–1920; 1922–1934; 1938	
LVOV	A	L	1785–1788; 1819–1820	19/XIII/226; 20/XIII/201
PRUCHNIK	U	M	1898–1939	
PRZEMYŚL	A	Y	1905–1906; 1908–1949	91; 1081–1083
PRUDNIK	**OPOLE**			
KOBLENZ	G	B	1824–1874	
KOBLENZ	G	D	1824–1827; 1833–1939	
KOBLENZ	G	N	1812–1824	
PRUSZKÓW	**WARSZAWA**			
PRUSZKÓW	U	B	1907; 1911; 1918–1939	

Repository type: **A** = Archive **G** = LDS Films of German-Held Records **J** = Jewish Historical Institute **U** = Urząd Stanu Cywilnego

TOWN NAME	VOIVODSHIP (Province)			Zespół/Sygnatura (Poland)
Repository Location	Repository Document Type	Code	Years	Fond/Opis/Delo (Belarus, Ukraine, Lithuania)
PRUSZKÓW	U	D	1904–1937	
PRUSZKÓW	U	M	1904–1939	
PRZASNYSZ	**OSTROŁĘKA**			
PUŁTUSK	A	B	1826–1893	106
PRZASNYSZ	U	B	1894–1939	
PUŁTUSK	A	D	1826–1893	106
PRZASNYSZ	U	D	1894–1939	
PUŁTUSK	A	M	1826–1893	106
PRZASNYSZ	U	M	1894–1939	
PRZEDBÓRZ	**PIOTRKÓW TRYBUNALSKI**			
KIELCE	A	B	1826–1871	563
PIOTRKÓW TRYBUNALSKI	A	B	1872–1888; 1890–1891	334/1–19
PRZEDBÓRZ	U	B	1892–1913; 1916–1941	
PIOTRKÓW TRYBUNALSKI	A	C	1874–1931	687
KIELCE	A	D	1826–1871	563
PIOTRKÓW TRYBUNALSKI	A	D	1872–1888; 1890–1891	334/1–19
PRZEDBÓRZ	U	D	1892–1913; 1916–1941	
KIELCE	A	M	1826–1871	563
PIOTRKÓW TRYBUNALSKI	A	M	1872–1888; 1890–1891	334/1–19
PRZEDBÓRZ	U	M	1892–1913; 1916–1941	
PIOTRKÓW TRYBUNALSKI	A	Y	1931–1951	367–371
PIOTRKÓW TRYBUNALSKI	A	Z	1822–1939	687
PRZEDECZ	**KONIN**			
PRZEDECZ	U	B	1902–1916; 1919–1934	
WARSZAWA	J	C	1919/1939	105
PRZEDECZ	U	D	1888–1916	
WARSZAWA	J	E	1919/1939	105
PRZEDMIEŚCIE DUBIECKIE	**PRZEMYŚL**			
PRZEMYŚL	A	C	1932–1950	200/47–49
PRZEMOCZE	**SZCZECIN**			
KOBLENZ	G	B	1812–1849	
KOBLENZ	G	D	1812–1849	
KOBLENZ	G	M	1812–1849	
KOBLENZ	G	N	1761–1849	
PRZEMYŚL	**PRZEMYŚL**			
PRZEMYŚL	A	A	1819–1875	129/9–16
PRZEMYŚL	A	B	1790–1827; 1853–1883	154/1, 6–9, 12
PRZEMYŚL	U	B	1884–1942	
PRZEMYŚL	A	D	1790–1884	154/1, 3–5, 10, 13
PRZEMYŚL	U	D	1885–1942	
PRZEMYŚL	A	G	1931–1951	208/19–20, 67–70, 72–73, 75–76, 78–81
PRZEMYŚL	A	K	1791; 1799–1887	129/169–173
LVOV	A	L	1785–1788; 1819–1820	19/XIII/235; 20/XIII/181
PRZEMYŚL	A	M	1790–1876	154/1–2
PRZEMYŚL	U	M	1882–1899; 1903–1942	
PRZEMYŚL	A	T	1819–1844	129/127–129
PRZEMYŚL	A	Y	1882–1951	92; 634; 1008–1016
PRZEMYŚL REGION	**PRZEMYŚL**			
PRZEMYŚL	A	C	1929–1930; 1953–1954	208/18, 66, 71, 74, 77, 82
PRZEROŚL	**SUWAŁKI**			
SUWAŁKI	A	B	1813–1825; 1827–1879; 1880/1884; 1885–1889	161; 201
PRZEROŚL	U	B	1896; 1898–1899; 1901; 1903; 1919–1924	
SUWAŁKI	A	D	1813–1825; 1827–1879; 1880/1884; 1885–1889	161; 201
PRZEROŚL	U	D	1896; 1898–1899; 1901–1903; 1919–1924	
SUWAŁKI	A	M	1813–1825; 1827–1879; 1880/1884; 1885–1889	161; 201
PRZEROŚL	U	M	1896; 1898–1899; 1901–1903; 1919–1924	
WARSZAWA	A	T	1826–1844	KRSW 4980–4981
PRZEWORSK	**PRZEMYŚL**			
PRZEMYŚL	A	A	1795–1914	137/184–203, 1186, 1327
PRZEMYŚL	A	B	1815–1850	137/523
PRZEMYŚL	A	C	1910–1921	137/1318
PRZEMYŚL	A	D	1815–1850; 1913–1936	137/523, 1320
PRZEMYŚL	A	E	1814–1853; 1928; 1930; 1935; 1938	137/521–522, 1302–1305
PRZEMYŚL	A	H	1940–1943	137/1416
PRZEWORSK	A	H	1945–1947	8/5, 9–10, 12
PRZEMYŚL	A	K	1782–1863; 1867; 1914	137/28, 51–55, 494–516, 524, 1173
PRZEMYŚL	A	M	1815–1850	137/523

A Army/recruit lists; **B** Birth; **C** Census; **D** Death; **E** Voter lists; **G** Immigration; **H** Holocaust; **J** Judaica; **K** Kahal; **L** Land; **M** Marriage; **N** Name changes; **O** Police files; **P** Pogroms; **R** Reference; **S** School records; **T** Tax lists; **V** Divorce; **W** Occupation lists; **X** Jewish hospital; **Y** Notary records; **Z** Local government records

TOWN NAME / Repository Location	VOIVODSHIP (Province) / Repository Document Type	Code	Years	Zespół/Sygnatura (Poland) Fond/Opis/Delo (Belarus, Ukraine, Lithuania)
PRZEWORSK	A	S	1921–1960	69/4–28, 34–41
PRZEMYŚL	A	T	1824–1863	137/517–520
PRZEMYŚL	A	X	1814–1864	137/299–301
PRZEMYŚL	A	Y	1860–1874; 1877–1935	93; 1046–1053
PRZEWORSK REGION	**PRZEMYŚL**			
PRZEWORSK	A	S	1913–1953	68/7–11, 15–46, 52–60
PRZYBYSZEW	**RADOM**			
GÓRA KALWARIA	A	B	1808–1836	163; 126
GÓRA KALWARIA	A	D	1808–1836	163; 126
GÓRA KALWARIA	A	M	1808–1836	163; 126
PRZYBYSZÓW	**KROSNO**			
SANOK	A	C	1937–1939	23/32
PRZYRÓW	**CZĘSTOCHOWA**			
ŁÓDŹ	A	A	1898	17
CZĘSTOCHOWA	A	B	1826–1895	95
PRZYRÓW	U	B	1896–1914; 1920–1942	
CZĘSTOCHOWA	A	D	1826–1895	95
PRZYRÓW	U	D	1896–1942	
CZĘSTOCHOWA	A	G	1921–1924	73
ŁÓDŹ	A	K	1822–1867	1
CZĘSTOCHOWA	A	K	1915–1924	73
CZĘSTOCHOWA	A	M	1826–1895	95
PRZYRÓW	U	M	1896–1902; 1907; 1913; 1915–1942	
ŁÓDŹ	A	X	1822–1867	1
PRZYSUCHA	**RADOM**			
KIELCE	A	B	1826–1865	597
RADOM	A	B	1869–1894	471/1
PRZYSUCHA	U	B	1895; 1897–1907; 1909–1917; 1920–1938	
KIELCE	A	D	1826–1865	597
RADOM	A	D	1869–1881; 1883–1894	471/1
PRZYSUCHA	U	D	1895; 1897–1917; 1920–1925; 1928–1932; 1934; 1936; 1938	
KIELCE	A	M	1826–1865	597
RADOM	A	M	1869–1894	471/1
PRZYSUCHA	U	M	1895; 1897–1907; 1909–1910; 1928–1932; 1934; 1936; 1938	
PRZYTYK	**RADOM**			
RADOM	A	B	1826–1939	189
RADOM	A	D	1826–1939	189
RADOM	A	M	1826–1918; 1921–1923; 1930–1939	189
PRZYTYK	U	M	1922–1937	
PSZCZEW	**GORZÓW WIELKOPOLSKI**			
BERLIN	G	B	1817–1847	
BERLIN	G	D	1817–1847	
BERLIN	G	M	1817–1847	
LEIPZIG	G	N	1877–1918	
PSZCZYNA	**KATOWICE**			
PSZCZYNA	A	B	1816; 1819; 1831; 1848–1874	26/I/1395, 1397–1398
PSZCZYNA	U	B	1876–1945	
PSZCZYNA	A	D	1816; 1831; 1848–1874	26/I/1395, 1397–1398
PSZCZYNA	U	D	1876–1945	
PSZCZYNA	A	H	1939–1940	26/I/3400
PSZCZYNA	A	M	1851–1874	26/I/1397–1398
PSZCZYNA	U	M	1876–1945	
PSZCZYNA REGION	**KATOWICE**			
PSZCZYNA	A	H	1941	157/I/2
PUCHACZÓW	**LUBLIN**			
LUBLIN	A	T	1866	NPK/16
PUCK	**GDAŃSK**			
GDAŃSK	A	O	1925; 1928	46/9
PUŁAWY	**LUBLIN**			
LUBLIN	A	B	1838–1893	113
PUŁAWY	U	B	1894–1939	
PUŁAWY	U	D	1894–1914; 1916–1939	
LUBLIN	A	K	1887; 1895–1897; 1899; 1901–1914; 1927	RGL IV ADM; UWL WSP/811–819
LVOV	A	L	1785–1788; 1819–1820	19/V/75; 20/V/172
LUBLIN	A	M	1866–1893	113

Repository type: **A** = Archive **G** = LDS Films of German-Held Records **J** = Jewish Historical Institute **U** = Urząd Stanu Cywilnego

TOWN NAME	VOIVODSHIP (Province)			
Repository Location	Repository Document Type	Code	Years	Zespół/Sygnatura (Poland) Fond/Opis/Delo (Belarus, Ukraine, Lithuania)
PUŁAWY		U	M	1894–1914; 1916–1939	
LUBLIN		A	T	1887; 1895–1897; 1899; 1901–1914; 1927; 1929	RGL IV ADM; UWL WSP/811; 414
PUŁTUSK	**CIECHANÓW**				
PUŁTUSK		A	B	1875–1892	84
PUŁTUSK		U	B	1893–1937	
PUŁTUSK		A	D	1875–1892	84
PUŁTUSK		U	D	1893–1937	
PUŁTUSK		A	M	1875–1892	84
PUŁTUSK		U	M	1893–1937	
PUŃSK	**SUWAŁKI**				
SUWAŁKI		A	B	1808–1825; 1833–1872; 1874–1875; 1878–1882; 1884–1885; 1889	162; 202
PUŃSK		U	B	1890–1901; 1923–1927; 1935–1938	
SUWAŁKI		A	D	1808–1825; 1833–1872; 1874–1875; 1878–1882; 1884–1885; 1889	162; 202
PUŃSK		U	D	1890–1901; 1923–1927; 1935–1938	
SUWAŁKI		A	K	1926–1929	31/129, 137
SUWAŁKI		A	M	1808–1825; 1833–1872; 1874–1875; 1878–1882; 1884–1885; 1889	162; 202
PUŃSK		U	M	1890–1901; 1923–1927; 1935–1938	
PUTZIG	**SEE PUCK**				
PYZDRY	**KONIN**				
POZNAŃ		A	B	1826–1894	3751/1, 3–4, 6, 8–30, 48–81
PYZDRY		U	B	1895–1938	
POZNAŃ		A	D	1826–1894	3751/2, 5A, 7–30, 48–81
PYZDRY		U	D	1895–1938	
POZNAŃ		A	M	1826–1894	3751/1, 5–6, 8–81
PYZDRY		U	M	1895–1938	
RACIĄŻ	**CIECHANÓW**				
PŁOCK		A	B	1826–1875	202
DZIAŁDOWO		A	B	1876–1894	34
RACIĄŻ		U	B	1895–1913; 1917–1939	
PŁOCK		A	D	1826–1875	202
DZIAŁDOWO		A	D	1876–1894	34
RACIĄŻ		U	D	1895–1913; 1917–1939	
PŁOCK		A	M	1826–1875	202
DZIAŁDOWO		A	M	1876–1894	34
DZIAŁDOWO		A	M	1876–1893 (MARRIAGE APPLICATIONS)	34
RACIĄŻ		U	M	1895–1913; 1916–1939	
PŁOCK		A	Y	1896–1908; 1916–1939	293–295
RACIBÓRZ	**KATOWICE**				
RACIBÓRZ		A	B	1847–1939	3/488
RACIBÓRZ		A	D	1847–1884	3/490
RACIBÓRZ		A	M	1847–1874	3/489
RACŁAWÓWKA	**RZESZÓW**				
RZESZÓW		A	E	1935	382/1
RZESZÓW		A	H	1940–1941	382/34
RACZKI	**SUWAŁKI**				
WARSZAWA		A	T	1821–1841	KRSW 5022–5023
RĄCZYNA	**PRZEMYŚL**				
PRZEWORSK		A	S	1893–1944	83/1–48
RADŁÓW	**TARNÓW**				
RADŁÓW		U	B	1882–1916	
RADŁÓW		U	D	1882–1942	
RADOGOSZCZ	**ŁÓDŹ**				
ŁÓDŹ		A	Z	1910	1; 227
RADOLIN	**PIŁA**				
PIŁA		A	C	1816–1847	13
RADOM	**RADOM**				
RADOM		A	A	1842–1848; 1867–1873; 1918–1921	1
RADOM		A	B	1826–1894	190/1
RADOM		U	B	1895–1940	
RADOM		A	D	1826–1894	190
RADOM		U	D	1895–1940	
RADOM		A	E	1906–1907; 1916; 1918; 1928; 1934; 1939	1; 206
RADOM		A	G	1868–1930	1
RADOM		A	H	1939–1943	206; 209; 331; 387

A Army/recruit lists; **B** Birth; **C** Census; **D** Death; **E** Voter lists; **G** Immigration; **H** Holocaust; **J** Judaica; **K** Kahal; **L** Land; **M** Marriage; **N** Name changes; **O** Police files; **P** Pogroms; **R** Reference; **S** School records; **T** Tax lists; **V** Divorce; **W** Occupation lists; **X** Jewish hospital; **Y** Notary records; **Z** Local government records

TOWN NAME	VOIVODSHIP (Province)			Zespół/Sygnatura (Poland) Fond/Opis/Delo (Belarus, Ukraine, Lithuania)
Repository Location	Repository Type	Document Code	Years	
WARSZAWA	J	K	1940–1943	212
RADOM	A	L	1865–1916; 1936; 1945	1
RADOM	A	M	1826–1894	190
RADOM	U	M	1895–1940	
RADOM	A	N	1821–1860	1
RADOM	A	S	1865–1876; 1878–1912; 1929–1939	1; 123
RADOM	A	T	1868–1914; 1916–1918	1
RADOM	A	W	1925–1930; 1934; 1938; 1941–1942	1; 351
RADOM	A	X	1833–1914	39; 195–196
RADOM	A	Y	1818–1950	72–75; 77–104; 491–498
RADOMSKO	**PIOTRKÓW TRYBUNALSKI**			
ŁÓDŹ	A	A	1891–1902	17
PIOTRKÓW TRYBUNALSKI	A	B	1871–1895	335/3–26
RADOMSKO	U	B	1896–1906; 1910–1929	
PIOTRKÓW TRYBUNALSKI	A	C	1793–1944	103
PIOTRKÓW TRYBUNALSKI	A	D	1856–1895	335/1, 5–26
RADOMSKO	U	D	1896–1897; 1899–1908; 1910–1928	
PIOTRKÓW TRYBUNALSKI	A	H	1939–1944	103
PIOTRKÓW TRYBUNALSKI	A	L	1818–1981	378
PIOTRKÓW TRYBUNALSKI	A	M	1870–1895	335/2, 5–26
RADOMSKO	U	M	1896–1897; 1899–1908; 1910–1924	
ŁÓDŹ	A	O	1905–1906	43
PIOTRKÓW TRYBUNALSKI	A	T	1873–1916	700
PIOTRKÓW TRYBUNALSKI	A	Y	1808–1952	127–138, 175–180, 373–375, 689
PIOTRKÓW TRYBUNALSKI	A	Z	1793–1949	103
ŁÓDŹ	A	Z	1873/1914	1
RADOMYŚL NAD SANEM	**TARNOBRZEG**			
RADOMYŚL NAD SANEM	U	B	1882–1940	
RADOMYŚL NAD SANEM	U	D	1937–1940	
LVOV	A	L	1785–1788; 1819–1820	19/V/240; 20/V/221
PRZEMYŚL	A	Y	1875–1879; 1887–1923	94; 969–972
RADOSZYCE	**KIELCE**			
KIELCE	A	B	1826–1893	565
RADOSZYCE	U	B	1894–1897; 1899; 1902; 1904–1918; 1937–1941	
KIELCE	A	D	1826–1893	565
RADOSZYCE	U	D	1894–1897; 1899; 1902; 1904–1918; 1937–1941	
KIELCE	A	M	1826–1893	565
RADOSZYCE	U	M	1894–1897; 1899; 1902; 1904–1918; 1937–1941	
RADYMNO	**PRZEMYŚL**			
PRZEMYŚL	A	B	1877	154/3
RADYMNO	U	B	1892–1893; 1895–1913; 1915–1932; 1936–1938	
PRZEMYŚL	A	D	1877	154/3
RADYMNO	U	D	1892–1893; 1895–1911; 1913; 1915–1916; 1918–1922; 1924–1925; 1928–1932; 1937–1938	
LVOV	A	L	1785–1788; 1819–1820	19/XIII/253; 20/XIII/217
RADYMNO	U	M	1893; 1897–1907; 1909–1913; 1915–1916; 1918–1919; 1922–1923; 1928; 1930–1932; 1935; 1938	
PRZEMYŚL	A	M	1920; 1925	154/1–2
RADZANÓW	**CIECHANÓW**			
DZIAŁDOWO	A	B	1826–1828; 1834–1842; 1846–1848; 1850–1873; 1875–1888; 1890–1894	53
RADZANÓW	U	B	1929–1931; 1933–1935	
DZIAŁDOWO	A	D	1826–1828; 1834–1842; 1846–1848; 1850–1873; 1875–1888; 1890–1894	53
RADZANÓW	U	D	1929–1931; 1933–1935	
DZIAŁDOWO	A	M	1826–1828; 1834–1842; 1846–1848; 1850–1873; 1875–1888; 1890–1894	53
DZIAŁDOWO	A	M	1843; 1845; 1847; 1849; 1852; 1856; 1861–1862; 1865; 1870 (MARR. APPLICATIONS)	53
RADZANÓW	U	M	1929–1931; 1933–1935	
RADZIEJÓW KUJAWSKI	**WŁOCŁAWEK**			
WŁOCŁAWEK	A	B	1831–1892	
WŁOCŁAWEK	A	D	1826–1892	
WŁOCŁAWEK	A	M	1826–1892	
WŁOCŁAWEK	A	M	1842–1844; 1854; 1858–1867 (MARRIAGE APPLICATIONS)	
RADZIŁÓW	**ŁOMŻA**			
ŁOMŻA	A	B	1826–1895	270

Repository type: **A** = Archive **G** = LDS Films of German-Held Records **J** = Jewish Historical Institute **U** = Urząd Stanu Cywilnego

TOWN NAME	VOIVODSHIP (Province)				
Repository Location	Repository Document Type	Code	Years		Zespół/Sygnatura (Poland) Fond/Opis/Delo (Belarus, Ukraine, Lithuania)

RADZIŁÓW	U	B	1897–1901; 1903–1906; 1908–1910; 1915–1920; 1924; 1926; 1930–1931; 1935	
ŁOMŻA	A	D	1826–1895	270
RADZIŁÓW	U	D	1897; 1901; 1903–1904; 1906; 1908; 1910–1911; 1915; 1920; 1922; 1924; 1926–1929; 1934–1935	
ŁOMŻA	A	M	1826–1895	270
RADZIŁÓW	U	M	1897; 1900–1901; 1903; 1906–1908; 1910; 1915–1920; 1922–1924; 1926–1929; 1934–1935	
RADZYMIN	**CIECHANÓW**			
NOWY DWÓR MAZOWIECKI	A	B	1829; 1879–1914	393
NOWY DWÓR MAZOWIECKI	A	D	1882; 1914	393
NOWY DWÓR MAZOWIECKI	A	M	1863–1894; 1914	393
RADZYMIN	U	B	1938–1939	
NOWY DWÓR MAZOWIECKI	A	C	1926–1940	63
RADZYMIN	U	D	1938–1939	
NOWY DWÓR MAZOWIECKI	A	M	1846	163
RADZYMIN	U	M	1938–1939	
RADZYŃ CHEŁMIŃSKI	**TORUŃ**			
TORUŃ	A	B	1827–1846	616/1
TORUŃ	A	D	1845–1846	616/1
TORUŃ	A	M	1824–1844	616/1
RADZYŃ PODLASKI	**BIAŁA PODLASKA**			
LUBLIN	A	B	1826–1862	113
RADZYŃ PODLASKI	U	B	1918–1938	
LUBLIN	A	C	1909–1916	
LUBLIN	A	D	1826–1880	113
RADZYŃ PODLASKI	U	D	1918–1938	
LUBLIN	A	E	1872–1866; 1913–1914	RGL IV ADM
LUBLIN	A	K	1863–1866; 1872–1896; 1913–1914; 1922–1936	NPRADZYN/12; RGL IV ADM; UWL WSP/820–822
LUBLIN	A	M	1826–1862	113
RADZYŃ PODLASKI	U	M	1918–1938	
LUBLIN	A	T	1872–1896; 1913–1914; 1927	RGL IV ADM; UWL WSP/820
RAJGRÓD	**ŁOMŻA**			
ŁOMŻA	A	B	1826–1855; 1873; 1878; 1885–1886; 1889; 1893	271
RAJGRÓD	U	B	1895; 1897; 1900; 1902–1907; 1929	
ŁOMŻA	A	D	1826–1855; 1873; 1878; 1885–1886; 1889; 1893	271
RAJGRÓD	U	D	1895; 1897; 1900; 1902–1907; 1929	
BIAŁYSTOK	A	K	1914–1915	6/186
ŁOMŻA	A	M	1826–1855; 1880–1892	271
ŁOMŻA	A	M	1826–1843; 1869–1874; 1880–1890; 1863–1866 (MARRIAGE SUPPLEMENTS)	271
RAJGRÓD	U	M	1897; 1900; 1902–1907; 1929	
WARSZAWA	A	T	1820–1833	KRSW 5029–5030
RASTENBURG	**SEE KĘTRZYN**			
RASZKÓW	**KALISZ**			
POZNAŃ	A	K	1836–1858	327/291
KALISZ	A	S	1849–1857	30/32
RATIBOR	**SEE RACIBÓRZ**			
RAWA MAZOWIECKA	**SKIERNIEWICE**			
ŁÓDŹ	A	A	1897–1902	17
RAWA MAZOWIECKA	A	B	1809/1839; 1841–1852; 1853/1862; 1865–1866; 1869–1873	45; 165
ŁÓDŹ	A	B	1875–1877; 1881–1890; 1893	270
RAWA MAZOWIECKA	U	B	1896; 1899; 1902; 1904–1905; 1907; 1909; 1914; 1918–1920; 1930–1931; 1933; 1936–1937	
RAWA MAZOWIECKA	A	D	1809/1839; 1841–1852; 1853/1862; 1865–1866; 1869–1873	45; 165
ŁÓDŹ	A	D	1875–1877; 1881–1889; 1893	270
RAWA MAZOWIECKA	U	D	1899; 1909; 1918–1920	
ŁÓDŹ	A	K	1913–1914	
RAWA MAZOWIECKA	A	M	1809/1839; 1841–1852; 1853/1862; 1865–1866; 1869–1873	45; 165
ŁÓDŹ	A	M	1875–1877; 1881–1887	270
RAWA MAZOWIECKA	U	M	1896; 1899; 1908–1909; 1918–1929	
ŁÓDŹ	A	S	1836/1913	83
ŁÓDŹ	A	T	1846–1857	1
ŁÓDŹ	A	W	1893–1913	19

A Army/recruit lists; **B** Birth; **C** Census; **D** Death; **E** Voter lists; **G** Immigration; **H** Holocaust; **J** Judaica; **K** Kahal; **L** Land; **M** Marriage; **N** Name changes; **O** Police files; **P** Pogroms; **R** Reference; **S** School records; **T** Tax lists; **V** Divorce; **W** Occupation lists; **X** Jewish hospital; **Y** Notary records; **Z** Local government records

TOWN NAME Repository Location	VOIVODSHIP (Province) Repository Document Type	Code	Years	Zespół/Sygnatura (Poland) Fond/Opis/Delo (Belarus, Ukraine, Lithuania)
RAWA MAZOWIECKA	A	Y	1809–1836; 1838–1914; 1916–1946	146–147; 240–250
RAWICZ	**LESZNO**			
LESZNO	A	C	1835–1900	27
LESZNO	A	H	1939–1944	27
POZNAŃ	A	K	1839–1914	331/144–146
RAWITSCH	**SEE RAWICZ**			
REGENWALDE	**SEE RESKO**			
REICHENBACH	**SEE DZIERŻONIÓW**			
REJOWIEC	**CHEŁM**			
LUBLIN	A	B	1826–1885; 1888–1892	113
REJOWIEC	U	B	1893–1896; 1920–1941	
LUBLIN	A	D	1826–1877; 1882; 1884–1885; 1888	113
REJOWIEC	U	D	1894–1896; 1920–1941	
LUBLIN	A	H	1941	36
LUBLIN	A	K	1871–1915; 1927–1937	RGL ADM; RGCH/481; UWL WSP/767
LUBLIN	A	M	1826–1877; 1888; 1891–1892	113
REJOWIEC	U	M	1893–1896; 1920–1941	
RESKO	**SZCZECIN**			
SZCZECIN	A	C	1812	AMTSGERICHT REGENSWALDE 11/1
SZCZECIN	A	D	1813–1847; 1849; 1851–1894; 1935	AMTSGERICHT REGENSWALDE 11/1
SZCZECIN	A	M	1814–1847; 1851–1894; 1935	AMTSGERICHT REGENSWALDE 11/1
RESZEL	**OLSZTYN**			
OLSZTYN	A	C	1812–1852; 1882; 1890; 1914; 1920; 1923	23/I; 265/I
RIESENBURG	**SEE PRABUTY**			
ROESSEL	**SEE RESZEL**			
ROGIENICE WYPYCHY	**ŁOMŻA**			
ŁOMŻA	A	C	1933–1951	160
ROGOŹNO	**TORUŃ**			
POZNAŃ	A	B	1817/1839; 1840–1847	3589/1–6, 11, 14, 17, 20, 23, 26, 29, 32, 35, 38, 41
POZNAŃ	A	D	1817/1839; 1840–1847	3589/1–5, 8, 10, 13, 16, 19, 22, 25, 28, 31, 34, 37, 40, 43
POZNAŃ	A	M	1817/1839; 1840–1847	3589/15, 7, 12, 15, 18, 21, 24, 27, 30, 33, 36, 39, 42
ROPCZYCE	**RZESZÓW**			
PRZEMYŚL	A	A	1919–1935	681/31
RZESZÓW	A	H	1940–1943	135/17–18
LVOV	A	L	1785–1788; 1819–1820	19/VII/389; 20/VII/284
PRZEMYŚL	A	Y	1873–1874; 1876–1934	96; 1090–1094
ROSENBERG	**SEE SUSZ**			
ROSSEL	**SEE RESZEL**			
ROSSOSZ	**BIAŁA PODLASKA**			
ROSSOSZ	U	B	1920–1939	
ROSSOSZ	U	D	1920–1939	
LUBLIN	A	K	1924–1928	SPB/207
ROSSOSZ	U	M	1920–1939	
RÓŻAN	**OSTROŁĘKA**			
RÓŻAN	U	B	1898–1916; 1919–1933; 1936–1938	
RÓŻAN	U	D	1898–1916; 1919–1933; 1936–1938	
RÓŻAN	U	M	1898–1916; 1919–1933; 1936–1938	
ROZBÓRZ	**PRZEMYŚL**			
PRZEWORSK	A	S	1884–1952	70/5–13, 18–55
ROŻNIATÓW	**PRZEMYŚL**			
PRZEWORSK	A	S	1904–1957	71/1–47
ROZPRZA	**PIOTRKÓW TRYBUNALSKI**			
ŁÓDŹ	A	A	1891–1896	17
PIOTRKÓW TRYBUNALSKI	A	B	1848; 1853–1865; 1873–1898; 1908–1928	336/2–27, 30
ROZPRZA	U	B	1895–1940	
PIOTRKÓW TRYBUNALSKI	A	C	1868–1931	32
PIOTRKÓW TRYBUNALSKI	A	D	1826–1867; 1873–1895; 1899–1922	336/1–24, 29
ROZPRZA	U	D	1896–1940	
PIOTRKÓW TRYBUNALSKI	A	M	1848; 1858–1895	336/2–24, 28
ROZPRZA	U	M	1896–1940	
ŁÓDŹ	A	S	1891–1899	83
PIOTRKÓW TRYBUNALSKI	A	Z	1805–1875	10

Repository type: **A** = Archive **G** = LDS Films of German-Held Records **J** = Jewish Historical Institute **U** = Urząd Stanu Cywilnego

TOWN NAME	VOIVODSHIP (Province)			
Repository Location	Repository Document Type	Code	Years	Zespół/Sygnatura (Poland) Fond/Opis/Delo (Belarus, Ukraine, Lithuania)
ŁÓDŹ	A	Z	1822–1866	1
ROZWADÓW	**TARNOBRZEG**			
PRZEMYŚL	A	K	1897	74/33
LVOV	A	L	1785–1788; 1819–1820	19/V/185; 20/V/192
PRZEMYŚL	A	S	1890–1894	74/27
PRZEMYŚL	A	Y	1859–1893; 1915–1934	97; 1169–1173
RUDA ŁAŃCUCKA	**RZESZÓW**			
RZESZÓW	A	C	1932–1939	269/111–123
RUDA PABIANICKA	**ŁÓDŹ**			
ŁÓDŹ	A	C	1923–1940	223
RUDNIK	**TARNOBRZEG**			
PRZEWORSK	A	T	1937; 1944–1948	18/8, 83–88
RUGENWALDE	**SEE DARŁOWO**			
RUMMELSBURG	**SEE MIASTKO**			
RUSKA WIEŚ	**PRZEMYŚL**			
PRZEMYŚL	A	C	1931–1939	200/50
LVOV	A	L	1785–1788; 1819–1820	19/V/8; 20/V/208
RUSZELCZYCE	**PRZEMYŚL**			
PRZEMYŚL	A	C	1913–1930; 1943; 1945–1957	203/22, 32, 49, 60, 69, 78, 87
RUTKI	**ŁOMŻA**			
ŁOMŻA	A	B	1860–1894	171
ŁOMŻA	A	D	1860–1894	171
ŁOMŻA	A	M	1860–1894	171
RUZOMBEROK	**SEE SUSZ**			
RYBITWY	**LUBLIN**			
RYBITWY	U	B	1882–1912; 1920–1937	
RYBITWY	U	D	1882–1912; 1920–1937	
RYBITWY	U	M	1882–1912; 1920–1937	
RYBNIK	**KATOWICE**			
RACIBÓRZ	A	C	1837–1874	78/1492–1494
KATOWICE	A	K	1923–1932	27/I–VI/1998–1999
RYBNIK REGION	**KATOWICE**			
RACIBÓRZ	A	B	1810–1874	118/1–31
RACIBÓRZ	A	D	1810–1874	118/1–31
RACIBÓRZ	A	K	1812–1911	78/1477–1483, 1488–1494
RACIBÓRZ	A	M	1810–1874	118/1–31
RACIBÓRZ	A	S	1820–1900	78/1484–1487
RYCHTAL	**KALISZ**			
KALISZ	A	C	1877–1890	31/4
KALISZ	A	E	1879; 1881; 1883; 1887; 1889; 1922; 1925; 1927; 1929–1931	31/4–6, 50–52
KALISZ	A	T	1918–1932	
RYCHWAŁ	**KONIN**			
POZNAŃ	A	B	1826–1855	3752/1–30
POZNAŃ	A	D	1826–1855	3752/1–30
POZNAŃ	A	G	1925/1939; 1945–1950	4302/16–17, 119, 123
POZNAŃ	A	M	1826–1855	3752/1–30
RYCZYWÓL	**RADOM**			
RADOM	A	B	1826–1840; 1842–1889; 1891–1892	191
RYCZYWÓL	U	B	1893–1905	
RADOM	A	D	1826–1840; 1842–1889; 1891–1892	191
RYCZYWÓL	U	D	1893–1905	
RADOM	A	M	1826–1840; 1842–1889; 1891–1892	191
RYCZYWÓL	U	M	1893–1905	
RYKI	**LUBLIN**			
RYKI	U	B	1882–1915; 1920–1939	
RYKI	U	D	1890–1930; 1936–1940	
RYKI	U	M	1884–1915; 1922–1939	
RYMANÓW	**KROSNO**			
RYMANÓW	U	B	1939–1941	
RYMANÓW	U	D	1938–1941	
SANOK	A	G	1942–1945	46/38–41
SANOK	A	H	1942–1945	46/38–41
LVOV	A	L	1785–1788; 1819–1820	19/XV/213; 20/XV/225
RYMANÓW	U	M	1939	

A Army/recruit lists; **B** Birth; **C** Census; **D** Death; **E** Voter lists; **G** Immigration; **H** Holocaust; **J** Judaica; **K** Kahal; **L** Land; **M** Marriage; **N** Name changes; **O** Police files; **P** Pogroms; **R** Reference; **S** School records; **T** Tax lists; **V** Divorce; **W** Occupation lists; **X** Jewish hospital; **Y** Notary records; **Z** Local government records

TOWN NAME Repository Location	VOIVODSHIP (Province) Repository Type	Document Code	Years	Zespół/Sygnatura (Poland) Fond/Opis/Delo (Belarus, Ukraine, Lithuania)
PRZEMYŚL	A	Y	1928–1933	660
RYNARZEWO	**BYDGOSZCZ**			
BYDGOSZCZ	A	B	1823–1852; 1874–1893	385; 1770
BYDGOSZCZ	A	D	1824–1849; 1874–1893	385; 1770
BYDGOSZCZ	A	M	1824–1851; 1874–1893	385; 1770
RYPIN	**WŁOCŁAWEK**			
WŁOCŁAWEK	A	B	1808–1822; 1826–1894	563
RYPIN	U	B	1895–1938	
WŁOCŁAWEK	A	D	1808–1822; 1826–1894	563
RYPIN	U	D	1895–1938	
WŁOCŁAWEK	A	M	1808–1822; 1826–1894	563
RYPIN	U	M	1895–1938	
RZEPEDŻ	**KROSNO**			
SANOK	A	C	1937–1939	23/32
RZEPIENNIK STRZYŻEWSKI	**TARNÓW**			
RZEPIENNIK STRZYŻEWSKI	U	B	1922–1945	
RZEPIENNIK STRZYŻEWSKI	U	D	1922–1945	
RZEPIENNIK STRZYŻEWSKI	U	M	1922–1945	
RZESZÓW	**RZESZÓW**			
RZESZÓW	A	A	1860/1918	1/1539–1547; 1556; 1697–1698; 2723–2725
LVOV	A	B	1841–1866	701/1/299
RZESZÓW	A	B	1866–1939 (ALPHA INDEX: 1913–1939)	533/20, 44, 55–57; 1/2735–2743
RZESZÓW	U	B	1888–1943	
RZESZÓW	A	C	1800/1850; 1869–1910; 1921; 1935–1942	533/1/32, 53, 489, 1497–1538, 2713
RZESZÓW	A	D	1842–1883; 1889; 1915–1942; (ALPHA INDEX: 1935–1942)	533/18, 20, 42–43, 50–52, 58–60; 1/3774–3775
RZESZÓW	U	D	1884–1888; 1894–1906; 1913–1943	
RZESZÓW	A	E	1925; 1939	1/105–110; 2053–2058
RZESZÓW	A	H	1940–1944	533/1/53; 3755
RZESZÓW	A	K	1858; 1882–1917; 1919–1923	533/1; 7; 2015; 2380–2384; 2471
RZESZÓW	A	L	1800/1850; 1940–1944; 1947	1/1488, 1496, 3698, 3701, 3755–3756; 36/498
LVOV	A	L	1785–1788	19/V/1
RZESZÓW	U	M	1882–1886; 1888–1943	
RZESZÓW	A	M	1895–1942	533/2–17, 21–41, 45, 47–49, 54
RZESZÓW	A	N	1918–1932	533/43
LVOV	A	S	1832–1839; 1879; 1891-1904; 1918-1920	
PRZEMYŚL	A	Y	1859–1951	98; 779; 1174–1193
RZESZÓW	A	Z	1841–1931 (COURT RECORDS/WILLS)	533/1
RZESZÓW REGION	**RZESZÓW**			
RZESZÓW	A	A	1894–1917	313/28–50; 516/11–24
RZESZÓW	A	B	1939	1/2738, 2741
RZESZÓW	A	E	1894–1917	516/11–24, 32–50
SAALFELD	**SEE ZALEWO**			
SAGAN	**SEE ŻAGAŃ**			
SANDOMIERZ	**TARNOBRZEG**			
SANDOMIERZ	A	B	1826–1893	173
SANDOMIERZ	U	B	1894–1942	
SANDOMIERZ	A	D	1826–1893	173
SANDOMIERZ	U	D	1894–1942	
SANDOMIERZ	A	G	1939–1942	111/1988, 2125
SANDOMIERZ	A	H	1940–1941;1945	111/1809
SANDOMIERZ	A	M	1826–1893	173
SANDOMIERZ	U	M	1894–1942	
SANOK	**KROSNO**			
SANOK	A	A	1869; 1874–1879; 1881–1899; 1901–1909; 1937–1939	135/570; 155/24
SANOK	A	B	1874–1879; 1881; 1884; 1888; 1891–1894; 1897; 1902–1908; 1940	155/21
SANOK	U	B	1897–1940	
SANOK	A	C	1918; 1927–1939	135/550–551, 553–557; 574
SANOK	A	D	1874–1879; 1881; 1884; 1888; 1891–1894; 1897; 1902–1908; 1910	155/21
SANOK	U	D	1914–1938	
SANOK	A	G	1879; 1881–1882; 1885–1886; 1888; 1890–1894; 1897–1909	155/22

Repository type: **A** = Archive **G** = LDS Films of German-Held Records **J** = Jewish Historical Institute **U** = Urząd Stanu Cywilnego

TOWN NAME	VOIVODSHIP (Province)			Zespół/Sygnatura (Poland)
Repository Location	Repository Document Type	Code	Years	Fond/Opis/Delo (Belarus, Ukraine, Lithuania)
SANOK	A	H	1938–1947	42/74
SANOK	A	K	1893	135/231
SANOK	A	L	1928; 1931–1939	135/572; 574
LVOV	A	L	1785–1788	19/XV/48
SANOK	A	M	1874–1879; 1881; 1884; 1888; 1891–1894; 1897; 1902–1908; 1910	155/21
SANOK	U	M	1915–1939	
PRZEMYŚL	A	Y	1900–1901; 1911–1912; 1929–1934	633; 993–995
SARNAKI	**BIAŁA PODLASKA**			
SIEDLCE	A	B	1836–1849; 1853; 1855–1858	217/1–18, 31
LUBLIN	A	B	1859–1875; 1877–1879; 1885–1887; 1890–1891; 1893–1894	113
SARNAKI	U	B	1896–1909; 1911–1912; 1914; 1926; 1930–1931	
SIEDLCE	A	D	1836–1849; 1853; 1855–1858	217/1–18, 31
LUBLIN	A	D	1859–1875; 1877–1879; 1885–1887; 1890–1891; 1893–1894	113
SARNAKI	U	D	1896–1909; 1911–1912; 1914; 1926; 1930–1931	
LUBLIN	A	K	1913–1914; 1927	RGL IV ADM; UWL WSP/794
SIEDLCE	A	M	1836–1844; 1846–1847; 1849; 1853; 1855–1858	217/1–18, 31
LUBLIN	A	M	1859–1875; 1877–1879; 1885–1887; 1890–1891; 1893–1894	113
SARNAKI	U	M	1896–1909; 1911–1912; 1914; 1926; 1930–1931	
SARNE	**SEE SARNOWA**			
SARNOWA	**LESZNO**			
LESZNO	A	C	1835–1842	29
POZNAŃ	A	C	1858–1910	314/148
POZNAŃ	A	K	1816–1817	314/148A
SAWIN	**CHEŁM**			
SAWIN	U	B	1919–1939	
SAWIN	U	D	1920; 1923–1934; 1936–1939	
LUBLIN	A	K	1912–1915; 1927	RGL IV ADM; UWL WSP/768
SAWIN	U	M	1922–1939	
SCHIPPENBEIL	**SEE SĘPOPOL**			
SCHIVELBEIN	**SEE ŚWIDWIN**			
SCHLICHTINGSHEIM	**SEE SZLICHTYNGOWA**			
SCHLOCHAU	**SEE CZŁUCHÓW**			
SCHNEIDEMUHL	**SEE PIŁA**			
SCHOENLANKE	**SEE PIŁA**			
SCHWEIDNITZ	**SEE ŚWIDNICA**			
SCHWERIN	**SEE SKWIERZYNA**			
SCHWIEBUS	**SEE ŚWIEBODZIN**			
SECEMIN	**CZĘSTOCHOWA**			
JĘDRZEJÓW	A	B	1826–1866; 1868–1869	221
JĘDRZEJÓW	A	D	1826–1866; 1868–1869	221
JĘDRZEJÓW	A	M	1826–1844; 1846–1847; 1849–1866; 1868–1869	221
SEJNY	**SUWAŁKI**			
SUWAŁKI	A	B	1808–1825; 1828–1829; 1836; 1838; 1840; 1844; 1847; 1849–1850; 1852; 1857–1858; 1859/1865; 1866–1875; 1880/1894	163; 207
SEJNY	U	B	1896–1898; 1901; 1903; 1910–1912; 1920–1938	
SUWAŁKI	A	D	1808–1825; 1826/1865; 1866–1875; 1880/1893; 1894	163; 207
SEJNY	U	D	1896–1898; 1901; 1903; 1910–1912; 1920–1938	
VILNIUS	A	G	1885–1917	1010
SUWAŁKI	A	K	1926–1938	31/138–143
SUWAŁKI	A	L	1944–1949	313/155
SUWAŁKI	A	M	1808–1826; 1828–1829; 1836; 1838; 1840; 1844; 1847/1865; 1866–1875; 1880; 1882; 1886–1887; 1889; 1893–1894	163; 207
SEJNY	U	M	1896–1898; 1901; 1903; 1910–1912; 1920–1938	
WARSZAWA	A	T	1823–1832; 1846/1865	KRSW 5118–5120; 5130–5131
SUWAŁKI	A	Y	1808–1939	227–240
SENSBURG	**SEE MRĄGOWO**			
SĘPOPOL	**OLSZTYN**			
BERLIN	G	B	1847–1874	

A Army/recruit lists; **B** Birth; **C** Census; **D** Death; **E** Voter lists; **G** Immigration; **H** Holocaust; **J** Judaica; **K** Kahal; **L** Land; **M** Marriage; **N** Name changes;
O Police files; **P** Pogroms; **R** Reference; **S** School records; **T** Tax lists; **V** Divorce; **W** Occupation lists; **X** Jewish hospital; **Y** Notary records; **Z** Local government records

TOWN NAME	VOIVODSHIP (Province)			Zespół/Sygnatura (Poland)
Repository Location	Repository Type	Document Code	Years	Fond/Opis/Delo (Belarus, Ukraine, Lithuania)
BERLIN	G	D	1847–1874	
BERLIN	G	M	1847–1874	
SEROCK	**WARSZAWA**			
NOWY DWÓR MAZOWIECKI	A	B	1874–1879; 1881; 1883–1884; 1886–1894	469
SEROCK	U	B	1895–1904; 1917–1924; 1930–1936	
NOWY DWÓR MAZOWIECKI	A	D	1875–1879; 1881; 1883–1884; 1886–1894	469
SEROCK	U	D	1895–1900; 1902–1904; 1917–1922; 1929–1932; 1934–1936	
NOWY DWÓR MAZOWIECKI	A	M	1875–1879; 1881; 1883–1884; 1886–1894	469
SEROCK	U	M	1895–1900; 1902–1904; 1917–1923; 1930–1932; 1934–1935	
SEROCZYN	**SIEDLCE**			
SIEDLCE	A	B	1841; 1843–1865; 1867–1877; 1879–1881; 1883–1888; 1890–1893	219/1–48
SIEDLCE	A	D	1841; 1843–1865; 1867–1877; 1879–1881; 1883–1888; 1890–1893	219/1–48
LUBLIN	A	K	1913–1915; 1923–1927	RGL IV ADM; UWL WSP/1565
SIEDLCE	A	M	1841; 1843–1865; 1867–1877; 1879–1881; 1883–1888; 1890–1893	219/1–48
LUBLIN	A	T	1913–1915; 1923–1927	RGL IV ADM; UWL WSP/1565
SIANÓW	**KOSZALIN**			
KOSZALIN	A	B	1841–1874	543/I/6–7
KOSZALIN	A	D	1847–1848; 1851–1871	543/I/10–11
KOSZALIN	A	M	1841–1874	543/I/8–9
SIEDLCE	**SIEDLCE**			
SIEDLCE	A	B	1828; 1834–1845; 1851–1852; 1856–1857; 1861–1863; 1865; 1867–1868; 1873; 1875–1877; 1885–1891; 1894	221/1–46
SIEDLCE	U	B	1902–1911; 1913; 1917; 1921–1923; 1926; 1929; 1933–1934; 1937–1938; 1940–1942; 1945	
SIEDLCE	A	C	1921–1950	36/119–2356; 2362
SIEDLCE	A	D	1828; 1834–1845; 1851–1852; 1856–1857; 1861–1863; 1865; 1867–1868; 1873; 1875–1877; 1885–1891; 1894	221/1–46
SIEDLCE	U	D	1902–1911; 1913; 1917; 1921–1923; 1926; 1929; 1933–1934; 1937–1941; 1943	
LUBLIN	A	E	1872–1914	RGL IV ADM
SIEDLCE	A	H	1939–1944	36/83, 2357, 2362–2363
SIEDLCE	A	J	1876/1936	334/1
LUBLIN	A	K	1872–1914; 1922–1936	RGL IV ADM; 403/823–824
SIEDLCE	A	M	1828; 1834–1845; 1851–1852; 1856–1857; 1861–1863; 1865; 1867–1868; 1873; 1875–1877; 1885–1891; 1894	221/1–46
SIEDLCE	U	M	1902–1911; 1913; 1917; 1921–1923; 1926; 1929; 1933–1934; 1937–1938; 1940–1942; 1945	
LUBLIN	A	T	1872–1914; 1922–1936	RGL IV ADM; UWL WSP/823
SIEDLECZKA	**PRZEMYŚL**			
PRZEWORSK	A	S	1912–1948	72/1–12, 14–18
SIEDLISKO	**ZIELONA GÓRA**			
LEIPZIG	G	B	1847–1874	
LEIPZIG	G	D	1847–1874	
LEIPZIG	G	M	1847–1874	
SIEDLISZCZE	**CHEŁM**			
LUBLIN	A	B	1827; 1829; 1874–1883; 1885; 1888	113
SIEDLISZCZE	U	B	1923–1939	
LUBLIN	A	D	1827; 1829; 1874–1883; 1885; 1888	113
SIEDLISZCZE	U	D	1923–1939	
LUBLIN	A	H	1941	37
LUBLIN	A	K	1869–1909; 1913–1915; 1923–1930	RGL ADM; RGCH/536; UWL WSP/1557
LUBLIN	A	M	1827; 1829; 1874–1883; 1885; 1888	113
SIEDLISZCZE	U	M	1923–1939	
LUBLIN	A	T	1869–1909; 1913–1915; 1923–1930	RGL ADM; RGCH/536; UWL WSP/1557
SIEMIANOWICE ŚLĄSKIE	**KATOWICE**			
KOBLENZ	G	G	1856–1862	
KATOWICE	A	K	1868–1921	27/I–VI/2000; 1/I/103, 509
KATOWICE	A	M	1847–1849	674/I/437
SIEMIATYCZE	**BIAŁYSTOK**			
BIAŁYSTOK	A	K	1861	564

Repository type: **A** = Archive   **G** = LDS Films of German-Held Records   **J** = Jewish Historical Institute   **U** = Urząd Stanu Cywilnego

TOWN NAME	VOIVODSHIP (Province)			
Repository Location	Repository Document Type	Code	Years	Zespół/Sygnatura (Poland) Fond/Opis/Delo (Belarus, Ukraine, Lithuania)
SIENIAWA	**PRZEMYŚL**			
SIENIAWA	U	B	1882–1888; 1891–1916; 1918–1925; 1927–1937; 1939	
SIENIAWA	U	D	1891; 1893–1898; 1901; 1903–1942	
LVOV	A	L	1785–1788; 1819–1820	29/XV/223; 20/XV/236
SIENIAWA	U	M	1882–1912; 1915–1924; 1926–1927; 1930–1933; 1935–1939	
SIENNICA	**SIEDLCE**			
SIEDLCE	A	B	1826–1829; 1831–1836	179/1–10
SIEDLCE	A	D	1826–1829; 1831–1836	179/1–10
SIEDLCE	A	M	1826–1829; 1831–1836	179/1–10
SIENNICA RÓŻANA	**INCLUDED IN KRASNYSTAW**			
SIENNO	**RADOM**			
STARACHOWICE	A	B	1826–1873	169
RADOM	A	B	1874–1894	477/1
SIENNO	U	B	1895–1912; 1919–1942	
STARACHOWICE	A	D	1826–1873	169
RADOM	A	D	1874–1894	477/1
SIENNO	U	D	1895–1912; 1919–1938	
STARACHOWICE	A	M	1826–1873	169
RADOM	A	M	1874–1894	477/1
SIENNO	U	M	1895–1912; 1916–1922; 1925–1938	
SIERADZ	**SIERADZ**			
SIERADZ	U	B	1914–1935; 1938–1940	
SIERADZ	U	D	1914–1935; 1938–1940	
SIERADZ	A	L	1931–1940	4
SIERADZ	U	M	1914–1925; 1938–1939	
SIERAKÓW	**POZNAŃ**			
POZNAŃ	A	B	1830	3590/1–2
POZNAŃ	A	D	1830	3590/1–2
POZNAŃ	A	K	1834–1915	313/2127, 2131–2132, 2134
POZNAŃ	A	M	1830	3590/1–2
SIERPC	**PŁOCK**			
PŁOCK	A	B	1826–1894	203
SIERPC	U	B	1895–1907; 1911; 1914–1936	
PŁOCK	A	D	1826–1894	203
SIERPC	U	D	1895–1907; 1911; 1914–1936	
PŁOCK	A	M	1826–1894	203
SIERPC	U	M	1895–1907; 1911; 1914–1936	
PŁOCK	A	Y	1824–1939	281–292
SIETESZ	**PRZEMYŚL**			
PRZEWORSK	A	S	1902–1952	73/2–12, 18–43, 45–50
SIEWIERZ	**KATOWICE**			
SIEWIERZ	U	B	1930–1940	
SIEWIERZ	U	D	1930–1941	
KATOWICE	A	H	1939–1944	890/1541, 1594–1595
KATOWICE	A	K	1905–1908; 1913; 1917	890/784, 938, 1011
SIEWIERZ	U	M	1930–1941	
SILESIA REGION	**KATOWICE**			
KATOWICE	A	B	1925–1939	27/I–VI/1987
KATOWICE	A	D	1925–1939	27/I–VI/1987
KATOWICE	A	K	1923; 1925–1939	27/I–VOL. VI/1985–1987
KATOWICE	A	M	1925–1939	27/I–VI/1987
SKALBMIERZ	**KIELCE**			
SKALBMIERZ	U	B	1932–1942	
PIŃCZÓW	A	C	1902–1931; 1940–1950	110
SKALBMIERZ	U	D	1932–1942	
SKALBMIERZ	U	M	1932–1942	
SKARZYSKO–KAMIENNA	**KIELCE**			
SKARZYSKO	U	B	1911–1913; 1924–1940	
SKARZYSKO	U	D	1911–1913; 1924–1940	
SKARZYSKO	U	M	1911–1913; 1924–1940	
SKAWINA	**KRAKÓW**			
KRAKÓW	U	B	1877/1941	
KRAKÓW	U	D	1877/1941	
KRAKÓW	U	M	1877/1941	

A Army/recruit lists; **B** Birth; **C** Census; **D** Death; **E** Voter lists; **G** Immigration; **H** Holocaust; **J** Judaica; **K** Kahal; **L** Land; **M** Marriage; **N** Name changes; **O** Police files; **P** Pogroms; **R** Reference; **S** School records; **T** Tax lists; **V** Divorce; **W** Occupation lists; **X** Jewish hospital; **Y** Notary records; **Z** Local government records

TOWN NAME	VOIVODSHIP (Province)			Zespół/Sygnatura (Poland)
Repository Location	Repository Document Type	Code	Years	Fond/Opis/Delo (Belarus, Ukraine, Lithuania)
KRAKÓW	A	Z	1578; 1772–1944	114
SKIERNIEWICE	**SKIERNIEWICE**			
ŁÓDŹ	A	B	1826–1877	270
SKIERNIEWICE	U	B	1880–1892; 1894–1908; 1910–1914; 1916–1917; 1919–1928; 1930–1932; 1934–1935; 1937–1939	
RAWA MAZOWIECKA	A	C	1867–1939	19/12–117, 132–182, 191–314
ŁÓDŹ	A	D	1826–1877	270
SKIERNIEWICE	U	D	1882; 1892; 1894–1908; 1910–1914; 1916–1917; 1919–1928; 1930–1932; 1934–1935; 1937–1939	
ŁÓDŹ	A	M	1826–1877	270
SKIERNIEWICE	U	M	1881–1892; 1894–1908; 1910–1914; 1916–1917; 1919–1928; 1930–1932; 1934–1935; 1937–1939	
RAWA MAZOWIECKA	A	Y	1873–1948	41–46; 151
SKOKI	**POZNAŃ**			
POZNAŃ	A	K	1835–1918	338/272–274; 4066/31
SKOPÓW	**PRZEMYŚL**			
PRZEMYŚL	A	C	1931/1943	203/23, 33, 50, 61, 70, 79, 88
SKULSK	**KONIN**			
POZNAŃ	A	B	1826–1829; 1831–1834; 1836–1846; 1848–1851; 1853–1855; 1883–1884	3753/1–46
SKULSK	U	B	1897–1898; 1900; 1915; 1917; 1921–1922; 1925–1926	
POZNAŃ	A	D	1826–1829; 1831–1834; 1836–1846; 1848–1851; 1853–1855; 1883–1884	3753/1–46
SKULSK	U	D	1887; 1897–1898; 1900; 1915; 1917; 1921–1922; 1925–1926	
POZNAŃ	A	M	1826–1829; 1831–1834; 1836–1846; 1848–1851; 1853–1855; 1883–1884	3753/1–46
SKULSK	U	M	1887; 1897–1898; 1900; 1915; 1917; 1921–1922; 1925–1926	
SKWIERZYNA	**GORZÓW WIELKOPOLSKI**			
KOBLENZ	G	B	1808–1846; 1861–1866	
GORZÓW WIELKOPOLSKI	A	C	1834–1841; 1848	MAGISTRAT SCHWERIN 185/294, 296
KOBLENZ	G	D	1808–1837; 1838/1844; 1845–1847; 1861–1866; 1875–1918	
GORZÓW WIELKOPOLSKI	A	K	1835	MAGISTRAT SCHWERIN 185/295
KOBLENZ	G	M	1808–1837; 1838/1847; 1861–1866	
KOBLENZ	G	N	1835–1862	
GORZÓW WIELKOPOLSKI	A	R	1834–1847	MAGISTRAT SCHWERIN 185/297
GORZÓW WIELKOPOLSKI	A	S	1826–1835; 1856–1858	MAGISTRAT SCHWERIN 185/398–401
GORZÓW WIELKOPOLSKI	A	Z	1807–1831	MAGISTRAT SCHWERIN 185/298
SŁAWATYCZE	**BIAŁA PODLASKA**			
LUBLIN	A	B	1847–1855; 1864–1895	113
SŁAWATYCZE	U	B	1896–1939	
LUBLIN	A	D	1847–1855; 1864–1895	113
SŁAWATYCZE	U	D	1896–1939	
LUBLIN	A	K	1911–1915; 1927	RGCH/443; UWL WSP/833
LUBLIN	A	M	1847–1855; 1864–1895	113
SŁAWATYCZE	U	M	1896–1939	
SŁAWKÓW	**KATOWICE**			
SŁAWKÓW	U	B	1904–1940	
SŁAWKÓW	U	D	1904–1940	
SŁAWKÓW	U	M	1904–1940	
ŚLESIN	**KONIN**			
POZNAŃ	A	B	1826–1867; 1878; 1881; 1884–1887; 1890–1891; 1894–1898	3757/1–50
ŚLESIN	U	B	1901; 1906; 1912; 1939–1940	
POZNAŃ	A	D	1826–1867; 1878; 1881; 1884–1887; 1890–1891; 1894–1898	3757/1–50
ŚLESIN	U	D	1901; 1906; 1912; 1939–1940	
POZNAŃ	A	G	1918–1939	25/106–116
POZNAŃ	A	M	1826–1867; 1878; 1881; 1884–1887; 1890–1891; 1894–1898	3757/1–50
ŚLESIN	U	M	1901; 1906; 1912; 1939–1940	
SŁOCINA	**RZESZÓW**			
RZESZÓW	A	C	1931–1943	383/60–72, 75–76, 81–83, 131–135

Repository type: **A** = Archive **G** = LDS Films of German-Held Records **J** = Jewish Historical Institute **U** = Urząd Stanu Cywilnego

TOWN NAME	VOIVODSHIP (Province)				Zespół/Sygnatura (Poland)
Repository Location	Repository Document				Fond/Opis/Delo (Belarus,
	Type	Code	Years		Ukraine, Lithuania)
SŁUPCA	**KONIN**				
POZNAŃ	A	B	1869–1894		3754/1–27
SŁUPCA	U	B	1895–1939		
POZNAŃ	A	D	1869–1894		3754/1–11, 13–27
SŁUPCA	U	D	1895–1939		
LUBLIN	A	H	1941		LUBLIN JUDENRAT/169
POZNAŃ	A	M	1869–1894		3754/1–11, 13–27
SŁUPCA	U	M	1895–1939		
POZNAŃ	A	S	1937–1939		805/192–193
SŁUPCZA	**TARNOBRZEG**				
LUBLIN	A	H	1941		150–172
SŁUPIA NOWA	**SEE NOWA SŁUPIA**				
SŁUPSK	**SŁUPSK**				
SŁUPSK	A	B	1813–1842; 1857–1882		6/5496, 5505–5506, 5508
SŁUPSK REGION	**SŁUPSK**				
SŁUPSK	A	B	1874–1894		266–360
SŁUPSK	A	D	1874–1894		266–360
SŁUPSK	A	M	1874–1894		266–360
SMOLNIK	**KROSNO**				
SANOK	A	C	1931–1945		31/2–8(6)
ŚNIADOWO	**ŁOMŻA**				
ŁOMŻA	A	B	1824; 1826–1827; 1829; 1833–1834; 1836–1837; 1841–1849; 1852; 1854–1860; 1863; 1867–1869; 1871–1872; 1876–1884; 1886–1891; 1893–1894		172
ŚNIADOWO	U	B	1895–1896; 1899–1906		
ŁOMŻA	A	C	1901–1937		161
ŁOMŻA	A	D	1824; 1827; 1829; 1833–1834; 1836–1837; 1841–1852; 1854–1860; 1863; 1867–1869; 1871–1872; 1876–1884; 1886–1891; 1893–1894		172
ŚNIADOWO	U	D	1895–1896; 1899–1906		
ŁOMŻA	A	M	1824; 1826–1827; 1829; 1833–1834; 1836–1837; 1841–1849; 1852; 1854–1860; 1863; 1867–1869; 1871–1872; 1876–1884; 1893–1894		172
ŚNIADOWO	U	M	1895–1896; 1899–1906		
SOBIENIE–JEZIORY	**SIEDLCE**				
SOBIENIE–JEZIORY	U	B	1882–1915; 1923–1940		
SOBIENIE–JEZIORY	U	D	1899–1915; 1923–1941		
LUBLIN	A	E	1913–1914		RGL IV ADM
LUBLIN	A	K	1913–1914; 1927–1936		RGL IV ADM; UWL WSP/775
SOBIENIE–JEZIORY	U	M	1882–1914; 1923–1928; 1933; 1935–1939		
LUBLIN	A	T	1913–1914; 1927–1936		RGL IV ADM; UWL WSP/775
SOBKÓW	**KIELCE**				
JĘDRZEJÓW	A	B	1820; 1826–1827; 1829–1876; 1881–1884; 1887–1889; 1891–1894		75
SOBKÓW	U	B	1901; 1904–1905; 1927–1940		
JĘDRZEJÓW	A	D	1820; 1826–1827; 1829–1859; 1861–1876; 1881–1884; 1886–1889; 1891–1894		75
SOBKÓW	U	D	1901; 1904–1905; 1927–1940		
JĘDRZEJÓW	A	M	1810; 1820; 1826–1827; 1829–1859; 1861–1876; 1881–1885; 1888; 1891–1894		75
SOBKÓW	U	M	1901; 1904–1905; 1927–1940		
SOBOLEW	**SIEDLCE**				
LUBLIN	A	K	1922–1936		UWL WSP/776
LUBLIN	A	T	1922–1936		UWL WSP/776
SOBOTA	**SKIERNIEWICE**				
ŁÓDŹ	A	B	1826–1885		270
ŁOWICZ	A	B	1826; 1856–1858; 1861–1872; 1874–1937		236
SOBOTA	U	B	1886–1939		
ŁÓDŹ	A	D	1826–1885		270
ŁOWICZ	A	D	1826; 1856–1858; 1861–1872; 1874–1937		236
SOBOTA	U	D	1894–1939		
ŁÓDŹ	A	M	1826–1885		270
ŁOWICZ	A	M	1826; 1856–1858; 1861–1872; 1874–1937		236
SOBOTA	U	M	1894–1939		
SOBÓTKA	**WROCŁAW**				
POZNAŃ	A	B	1846		3591/1

A Army/recruit lists; **B** Birth; **C** Census; **D** Death; **E** Voter lists; **G** Immigration; **H** Holocaust; **J** Judaica; **K** Kahal; **L** Land; **M** Marriage; **N** Name changes; **O** Police files; **P** Pogroms; **R** Reference; **S** School records; **T** Tax lists; **V** Divorce; **W** Occupation lists; **X** Jewish hospital; **Y** Notary records; **Z** Local government records

TOWN NAME	VOIVODSHIP (Province)				Zespół/Sygnatura (Poland)
Repository Location	Repository Type	Document Code	Years		Fond/Opis/Delo (Belarus, Ukraine, Lithuania)
SOCHOCIN	**CIECHANÓW**				
NOWY DWÓR MAZOWIECKI	A	B	1826–1903; 1914–1915; 1919–1923; 1930; 1932–1933		97
NOWY DWÓR MAZOWIECKI	A	D	1826–1903; 1914–1915; 1919–1923; 1930; 1932–1933		97
NOWY DWÓR MAZOWIECKI	A	M	1826–1903; 1914–1915; 1919–1923; 1930; 1932–1933		97
SOKÓŁKA	**BIAŁYSTOK**				
BIAŁYSTOK	A	A	1863–1874		724
VILNIUS	A	B	1835		1108/1/15
MINSK	A	C	1795–1882		
VILNIUS	A	D	1835		1108/1/15
VILNIUS	A	M	1835		1108/1/15
GRODNO2	A	S	1939–1941		302
BIAŁYSTOK	A	T	1945–1950		727
BIAŁYSTOK	A	Y	1883–1936		302–309
SOKOŁÓW MAŁOPOLSKI	**RZESZÓW**				
RZESZÓW	A	B	1825–1890; 1912		990/1–5
SOKOŁÓW MAŁOPOLSKI	U	B	1894–1936		
RZESZÓW	A	C	1932–1937		193/35–40
RZESZÓW	A	D	1877–1893		990/6
SOKOŁÓW MAŁOPOLSKI	U	D	1894–1939		
RZESZÓW	A	E	1939		193/34
RZESZÓW	A	G	1932–1937		193/35–40
LVOV	A	L	1785–1788		19/V/278
SOKOŁÓW MAŁOPOLSKI	U	M	1882–1939		
PRZEMYŚL	A	Y	1872–1873; 1875–1892; 1904–1934		101; 1056–1063
SOKOŁÓW PODLASKI	**SIEDLCE**				
SIEDLCE	A	B	1826–1888		227/1–43, 63–88
SOKOŁÓW PODLASKI	U	B	1889–1941		
SIEDLCE	A	D	1826–1888		227/1–43, 63–88
SOKOŁÓW PODLASKI	U	D	1889–1941		
LUBLIN	A	K	1913–1914; 1921–1936		RGL IV ADM; 403/825–827
SIEDLCE	A	M	1826–1888		227/1–43, 63–88
SOKOŁÓW PODLASKI	U	M	1889–1941		
LUBLIN	A	T	1913–1914; 1921–1935		RGL IV ADM; UWL WSP/825
SOKOŁY	**ŁOMŻA**				
BIAŁYSTOK	A	B	1826–1830; 1832; 1834; 1839–1841; 1846; 1848–1849; 1851; 1853; 1859; 1863; 1865; 1867; 1869–1872; 1875; 1878; 1881		265
SOKOŁY	U	B	1882–1887; 1890; 1909–1910; 1916–1920; 1927–1930; 1932–1934		
BIAŁYSTOK	A	D	1826–1830; 1834; 1839–1841; 1846; 1848–1849; 1851; 1853; 1859; 1863; 1865; 1867; 1869–1872; 1878; 1881		265
SOKOŁY	U	D	1886–1887; 1892–1893; 1910; 1916–1917; 1920; 1930; 1932; 1934		
BIAŁYSTOK	A	M	1826–1830; 1834; 1839–1841; 1846; 1848; 1851; 1853; 1859; 1863; 1865; 1867; 1869–1872; 1875; 1878; 1881		265
SOKOŁY	U	M	1887; 1890; 1892–1893; 1902–1903; 1909–1912; 1916–1918; 1920; 1927–1930; 1932; 1934; 1936		
WARSZAWA	A	T	1827–1846		KRSW 5134
SOLDIN	**SEE MYŚLIBÓRZ**				
SOLEC KUJAWSKI	**BYDGOSZCZ**				
BYDGOSZCZ	A	B	1823–1847; 1874–1893		388; 1775
BYDGOSZCZ	A	D	1823–1847; 1874–1893		388; 1775
BYDGOSZCZ	A	M	1823–1847; 1874–1893		388; 1775
BYDGOSZCZ	A	Z	1811–1910		197
SOLEC NAD WISŁĄ	**RADOM**				
RADOM	A	B	1886–1891		551/1
SOLEC NAD WISŁĄ	U	B	1892–1910; 1921–1940		
RADOM	A	D	1886–1891		551/1
SOLEC NAD WISŁĄ	U	D	1892–1910; 1921–1940		
RADOM	A	M	1886–1891		551/1
SOLEC NAD WISŁĄ	U	M	1892–1910; 1921–1940		
SOLINKA	**KROSNO**				
SANOK	A	C	1934–1944		30/30

Repository type: **A** = Archive **G** = LDS Films of German-Held Records **J** = Jewish Historical Institute **U** = Urząd Stanu Cywilnego

TOWN NAME	VOIVODSHIP (Province)			
Repository Location	Repository Document			Zespół/Sygnatura (Poland) Fond/Opis/Delo (Belarus, Ukraine, Lithuania)
	Type	Code	Years	
SOMPOLNO	**KONIN**			
POZNAŃ	A	B	1826–1829; 1833–1894	3755/1–65
SOMPOLNO	U	B	1895–1938	
POZNAŃ	A	D	1826–1829; 1833–1894	3755/1–65
SOMPOLNO	U	D	1895–1938	
POZNAŃ	A	M	1826; 1828–1829; 1833–1894	3755/1–65
SOMPOLNO	U	M	1895–1938	
SOPOT	**GDAŃSK**			
GDAŃSK	A	K	1856–1934	7/133–134; 521/1154
SORAU	**SEE ŻARY**			
SOŚNICOWICE	**KATOWICE**			
GLIWICE	A	B	1812–1847	1/I/5851
GLIWICE	A	D	1812–1847	1/I/5851
KOBLENZ	G	K	1831–1893 (CEMETERY RECORDS); 1806–1865 (CIRCUMCISION RECORDS)	
SOSNOWIEC	**KATOWICE**			
ŁÓDŹ	A	A	1907–1911	17
SOSNOWIEC	U	B	1901–1943; 1945	
KATOWICE	A	C	1806–1907; 1919–1928; 1931–1939	776/912–917, 2996–3005, 3007–3010, 3024–3030, 3032–3042
SOSNOWIEC	U	D	1901–1943; 1945	
KATOWICE	A	E	1912; 1934; 1939	776/670, 1768–1788
ŁÓDŹ	A	G	1895/1908	1
KATOWICE	A	G	1927	776/3067–3068
KATOWICE	A	H	1939–1944	776/5649, 5834, 6366, 6368–6374, 6398, 6408, 6555, 6566–6568, 6581, 6614–6615, 6803, 6809–6810, 6858–6859, 6884, 7051
ŁÓDŹ	A	K	1896/1913	1
KATOWICE	A	K	1903; 1905–1915; 1921–1927; 1929–1939	776/26, 343, 411, 459, 517, 524, 562, 575, 635, 736, 763, 771, 986, 2681, 4171, 4189; 770/4, 187, 190, 192, 227, 580; 777/103–131
KATOWICE	A	L	1918; 1929	776/1076, 3054–3060
SOSNOWIEC	U	M	1901–1943; 1945	
ŁÓDŹ	A	O	1906–1912	42
KATOWICE	A	P	1918–1925	776/1561
ŁÓDŹ	A	S	1890–1913	83
KATOWICE	A	S	1903–1914; 1916–1920; 1923–1933	776/10, 71, 173, 230, 310, 444, 732, 847, 4800–4842, 4934–4935, 5519
KATOWICE	A	W	1941–1943	776/5855–5858, 6172
KATOWICE	A	X	1915–1923; 1926–1937	776/1152–1153, 4670–4672, 4702, 5031–5033, 5081–5082
KATOWICE	A	Y	1885–1939	825/1–12; 826/1–16; 827/1–21; 828/1–15; 829/1–45; 830/1–23; 831/1–13; 832/1–15; 833/1–20; 834/1–137; 835/1–69; 836/1–7; 837/1–15; 838/1–49
KATOWICE	A	Z	1907; 1915–1939; 1940–1943	776/290, 1309, 2080–2081, 2364, 2589, 2612, 2703, 3235, 3249, 3275–3276, 3353–3359, 5165–5166, 5197–5243, 5482–5483, 6261, 6385, 6444, 6802
SPROTTAU	**SEE SZPROTAWA**			
ŚREM	**POZNAŃ**			
POZNAŃ	A	B	1817–1847	3592/1–2, 5
POZNAŃ	A	D	1817–1847	3592/1–2, 4
POZNAŃ	A	K	1919–1934	4390/706–707
POZNAŃ	A	M	1817–1847	3592/1–3, 7–12
POZNAŃ	A	S	1907–1921	4390/179
ŚRODA ŚLĄSKA	**WROCŁAW**			
KOBLENZ	G	B	1818–1848	
WROCŁAW	A	B	1880; 1883–1885; 1887–1890	556/II
WROCŁAW	A	C	1604; 1809–1945	172/II
WARSZAWA	J	C	1807/1891	PROVINCE: ŚLĄSK
KOBLENZ	G	C	1841	
WARSZAWA	J	K	1807/1891	PROVINCE: ŚLĄSK
KOBLENZ	G	M	1841–1847	
WROCŁAW	A	M	1875; 1878; 1881–1882; 1885; 1889–1893	556/II
WARSZAWA	J	T	1807/1891	PROVINCE: ŚLĄSK

A Army/recruit lists; **B** Birth; **C** Census; **D** Death; **E** Voter lists; **G** Immigration; **H** Holocaust; **J** Judaica; **K** Kahal; **L** Land; **M** Marriage; **N** Name changes; **O** Police files; **P** Pogroms; **R** Reference; **S** School records; **T** Tax lists; **V** Divorce; **W** Occupation lists; **X** Jewish hospital; **Y** Notary records; **Z** Local government records

TOWN NAME	VOIVODSHIP (Province)			Zespół/Sygnatura (Poland)
Repository Location	Repository Type	Document Code	Years	Fond/Opis/Delo (Belarus, Ukraine, Lithuania)
WARSZAWA	J	Y	1807/1891	PROVINCE: ŚLĄSK
WARSZAWA	J	Z	1807/1891	PROVINCE: ŚLĄSK
ŚRODA WIELKOPOLSKA	**POZNAŃ**			
LEIPZIG	G	B	1840–1847	
LEIPZIG	G	D	1840–1847	
POZNAŃ	A	K	1835–1915	336/511–514
LEIPZIG	G	M	1840–1847	
POZNAŃ	A	N	1878–1916	336/520–522
STALOWA WOLA	**TARNOBRZEG**			
SANDOMIERZ	A	C	1939–1950	524
SANDOMIERZ	A	H	1943	524/14
STANISŁAWÓW	**SIEDLCE**			
SIEDLCE	A	B	1826–1832; 1834–1836; 1885–1893	178/1–17
STANISŁAWÓW	U	B	1894–1913; 1916; 1922–1935	
SIEDLCE	A	D	1826–1832; 1834–1836; 1885–1893	178/1–17
STANISŁAWÓW	U	D	1894–1913; 1916; 1922–1935	
SIEDLCE	A	M	1826–1832; 1834–1836; 1885–1893	178/17
STANISŁAWÓW	U	M	1894–1913; 1916; 1922–1935	
STANY	**TARNOBRZEG**			
PRZEWORSK	A	G	1947–1951	120/13–16
PRZEWORSK	A	T	1947–1948	120/24–29
STARACHOWICE	**KIELCE**			
STARACHOWICE	U	B	1908–1941	
STARACHOWICE	U	D	1908–1941	
KIELCE	A	G	1932–1950	5
STARACHOWICE	U	M	1908–1941	
STARACHOWICE	A	Z	1940	5
STARGARD SZCZECIŃSKI	**SZCZECIN**			
BERLIN	G	B	1812–1849	
BERLIN	G	C	1742/1936	
BERLIN	G	D	1812–1849	
SZCZECIN	A	K	1870–1874; 1913–1930	MAGISTRAT STARGARD 961–962; GMINY ZYDOWSKIE; POMORZA ZACHODNIEGO 79–85; REGIERUNG STETTIN I/10737, 10748–10750
BERLIN	G	M	1812–1849	
SZCZECIN	A	Z	1766–1876	MAGISTRAT STARGARD 963–977
STAROGARD	**GDAŃSK**			
GDAŃSK	A	K	1923–1927	1632/17
KATOWICE	A	K	1922–1924	27/I–VI/1990
STARY SĄCZ	**NOWY SĄCZ**			
STARY SĄCZ	U	B	1883–1898; 1900–1902; 1904–1906; 1908; 1918–1925; 1927; 1929–1931; 1935–1936; 1940–1941	
NOWY SĄCZ	A	C	1870; 1910; 1938–1939	22–23/317–318; 437
STARY SĄCZ	U	D	1883–1889; 1891–1892; 1894; 1896–1907; 1909–1925; 19281932–1941	
STARY SĄCZ	U	M	1882–1893; 1895–1899; 1906–1910; 1918–1931; 1935–1939; 1941	
STARY ŻMIGRÓD	**SEE NOWY ŻMIGRÓD**			
STASZÓW	**TARNOBRZEG**			
SANDOMIERZ	A	B	1826–1894	253
STASZÓW	U	B	1895–1912; 1917–1942	
SANDOMIERZ	A	D	1826–1894	253
STASZÓW	U	D	1895–1912; 1917–1942	
WARSZAWA	J	K	1940–1943	212
SANDOMIERZ	A	M	1826–1894	253
STASZÓW	U	M	1895–1912; 1917–1942	
STAW	**KALISZ**			
KALISZ	A	C	1872–1951	53/500–540
KALISZ	A	E	1907; 1909	321/18–19, 21
KALISZ	A	W	1835–1853; 1856–1864	1/112, 442
STAWISZYN	**KALISZ**			
POZNAŃ	A	B	1826–1865	3756/1, 3
KALISZ	A	B	1866–1894	755/1–4
STAWISZYN	U	B	1895–1931	
KALISZ	A	C	1917–1924	32/189–191, 227–233

Repository type: **A** = Archive **G** = LDS Films of German-Held Records **J** = Jewish Historical Institute **U** = Urząd Stanu Cywilnego

TOWN NAME				
	VOIVODSHIP (Province)			
Repository Location	Repository Document Type	Code	Years	Zespół/Sygnatura (Poland) Fond/Opis/Delo (Belarus, Ukraine, Lithuania)
POZNAŃ	A	D	1826–1861	3756/2
KALISZ	A	D	1855–1879	755/1–4
STAWISZYN	U	D	1882–1939	
KALISZ	A	E	1907; 1909; 1922; 1927; 1930; 1935; 1938	32/67–80; 321/18–19, 21
KALISZ	A	G	1917–1919	32/189–191
KALISZ	A	L	1855; 1917; 1931	32/189–190, 196; 1/449
POZNAŃ	A	M	1847–1854	3756/4
KALISZ	A	M	1862–1879	755/1–4
STAWISZYN	U	M	1882–1939	
KALISZ	A	T	1936–1939	32
KALISZ	A	W	1832–1864	1/113, 446, 448
STERDYŃ	**SIEDLCE**			
STERDYŃ	U	B	1882–1941	
STERDYŃ	U	D	1882–1941	
LUBLIN	A	E	1913–1914	RGL IV ADM
LUBLIN	A	K	1913–1914; 1922–1936	RGL IV ADM; UWL WSP/827
STERDYŃ	U	M	1882–1941	
LUBLIN	A	T	1913–1914; 1922–1936	RGL IV ADM; UWL WSP/827
STETTIN	**SEE SZCZECIN**			
STOCZEK	**SIEDLCE**			
LUBLIN	A	K	1923–1927; 1931–1935	UWL WSP/810, 829; SPŁUK/631
LUBLIN	A	T	1923–1927; 1931–1935	UWL WSP/810, 829; SPŁUK/631
STOCZEK ŁUKOWSKI	**SIEDLCE**			
STOCZEK ŁUKOWSKI	U	B	1894–1910; 1912–1915; 1921–1939	
STOCZEK ŁUKOWSKI	U	D	1894–1939	
STOCZEK ŁUKOWSKI	U	M	1894; 1906–1909; 1911–1915; 1923–1939	
STOLP	**SEE SŁUPSK**			
STOPNICA	**KIELCE**			
PIŃCZÓW	A	B	1875–1894	374
STOPNICA	U	B	1895–1940	
PIŃCZÓW	A	D	1875–1894	374
STOPNICA	U	D	1895–1940	
PIŃCZÓW	A	M	1875–1894	374
STOPNICA	U	M	1895–1940	
STORCHNEST	**SEE OSIECZNA**			
STRACHOCINA	**KROSNO**			
SANOK	A	C	1931–1949	21/85–87
STRASBURG	**SEE BRODNICA**			
STRIEGAU	**SEE STRIEGAU**			
STROMIEC	**RADOM**			
STROMIEC	U	B	1907–1940	
STROMIEC	U	D	1907–1940	
STROMIEC	U	M	1907–1940	
STRYKÓW	**ŁÓDŹ**			
ŁÓDŹ	A	A	1899	17
ŁÓDŹ	A	B	1826–1870; 1882–1893	270
STRYKÓW	U	B	1894–1897; 1899; 1901–1905; 1908–1929; 1931–1932; 1934; 1938	
ŁÓDŹ	A	D	1826–1870; 1882–1893	270
STRYKÓW	U	D	1894–1897; 1899; 1901–1905; 1908–1929; 1931–1932; 1934–1938	
ŁÓDŹ	A	K	1907–1913	1
ŁÓDŹ	A	M	1826–1870; 1882–1893	270
STRYKÓW	U	M	1894–1897; 1899; 1901–1905; 1908–1929; 1931–1932; 1934–1938	
ŁÓDŹ	A	Z	1821–1866	1
PIOTRKÓW TRYBUNALSKI	A	Z	1929–1950	148
STRZEGOM	**WAŁBRZYCH**			
KOBLENZ	G	B	1830–1839	
WROCŁAW	A	B	1874–1877; 1879–1882; 1884–1885; 1887–1889	557/II
KOBLENZ	G	D	1830–1839	
WROCŁAW	A	D	1874–1878; 1881–1886; 1888–1890; 1892–1893	557/II
WARSZAWA	J	K	1842/1930	PROVINCE: ŚLĄSK
KOBLENZ	G	M	1830–1839	
WROCŁAW	A	M	1874–1885; 1887–1892	557/II
WARSZAWA	J	T	1842/1930	PROVINCE: ŚLĄSK

A Army/recruit lists; **B** Birth; **C** Census; **D** Death; **E** Voter lists; **G** Immigration; **H** Holocaust; **J** Judaica; **K** Kahal; **L** Land; **M** Marriage; **N** Name changes; **O** Police files; **P** Pogroms; **R** Reference; **S** School records; **T** Tax lists; **V** Divorce; **W** Occupation lists; **X** Jewish hospital; **Y** Notary records; **Z** Local government records

TOWN NAME	VOIVODSHIP (Province)			Zespół/Sygnatura (Poland)
Repository Location	Repository Document Type	Code	Years	Fond/Opis/Delo (Belarus, Ukraine, Lithuania)

Town / Repository	Type	Code	Years	Signature
STRZELCE KRAJEŃSKIE	**GORZÓW WIELKOPOLSKI**			
BERLIN	G	B	1847–1853	
BERLIN	G	D	1794–1913	
SZCZECIN	A	K	1907–1939	JUDISCHE GEMEINDE FRIEDEBERG NM 110/1–4
BERLIN	G	M	1847–1853	
STRZELCE OPOLSKIE	**OPOLE**			62
OPOLE	A	B	1847–1874	PROVINCE: ŚLĄSK
WARSZAWA	J	K	1855/1920	PROVINCE: ŚLĄSK
WARSZAWA	J	Y	1855/1920	PROVINCE: ŚLĄSK
WARSZAWA	J	Z	1855/1920	
STRZELNO	**BYDGOSZCZ**			
INOWROCŁAW	A	G	1838–1917; 1920–1925	62/315–319, 321, 868
INOWROCŁAW	A	K	1839/1917	62
INOWROCŁAW	A	S	1867/1920	62
INOWROCŁAW	A	T	1900–1918	62/47–51
INOWROCŁAW	A	Y	1864–1867	62
STRZEMIESZYCE WIELKIE	**KATOWICE**			
STRZEMIESZYCE WIELKIE	U	B	1931–1942	
STRZEMIESZYCE WIELKIE	U	D	1931–1942	
STRZEMIESZYCE WIELKIE	U	M	1931–1942	
STRZYŻÓW	**RZESZÓW**			
RZESZÓW	A	A	1861–1927	740/20; 71–72
LVOV	A	L	1785–1788; 1819–1820	19/II/139; 20/II/282
PRZEMYŚL	A	Y	1873–1875; 1878–1947	102; 1246–1249
STUDZIANKA	**BIAŁA PODLASKA**			
STUDZIANKA	U	B	1907–1911	
STUDZIANKA	U	D	1907–1911	
STUDZIANKA	U	M	1907–1911	
STUHM	**SEE SZTUM**			
SUKOWATE	**KROSNO**			
SANOK	A	C	1938–1943	30/29
SULEJÓW	**PIOTRKÓW TRYBUNALSKI**			
ŁÓDŹ	A	A	1902	17
ŁÓDŹ	A	B	1826–1855; 1866–1883	270
PIOTRKÓW TRYBUNALSKI	A	B	1884–1898	337/1–4
SULEJÓW	U	B	1899–1940	
ŁÓDŹ	A	D	1826–1855; 1866–1883	270
PIOTRKÓW TRYBUNALSKI	A	D	1884–1898	337/1–4
SULEJÓW	U	D	1899–1940	
ŁÓDŹ	A	M	1826–1855; 1866–1883	270
PIOTRKÓW TRYBUNALSKI	A	M	1884–1898	337/1–4
SULEJÓW	U	M	1899–1940	
ŁÓDŹ	A	S	1875–1897	83–84
ŁÓDŹ	A	W	1899–1913	19
ŁÓDŹ	A	Z	1864–1866	1
SULMIERZYCE	**KALISZ**			
KALISZ	A	C	1931–1935	33/944–945
KALISZ	A	G	1907; 1909	33
KALISZ	A	L	1841–1942	91/242–251
ŁÓDŹ	A	A	1902	17
PIOTRKÓW TRYBUNALSKI	A	B	1873–1895	338/4–26
SULMIERZYCE	U	B	1900–1915	
PIOTRKÓW TRYBUNALSKI	A	D	1826–1869; 1873–1895	338/1, 4–26
SULMIERZYCE	U	D	1900–1915	
PIOTRKÓW TRYBUNALSKI	A	M	1863–1895	338/2–26
SULMIERZYCE	U	M	1900–1915	
ŁÓDŹ	A	Z	1845–1866	1
SUPRAŚL	**BIAŁYSTOK**			
SUPRAŚL	U	M	1939	
SURAŻ	**BIAŁYSTOK**			
SURAŻ	U	B	1882–1914	
SURAŻ	U	D	1882–1914	
SURAŻ	U	M	1882–1914	
SUSZ	**ELBLĄG**			
OLSZTYN	A	B	1847–1874	320/I

Repository type: **A** = Archive **G** = LDS Films of German-Held Records **J** = Jewish Historical Institute **U** = Urząd Stanu Cywilnego

TOWN NAME		VOIVODSHIP (Province)			
Repository Location	Repository Type	Document Code	Years		Zespół/Sygnatura (Poland) Fond/Opis/Delo (Belarus, Ukraine, Lithuania)
SUWAŁKI		**SUWAŁKI**			
SUWAŁKI	A	A	1938–1939		31/205
SUWAŁKI	A	B	1808–1825; 1826/1834; 1835–1840; 1842–1854; 1856–1888; 1891–1892		165; 204
SUWAŁKI	U	B	1893–1894; 1896; 1900–1902; 1905; 1908–1914; 1920–1938		
SUWAŁKI	A	C	1846–1867		14/208–219; 533–536; 773
SUWAŁKI	A	D	1826/1834; 1835–1840; 1842–1854; 1856–1877; 1878/1883; 1884–1888; 1891–1892		165/204
SUWAŁKI	U	D	1893–1894; 1896; 1900–1902; 1905; 1908–1914; 1920–1938		
SUWAŁKI	A	E	1847–1867		14/208–215
GRODNO2	A	G	1921–1938 (IMMIGRATION TO POLAND)		208
SUWAŁKI	A	K	1840–1867; 1917; 1926–1937		14/129, 207–215, 466, 605, 703–716; 31/144–148, 155–156, 158, 303
SUWAŁKI	A	L	1857/1876; 1945–1949 (CONFISCATED PROPERTY)		14/89–92, 94, 96–104, 106–113, 117–119, 123–126, 131–132, 136–139, 141, 145, 151; 313/155
SUWAŁKI	A	M	1808–1825; 1826/1834; 1835–1840; 1842–1854; 1856–1877; 1878/1883; 1884–1893		165; 204
SUWAŁKI	U	M	1894; 1896; 1900–1902; 1905; 1908–1914; 1920–1938		
GRODNO2	A	O	1934–1939 (MEMBERSHIP IN JEWISH ORGANIZATIONS)		209
SUWAŁKI	A	S	1847–1867; 1931–1937		14/208–215; 31/131
WARSZAWA	A	T	1822–1828; 1832–1834		KRSW 5042; 5044
SUWAŁKI	A	W	1812–1871; 1920–1936		31/198; 14/152–190
SUWAŁKI	A	X	1847–1870		14/377; 27/5–20
GRODNO	A	X	1863–1869		1060 (16 BOOKS)
BIAŁYSTOK	A	X	1870–1915		26/85–99, 209–220
SUWAŁKI	A	Y	1826–1939		245–270
SUWAŁKI	A	Z	1807–1866		14
SUWAŁKI REGION		**SUWAŁKI**			
VILNIUS	A	G	1885–1917 (EXTERNAL PASSPORTS)		1010/1/202, 1557, 2098, 2102, 2105–2106, 2123, 2802; 1010/2/93–99, 106, 110, 112, 115, 118, 123–127
VILNIUS	A	K	1897; 1911–1914		1108; 1466
SUWAŁKI	A	T	1847; 1867; 1903–1915		14/208–215; 24/1–17
SWARZĘDZ		**POZNAŃ**			
POZNAŃ	A	K	1734–1792; 1823; 1825–1831; 1902–1916		4389/114–115; 906/16–17; 329/1232
WARSZAWA	J	K	1781/1851		PROVINCE: POZNAŃ
POZNAŃ	A	S	1824–1927		4389/121–123
WARSZAWA	J	T	1781/1851		PROVINCE: POZNAŃ
WARSZAWA	J	Z	1781/1851		PROVINCE: POZNAŃ
ŚWIDNICA		**WAŁBRZYCH**			
KOBLENZ	G	B	1854–1875		
WROCŁAW	A	B	1874–1893		557/II
KOBLENZ	G	D	1854–1875		
WROCŁAW	A	D	1874–1893		557/II
KOBLENZ	G	M	1854–1875		
WROCŁAW	A	M	1874–1893		557/II
ŚWIDWIN		**KOSZALIN**			
SZCZECIN	A	E	1871–1899		MAGISTRAT SCHINELBEING 32
ŚWIEBODZIN		**ZIELONA GÓRA**			
WARSZAWA	J	K	1934–1935		PROVINCE: ŚLĄSK
ŚWIECIE		**BYDGOSZCZ**			
BYDGOSZCZ	A	C	1923–1931		199
BYDGOSZCZ	A	E	1920–1931		199
ŚWIERKOCIN		**GORZÓW WIELKOPOLSKI**			
GORZÓW WIELKOPOLSKI	A	B	1828–1836		AMTSGERICHT LANDSBERG W.28/1370
GORZÓW WIELKOPOLSKI	A	D	1830; 1835		AMTSGERICHT LANDSBERG W.28/1370
GORZÓW WIELKOPOLSKI	A	M	1827; 1830; 1836		AMTSGERICHT LANDSBERG W.28/1370
ŚWIERŻE		**CHEŁM**			
LUBLIN	A	B	1826–1865		113
ŚWIERŻE	U	B	1882–1914; 1916–1944		
LUBLIN	A	D	1826–1865		113
ŚWIERŻE	U	D	1882–1914; 1916–1944		

A Army/recruit lists; **B** Birth; **C** Census; **D** Death; **E** Voter lists; **G** Immigration; **H** Holocaust; **J** Judaica; **K** Kahal; **L** Land; **M** Marriage; **N** Name changes; **O** Police files; **P** Pogroms; **R** Reference; **S** School records; **T** Tax lists; **V** Divorce; **W** Occupation lists; **X** Jewish hospital; **Y** Notary records; **Z** Local government records

| TOWN NAME | VOIVODSHIP (Province) | | | Zespół/Sygnatura (Poland) |
Repository Location	Repository Type	Document Code	Years	Fond/Opis/Delo (Belarus, Ukraine, Lithuania)
LUBLIN	A	K	1871–1910; 1912–1915; 1926–1927	RGL ADM; RGCH/482; UWL WSP/1558
LUBLIN	A	M	1826–1865	113
ŚWIERŻE	U	M	1882–1914; 1916–1944	
LUBLIN	A	T	1871–1910; 1912–1915; 1926–1927	RGL ADM; RGCH/482; UWL WSP/1558
ŚWIĘTOCHŁOWICE	**KATOWICE**			
KATOWICE	A	B	1844–1849	674/I/368–G, H, I
KATOWICE	A	C	1928–1938	83/I/26, 32
KATOWICE	A	D	1847	674/I/601
KATOWICE	A	G	1930–1939	91/I/51
KATOWICE	A	H	1943	83/I/113
KATOWICE	A	S	1924–1939	72
ŚWIĘTONIOWA	**PRZEMYŚL**			
PRZEWORSK	A	S	1911–1958	80/4–22
SWINEMUNDE	**SEE ŚWINOUJŚCIE**			
ŚWINIARSKO	**INCLUDED IN NOWY SĄCZ**			
ŚWINOUJŚCIE	**SZCZECIN**			
SZCZECIN	A	K	1847–1933	GMINY ZYDOWSKIE POMORZA ZACHODNIEGO–ZBIDOR, SZCZATKOW/95–132
SWOSZOWICE	**KRAKÓW**			
KRAKÓW	U	B	1877/1941	
KRAKÓW	U	D	1877/1941	
KRAKÓW	U	M	1877/1941	
SYCÓW	**KALISZ**			
WARSZAWA	J	D	1886–1903	
WARSZAWA	J	E	1846/1914	PROVINCE: ŚLĄSK
KOBLENZ	G	K	1820–1867 (CEMETERY RECORDS)	
WARSZAWA	J	T	1846/1914	PROVINCE: ŚLĄSK
WARSZAWA	J	X	1846/1914	PROVINCE: ŚLĄSK
WARSZAWA	J	Y	1846/1914	PROVINCE: ŚLĄSK
SZADEK	**SIERADZ**			
ŁÓDŹ	A	B	1826–1854; 1882–1893	270
SZADEK	U	B	1894–1939	
ŁÓDŹ	A	D	1826–1854; 1882–1893	270
SZADEK	U	D	1894–1939	
SIERADZ	A	H	1940–1942	7
ŁÓDŹ	A	M	1826–1854; 1882–1893	270
SZADEK	U	M	1894–1939	
SZCZAWNE	**KROSNO**			
SANOK	A	C	1937–1939	23/32
SZCZAWNICA KROŚCIENKO	**NOWY SĄCZ**			
SZCZAWNICA KROŚCIENKO	U	B	1890–1938	
SZCZAWNICA KROŚCIENKO	U	D	1890–1938	
SZCZAWNICA KROŚCIENKO	U	M	1890–1938	
SZCZEBRZESZYN	**ZAMOŚĆ**			
LUBLIN	A	B	1826–1827; 1858–1875	113
ZAMOŚĆ	A	B	1876–1893	209/1–18
SZCZEBRZESZYN	U	B	1894–1938	
LUBLIN	A	C	1866	ZPZ/132
LUBLIN	A	D	1826–1827; 1858–1875	113
ZAMOŚĆ	A	D	1876–1893	209/1–18
SZCZEBRZESZYN	U	D	1894–1938	
LUBLIN	A	K	1870–1904; 1906; 1908–1915; 1922–1927	RGL IV; RGCH/483; UWL WSP/840
LUBLIN	A	M	1826–1827; 1858–1875	113
ZAMOŚĆ	A	M	1876–1893	209/1–18
SZCZEBRZESZYN	U	M	1894–1938	
ZAMOŚĆ	A	S	1927–1937	12/511
LUBLIN	A	T	1870–1904; 1906; 1908–1915; 1922–1927	RGL IV; RGCH/483; UWL WSP/840
ZAMOŚĆ	A	Y	1824–1954	107–116
SZCZECIN	**SZCZECIN**			
SZCZECIN	A	B	1874–1896	STANDESAMIT STETTIN
KOBLENZ	G	C	1938	
SZCZECIN	A	D	1874–1896	STANDESAMIT STETTIN
LUBLIN	A	H	1940–1942	JUDENRAT LUBLIN/166–167
SZCZECIN	A	K	1894–1930	REGIERUNG STETTIN I/10751–10752; GMINY ZYDOWSKIE, POMORZA ZACHODNIEGO 86–94

Repository type: **A** = Archive   **G** = LDS Films of German-Held Records   **J** = Jewish Historical Institute   **U** = Urząd Stanu Cywilnego

TOWN NAME				Zespół/Sygnatura (Poland)
	VOIVODSHIP (Province)			
Repository Location	Repository Document Type	Code	Years	Fond/Opis/Delo (Belarus, Ukraine, Lithuania)

SZCZECIN				
SZCZECIN	A	M	1874–1896	STANDESAMIT STETTIN
KOBLENZ	G	N	1841–1847; 1850–1880	
SZCZECIN	A	R	1829–1943	BIBLIOTEKA IN SZCZECIN ARCHIVES
SZCZECINEK	**KOSZALIN**			
KOSZALIN	A	K	1816–1917	358/418–426, 451–466, 483–485
SZCZEKOCINY	**CZĘSTOCHOWA**			
JĘDRZEJÓW	A	B	1826–1838	224
CZĘSTOCHOWA	A	B	1826–1895	281
SZCZEKOCINY	U	B	1896–1901; 1903–1909; 1912–1913; 1916–1942	
JĘDRZEJÓW	A	D	1826–1843	224
CZĘSTOCHOWA	A	D	1826–1895	281
SZCZEKOCINY	U	D	1896–1901; 1903–1909; 1912–1913; 1916–1942	
JĘDRZEJÓW	A	M	1826–1842; 1857–1865	224
CZĘSTOCHOWA	A	M	1826–1895	281
SZCZEKOCINY	U	M	1896–1901; 1903–1909; 1912–1913; 1916–1942	
SZCZEPANKOWO	**ŁOMŻA**			
ŁOMŻA	A	M	1820–1821	162
SZCZERCÓW	**PIOTRKÓW TRYBUNALSKI**			
ŁÓDŹ	A	B	1826–1874	270
PIOTRKÓW TRYBUNALSKI	A	B	1875–1894	339/1–20
SZCZERCÓW	U	B	1895–1911; 1913; 1915–1924; 1926–1927; 1929–1933; 1935	
ŁÓDŹ	A	D	1826–1874	270
PIOTRKÓW TRYBUNALSKI	A	D	1875–1894	339/1–20
SZCZERCÓW	U	D	1895–1911; 1913; 1915–1924; 1926–1927; 1929–1933; 1935	
ŁÓDŹ	A	M	1826–1874	270
PIOTRKÓW TRYBUNALSKI	A	M	1875–1894	339/1–20
SZCZERCÓW	U	M	1895–1911; 1913; 1915–1924; 1926–1927; 1929–1933; 1935	
SZCZUCIN	**TARNÓW**			
SZCZUCIN	U	B	1849–1876; 1878–1881; 1883–1884; 1886–1887; 1889–1890; 1892–1893; 1895–1899; 1901–1904; 1908–1938	
SZCZUCIN	U	D	1849–1877; 1891; 1898–1900; 1906; 1917; 1919; 1921; 1923–1926; 1929; 1931–1937	
LVOV	A	L	1785–1788; 1819–1820	19/VII/102; 20/VII/397
SZCZUCIN	U	M	1850; 1888; 1895–1897; 1899; 1902; 1914–1916; 1920–1922; 1927–1928; 1933–1938	
SZCZUCZYN	**ŁOMŻA**			
EŁK	A	A	1874/1917	214
ŁOMŻA	A	B	1826/1849; 1850–1865; 1866/1869; 1870–1894	272
SZCZUCZYN	U	B	1898–1899; 1901–1906; 1909; 1913–1914; 1925; 1931–1939	
EŁK	A	C	1894	212/189
ŁOMŻA	A	D	1826/1849; 1850–1865; 1866/1869; 1870–1894	272
SZCZUCZYN	U	D	1896; 1900; 1904–1906; 1913–1914; 1918–1919; 1921–1939	
EŁK	A	E	1882–1883; 1898–1913	212/394, 402, 414, 425, 453, 459, 478, 560–561, 564, 566, 957, 1377, 1451, 1591, 1599, 1648, 1650, 1753, 1758, 1812–1813, 1915–1916, 1920–1923, 1939–1940, 1997–2302
ŁOMŻA	A	M	1826–1831; 1850–1894	272
SZCZUCZYN	U	M	1898; 1900; 1913–1914; 1918–1920; 1922–1939	
WARSZAWA	A	T	1823–1830	KRSW 5094
EŁK	A	Y	1807–1914; 1916–1939	56–62; 141; 186
SZCZUROWA	**TARNÓW**			
SZCZUROWA	U	B	1902–1942	
SZCZUROWA	U	D	1902–1942	
SZCZUROWA	U	M	1902–1942	
SZCZYTNO	**OLSZTYN**			
OLSZTYN	A	B	1874; 1878; 1883; 1885–1889; 1894	720/I
OLSZTYN	A	C	1908	268/I
OLSZTYN	A	D	1874; 1877–1878; 1880; 1883–1890; 1893–1894	720/I
OLSZTYN	A	M	1883; 1885; 1887–1892; 1894	720/I
SZLICHTYNGOWA	**LESZNO**			
KOBLENZ	G	B	1802–1876	

A Army/recruit lists; **B** Birth; **C** Census; **D** Death; **E** Voter lists; **G** Immigration; **H** Holocaust; **J** Judaica; **K** Kahal; **L** Land; **M** Marriage; **N** Name changes; **O** Police files; **P** Pogroms; **R** Reference; **S** School records; **T** Tax lists; **V** Divorce; **W** Occupation lists; **X** Jewish hospital; **Y** Notary records; **Z** Local government records

TOWN NAME	VOIVODSHIP (Province)			Zespół/Sygnatura (Poland)
Repository Location	Repository Document Type	Code	Years	Fond/Opis/Delo (Belarus, Ukraine, Lithuania)
STARY KISIELIN				
STARY KISIELIN	A	B	1835–1847	132
KOBLENZ	G	D	1802–1876	
STARY KISIELIN	A	D	1835–1847	132
LESZNO	A	K	1763–1936 (CEMETERY RECORDS)	
KOBLENZ	G	M	1811–1876	
STARY KISIELIN	A	M	1835–1847	132
STARY KISIELIN	A	Z	1820–1931	361
SZPROTAWA	**ZIELONA GÓRA**			
KOBLENZ	G	B	1811–1847	
KOBLENZ	G	D	1811–1847	
STARY KISIELIN	A	G	1813–1845	
KOBLENZ	G	K	1817–1933 (CEMETERY RECORDS)	
KOBLENZ	G	M	1811–1847	
ŻARY	A	Z	1812–1861	1
SZREŃSK	**CIECHANÓW**			
DZIAŁDOWO	A	B	1827–1834; 1837–1846; 1848–1885	29
SZREŃSK	U	B	1886–1937	
DZIAŁDOWO	A	D	1826–1885	29
SZREŃSK	U	D	1886–1937	
DZIAŁDOWO	A	M	1827–1834; 1837–1846; 1848–1885; 1852 (MARRIAGE APPLICATIONS)	29
SZREŃSK	U	M	1886–1937	
SZTABIN	**SUWAŁKI**			
VILNIUS	A	G	1885–1917	1010
SZTUM	**ELBLĄG**			
GDAŃSK	A	B	1812–1848	1497/65
GDAŃSK	A	D	1812–1848	1497/65
GDAŃSK	A	M	1812–1848	1497/65
SZUBIN	**BYDGOSZCZ**			
BYDGOSZCZ	A	B	1820–1847; 1874–1893	377
BYDGOSZCZ	A	D	1820–1834; 1874–1893	377
BYDGOSZCZ	A	G	1920–1935	198
BYDGOSZCZ	A	M	1820–1834; 1874–1893	377
BYDGOSZCZ	A	Z	1833–1923	198
SZYDŁÓW	**KIELCE**			
PIŃCZÓW	A	B	1854–1877; 1879–1882; 1884–1896	392
SZYDŁÓW	U	B	1897–1904; 1906–1913; 1922–1925; 1929–1930; 1933–1937	
PIŃCZÓW	A	D	1854–1877; 1879–1882; 1884–1896	392
SZYDŁÓW	U	D	1897–1904; 1906–1913; 1922–1925; 1929–1930; 1933–1937	
PIŃCZÓW	A	M	1854–1877; 1879–1882; 1884–1896	392
SZYDŁÓW	U	M	1897–1904; 1906–1913; 1922–1925; 1929–1930; 1933–1937	
SZDŁOWIEC	**RADOM**			
RADOM	A	B	1826–1894	192
SZDŁOWIEC	U	B	1895–1913; 1916–1917; 1919; 1921–1940	
RADOM	A	D	1826–1894	192
SZDŁOWIEC	U	D	1895–1913; 1916–1917; 1919; 1921–1940	
RADOM	A	M	1826–1894	192
SZDŁOWIEC	U	M	1895–1913; 1916–1917; 1919; 1921–1940	
TARCZYN	**WARSZAWA**			
GÓRA KALWARIA	A	B	1808–1837; 1844–1873; 1875–1894	165; 125
TARCZYN	U	B	1895–1937	
GÓRA KALWARIA	A	D	1808–1837; 1844–1873; 1875–1894	165; 125
TARCZYN	U	D	1895–1937	
GÓRA KALWARIA	A	M	1808–1837; 1844–1873; 1875–1894	165; 125
TARCZYN	U	M	1895–1937	
TARŁÓW	**TARNOBRZEG**			
STARACHOWICE	A	B	1826–1887	172
SANDOMIERZ	A	B	1889–1893	647
STARACHOWICE	A	D	1826–1887	172
SANDOMIERZ	A	D	1889–1893	647
STARACHOWICE	A	M	1826–1887	172
SANDOMIERZ	A	M	1889–1893	647
TARNAWA GÓRNA	**KROSNO**			
SANOK	A	C	1909–1952	27/33

Repository type: **A** = Archive **G** = LDS Films of German-Held Records **J** = Jewish Historical Institute **U** = Urząd Stanu Cywilnego

TOWN NAME	VOIVODSHIP (Province)				Zespół/Sygnatura (Poland)
Repository Location	Repository Document Type	Code	Years		Fond/Opis/Delo (Belarus, Ukraine, Lithuania)
TARNOBRZEG	**TARNOBRZEG**				
PRZEMYŚL	A	B	1892–1909; 1916; 1918		74/30
TARNOBRZEG	U	B	1903–1932; 1935; 1937		
PRZEMYŚL	A	D	1892–1909; 1916; 1918		74/30
TARNOBRZEG	U	D	1903–1932; 1935; 1937		
SANDOMIERZ	A	G	1843–1948		525/80
PRZEMYŚL	A	K	1889–1898; 1916		74/26, 28, 31
LVOV	A	L	1785–1788; 1819–1820		19/V/252; 20/V/51
PRZEMYŚL	A	M	1892–1909; 1916; 1918		74/30
TARNOBRZEG	U	M	1903–1932; 1935; 1937		
KRAKÓW	A	T	18TH/19TH CENTURY		120
KRAKÓW	A	Z	1695/1830		120
TARNOGÓRA	**ZAMOŚĆ**				
LUBLIN	A	B	1865–1870; ALSO INCLUDED IN IZBICA		113
ZAMOŚĆ	A	B	1871–1872		209/1–2
LUBLIN	A	D	1865–1870; ALSO INCLUDED IN IZBICA		113
ZAMOŚĆ	A	D	1871–1872		209/1–2
LUBLIN	A	M	1865–1870; ALSO INCLUDED IN IZBICA		113
ZAMOŚĆ	A	M	1871–1872		209/1–2
TARNOGRÓD	**ZAMOŚĆ**				
LUBLIN	A	B	1870–1875		113
ZAMOŚĆ	A	B	1877–1881; 1883–1893		209/1–16
TARNOGRÓD	U	B	1894–1913; 1915–1926; 1928–1938		
LUBLIN	A	D	1870–1875		113
ZAMOŚĆ	A	D	1877–1881; 1883–1893		209/1–16
TARNOGRÓD	U	D	1894–1913; 1915–1926; 1928–1938		
LUBLIN	A	E	1872–1909		RGL IV ADMIN
LUBLIN	A	K	1872–1909; 1924–1934		RGL IV ADMIN; RGCH/506
LUBLIN	A	M	1870–1875		113
ZAMOŚĆ	A	M	1877–1881; 1883–1893		209/1–16
TARNOGRÓD	U	M	1894–1913; 1915–1926; 1928–1938		
TARNÓW	**TARNÓW**				
KRAKÓW	A	B	1808–1849		526/III/131/2–3, 6–7
TARNÓW	A	B	1849–1876; 1879–1899		276/USCT 1–11, 37
TARNÓW	A	B	1861–1895 (ALPHA INDEX)		276/USCT 12–17
TARNÓW	A	B	1877–1898 (ILLEGITIMATE BIRTHS)		276/USCT 23
TARNÓW	U	B	1896–1941		
KRAKÓW	A	D	1808–1855		526/III/131/1, 4–5, 8
TARNÓW	A	D	1850–1942 (ALPHA INDEX)		276/USCT 33–36
TARNÓW	A	D	1855–1899		276/USCT 25–32
TARNÓW	U	D	1900–1941		
TARNÓW	A	H	1945		15/STT49
LVOV	A	L	1785–1788; 1819–1820		19/VII/1; 20/VII/322
TARNÓW	A	M	1849–1899		276/USCT 18–22
TARNÓW	A	M	1877–1899 (ALPHA INDEX)		276/USCT 24
TARNÓW	U	M	1899–1941		
TARNÓW	A	W	1940–1942		214
TARNÓW	A	Z	1837–1944		1
TARNOWSKIE GÓRY	**KATOWICE**				
KATOWICE	A	A	1856–1890		91/2356–2377, 2402–2416
TARNOWSKIE GÓRY	A	B	1813–1856		173/1; 91/2028
TARNOWSKIE GÓRY	A	C	1817–1896; 1904–1914; 1920–1922		91/212–225, 452–454, 469, 492, 2028–2034
TARNOWSKIE GÓRY	A	D	1847–1868		173/2
TARNOWSKIE GÓRY	A	K	1781–1914		91/2027–2051
KATOWICE	A	K	1922–1931		27/I–VI/2001A, 2002
TARNOWSKIE GÓRY	A	M	1813–1874		173/3; 91/2028
TARNOWSKIE GÓRY	A	S	1845		91/1838
TCZEW	**GDAŃSK**				
GDAŃSK	A	B	1828–1874; 1888 (ONE RECORD); 1897 (ONE RECORD)		1497/61–62
GDAŃSK	A	D	1828–1874		1497/61, 64
GDAŃSK	A	M	1828–1874		1497/61, 63
TEMPELBURG	**SEE CZAPLINEK**				
TEMPOCZÓW	**KIELCE**				
TEMPOCZÓW	U	B	1932–1942		
TEMPOCZÓW	U	D	1932–1942		
TEMPOCZÓW	U	M	1932–1942		

A Army/recruit lists; **B** Birth; **C** Census; **D** Death; **E** Voter lists; **G** Immigration; **H** Holocaust; **J** Judaica; **K** Kahal; **L** Land; **M** Marriage; **N** Name changes; **O** Police files; **P** Pogroms; **R** Reference; **S** School records; **T** Tax lists; **V** Divorce; **W** Occupation lists; **X** Jewish hospital; **Y** Notary records; **Z** Local government records

TOWN NAME	VOIVODSHIP (Province)			Zespół/Sygnatura (Poland)
Repository Location	Repository Type	Document Code	Years	Fond/Opis/Delo (Belarus, Ukraine, Lithuania)
TERESPOL	**BIAŁA PODLASKA**			
LUBLIN	A	B	1826–1864	113
TERESPOL	U	B	1882–1938	
LUBLIN	A	D	1826–1864	113
TERESPOL	U	D	1882–1938	
LUBLIN	A	K	1909–1914; 1924–1935	RGCH/437; SPB/208; UWL WSP/759
LUBLIN	A	M	1826–1864	113
TERESPOL	U	M	1882–1938	
LUBLIN	A	T	1912–1914; 1924–1935; 1945–1950	RGCH/445; SPB/208; UWL WSP/759
THORN	**SEE TORUŃ**			
TIKTIN	**SEE TYKOCIN**			
TIRSCHTIEGEL	**SEE TRZCIEL**			
TŁUSZCZ	**OSTROŁĘKA**			
TŁUSZCZ	U	B	1918–1919	
TŁUSZCZ	U	D	1918–1919	
TŁUSZCZ	U	M	1920–1939	
TOMASZÓW LUBELSKI	**ZAMOŚĆ**			
LUBLIN	A	B	1826–1875	113
ZAMOŚĆ	A	B	1869–1893	209/OA; OB; OC; 1–9; 9A; 10–20
TOMASZÓW LUBELSKI	U	B	1894–1913; 1919–1939	
ZAMOŚĆ	A	C	1890–1949	24
LUBLIN	A	D	1826–1875	113
ZAMOŚĆ	A	D	1876–1893	209/OD; 1–9; 9A; 10–15; 17; 19–20
TOMASZÓW LUBELSKI	U	D	1894–1913; 1919–1939	
LUBLIN	A	E	1870–1914	RGL IV ADM; RGCH/488
LUBLIN	A	K	1859–1860; 1870–1914; 1921–1928	POL.RGL/719; RGL IV ADM; RGCH/488; UWL WSP/835
LUBLIN	A	M	1826–1875	113
ZAMOŚĆ	A	M	1866–1893	209/1–15, 17–20
TOMASZÓW LUBELSKI	U	M	1894–1913; 1919–1939	
LUBLIN	A	T	1870–1914	RGL IV ADM; RGCH/488
ZAMOŚĆ	A	T	1927–1952	24
ZAMOŚĆ	A	Y	1810–1936	117–126
ZAMOŚĆ	A	Z	1892–1950	24
TOMASZÓW MAZOWIECKI	**PIOTRKÓW TRYBUNALSKI**			
ŁÓDŹ	A	A	1865–1914	17
ŁÓDŹ	A	B	1830–1881	270
PIOTRKÓW TRYBUNALSKI	A	B	1873–1892	340/1–2, 7–15
TOMASZÓW MAZOWIECKI	U	B	1893–1942	
TOMASZÓW MAZOWIECKI	A	C	1824–1942	7/1042, 1070–1075, 1077, 1081, 1089–1091, 1095, 1108, 2974–3155
ŁÓDŹ	A	D	1830–1881	270
PIOTRKÓW TRYBUNALSKI	A	D	1886–1892	340/5–13, 18
TOMASZÓW MAZOWIECKI	U	D	1893–1942	
PIOTRKÓW TRYBUNALSKI	A	G	1927–1939	1
PIOTRKÓW TRYBUNALSKI	A	H	1939–1944	7
PIOTRKÓW TRYBUNALSKI	A	L	1807–1985	247
ŁÓDŹ	A	M	1830–1881	270
PIOTRKÓW TRYBUNALSKI	A	M	1871–1894	340/3–4, 7–13, 16–17
TOMASZÓW MAZOWIECKI	U	M	1895–1943	
PIOTRKÓW TRYBUNALSKI	A	O	1927–1939	1
ŁÓDŹ	A	S	1828/1914	83
TOMASZÓW MAZOWIECKI	A	T	1915–1943	7/3–2505; 5/2, 47, 51, 61, 64, 86, 96, 106, 108, 110, 117, 134, 144, 149, 151, 154, 159, 161–162, 165, 169, 171; 174, 182, 194, 196–197, 199, 200, 204
ŁÓDŹ	A	W	1828/1914	19
ŁÓDŹ	A	X	1896–1911	15
PIOTRKÓW TRYBUNALSKI	A	Y	1826–1951	32; 41–42; 111–113; 122; 135; 251–256
PIOTRKÓW TRYBUNALSKI	A	Z	1820–1944	7
TORUŃ	**TORUŃ**			
TORUŃ	A	K	1725–1859	283/1
TORUŃ	A	N	1818–1920	1/1
TOSZEK	**KATOWICE**			
GLIWICE	A	B	1812–1847	1/I/5851
GLIWICE	A	D	1812–1847	1/I/5851
WARSZAWA	J	K	1831/1877	PROVINCE: ŚLĄSK
KOBLENZ	G	M	1886	

Repository type: **A** = Archive **G** = LDS Films of German-Held Records **J** = Jewish Historical Institute **U** = Urząd Stanu Cywilnego

TOWN NAME	VOIVODSHIP (Province)			Zespół/Sygnatura (Poland)
Repository Location	Repository Type	Document Code	Years	Fond/Opis/Delo (Belarus, Ukraine, Lithuania)
TOSZEK REGION	**KATOWICE**			
GLIWICE	A	K	1812–1900	1/I/5813–5863
TRACHENBERG	**SEE ŻMIGRÓD**			
TRÓJCZYCE	**PRZEMYŚL**			
PRZEMYŚL	A	C	1930/1942	207/30–31
TRYŃCZA	**PRZEMYŚL**			
PRZEWORSK	A	S	1915–1959	74/1–29, 32–46
TRZCIANKA	**PIŁA**			
POZNAŃ	A	B	1815–1847; 1855–1908	3593/2, 6
POZNAŃ	A	D	1815–1847; 1855–1908	3593/1, 5–7
POZNAŃ	A	M	1815–1847; 1855–1908	3593/3, 6
TRZCIANNE	**ŁOMŻA**			
TRZCIANNE	U	B	1889–1899	
TRZCIEL	**GORZÓW WIELKOPOLSKI**			
GORZÓW WIELKOPOLSKI	A	D	1817–1823; 1825–1834; 1844–1845	AMTSGERICHT TIRSCHTIEGEL 249/5227–5229, 5232
GORZÓW WIELKOPOLSKI	A	M	1817–1823; 1825–1834; 1844–1845	AMTSGERICHT TIRSCHTIEGEL 249/5226, 5228–5229, 5231
KOBLENZ	G	N	1834–1848	
TRZEBINIA	**KATOWICE**			
TRZEBINIA	U	B	1895; 1897; 1913; 1941	
TRZEBINIA	U	D	1941; 1945	
TRZEBINIA	U	M	1886; 1909–1911; 1941; 1945	
TRZEMESZNO	**BYDGOSZCZ**			
INOWROCŁAW	A	B	1832; 1837–1847	113/1–2
INOWROCŁAW	A	D	1832; 1837–1847	113/1–2
INOWROCŁAW	A	K	1833/1910	63
INOWROCŁAW	A	M	1832; 1837–1847	113/1–2
INOWROCŁAW	A	S	1843/1920	64
INOWROCŁAW	A	Y	1843–1907	63
TUCHEL	**SEE TUCHOLA**			
TUCHOLA	**BYDGOSZCZ**			
BYDGOSZCZ	A	B	1812–1834; 1874–1893	1674
BYDGOSZCZ	A	D	1812–1834; 1874–1893	1674
BYDGOSZCZ	A	M	1812–1834; 1874–1893	1674
BYDGOSZCZ	A	Z	1786–1919	1674
TULISZKÓW	**KONIN**			
ŁÓDŹ	A	Z	1905	92
TUREK	**KONIN**			
POZNAŃ	A	B	1837	3758/1
POZNAŃ	A	D	1837	3758/1
ŁÓDŹ	A	G	1908–1909	92
POZNAŃ	A	M	1837	3758/1
ŁÓDŹ	A	Z	1913–1914	92
TUROBIN	**ZAMOŚĆ**			
LUBLIN	A	B	1826–1831; 1833–1869; 1873–1875	113
ZAMOŚĆ	A	B	1870–1871; 1876–1889; 1891–1893	209/1–18
TUROBIN	U	B	1894–1904; 1906–1913; 1920–1933; 1935–1937	
LUBLIN	A	C	1910	ZPK/128
LUBLIN	A	D	1826–1832; 1834–1869; 1873–1875	113
ZAMOŚĆ	A	D	1870–1871; 1876–1889; 1891–1893	209/1–18
TUROBIN	U	D	1894–1904; 1906–1913; 1920–1933; 1935–1937	
LUBLIN	A	K	1870–1914; 1922–1927; 1936	RGL IV ADM.; UWL WSP/790
LUBLIN	A	M	1826–1832; 1834–1869; 1873–1875	113
ZAMOŚĆ	A	M	1870–1871; 1876–1889; 1891–1893	209/1–18
TUROBIN	U	M	1894–1904; 1906–1913; 1920–1933; 1935–1937	
LUBLIN	A	T	1870–1914; 1922–1927; 1936	RGL IV ADM.; UWL WSP/790
TUROŚL	**ŁOMŻA**			
ŁOMŻA	A	C	1931–1939	159
TUSZYN	**PIOTRKÓW TRYBUNALSKI**			
ŁÓDŹ	A	A	1890	17
ŁÓDŹ	A	B	1826–1856	270
PIOTRKÓW TRYBUNALSKI	A	B	1857–1895	341/2–26
TUSZYN	U	B	1896–1939	
ŁÓDŹ	A	D	1826–1856	270
PIOTRKÓW TRYBUNALSKI	A	D	1873–1895	341/5–26

A Army/recruit lists; **B** Birth; **C** Census; **D** Death; **E** Voter lists; **G** Immigration; **H** Holocaust; **J** Judaica; **K** Kahal; **L** Land; **M** Marriage; **N** Name changes; **O** Police files; **P** Pogroms; **R** Reference; **S** School records; **T** Tax lists; **V** Divorce; **W** Occupation lists; **X** Jewish hospital; **Y** Notary records; **Z** Local government records

TOWN NAME	VOIVODSHIP (Province)				
Repository Location	Repository Document Type	Code	Years		Zespół/Sygnatura (Poland) Fond/Opis/Delo (Belarus, Ukraine, Lithuania)
TUSZYN					
ŁÓDŹ	U	D	1896–1939		
PIOTRKÓW TRYBUNALSKI	A	M	1826–1856		270
TUSZYN	A	M	1859–1895		341/1, 5–26
PABIANICE	U	M	1896–1939		
	A	Z	1901–1913		158
TWARDOGÓRA	**WROCŁAW**				
KOBLENZ	G	B	1819–1874		
WROCŁAW	A	B	1874–1893		556/II
WARSZAWA	J	C	1937		PROVINCE: ŚLĄSK
KOBLENZ	G	D	1812–1874		
WROCŁAW	A	D	1874–1892		556/II
KOBLENZ	G	M	1819–1874		
WROCŁAW	A	M	1874–1893		556/II
TYCZYN	**RZESZÓW**				
RZESZÓW	A	B	1877–1880		884/1
TYCZYN	U	B	1881–1902; 1913–1942		
LVOV	A	D	1792–1876		701/1/358
TYCZYN	U	D	1877–1902		
LVOV	A	L	1785–1788; 1819–1820		19/V/84; 20/V/224
TYCZYN	U	M	1877–1942		
RZESZÓW	A	S	1898–1946		180/15–62
PRZEMYŚL	A	Y	1872–1939		104; 1115–1127
RZESZÓW	A	Z	1722; 1732		255/29–30
TYKOCIN	**BIAŁYSTOK**				
BIAŁYSTOK	A	B	1826–1844; 1846–1847; 1852–1853; 1856–1862; 1864; 1866–1876; 1880–1881; 1883–1885; 1890		266
TYKOCIN	U	B	1891–1914; 1921–1935; 1939		
BIAŁYSTOK	A	D	1827–1831; 1833; 1835–1839; 1841–1842; 1844; 1846–1847; 1852–1853; 1856–1883; 1885; 1890		266
TYKOCIN	U	D	1907–1912; 1922–1927		
BIAŁYSTOK	A	G	1899		67/6
BIAŁYSTOK	A	K	1910–1912		6/163, 166
BIAŁYSTOK	A	L	1904		67/7
BIAŁYSTOK	A	M	1827–1831; 1833; 1835–1839; 1841–1842; 1844; 1846–1847; 1852–1853; 1856–1862; 1864; 1866; 1868; 1871–1876; 1880–1881; 1883; 1885; 1890		266
TYKOCIN	U	M	1891–1913; 1916; 1922–1934; 1936		
BIAŁYSTOK	A	Y	1928–1939		310–311
ŁOMŻA	A	E	1906–1907		22
TYRAWA WOŁOSKA	**KROSNO**				
PRZEMYŚL	A	K	1937		154/1
LVOV	A	L	1785–1788; 1819–1820		19/XV/III
TYSZOWCE	**ZAMOŚĆ**				
LUBLIN	A	B	1826–1875		113
ZAMOŚĆ	A	B	1876–1893		209/1–15
TYSZOWCE	U	B	1894–1915; 1920–1923; 1925–1926; 1928–1938		
LUBLIN	A	D	1826–1875		113
ZAMOŚĆ	A	D	1876–1893		209/1–15
TYSZOWCE	U	D	1894–1915; 1920–1923; 1925–1926; 1928–1938		
LUBLIN	A	K	1873–1905; 1910–1915		RGL IV ADM; RGCH/486
LUBLIN	A	M	1826–1875		113
ZAMOŚĆ	A	M	1876–1877; 1879–1893		209/1–15
TYSZOWCE	U	M	1894–1915; 1920–1923; 1925–1926; 1928–1938		
ZAMOŚĆ	A	Y	1927–1934		127–130/1–38
UBIESZYN	**PRZEMYŚL**				
PRZEWORSK	A	S	1906–1953		75/1–30, 33–37
UCHANIE	**ZAMOŚĆ**				
LUBLIN	A	B	1826–1864; 1867; 1869–1872		113
ZAMOŚĆ	A	B	1866; 1876–1880 (SEE ALSO JAROSŁAWIEC)		209/0–3
UCHANIE	U	B	1889; 1891–1901; 1905–1906; 1908–1911; 1924–1938		
LUBLIN	A	D	1826–1864; 1867; 1869–1872		113
ZAMOŚĆ	A	D	1866; 1876–1880 (SEE ALSO JAROSŁAWIEC)		209/0–2
UCHANIE	U	D	1889; 1891–1901; 1905–1906; 1908–1911; 1924–1938		
LUBLIN	A	K	1869–1908; 1927		RGL IV ADM; UWL WSP/782
LUBLIN	A	M	1826–1864; 1867; 1869–1872		113
ZAMOŚĆ	A	M	1866; 1876–1879 (SEE ALSO JAROSŁAWIEC)		209/0–2

Repository type: **A** = Archive **G** = LDS Films of German-Held Records **J** = Jewish Historical Institute **U** = Urząd Stanu Cywilnego

TOWN NAME Repository Location	VOIVODSHIP (Province) Repository Document Type Code Years			Zespół/Sygnatura (Poland) Fond/Opis/Delo (Belarus, Ukraine, Lithuania)
UCHANIE	U	M	1889; 1891–1901; 1905–1906; 1908–1911; 1924–1938	
LUBLIN	A	T	1869–1908; 1927	RGL IV ADM; UWL WSP/782
UJAZD	**PIOTRKÓW TRYBUNALSKI**			
ŁÓDŹ	A	B	1826–1870; 1876	270
PIOTRKÓW TRYBUNALSKI	A	B	1826–1834; 1838–1839; 1841; 1847–1857; 1868–1937; 1940	342/1, 3–75
UJAZD	U	B	1903–1937	
ŁÓDŹ	A	D	1826–1870; 1876	270
PIOTRKÓW TRYBUNALSKI	A	D	1826–1834; 1838–1839; 1841; 1847–1937; 1940	342/2–63, 84–87
UJAZD	U	D	1894–1937	
ŁÓDŹ	A	M	1826–1870; 1876	270
PIOTRKÓW TRYBUNALSKI	A	M	1826–1834; 1838–1839; 1841; 1847–1857; 1860–1937; 1940	342/3–63, 76–83
UJAZD	U	M	1900; 1914; 1916; 1920–1937	
ŁÓDŹ	A	Z	1825–1865; 1897–1912	1
UJEZNA	**PRZEMYŚL**			
PRZEWORSK	A	S	1899–1950	76/1–21, 23–57
UJKOWICE	**PRZEMYŚL**			
PRZEMYŚL	A	C	1932–1933	207/32–33
LVOV	A	L	1785–1788; 1819–1820	19/XIII/332; 20/XIII/280
UJŚCIE	**PIŁA**			
POZNAŃ	A	S	1824–1915	1029/114–116
ULANÓW	**TARNOBRZEG**			
PRZEWORSK	A	A	1887–1927; 1935	19/8; 20/19
PRZEWORSK	A	C	1931–1939; 1949–1950	19/5–7; 20/8–18, 73
PRZEWORSK	A	E	1949	20/72
PRZEWORSK	A	G	1938–1939	20/20–21
PRZEWORSK	A	T	1922–1944; 1948/1952	19/14–18, 57, 64; 20/22–42, 102–115
PRZEMYŚL	A	Y	1875–1934	105; 1095–1099
UNIERZYŻ	**CIECHANÓW**			
UNIERZYŻ	U	B	1921–1928; 1930–1931; 1933; 1935–1937	
UNIERZYŻ	U	D	1917; 1921–1927; 1929–1930; 1932–1933	
UNIERZYŻ	U	M	1921; 1923–1927; 1930–1932; 1937	
UNRUHSTADT	**SEE KARGOWA**			
URZĘDÓW	**LUBLIN**			
LUBLIN	A	K	1922–1935	UWL WSP/786
LUBLIN	A	T	1922–1935	UWL WSP/786
USTRZYKI DOLNE	**KROSNO**			
LVOV	A	L	1785–1788; 1819–1820	19/XV/96; 20/XV/67
PRZEMYŚL	A	Y	1894–1896	732
VRONIK	**SEE WRONKI**			
WADOWICE	**TARNÓW**			
BERLIN	G	M	1877–1929	
WĄGROWIEC	**PIŁA**			
POZNAŃ	A	K	1826–1916	338/275–278, 280–282
WALAWA	**PRZEMYŚL**			
PRZEMYŚL	A	C	1946–1951	212/29, 45, 51, 70–71
WAŁBRZYCH	**WAŁBRZYCH**			
WAŁBRZYCH	U	B	1934–1938	
WAŁBRZYCH	U	D	1934–1938	
WARSZAWA	J	K	1853/1928	PROVINCE: ŚLĄSK
WAŁBRZYCH	U	M	1934–1938	
WAŁCZ	**PIŁA**			
BERLIN	G	B	1812–1874	
BERLIN	G	D	1812–1874	
BERLIN	G	M	1812–1874	
WAŁCZ REGION	**PIŁA**			
KOSZALIN	A	C	1844–1847	20/I/163
KOSZALIN	A	K	1818–1846	20/I/159–170
KOSZALIN	A	S	1828–1849	20/I/161
WALDENBURG	**SEE WAŁBRZYCH**			
WALDWINKEL	**SEE WALDWINKEL**			
WANGERIN	**SEE WĘGORZYNO**			

A Army/recruit lists; **B** Birth; **C** Census; **D** Death; **E** Voter lists; **G** Immigration; **H** Holocaust; **J** Judaica; **K** Kahal; **L** Land; **M** Marriage; **N** Name changes; **O** Police files; **P** Pogroms; **R** Reference; **S** School records; **T** Tax lists; **V** Divorce; **W** Occupation lists; **X** Jewish hospital; **Y** Notary records; **Z** Local government records

TOWN NAME	VOIVODSHIP (Province)			Zespół/Sygnatura (Poland)
Repository Location	Repository Type	Document Code	Years	Fond/Opis/Delo (Belarus, Ukraine, Lithuania)

WANGROWITZ	**SEE WĄGROWIEC**			
WARKA	**RADOM**			
GÓRA KALWARIA	A	B	1808–1872	166; 124
RADOM	A	B	1873–1894	467
WARKA	U	B	1895–1913; 1917–1919; 1921–1935; 1939	
GÓRA KALWARIA	A	D	1808–1872	166; 124
RADOM	A	D	1873–1894	467
WARKA	U	D	1895–1913; 1918–1919; 1921–1935; 1939	
GÓRA KALWARIA	A	M	1808–1872	166; 124
RADOM	A	M	1873–1894	467
WARKA	U	M	1895–1913; 1917–1919; 1921–1935; 1939	
WARSZAWA	**WARSZAWA**			
WARSAW2	A	B	1846–1848; 1860; 1868–1889; 1891–1894; 1908; 1911	180/I
WARSAW2	A	D	1846; 1860; 1868–1889; 1891–1894; 1909	180/I
WARSZAWA	J	H	1939–1942 (INCLUDES LIST OF 13, 000 DEATHS IN WARSZAWA GHETTO)	201
WARSZAWA	J	K	1857–1878; 1940–1943	212
WARSZAWA	A	L	1804/1863	662/III
WARSAW2	A	M	1826–1893	180/I
KRAKÓW	A	R	1937–1938	
WARSAW2	A	S	1852–1918	214; 216; 305; 311
WARSAW2	A	Y	1808–1939	665–1660
WARSZAWA/MOKOTOW REGION	**WARSZAWA**			
WARSZAWA	U	B	1917; 1936–1938 (INCLUDED IN WARSZAWA)	
WARSZAWA	U	D	1917; 1936–1938	
WARSZAWA	U	M	1917; 1936–1938	
WARSZAWA/PRAGA POLNOC REGION	**WARSZAWA**			
WARSZAWA	U	B	1934; 1936	
WARSZAWA	U	D	1934; 1936	
WARSZAWA	U	M	1934; 1936	
WARSZAWA/PRAGA POLUDNIE REGION	**WARSZAWA**			
WARSZAWA	U	B	1917; 1920–1938	
WARSZAWA	U	D	1934; 1936	
WARSZAWA	U	M	1909–1917; 1920; 1922–1939	
WARSZAWA/SRODMIESCIE REGION	**WARSZAWA**			
WARSZAWA	U	M	1894–1939	
WARSZAWA	U	B	1894–1939	
WARSZAWA	U	D	1894–1939	
WARTA	**SIERADZ**			
ŁÓDŹ	A	B	1809–1855; 1858	270
WARTA	U	B	1897–1935	
ŁÓDŹ	A	D	1809–1855; 1858	270
WARTA	U	D	1897–1935	
ŁÓDŹ	A	M	1809–1855; 1858	270
WARTA	U	M	1897–1935	
ŁÓDŹ	A	W	1912–1914	92
WARTENBURG	**SEE BARCZEWO**			
WASILKÓW	**BIAŁYSTOK**			
WASILKÓW	U	B	1889; 1891–1892; 1895–1896; 1898; 1900; 1903; 1905–1911; 1914; 1916–1926; 1929–1939	
WASILKÓW	U	D	1921–1926	
WASILKÓW	U	M	1921–1926; 1930–1934	
WĄSOSZ	**ŁOMŻA**			
ŁOMŻA	A	B	1840–1875; 1878; 1881/1886; 1887–1890; 1892–1899	273
ŁOMŻA	A	D	1840–1875; 1878; 1881/1886; 1887–1890; 1892–1899	273
ŁOMŻA	A	M	1840–1875; 1878; 1881/1886; 1887–1890; 1892–1899	273
WĄWOLNICA	**LUBLIN**			
LUBLIN	A	B	1851–1879	113
LUBLIN	A	D	1826–1911	113
LUBLIN	A	K	1867–1913; 1922–1927	RGL IV ADM; UWL WSP/819
LUBLIN	A	M	1854–1890	113
LUBLIN	A	T	1867–1913; 1922–1927	RGL IV ADM; UWL WSP/819

Repository type: **A** = Archive   **G** = LDS Films of German-Held Records   **J** = Jewish Historical Institute   **U** = Urząd Stanu Cywilnego

TOWN NAME	VOIVODSHIP (Province)			Zespół/Sygnatura (Poland)
Repository Location	Repository Document Type	Code	Years	Fond/Opis/Delo (Belarus, Ukraine, Lithuania)
WĘGLÓWKA	**INCLUDED IN KORCZYNA**			
WĘGORZEWO	**SUWAŁKI**			
LEIPZIG	G	B	1847–1874	
OLSZTYN	A	C	1818–1820; 1835	26/I
LEIPZIG	G	D	1847–1874	
LEIPZIG	G	M	1847–1874	
WĘGORZYNO	**SZCZECIN**			
LEIPZIG	G	B	1841–1874	
LEIPZIG	G	D	1841–1874	
SZCZECIN	A	K	1904–1924	MAGISTRAT WANGERIN 71
WĘGRÓW	**SIEDLCE**			
SIEDLCE	A	B	1826–1889	234/1–30
WĘGRÓW	U	B	1890–1942	
SIEDLCE	A	D	1826–1888	234/1–30
WĘGRÓW	U	D	1889–1942	
BIAŁYSTOK	A	K	1900–1912; 1914–1915	6/141, 174
LUBLIN	A	K	1922–1927	403/828–829
SIEDLCE	A	M	1826–1888	234/1–30
WĘGRÓW	U	M	1889–1936; 1938–1941	
WEJHEROWO	**GDAŃSK**			
GDAŃSK	A	D	1848–1881	1497/60
GDAŃSK	A	H	1940–1942	37/264
GDAŃSK	A	M	1847–1874	1497/59
WIĄZOWNA	**WARSZAWA**			
WIĄZOWNA	U	B	1920; 1925–1928; 1930–1939	
WIĄZOWNA	U	D	1920; 1925–1928; 1930–1939	
WIĄZOWNA	U	M	1920; 1925–1928; 1930–1939	
WIDACZÓW	**PRZEMYŚL**			
PRZEWORSK	A	S	1893–1949	77/1–4, 7
WIDAWA	**SIERADZ**			
ŁÓDŹ	A	A	1901–1902	92, 107–108
ŁÓDŹ	A	B	1826–1850; 1852–1891	270
WIDAWA	U	B	1898–1914; 1930; 1935	
ŁÓDŹ	A	D	1826–1850; 1852–1891	270
WIDAWA	U	D	1930; 1935	
ŁÓDŹ	A	M	1826–1850; 1852–1875	270
WIDAWA	U	M	1923; 1930; 1935; 1938	
PABIANICE	A	Z	1939–1953	24
WIDUCHOWA	**SZCZECIN**			
SZCZECIN	A	K	1840–1862	REGIERUNG STETTIN I/10733
WIECBORK	**BYDGOSZCZ**			
BYDGOSZCZ	A	B	1825–1847; 1874–1894	389; 1804
BYDGOSZCZ	A	D	1825–1847; 1874–1894	389; 1804
BYDGOSZCZ	A	M	1825–1847; 1874–1894	389; 1804
BYDGOSZCZ	A	Z	1812–1905	1676
WIELICZKA	**KRAKÓW**			
KRAKÓW	U	B	1877/1941	
KRAKÓW	A	C	1867/1945	117
KRAKÓW	U	D	1877/1941	
LVOV	A	L	1785–1788; 1819–1820	19/I/336; 20/I/30
KRAKÓW	U	M	1877/1941	
KRAKÓW	A	Z	1777–1945	117
WIELISZEW	**WARSZAWA**			
NOWY DWÓR MAZOWIECKI	A	B	1824; 1826–1828; 1830–1835; 1837; 1842–1846; 1850–1851; 1863–1865; 1871–1874; 1876–1877; 1880–1882; 1884; 1890; 1897; 1900; 1906; 1918; 1933; 1935	383
NOWY DWÓR MAZOWIECKI	A	D	1824; 1826–1828; 1830–1835; 1837; 1842–1846; 1850–1851; 1863–1865; 1871–1874; 1876–1877; 1880–1882; 1884; 1890; 1897; 1900; 1906; 1918; 1933; 1935	383
NOWY DWÓR MAZOWIECKI	A	M	1822; 1824; 1826–1828; 1830–1835; 1837; 1842–1846; 1850–1851; 1863–1865; 1871–1874; 1876–1877; 1880–1882; 1884; 1890; 1897; 1900; 1906; 1920; 1933; 1935	383
WIELKIE OCZY	**PRZEMYŚL**			
LVOV	A	B	1791–1853	701/1/259

A Army/recruit lists; **B** Birth; **C** Census; **D** Death; **E** Voter lists; **G** Immigration; **H** Holocaust; **J** Judaica; **K** Kahal; **L** Land; **M** Marriage; **N** Name changes; **O** Police files; **P** Pogroms; **R** Reference; **S** School records; **T** Tax lists; **V** Divorce; **W** Occupation lists; **X** Jewish hospital; **Y** Notary records; **Z** Local government records

| TOWN NAME | VOIVODSHIP (Province) | | | Zespół/Sygnatura (Poland) |
Repository Location	Repository Document Type	Code	Years	Fond/Opis/Delo (Belarus, Ukraine, Lithuania)
WARSZAWA	A	B	1843–1874	1481
LVOV	A	D	1791–1853	701/1/259
WARSZAWA	A	D	1843–1874	1481
WIELOWIEŚ	**KATOWICE**			
GLIWICE	A	B	1812–1847	1/I/5851
GLIWICE	A	D	1812–1847	1/I/5851
WARSZAWA	J	D	1838–1852	
GLIWICE	A	K	1812–1900	1/I/5813–5863
WARSZAWA	J	K	1838/1926	PROVINCE: ŚLĄSK
KOBLENZ	G	M	1828–1851	
KOBLENZ	G	N	1762–1820; 1845/1889	
WIELUŃ	**SIERADZ**			
ŁÓDŹ	A	B	1826–1870; 1882–1893	270
WIELUŃ	U	B	1894–1940	
ŁÓDŹ	A	D	1826–1870; 1882–1893	270
WIELUŃ	U	D	1894–1940	
ŁÓDŹ	A	G	1914	92
ŁÓDŹ	A	M	1826–1870; 1882–1893	270
WIELUŃ	U	M	1894–1940	
ŁÓDŹ	A	Z	1895–1914	115
WIENIAWA	**LUBLIN**			
LUBLIN	A	B	1826–1894	113 (INCLUDED IN LUBLIN)
LUBLIN	A	D	1826–1894	113 (INCLUDED IN LUBLIN)
LUBLIN	A	E	1867–1914	RGL IV ADM.
LUBLIN	A	K	1867–1914	RGL IV ADM.
LUBLIN	A	M	1826–1894	113 (INCLUDED IN LUBLIN)
LUBLIN	A	T	1795; 1867–1914 (AFTER 1917, SEE LUBLIN)	RGL IV ADM; AML/482
WIERUSZÓW	**KALISZ**			
KALISZ	A	B	1831; 1836; 1871–1882	768/1–10
ŁÓDŹ	A	B	1838–1877	270
WIERUSZÓW	U	B	1883–1905; 1907; 1909–1939	
KALISZ	A	D	1831; 1875; 1878–1882	768/1–10
ŁÓDŹ	A	D	1838–1874	270
WIERUSZÓW	U	D	1883–1911; 1917–1927; 1932–1933; 1935	
KALISZ	A	M	1836; 1871–1884	768/1–10
ŁÓDŹ	A	M	1838–1870	270
WIERUSZÓW	U	M	1885–1927; 1933; 1935	
WIERZBNIK	**SEE STARACHOWICE**			
WIESZOWA	**KATOWICE**			
TARNOWSKIE GÓRY	A	B	1847–1848	174/1
TARNOWSKIE GÓRY	A	D	1847–1848	174/1
WILCZYN	**KONIN**			
POZNAŃ	A	B	1827/1859	3759/1–25
WILCZYN	U	B	1922	
POZNAŃ	A	D	1827/1859	3759/1–25
WILCZYN	U	D	1905; 1909	
POZNAŃ	A	M	1827/1859	3759/1–25
WILCZYN	U	M	1913; 1935	
WIRSITZ	**SEE WYRZYSK**			
WISKITKI	**SKIERNIEWICE**			
ŻYRARDÓW	A	B	1826–1887	63
WISKITKI	U	B	1888–1938	
ŻYRARDÓW	A	D	1826–1887	63
WISKITKI	U	D	1888–1938	
ŻYRARDÓW	A	M	1826–1887	63
WISKITKI	U	M	1888–1938	
WIŚLICA	**KIELCE**			
PIŃCZÓW	A	B	1826–1835; 1837–1844; 1846–1850; 1852–1853; 1855–1872; 1874; 1882–1884; 1886–1887	51
WIŚLICA	U	B	1888–1939	
PIŃCZÓW	A	D	1826–1835; 1837–1844; 1846–1850; 1852–1853; 1855–1872; 1874–1882; 1884; 1886–1887	51
WIŚLICA	U	D	1888–1939	
PIŃCZÓW	A	M	1826–1835; 1837–1844; 1846–1850; 1852–1853; 1855–1872; 1874–1882; 1884; 1886–1887	51
WIŚLICA	U	M	1888–1939	

Repository type: **A** = Archive   **G** = LDS Films of German-Held Records   **J** = Jewish Historical Institute   **U** = Urząd Stanu Cywilnego

TOWN NAME		VOIVODSHIP (Province)			
Repository Location	Repository Document Type	Code	Years		Zespół/Sygnatura (Poland) Fond/Opis/Delo (Belarus, Ukraine, Lithuania)

WIŚNICZ		**TARNÓW**		
BOCHNIA	A	B	1814–1897	76/OMW 1–7
WIŚNICZ	U	B	1898–1942	
KRAKÓW	A	D	1826–1853	526/MIW
BOCHNIA	A	D	1859–1895	76/OMW 8–9
WIŚNICZ	U	D	1896–1937	
BOCHNIA	A	M	1827–1876	76/OMW 3
WIŚNICZ	U	M	1882–1942	
WIŚNICE		**BIAŁA PODLASKA**		
LUBLIN	A	B	1826–1849	113
WIŚNICE	U	B	1898–1907; 1922–1939	
LUBLIN	A	D	1826–1882	113
WIŚNICE	U	D	1932; 1934	
LUBLIN	A	E	1913–1914	RGCH/544
LUBLIN	A	K	1913–1914; 1925–1927	RGCH/544; UWL WSP/834
LUBLIN	A	M	1826–1870	113
WIŚNICE	U	M	1898–1907; 1922–1939	
LUBLIN	A	T	1913–1914; 1925–1927	RGCH/544; UWL WSP/834
WITKÓW		**ZAMOŚĆ**		
WARSZAWA	J	K	1820–1868	
WITKOWO		**KONIN**		
WARSZAWA	J	B	1823–1829	PROVINCE: POZNAŃ
WIŻAJNY		**SUWAŁKI**		
SUWAŁKI	A	B	1808–1825; 1829–1830; 1832–1838; 1840–1842; 1844–1848; 1851–1853; 1855–1869; 1873–1874; 1877; 1879–1880; 1892	169; 206
WIŻAJNY	U	B	1896–1897; 1900; 1921–1938	
SUWAŁKI	A	D	1808–1825; 1829–1830; 1832–1838; 1840–1842; 1844–1848; 1851–1853; 1855–1869; 1873–1874; 1877; 1879–1880; 1892	169; 206
WIŻAJNY	U	D	1896–1897; 1900; 1921–1938	
SUWAŁKI	A	K	1926–1938	31/149–152
SUWAŁKI	A	M	1808–1825; 1829–1830; 1832–1838; 1840–1842; 1844–1848; 1851–1853; 1855–1869; 1873–1874; 1877; 1879–1880; 1892	169; 206
WIŻAJNY	U	M	1896–1897; 1900; 1921–1938	
SUWAŁKI	A	R	1890–1939	527
WIZNA		**ŁOMŻA**		
ŁOMŻA	A	B	1826–1836; 1838–1865; 1868–1873; 1876; 1878; 1882; 1884; 1887–1888; 1890–1894	173
WIZNA	U	B	1900; 1911–1913; 1919–1920; 1934–1935	
ŁOMŻA	A	D	1826–1836; 1838–1865; 1868–1873; 1876; 1878; 1882; 1884; 1887–1888; 1890–1894	173
WIZNA	U	D	1899–1900; 1911–1913; 1919–1920; 1934–1935	
ŁOMŻA	A	M	1826–1836; 1838–1865; 1868–1873; 1876; 1878; 1882; 1884; 1887–1888; 1890–1894	173
WIZNA	U	M	1899–1900; 1908; 1911–1913; 1919–1920; 1934–1935	
WŁOCŁAWEK		**WŁOCŁAWEK**		
WŁOCŁAWEK	U	B	1913–1917; 1930–1932	
WŁOCŁAWEK	U	D	1913–1917; 1930–1932	
WARSZAWA	J	K	1919–1939	105/113
WŁOCŁAWEK	A	M	1872 (MARRIAGE APPLICATIONS)	563
WŁOCŁAWEK	U	M	1913–1917; 1930–1932	
WŁODAWA		**CHEŁM**		
WŁODAWA	U	B	1887–1914; 1919–1938	
WŁODAWA	U	D	1884–1910; 1920–1936	
WŁODAWA	U	M	1888–1914; 1919–1939	
LUBLIN	A	B	1844–1873; 1932–1934	113
LUBLIN	A	D	1826–1836	113
LVOV2	A	H	1943	35/13/102
LUBLIN	A	K	1924–1935	403/830–834, 1582
LUBLIN	A	M	1846–1859	113
WŁOSZCZOWA		**KIELCE**		
JĘDRZEJÓW	A	B	1823; 1826–1828; 1832; 1836–1838; 1851–1855; 1857–1878; 1880–1894	226

A Army/recruit lists; **B** Birth; **C** Census; **D** Death; **E** Voter lists; **G** Immigration; **H** Holocaust; **J** Judaica; **K** Kahal; **L** Land; **M** Marriage; **N** Name changes; **O** Police files; **P** Pogroms; **R** Reference; **S** School records; **T** Tax lists; **V** Divorce; **W** Occupation lists; **X** Jewish hospital; **Y** Notary records; **Z** Local government records

TOWN NAME	VOIVODSHIP (Province)			Zespół/Sygnatura (Poland)
Repository Location	Repository Document Type	Code	Years	Fond/Opis/Delo (Belarus, Ukraine, Lithuania)
WŁOSZCZOWA	U	B	1895–1921; 1923–1934; 1936–1937; 1939–1941	
JĘDRZEJÓW	A	D	1823; 1826–1828; 1832; 1836–1838; 1851–1852; 1854–1855; 1857–1878; 1880–1894	226
WŁOSZCZOWA	U	D	1895–1921; 1923–1934; 1936–1937; 1939–1941	
JĘDRZEJÓW	A	G	1923; 1927	159
WARSZAWA	J	K	1940–1943	212
JĘDRZEJÓW	A	M	1823; 1826–1828; 1832; 1836–1838; 1851–1852; 1854–1855; 1857–1878; 1880–1894	226
WŁOSZCZOWA	U	M	1895–1921; 1923–1934; 1936–1937; 1939–1941	
WODYNIE	**SIEDLCE**			
SIEDLCE	A	B	1826–1839	238/1–14
SIEDLCE	A	D	1826–1837; 1839	238/1–14
SIEDLCE	A	M	1826–1839	238/1–14
WODZISŁAW	**KATOWICE**			
CIESZYN	A	A	1742–1752; 1809–1919	84/I/48–51
JĘDRZEJÓW	A	B	1826–1838; 1840–1887	80
WODZISŁAW	U	B	1888–1912; 1922–1938; 1940–1942	
JĘDRZEJÓW	A	D	1826–1838; 1840–1887	80
WODZISŁAW	U	D	1888–1912; 1922–1938; 1940–1941	
JĘDRZEJÓW	A	M	1826–1830; 1832–1838; 1840–1867; 1869–1887	80
WODZISŁAW	U	M	1888–1912; 1922–1938; 1940–1942	
WOHLAU	**SEE WOŁÓW**			
WOHYŃ	**BIAŁA PODLASKA**			
LUBLIN	A	B	1826–1831; 1833–1843; 1856–1863; 1870–1878	113
LUBLIN	A	D	1826–1831; 1833–1843; 1856–1863; 1870–1878	113
LUBLIN	A	K	1913–1914; 1922–1937	RGL IV ADM; UWL WSP/822
LUBLIN	A	M	1826–1831; 1833–1843; 1856–1863; 1870–1878	113
LUBLIN	A	T	1913–1914; 1922–1937	RGL IV ADM; UWL WSP/822
WOJNICZ	**TARNÓW**			
BOCHNIA	A	B	1829–1875	76/OMB 1–3
WOJNICZ	U	B	1882–1942	
WOJNICZ	U	D	1882–1942	
BOCHNIA	M	D	1885; 1913	
LVOV	A	L	1785–1788; 1819–1820	19/1/324; 20/1/54
WOJNICZ	U	M	1882–1925	
WOJSŁAWICE	**CHEŁM**			
LUBLIN	A	B	1826; 1834; 1836; 1839; 1841–1877; 1884; 1886; 1888–1890	113
WOJSŁAWICE	U	B	1892–1894; 1896–1898; 1911; 1913; 1930; 1937	
LUBLIN	A	D	1826; 1834; 1836; 1839; 1841–1877; 1884; 1886; 1888–1890	113
WOJSŁAWICE	U	D	1892–1894; 1896–1898; 1911; 1913; 1930; 1937	
LUBLIN	A	K	1868–1910; 1914; 1927	RGL IV ADM; ZPCH/34; UWL WSP/769
LUBLIN	A	M	1826; 1834; 1836; 1839; 1841–1877; 1884; 1886; 1888–1890	113
WOJSŁAWICE	U	M	1892–1894; 1896–1898; 1911; 1913; 1930; 1937	
LUBLIN	A	T	1868–1910; 1914; 1927	RGL ADM; ZPCH/34; UWL WSP/769
WOLA KRZYWIECKA	**PRZEMYŚL**			
PRZEMYŚL	A	C	1930–1950	203/25, 35, 63, 72, 81, 90
WOLA MICHOWA	**KROSNO**			
SANOK	A	C	1931–1946	31/2–8(7)
WOLANÓW	**RADOM**			
RADOM	A	B	1826–1858; 1860–1894	193
WOLANÓW	U	B	1895–1917; 1919–1941	
RADOM	A	D	1826–1858; 1860–1894	193
WOLANÓW	U	D	1895–1917; 1919–1940	
RADOM	A	M	1826–1858; 1860–1894	193
WOLANÓW	U	M	1895–1917; 1919–1942	
WOLBÓRZ	**PIOTRKÓW TRYBUNALSKI**			
ŁÓDŹ	A	B	1826–1867	270
WOLBÓRZ	U	B	1882–1885; 1887–1900; 1902–1941	
PIOTRKÓW TRYBUNALSKI	A	C	1841–1931	241/11, 36
ŁÓDŹ	A	D	1826–1867	270
WOLBÓRZ	U	D	1882–1885; 1887–1900; 1902–1941	
ŁÓDŹ	A	M	1826–1867	270
WOLBÓRZ	U	M	1882–1885; 1887–1900; 1902–1941	
PIOTRKÓW TRYBUNALSKI	A	Z	1808–1876	11

Repository type: **A** = Archive   **G** = LDS Films of German-Held Records   **J** = Jewish Historical Institute   **U** = Urząd Stanu Cywilnego

TOWN NAME	VOIVODSHIP (Province)			
Repository Location	Repository Document Type	Code	Years	Zespół/Sygnatura (Poland) Fond/Opis/Delo (Belarus, Ukraine, Lithuania)
ŁÓDŹ	A	Z	1906–1915	1
WOLBROM	**KATOWICE**			
KATOWICE	A	B	1826–1838; 1842–1870; 1882–1886	42
WOLBROM	U	B	1898–1902; 1906; 1908; 1910–1940	
KATOWICE	A	D	1826–1870; 1883–1888	42
WOLBROM	U	D	1890–1896; 1898–1904; 1906; 1908; 1911; 1915–1919; 1925–1942	
KATOWICE	A	M	1826–1870; 1882–1892	42
WOLBROM	U	M	1893–1901; 1903–1907; 1909–1913; 1938–1941	
WOŁCZYN	**OPOLE**			
WARSZAWA	J	B	1833–1838	
KOBLENZ	G	B	1835–1890	
OPOLE	A	B	1874–1892	858
WARSZAWA	J	D	1833–1838	
KOBLENZ	G	D	1835–1890	
OPOLE	A	D	1874–1892	858
WARSZAWA	J	E	1833/1926	PROVINCE: ŚLĄSK
WARSZAWA	J	K	1833/1926	PROVINCE: ŚLĄSK
WARSZAWA	J	T	1833/1926	PROVINCE: ŚLĄSK
WARSZAWA	J	W	1833/1926	PROVINCE: ŚLĄSK
WARSZAWA	J	Y	1833/1926	PROVINCE: ŚLĄSK
WARSZAWA	J	Z	1833/1926	PROVINCE: ŚLĄSK
WOLDENBERG	**SEE DOBIEGNIEW**			
WOLIN	**SZCZECIN**			
BERLIN	G	B	1813–1874	
BERLIN	G	D	1813–1874	
SZCZECIN	A	K	1875–1935	GMINY ZYDOWSKIE POMORZA ZACHODNIEGO/133–137
BERLIN	G	M	1813–1874	
WÓLKA MAŁKOWA	**PRZEMYŚL**			
PRZEWORSK	A	S	1900–1956	81/1–9, 12–31, 34–35
WOLLSTEIN	**SEE WOLSZTYN**			
WOŁOMIN	**WARSZAWA**			
NOWY DWÓR MAZOWIECKI	A	C	1920–1924; 1927–1928; 1930–1931; 1933	162
WOŁÓW	**WROCŁAW**			
WARSZAWA	J	K	1858/1885	PROVINCE: ŚLĄSK
WARSZAWA	J	Z	1858/1885	PROVINCE: ŚLĄSK
WOLSZTYN	**ZIELONA GÓRA**			
POZNAŃ	A	K	1698–1865	906/18–29
WONGROWITZ	**SEE WĄGROWIEC**			
WOŹNIKI	**CZĘSTOCHOWA**			
KATOWICE	A	K	1922–1924	27/I–VI/2003
WROCŁAW	**WROCŁAW**			
KOBLENZ	G	B	1760–1939	
WROCŁAW	A	B	1874–1893	556/II
WARSZAWA	J	C	1794/1939	103
KOBLENZ	G	D	1760–1939	
WARSZAWA	J	D	1816; 1831–1893	103
WROCŁAW	A	D	1874–1893	556/II
WROCŁAW	U	D	1906	
WARSZAWA	J	E	1794/1939	103
WROCŁAW	A	K	1604; 1809–1945	172/II
WARSZAWA	J	K	1794/1939	103; 105
WARSZAWA	J	L	1794/1939	103
KOBLENZ	G	M	1760–1939	
WROCŁAW	A	M	1874–1893	556/II
WROCŁAW	A	N	1604; 1809–1945	172/II
WARSZAWA	J	S	1794/1939	103
WARSZAWA	J	T	1794/1939	103
WARSZAWA	J	W	1794/1939	103
WARSZAWA	J	X	1794/1939	103
WARSZAWA	J	Y	1794/1939	103
WARSZAWA	J	Z	1794/1939	103
WRONKI	**PIŁA**			
POZNAŃ	A	N	1832/1842	

A Army/recruit lists; **B** Birth; **C** Census; **D** Death; **E** Voter lists; **G** Immigration; **H** Holocaust; **J** Judaica; **K** Kahal; **L** Land; **M** Marriage; **N** Name changes; **O** Police files; **P** Pogroms; **R** Reference; **S** School records; **T** Tax lists; **V** Divorce; **W** Occupation lists; **X** Jewish hospital; **Y** Notary records; **Z** Local government records

TOWN NAME	VOIVODSHIP (Province)			Zespół/Sygnatura (Poland)
Repository Location	Repository Document Type	Code	Years	Fond/Opis/Delo (Belarus, Ukraine, Lithuania)
WRZEŚNIA	**POZNAŃ**			
BERLIN	G	D	1867–1869	
BERLIN	G	M	1859–1860	
BERLIN	G	N	1834	
POZNAŃ	A	S	1832–1916	339/61–63
WSCHOWA	**LESZNO**			
BERLIN	G	B	1802/1811; 1812–1876	
STARY KISIELIN	A	B	1838	124
BERLIN	G	D	1802/1811; 1812–1876	
STARY KISIELIN	A	D	1838	124
BERLIN	G	K	1763–1936 (CEMETERY RECORDS)	
WARSZAWA	J	K	1827/1938	PROVINCE: POZNAŃ
BERLIN	G	M	1802/1811; 1812–1876	
STARY KISIELIN	A	M	1838	124
BERLIN	G	N	1800; 1840–1919	
WARSZAWA	J	S	1827/1938	PROVINCE: POZNAŃ
WARSZAWA	J	Y	1827/1938	PROVINCE: POZNAŃ
STARY KISIELIN	A	Z	1793–1841	363
WARSZAWA	J	Z	1827/1938	PROVINCE: POZNAŃ
WYLATOWO	**BYDGOSZCZ**			
INOWROCŁAW	A	B	1832–1847	114/1–2
INOWROCŁAW	A	D	1832–1847	114/1–2
INOWROCŁAW	A	M	1832–1847	114/1–2
WYRZYSK	**PIŁA**			
BYDGOSZCZ	A	B	1818–1847	384
BYDGOSZCZ	A	D	1818–1847	384
BYDGOSZCZ	A	M	1818–1847	384
BYDGOSZCZ	A	Z	1923–1936	200
WYSOCZANY	**KROSNO**			
SANOK	A	C	1937–1939	23/32
WYSOKIE	**ZAMOŚĆ**			
LUBLIN	A	B	1820; 1826–1836; 1872–1875	113
ZAMOŚĆ	A	B	1876; 1879; 1882–1891	209/1–12
WYSOKIE	U	B	1908–1913	
LUBLIN	A	C	1910	ZPK/129
LUBLIN	A	D	1826–1836; 1872–1875	113
ZAMOŚĆ	A	D	1876; 1879; 1882–1891	209/1/12
WYSOKIE	U	D	1908–1913	
LUBLIN	A	K	1870–1914; 1928	RGL IV ADM; UWL WSP/1560
LUBLIN	A	M	1826–1836; 1872–1875	113
ZAMOŚĆ	A	M	1876; 1879; 1882–1891	209/1–12
WYSOKIE	U	M	1908–1913	
LUBLIN	A	T	1870–1914; 1928	RGL IV ADM; UWL WSP/1560
WYSOKIE MAZOWIECKIE	**ŁOMŻA**			
ŁOMŻA	A	B	1826–1829; 1833–1896; 1912; 1919; 1926–1934	177
WYSOKIE MAZOWIECKIE	U	B	1900; 1905; 1910; 1921; 1923; 1925–1926; 1928; 1930; 1933–1937; 1939	
ŁOMŻA	A	D	1826–1829; 1833–1837; 1840–1841; 1844–1880; 1882; 1891; 1893; 1912; 1927	177
WYSOKIE MAZOWIECKIE	U	D	1900; 1905; 1910; 1921; 1923; 1925–1926; 1928; 1930; 1933–1937; 1939	
ŁOMŻA	A	M	1833–1837; 1839–1866; 1868; 1872–1876; 1878–1879; 1882; 1891; 1893; 1912; 1916–1939	177
WYSOKIE MAZOWIECKIE	U	M	1900; 1905; 1910; 1923; 1926; 1928; 1930; 1933–1937	
ŁOMŻA	A	Y	1909–1915	212
WYSZANÓW	**KALISZ**			
POZNAŃ	A	B	1835–1836	3594/1–2
POZNAŃ	A	D	1835–1836	3594/1–2
POZNAŃ	A	M	1835–1836	3594/1–2
WYSZKÓW	**OSTROŁĘKA**			
PUŁTUSK	A	B	1874–1886; 1888–1892	98
WYSZKÓW	U	B	1893–1918; 1920–1934	
PUŁTUSK	A	D	1874–1886; 1888–1892	98
WYSZKÓW	U	D	1893–1934	
PUŁTUSK	A	M	1874–1886; 1888–1892	98
WYSZKÓW	U	M	1893–1934	

Repository type: **A** = Archive **G** = LDS Films of German-Held Records **J** = Jewish Historical Institute **U** = Urząd Stanu Cywilnego

TOWN NAME		VOIVODSHIP (Province)			
Repository Location	Repository Document Type	Code	Years		Zespół/Sygnatura (Poland) Fond/Opis/Delo (Belarus, Ukraine, Lithuania)
WYSZOGRÓD		**PŁOCK**			
PŁOCK	A	B	1826–1873; 1875–1894		176
WYSZOGRÓD	U	B	1895–1938		
PŁOCK	A	C	1945–1950		6
PŁOCK	A	D	1826–1873; 1875–1894		176
WYSZOGRÓD	U	D	1895–1938		
PŁOCK	A	M	1826–1873; 1875–1894		176
WYSZOGRÓD	U	M	1895–1938		
ZĄBKOWICE		**WAŁBRZYCH**			
WARSZAWA	J	K	1860/1928		PROVINCE: ŚLĄSK
WARSZAWA	J	S	1860/1928		PROVINCE: ŚLĄSK
WARSZAWA	J	Y	1860/1928		PROVINCE: ŚLĄSK
ŻABNO		**TARNÓW**			
TARNÓW	A	B	1879; 1885–1887; 1891–1895		309/GJZ1, 4
ŻABNO	U	B	1896–1940		
TARNÓW	A	D	1882–1883; 1885–1893		309/GJZ2, 5
ŻABNO	U	D	1894–1940		
LVOV	A	L	1785–1788; 1819–1820		19/VII/52; 20/VII/128
TARNÓW	A	M	1885; 1887; 1894		309/GJZ3
ŻABNO	U	M	1895–1940		
ZABRZE		**KATOWICE**			
KATOWICE	A	B	1847–1849		674/I/369
GLIWICE	A	C	1937		95/II/55
KATOWICE	A	D	1847–1848		674/I/602
GLIWICE	A	E	1917–1923		29/II/160
WARSZAWA	J	K	1870/1934		107/159
GLIWICE	A	K	1896–1922		35/I/280, 298, 311, 322
KATOWICE	A	M	1848–1849		674/I/443
KOBLENZ	G	M	1882–1883		
GLIWICE	A	S	1847–1912		29/II/245–249
ŻAGAŃ		**ZIELONA GÓRA**			
WARSZAWA	J	C	1855/1930		PROVINCE: ŚLĄSK
ŻARY	A	L	1897–1944		119
WARSZAWA	J	S	1855/1930		PROVINCE: ŚLĄSK
WARSZAWA	J	Y	1855/1930		PROVINCE: ŚLĄSK
WARSZAWA	J	Z	1855/1930		PROVINCE: ŚLĄSK
ZAGÓRÓW		**KONIN**			
POZNAŃ	A	B	1826–1865; 1882; 1886–1891; 1893–1894		3760/1–35, 54A–81
ZAGÓRÓW	U	B	1895; 1897–1911; 1913–1919; 1923–1925; 1927–1929; 1931–1932; 1935–1938		
POZNAŃ	A	D	1826–1865; 1882; 1886–1891; 1893–1894		3760/1–35, 54A–81
ZAGÓRÓW	U	D	1895; 1897–1911; 1913–1919; 1923–1925; 1927–1929; 1931–1932; 1935–1938		
POZNAŃ	A	M	1826–1865; 1882; 1886–1891; 1893–1894		3760/1–81
ZAGÓRÓW	U	M	1895; 1897–1911; 1913–1919; 1923–1925; 1927–1929; 1931–1932; 1935–1938		
ZAGÓRZE		**KATOWICE**			
ZAGÓRZE	U	B	1890–1921; 1927–1928		
ZAGÓRZE	U	D	1890–1928		
ZAGÓRZE	U	M	1890–1920; 1922–1924		
ZAKLICZYN		**TARNÓW**			
ZAKLICZYN	U	B	1894–1942		
ZAKLICZYN	U	D	1896–1942		
LVOV	A	L	1785–1788; 1819–1820		19/1/272; 20/1/269
ZAKLIKÓW		**TARNOBRZEG**			
LUBLIN	A	B	1826–1854; 1885–1893		113
ZAKLIKÓW	U	B	1894–1912; 1916–1918; 1924–1940		
LUBLIN	A	D	1826–1863; 1882–1893		113
ZAKLIKÓW	U	D	1894–1914; 1916–1930; 1932–1940		
LUBLIN	A	M	1826–1854		113
ZAKLIKÓW	U	M	1916–1940		
LUBLIN	A	T	1870–1914; 1927–1929		RGL IV ADM; UWL WSP/787
ZAKROCZYM		**WARSZAWA**			
NOWY DWÓR MAZOWIECKI	A	B	1825–1876; 1879–1889; 1891–1903; 1905–1912; 1916–1920		143
NOWY DWÓR MAZOWIECKI	A	D	1825–1876; 1879–1889; 1891–1903; 1905–1912; 1916–1920		143

A Army/recruit lists; **B** Birth; **C** Census; **D** Death; **E** Voter lists; **G** Immigration; **H** Holocaust; **J** Judaica; **K** Kahal; **L** Land; **M** Marriage; **N** Name changes; **O** Police files; **P** Pogroms; **R** Reference; **S** School records; **T** Tax lists; **V** Divorce; **W** Occupation lists; **X** Jewish hospital; **Y** Notary records; **Z** Local government records

TOWN NAME Repository Location	VOIVODSHIP (Province) Repository Document Type Code	Years	Zespół/Sygnatura (Poland) Fond/Opis/Delo (Belarus, Ukraine, Lithuania)
NOWY DWÓR MAZOWIECKI	A M	1825–1876; 1879–1889; 1891–1903; 1905–1912; 1916–1920	143
ZALESIE	**PRZEMYŚL**		
PRZEWORSK	A S	1938	78/1–8, 10–15
ZALEWO	**OLSZTYN**		
OLSZTYN	A B	1874–1878; 1880; 1885; 1887–1890; 1893–1894	750/I
OLSZTYN	A D	1874–1883; 1886; 1888–1890	750/I
OLSZTYN	A M	1876–1883; 1886; 1888–1890; 1893–1894	750/I
ZAŁUBINCZE	**INCLUDED IN NOWY SĄCZ**		
ZAMBRÓW	**ŁOMŻA**		
ŁOMŻA	A B	1824–1865; 1867–1881; 1883; 1885–1890; 1892–1894; 1896–1898; 1901–1904; 1907–1910; 1912; 1914; 1922–1923; 1925–1927; 1934–1935	174
ŁOMŻA	A D	1824–1865; 1867–1881; 1883; 1885–1890; 1892–1894; 1896–1898; 1901; 1903–1904; 1907–1910; 1912; 1914; 1922–1923; 1925–1927; 1934–1935	174
BIAŁYSTOK	A K	1912	5/119
ŁOMŻA	A M	1824–1865; 1867–1881; 1883; 1885–1890; 1892–1894; 1896–1898; 1901; 1903–1904; 1907–1910; 1912; 1914; 1922–1923; 1925–1927; 1934–1935	174
ZAMOŚĆ	**ZAMOŚĆ**		
LUBLIN	A B	1826–1865; 1872–1882	113
ZAMOŚĆ	A B	1866–1890	209/1; 4; 6–7; 10
ZAMOŚĆ	U B	1891–1941	
ZAMOŚĆ	A C	1880–1951	25
LUBLIN	A D	1826–1830; 1832–1864; 1874–1878	113
ZAMOŚĆ	A D	1876–1890	209/3; 9; 11
ZAMOŚĆ	U D	1891–1942	
LUBLIN	A K	1867–1906; 1910–1911; 1913–1915; 1922–1936	RGL IV; RGCH/484; 403/838–840
LUBLIN	A M	1826–1830; 1832–1864	113
ZAMOŚĆ	A M	1865–1888	209
ZAMOŚĆ	U M	1889–1941	
ZAMOŚĆ	A S	1926–1939	12; 576–579
LUBLIN	A T	1867–1906; 1910–1911; 1913–1915; 1928–1936	RGL IV; RGCH/484; UWL WSP/838
ZAMOŚĆ	A T	1937–1948	9
ZAMOŚĆ	A Y	1810–1824; 1873–1939	131–146
ZAMOŚĆ	A Z	1821–1939	25
ZANIEMYŚL	**POZNAŃ**		
KOBLENZ	G B	1817–1839	
KOBLENZ	G D	1817–1839	
KOBLENZ	G M	1817–1839	
KOBLENZ	G N	1834–1853	
ZANOW	**SEE SIANÓW**		
ZARĘBY	**ŁOMŻA**		
WARSZAWA	J B	1808–1939	
PUŁTUSK	A B	1837–1873	273
ŁOMŻA	A B	1874–1880; 1893–1894	420
ZARĘBY	U B	1895–1935	
WARSZAWA	J D	1808–1939	
PUŁTUSK	A D	1837–1873	273
ŁOMŻA	A D	1874–1880; 1893–1894	420
ZARĘBY	U D	1895–1935	
WARSZAWA	J M	1808–1939	
PUŁTUSK	A M	1837–1873	273
ŁOMŻA	A M	1874–1880; 1893–1894	420
ZARĘBY	U M	1895–1935	
ŻARKI	**CZĘSTOCHOWA**		
CZĘSTOCHOWA	A B	1826–1888; 1895	295
ŻARKI	U B	1896–1902; 1905–1917; 1921–1942	
CZĘSTOCHOWA	A D	1826–1895	295
ŻARKI	U D	1896–1942	
KATOWICE	A K	1918–1919; 1922; 1928–1937	770/189, 511; 880/491–521
KATOWICE	A L	1914	794/196
CZĘSTOCHOWA	A M	1826–1895	295
ŻARKI	U M	1896–1898; 1900–1908; 1913–1914; 1920–1929; 1934–1942	

Repository type: **A** = Archive   **G** = LDS Films of German-Held Records   **J** = Jewish Historical Institute   **U** = Urząd Stanu Cywilnego

TOWN NAME	VOIVODSHIP (Province)			Zespół/Sygnatura (Poland)
Repository Location	Repository Document Type	Code	Years	Fond/Opis/Delo (Belarus, Ukraine, Lithuania)
CZĘSTOCHOWA	A	S	1919; 1925–1927; 1932–1933	174; 249–250
ŻARNÓW	**PIOTRKÓW TRYBUNALSKI**			
KIELCE	A	B	1826–1873	591
PIOTRKÓW TRYBUNALSKI	A	B	1865–1895	878
ŻARNÓW	U	B	1898–1942	
KIELCE	A	D	1826–1873	591
PIOTRKÓW TRYBUNALSKI	A	D	1845–1895	878
ŻARNÓW	U	D	1898–1942	
KIELCE	A	M	1826–1873	591
PIOTRKÓW TRYBUNALSKI	A	M	1845–1895	878
ŻARNÓW	U	M	1898–1942	
ŻARNOWIEC	**KATOWICE**			
KATOWICE	A	B	1811–1852; 1858–1868; 1882–1892	41
ŻARNOWIEC	U	B	1893–1938	
KATOWICE	A	D	1811–1852; 1858–1868; 1882–1892	41
ŻARNOWIEC	U	D	1893–1938	
KATOWICE	A	M	1811–1852; 1858–1868; 1882–1892	41
ŻARNOWIEC	U	M	1893–1938	
ŻARSZYN	**KROSNO**			
SANOK	A	C	1945–1951	21/50–52
LVOV	A	L	1785–1788; 1819–1820	19/XV/263
ŻARY	**ZIELONA GÓRA**			
ŻARY	A	L	1865–1940	90
ZASÓW	**TARNÓW**			
PRZEMYŚL	A	Y	1873	106
ZAWICHOST	**TARNOBRZEG**			
SANDOMIERZ	A	B	1826–1894	174
ZAWICHOST	U	B	1895–1913; 1915–1941	
SANDOMIERZ	A	D	1826–1894	174
ZAWICHOST	U	D	1895–1913; 1921–1941	
SANDOMIERZ	A	M	1826–1894	174
ZAWICHOST	U	M	1895–1913; 1915–1941	
ZAWIERCIE	**KATOWICE**			
ŁÓDŹ	A	A	1891–1901	17
ZAWIERCIE	U	B	1882–1941	
ZAWIERCIE	U	D	1882–1941	
ŁÓDŹ	A	K	1908–1910	1
KATOWICE	A	K	1925–1938	880/136–140, 176, 461–490; 770/188
ZAWIERCIE	U	M	1882–1941	
ŁÓDŹ	A	O	1905–1906	112
KATOWICE	A	P	1930–1936	880/239
KATOWICE	A	Y	1903–1914	1019/1–39; 1020/1–37
ZBĄSZYNEK	**ZIELONA GÓRA**			
GORZÓW WIELKOPOLSKI	A	B	1817–1819; 1837–1843; 1881	AMTSGERICHT TIRSCHTIEGEL 249/5230
GORZÓW WIELKOPOLSKI	A	D	1817–1819; 1837–1843; 1881	AMTSGERICHT TIRSCHTIEGEL 249/5232
GORZÓW WIELKOPOLSKI	A	M	1817–1819; 1837–1843; 1881	AMTSGERICHT TIRSCHTIEGEL 249/5231
ZDUŃSKA WOLA	**SIERADZ**			
ŁÓDŹ	A	B	1826–1893	270
ZDUŃSKA WOLA	U	B	1894–1942	
ŁÓDŹ	A	D	1826–1893	270
ZDUŃSKA WOLA	U	D	1894–1942	
ŁÓDŹ	A	M	1826–1893	270
ZDUŃSKA WOLA	U	M	1894–1939	
ZDUNY	**KALISZ**			
POZNAŃ	A	D	1818–1847	3597/1–2
KALISZ	A	L	1841–1943	91/272–275
POZNAŃ	A	M	1818–1847	3597/1
ŻELECHÓW	**SIEDLCE**			
ŻELECHÓW	U	B	1905	
LUBLIN	A	K	1913–1915; 1922–1936	RGL IV; UWL WSP/777
WARSZAWA	A	T	1886–1911	ZPG/531
LUBLIN	A	T	1913–1915; 1922–1936	RGL IV; UWL WSP/777
ZELÓW	**PIOTRKÓW TRYBUNALSKI**			
ZELÓW	U	B	1924–1925	

A Army/recruit lists; **B** Birth; **C** Census; **D** Death; **E** Voter lists; **G** Immigration; **H** Holocaust; **J** Judaica; **K** Kahal; **L** Land; **M** Marriage; **N** Name changes; **O** Police files; **P** Pogroms; **R** Reference; **S** School records; **T** Tax lists; **V** Divorce; **W** Occupation lists; **X** Jewish hospital; **Y** Notary records; **Z** Local government records

TOWN NAME	VOIVODSHIP (Province)				Zespół/Sygnatura (Poland)
Repository Location	Repository Type	Document Code	Years		Fond/Opis/Delo (Belarus, Ukraine, Lithuania)
ZELÓW	U	D	1924–1925		
ZELW	U	M	1924–1925		
ZGIERZ	**ŁÓDŹ**				
ŁÓDŹ	A	A	1890–1902		17
ŁÓDŹ	A	B	1826–1893		270
ZGIERZ	U	B	1894–1939		
ŁÓDŹ	A	D	1826–1893		270
ZGIERZ	U	D	1894–1939		
ŁÓDŹ	A	G	1867/1914		1
ŁÓDŹ	A	K	1878–1913		1
ŁÓDŹ	A	M	1826–1893		270
ZGIERZ	U	M	1894–1939		
ŁÓDŹ	A	O	1905–1906		41
ŁÓDŹ	A	S	1885–1913		83
PABIANICE	A	Z	1825–1864		150
ZGORZELEC	**JELENIA GÓRA**				
KOBLENZ	G	B	1864–1932		
KOBLENZ	G	D	1864–1932		
WROCŁAW	A	K	1800–1945		132
KOBLENZ	G	M	1864–1932		
ZIEGENHALS	**SEE GŁUCHOŁAZY**				
ZIELONA GÓRA	**ZIELONA GÓRA**				
WARSZAWA	J	E	1804/1916		PROVINCE: ŚLĄSK
WARSZAWA	J	K	1804/1916		PROVINCE: ŚLĄSK
STARY KISIELIN	A	K	1834/1908		CITY ACTS OF ZIELONA GÓRA
STARY KISIELIN	A	L	1865–1945		184
WARSZAWA	J	Y	1804/1916		PROVINCE: ŚLĄSK
WARSZAWA	J	Z	1804/1916		PROVINCE: ŚLĄSK
ZIELUŃ	**CIECHANÓW**				
ZIELUŃ	U	B	1916–1935		
ZIELUŃ	U	D	1916–1935		
KRAKÓW	A	G	1824		IT1592
ZIELUŃ	U	M	1916–1935		
ZŁOCZEW	**SIERADZ**				
ŁÓDŹ	A	B	1826–1880;1882–1893		270
ZŁOCZEW	U	B	1894–1939		
ŁÓDŹ	A	D	1826–1872;1889–1893		270
ZŁOCZEW	U	D	1894–1934;1938–1939		
ŁÓDŹ	A	M	1826–1872		270
ZŁOCZEW	U	M	1894;1900–1935		
ZŁOTÓW	**PIŁA**				
BERLIN	G	B	1813–1846		
BERLIN	G	D	1813–1846		
KOSZALIN	A	K	1785–1901		31/I/30,32,35,60–70
SZCZECIN	A	K	1833–1938		GMINA ZYDOWSKIE POMORZA ZACHONDNIEGO 133/137
BERLIN	G	M	1813–1846		
ZŁOTÓW REGION	**PIŁA**				
KOSZALIN	A	C	1834–1915		124/I/350–360
KOSZALIN	A	K	1834–1915		124/I/350–360
KOSZALIN	A	S	1834–1915		124/I/350–360
ŻMIGRÓD	**WROCŁAW**				
WARSZAWA	J	K	1860/1935		PROVINCE: ŚLĄSK
WARSZAWA	J	Y	1860/1935		PROVINCE: ŚLĄSK
WARSZAWA	J	Z	1860/1935		PROVINCE: ŚLĄSK
ZOBTEN	**SEE SOBÓTKA**				
ŻÓŁKIEWKA	**ZAMOŚĆ**				
LUBLIN	A	B	1826–1870;1875		113
ZAMOŚĆ	A	B	1871–1880		209/1–10
ŻÓŁKIEWKA	U	B	1883–1905;1907–1914;1918–1928; 1930–1936		
LUBLIN	A	C	1910		ZPK/130
LUBLIN	A	D	1826–1870;1875		113
ZAMOŚĆ	A	D	1871–1880		209/1–10
ŻÓŁKIEWKA	U	D	1883–1905;1907–1914;1918–1928; 1930–1936		
LUBLIN	A	E	1873–1914		RGL IV ADM.
LUBLIN	A	K	1873–1914;1927		RGL IV ADM;UWL WSP/791
LUBLIN	A	M	1826–1870;1875		113

Repository type: **A** = Archive   **G** = LDS Films of German-Held Records   **J** = Jewish Historical Institute   **U** = Urząd Stanu Cywilnego

TOWN NAME	VOIVODSHIP (Province)			Zespół/Sygnatura (Poland)
Repository Location	Repository Document Type	Code	Years	Fond/Opis/Delo (Belarus, Ukraine, Lithuania)
ZAMOŚĆ	A	M	1871–1880	209/1–10
ŻÓŁKIEWKA	U	M	1883–1905;1907–1914;1918–1928; 1930–1936	
LUBLIN	A	T	1873–1914;1927	
ŻOŁYNIA	**RZESZOW**			
ŻOŁYNIA	U	B	1922–1939	
ŻOŁYNIA	U	D	1922–1939	
PRZEMYŚL	A	M	1916–1922	154/1
ŻOŁYNIA	U	M	1923–1939	
ŻORY	**KATOWICE**			
RACIBÓRZ	A	C	1930–1932; 1945–1947	
KOBLENZ	G	D	1837–1879	
ZUBEŃSKO	**KROSNO**			
SANOK	A	C	1932–1946	31/2–8(8)
ZUELZ	**SEE BIAŁA**			
ŻURAWICA	**PRZEMYŚL**			
PRZEMYŚL	A	C	1925–1951	212/52–55, 59–61, 63, 74–75
LVOV	A	L	1785–1788; 1819–1820	19/XIII/352; 20/XIII/74
ŻUROMIN	**CIECHANÓW**			
DZIAŁDOWO	A	B	1826–1904	31
ŻUROMIN	U	B	1905–1907; 1909–1913; 1916–1937	
DZIAŁDOWO	A	D	1826–1904	31
ŻUROMIN	U	D	1905–1907; 1909–1913; 1916–1937	
DZIAŁDOWO	A	M	1826–1829; 1841–1904	31
DZIAŁDOWO	A	M	1843–1871; 1873–1879; 1901; 1903–1904; 1906; 1916–1938 (MARRIAGE APPLICATIONS)	31
ŻUROMIN	U	M	1905–1907; 1909–1913; 1916–1937	
ZWIERZYNIEC	**ZAMOŚĆ**			
LUBLIN	A	K	1927–1928	UWL WSP/1566
LUBLIN	A	T	1927–1928	UWL WSP/1566
ZWOLEŃ	**RADOM**			
RADOM	A	B	1826–1883; 1886–1894	194
ZWOLEŃ	U	B	1895–1914; 1916–1935; 1937	
RADOM	A	D	1826–1883; 1886–1894	194
ZWOLEŃ	U	D	1895–1914; 1916–1935; 1937	
RADOM	A	M	1826–1883; 1886–1894	194
ZWOLEŃ	U	M	1895–1914; 1916–1935; 1937	
ŻYWIEC	A	L	1932	13/42
ŻYWIEC	A	W	1918–1939	232/STZ-II/171
ŻYCHLIN	**PŁOCK**			
KUTNO	A	A	1862	3/23
KUTNO	A`	B	1873	82
BERLIN	G	B	1903–1913	
KUTNO	A	C	1858–1859; 1865; 1872	21/22, 164, 166–167, 169, 178; 3/173
WARSZAWA	J	C	1918–1939	106/111
KUTNO	A	D	1873	82
WARSZAWA	J	K	1918–1939	106/111
KUTNO	A	M	1873	82
WARSZAWA	J	T	1918–1939	106/111
KUTNO	A	Y	1929–1951	79/1ű29
KUTNO	A	Z	1908	21/134
ŻYRARDÓW	**SKIERNIEWICE**			
ŻYRARDÓW	A	B	1886–1887	308
ŻYRARDÓW	U	B	1888–1914; 1916–1940	
ŻYRARDÓW	A	D	1886–1887	308
ŻYRARDÓW	U	D	1886–1998	
ŻYRARDÓW	A	M	1886–1887	308
ŻYRARDÓW	U	M	1888–1914; 1916–1940	
ŻYWIEC	**BIELSKO BIAŁA**			
ŻYWIEC	A	A	1884; 1886–1889; 1912; 1915; 1919–1925	14/1; 1/34–35
ŻYWIEC	A	G	1915–1931	1/86
ŻYWIEC	A	L	1932	13/42
ŻYWIEC	A	W	1918–1939	232/STZ-II/171
ŻYWIEC REGION	**BIELSKO BIAŁA**			
KRAKÓW	A	A	1919–1933	232/STZ-II/276–306
KRAKÓW	A	C	1919–1939	232/STZ-II/116–134, 136
ŻYWIEC	A	C	1939–1940; 1945–1947	17/5; 15/148; 13/42
KRAKÓW	A	G	1920–1939	232/STZ-II/111

A Army/recruit lists; **B** Birth; **C** Census; **D** Death; **E** Voter lists; **G** Immigration; **H** Holocaust; **J** Judaica; **K** Kahal; **L** Land; **M** Marriage; **N** Name changes; **O** Police files; **P** Pogroms; **R** Reference; **S** School records; **T** Tax lists; **V** Divorce; **W** Occupation lists; **X** Jewish hospital; **Y** Notary records; **Z** Local government records

ARCHIVAL HOLDINGS INDEXED BY REPOSITORY
Polish State Archives

by Miriam Weiner

TOWN NAME Document Type Years	VOIVODSHIP/OBLAST (Province)	COUNTRY Zespół/Sygnatura (Poland) Fond/Opis/Delo (Belarus, Ukraine, Lithuania)

BIAŁYSTOK Archives

BIAŁYSTOK	**BIAŁYSTOK**	**POLAND**
A 1903–1917		42
B 1835; 1839; 1846; 1848; 1855–1866; 1869; 1871–1872; 1874–1875; 1877–1884; 1886; 1888–1894		264
C 1847–1850		64/24
D 1846; 1852; 1854–1877; 1879–1882; 1884–1886; 1888–1890; 1892–1894		264
K 1913		447/1–2
L 1853; 1910		733/2; 30/3
M 1854; 1856–1894		264
V 1858–1862; 1864–1873; 1875–1876; 1878–1882; 1884–1894		264
X 1913		441
Y 1882–1914; 1919–1939		280–298
Z 1941–1944 (MORTGAGE REGISTRATIONS)		561/338
BIELSK PODLASKI	**BIAŁYSTOK**	**POLAND**
B 1835; 1842; 1871		545
D 1835		545
M 1835; 1868		545
Y 1883–1909		553–560
BRAŃSK	**BIAŁYSTOK**	**POLAND**
T 1946–1950		566
Y 1924–1932		862
CHOROSZCZ	**BIAŁYSTOK**	**POLAND**
A 1903–1914		42
B 1882–1888; 1890–1892		935
CIECHANOWIEC	**ŁOMZA**	**POLAND**
B 1839; 1843–1847; 1849–1851; 1853–1859; 1865; 1867–1870		544
D 1839; 1843–1847; 1849–1851; 1853–1859; 1865; 1867–1870		544
M 1839; 1843–1847; 1849–1851; 1853–1859; 1865; 1867; 1869–1870		544
GRAJEWO	**ŁOMZA**	**POLAND**
K 1911		6/167
GRODNO REGION	**GRODNO**	**BELARUS**
A 1804–1883		41/13
LAZDIJAI	**LAZDIJAI**	**LITHUANIA**
B 1808–1825; 1827–1854		
D 1818–1825; 1827–1854		
M 1808–1825; 1827–1854		
ŁOMŻA	**ŁOMŻA**	**POLAND**
K 1868–1883; 1887–1889; 1893–1906		6/120; 15/92,129
X 1902–1909		15/311
ŁOMŻA REGION	**ŁOMŻA**	**POLAND**
K 1910–1912; 1914–1915		6/143,195
MAKÓW MAZOWIECKI	**OSTROŁEKA**	**POLAND**
K 1914–1915		6/200,203,208
ORLA	**BIAŁYSTOK**	**POLAND**
B 1836; 1846		545
D 1836		545
M 1836; 1860		545
OSTROŁEKA	**OSTROŁEKA**	**POLAND**
K 1910		6/148

A Army/recruit lists; **B** Birth; **C** Census; **D** Death; **E** Voter lists; **G** Immigration; **H** Holocaust; **J** Judaica; **K** Kahal; **L** Land; **M** Marriage; **N** Name changes; **O** Police files; **P** Pogroms; **R** Reference; **S** School records; **T** Tax lists; **V** Divorce; **W** Occupation lists; **X** Jewish hospital; **Y** Notary records; **Z** Local government records

TOWN NAME Document Type Years	VOIVODSHIP/OBLAST (Province)	COUNTRY Zespół /Sygnatura (Poland) Fond/Opis/Delo (Belarus, Ukraine, Lithuania)
RAJGRÓD	**ŁOMŻA**	**POLAND**
K 1914–1915		6/186
SIEMIATYCZE	**BIAŁYSTOK**	**POLAND**
K 1861		564
SOKÓŁKA	**BIAŁYSTOK**	**POLAND**
A 1863–1874		724
Y 1883–1936		302–309
SOKOŁY	**ŁOMŻA**	**POLAND**
B 1826–1830; 1832; 1834; 1839–1841; 1846; 1848–1849; 1851; 1853; 1859; 1863; 1865; 1867; 1869–1872;1875;1878; 1881		265
D 1826–1830; 1834; 1839–1841; 1846; 1848–1849; 1851; 1853; 1859; 1863; 1865; 1867; 1869–1872; 1878; 1881		265
M 1826–1830; 1834; 1839–1841; 1846; 1848–1851; 1853; 1859; 1863; 1865; 1867; 1869–1872; 1875; 1878; 1881		265
SUWAŁKI	**SUWAŁKI**	**POLAND**
X 1870–1915		26/85–99,209–220
TIKTIN	**SEE TYKOCIN**	
TYKOCIN	**BIAŁYSTOK**	**POLAND**
B 1826–1844; 1846–1847; 1852–1853; 1856–1862; 1864; 1866–1876; 1880–1881; 1883–1885; 1890		266
D 1827–1831; 1833; 1835–1839; 1841–1842; 1844; 1846–1847; 1852–1853; 1856–1883; 1885; 1890		266
G 1899		67/6
K 1910–1912		6/163,166
L 1904		67/7
M 1827–1831; 1833; 1835–1839; 1841–1842; 1844; 1846–1847; 1852–1853; 1856–1862; 1864; 1866; 1868; 1871–1876; 1880–1881; 1883; 1885; 1890		266
Y 1928–1939		310–311
WĘGRÓW	**SIEDLCE**	**POLAND**
K 1900–1912; 1914–1915		6/141,174
ZAMBRÓW	**ŁOMŻA**	**POLAND**
K 1912		5/119

BIELSKO BIAŁA Branch Archives

BIELSKO BIAŁA	**BIELSKO BIAŁA**	**POLAND**
G 1946–1947		5/355–356,358–360,367

BOCHNIA Branch Archives

BOCHNIA	**TARNÓW**	**POLAND**
A 1937 (ALPHA INDEX)		1 ZMB/501
C 1830–1952		1 ZMB/141,144,499–499A; 1/535
G 1922–1943		1 ZMB/496,500
H 1940; 1943		1/ZMB 766
L 1926		1/ZMB 503
T 1941–1945		1/824,835
W 1830/1952		1/ZMB 499
Z 1924–1933 (LIST OF BUSINESSES)		ZMB/535
WIŚNICZ	**TARNÓW**	**POLAND**
B 1814–1897		76/OMW 1–7
D 1859–1895		76/OMW 8–9
M 1827–1876		76/OMW 3
WOJNICZ	**TARNÓW**	**POLAND**
B 1829–1875		76/OMB 1–3

BYDGOSZCZ Archives

BYDGOSZCZ	**BYDGOSZCZ**	**POLAND**
B 1823–1894		378; 1663
D 1823–1894		378; 1663
K 1874–1939		224
M 1823–1894		378; 1663
S 1826–1921		2
Z 1773–1919		189
FORDON	**BYDGOSZCZ**	**POLAND**
B 1820–1892		380; 1685
D 1820–1892		380; 1685
M 1820–1892		380; 1685

A Army/recruit lists; **B** Birth; **C** Census; **D** Death; **E** Voter lists; **G** Immigration; **H** Holocaust; **J** Judaica; **K** Kahal; **L** Land; **M** Marriage; **N** Name changes; **O** Police files; **P** Pogroms; **R** Reference; **S** School records; **T** Tax lists; **V** Divorce; **W** Occupation lists; **X** Jewish hospital; **Y** Notary records; **Z** Local government records

TOWN NAME Document Type Years	VOIVODSHIP/OBLAST (Province)	COUNTRY Zespół/Sygnatura (Poland) Fond/Opis/Delo (Belarus, Ukraine, Lithuania)
KORONOWO	**BYDGOSZCZ**	**POLAND**
B 1847–1894		381; 1713
G 1920–1935		192
LOBSENS	**SEE ŁOBŻENICA**	**POLAND**
ŁOBŻENICA	**PIŁA**	**POLAND**
G 1885–1912		194
K 1837–1915; 1923–1930		194
S 1857–1911		194
NAKŁO NAD NOTECIĄ	**BYDGOSZCZ**	**POLAND**
B 1823–1889		383; 1741
C 1857–1945		195
D 1823–1887		383; 1741
M 1823–1887		383; 1741
RYNARZEWO	**BYDGOSZCZ**	**POLAND**
B 1823–1852; 1874–1893		385; 1770
D 1824–1849; 1874–1893		385; 1770
M 1824–1851; 1874–1893		385; 1770
SOLEC KUJAWSKI	**BYDGOSZCZ**	**POLAND**
B 1823–1847; 1874–1893		388; 1775
D 1823–1847; 1874–1893		388; 1775
M 1823–1847; 1874–1893		388; 1775
Z 1811–1910		197
ŚWIECIE	**BYDGOSZCZ**	**POLAND**
C 1923–1931		199
E 1920–1931		199
SZUBIN	**BYDGOSZCZ**	**POLAND**
B 1820–1847; 1874–1893		377
D 1820–1834; 1874–1893		377
G 1920–1935		198
M 1820–1834; 1874–1893		377
Z 1833–1923		198
TUCHEL	**SEE TUCHOLA**	
TUCHOLA	**BYDGOSZCZ**	**POLAND**
B 1812–1834; 1874–1893		1674
D 1812–1834; 1874–1893		1674
M 1812–1834; 1874–1893		1674
Z 1786–1919		1674
WIECBORK	**BYDGOSZCZ**	**POLAND**
B 1825–1847; 1874–1894		389; 1804
D 1825–1847; 1874–1894		389; 1804
M 1825–1847; 1874–1894		389; 1804
Z 1812–1905		1676
WIRSITZ	**SEE WYRZYSK**	
WYRZYSK	**PIŁA**	**POLAND**
B 1818–1847		384
D 1818–1847		384
M 1818–1847		384
Z 1923–1936		200

CIESZYN Branch Archives

TOWN NAME Document Type Years	VOIVODSHIP/OBLAST	COUNTRY
CIESZYN	**BIELSKO BIAŁA**	**POLAND**
A 1662/1945		13/I/214–219,245–264
B 1841–1849		13/I/470
C 1851–1905; 1911–1931		13/I/476
D 1838–1846		13/I
E 1861–1902; 1922; 1935–1938		13/I/130–147,154–179
K 1839–1843		13/I/1155
L 1839–1843		13/I/1155
Z 1919–1945		13/I
GOLESZÓW	**BIELSKO BIAŁA**	**POLAND**
A 1894–1936		102/II/7,18
H 1941–1944 (DEATH BOOK)		102/II/40
STRUMIEŃ	**BIELSKO BIAŁA**	**POLAND**
A 1857–1868		10/I/19–26

A Army/recruit lists; **B** Birth; **C** Census; **D** Death; **E** Voter lists; **G** Immigration; **H** Holocaust; **J** Judaica; **K** Kahal; **L** Land; **M** Marriage; **N** Name changes; **O** Police files; **P** Pogroms; **R** Reference; **S** School records; **T** Tax lists; **V** Divorce; **W** Occupation Lists; **X** Jewish hospital; **Y** Notary records; **Z** Local government records

TOWN NAME Document Type Years	VOIVODSHIP/OBLAST (Province)	COUNTRY Zespół/Sygnatura (Poland) Fond/Opis/Delo (Belarus, Ukraine, Lithuania)
STRUMIEŃ REGION	**BIELSKO BIAŁA**	**POLAND**
C 1861–1867		10/I/95–116
WISŁA REGION	**BIELSKO BIAŁA**	**POLAND**
H 1940–1943		116/II/1–7
WODZISŁAW	**KATOWICE**	**POLAND**
A 1742–1752; 1809–1919		84/I/48–51

CZĘSTOCHOWA Archives

CZĘSTOCHOWA	**CZĘSTOCHOWA**	**POLAND**
B 1826–1895		58
C 1915–1939		1
D 1826–1895		58
K 1933–1939		60
L 1918–1939		1
M 1826–1895		58
S 1915–1917		1
W 1940–1941; 1945		1
X 1915–1917		1
Z 1835/1914		1
GORZÓW ŚLĄSKI	**CZĘSTOCHOWA**	**POLAND**
B 1874–1884		226
D 1874–1884		226
M 1874–1884		226
JANÓW	**CZĘSTOCHOWA**	**POLAND**
B 1863–1895		309
C 1914		67
D 1880–1895		309
M 1880–1895		309
KŁOBUCK	**CZĘSTOCHOWA**	**POLAND**
B 1826–1895		107
D 1826–1895		107
M 1826–1895		107
KRZEPICE	**CZĘSTOCHOWA**	**POLAND**
B 1830–1895		113
D 1830–1895		113
M 1830–1895		113
S 1924		97
LELÓW	**CZĘSTOCHOWA**	**POLAND**
B 1873–1895		246
D 1873–1895		246
M 1873–1895		246
MSTÓW	**CZĘSTOCHOWA**	**POLAND**
B 1826–1895		92
D 1826–1895		92
M 1826–1895		92
OLESNO	**CZĘSTOCHOWA**	**POLAND**
B 1874–1884		258
D 1874–1884		258
M 1874–1884		258
PRASZKA	**CZĘSTOCHOWA**	**POLAND**
B 1869–1895		267
D 1869–1895		267
M 1869–1895		267
PRZYRÓW	**CZĘSTOCHOWA**	**POLAND**
B 1826–1895		95
D 1826–1895		95
G 1921–1924		73
K 1915–1924		73
M 1826–1895		95
SZCZEKOCINY	**CZĘSTOCHOWA**	**POLAND**
B 1826–1895		281
D 1826–1895		281
M 1826–1895		281

A Army/recruit lists; **B** Birth; **C** Census; **D** Death; **E** Voter lists; **G** Immigration; **H** Holocaust; **J** Judaica; **K** Kahal; **L** Land; **M** Marriage; **N** Name changes;
O Police files; **P** Pogroms; **R** Reference; **S** School records; **T** Tax lists; **V** Divorce; **W** Occupation lists; **X** Jewish hospital; **Y** Notary records; **Z** Local government records

TOWN NAME Document Type Years	VOIVODSHIP/OBLAST (Province)	COUNTRY Zespół/Sygnatura (Poland) Fond/Opis/Delo (Belarus, Ukraine, Lithuania)
ŻARKI	**CZĘSTOCHOWA**	**POLAND**
B 1826–1888; 1895		295
D 1826–1895		295
M 1826–1895		295
S 1919; 1925–1927; 1932–1933		174; 249–250

DZIAŁDOWO Branch Archives

BIEŻUŃ	**CIECHANÓW**	**POLAND**
B 1857–1858; 1877–1884		77
D 1857–1858; 1878–1884		77
M 1857–1858		77
KUCZBORK	**CIECHANÓW**	**POLAND**
B 1826–1863; 1865–1892; 1894–1907		151
D 1826–1832; 1839–1846; 1848–1852; 1854–1863; 1865–1892; 1894–1907		151
M 1826–1832; 1839–1846; 1848–1852; 1854–1863; 1865–1892; 1894–1907		56
RACIĄŻ	**CIECHANÓW**	**POLAND**
B 1876–1894		34
D 1876–1894		34
M 1876–1894		34
M 1876–1893 (MARRIAGE APPLICATIONS)		34
RADZANÓW	**CIECHANÓW**	**POLAND**
B 1826–1828; 1834–1842; 1846–1848; 1850–1873; 1875–1888; 1890–1894		53
D 1826–1828; 1834–1842; 1846–1848; 1850–1873; 1875–1888; 1890–1894		53
M 1826–1828; 1834–1842; 1846–1848; 1850–1873; 1875–1888; 1890–1894		53
M 1843; 1845; 1847; 1849; 1852; 1856; 1861–1862; 1865; 1870 (MARRIAGE APPLICATIONS)		53
SZREŃSK	**CIECHANÓW**	**POLAND**
B 1827–1834; 1837–1846; 1848–1885		29
D 1826–1885		29
M 1827–1834; 1837–1846; 1848–1885 1852 (MARRIAGE APPLICATIONS)		29
ŻUROMIN	**CIECHANÓW**	**POLAND**
B 1826–1904		31
D 1826–1904		31
M 1826–1829; 1841–1904		31

ELBLĄG Branch Archives (in Malbork)

MALBORK	**ELBLĄG**	**POLAND**
C 1855/1940		60; 91/1–107
E 1885; 1896; 1908		60; 91/109–115
J 1856–1937		60/63–64
K 1818–1897		90/23–24,45,60; 92/1–61

EŁK Branch Archives

GRAJEWO	**ŁOMŻA**	**POLAND**
Y 1902–1914; 1919–1939		63–64,140,185
SZCZUCZYN	**ŁOMŻA**	**POLAND**
A 1874/1917		214
C 1894		212/189
E 1882–1883; 1898–1913		212/394,402,414,425,453,459,478,560–561,564, 566,957,1377,1451,1591,1599,1648, 1650,1753, 1758,1812–1813,1915–1916, 1920–1923, 1939–1940,1997–2302

GDAŃSK Archives

BERENT	**SEE KOŚCIERZYNA**	
DANZIG	**SEE GDAŃSK**	
DIRSCHAU	**SEE TCZEW**	
ELBING	**SEE ELBLĄG**	
ELBLĄG	**ELBLĄG**	**POLAND**
B 1801–1808; 1812–1874		369/2/4899; 372/47,50–51
C 1812/1900		369/2/4901
D 1812–1874		372/47–48,50–51
K 1772/1912; 1939		373/72
M 1801–1808; 1812–1874		369/2/4899; 372/47; 49–51

A Army/recruit lists; **B** Birth; **C** Census; **D** Death; **E** Voter lists; **G** Immigration; **H** Holocaust; **J** Judaica; **K** Kahal; **L** Land; **M** Marriage; **N** Name changes; **O** Police files; **P** Pogroms; **R** Reference; **S** School records; **T** Tax lists; **V** Divorce; **W** Occupation Lists; **X** Jewish hospital; **Y** Notary records; **Z** Local government records

TOWN NAME Document Type Years	VOIVODSHIP/OBLAST (Province)	COUNTRY Zespół/Sygnatura (Poland) Fond/Opis/Delo (Belarus, Ukraine, Lithuania)
GDAŃSK	**GDAŃSK**	**POLAND**
G 1932–1939		260/2171–2177
H 1933–1941		96/85; 264/23,27
K 1545/1793; 1807–1814		10; 98/276; 300
O 1922–1932		14/5945
P 1938		2384/50/VI/20
T 1377/1794; 1807–1814		300/12
W 1405/1814		300; 58/50,78–79
Z 1559–1794; 1807–1814		300; 93/55E
GDAŃSK REGION	**GDAŃSK**	**POLAND**
B 1828/1846; 1847–1879; 1880/1934		1497/1–2,5–16,46,48,50,56,61–62,65,71–76
D 1828/1840; 1841–1879; 1880/1934		1497/1; 35–46; 53–54; 58; 60–61; 64–65; 71–76
H 1939–1941		263/2
L 1939–1941		264/23,27
M 1828/1846; 1847–1879; 1880/1934		1497/1,3–4,17–34,46–47,49,51–52,57,59,61,63, 65,67– 76
GDYNIA	**GDAŃSK**	**POLAND**
G 1925–1939		1036/42–44,47,78–79,149–151,1067,1091–1093; 124/2299–2301
H 1939–1941		264/23,27
L 1939–1941		264/23,27
KARTHAUS	**SEE KARTUZY**	
KARTUZY	**GDAŃSK**	**POLAND**
O 1921–1923		44/21,28,32
KOŚCIERZYNA	**GDAŃSK**	**POLAND**
B 1847–1884		1497/56
D 1847–1874		1497/58
M 1848–1874		1497/57
LAUENBERG	**SEE LĘBORK**	
LĘBORK	**SŁUPSK**	**POLAND**
K 1886–1940		1953/592
MALBORK	**ELBLĄG**	**POLAND**
B 1847–1934		1497/46,48,50
D 1847/1906		1497/46,53–54
K 1906–1940		508/2533–2534,2536
M 1847–1916		1497/46–47,49,51–52
MARIENBERG	**SEE MALBORK**	
NEUSTADT	**SEE WEJHEROWO**	
NEUTEICH	**SEE NOWY STAW**	
NOWY STAW	**ELBLĄG**	**POLAND**
C 1900–1929		518/9
PREUSSISCH STARGARD	**SEE STAROGARD**	
PUCK	**GDAŃSK**	**POLAND**
O 1925; 1928		46/9
PUTZIG	**SEE PUCK**	**POLAND**
SOPOT	**GDAŃSK**	**POLAND**
K 1856–1934		7/133–134; 521/1154
STAROGARD	**GDAŃSK**	**POLAND**
K 1923–1927		1632/17
STUHM	**SEE SZTUM**	
SZTUM	**ELBLĄG**	**POLAND**
B 1812–1848		1497/65
D 1812–1848		1497/65
M 1812–1848		1497/65
TCZEW	**GDAŃSK**	**POLAND**
B 1828–1874; 1888(ONE RECORD); 1897(ONE RECORD)		1497/61–62
D 1828–1874		1497/61,64
M 1828–1874		1497/61,63
WEJHEROWO	**GDAŃSK**	**POLAND**
D 1848–1881		1497/60
H 1940–1942		37/264
M 1847–1874		1497/59

A Army/recruit lists; **B** Birth; **C** Census; **D** Death; **E** Voter lists; **G** Immigration; **H** Holocaust; **J** Judaica; **K** Kahal; **L** Land; **M** Marriage; **N** Name changes;
O Police files; **P** Pogroms; **R** Reference; **S** School records; **T** Tax lists; **V** Divorce; **W** Occupation lists; **X** Jewish hospital; **Y** Notary records; **Z** Local government records

TOWN NAME Document Type Years	VOIVODSHIP/OBLAST (Province)	COUNTRY Zespół/Sygnatura (Poland) Fond/Opis/Delo (Belarus, Ukraine, Lithuania)

GLIWICE Branch Archives

GLEIWITZ	**SEE GLIWICE**	
GLIWICE	**KATOWICE**	**POLAND**
B 1812–1847		1/I/5852
C 1812–1822; 1846–1874		1/I/5861–5863
D 1812–1849		1/I/5855
E 1811–1861		1/I/5840
M 1812–1847		1/I/5859
GLIWICE REGION	**KATOWICE**	**POLAND**
K 1812–1900		1/I/5813–5863
SOŚNICOWICE	**KATOWICE**	**POLAND**
B 1812–1847		1/I/5851
D 1812–1847		1/I/5851
TOSZEK	**KATOWICE**	**POLAND**
B 1812–1847		1/I/5851
D 1812–1847		1/I/5851
TOSZEK REGION	**KATOWICE**	**POLAND**
K 1812–1900		1/I/5813–5863
WIELOWIEŚ	**KATOWICE**	**POLAND**
B 1812–1847		1/I/5851
D 1812–1847		1/I/5851
K 1812–1900		1/I/5813–5863
ZABRZE	**KATOWICE**	**POLAND**
C 1937		95/II/55
E 1917–1923		29/II/160
K 1896–1922		35/I/280,298,311,322
S 1847–1912		29/II/245–249

GÓRA KALWARIA Branch Archives

CZERSK	**WARSZAWA**	**POLAND**
B 1828–1836		128
D 1828–1836		128
M 1828–1836		128
GÓRA KALWARIA	**WARSZAWA**	**POLAND**
B 1808–1810; 1813–1816; 1818; 1820–1893		171; 127
D 1806–1810; 1813–1816; 1818; 1820–1893		171; 127
M 1808–1810; 1813–1816; 1818; 1820–1893		171; 127
Y 1808–1834; 1876–1939		92–94; 101; 116–119
GOSZCZYN	**RADOM**	**POLAND**
B 1808–1837		150; 35
C 1885–1931		61
D 1808–1836		150; 35
M 1808–1836		150; 35
GROJEC	**RADOM**	**POLAND**
B 1808–1811; 1813–1875		151; 36
C 1870–1931		87
D 1808–1811; 1813–1875		151; 36
M 1808–1811; 1813–1875		151; 36
MOGIELNICA	**RADOM**	**POLAND**
B 1808–1813; 1815; 1818–1873		159; 37
C 1885–1931		130
D 1808–1813; 1815; 1818–1873		159; 37
M 1808–1813; 1815; 1818–1873		159; 37
PIASECZNO	**WARSZAWA**	**POLAND**
B 1808–1825; 1829; 1833–1836; 1869–1894; 1910		173; 123
C 1842–1852; 1889–1933		129
D 1808–1825; 1829; 1833–1836; 1869–1882; 1884; 1886–1887; 1889–1893; 1910		173; 123
M 1808–1825; 1829; 1833–1836; 1869–1882; 1884; 1886–1887; 1889–1893; 1910		173; 123
PRZYBYSZEW	**RADOM**	**POLAND**
B 1808–1836		163; 126
D 1808–1836		163; 126
M 1808–1836		163; 126
TARCZYN	**WARSZAWA**	**POLAND**
B 1808–1837; 1844–1873; 1875–1894		165; 125

A Army/recruit lists; **B** Birth; **C** Census; **D** Death; **E** Voter lists; **G** Immigration; **H** Holocaust; **J** Judaica; **K** Kahal; **L** Land; **M** Marriage; **N** Name changes; **O** Police files; **P** Pogroms; **R** Reference; **S** School records; **T** Tax lists; **V** Divorce; **W** Occupation Lists; **X** Jewish hospital; **Y** Notary records; **Z** Local government records

TOWN NAME Document Type Years	VOIVODSHIP/OBLAST (Province)	COUNTRY Zespół/Sygnatura (Poland) Fond/Opis/Delo (Belarus, Ukraine, Lithuania)
D 1808–1837; 1844–1873; 1875–1894 M 1808–1837; 1844–1873; 1875–1894		165; 125 165; 125
WARKA	**RADOM**	**POLAND**
B 1808–1872 D 1808–1872 M 1808–1872		166; 124 166; 124 166; 124

GORZÓW WIELKOPOLSKI Branch Archives

BRÓJCE	**GORZÓW WIELKOPOLSKI**	**POLAND**
B 1817–1823; 1825–1831; 1833–1835; 1841; 1845–1847 D 1817–1823; 1825–1831; 1833–1835; 1841; 1845–1847 M 1817–1823; 1825–1831; 1833–1835; 1841; 1845–1847		AMTSGERICHT MESERITZ 247/5593 AMTSGERICHT MESERITZ 247/5595 AMTSGERICHT MESERITZ 247/5594
GORZÓW WIELKOPOLSKI	**GORZÓW WIELKOPOLSKI**	**POLAND**
B 1837–1865; 1870–1872 D 1847–1874 E 1927; 1935 K 1656/1842 M 1847–1870; 1872–1874		AMTSGERICHT LANDSBERG/W.28/1338–1343 AMTSGERICHT LANDSBERG/W.28/ 1337A–1337F MAGISTRAT LANDSBERG/W.30/6637 MAGISTRAT LANDSBERG/W.30/ 1978–2016,6636–6648 AMTSGERICHT LANDSBERG/W.28/1346–1347B
LANDSBERG AN DER WARTHE	**SEE GORZÓW WIELKOPOLSKI**	
MESERITZ	**SEE MIĘDZYRZECZ**	
MIĘDZYRZECZ	**GORZÓW WIELKOPOLSKI**	**POLAND**
B 1817–1825; 1828; 1835; 1837; 1839–1841; 1843–1844; 1846–1864 D 1817–1825; 1828; 1835; 1837; 1839–1841; 1843–1844; 1846–1864 M 1817–1825; 1828; 1835; 1837; 1839–1841; 1843–1844; 1846–1864		AMTSGERICHT MESERITZ 247/5590 AMTSGERICHT MESERITZ 247/5592 AMTSGERICHT MESERITZ 247/5591
NEU BENTSCHEN	**SEE ZBĄSZYNEK**	
SKWIERZYNA	**GORZÓW WIELKOPOLSKI**	**POLAND**
C 1834–1841; 1848 K 1835 R 1834–1847 S 1826–1835; 1856–1858 Z 1807–1831		MAGISTRAT SCHWERIN 185/294,296 MAGISTRAT SCHWERIN 185/295 MAGISTRAT SCHWERIN 185/297 MAGISTRAT SCHWERIN 185/398–401 MAGISTRAT SCHWERIN 185/298
ŚWIERKOCIN	**GORZÓW WIELKOPOLSKI**	**POLAND**
B 1828–1836 D 1830; 1835 M 1827; 1830; 1836		AMTSGERICHT LANDSBERG W.28/1370 AMTSGERICHT LANDSBERG W.28/1370 AMTSGERICHT LANDSBERG W.28/1370
TIRSCHTIEGEL	**SEE TRZCIEL**	**POLAND**
TRZCIEL	**GORZÓW WIELKOPOLSKI**	**POLAND**
D 1817–1823; 1825–1834; 1844–1845 M 1817–1823; 1825–1834; 1844–1845		AMTSGERICHT TIRSCHTIEGEL 249/ 5227–5229,5232 AMTSGERICHT TIRSCHTIEGEL 249/ 5226,5228–5229,5231
ZBĄSZYNEK	**ZIELONA GÓRA**	**POLAND**
B 1817–1819; 1837–1843; 1881 D 1817–1819; 1837–1843; 1881 M 1817–1819; 1837–1843; 1881		AMTSGERICHT TIRSCHTIEGEL 249/5230 AMTSGERICHT TIRSCHTIEGEL 249/5232 AMTSGERICHT TIRSCHTIEGEL 249/5231

INOWROCŁAW Branch Archives

GĘBICE	**BYDGOSZCZ**	**POLAND**
B 1832–1845; 1847–1848 D 1832–1845; 1847–1848 M 1832–1845; 1847–1848		110/1–2 110/1–2 110/1–2
GNIEWKOWO	**BYDGOSZCZ**	**POLAND**
B 1815–1847 D 1816–1847 L 1836–1920 M 1825–1847 S 1844/1907 T 1836–1920		111 111 56/362–545,907–912 111 56 56/787–788,1161–1234
INOWROCŁAW	**BYDGOSZCZ**	**POLAND**
C 19TH CENTURY–1950 K 1938 Y 1834–1868		57 2 1

A Army/recruit lists;   **B** Birth;   **C** Census;   **D** Death;   **E** Voter lists;   **G** Immigration;   **H** Holocaust;   **J** Judaica;   **K** Kahal;   **L** Land;   **M** Marriage;   **N** Name changes;
O Police files;   **P** Pogroms;   **R** Reference;   **S** School records;   **T** Tax lists;   **V** Divorce;   **W** Occupation lists;   **X** Jewish hospital;   **Y** Notary records;   **Z** Local government records

TOWN NAME Document Type Years	VOIVODSHIP/OBLAST (Province)	COUNTRY Zespół/Sygnatura (Poland) Fond/Opis/Delo (Belarus, Ukraine, Lithuania)
KRUSZWICA	**BYDGOSZCZ**	**POLAND**
B 1847–1854		59
D 1847–1854		59
KWIECISZEWO	**BYDGOSZCZ**	**POLAND**
B 1832–1848; 1873		112/1–2
D 1832–1848; 1873		112/1–2
M 1832–1848; 1873		112/1–2
MOGILNO	**BYDGOSZCZ**	**POLAND**
B 1823–1874; 1875/1907		61/854
C 1834/1909; 1920–1939		61
D 1829–1846		61
E 1919–1935		61
K 1879/1919		5
M 1829–1846		61
T 1810–1939		61/110–174,1124–1169
PAKOŚĆ	**BYDGOSZCZ**	**POLAND**
B 1825–1847		196
D 1825–1847		196
E 1903–1914; 1933–1935		60
G 1847/1906		60
K 1854–1893		128
M 1823–1847		196
STRZELNO	**BYDGOSZCZ**	**POLAND**
G 1838–1917; 1920–1925		62/315–319,321,868
K 1839/1917		62
S 1867/1920		62
T 1900–1918		62/47–51
Y 1864–1867		62
TRZEMESZNO	**BYDGOSZCZ**	**POLAND**
B 1832; 1837–1847		113/1–2
D 1832; 1837–1847		113/1–2
K 1833/1910		63
M 1832; 1837–1847		113/1–2
S 1843/1920		64
Y 1843–1907		63
WYLATOWO	**BYDGOSZCZ**	**POLAND**
B 1832–1847		114/1–2
D 1832–1847		114/1–2
M 1832–1847		114/1–2

JĘDRZEJÓW Branch Archives

TOWN NAME Document Type Years	VOIVODSHIP/OBLAST (Province)	COUNTRY
JĘDRZEJÓW	**KIELCE**	**POLAND**
B 1875–1893		333
C 1886–1943		6
D 1876–1892		333
L 1940–1941		6
M 1875–1893		333
T 1941–1944		6
MAŁOGOSZCZ	**KIELCE**	**POLAND**
B 1826–1827; 1829; 1832–1855; 1857–1860; 1863–1867; 1885–1889		59
D 1826–1855; 1857–1860; 1863–1867; 1886–1889		59
M 1826–1827; 1829; 1832–1855; 1857–1860; 1863–1867; 1886–1889		59
MIECHÓW	**KIELCE**	**POLAND**
B 1870–1880; 1888–1890		397
D 1870–1880; 1888–1891		397
M 1870–1880; 1888–1891		397
SECEMIN	**CZĘSTOCHOWA**	**POLAND**
B 1826–1866; 1868–1869		221
D 1826–1866; 1868–1869		221
M 1826–1844; 1846–1847; 1849–1866; 1868–1869		221
SOBKÓW	**KIELCE**	**POLAND**
B 1820; 1826–1827; 1829–1876; 1881–1884; 1887–1889; 1891–1894		75
D 1820; 1826–1827; 1829–1859; 1861–1876; 1881–1884; 1886–1889; 1891–1894		75
M 1810; 1820; 1826–1827; 1829–1859; 1861–1876; 1881–1885; 1888; 1891–1894		75
SZCZEKOCINY	**CZĘSTOCHOWA**	**POLAND**
B 1826–1838		224

A Army/recruit lists; **B** Birth; **C** Census; **D** Death; **E** Voter lists; **G** Immigration; **H** Holocaust; **J** Judaica; **K** Kahal; **L** Land; **M** Marriage; **N** Name changes; **O** Police files; **P** Pogroms; **R** Reference; **S** School records; **T** Tax lists; **V** Divorce; **W** Occupation Lists; **X** Jewish hospital; **Y** Notary records; **Z** Local government records

TOWN NAME	VOIVODSHIP/OBLAST (Province)	COUNTRY
Document Type Years		Zespół/Sygnatura (Poland) Fond/Opis/Delo (Belarus, Ukraine, Lithuania)

D	1826–1843		224
M	1826–1842; 1857–1865		224
WŁOSZCZOWA		**KIELCE**	**POLAND**
B	1823; 1826–1828; 1832; 1836–1838; 1851–1855; 1857–1878; 1880–1894		226
D	1823; 1826–1828; 1832; 1836–1838; 1851–1852; 1854–1855; 1857–1878; 1880–1894		226
G	1923; 1927		159
M	1823; 1826–1828; 1832; 1836–1838; 1851–1852; 1854–1855; 1857–1878; 1880–1894		226
WODZISŁAW		**KIELCE**	**POLAND**
B	1826–1838; 1840–1887		80
D	1826–1838; 1840–1887		80
M	1826–1830; 1832–1838; 1840–1867; 1869–1887		80

JELENIA GÓRA Branch Archives

FRIEDEBERG		**SEE MIRSK**	
HIRSCHBERG		**SEE JELENIA GÓRA**	**POLAND**
JELENIA GÓRA		**JELENIA GÓRA**	**POLAND**
B	1820–1831		3/I/3070
C	1820–1869		3/I/228
D	1820–1831		3/I/3070
E	1869–1936		3/I/7745–7749
K	1886–1909 (CEMETERY RECORDS)		3/I/7742
M	1820–1831		3/I/3070
KAMIENNA GORA		**JELENIA GÓRA**	**POLAND**
B	1848–1888		94/I/193
K	1846–1887		7/I/1143
M	1827–1874		7/I/1549
LANDESHUT		**SEE KAMIENNA GORA**	
LIEBAU		**SEE LUBAWKA**	
LIEBENTHAL		**SEE LUBOMIERZ**	
LOWENBERG		**SEE LWÓWEK SLASKI**	
LUBAWKA		**JELENIA GÓRA**	**POLAND**
C	1856		9/I/623
LUBOMIERZ		**JELENIA GÓRA**	**POLAND**
L	1813–1884; 1888–1944		13/I/42–52
LWÓWEK SLASKI		**JELENIA GÓRA**	**POLAND**
C	1742–1816; 1849–1889		10/I/120–123
MIRSK		**JELENIA GÓRA**	**POLAND**
C	1833–1902		12/2166
T	1860–1931; 1933–1935; 1937–1938; 1941–1942		12/I/1522–1758

KALISZ Archives

BŁASZKI		**SIERADZ**	**POLAND**
C	1872; 1917–1951		1/900–918; 53/1–56
E	1907; 1909		1/18–19
L	1848–1861		1/650
W	1831–1846		1/84
BRUDZEW		**KALISZ**	**POLAND**
C	1872; 1917–1951		1/919–935; 53/57–121
E	1907; 1909		1/18–19,21
CHOCZ		**KALISZ**	**POLAND**
C	1872		1/936–941
E	1907; 1909		321/18–19,21
W	1834–1848		1/90
GRABÓW		**KALISZ**	**POLAND**
C	1946		18/30
K	1886–1912		18/31
IWANOWICE		**KALISZ**	**POLAND**
C	1872; 1874–1931		1/942–944; 53/241–244
E	1907; 1909		321/18–19,21
W	1831–1865		1/92
KALISZ		**KALISZ**	**POLAND**
A	1836–1856		610/37–85
B	1875–1894; 1922–1923		693/74–93; 3/223

A Army/recruit lists; **B** Birth; **C** Census; **D** Death; **E** Voter lists; **G** Immigration; **H** Holocaust; **J** Judaica; **K** Kahal; **L** Land; **M** Marriage; **N** Name changes; **O** Police files; **P** Pogroms; **R** Reference; **S** School records; **T** Tax lists; **V** Divorce; **W** Occupation lists; **X** Jewish hospital; **Y** Notary records; **Z** Local government records

TOWN NAME Document Type Years	VOIVODSHIP/OBLAST (Province)	COUNTRY Zespół/Sygnatura (Poland) Fond/Opis/Delo (Belarus, Ukraine, Lithuania)
C 1872; 1919		1/945–948; 11/114
D 1875–1894; 1922–1923		693/74–93; 3/223
E 1907; 1909		321/18–19,21
G 1836–1856; 1909; 1923–1951		610/37–85; 645/1/19
K 1843–1851 (CIRCUMCISIONS,MARRIAGES,FUNERALS)		1/457
L 1852–1863; 1886–1954		1/427,433,672,866; 3/222; 203
M 1875–1894; 1922–1923		693/74–93; 3/223
N 1833–1846		1/74
S 1863–1864; 1934		1/473; 3/216
W 1846–1852; 1863–1866; 1892–1893		1/335,428,434,605,627,647,900
Y 1808–1951		94–139; 413–432
Z 1832–1862 (RELIGION CONVERSIONS); 1865 (LIST OF RABBIS)		1/125,139,214,689,821
KALISZ REGION	**KALISZ**	**POLAND**
W 1855–1865		1/901
KĘPNO	**KALISZ**	**POLAND**
C 1910; 1916; 1918; 1921; 1927–1930		20/65,237
KOŹMIN	**KALISZ**	**POLAND**
K 1810–1839		22/373–374
L 1861–1943		91/130–173
S 1826–1872		22/219,332
T 1800–1918		
KOŹMINEK	**KALISZ**	**POLAND**
C 1872–1948		1/957–964; 53/303–365
E 1907; 1909		321/18–19,21
W 1831–1866		1/98,436
KROTOSZYN	**KALISZ**	**POLAND**
C 1823–1950		14/128–129,171–172,489; 23
L 1885–1944		91/174–175
Y 1830–1951		151–166; 778–788
Z 1884–1943		91/128–129
OPATÓWEK	**KALISZ**	**POLAND**
C 1872–1951		1/965–966; 53/394–457
E 1907; 1909		321/18–19,21
W 1831–1856		1/103,105
OSTRÓW WIELKOPOLSKI	**KALISZ**	**POLAND**
C 1875–1945		8/61–64; 72/1–34
E 1907; 1909		321/18–19,21
P 1920–1921		3/1
OSTRZESZÓW	**KALISZ**	**POLAND**
C 1919–1930		9/155; 27/304
E 1923–1930		27/166–167
K 1927		27/247
Y 1882–1915		176–182
PLESZEW	**KALISZ**	**POLAND**
C 1834–1903		28/1775,1808–1809
S 1855–1906		28/352
Y 1835–1919		183–194
Z 1821–1920 (COURT RECORDS)		92
POGORZELA	**LESZNO**	**POLAND**
C 1921–1935		29/361–364,366,368–369
E 1918–1930		29/363–369
L 1834–1943		91/201–221
T 1883–1921		29/189–190
RASZKÓW	**KALISZ**	**POLAND**
S 1849–1857		30/32
RYCHTAL	**KALISZ**	**POLAND**
C 1877–1890		31/4
E 1879; 1881; 1883; 1887; 1889; 1922; 1925; 1927; 1929–1931		31/4–6,50–52
T 1918–1932		
STAW	**KALISZ**	**POLAND**
C 1872–1951		53/500–540
E 1907; 1909		321/18–19,21
W 1835–1853; 1856–1864		1/112,442
STAWISZYN	**KALISZ**	**POLAND**
B 1866–1894		755/1–4
C 1917–1924		32/189–191,227–233

A Army/recruit lists; **B** Birth; **C** Census; **D** Death; **E** Voter lists; **G** Immigration; **H** Holocaust; **J** Judaica; **K** Kahal; **L** Land; **M** Marriage; **N** Name changes; **O** Police files; **P** Pogroms; **R** Reference; **S** School records; **T** Tax lists; **V** Divorce; **W** Occupation Lists; **X** Jewish hospital; **Y** Notary records; **Z** Local government records

TOWN NAME Document Type Years	VOIVODSHIP/OBLAST (Province)	COUNTRY Zespół/Sygnatura (Poland) Fond/Opis/Delo (Belarus, Ukraine, Lithuania)
D 1855–1879		755/1–4
E 1907; 1909; 1922; 1927; 1930; 1935; 1938		32/67–80; 321/18–19,21
G 1917–1919		32/189–191
L 1855; 1917; 1931		32/189–190,196; 1/449
M 1862–1879		755/1–4
T 1936–1939		32
W 1832–1864		1/113,446,448
SULMIERZYCE	**KALISZ**	**POLAND**
C 1931–1935		33/944–945
G 1907; 1909		33
L 1841–1942		91/242–251
WIERUSZÓW	**KALISZ**	**POLAND**
B 1831; 1836; 1871–1882		768/1–10
D 1831; 1875; 1878–1882		768/1–10
M 1836; 1871–1884		768/1–10
ZDUNY	**KALISZ**	**POLAND**
L 1841–1943		91/272–275

KATOWICE Archives

BĘDZIN	**KATOWICE**	**POLAND**
B 1826–1883; 1909–1911		788/1–35; 773/334
C 1826–1865; 1931		773/965
D 1826–1883		788/1–35
E 1916–1919; 1925; 1928		773/731–741
G 1920–1921		773/959
H 1943–1944		773/1194
K 1844–1873; 1881; 1892–1903; 1909; 1919–1923		773/33–35,169,235,307,339–384; 770/508–509
L 1892–1912; 1914; 1942		773/239–240,249–250,255,261,279,295,310, 312,333,337–338,344–345,350–351,356, 359–361,370,1206
M 1826–1883		788/1–35
Y 1870–1938		811/1–278; 812/1–19; 813/1–10; 814/1–2; 815/1–35; 816/1–20; 817/1–32; 818/1–16; 819/1–11; 820/1–84; 821/1–6; 822/1–72
BEUTHEN	**KATOWICE**	**POLAND**
SEE BYTOM		
BIELSKO BIAŁA	**BIELSKO BIAŁA**	**POLAND**
K 1922–1932		27/1/VI; 1988–1989
BIERUŃ STARY	**KATOWICE**	**POLAND**
K 1922–1924		27/I–VI/1990
BYTOM	**KATOWICE**	**POLAND**
B 1847–1849; 1861–1885		674/I/362–364,374–397; 749/I/1–96
C 1792–1804; 1820–1864; 1908–1915; 1938		645/I/3123,3126–3128; 164
D 1847–1885		674/I/592–594; 604–615; 749/I/1–96
M 1847–1885		674/I/443–514; 749/I/1–96
T 1850; 1861–1863; 1867; 1879–1881; 1884–1895; 1899; 1903; 1907; 1910		645/1/82–98; 3126
BYTOM REGION	**KATOWICE**	**POLAND**
B 1847–1849; 1861–1885		674/I/362–364,374–397; 750/I/1–39; 753/I/1–36; 754/I/1–6
D 1874–1885		750/I; 753–754/I
CHEŁM WIEŁKI	**KATOWICE**	**POLAND**
S 1908–1928		9/I/5–6
CHORZÓW	**KATOWICE**	**POLAND**
B 1847–1849; 1872		674/I/365,368A,685
C 1938		646/I/2109
D 1847–1849; 1872–1885		674/I/595A,596,598A,709
K 1871–1879; 1886; 1911–1933		27/VOL.I–VI/1994–1995; 61/I/85;646/I/1581,1583
M 1847–1849		647/1/434,439A
CIESZYN	**BIELSKO BIAŁA**	
L 1637–1784		
K 1929–1939		27/I/596
DĄBROWA GÓRNICZA	**KATOWICE**	**POLAND**
C 1864–1935		775/40,46–47,54,68,76–77,81,83,91,97,104, 118,124,1 32,142–147,160–162,175–178, 205–207,229
K 1883–1884; 1888–1900; 1911–1914		775/157,171,191

A Army/recruit lists; **B** Birth; **C** Census; **D** Death; **E** Voter lists; **G** Immigration; **H** Holocaust; **J** Judaica; **K** Kahal; **L** Land; **M** Marriage; **N** Name changes;
O Police files; **P** Pogroms; **R** Reference; **S** School records; **T** Tax lists; **V** Divorce; **W** Occupation lists; **X** Jewish hospital; **Y** Notary records; **Z** Local government records

TOWN NAME Document Type Years	VOIVODSHIP/OBLAST (Province)	COUNTRY Zespół/Sygnatura (Poland) Fond/Opis/Delo (Belarus, Ukraine, Lithuania)
S 1875–1880; 1908; 1912–1914		775/128,174,196,220
Y 1908–1938		824/1–107
Z 1893–1894; 1898–1900; 1915		775/50–51,66,261
DZIEDZICE	**KATOWICE**	**POLAND**
K 1925–1932		27/VOL.I–VI/1991
HINDENBURG	**SEE ZABRZE**	**POLAND**
KATOWICE	**KATOWICE**	**POLAND**
B 1848–1899		674/I/368,372–373
K 1922–1931,1935–1939		27/I–VI/1992–1993; 40/I/180
M 1860		1/I/101
N 1921; 1930–1931		27/I–VI/1440–1442,1477–1503
S 1843–1909; 1922–1939		27/I/1; 64/I/1–169
KATOWICE REGION	**KATOWICE**	**POLAND**
D 1844–1849		674/I/370–371
E 1922–1935		18/I/1–24
KRÓLEWSKA HUTA	**KATOWICE**	**POLAND**
K 1922–1932		27/I–VI/1994–1995
KROMOŁÓW	**KATOWICE**	**POLAND**
B 1826–1854; 1909		887/196; 898/1–29
D 1826–1854		898/1–29
K 1908–1913		887/176,225–227
M 1826–1854		898/1–29
S 1912		887/266
ŁAGIEWNIKI	**KATOWICE**	**POLAND**
B 1874–1885		751/I
M 1874–1885		751/I
S 1932		65/I/4–5; 81/I/134–137
ŁAZY	**KATOWICE**	**POLAND**
K 1930–1938		880/140
MICHAŁKOWICE	**OPOLE**	**POLAND**
B 1844–1847		674/I/368C,368D
D 1844–1847		674/I/368C,599
MIECHOWICE	**KATOWICE**	**POLAND**
B 1848; 1874–1885		674/I/368E; 752/1
D 1848; 1874–1885		674/I/368E; 752/1
M 1848; 1874–1885		674/I/368E; 752/1
MIKOŁÓW	**KATOWICE**	**POLAND**
B 1849–1874		113/I/62
K 1921		27/I–VI/1996
S 1938–1939		27/I–XIII/847
MYSŁOWICE	**KATOWICE**	**POLAND**
B 1847–1874		82/I/416; 5/I/269–274
C 1785–1834		82/I/72
D 1847–1874		82/I/416; 5/I/290–291
E 1930; 1935		82/I/759–761,766–768
G 1925–1933		82/I/742
H 1940–1943		82/I/682–683
K 1853; 1922–1932		27/I–VI/1997; 82/I/15
L 1845		82/I/127
M 1847–1874		82/I/416; 5/I/276–289
S 1908–1917		9/I/7
NOWA WIEŚ	**KATOWICE**	**POLAND**
B 1911–1920		107/I
NOWY BYTOM	**KATOWICE**	**POLAND**
S 1933		65/I/9–10
OLKUSZ	**KATOWICE**	**POLAND**
B 1827–1870; 1882–1893		27
D 1827–1870; 1882–1893		27
M 1827–1870; 1882–1893		27
PILICA	**KATOWICE**	**POLAND**
B 1826–1870; 1889; 1892		29
D 1826–1870; 1889; 1892		29
M 1826–1870; 1889; 1892		29
RYBNIK	**KATOWICE**	**POLAND**
K 1923–1932		27/I–VI/1998–1999

A Army/recruit lists; **B** Birth; **C** Census; **D** Death; **E** Voter lists; **G** Immigration; **H** Holocaust; **J** Judaica; **K** Kahal; **L** Land; **M** Marriage; **N** Name changes; **O** Police files; **P** Pogroms; **R** Reference; **S** School records; **T** Tax lists; **V** Divorce; **W** Occupation Lists; **X** Jewish hospital; **Y** Notary records; **Z** Local government records

TOWN NAME Document Type Years	VOIVODSHIP/OBLAST (Province)	COUNTRY Zespół/Sygnatura (Poland) Fond/Opis/Delo (Belarus, Ukraine, Lithuania)
SIEMIANOWICE ŚLĄSKIE	**KATOWICE**	**POLAND**
K 1868–1921		27/I–VI/2000; 1/I/103,509
M 1847–1849		674/I/437
SIEWIERZ	**KATOWICE**	**POLAND**
H 1939–1944		890/1541,1594–1595
K 1905–1908; 1913; 1917		890/784,938,1011
SILESIA REGION	**KATOWICE**	**POLAND**
B 1925–1939		27/I–VI/1987
D 1925–1939		27/I–VI/1987
K 1923; 1925–1939		27/I–VOL. VI/1985–1987
M 1925–1939		27/I–VI/1987
SKOCZÓW	**BIELSKO BIAŁA**	**POLAND**
K 1927		27/I–VI/2001
SOSNOWIEC	**KATOWICE**	**POLAND**
C 1806–1907; 1919–1928; 1931–1939		776/912–917,2996–3005,3007–3010,3024–3030, 3032–3042
E 1912; 1934; 1939		776/670,1768–1788
G 1927		776/3067–3068
H 1939–1944		776/5649,5834,6366,6368–6374,6398,6408, 6555,6566–6568,6581,6614–6615,6803, 6809–6810,6858–6859,6884,7051
K 1903; 1905–1915; 1921–1927; 1929–1939		776/26,343,411,459,517,524,562,575,635, 736,763,771,986,2681,4171,4189; 770/4, 187,190,192,227,580; 777/103–131
L 1918; 1929		776/1076,3054–3060
P 1918–1925		776/1561
S 1903–1914; 1916–1920; 1923–1933		776/10,71,173,230,310,444,732,847,4800–4842, 4934–4935,5519
W 1941–1943		776/5855–5858,6172
X 1915–1923; 1926–1937		776/1152–1153,4670–4672,4702, 5031–5033,5081–5082
Y 1885–1939		825/1–12; 826/1–16; 827/1–21; 828/1–15; 829/1–45; 830/1–23; 831/1–13; 832/1–15; 833/1–20; 834/1–137; 835/1–69; 836/1–7; 837/1–15; 838/1–49
Z 1907; 1915–1939; 1940–1943		776/290,1309,2080–2081,2364,2589,2612, 2703,3235,3249,3275–3276,3353–3359, 5165–5166,5197–5243,5482–5483, 6261,6385,6444,6802
ŚWIĘTOCHŁOWICE	**KATOWICE**	**POLAND**
B 1844–1849		674/I/368–G,H,I
C 1928–1938		83/I/26,32
D 1847		674/I/601
G 1930–1939		91/I/51
H 1943		83/I/113
S 1924–1939		72
TARNOWSKIE GÓRY	**KATOWICE**	**POLAND**
K 1922–1931		27/I–VI/2001A,2002
WOLBROM	**KATOWICE**	**POLAND**
B 1826–1838; 1842–1870; 1882–1886		42
D 1826–1870; 1883–1888		42
M 1826–1870; 1882–1892		42
WOŹNIKI	**CZĘSTOCHOWA**	**POLAND**
K 1922–1924		27/I–VI/2003
ZABRZE	**KATOWICE**	**POLAND**
B 1847–1849		674/I/369
D 1847–1848		674/I/602
M 1848–1849		674/I/443
ŻARKI	**CZĘSTOCHOWA**	**POLAND**
K 1918–1919; 1922; 1928–1937		770/189,511; 880/491–521
L 1914		794/196
ŻARNOWIEC	**KATOWICE**	**POLAND**
B 1811–1852; 1858–1868; 1882–1892		41
D 1811–1852; 1858–1868; 1882–1892		41
M 1811–1852; 1858–1868; 1882–1892		41

A Army/recruit lists; **B** Birth; **C** Census; **D** Death; **E** Voter lists; **G** Immigration; **H** Holocaust; **J** Judaica; **K** Kahal; **L** Land; **M** Marriage; **N** Name changes;
O Police files; **P** Pogroms; **R** Reference; **S** School records; **T** Tax lists; **V** Divorce; **W** Occupation lists; **X** Jewish hospital; **Y** Notary records; **Z** Local government records

TOWN NAME Document Type Years	VOIVODSHIP/OBLAST (Province)	COUNTRY Zespół/Sygnatura (Poland) Fond/Opis/Delo (Belarus, Ukraine, Lithuania)
ZAWIERCIE	**KATOWICE**	**POLAND**
K 1925–1938		880/136–140,176,461–490; 770/188
P 1930–1936		880/239
Y 1903–1914		1019/1–39; 1020/1–37

KIELCE Archives

BODZENTYN	**KIELCE**	**POLAND**
B 1869–1895		421
D 1869–1895		421
M 1869–1895		421
CHĘCINY	**KIELCE**	**POLAND**
B 1826–1894		79
D 1826–1894		79
M 1826–1894		79
Z 1787–1791; 1824–1915		121
DALESZYCE	**KIELCE**	**POLAND**
B 1826–1870		83
D 1826–1893		83
M 1826–1893		83
DURACZÓW	**KIELCE**	**POLAND**
C 1939		524
GOWARCZÓW	**RADOM**	**POLAND**
B 1826–1859		553
D 1826–1859		553
M 1826–1859		553
KIELCE	**KIELCE**	**POLAND**
B 1868–1896		422
C 1868–1939		122
D 1868–1896		422
M 1868–1896		422
KLWÓW	**RADOM**	**POLAND**
B 1851–1860		594
D 1851–1860		594
M 1851–1860		594
KOŃSKIE	**KIELCE**	**POLAND**
B 1826–1894		555
C 1945–1950		519
D 1826–1894		555
G 1915–1940		447
M 1826–1894		555
ŁOPUSZNO	**KIELCE**	**POLAND**
B 1874–1894		810
D 1874–1894		810
M 1874–1894		810
OLKUSZ REGION	**KATOWICE**	**POLAND**
C 1843–1860		4
OPOCZNO	**PIÓTRKOW TRYBUNALSKI**	**POLAND**
B 1826–1874		582
D 1826–1874		582
M 1826–1874		582
OSTROWIEC ŚWIĘTOKRZYSKI	**KIELCE**	**POLAND**
C 1887–1930		214
E 1939		214
PRZEDBÓRZ	**PIÓTRKOW TRYBUNALSKI**	**POLAND**
B 1826–1871		563
D 1826–1871		563
M 1826–1871		563
PRZYSUCHA	**RADOM**	**POLAND**
B 1826–1865		597
D 1826–1865		597
M 1826–1865		597
RADOSZYCE	**KIELCE**	**POLAND**
B 1826–1893		565
D 1826–1893		565
M 1826–1893		565

A Army/recruit lists; **B** Birth; **C** Census; **D** Death; **E** Voter lists; **G** Immigration; **H** Holocaust; **J** Judaica; **K** Kahal; **L** Land; **M** Marriage; **N** Name changes; **O** Police files; **P** Pogroms; **R** Reference; **S** School records; **T** Tax lists; **V** Divorce; **W** Occupation Lists; **X** Jewish hospital; **Y** Notary records; **Z** Local government records

TOWN NAME Document Type Years	VOIVODSHIP/OBLAST (Province)	COUNTRY Zespół/Sygnatura (Poland) Fond/Opis/Delo (Belarus, Ukraine, Lithuania)
STARACHOWICE	**KIELCE**	**POLAND**
G 1932–1950		5
ŻARNÓW	**PIÓTRKOW TRYBUNALSKI**	**POLAND**
B 1826–1873		591
D 1826–1873		591
M 1826–1873		591

KOSZALIN Archives

BELGARD	**SEE BIAŁOGARD**	
BELGRAD	**SEE BIAŁOGARD**	
BIAŁOGARD	**KOSZALIN**	**POLAND**
B 1813–1847		52/I/48; 142/I/1680
D 1813–1847		52/I/48; 142/I/1680
M 1813–1847		52/I/48; 142/I/1680
CZAPLINEK	**KOSZALIN**	**POLAND**
C 1840		117/I/11
T 1810–1934		117/I/22–40
KOSZALIN	**KOSZALIN**	**POLAND**
B 1812–1874		52/I/10; 73/I/141
D 1812–1874		52/I/10; 73/I/143
M 1812–1874		52/I/10; 73/I/142
Z 1738–1816		33/I/446–450
KOSZAZOWO	**SEE KOSZALIN**	
NEUSTETTIN	**SEE SZCZECINEK**	
SIANÓW	**KOSZALIN**	**POLAND**
B 1841–1874		543/I/6–7
D 1847–1848; 1851–1871		543/I/10–11
M 1841–1874		543/I/8–9
SZCZECINEK	**KOSZALIN**	**POLAND**
K 1816–1917		358/418–426,451–466,483–485
WAŁCZ REGION	**PIŁA**	**POLAND**
C 1844–1847		20/I/163
K 1818–1846		20/I/159–170
S 1828–1849		20/I/161
ZANOW	**SEE SIANÓW**	
ZŁOTÓW	**PIŁA**	**POLAND**
K 1785–1901		31/I/30,32,35,60–70
ZŁOTÓW REGION	**PIŁA**	**POLAND**
C 1834–1915		124/I/350–360
K 1834–1915		124/I/350–360
S 1834–1915		124/I/350–360

KRAKÓW Archives

ANTONUVKA	**ROVNO**	**UKRAINE**
Z 1806–1855		
BĘDZIN	**KATOWICE**	**POLAND**
W 1936–1938		536/IT–2034
BIAŁA REGION	**BIELSKO BIAŁA**	**POLAND**
A 1892–1918		209/STB 295–298
C 1921–1924		209/STB 520
K 1877–1917		209/STB 307
BOCHNIA	**TARNÓW**	**POLAND**
B 1825–1869		526/MIB–O/1
CHRZANÓW	**KATOWICE**	**POLAND**
K 1787–1815		526/IT 222A–C
DĄBROWA TARNOWSKA	**TARNÓW**	**POLAND**
M 1919		526/MID/1
DUBNO	**ROVNO**	**UKRAINE**
T 1726		637/A SANG.RKPS 469G
KAŃCZUGA	**PRZEMYŚL**	**POLAND**
Z 1874–1936		526/UMI KM1; IT 2149

A Army/recruit lists;   **B** Birth;   **C** Census;   **D** Death;   **E** Voter lists;   **G** Immigration;   **H** Holocaust;   **J** Judaica;   **K** Kahal;   **L** Land;   **M** Marriage;   **N** Name changes;
O Police files;   **P** Pogroms;   **R** Reference;   **S** School records;   **T** Tax lists;   **V** Divorce;   **W** Occupation lists;   **X** Jewish hospital;   **Y** Notary records;   **Z** Local government records

TOWN NAME Document Type Years	VOIVODSHIP/OBLAST (Province)	COUNTRY Zespół/Sygnatura (Poland) Fond/Opis/Delo (Belarus, Ukraine, Lithuania)
KAZIMIERZ	**KRAKÓW**	**POLAND**
Z 1335–1860		34; 35/IUD/CAS.III/11 1–13
KRAKÓW	**KRAKÓW**	**POLAND**
B 1798–1854; 1869–1895		526/MIK 1–12; 335/M 1920–2102
C 1795–1853; 1857; 1870; 1880; 1890; 1900; 1910; 1921; 1939–1942		84–93; 684/TSCHN 1866; 33–VII/SMK 450–681
D 1798–1854; 1871–1889		335/M 1920–2102; 526/MIK 1–12
E 1865–1933		IT/1028,1060,1081–1082,1310,1936
H 1939–1945		33 VII/SMK 211,772–774; 655/IT 1395
K 1939–1940		IT 1815
L 1790–1794 (PROPERTY OWNERS IN KAZIMIERZ)		
M 1798–1852; 1878–1895		335/M 1920–2102; 526/MIK 1–12
R 1892; 1905; 1908; 1909; 1926; 1929–1930; 1932–1934		
S 1801–1933		482–493
T 1796–1809; 1815–1853		33–II; 33–III; WMK,V–59,102–105
V 1811–1853		335
W 1550–1860 (INCLUDES LIST OF JEWISH DOORKEEPERS)		35/III/11/9–12; 77/IT 638–640,649–650
Z 1300–1945		1343/PMI/1–219; 33–I/33–VIII,34,36,53
KRAKÓW REGION	**KRAKÓW**	**POLAND**
C 1790–1792; 1795–1796		301/191A
KSIĄŻ WIELKI REGION	**KIELCE**	**POLAND**
C 1790–1792		301/191A
LELÓW REGION	**CZĘSTOCHOWA**	**POLAND**
C 1790–1792		30/191A
LOKACHI	**VOLYNSK**	**UKRAINE**
Z 1723–1727		637/A.SANG.RKPS.457; 465
LVOV	**LVOV**	**UKRAINE**
R 1898; 1901–1902; 1908–1909		
MLINOV	**ROVNO**	**UKRAINE**
G 1710–1816		630
W 1830; 1833–1851		630
NOWY TARG	**NOWY SĄCZ**	**POLAND**
C 1870; 1880; 1940–1942		208/GDK 42–53
H 1940–1942		208/GDK 4
NOWY TARG REGION	**NOWY SĄCZ**	**POLAND**
C 1940		208/GDK 54
OPATÓW	**TARNOBRZEG**	**POLAND**
W 1720–1729		637/A SANG. RKPS 428
OSTROG	**ROVNO**	**UKRAINE**
K 1721–1725		637
OŚWIĘCIM REGION	**BIELSKO BIAŁA**	**POLAND**
A 1918–1931		228/STO 59–61
G 1918–1932		228/STO 37
W 1910–1918		228/STO 15
X 1911–1918		228/STO 10
PODGÓRZE	**KRAKÓW**	**POLAND**
B 1804–1893		526/MIK–P1
C 1857; 1870; 1880; 1890; 1900; 1910		93
D 1804–1894		526/MIK–P1
L 1838–1873		53
M 1804–1894		526/MIK–P1
R 1892; 1905; 1908; 1909		
PROSZOWICE	**KRAKÓW**	**POLAND**
Z 1474–1734		120
PROSZOWICE REGION	**KRAKÓW**	**POLAND**
C 1790–1792		30/191A
SKAWINA	**KRAKÓW**	**POLAND**
Z 1578; 1772–1944		114
TARNOBRZEG	**TARNOBRZEG**	**POLAND**
T 18TH/19TH CENTURY		120
Z 1695/1830		120
TARNÓW	**TARNÓW**	**POLAND**
B 1808–1849		526/III/131/2–3,6–7
D 1808–1855		526/III/131/1,4–5,8
WARSZAWA	**WARSZAWA**	**POLAND**
R 1937–1938		

A Army/recruit lists; **B** Birth; **C** Census; **D** Death; **E** Voter lists; **G** Immigration; **H** Holocaust; **J** Judaica; **K** Kahal; **L** Land; **M** Marriage; **N** Name changes; **O** Police files; **P** Pogroms; **R** Reference; **S** School records; **T** Tax lists; **V** Divorce; **W** Occupation Lists; **X** Jewish hospital; **Y** Notary records; **Z** Local government records

TOWN NAME Document Type Years	VOIVODSHIP/OBLAST (Province)	COUNTRY Zespół/Sygnatura (Poland) Fond/Opis/Delo (Belarus, Ukraine, Lithuania)
WIELICZKA	KRAKÓW	POLAND
C 1867/1945		117
Z 1777–1945		117
WIŚNICZ	TARNÓW	POLAND
D 1826–1853		526/MIW
ZABŁOCIE	BIELSKO BIAŁA	POLAND
B 1877–1916		1297/MGIZ 1–12
D 1877–1916		1297/MGIZ 29–45
M 1877–1916		1297/MGIZ 20–28
ZIELUŃ	CIECHANÓW	POLAND
G 1824		IT1592
ŻYWIEC	BIELSKO BIAŁA	POLAND
W 1918–1939		232/STZ–II/171
ŻYWIEC REGION	BIELSKO BIAŁA	POLAND
A 1919–1933		232/STZ–II/276–306
C 1919–1939		232/STZ–II/116–134,136
G 1920–1939		232/STZ–II/111

KRAŚNIK Branch Archives

POTOK GÓRNY	ZAMOŚĆ	POLAND
C 1882–1954		26

KUTNO Branch Archives

ŻYCHLIN	PŁOCK	POLAND
A 1862		3/23
B 1873		82
C 1858–1859; 1865; 1872		21/22,164,166–167,169,178; 3/173
D 1873		82
M 1873		82
Y 1929–1951		79/1–29
Z 1908		21/134

ŁĘCZYCA Branch Archives

ŁĘCZYCA	PŁOCK	POLAND
Z 1806–1950		10

LEGNICA Branch Archives

CHOJNÓW	LEGNICA	POLAND
H 1945–1949		488/99
HAYNAU	SEE CHOJNÓW	
JAWOR	LEGNICA	POLAND
K 1752/1936		2/9–14
LEGNICA	LEGNICA	POLAND
B 1875; 1881–1884; 1886–1892		300
D 1874–1884; 1886–1892		300
K 1742–1774; 1776–1844		3
M 1874–1875; 1877; 1885; 1887–1891		300
LEGNISZEWO	SEE LEGNICA	
LIEGNITZ	SEE LEGNICA	

LESZNO Archives

GOSTYŃ	LESZNO	POLAND
C 1885–1900		16
JUTROSIN	LESZNO	POLAND
B 1820–1885		17
D 1820–1885		17
M 1820–1885		17
KOŚCIAN	LESZNO	POLAND
C 1842–1881; 1939–1944		18

A Army/recruit lists; **B** Birth; **C** Census; **D** Death; **E** Voter lists; **G** Immigration; **H** Holocaust; **J** Judaica; **K** Kahal; **L** Land; **M** Marriage; **N** Name changes; **O** Police files; **P** Pogroms; **R** Reference; **S** School records; **T** Tax lists; **V** Divorce; **W** Occupation lists; **X** Jewish hospital; **Y** Notary records; **Z** Local government records

TOWN NAME Document Type Years	VOIVODSHIP/OBLAST (Province)	COUNTRY Zespół/Sygnatura (Poland) Fond/Opis/Delo (Belarus, Ukraine, Lithuania)
KRZYWIN	**LESZNO**	**POLAND**
C 1926–1932		20
LESZNO	**LESZNO**	**POLAND**
B 1808–1809; 1847–1874		83; 403
C 1795–1915; 1921		21
D 1812–1874		83; 403
J 1808–1939		403
M 1847–1874		83
LISSA	**SEE LESZNO**	
OSIECZNA	**LESZNO**	**POLAND**
B 1817–1847		23
D 1817–1847		23
M 1817–1847		23
RAWICZ	**LESZNO**	**POLAND**
C 1835–1900		27
H 1939–1944		27
RAWITSCH	**SEE RAWICZ**	
SARNE	**SEE SARNOWA**	
SARNOWA	**LESZNO**	**POLAND**
C 1835–1842		29
STORCHNEST	**SEE OSIECZNA**	
SZLICHTYNGOWA	**LESZNO**	**POLAND**
K 1763–1936 (CEMETERY RECORDS)		

ŁÓDŹ Archives

ALEKSANDRÓW ŁÓDZKI	**ŁÓDŹ**	**POLAND**
B 1826–1892		270
D 1826–1892		270
K 1822–1865; 1871–1914		1
M 1826–1892		270
BĘDKÓW	**PIOTRKÓW TRYBUNALSKI**	**POLAND**
B 1826–1846		270
D 1826–1846		270
M 1826–1846		270
Z 1849–1864; 1901; 1906		1
BĘDZIN	**KATOWICE**	**POLAND**
A 1891–1904		17
K 1841–1866; 1885–1915		1
O 1898–1914		42
S 1871–1914		83
X 1899–1912		15
Z 1908–1913		1
BEŁCHATÓW	**PIOTRKÓW TRYBUNALSKI**	**POLAND**
K 1890–1911		1
S 1890–1899		83
T 1843–1866		23
B 1824–1872		270
D 1824–1872		
M 1824–1854		
BIAŁA RAWSKA	**SKIERNIEWICE**	**POLAND**
A 1898–1901		131
B 1826–1874		270
D 1826–1874		270
K 1899–1913		1
M 1826–1868		270
BIELAWY	**SKIERNIEWICE**	**POLAND**
B 1826–1855		270
D 1826–1855		270
M 1826–1855		270
BŁASZKI	**SIERADZ**	**POLAND**
O 1904–1912		117
BOLESŁAWIEC	**KALISZ**	**POLAND**
B 1826–1838		270
D 1826–1838		270
M 1826–1838		270

A Army/recruit lists; **B** Birth; **C** Census; **D** Death; **E** Voter lists; **G** Immigration; **H** Holocaust; **J** Judaica; **K** Kahal; **L** Land; **M** Marriage; **N** Name changes; **O** Police files; **P** Pogroms; **R** Reference; **S** School records; **T** Tax lists; **V** Divorce; **W** Occupation Lists; **X** Jewish hospital; **Y** Notary records; **Z** Local government records

TOWN NAME Document Type Years	VOIVODSHIP/OBLAST (Province)	COUNTRY Zespół/Sygnatura (Poland) Fond/Opis/Delo (Belarus, Ukraine, Lithuania)
BOLIMÓW	SKIERNIEWICE	POLAND
B 1826–1858; 1882–1884; 1886–1890		270
D 1826–1858; 1882–1884; 1886–1890		270
M 1826–1858; 1882–1884; 1886–1890		270
BRDÓW	KONIN	POLAND
K 1891		92
BRUŻYCA	INCLUDED IN ALEKSANDRÓW ŁODZKI	
BRZEZINY	SKIERNIEWICE	POLAND
A 1891–1901		17
B 1826–1876		270
D 1826–1876		270
K 1885–1915		1
M 1826–1876		270
S 1889–1898; 1912–1913		83
BRZEŹNICA	ŁÓDŹ	POLAND
B 1826–1864		270
D 1826–1864		270
M 1826–1864		270
BURZENIN	SIERADZ	POLAND
B 1826–1864; 1883–1885; 1888–1894; 1896		270
D 1826–1864; 1883–1885; 1888–1894		270
M 1826–1864; 1883–1885; 1888–1894		270
CZĘSTOCHOWA	CZĘSTOCHOWA	POLAND
A 1891–1902		17
O 1905–1914		43
S 1843/1913		1; 83
W 1864/1914		1/19
X 1900–1913		15
Z 1908–1912		1
DĄBROWA GÓRNICZA	KATOWICE	POLAND
K 1907–1913		1
O 1906		42
Z 1896–1898		1
DZIAŁOSZYN	SIERADZ	POLAND
B 1828–1837		270
D 1828–1837		270
M 1828–1837		270
GŁOWNO	ŁÓDŹ	POLAND
B 1812–1893		270
D 1812–1893		270
K 1822–1866		1
M 1812–1893		270
O 1906		44
Z 1822/1866; 1897–1914		1
GROCHOLICE	PIOTRKÓW TRYBUNALSKI	POLAND
B 1826–1869		270
D 1826–1869		270
M 1826–1869		270
INOWŁÓDZ	PIOTRKÓW TRYBUNALSKI	POLAND
Z 1825–1866; 1900–1913		1
JANÓW	CZĘSTOCHOWA	POLAND
Z 1849–1866; 1893–1913		1
JEŻÓW	SKIERNIEWICE	POLAND
B 1826–1889		270
D 1826–1889		270
M 1826–1889		270
Z 1879–1912		1
KALISZ	KALISZ	POLAND
G 1881/1914; 1923–1957		19; 92
O 1881/1914		114–115
S 1894–1914		122
X 1822/1914		111
Z 1871–1914		92
KAMIEŃSK	PIOTRKÓW TRYBUNALSKI	POLAND
B 1826–1830; 1832–1857		270
D 1826–1830; 1832–1857		270

A Army/recruit lists; **B** Birth; **C** Census; **D** Death; **E** Voter lists; **G** Immigration; **H** Holocaust; **J** Judaica; **K** Kahal; **L** Land; **M** Marriage; **N** Name changes; **O** Police files; **P** Pogroms; **R** Reference; **S** School records; **T** Tax lists; **V** Divorce; **W** Occupation lists; **X** Jewish hospital; **Y** Notary records; **Z** Local government records

TOWN NAME Document Type Years	VOIVODSHIP/OBLAST (Province)	COUNTRY Zespół/Sygnatura (Poland) Fond/Opis/Delo (Belarus, Ukraine, Lithuania)
M 1826–1830; 1832–1857		270
Z 1821–1866; 1900–1912		1
KŁOBUCK	CZĘSTOCHOWA	POLAND
O 1897–1899		113
Z 1835–1866; 1899–1912		1
KOŁO	KONIN	POLAND
S 1893–1909		92; 122
Z 1893–1914		92,96
KONIECPOL	CZĘSTOCHOWA	POLAND
B 1826–1842; 1844–1855; 1890		270
D 1826–1842; 1844–1855; 1890		270
K 1899–1913		1
M 1826–1842; 1844–1855; 1890		270
Z 1841–1866; 1891–1901		1
KONIN	KONIN	POLAND
K 1893–1913		92,96
Z 1895–1914		92,96
KONSTANTYNÓW ŁÓDZKI	ŁÓDŹ	POLAND
B 1832–1889; 1891–1893		270
D 1832–1889; 1891–1893		270
K 1825–1860; 1895–1914		1
M 1832–1889; 1891–1893		270
Z 1895–1896		1,5
KROMOŁÓW	KATOWICE	POLAND
K 1860–1913		1
T 1860–1913		23
KRZEPICE	CZĘSTOCHOWA	POLAND
K 1822–1866		1
Z 1822–1866; 1888–1912		1
KUTNO	PŁOCK	POLAND
B 1808–1833		270
D 1808–1833		270
M 1808–1833		270
LĄDEK	KALISZ	POLAND
G 1903–1904		92
ŁASK	SIERADZ	POLAND
B 1827–1893		270
D 1827–1893		270
K 1899–1913		1
L 1816–1866		1
M 1827–1893		270
S 1889–1898		83
ŁĘCZYCA	PŁOCK	POLAND
K 1878–1912		92
Z 1887–1912		92
ŁÓDŹ	ŁÓDŹ	POLAND
A 1885/1935		221/11471–11482
B 1826–1893		221/270
C 1809–1822; 1827–1939		221/101,374,629–633,8709–8748,9873
D 1826–1893		221/270
G 1885/1935		221/8903–8904,8915–8916,8923–8999
H 1939–1944		221/278
J 1884–1888		221/7174–7178
K 1806–1807; 1818–1872; 1885–1939		221/1561,1565–1572,1598,2931,6790; 228
L 1836–1866; 1881; 1884–1913; 1915–1939		221/6021–6049,6827,7123
M 1826–1893		270
N 1844–1845		221/588
O 1903–1912		221/38,41
S 1818/1935		221/4630–4687,7167–7173,11949
T 1884/1935		221/5916–5948,11804,11806
X 1818/1914		221/7174–7178; 15
Z 1818/1914		1; 5; 221
LUTOMIERSK	SIERADZ	POLAND
B 1826–1876		270
D 1826–1876		270
M 1826–1876		270

A Army/recruit lists; **B** Birth; **C** Census; **D** Death; **E** Voter lists; **G** Immigration; **H** Holocaust; **J** Judaica; **K** Kahal; **L** Land; **M** Marriage; **N** Name changes; **O** Police files; **P** Pogroms; **R** Reference; **S** School records; **T** Tax lists; **V** Divorce; **W** Occupation Lists; **X** Jewish hospital; **Y** Notary records; **Z** Local government records

TOWN NAME Document Type Years	VOIVODSHIP/OBLAST (Province)	COUNTRY Zespół/Sygnatura (Poland) Fond/Opis/Delo (Belarus, Ukraine, Lithuania)
LUTOTÓW	**SIERADZ**	**POLAND**
Z 1913–1914		92
MSTÓW	**CZĘSTOCHOWA**	**POLAND**
K 1887–1892		1
NOWE MIASTO NAD PILICĄ	**RADOM**	**POLAND**
B 1826–1868		270
D 1826–1868		270
K 1820–1861; 1893–1912		1
M 1826–1868		270
OZORKÓW	**ŁÓDŹ**	**POLAND**
M 1844/1902		270
S 1906–1909		83
PABIANICE	**ŁÓDŹ**	**POLAND**
B 1831–1874; 1887–1893		270
D 1831–1874; 1884–1893		270
M 1831–1874; 1882–1893		270
O 1886–1914		39
S 1889–1909		83
PAJĘCZNO	**CZĘSTOCHOWA**	**POLAND**
B 1826–1893		270
D 1826–1893		270
K 1822–1862; 1903–1913		1
M 1826–1893		270
PIOTRKÓW TRYBUNALSKI	**PIOTRKÓW TRYBUNALSKI**	**POLAND**
A 1867–1917		17
B 1826–1873		270
D 1826–1873		270
G 1903–1911		1
K 1868/1914		1
O 1903–1911		41
S 1859/1914		83
T 1816–1866; 1869–1918		23
W 1871/1914		19
X 1822/1913		15
PŁAWNO	**CZĘSTOCHOWA**	**POLAND**
A 1897–1899		17
B 1826–1889; 1891–1893		270
D 1826–1889; 1891–1893		270
K 1822–1866; 1899–1914		1
M 1826–1889; 1891–1893		270
PODDĘBICE	**SIERADZ**	**POLAND**
B 1817–1870		270
D 1817–1870		270
M 1817–1870		270
PRASZKA	**CZĘSTOCHOWA**	**POLAND**
B 1826–1868		270
D 1826–1868		270
K 1870–1875		1
M 1826–1868		270
PRZYRÓW	**CZĘSTOCHOWA**	**POLAND**
A 1898		17
K 1822–1867		1
X 1822–1867		1
RADOGOSZCZ	**ŁÓDŹ**	**POLAND**
Z 1910		1; 227
RADOMSKO	**PIOTRKÓW TRYBUNALSKI**	**POLAND**
A 1891–1902		17
O 1905–1906		43
Z 1873/1914		1
RAWA MAZOWIECKA	**SKIERNIEWICE**	**POLAND**
A 1897–1902		17
B 1875–1877; 1881–1890; 1893		270
D 1875–1877; 1881–1889; 1893		270
K 1913–1914		
M 1875–1877; 1881–1887		270
S 1836/1913		83
T 1846–1857		1

A Army/recruit lists; **B** Birth; **C** Census; **D** Death; **E** Voter lists; **G** Immigration; **H** Holocaust; **J** Judaica; **K** Kahal; **L** Land; **M** Marriage; **N** Name changes; **O** Police files; **P** Pogroms; **R** Reference; **S** School records; **T** Tax lists; **V** Divorce; **W** Occupation lists; **X** Jewish hospital; **Y** Notary records; **Z** Local government records

TOWN NAME Document Type Years	VOIVODSHIP/OBLAST (Province)	COUNTRY Zespół/Sygnatura (Poland) Fond/Opis/Delo (Belarus, Ukraine, Lithuania)	
W 1893–1913		19	
ROZPRZA	**PIÓTRKOW TRYBUNALSKI**		**POLAND**
A 1891–1896		17	
S 1891–1899		83	
Z 1822–1866		1	
RUDA PABIANICKA	**ŁÓDŹ**		**POLAND**
C 1923–1940		223	
SKIERNIEWICE	**SKIERNIEWICE**		**POLAND**
B 1826–1877		270	
D 1826–1877		270	
M 1826–1877		270	
SOBOTA	**SKIERNIEWICE**		**POLAND**
B 1826–1885		270	
D 1826–1885		270	
M 1826–1885		270	
SOSNOWIEC	**KATOWICE**		**POLAND**
A 1907–1911		17	
G 1895/1908		1	
K 1896/1913		1	
O 1906–1912		42	
S 1890–1913		83	
STRYKÓW	**ŁÓDŹ**		**POLAND**
A 1899		17	
B 1826–1870; 1882–1893		270	
D 1826–1870; 1882–1893		270	
K 1907–1913		1	
M 1826–1870; 1882–1893		270	
Z 1821–1866		1	
SULEJÓW	**PIOTRKÓW TRYBUNALSKI**		**POLAND**
A 1902		17	
B 1826–1855; 1866–1883		270	
D 1826–1855; 1866–1883		270	
M 1826–1855; 1866–1883		270	
S 1875–1897		83–84	
W 1899–1913		19	
Z 1864–1866		1	
SULMIERZYCE	**PIOTRKÓW TRYBUNALSKI**		**POLAND**
A 1902		17	
Z 1845–1866		1	
SZADEK	**SIERADZ**		**POLAND**
B 1826–1854; 1882–1893		270	
D 1826–1854; 1882–1893		270	
M 1826–1854; 1882–1893		270	
SZCZERCÓW	**PIOTRKÓW TRYBUNALSKI**		**POLAND**
B 1826–1874		270	
D 1826–1874		270	
M 1826–1874		270	
TOMASZÓW MAZOWIECKI	**PIOTRKÓW TRYBUNALSKI**		**POLAND**
A 1865–1914		17	
B 1830–1881		270	
D 1830–1881		270	
M 1830–1881		270	
S 1828/1914		83	
W 1828/1914		19	
X 1896–1911		15	
TULISZKÓW	**KONIN**		**POLAND**
Z 1905		92	
TUREK	**KONIN**		**POLAND**
G 1908–1909		92	
Z 1913–1914		92	
TUSZYN	**PIOTRKÓW TRYBUNALSKI**		**POLAND**
A 1890		17	
B 1826–1856		270	
D 1826–1856		270	
M 1826–1856		270	

A Army/recruit lists; **B** Birth; **C** Census; **D** Death; **E** Voter lists; **G** Immigration; **H** Holocaust; **J** Judaica; **K** Kahal; **L** Land; **M** Marriage; **N** Name changes; **O** Police files; **P** Pogroms; **R** Reference; **S** School records; **T** Tax lists; **V** Divorce; **W** Occupation Lists; **X** Jewish hospital; **Y** Notary records; **Z** Local government records

TOWN NAME Document Type Years	VOIVODSHIP/OBLAST (Province)	COUNTRY Zespół/Sygnatura (Poland) Fond/Opis/Delo (Belarus, Ukraine, Lithuania)
UJAZD	**PIOTRKÓW TRYBUNALSKI**	**POLAND**
B 1826–1870; 1876		270
D 1826–1870; 1876		270
M 1826–1870; 1876		270
Z 1825–1865; 1897–1912		1
WARTA	**SIERADZ**	**POLAND**
B 1809–1855; 1858		270
D 1809–1855; 1858		270
M 1809–1855; 1858		270
W 1912–1914		92
WIDAWA	**SIERADZ**	**POLAND**
A 1901–1902		92, 107–108
B 1826–1850; 1852–1891		270
D 1826–1850; 1852–1891		270
M 1826–1850; 1852–1875		270
WIELUŃ	**SIERADZ**	**POLAND**
B 1826–1870; 1882–1893		270
D 1826–1870; 1882–1893		270
G 1914		92
M 1826–1870; 1882–1893		270
Z 1895–1914		115
WIERUSZÓW	**KALISZ**	**POLAND**
B 1838–1877		270
D 1838–1874		270
M 1838–1870		270
WOLBÓRZ	**PIOTRKÓW TRYBUNALSKI**	**POLAND**
B 1826–1867		270
D 1826–1867		270
M 1826–1867		270
Z 1906–1915		1
ZAWIERCIE	**KATOWICE**	**POLAND**
A 1891–1901		17
K 1908–1910		1
O 1905–1906		112
ZDUŃSKA WOLA	**SIERADZ**	**POLAND**
B 1826–1893		270
D 1826–1893		270
M 1826–1893		270
ZGIERZ	**ŁÓDŹ**	**POLAND**
A 1890–1902		17
B 1826–1893		270
D 1826–1893		270
G 1867/1914		1
K 1878–1913		1
M 1826–1893		270
O 1905–1906		41
S 1885–1913		83
ZŁOCZEW	**SIERADZ**	**POLAND**
B 1826–1880; 1882–1893		270
D 1826–1872; 1889–1893		270
M 1826–1872		270

ŁOMŻA Branch Archives

CIECHANOWIEC	**ŁOMŻA**	**POLAND**
B 1826–1829; 1833–1839 (INCLUDED IN WYSOKIE MAZOWIECKI)		177
CZYŻEW–OSADA	**ŁOMŻA**	**POLAND**
B 1860–1893		175; 415
D 1860–1893		175; 415
M 1860–1893		175; 415
Y 1869–1939		409–413
GAWRYCHY	**ŁOMŻA**	**POLAND**
C 1933–1939		157
GRAJEWO	**ŁOMŻA**	**POLAND**
B 1832–1894		269
D 1832–1894		269
M 1832–1894		269

A Army/recruit lists; **B** Birth; **C** Census; **D** Death; **E** Voter lists; **G** Immigration; **H** Holocaust; **J** Judaica; **K** Kahal; **L** Land; **M** Marriage; **N** Name changes; **O** Police files; **P** Pogroms; **R** Reference; **S** School records; **T** Tax lists; **V** Divorce; **W** Occupation lists; **X** Jewish hospital; **Y** Notary records; **Z** Local government records

TOWN NAME Document Type Years	VOIVODSHIP/OBLAST (Province)	COUNTRY Zespół/Sygnatura (Poland) Fond/Opis/Delo (Belarus, Ukraine, Lithuania)
JABŁONKA	**ŁOMŻA**	**POLAND**
B 1827; 1834–1836; 1844; 1846–1849; 1852; 1857; 1859–1861; 1863–1866; 1869; 1871		176
D 1826–1857; 1859–1861; 1863–1866; 1869; 1871		176
M 1827; 1834–1836; 1844; 1846–1849; 1852; 1857; 1859–1861; 1863–1866; 1869; 1871		176
KOLNO	**ŁOMŻA**	**POLAND**
A 1872; 1898; 1915		25
Y 1892–1932		206–209
ŁOMŻA	**ŁOMŻA**	**POLAND**
A 1867–1918		12
B 1827–1867; 1869–1890		169
C 1896–1897		19
D 1827–1891		169
L 1896–1897; 1935–1939		19; 64
M 1827–1893		169
S 1825–1839		257–259; 261–262; 267
W 1867–1918		7; 21
X 1850–1868		275
Y 1903; 1938		210–211
Z 1935–1939		64
MAŁY PŁOCK	**ŁOMŻA**	**POLAND**
C 1899–1939		158
NOWOGRÓD	**ŁOMŻA**	**POLAND**
B 1826–1843; 1845–1864; 1866–1894		170
D 1826–1856; 1859–1860; 1862–1864; 1866–1891; 1894		170
M 1826–1831; 1835–1837; 1839–1840; 1843–1894		170
PIĄTNICA	**INCLUDED IN ŁOMŻA**	
RADZIŁÓW	**ŁOMŻA**	**POLAND**
B 1826–1895		270
D 1826–1895		270
M 1826–1895		270
RAJGRÓD	**ŁOMŻA**	**POLAND**
B 1826–1855; 1880–1892		271
D 1826–1855; 1880–1892		271
M 1826–1855; 1880–1892		271
ROGIENICE WYPYCHY	**ŁOMŻA**	**POLAND**
C 1933–1951		160
RUTKI	**ŁOMŻA**	**POLAND**
B 1860–1894		171
D 1860–1894		171
M 1860–1894		171
ŚNIADOWO	**ŁOMŻA**	**POLAND**
B 1824; 1826–1827; 1829; 1833–1834; 1836–1837; 1841–1849; 1852; 1854–1860; 1863; 1867–1869; 1871–1872; 1876–1884; 1886–1891; 1893–1894		172
C 1901–1937		161
D 1824; 1827; 1829; 1833–1834; 1836–1837; 1841–1852; 1854–1860; 1863; 1867–1869; 1871–1872; 1876–1884; 1886–1891; 1893–1894		172
M 1824; 1826–1827; 1829; 1833–1834; 1836–1837; 1841–1849; 1852; 1854–1860; 1863; 1867–1869; 1871–1872; 1876–1884; 1893–1894		172
SZCZEPANKOWO	**ŁOMŻA**	**POLAND**
M 1820–1821		162
SZCZUCZYN	**ŁOMŻA**	**POLAND**
B 1826/1849; 1850–1865; 1866/1869; 1870–1894		272
D 1826/1849; 1850–1865; 1866/1869; 1870–1894		272
M 1826–1831; 1850–1894		272
TUROŚL	**ŁOMŻA**	**POLAND**
C 1931–1939		159
TYKOCIN	**ŁOMŻA**	**POLAND**
E 1906–1907		22
WĄSOSZ	**ŁOMŻA**	**POLAND**
B 1840–1875; 1878; 1881/1886; 1887–1890; 1892–1899		273
D 1840–1875; 1878; 1881/1886; 1887–1890; 1892–1899		273
M 1840–1875; 1878; 1881/1886; 1887–1890; 1892–1899		273
WIZNA	**ŁOMŻA**	**POLAND**
B 1826–1836; 1838–1865; 1868–1873; 1876; 1878; 1882; 1884; 1887–1888; 1890–1894		173
D 1826–1836; 1838–1865; 1868–1873; 1876; 1878; 1882; 1884; 1887–1888; 1890–1894		173
M 1826–1836; 1838–1865; 1868–1873; 1876; 1878; 1882; 1884; 1887–1888; 1890–1894		173

A Army/recruit lists; **B** Birth; **C** Census; **D** Death; **E** Voter lists; **G** Immigration; **H** Holocaust; **J** Judaica; **K** Kahal; **L** Land; **M** Marriage; **N** Name changes; **O** Police files; **P** Pogroms; **R** Reference; **S** School records; **T** Tax lists; **V** Divorce; **W** Occupation Lists; **X** Jewish hospital; **Y** Notary records; **Z** Local government records

TOWN NAME Document Type Years	VOIVODSHIP/OBLAST (Province)	COUNTRY Zespół/Sygnatura (Poland) Fond/Opis/Delo (Belarus, Ukraine, Lithuania)
WYSOKIE MAZOWIECKIE	**ŁOMŻA**	**POLAND**
B 1826–1829; 1833–1896; 1912; 1919; 1926–1934		177
D 1826–1829; 1833–1837; 1840–1841; 1844–1880; 1882; 1891; 1893; 1912; 1927		177
M 1833–1837; 1839–1866; 1868; 1872–1876; 1878–1879; 1882; 1891; 1893; 1912; 1916–1939		177
Y 1909–1915		212
ZAMBRÓW	**ŁOMŻA**	**POLAND**
B 1824–1865; 1867–1881; 1883; 1885–1890; 1892–1894; 1896–1898; 1901–1904; 1907–1910; 1912; 1914; 1922–1923; 1925–1927; 1934–1935		174
D 1824–1865; 1867–1881; 1883; 1885–1890; 1892–1894; 1896–1898; 1901; 1903–1904; 1907–1910; 1912; 1914; 1922–1923; 1925–1927; 1934–1935		174
M 1824–1865; 1867–1881; 1883; 1885–1890; 1892–1894; 1896–1898; 1901; 1903–1904; 1907–1910; 1912; 1914; 1922–1923; 1925–1927; 1934–1935		174
ZARĘBY	**ŁOMŻA**	**POLAND**
B 1874–1880; 1893–1894		420
D 1874–1880; 1893–1894		420
M 1874–1880; 1893–1894		420

ŁOWICZ Branch Archives

BIELAWY	**SKIERNIEWICE**	**POLAND**
B 1820–1821; 1856–1884; 1896–1912; 1935		234
D 1820–1821; 1856–1884; 1896–1912; 1935		234
M 1820–1821; 1856–1884; 1896–1912; 1935		234
BOLIMÓW	**SKIERNIEWICE**	**POLAND**
B 1889–1937		295
D 1889–1937		295
E 1940		14/119–120
L 1940		14/119–120
M 1889–1937		295
W 1940		14/119–120
CHRUŚLIN	**SKIERNIEWICE**	**POLAND**
B 1870		235
D 1870		235
M 1870		235
ŁOWICZ	**SKIERNIEWICE**	**POLAND**
A 1873–1874		224/1–2
B 1826–1832; 1835–1893		296
D 1873–1893		
G 1918–1947		
L 1812–1861		276
M 1873–1893		
Z 1915–1916; 1918–1920; 1940–1941		7/52,90,105,108,144,254,358–359,3045–3046
ŁYSZKOWICE	**SKIERNIEWICE**	**POLAND**
B 1918–1939		305
D 1918–1939		305
M 1918–1939		305
SOBOTA	**SKIERNIEWICE**	**POLAND**
B 1826; 1856–1858; 1861–1872; 1874–1937		236
D 1826; 1856–1858; 1861–1872; 1874–1937		236
M 1826; 1856–1858; 1861–1872; 1874–1937		236

LUBLIN Archives

ADAMÓW	**SIEDLCE**	**POLAND**
K 1925–1935		SPŁUK/627
T 1925–1935		SPŁUK/627
ANNOPOL	**TARNOBRZEG**	**POLAND**
B 1826–1855		113
D 1826–1855		113
E 1867–1912		RGL IV ADM.
K 1867–1912; 1922–1935		RGL IV ADM; UWL WSP/783
M 1826–1855		113
T 1867–1912; 1922–1935		RGL IV ADM; UWL WSP/783
BARANÓW	**LUBLIN**	**POLAND**
B 1826–1851; 1853–1855; 1859; 1862; 1864; 1868; 1872–1889; 1891–1893		113
D 1826–1851; 1853–1860; 1862; 1864; 1868; 1871–1889; 1891–1893		113
M 1826–1851; 1853–1855; 1857; 1859; 1862; 1864; 1868; 1872–1889; 1891–1893		113

A Army/recruit lists; **B** Birth; **C** Census; **D** Death; **E** Voter lists; **G** Immigration; **H** Holocaust; **J** Judaica; **K** Kahal; **L** Land; **M** Marriage; **N** Name changes; **O** Police files; **P** Pogroms; **R** Reference; **S** School records; **T** Tax lists; **V** Divorce; **W** Occupation lists; **X** Jewish hospital; **Y** Notary records; **Z** Local government records

TOWN NAME Document Type Years	VOIVODSHIP/OBLAST (Province)	COUNTRY Zespół/Sygnatura (Poland) Fond/Opis/Delo (Belarus, Ukraine, Lithuania)
BELZ	**LVOV**	**UKRAINE**
T 1755–1786		62
BEŁŻCE	**LUBLIN**	**POLAND**
B 1826–1868		113
D 1826–1868		113
E 1869–1914		RGL IV ADM.
H 1939–1944		KREISHAUPTMANSCHAFT LUBLIN
K 1811–1856 (CEMETERY RECORDS); 1869–1914; 1919–1938		27/18; RGL IV; SPL/645; UWL WSP/801
M 1826–1868		113
N 1821–1847		27/28
T 1869–1914; 1919–1938		RGL IV; SPL/645; UWL WSP/801
BIAŁA PODLASKA	**BIAŁA PODLASKA**	**POLAND**
B 1826–1894		113
C 1833/1950		20
D 1826–1894		113
E 1913–1915		RGCH/458
K 1913–1915; 1924–1937		RGCH/458; 403/754–759; 404/203–208; 49
M 1826–1894		113
T 1913–1915; 1927–1936		RGCH/458; UWL WSP/754
BIŁGORAJ	**ZAMOŚĆ**	**POLAND**
B 1870–1875		113
D 1870–1875		113
E 1870–1909; 1911–1915		RGL ADM; RGCH/484
H 1942		DIST.LUBLIN/749
K 1870–1909; 1911–1915; 1922–1937		RGL ADM; RGCH/484; 403/760–766
M 1869–1875		113
T 1870–1909; 1911–1915; 1927		RGL ADM; RGCH/484; UWL WSP/760
BISKUPICE	**LUBLIN**	**POLAND**
B 1826–1888		113
D 1826–1888		113
E 1869–1914		RGL IV ADM.
G 1940–1941		2–6; 140
H 1939–1942 (JUDENRAT)		618/2–6; 501/140
K 1869–1914; 1919–1936		RGL IV ADM; SPL/646
M 1826–1888		113
T 1869–1914; 1919–1936		RGL IV ADM; SPL/646
W 1940–1941		2–6
BOBROWNIKI	**LUBLIN**	**POLAND**
B 1892–1893		113
D 1892–1893		113
E 1867–1893 (AFTER 1893, INCLUDED IN IRENA)		RGL IV ADM.
K 1867–1893 (AFTER 1893, INCLUDED IN IRENA)		RGL IV ADM.
M 1892–1893		113
T 1867–1893 (AFTER 1893, INCLUDED IN IRENA)		RGL IV ADM.
BREST	**BREST**	**BELARUS**
C 1915		ZPB/7
BYCHAWA	**LUBLIN**	**POLAND**
B 1826–1893		113
D 1826–1893		113
E 1871–1914		RGL IV ADM
H 1940–1942		KREISHAUPTMANSCHAFT LUBLIN
K 1797–1808; 1871–1914; 1919–1936		RGL IV ADM; SPL/647
M 1826–1893		113
T 1871–1914; 1919–1936		RGL IV ADM; SPL/647
CHEŁM	**CHEŁM**	**POLAND**
B 1826–1890; 1892		113
D 1823–1894		113
E 1870–1915		RGL ADM; RGCH/480
G 1919/1950		117–118
K 1842; 1870–1915; 1922; 1927–1936		RGL ADM; RGCH/480; UWL WSP/766; 416
M 1826–1890; 1892		113
T 1744–1786; 1870–1915; 1927–1936		RGL ADM; RGCH/480; UWL WSP/766
CHODEL	**LUBLIN**	**POLAND**
B 1870–1888		113
D 1870–1888		113
E 1869–1912		RGL IV ADM.
H 1941		498
K 1869–1912; 1919–1938		RGL IV ADM; SPL/648

A Army/recruit lists; **B** Birth; **C** Census; **D** Death; **E** Voter lists; **G** Immigration; **H** Holocaust; **J** Judaica; **K** Kahal; **L** Land; **M** Marriage; **N** Name changes;
O Police files; **P** Pogroms; **R** Reference; **S** School records; **T** Tax lists; **V** Divorce; **W** Occupation Lists; **X** Jewish hospital; **Y** Notary records; **Z** Local government records

TOWN NAME Document Type Years	VOIVODSHIP/OBLAST (Province)	COUNTRY Zespół/Sygnatura (Poland) Fond/Opis/Delo (Belarus, Ukraine, Lithuania)
M 1870–1888		113
T 1869–1912; 1919–1938		RGL IV ADM; SPL/648
CZAJKI	**LUBLIN**	**POLAND**
T INCLUDED IN: KRASNYSTAW		
CZEMIERNIKI	**BIAŁA PODLASKA**	**POLAND**
B 1828–1855; 1858–1874; 1877–1878; 1882		113
D 1828–1855; 1858–1874; 1877–1878; 1882		113
E 1868–1912		RGL IV ADM.
K 1868–1912; 1921–1927		RGL IV ADM; UWL WSP/796
M 1828–1855; 1858–1874; 1877–1878; 1882		113
T 1868–1912; 1921–1927		RGL IV ADM; UWL WSP/796
DUBIENKA	**CHEŁM**	**POLAND**
B 1826–1853; 1857–1894		113
D 1826–1853; 1857–1894		113
E 1867–1907		RGL IV ADM.
K 1867–1907; 1927; 1929–1933		RGL IV; UWL WSP/779; SPH/509
M 1826–1853; 1857–1894		113
T 1795–1797; 1867–1907; 1927; 1929–1933		RGL IV; UWL WSP/779; SPH/509
W 1785		30
FIRLEJ	**LUBLIN**	**POLAND**
B 1826–1831		113
D 1826–1831		113
M 1826–1831		113
FRAMPOL	**ZAMOŚĆ**	**POLAND**
B 1871–1875		113
D 1871–1875		113
E 1878–1914		RGL IV ADM
K 1878–1914; 1927		RGL IV ADM; UWL WSP/761
M 1871–1875		113
T 1878–1914; 1927		RGL IV ADM; UWL WSP/761
GARWOLIN	**SIEDLCE**	**POLAND**
E 1895; 1913–1915		RGL IV ADM
K 1895; 1913–1915; 1921–1936		RGL IV ADM; 403/770
T 1895; 1913–1915; 1927–1936		RGL IV ADM; UWL WSP/770
GŁUSK	**LUBLIN**	**POLAND**
B 1826–1886		113
C 1854		6
D 1826–1905		113
E 1869–1914		RGL IV ADM.
K 1845; 1869–1914; 1920–1928		22; RGL IV; SPL/649; UWL WSP/805
M 1826–1886		113
T 1869–1914; 1920–1928		RGL IV; SPL/649
W 1819–1866		1
GORAJ LUBELSKI	**ZAMOŚĆ**	**POLAND**
E 1875–1914		RGL IV ADM
K 1875–1914; 1927–1928		RGL IV ADM; UWL WSP/762,1556
T 1875–1914; 1927–1928		RGL IV ADM; UWL WSP/762,1556
GORZKÓW	**ZAMOŚĆ**	**POLAND**
B 1826–1843; 1845–1870; 1875		113
C 1910		ZPK/123
D 1826–1843; 1845–1870; 1875		113
E 1873–1913		RGL IV ADM
K 1873–1913; 1925–1927		RGL IV ADM; UWL WSP/1559
M 1826–1843; 1845–1870; 1875		113
T 1866; 1873–1913; 1925–1927 & ALSO INCLUDED IN KRASNYSTAW		NPK/16; RGL IV ADM; UWL WSP/1559
GRABOWIEC	**ZAMOŚĆ**	**POLAND**
B 1826–1875		113
D 1826–1875		113
E 1867–1912		RGL IV ADM.
K 1867–1912; 1921–1935		RGL IV ADM.; UWL WSP/780
M 1826–1875		113
T 1867–1912; 1921–1935		RGL IV ADM.; UWL WSP/780
HORODŁO	**ZAMOŚĆ**	**POLAND**
B 1826–1854		113
D 1826–1854		113
E 1867–1912; 1916–1917		RGL IV ADM.; RGCH/654
K 1867–1912; 1916–1917; 1927		RGL IV; RGCH/654; UWL WSP/781

A Army/recruit lists; **B** Birth; **C** Census; **D** Death; **E** Voter lists; **G** Immigration; **H** Holocaust; **J** Judaica; **K** Kahal; **L** Land; **M** Marriage; **N** Name changes; **O** Police files; **P** Pogroms; **R** Reference; **S** School records; **T** Tax lists; **V** Divorce; **W** Occupation lists; **X** Jewish hospital; **Y** Notary records; **Z** Local government records

TOWN NAME Document Type Years	VOIVODSHIP/OBLAST (Province)	COUNTRY Zespół/Sygnatura (Poland) Fond/Opis/Delo (Belarus, Ukraine, Lithuania)
L 1742; 1744		33
M 1826–1854		113
T 1867–1912; 1916–1917; 1927		RGL IV; RGCH/654; UWL WSP/781
Z 1600/1809		33
HRUBIESZÓW	**ZAMOŚĆ**	**POLAND**
B 1826–1875		113
D 1826–1875		113
E 1870–1909		RGL IV ADM.
K 1870–1909; 1921–1936		RGL IV; 403/778–782; 405/511
M 1826–1875		113
T 1870–1909; 1927–1936		RGL IV; UWL WSP/778; SPH/511
IRENA	**LUBLIN**	**POLAND**
B 1869–1891		113
D 1869–1891		113
E 1860–1864; 1868–1911		POLISH RGL/1716; RGL ADM.
K 1860–1864; 1868–1911; 1922–1927		POL. RGL/1716; RGL IV; UWL WSP/812
M 1869–1891		113
T 1860–1864; 1868–1911; 1922–1927		POL. RGL/1716; RGL IV; UWL WSP/812
IZBICA	**ZAMOŚĆ**	**POLAND**
B 1826–1872; 1875		113
C 1910		ZPK/124
D 1826–1861; 1863–1864		113
E 1873–1915		RGL IV ADM.
G 1859		22/51
K 1873–1915; 1927		RGL IV ADM; UWL WSP/789
M 1826–1864		113
T 1873–1915; 1927		RGL IV ADM; UWL WSP/789
JANÓW LUBELSKI	**TARNOBRZEG**	**POLAND**
C 1900–1942		TOWN ACTS (SEE KRAŚNIK)
E 1870–1914		RGL IV ADM.
K 1870–1914; 1924–1935		RGL IV ADM.; SPJ/13
T 1870–1914; 1924–1925		RGL IV ADM.; SPJ/13
JANÓW PODLASKI	**BIAŁA PODLASKA**	**POLAND**
B 1826–1892		113
D 1826–1892		113
K 1927		UWL WSP/793
M 1826–1892		113
T 1927		UWL WSP/793
JANOWIEC	**LUBLIN**	**POLAND**
B 1817–1894		113
C 1774		22/299A
D 1817–1894		113
M 1817–1894		113
JARCZÓW	**ZAMOŚĆ**	**POLAND**
B 1826–1875		113
D 1826–1875		113
E 1892–1913		RGL IV ADM
K 1892–1913		RGL IV ADM
M 1826–1875		113
T 1892–1913		RGL IV ADM
JAROSŁAWIEC	**ZAMOŚĆ**	**POLAND**
B 1874–1875		113
D 1874–1875		113
M 1874–1875		113
JÓZEFÓW	**ZAMOŚĆ**	**POLAND**
B 1826–1875		113
D 1826–1875		113
E 1867–1914		RGL IV ADMIN.
K 1867–1914; 1922–1927		RGL ADM; UWL WSP/763
M 1826–1875		113
T 1867–1914; 1922–1927		RGL ADM; UWL WSP/763
JÓZEFÓW NAD WISLĄ	**LUBLIN**	**POLAND**
B 1826–1895		113
D 1826–1893		113
E 1872–1914		RGL IV ADM.
K 1872–1914; 1927		RGL IV ADM; UWL WSP/813
M 1826–1893		113

A Army/recruit lists; **B** Birth; **C** Census; **D** Death; **E** Voter lists; **G** Immigration; **H** Holocaust; **J** Judaica; **K** Kahal; **L** Land; **M** Marriage; **N** Name changes; **O** Police files; **P** Pogroms; **R** Reference; **S** School records; **T** Tax lists; **V** Divorce; **W** Occupation Lists; **X** Jewish hospital; **Y** Notary records; **Z** Local government records

TOWN NAME Document Type Years	VOIVODSHIP/OBLAST (Province)	COUNTRY Zespół/Sygnatura (Poland) Fond/Opis/Delo (Belarus, Ukraine, Lithuania)
T 1872–1914; 1927		RGL IV ADM; UWL WSP/813
KAMIONKA	**LUBLIN**	**POLAND**
B 1826–1894		113
D 1826–1894		113
E 1867–1914		RGL IV ADM.
K 1867–1914; 1922–1927		RGL IV ADM; UWL WSP/797
M 1826–1894		113
T 1867–1914; 1922–1927		RGL IV ADM; UWL WSP/797
KAZIMIERZ	**KRAKÓW**	**POLAND**
C 1865		37/114
KAZIMIERZ DOLNY	**LUBLIN**	**POLAND**
B 1826–1842; 1848; 1859; 1863		91; 113
C 1864–1865		93,114
D 1826–1842; 1848; 1859; 1863		92; 113
E 1867–1914		RGL IV ADM.
K 1849–1850; 1858–1914; 1922–1927		160–169; RGL IV; UWL WSP/812
M 1826–1842; 1848; 1863		113
T 1858–1914		RGL IV ADM.; 176
Z 1799–1809		44–45; 47; 63–64
KOCK	**LUBLIN**	**POLAND**
B 1826–1894		113
C 1877/1915		
D 1826–1894		113
E 1913		RGL IV ADM.
K 1913; 1927		RGL IV; UWL WSP/808
M 1826–1894		113
T 1913; 1924–1935		RGL IV; UWL WSP/808; SPŁUK/628
KODEŃ	**BIAŁA PODLASKA**	**POLAND**
B 1826–1893		113
D 1826–1893		113
K 1924; 1927		SPB/204; UWL WSP/755
M 1826–1893		113
T 1924; 1927		SPB/204; UWL WSP/755
KOMARÓW	**ZAMOŚĆ**	**POLAND**
B 1826–1872		113
D 1826–1872		113
E 1872–1899; 1902; 1905; 1910; 1912–1913		RGL IV ADM
K 1872–1899; 1902; 1905; 1910; 1912–1913; 1927		RGL IV ADM; UWL WSP/836
M 1826–1872		113
T 1872–1899; 1902; 1905; 1910; 1912–1913; 1927		RGL IV ADM; UWL WSP/836
KOŃSKOWOLA	**LUBLIN**	**POLAND**
B 1826–1893		113
D 1826–1893		113
E 1873–1913		RGL IV ADM.
K 1873–1913; 1923–1927		RGL IV ADM.; UWL WSP/815
M 1826–1893		113
T 1873–1913; 1923–1927		RGL IV ADM.; UWL WSP/815
KONSTANTYNÓW	**BIAŁA PODLASKA**	**POLAND**
B 1826–1888		113
D 1826–1888		113
K 1922–1927		UWL WSP/794
M 1826–1888		113
T 1922–1927		UWL WSP/794
KOSÓW LACKI	**SIEDLCE**	**POLAND**
E 1913–1914		RGL IV ADM
K 1913–1914; 1922–1936		RGL IV ADM; UWL WSP/826
T 1913–1914; 1922–1936		RGL IV ADM; UWL WSP/826
KRAŚNICZYN	**CHEŁM**	**POLAND**
B 1826–1836		113
C 1910 (INCLUDED IN KRASNYSTAW)		ZPK/125
D 1826–1836		113
E 1910–1914 & ALSO INCLUDED IN KRASNYSTAW		RGL IV ADM
K 1910–1914 & ALSO INCLUDED IN KRASNYSTAW		RGL IV ADM
M 1826–1836		113
T 1910–1914 & ALSO INCLUDED IN KRASNYSTAW		RGL IV ADM
KRAŚNIK	**LUBLIN**	**POLAND**
B 1826–1855; 1866–1875; 1882–1884		113

A Army/recruit lists; **B** Birth; **C** Census; **D** Death; **E** Voter lists; **G** Immigration; **H** Holocaust; **J** Judaica; **K** Kahal; **L** Land; **M** Marriage; **N** Name changes;
O Police files; **P** Pogroms; **R** Reference; **S** School records; **T** Tax lists; **V** Divorce; **W** Occupation lists; **X** Jewish hospital; **Y** Notary records; **Z** Local government records

TOWN NAME Document Type Years	VOIVODSHIP/OBLAST (Province)	COUNTRY Zespół/Sygnatura (Poland) Fond/Opis/Delo (Belarus, Ukraine, Lithuania)
D 1826–1886		113
E 1869–1914		RGL IV ADM
K 1869–1914; 1922–1935		RGL IV ADM; UWL WSP/785
M 1826–1886		113
T 1869–1914; 1922–1935		RGL IV ADM; UWL WSP/785
KRASNOBRÓD	**ZAMOŚĆ**	**POLAND**
B 1827–1873		113
D 1827–1873		113
E 1867–1910		RGL IV ADM
K 1867–1910; 1922–1926		RGL IV ADM; UWL WSP/839
M 1827–1873		113
T 1867–1910; 1922–1926		RGL IV ADM; UWL WSP/839
KRASNYSTAW	**CHEŁM**	**POLAND**
B 1826–1833; 1835–1893		113
C 1910		ZPK/125
D 1826–1833; 1835–1893		113
E 1868–1914		RGL IV ADM.
K 1868–1914; 1922–1927		RGL IV ADM; 403/788–791
M 1826–1833; 1835–1893		113
T 1710; 1868–1914; 1922–1927; 1936		RGL IV ADM; UWL WSP/788
KRYŁÓW	**ZAMOŚĆ**	**POLAND**
B 1826–1874		113
D 1826–1874		113
E 1867–1906		RGL IV ADM.
K 1867–1906		RGL IV ADM.
M 1826–1874		113
T 1867–1906		RGL IV ADM.
KRZESZÓW	**TARNOBRZEG**	**POLAND**
B 1826–1832		113
C 1786; 1795		71/1604–1605
E 1872–1909		RGL IV ADM.
K 1872–1909; 1924–1934		RGL IV ADM; UWL WSP/764
M 1826–1834		113
T 1872–1909; 1924–1934		RGL IV ADM; UWL WSP/764
KURÓW	**LUBLIN**	**POLAND**
B 1828–1894		113
D 1828–1894		113
E 1873–1915		RGL IV ADM
K 1873–1915; 1922–1935		RGL IV ADM; UWL WSP/816
M 1828–1894		113
T 1873–1915; 1922–1935		RGL IV ADM; UWL WSP/816
ŁASKARZEW	**SIEDLCE**	**POLAND**
K 1927		UWL WSP/771
T 1927		UWL WSP/771
ŁASZCZÓW	**ZAMOŚĆ**	**POLAND**
B 1826–1875		113
D 1826–1875		113
E 1868–1903; 1906–1916		RGL IV ADM; RGCH/489
K 1868–1903; 1906–1916; 1923–1929		RGL IV; RGCH/489; UWL WSP/837
M 1826–1875		113
T 1868–1903; 1906–1916; 1923–1929		RGL IV; RGCH/489; UWL WSP/837
ŁĘCZNA	**LUBLIN**	**POLAND**
B 1826–1894		113
C 1812–1856		44
D 1826–1894		113
E 1872–1914		RGL IV ADM.
K 1872–1914; 1922–1937		RGL IV ADM; UWL WSP/798
M 1826–1894		113
T 1816–1827; 1872–1914; 1922–1937		RGL IV ADM; UWL WSP/798
ŁOMAZY	**BIAŁA PODLASKA**	**POLAND**
B 1826–1854; 1856–1872		113
D 1826–1854; 1856–1872		113
E 1913–1915		RGCH/490
K 1913–1915; 1923–1928		RGCH/490; SPB/205
M 1826–1854; 1856–1872		113
T 1913–1915; 1923–1928		RGCH/490; SPB/205
ŁOPIENNIK	**LUBLIN**	**POLAND**
T INCLUDED IN KRASNYSTAW		

A Army/recruit lists; **B** Birth; **C** Census; **D** Death; **E** Voter lists; **G** Immigration; **H** Holocaust; **J** Judaica; **K** Kahal; **L** Land; **M** Marriage; **N** Name changes; **O** Police files; **P** Pogroms; **R** Reference; **S** School records; **T** Tax lists; **V** Divorce; **W** Occupation Lists; **X** Jewish hospital; **Y** Notary records; **Z** Local government records

TOWN NAME Document Type Years	VOIVODSHIP/OBLAST (Province)	COUNTRY Zespół/Sygnatura (Poland) Fond/Opis/Delo (Belarus, Ukraine, Lithuania)
ŁOSICE	**BIAŁA PODLASKA**	**POLAND**
B 1864–1869; 1871–1875; 1887; 1891–1894		113
D 1864–1869; 1871–1875; 1887; 1891–1894		113
K 1927		UWL WSP/756
M 1864–1869; 1871–1875; 1887; 1891–1894		113
T 1927		UWL WSP/756
LUBARTÓW	**LUBLIN**	**POLAND**
A 1919–1939		
B 1826–1939		570–592
C 1823–1827; 1917–1940		113
D 1826–1939		AMLUB/12; 11; 505–519
E 1873–1914; 1919–1939		113
G 1940–1943		RGL IV ADM; 445–460
H 1940–1944		833–834
K 1766; 1873–1914; 1919–1937		AM LUB/833
M 1826–1939		RGL IV ADM; 403/795–799; 476–486
T 1873–1914; 1922–1935		113
Z 1545–1570; 1714–1827		RGL IV ADM; UWL WSP/795
		43
LUBLIN	**LUBLIN**	**POLAND**
A 1886–1915		22/983–1010
B 1826–1894; 1941		113; 22/746
C 1774; 1819; 1849; 1852–1853; 1858–1871; 1876–1915; 1920–1921; 1940–1950		22/71, 749, 1155, 1172–1174, 1176–1177, 1179, 1186–1187, 1199, 1222–1734,3430,3486; 20/299A
D 1826–1894; 1907–1942		113; 22/746
E 1849; 1894–1918; 1924		AML/2415; 22/545–550; SPL/650
G 1876–1895; 1940–1942		22/1735–5237; 43–49; 170–172
H 1939–1943		20–21; 43–49,150–172; 131; 301–304; 333; 498/891–898
K 1775–1782; 1812–1915; 1919–1939		22/536–539,551–630,8271; 289; 403/800–806; 410; 645–651; 411/49
L 1940		300
M 1826–1894; 1941		113
S 1861; 1869; 1871–1913		22/418–516,540,2415,5869–5895
T 1716; 1790; 1831; 1854; 1862–1915; 1924–1936		AML/2415; UWL WSP/800
W 1735; 1752; 1812–1869		22/262–263,265,1083–1386
X 1837–1880		22/1105–1106,2219–2222,2231
Z 1736; 1765; 1791; 1844–1868		488; 1533–1737
ŁUKÓW	**SIEDLCE**	**POLAND**
B 1826–1872		113
C 1869–1877; 1944–1950		ZPLUG/164
D 1826–1872		113
E 1913–1914		RGL IV ADM.
K 1913–1914; 1923–1936		RGL IV ADM; UWL WSP/807–810; SPŁUK/629; 413/637–641
M 1826–1872		113
T 1913–1914; 1925–1936		RGL IV; UWL WSP/807; SPŁUK/629
ŁYSOBYKI	**LUBLIN**	**POLAND**
B 1826–1876; 1881		113
D 1826–1876; 1881		113
E 1913–1914		RGL IV ADM.
K 1913–1914; 1927; 1931–1935		RGL IV; UWL WSP/809; SPŁUK/630
M 1826–1876; 1881		113
T 1913–1914; 1927; 1931–1935		RGL IV; UWL WSP/809; SPŁUK/630
MACIEJOWICE	**SIEDLCE**	**POLAND**
E 1914		RGL IV ADM
K 1914; 1921–1936		RGL IV ADM; UWL WSP/772
T 1914; 1921–1936		RGL IV ADM; UWL WSP/772
MARKUSZÓW	**LUBLIN**	**POLAND**
B 1826–1894		113
D 1826–1894		113
E 1868–1912		RGL IV ADM
K 1868–1912; 1927–1929		RGL IV ADM; UWL WSP/817
M 1826–1894		113
T 1868–1912; 1927–1929		RGL IV ADM; UWL WSP/817
MICHÓW	**LUBLIN**	**POLAND**
B 1826–1894		113
D 1826–1894		113
E 1873–1914		RGL IV ADM.

A Army/recruit lists; **B** Birth; **C** Census; **D** Death; **E** Voter lists; **G** Immigration; **H** Holocaust; **J** Judaica; **K** Kahal; **L** Land; **M** Marriage; **N** Name changes;
O Police files; **P** Pogroms; **R** Reference; **S** School records; **T** Tax lists; **V** Divorce; **W** Occupation lists; **X** Jewish hospital; **Y** Notary records; **Z** Local government records

TOWN NAME Document Type Years	VOIVODSHIP/OBLAST (Province)	COUNTRY Zespół/Sygnatura (Poland) Fond/Opis/Delo (Belarus, Ukraine, Lithuania)
K 1873–1914; 1927–1936		RGL IV ADM; UWL WSP/799
M 1826–1894		113
T 1873–1914; 1927–1936		RGL IV ADM; UWL WSP/799
MIĘDZYRZEC PODLASKI	**BIAŁA PODLASKA**	**POLAND**
B 1826–1893		113
D 1826–1893		113
E 1872; 1913–1914		RGL IV ADM
K 1863–1866; 1872; 1913–1914; 1927–1936		RGL IV ADM; NPRADZYN/12; UWL WSP/821
M 1826–1893		113
T 1872; 1913–1914; 1920–1943		RGL IV; UWL WSP/821
MODLIBORZYCE	**TARNOBRZEG**	**POLAND**
E 1868–1911		RGL IV ADM
K 1868–1911; 1922–1935		RGL IV ADM; UWL WSP/786
T 1790–1808; 1868–1911; 1922–1935		RGL IV ADM; UWL WSP/786
Z 1641–1809		47
MOKOBODY	**SIEDLCE**	**POLAND**
E 1913–1915		RGL IV ADM
K 1913–1915; 1926–1927		RGL IV ADM; UWL WSP/1564
T 1913–1915; 1926–1927		RGL IV ADM; UWL WSP/1564
MORDY	**SIEDLCE**	**POLAND**
E 1913–1914		RGL IV ADM
K 1913–1914; 1922–1929		RGL IV ADM; UWL WSP/824
T 1913–1914; 1922–1929		RGL IV ADM; UWL WSP/824
OPOLE LUBELSKIE	**LUBLIN**	**POLAND**
B 1826–1879		113
D 1826–1850; 1855–1873		113
E 1870–1914		RGL IV ADM
K 1870–1914; 1926–1929		RGL IV ADM; UWL WSP/818
M 1826–1875		113
T 1870–1914; 1926–1929		RGL IV ADM; UWL WSP/818
Z 1510/1811		48
OSIECK	**SIEDLCE**	**POLAND**
K 1923–1936		UWL WSP/773
T 1923–1936		UWL WSP/773
OSTRÓW LUBELSKI	**LUBLIN**	**POLAND**
B 1941		AMO/135
C 1890; 1919; 1921; 1927		AMO/166–167,169–170; 901/136
D 1941		AMO/135
E 1912–1915; 1919; 1922; 1927–1928; 1934–1935; 1939		30–44; RGCH/657
G 1922–1929		72–76
H 1940–1942		901/134
K 1912–1915; 1922–1935		RGCH/657; UWL WSP/831; AMO 128–133
M 1941		AMO/135
T 1912–1915; 1924–1935		RGCH/657; UWL WSP/831
PARCZEW	**BIAŁA PODLASKA**	**POLAND**
B 1826–1832; 1846–1855		113
D 1825–1853		113
E 1906; 1913–1915		RGL IV ADM
K 1906; 1913–1915; 1927–1929		RGL IV ADM; UWL WSP/832
S 1630		25
T 1906; 1913–1915; 1927–1929		RGL IV ADM; UWL WSP/832
Z 1570–1629		63
PARYSÓW	**SIEDLCE**	**POLAND**
E 1913–1915		RGL IV ADM
K 1913–1915; 1922–1936		RGL IV ADM; UWL WSP/772
T 1913–1915; 1922–1936		RGL IV ADM; UWL WSP/772
PIASKI	**LUBLIN**	**POLAND**
B 1826–1893		113
D 1826–1893		113
E 1869–1915		RGL IV ADM.
H 1940–1942		KREISHAUPTMANSCHAFT LUBLIN
K 1869–1915; 1919–1939		RGL IV ADM; SPL/651
M 1826–1893		113
T 1869–1915; 1919–1939		RGL IV ADM; SPL/651
PISZCZAC	**BIAŁA PODLASKA**	**POLAND**
B 1815; 1820; 1823; 1825–1871; 1874–1892		113
D 1815; 1820; 1823; 1825–1871; 1874–1892		113

A Army/recruit lists; **B** Birth; **C** Census; **D** Death; **E** Voter lists; **G** Immigration; **H** Holocaust; **J** Judaica; **K** Kahal; **L** Land; **M** Marriage; **N** Name changes; **O** Police files; **P** Pogroms; **R** Reference; **S** School records; **T** Tax lists; **V** Divorce; **W** Occupation Lists; **X** Jewish hospital; **Y** Notary records; **Z** Local government records

TOWN NAME Document Type Years	VOIVODSHIP/OBLAST (Province)	COUNTRY Zespół/Sygnatura (Poland) Fond/Opis/Delo (Belarus, Ukraine, Lithuania)
E 1912–1914		RGCH/444
K 1912–1914; 1923–1926		RGCH/444; UWL WSP/757
M 1815; 1820; 1823; 1825–1871; 1874–1892		113
T 1912–1914; 1923–1926		RGCH/444; UWL WSP/757
PRAWDA	**SIEDLCE**	**POLAND**
T (INCLUDED IN GARWOLIN)		RGL IV ADM; UWL WSP/770
PUCHACZÓW	**LUBLIN**	**POLAND**
T 1866		NPK/16
PUŁAWY	**LUBLIN**	**POLAND**
B 1838–1893		113
E 1887; 1895–1897; 1899; 1901–1914		RGL IV ADM
K 1887; 1895–1897; 1899; 1901–1914; 1927		RGL IV ADM; UWL WSP/811–819
M 1866–1893		113
T 1887; 1895–1897; 1899; 1901–1914; 1927; 1929		RGL IV ADM; UWL WSP/811; 414
RADZYŃ PODLASKI	**BIAŁA PODLASKA**	**POLAND**
B 1826–1862		113
C 1909–1916		
D 1826–1880		113
E 1872–1866; 1913–1914		RGL IV ADM
K 1863–1866; 1872–1896; 1913–1914; 1922–1936		NPRADZYN/12; RGL IV ADM; UWL WSP/820–822
M 1826–1862		113
T 1872–1896; 1913–1914; 1927		RGL IV ADM; UWL WSP/820
REJOWIEC	**CHEŁM**	**POLAND**
B 1826–1885; 1888–1892		113
D 1826–1877; 1882; 1884–1885; 1888		113
E 1871–1915		RGL ADM; RGCH/481
H 1941		36
K 1871–1915; 1927–1937		RGL ADM; RGCH/481; UWL WSP/767
M 1826–1877; 1888; 1891–1892		113
T 1871–1915; 1927–1937		RGL ADM; RGCH/481; UWL WSP/767
ROSSOSZ	**BIAŁA PODLASKA**	**POLAND**
K 1924–1928		SPB/207
T 1924–1928		SPB/207
SARNAKI	**BIAŁA PODLASKA**	**POLAND**
B 1859–1875; 1877–1879; 1885–1887; 1890–1891; 1893–1894		113
D 1859–1875; 1877–1879; 1885–1887; 1890–1891; 1893–1894		113
E 1913–1914		RGL IV ADM
K 1913–1914; 1927		RGL IV ADM; UWL WSP/794
M 1859–1875; 1877–1879; 1885–1887; 1890–1891; 1893–1894		113
T 1913–1914; 1927		RGL IV ADM; UWL WSP/794
SAWIN	**CHEŁM**	**POLAND**
E 1912–1915		RGL IV ADM
K 1912–1915; 1927		RGL IV ADM; UWL WSP/768
T 1912–1915; 1927		RGL IV ADM; UWL WSP/768
SEROCZYN	**SIEDLCE**	**POLAND**
E 1913–1915		RGL IV ADM
K 1913–1915; 1923–1927		RGL IV ADM; UWL WSP/1565
T 1913–1915; 1923–1927		RGL IV ADM; UWL WSP/1565
SIEDLCE	**SIEDLCE**	**POLAND**
E 1872–1914		RGL IV ADM
K 1872–1914; 1922–1936		RGL IV ADM; 403/823–824
T 1872–1914; 1922–1936		RGL IV ADM; UWL WSP/823
SIEDLISZCZE	**CHEŁM**	**POLAND**
B 1827; 1829; 1874–1883; 1885; 1888		113
D 1827; 1829; 1874–1883; 1885; 1888		113
E 1869–1909; 1913–1915		RGL IV ADM; RGCH/536
H 1941		37
K 1869–1909; 1913–1915; 1923–1930		RGL ADM; RGCH/536; UWL WSP/1557
M 1827; 1829; 1874–1883; 1885; 1888		113
T 1869–1909; 1913–1915; 1923–1930		RGL ADM; RGCH/536; UWL WSP/1557
SIENNICA RÓŻANA	**INCLUDED IN KRASNYSTAW**	**POLAND**
SŁAWATYCZE	**BIAŁA PODLASKA**	**POLAND**
B 1847–1855; 1864–1895		113
D 1847–1855; 1864–1895		113
E 1911–1915		RGCH/443
K 1911–1915; 1927		RGCH/443; UWL WSP/833

A Army/recruit lists; **B** Birth; **C** Census; **D** Death; **E** Voter lists; **G** Immigration; **H** Holocaust; **J** Judaica; **K** Kahal; **L** Land; **M** Marriage; **N** Name changes;
O Police files; **P** Pogroms; **R** Reference; **S** School records; **T** Tax lists; **V** Divorce; **W** Occupation lists; **X** Jewish hospital; **Y** Notary records; **Z** Local government records

TOWN NAME Document Type Years	VOIVODSHIP/OBLAST (Province)	COUNTRY Zespół/Sygnatura (Poland) Fond/Opis/Delo (Belarus, Ukraine, Lithuania)
M 1847–1855; 1864–1895		113
T 1911–1915; 1927		RGCH/443; UWL WSP/833
SŁUPCA	**KONIN**	**POLAND**
H 1941		LUBLIN JUDENRAT/169
SŁUPCZA	**TARNOBRZEG**	**POLAND**
H 1941		150–172
SOBIENIE–JEZIORY	**SIEDLCE**	**POLAND**
E 1913–1914		RGL IV ADM
K 1913–1914; 1927–1936		RGL IV ADM; UWL WSP/775
T 1913–1914; 1927–1936		RGL IV ADM; UWL WSP/775
SOBOLEW	**SIEDLCE**	**POLAND**
K 1922–1936		UWL WSP/776
T 1922–1936		UWL WSP/776
SOKOŁÓW PODLASKI	**SIEDLCE**	**POLAND**
E 1913–1914		RGL IV ADM
K 1913–1914; 1921–1936		RGL IV ADM; 403/825–827
T 1913–1914; 1921–1935		RGL IV ADM; UWL WSP/825
STERDYŃ	**SIEDLCE**	**POLAND**
E 1913–1914		RGL IV ADM
K 1913–1914; 1922–1936		RGL IV ADM; UWL WSP/827
T 1913–1914; 1922–1936		RGL IV ADM; UWL WSP/827
STOCZEK	**SIEDLCE**	**POLAND**
K 1923–1927; 1931–1935		UWL WSP/810,829; SPŁUK/631
T 1923–1927; 1931–1935		UWL WSP/810,829; SPŁUK/631
ŚWIERŻE	**CHEŁM**	**POLAND**
B 1826–1865		113
D 1826–1865		113
E 1871–1910; 1912–1915		RGL IV ADM; RGCH/482
K 1871–1910; 1912–1915; 1926–1927		RGL ADM; RGCH/482; UWL WSP/1558
M 1826–1865		113
T 1871–1910; 1912–1915; 1926–1927		RGL ADM; RGCH/482; UWL WSP/1558
SZCZEBRZESZYN	**ZAMOŚĆ**	**POLAND**
B 1826–1827; 1858–1875		113
C 1866		ZPZ/132
D 1826–1827; 1858–1875		113
E 1870–1904; 1906; 1908–1915		RGL IV ADM; RGCH/483
K 1870–1904; 1906; 1908–1915; 1922–1927		RGL IV; RGCH/483; UWL WSP/840
M 1826–1827; 1858–1875		113
T 1870–1904; 1906; 1908–1915; 1922–1927		RGL IV; RGCH/483; UWL WSP/840
SZCZECIN	**SZCZECIN**	**POLAND**
H 1940–1942		JUDENRAT LUBLIN/166–167
TARNOGÓRA	**ZAMOŚĆ**	**POLAND**
B 1865–1870; ALSO INCLUDED IN IZBICA		113
D 1865–1870; ALSO INCLUDED IN IZBICA		113
M 1865–1870; ALSO INCLUDED IN IZBICA		113
TARNOGRÓD	**ZAMOŚĆ**	**POLAND**
B 1870–1875		113
D 1870–1875		113
E 1872–1909		RGL IV ADMIN
K 1872–1909; 1924–1934		RGL IV ADMIN; RGCH/506
M 1870–1875		113
T 1872–1909; 1924–1934		RGL IV ADMIN; RGCH/506
TERESPOL	**BIAŁA PODLASKA**	**POLAND**
B 1826–1864		113
D 1826–1864		113
E 1912–1914		RGCH/445
K 1909–1914; 1924–1935		RGCH/437; SPB/208; UWL WSP/759
M 1826–1864		113
T 1912–1914; 1924–1935; 1945–1950		RGCH/445; SPB/208; UWL WSP/759
TOMASZÓW LUBELSKI	**ZAMOŚĆ**	**POLAND**
B 1826–1875		113
D 1826–1875		113
E 1870–1914		RGL IV ADM; RGCH/488
K 1859–1860; 1870–1914; 1921–1928		POL.RGL/719; RGL IV ADM; RGCH/488; UWL/WSP/835
M 1826–1875		113

A Army/recruit lists; **B** Birth; **C** Census; **D** Death; **E** Voter lists; **G** Immigration; **H** Holocaust; **J** Judaica; **K** Kahal; **L** Land; **M** Marriage; **N** Name changes; **O** Police files; **P** Pogroms; **R** Reference; **S** School records; **T** Tax lists; **V** Divorce; **W** Occupation Lists; **X** Jewish hospital; **Y** Notary records; **Z** Local government records

TOWN NAME Document Type Years	VOIVODSHIP/OBLAST (Province)	COUNTRY Zespół/Sygnatura (Poland) Fond/Opis/Delo (Belarus, Ukraine, Lithuania)
T 1870–1914		RGL IV ADM; RGCH/488
TUROBIN	**ZAMOŚĆ**	**POLAND**
B 1826–1831; 1833–1869; 1873–1875		113
C 1910		ZPK/128
D 1826–1832; 1834–1869; 1873–1875		113
E 1870–1914		RGL IV ADM.
K 1870–1914; 1922–1927; 1936		RGL IV ADM.; UWL WSP/790
M 1826–1832; 1834–1869; 1873–1875		113
T 1870–1914; 1922–1927; 1936		RGL IV ADM.; UWL WSP/790
TYSZOWCE	**ZAMOŚĆ**	**POLAND**
B 1826–1875		113
D 1826–1875		113
E 1873–1905; 1910–1915		RGL IV ADM; RGCH/486
K 1873–1905; 1910–1915		RGL IV ADM; RGCH/486
M 1826–1875		113
T 1873–1905; 1910–1915		RGL IV ADM; RGCH/486
UCHANIE	**ZAMOŚĆ**	**POLAND**
B 1826–1864; 1867; 1869–1872		113
D 1826–1864; 1867; 1869–1872		113
E 1869–1908		RGL IV ADM
K 1869–1908; 1927		RGL IV ADM; UWL WSP/782
M 1826–1864; 1867; 1869–1872		113
T 1869–1908; 1927		RGL IV ADM; UWL WSP/782
URZĘDÓW	**LUBLIN**	**POLAND**
K 1922–1935		UWL WSP/786
T 1922–1935		UWL WSP/786
WĄWOLNICA	**LUBLIN**	**POLAND**
B 1851–1879		113
D 1826–1911		113
E 1867–1913		RGL IV ADM
K 1867–1913; 1922–1927		RGL IV ADM; UWL WSP/819
M 1854–1890		113
T 1867–1913; 1922–1927		RGL IV ADM; UWL WSP/819
WĘGRÓW	**SIEDLCE**	**POLAND**
K 1922–1927		403/828–829
T 1922–1927		UWL WSP/828
WIENIAWA	**LUBLIN**	**POLAND**
B 1826–1894		113 (INCLUDED IN LUBLIN RECORDS)
D 1826–1894		113 (INCLUDED IN LUBLIN RECORDS)
E 1867–1914		RGL IV ADM.
K 1867–1914		RGL IV ADM.
M 1826–1894		113 (INCLUDED IN LUBLIN RECORDS)
T 1795; 1867–1914 (AFTER 1917, INCLUDED IN LUBLIN)		RGL IV ADM; AML/482
WIŚNICE	**BIAŁA PODLASKA**	**POLAND**
B 1826–1849		113
D 1826–1882		113
E 1913–1914		RGCH/544
K 1913–1914; 1925–1927		RGCH/544; UWL WSP/834
M 1826–1870		113
T 1913–1914; 1925–1927		RGCH/544; UWL WSP/834
WŁODAWA	**CHEŁM**	**POLAND**
B 1844–1873; 1932–1934		113
D 1826–1836		113
K 1924–1935		403/830–834, 1582
M 1846–1859		113
WOHYŃ	**BIAŁA PODLASKA**	**POLAND**
B 1826–1831; 1833–1843; 1856–1863; 1870–1878		113
D 1826–1831; 1833–1843; 1856–1863; 1870–1878		113
E 1913–1914		RGL IV ADM
K 1913–1914; 1922–1937		RGL IV ADM; UWL WSP/822
M 1826–1831; 1833–1843; 1856–1863; 1870–1878		113
T 1913–1914; 1922–1937		RGL IV ADM; UWL WSP/822
WOJSŁAWICE	**CHEŁM**	**POLAND**
B 1826; 1834; 1836; 1839; 1841–1877; 1884; 1886; 1888–1890		113
D 1826; 1834; 1836; 1839; 1841–1877; 1884; 1886; 1888–1890		113
E 1868–1910		RGL IV ADM; ZPCH/34
K 1868–1910; 1914; 1927		RGL IV ADM; ZPCH/34; UWL WSP/769

A Army/recruit lists; **B** Birth; **C** Census; **D** Death; **E** Voter lists; **G** Immigration; **H** Holocaust; **J** Judaica; **K** Kahal; **L** Land; **M** Marriage; **N** Name changes;
O Police files; **P** Pogroms; **R** Reference; **S** School records; **T** Tax lists; **V** Divorce; **W** Occupation lists; **X** Jewish hospital; **Y** Notary records; **Z** Local government records

TOWN NAME Document Type Years	VOIVODSHIP/OBLAST (Province)	COUNTRY Zespół/Sygnatura (Poland) Fond/Opis/Delo (Belarus, Ukraine, Lithuania)
M 1826; 1834; 1836; 1839; 1841–1877; 1884; 1886; 1888–1890		113
T 1868–1910; 1914; 1927		RGL IV ADM; ZPCH/34; UWL WSP/769
WYSOKIE	**ZAMOŚĆ**	**POLAND**
B 1820; 1826–1836; 1872–1875		113
C 1910		ZPK/129
D 1826–1836; 1872–1875		113
E 1870–1914		RGL IV ADM.
K 1870–1914; 1928		RGL IV ADM; UWL WSP/1560
M 1826–1836; 1872–1875		113
T 1870–1914; 1928		RGL IV ADM; UWL WSP/1560
ZAKLIKÓW	**TARNOBRZEG**	**POLAND**
B 1826–1854; 1885–1893		113
D 1826–1863; 1882–1893		113
E 1870–1914		RGL IV ADM
K 1870–1914; 1927–1929		RGL IV ADM; UWL WSP/787
M 1826–1854		113
T 1870–1914; 1927–1929		RGL IV ADM; UWL WSP/787
ZAMOŚĆ	**ZAMOŚĆ**	**POLAND**
B 1826–1865; 1872–1882		113
D 1826–1830; 1832–1864; 1874–1878		113
E 1867–1906; 1910–1911; 1913–1915		RGL IV; RGCH/484
K 1867–1906; 1910–1911; 1913–1915; 1922–1936		RGL IV; RGCH/484; 403/838–840
M 1826–1830; 1832–1864		113
T 1867–1906; 1910–1911; 1913–1915; 1928–1936		RGL IV; RGCH/484; UWL WSP/838
ŻELECHÓW	**SIEDLCE**	**POLAND**
E 1913–1915		RGL IV ADM.
K 1913–1915; 1922–1936		RGL IV; UWL WSP/777
T 1913–1915; 1922–1936		RGL IV; UWL WSP/777
ŻÓŁKIEWKA	**ZAMOŚĆ**	**POLAND**
B 1826–1870; 1875		113
C 1910		ZPK/130
D 1826–1870; 1875		113
E 1873–1914		RGL IV ADM.
K 1873–1914; 1927		RGL IV ADM; UWL WSP/791
M 1826–1870; 1875		113
T 1873–1914; 1927		RGL IV ADM; UWL WSP/791
ZWIERZYNIEC	**ZAMOŚĆ**	**POLAND**
K 1927–1928		UWL WSP/1566
T 1927–1928		UWL WSP/1566

MŁAWA Branch Archives

CIECHANÓW	**CIECHANÓW**	**POLAND**
B 1826–1876; 1878–1895		572
D 1826–1876; 1878–1895		572
M 1826–1876; 1878–1895		572
Y 1849–1939		192–195; 197; 202–203; 206; 209–212; 214; 243
MŁAWA	**CIECHANÓW**	**POLAND**
B 1829–1830; 1832; 1834–1836; 1838–1841; 1843–1852; 1854; 1856–1874; 1876–1879; 1881–1883; 1885–1887; 1889–1891; 1893–1895		56
D 1829–1830; 1832; 1834–1836; 1838–1841; 1843–1852; 1854; 1856–1874; 1876–1879; 1881–1883; 1885–1887; 1889–1891; 1893–1895		56
M 1829–1830; 1832; 1834–1836; 1838–1841; 1843–1852; 1854; 1856–1874; 1876–1879; 1881–1883; 1885–1887; 1889–1891; 1893–1895		56
Y 1809–1952		191; 193; 196; 198–201; 204–205; 207–208; 213; 216–217; 227; 238–242; 300
PŁOŃSK	**CIECHANÓW**	**POLAND**
B 1877–1895		474
D 1877–1895		474
M 1877–1895		474

NOWY DWÓR MAZOWIECKI Branch Archives

CHOCISZEWO	**WARSZAWA**	**POLAND**
B 1809–1812		287
D 1809–1812		287
M 1809–1812		287

A Army/recruit lists; **B** Birth; **C** Census; **D** Death; **E** Voter lists; **G** Immigration; **H** Holocaust; **J** Judaica; **K** Kahal; **L** Land; **M** Marriage; **N** Name changes; **O** Police files; **P** Pogroms; **R** Reference; **S** School records; **T** Tax lists; **V** Divorce; **W** Occupation Lists; **X** Jewish hospital; **Y** Notary records; **Z** Local government records

TOWN NAME Document Type Years	VOIVODSHIP/OBLAST (Province)	COUNTRY Zespół/Sygnatura (Poland) Fond/Opis/Delo (Belarus, Ukraine, Lithuania)
CZERWIŃSK NAD WISŁA	**PŁOCK**	**POLAND**
B 1826–1854; 1858–1865		
D 1826–1854; 1858–1865		117
M 1826–1854; 1858–1865		117
		117
KRYSK	**CIECHANÓW**	**POLAND**
B 1826–1876		
D 1826–1876		81
M 1826–1876		81
		81
NOWY DWÓR MAZOWIECKI	**WARSZAWA**	**POLAND**
B 1824; 1826–1828; 1830–1835; 1837; 1842–1846; 1850–1851; 1859; 1863–1865; 1872–1874; 1876–1877; 1880–1882; 1884; 1890; 1897; 1900; 1906; 1918; 1933; 1935		383
C 1938–1939		124
D 1824; 1826–1828; 1830–1835; 1837; 1842–1846; 1850–1851; 1859; 1863–1865; 1871–1874; 1876–1877; 1880–1882; 1884; 1890; 1897; 1900; 1906; 1918; 1920–1921; 1933; 1935		383
M 1822; 1824; 1826–1828; 1830–1835; 1837; 1842–1846; 1850–1851; 1859; 1863–1865; 1871–1874; 1876–1877; 1880–1882; 1884; 1890; 1897; 1900; 1906; 1920; 1933; 1935		383
OKUNIEW	**WARSZAWA**	**POLAND**
B 1826–1829; 1833–1837		
D 1827–1829		110
M 1827		110
		110
PŁOŃSK	**CIECHANÓW**	**POLAND**
B 1826–1872; 1876		
D 1826–1872; 1876; 1906		96
M 1826–1872; 1876; 1906		96
R 1931; 1940		96
		62
RADZYMIN	**CIECHANÓW**	**POLAND**
B 1829; 1879–1914		
D 1882; 1914		393
M 1863–1894; 1914		393
C 1926–1940		393
M 1846		63
		163
SEROCK	**WARSZAWA**	**POLAND**
B 1874–1879; 1881; 1883–1884; 1886–1894		
D 1875–1879; 1881; 1883–1884; 1886–1894		469
M 1875–1879; 1881; 1883–1884; 1886–1894		469
		469
SOCHOCIN	**CIECHANÓW**	**POLAND**
B 1826–1903; 1914–1915; 1919–1923; 1930; 1932–1933		
D 1826–1903; 1914–1915; 1919–1923; 1930; 1932–1933		97
M 1826–1903; 1914–1915; 1919–1923; 1930; 1932–1933		97
		97
WIELISZEW	**WARSZAWA**	**POLAND**
B 1824; 1826–1828; 1830–1835; 1837; 1842–1846; 1850–1851; 1863–1865; 1871–1874; 1876–1877; 1880–1882; 1884; 1890; 1897; 1900; 1906; 1918; 1933; 1935		383
D 1824; 1826–1828; 1830–1835; 1837; 1842–1846; 1850–1851; 1863–1865; 1871–1874; 1876–1877; 1880–1882; 1884; 1890; 1897; 1900; 1906; 1918; 1933; 1935		383
M 1822; 1824; 1826–1828; 1830–1835; 1837; 1842–1846; 1850–1851; 1863–1865; 1871–1874; 1876–1877; 1880–1882; 1884; 1890; 1897; 1900; 1906; 1920; 1933; 1935		383
WOŁOMIN	**WARSZAWA**	**POLAND**
C 1920–1924; 1927–1928; 1930–1931; 1933		162
ZAKROCZYM	**WARSZAWA**	**POLAND**
B 1825–1876; 1879–1889; 1891–1903; 1905–1912; 1916–1920		
D 1825–1876; 1879–1889; 1891–1903; 1905–1912; 1916–1920		143
M 1825–1876; 1879–1889; 1891–1903; 1905–1912; 1916–1920		143
		143

NOWY SĄCZ Branch Archives

GRYBÓW	**NOWY SĄCZ**	**POLAND**
C 1928–1936 (LISTING OF ORPHANS); 1884; 1891; 1897; 1910; 1922; 1927–1928; 1930; 1935; 1938–1939		158; 12–15; 17–18
E 1891–1939		17
K 1901; 1906–1916		111; 154
Z 1878–1931		169
KRYNICA ZDRÓJ	**NOWY SĄCZ**	**POLAND**
A 1867–1890; 1918–1939		AMK 36; 247
D 1934–1938		AMK 233
L 1918–1939		18
T 1912–1917		18

A Army/recruit lists; **B** Birth; **C** Census; **D** Death; **E** Voter lists; **G** Immigration; **H** Holocaust; **J** Judaica; **K** Kahal; **L** Land; **M** Marriage; **N** Name changes;
O Police files; **P** Pogroms; **R** Reference; **S** School records; **T** Tax lists; **V** Divorce; **W** Occupation lists; **X** Jewish hospital; **Y** Notary records; **Z** Local government records

TOWN NAME Document Type Years	VOIVODSHIP/OBLAST (Province)	COUNTRY Zespół/Sygnatura (Poland) Fond/Opis/Delo (Belarus, Ukraine, Lithuania)
MUSZYNA	**NOWY SĄCZ**	**POLAND**
C 1937		84
NOWY SĄCZ	**NOWY SĄCZ**	**POLAND**
C 1870; 1900; 1910–1927; 1932–1939		183/13,15–17,204,232
E 1907; 1911		AMNS-1/259
H 1939–1944 (LIST OF DEPORTATIONS)		
T 1842–1843		15–16
Z 1914 (LIST OF LOANS)		MMNS-1/310
STARY SĄCZ	**NOWY SĄCZ**	**POLAND**
C 1870; 1910; 1938–1939		22–23/317–318; 437

OLSZTYN Archives

ALLENSTEIN	**SEE OLSZTYN**	
BARCZEWO	**OLSZTYN**	**POLAND**
B 1874–1894		699/I
C 1874; 1881/1897; 1900; 1903; 1906; 1935–1939		247/I
D 1874–1894		699/I
M 1874–1894		699/I
BISKUPIEC	**OLSZTYN**	**POLAND**
B 1878; 1880–1882; 1886; 1888; 1890–1891		854/I
D 1876; 1878–1880; 1882; 1886; 1888–1889; 1892		854/I
M 1876; 1878–1882; 1884–1885; 1889–1891		854/I
BISKUPIEC POMORSKI	**TORUŃ**	**POLAND**
C 1812–1892		248/I
BRANIEWO	**ELBLĄG**	**POLAND**
C 1904–1905; 1908; 1910–1912; 1914; 1916; 1922; 1938–1939		10/I
BRAUNSBERG	**SEE BRANIEWO**	
EŁK	**SUWAŁKI**	**POLAND**
C 1838; 1864–1874; 1901–1906		4/I
GIŻYCKO	**SUWAŁKI**	**POLAND**
C 1812; 1904–1905		4/I; 11/I
GÓROWO IŁAWIECKIE	**OLSZTYN**	**POLAND**
B 1874–1893		692/I
D 1874–1893		692/I
M 1874–1893		692/I
HEILSBERG	**SEE LIDZBARK WARMIŃSKI**	
HOHENSTEIN	**SEE OLSZTYNEK**	
IŁAWA	**OLSZTYN**	**POLAND**
B 1874–1894		311/I
D 1874–1894		311/I
M 1874–1894		311/I
JANOWO	**OLSZTYN**	**POLAND**
B 1810/1912		635/I
D 1810/1912		635/I
M 1810/1912		635/I
JOHANNISBURG	**SEE PISZ**	
KĘTRZYN	**OLSZTYN**	**POLAND**
B 1881–1882; 1890–1891		735/I
C 1825; 1833; 1864; 1932–1933; 1939		12/I; 254/I
D 1878–1879; 1886–1887; 1891		735/I
M 1877–1881; 1884–1886; 1890–1891		735/I
LANDSBERG OST PREUSSEN	**SEE GOROWO IŁAWIECKIE**	
LIDZBARK WARMIŃSKI	**OLSZTYN**	**POLAND**
D 1877–1878; 1887–1891		634/I
M 1875; 1877–1883; 1890–1891		634/I
LOTZEN	**SEE GIŻYCKO**	
LUBAWA	**OLSZTYN**	**POLAND**
B 1874–1893		796/I
D 1874–1893		796/I
M 1874–1893		796/I
LYCK	**SEE EŁK**	**POLAND**
MIŁAKOWO	**OLSZTYN**	**POLAND**
B 1875–1880; 1882–1887; 1889–1894		746/I

A Army/recruit lists; **B** Birth; **C** Census; **D** Death; **E** Voter lists; **G** Immigration; **H** Holocaust; **J** Judaica; **K** Kahal; **L** Land; **M** Marriage; **N** Name changes; **O** Police files; **P** Pogroms; **R** Reference; **S** School records; **T** Tax lists; **V** Divorce; **W** Occupation Lists; **X** Jewish hospital; **Y** Notary records; **Z** Local government records

TOWN NAME Document Type Years	VOIVODSHIP/OBLAST (Province)	COUNTRY Zespół/Sygnatura (Poland) Fond/Opis/Delo (Belarus, Ukraine, Lithuania)	
D 1875–1878; 1880–1882; 1884–1889; 1892; 1894		746/I	
M 1875–1876; 1878–1880; 1883–1889; 1891–1894		746/I	
MIŁOMŁYN	**OLSZTYN**	**POLAND**	
B 1874–1894		890/I	
MOHRUNGEN	**SEE MORĄG**		
MORĄG	**OLSZTYN**	**POLAND**	
B 1874–1894		744/I	
D 1874–1894		744/I	
M 1874–1894		744/I	
MRĄGOWO	**OLSZTYN**	**POLAND**	
B 1874–1893		869/I	
C 1840; 1842–1843; 1847; 1849; 1884/1936		16/I	
D 1874–1893		869/I	
M 1874–1893		869/I	
NEIDENBURG	**SEE NIDZICA**		
NIDZICA	**OLSZTYN**	**POLAND**	
B 1874–1881; 1883–1893		893/I	
D 1874–1893		893/I	
M 1874–1893		893/I	
OLSZTYN	**OLSZTYN**	**POLAND**	
B 1874–1884; 1886–1894		705/I	
C 1825; 1885–1886; 1890; 1893–1895; 1897; 1900; 1946–1947		19/I; 487/II	
D 1874–1889; 1893–1894		705/I	
M 1882; 1885; 1893–1894		705/I	
OLSZTYNEK	**OLSZTYN**	**POLAND**	
B 1874–1894		351/I	
D 1874–1894		351/I	
M 1874–1894		351/I	
ORTELSBURG	**SEE SZCZYTNO**		
PASSENHEIM	**SEE PASYM**		
PASYM	**OLSZTYN**	**POLAND**	
B 1874–1894		718/I	
D 1874–1880; 1882–1894		718/I	
M 1874–1894		718/I	
PISZ	**OLSZTYN**	**POLAND**	
C 1938		264/I	
PRABUTY	**ELBLĄG**	**POLAND**	
B 1812–1874		319/I	
D 1812–1874		319/I	
M 1847–1874		319/I	
RESZEL	**OLSZTYN**	**POLAND**	
C 1812–1852; 1882; 1890; 1914; 1920; 1923		23/I; 265/I	
RIESENBURG	**SEE PRABUTY**		
ROESSEL	**SEE RESZEL**		
ROSENBERG	**SEE SUSZ**		
ROSSEL	**SEE RESZEL**		
RUZOMBEROK	**SEE SUSZ**		
SAALFELD	**SEE ZALEWO**		
SENSBURG	**SEE MRĄGOWO**		
SUSZ	**ELBLĄG**	**POLAND**	
B 1847–1874		320/I	
SZCZYTNO	**OLSZTYN**	**POLAND**	
B 1874; 1878; 1883; 1885–1889; 1894		720/I	
C 1908		268/I	
D 1874; 1877–1878; 1880; 1883–1890; 1893–1894		720/I	
M 1883; 1885; 1887–1892; 1894		720/I	
WARTENBURG	**SEE BARCZEWO**		
WĘGORZEWO	**SUWAŁKI**	**POLAND**	
C 1818–1820; 1835		26/I	
ZALEWO	**OLSZTYN**	**POLAND**	
B 1874–1878; 1880; 1885; 1887–1890; 1893–1894		750/I	
D 1874–1883; 1886; 1888–1890		750/I	
M 1876–1883; 1886; 1888–1890; 1893–1894		750/I	

A Army/recruit lists; **B** Birth; **C** Census; **D** Death; **E** Voter lists; **G** Immigration; **H** Holocaust; **J** Judaica; **K** Kahal; **L** Land; **M** Marriage; **N** Name changes; **O** Police files; **P** Pogroms; **R** Reference; **S** School records; **T** Tax lists; **V** Divorce; **W** Occupation lists; **X** Jewish hospital; **Y** Notary records; **Z** Local government records

TOWN NAME Document Type Years	VOIVODSHIP/OBLAST (Province)	COUNTRY Zespół/Sygnatura (Poland) Fond/Opis/Delo (Belarus, Ukraine, Lithuania)

OPOLE Archives

BERGSTADT	SEE LEŚNICA		
BRIEG	SEE BRZEG		
BRZEG	OPOLE		POLAND
B	1778–1847		4
D	1810–1812; 1829–1868		4
M	1809–1811		4
T	1786–1842		4
COSEL	SEE KOŹLE		
FALKENBERG	SEE NIEMODLIN		
GŁUBCZYCE	OPOLE		POLAND
B	1830–1917		293
M	1870–1922		293
GRODKÓW	OPOLE		POLAND
B	1797/1874		11
C	1759/1933		
D	1815–1874		11
G	1842/1938		2; 11
M	1815/1927		11
T	1778/1942		
GROTTKAU	SEE GRODKÓW		
KLUCZBORK	OPOLE		POLAND
B	1814–1924		13
C	1845; 1927; 1947		13; 68
D	1814–1924		13
K	1818–1944		13
M	1814–1924		13
S	1818–1857		13
T	1802–1933		
W	1824–1927		13
KORFANTÓW	OPOLE		POLAND
B	1863–1865; 1868–1869; 1872; 1875		14/49
KOŹLE	OPOLE		POLAND
D	1826–1861		504
M	1812–1847		504
KRAPKOWICE	OPOLE		POLAND
B	1820–1873		58
C	1855–1857; 1860–1861; 1863–1864; 1870; 1872; 1876–1878; 1890–1894; 1908; 1910–1912		16/2348–2375
D	1820–1873		58
M	1827–1873		58
O	1938		16/1841
T	1894–1903; 1905–1914; 1916–1918		16/739–762
W	1937–1944		16/1792,1819
KRAPPITZ	SEE KRAPKOWICE		
KREUZBURG	SEE KREUZBURG		
LEOBSCHUETZ	SEE GŁUBCZYCE		
LESCHNITZ	SEE LEŚNICA		
LEŚNICA	OPOLE		POLAND
B	1818–1844		17
D	1818–1864		17
G	1870–1874		17
K	1837–1902 (CEMETERY RECORDS)		17
M	1818–1864		17
W	1834–1861		17
LEWIN BRZESKI	OPOLE		POLAND
C	1934–1940		5
J	1901; 1938–1941		5
L	1938–1939		5
LOWEN	SEE LEWIN BRZESKI		
NAMSLAU	SEE NAMYSŁÓW		
NAMYSŁÓW	OPOLE		POLAND
B	1834–1868		18
C	1799–1885		18

A Army/recruit lists; **B** Birth; **C** Census; **D** Death; **E** Voter lists; **G** Immigration; **H** Holocaust; **J** Judaica; **K** Kahal; **L** Land; **M** Marriage; **N** Name changes; **O** Police files; **P** Pogroms; **R** Reference; **S** School records; **T** Tax lists; **V** Divorce; **W** Occupation Lists; **X** Jewish hospital; **Y** Notary records; **Z** Local government records

TOWN NAME Document Type Years	VOIVODSHIP/OBLAST (Province)	COUNTRY Zespół/Sygnatura (Poland) Fond/Opis/Delo (Belarus, Ukraine, Lithuania)
E 1888–1910		
M 1834–1868; 18		18
S 1820		
NEISSE	**SEE NYSA**	18
NIEMODLIN	**OPOLE**	**POLAND**
B 1804–1823		
D 1804–1824		1
		1
NYSA	**OPOLE**	**POLAND**
B 1874–1894		
D 1874–1894		964
M 1874–1894		964
		964
OPOLE	**OPOLE**	**POLAND**
B 1756–1781; 1847		
E 1815–1860		60
K 1843–1940 (CEMETERY RECORDS)		22
M 1933–1937		22; 47
S 1820–1889		1
		22
OPPELN	**SEE OPOLE**	
STRZELCE OPOLSKIE	**OPOLE**	**POLAND**
B 1847–1874		
		62
WOŁCZYN	**OPOLE**	**POLAND**
B 1874–1892		
D 1874–1892		858
		858

OŚWIĘCIM Branch Archives

ANDRYCHÓW	**BIELSKO BIAŁA**	**POLAND**
C 1928–1931		28/17
H 1945		18/19–20
K 1931		28/62
L 1945–1950		28/26–37
W 1907–1936		28/8
BACHOWICE	**BIELSKO BIAŁA**	**POLAND**
A 1926–1935		6/17
GIERAŁTOWICZKI	**BIELSKO BIAŁA**	**POLAND**
C 1933–1941		6/67
GŁĘBOWICE	**BIELSKO BIAŁA**	**POLAND**
C 1932–1941		6/68
GRABOSZYCE	**BIELSKO BIAŁA**	**POLAND**
C 1919–1939		5/60–61
LANCKORONA	**BIELSKO BIAŁA**	**POLAND**
A 1885–1931		8/77–79
C 1806–1825; 1887–1939		8/7,75,196–198
E 1921–1931		8/206–208
L 1790–1945		8/6,87,96–97
OŚWIĘCIM	**BIELSKO BIAŁA**	**POLAND**
B 1890; 1895–1901; 1908–1928; 1930–1932		9/47–62,82–93,255–268
C 1945–1950		1/76,76A,138,143
M 1890; 1895–1901; 1908–1928; 1930–1932		9/47–62,82–93,255–268
PIOTROWICE	**BIELSKO BIAŁA**	**POLAND**
C 1919–1939		5/67–69
PRZECISZÓW	**BIELSKO BIAŁA**	**POLAND**
C 1919–1939		5/72–74
PRZYBRADZ	**BIELSKO BIAŁA**	**POLAND**
C 1931–1941		6/69
RYCZÓW	**BIELSKO BIAŁA**	**POLAND**
C 1935–1946		6/9–10
SPYTKOWICE	**BIELSKO BIAŁA**	**POLAND**
C 1919–1939; 1945		6/11–13
WADOWICE	**BIELSKO BIAŁA**	**POLAND**
C 1940–1945		6/72
WILAMOWICE	**BIELSKO BIAŁA**	**POLAND**
A 1879–1893		11/2
ZAWOJA	**BIELSKO BIAŁA**	**POLAND**
C 1919–1951		6/56,64

A Army/recruit lists; **B** Birth; **C** Census; **D** Death; **E** Voter lists; **G** Immigration; **H** Holocaust; **J** Judaica; **K** Kahal; **L** Land; **M** Marriage; **N** Name changes;
O Police files; **P** Pogroms; **R** Reference; **S** School records; **T** Tax lists; **V** Divorce; **W** Occupation lists; **X** Jewish hospital; **Y** Notary records; **Z** Local government records

TOWN NAME Document Type Years	VOIVODSHIP/OBLAST (Province)	COUNTRY Zespół/Sygnatura (Poland) Fond/Opis/Delo (Belarus, Ukraine, Lithuania)

OTWOCK Branch Archives

BOBROWNIKI		LUBLIN		POLAND
B	1826–1858		167	
D	1826–1858		167	
M	1826–1858		167	
KARCZEW		**WARSZAWA**		**POLAND**
B	1826–1892		42	
D	1826–1892		42	
M	1826–1892		42	
MIŃSK MAZOWIECKI		**SIEDLCE**		**POLAND**
C	1890–1930; 1935–1939		35	
E	1922–1923; 1927; 1930–1935; 1939		35	
H	1937–1939; 1942–1944; 1949		35; 40	
OTWOCK		**WARSZAWA**		**POLAND**
C	1940–1941		1	
H	1939		1	
L	1916/1950		1	

PABIANICE Branch Archives

ALEKSANDRÓW ŁÓDZKI		ŁÓDŹ		POLAND
L	1918–1939		147	
T	1914–1939		147	
ŁASK		**SIERADZ**		**POLAND**
C	1879–1939		7	
T	1925/1940		7,14	
Z	1892–1902; 1908–1909; 1904–1913		7	
LUTOMIERSK		**SIERADZ**		**POLAND**
Z	1821–1866; 1894–1913		148	
PABIANICE		**ŁÓDŹ**		**POLAND**
C	1836–1862		8	
G	1867/1914		8	
K	1901–1914		8	
TUSZYN		**PIOTRKÓW TRYBUNALSKI**		**POLAND**
Z	1901–1913		158	
WIDAWA		**SIERADZ**		**POLAND**
Z	1939–1953		24	
ZGIERZ		**ŁÓDŹ**		**POLAND**
Z	1825–1864		150	

PIŁA Branch Archives

RADOLIN		PIŁA		POLAND
C	1816–1847		13	

PIŃCZÓW Branch Archives

BUSKO–ZDRÓJ		KIELCE		POLAND
B	1875-1896			
C	1876–1922		11	
D	1875-1896			
M	1876-1896			
CHMIELNIK		**KIELCE**		**POLAND**
B	1876–1896		371	
D	1876–1896		371	
M	1876–1896		371	
DZIAŁOSZYCE		**KIELCE**		**POLAND**
B	1826–1864; 1873–1894		143	
D	1826–1864; 1873–1894		143	
M	1826–1894		143	
NOWY KORCZYN		**KIELCE**		**POLAND**
B	1826–1839; 1849; 1862; 1875–1884; 1886–1889; 1891–1895		372	
C	1902–1931		398	
D	1826–1839; 1849; 1862; 1875–1884; 1886–1889; 1891–1895		372	
M	1826–1839; 1849; 1862; 1875–1884; 1886–1889; 1891–1895		372	

A Army/recruit lists; **B** Birth; **C** Census; **D** Death; **E** Voter lists; **G** Immigration; **H** Holocaust; **J** Judaica; **K** Kahal; **L** Land; **M** Marriage; **N** Name changes; **O** Police files; **P** Pogroms; **R** Reference; **S** School records; **T** Tax lists; **V** Divorce; **W** Occupation Lists; **X** Jewish hospital; **Y** Notary records; **Z** Local government records

TOWN NAME Document Type Years	VOIVODSHIP/OBLAST (Province)	COUNTRY Zespół/Sygnatura (Poland) Fond/Opis/Delo (Belarus, Ukraine, Lithuania)
Z 1876–1922 (COURT RECORDS)		1062
PACANÓW	**KIELCE**	**POLAND**
B 1826/1874; 1875–1884; 1886–1896		373
D 1826/1874; 1875–1884; 1886–1896		373
M 1826/1874; 1875–1884; 1886–1896		373
PIŃCZÓW	**KIELCE**	**POLAND**
B 1826–1865; 1867–1875; 1878–1886; 1888–1890; 1892–1894		233
D 1826–1865; 1867–1875; 1878–1886; 1888–1890; 1892–1894		233
M 1826–1865; 1867–1875; 1878–1886; 1888–1890; 1892–1894		233
SKALBMIERZ	**KIELCE**	**POLAND**
C 1902–1931; 1940–1950		110
STOPNICA	**KIELCE**	**POLAND**
B 1875–1894		374
D 1875–1894		374
M 1875–1894		374
SZYDŁÓW	**KIELCE**	**POLAND**
B 1854–1877; 1879–1882; 1884–1896		392
D 1854–1877; 1879–1882; 1884–1896		392
M 1854–1877; 1879–1882; 1884–1896		392
WIŚLICA	**KIELCE**	**POLAND**
B 1826–1835; 1837–1844; 1846–1850; 1852–1853; 1855–1872; 1874; 1882–1884; 1886–1887		51
D 1826–1835; 1837–1844; 1846–1850; 1852–1853; 1855–1872; 1874–1882; 1884; 1886–1887		51
M 1826–1835; 1837–1844; 1846–1850; 1852–1853; 1855–1872; 1874–1882; 1884; 1886–1887		51

PIOTRKÓW TRYBUNALSKI Archives

TOWN NAME Document Type Years	VOIVODSHIP/OBLAST (Province)	COUNTRY
BEŁCHATÓW	**PIOTRKÓW TRYBUNALSKI**	**POLAND**
B 1873–1895		330
C 1906–1931		8/1–12
D 1873–1895		330/4–26
L 1796–1946		377
M 1855–1895		330/1–2,5–22,24–27
Y 1919–1952		167–175; 376
Z 1906–1944		8
BRZEZINY	**SKIERNIEWICE**	**POLAND**
G 1920–1950		115
Y 1808–1949		30–31; 33–40; 116; 120–121; 128–129; 258–261
Z 1843–1950		108
KAMIEŃSK	**PIOTRKÓW TRYBUNALSKI**	**POLAND**
B 1849–1893		331/6–9,11–43
D 1832–1840; 1848–1893		331/1–5,11–43
M 1860–1893		331/10–43
KOLUSZKI	**PIOTRKÓW TRYBUNALSKI**	**POLAND**
C 1940–1950		126
Z 1940–1950		126
NOWE MIASTO NAD PILICĄ	**RADOM**	**POLAND**
C 1817–1950		117
G 1817–1950		117
Y 1929–1947		130,257
Z 1817–1953		117
OPOCZNO	**PIOTRKÓW TRYBUNALSKI**	**POLAND**
B 1875; 1877–1894		332/23–38,40,42,44,46–47
D 1875–1887; 1889–1894		332/10–22,25–36,39,41,43,45–47
L 1820–1972		351
M 1875–1887; 1893–1894		332/1–9,25–36,46–47
Y 1810–1951		230–239
PIOTRKÓW TRYBUNALSKI	**PIOTRKÓW TRYBUNALSKI**	**POLAND**
A 1919–1939		1/1269–1845
B 1856–1894; 1938–1942		333/1–11,25–61,63,65–66
C 1865–1939		9/1671–1737; 1/1269–1845
D 1856–1889; 1891–1893; 1939; 1942		333/20–59,64,67–68
G 1919–1939		1
H 1939–1944		9
L 1800–1876; 1919–1939		381; 400; BIBL.2251
M 1856–1889; 1891–1893; 1938–1942		333/12–19,25–59,62
O 1915–1939		1; 352
R 1913; 1927; 1929; 1942		BIBL.3191

A Army/recruit lists; **B** Birth; **C** Census; **D** Death; **E** Voter lists; **G** Immigration; **H** Holocaust; **J** Judaica; **K** Kahal; **L** Land; **M** Marriage; **N** Name changes; **O** Police files; **P** Pogroms; **R** Reference; **S** School records; **T** Tax lists; **V** Divorce; **W** Occupation lists; **X** Jewish hospital; **Y** Notary records; **Z** Local government records

TOWN NAME Document Type Years	VOIVODSHIP/OBLAST (Province)	COUNTRY Zespół/Sygnatura (Poland) Fond/Opis/Delo (Belarus, Ukraine, Lithuania)
S 1858–1869		9/243
T 1868–1944		699
X 1875/1940		89
Y 1807–1951		47–70,150–166,361–366
Z 1803–1945		9
PRZEDBÓRZ	**PIOTRKÓW TRYBUNALSKI**	**POLAND**
B 1872–1888; 1890–1891		334/1–19
C 1874–1931		687
D 1872–1888; 1890–1891		334/1–19
M 1872–1888; 1890–1891		334/1–19
Y 1931–1951		367–371
Z 1822–1939		687
RADOMSKO	**PIOTRKÓW TRYBUNALSKI**	**POLAND**
B 1871–1895		335/3–26
C 1793–1944		103
D 1856–1895		335/1,5–26
H 1939–1944		103
L 1818–1981		378
M 1870–1895		335/2,5–26
T 1873–1916		700
Y 1808–1952		127–138,175–180,373–375,689
Z 1793–1949		103
ROZPRZA	**PIOTRKÓW TRYBUNALSKI**	**POLAND**
B 1848; 1853–1865; 1873–1898; 1908–1928		336/2–27,30
C 1868–1931		32
D 1826–1867; 1873–1895; 1899–1922		336/1–24,29
M 1848; 1858–1895		336/2–24,28
Z 1805–1875		10
STRYKÓW	**ŁÓDŹ**	**POLAND**
Z 1929–1950		148
SULEJÓW	**PIOTRKÓW TRYBUNALSKI**	**POLAND**
B 1884–1898		337/1–4
D 1884–1898		337/1–4
M 1884–1898		337/1–4
SULMIERZYCE	**PIOTRKÓW TRYBUNALSKI**	**POLAND**
B 1873–1895		338/4–26
D 1826–1869; 1873–1895		338/1,4–26
M 1863–1895		338/2–26
SZCZERCÓW	**PIOTRKÓW TRYBUNALSKI**	**POLAND**
B 1875–1894		339/1–20
D 1875–1894		339/1–20
M 1875–1894		339/1–20
TOMASZÓW MAZOWIECKI	**PIOTRKÓW TRYBUNALSKI**	**POLAND**
B 1873–1892		340/1–2,7–15
D 1886–1892		340/5–13,18
G 1927–1939		1
H 1939–1944		7
L 1807–1985		247
M 1871–1894		340/3–4,7–13,16–17
O 1927–1939		1
Y 1826–1951		32; 41–42; 111–113; 122; 135; 251–256
Z 1820–1944		7
TUSZYN	**PIOTRKÓW TRYBUNALSKI**	**POLAND**
B 1857–1895		341/2–26
D 1873–189533		341/5–26
M 1859–1895		341/1,5–26
UJAZD	**PIOTRKÓW TRYBUNALSKI**	**POLAND**
B 1826–1834; 1838–1839; 1841; 1847–1857; 1868–1937; 1940		342/1,3–75
D 1826–1834; 1838–1839; 1841; 1847–1937; 1940		342/2–63,84–87
M 1826–1834; 1838–1839; 1841; 1847–1857; 1860–1937; 1940		342/3–63,76–83
WOLBÓRZ	**PIOTRKÓW TRYBUNALSKI**	**POLAND**
C 1841–1931		241/11,36
Z 1808–1876		11
ŻARNÓW	**PIOTRKÓW TRYBUNALSKI**	**POLAND**
B 1865–1895		878
D 1845–1895		878
M 1845–1895		878

A Army/recruit lists; **B** Birth; **C** Census; **D** Death; **E** Voter lists; **G** Immigration; **H** Holocaust; **J** Judaica; **K** Kahal; **L** Land; **M** Marriage; **N** Name changes; **O** Police files; **P** Pogroms; **R** Reference; **S** School records; **T** Tax lists; **V** Divorce; **W** Occupation Lists; **X** Jewish hospital; **Y** Notary records; **Z** Local government records

TOWN NAME Document Type Years	VOIVODSHIP/OBLAST (Province)	COUNTRY Zespół/Sygnatura (Poland) Fond/Opis/Delo (Belarus, Ukraine, Lithuania)

PŁOCK Archives

BIELSK		PŁOCK	POLAND
B	1826–1870		172
D	1826–1839; 1841; 1843–1870		172
M	1826–1870		172
BIEŻUŃ		CIECHANÓW	POLAND
B	1826–1856		201
D	1826–1856		201
M	1826–1856		201
BODZANÓW		PŁOCK	POLAND
B	1826–1832; 1834–1836; 1838–1883; 1886–1894		173
D	1826–1832; 1834–1836; 1838–1883; 1886–1894		173
M	1826–1832; 1834–1836; 1838–1883; 1886–1894		173
DROBIN		PŁOCK	POLAND
B	1826–1894		174
D	1826–1894		174
M	1826–1894		174
GĄBIN		PŁOCK	POLAND
T	1820–1871		2
Y	1868–1939		272–277; 472–473
GOSTYŃ		LESZNO	POLAND
Y	1820–1857; 1876–1939		268–271; 278–279; 281; 469–470
PŁOCK		PŁOCK	POLAND
B	1808–1887		175; 373
C	1830–1930; 1937–1949		90/133
D	1811–1894		175; 373
M	1811–1863; 1865–1871; 1873–1890		175; 373
Y	1808–1946		225–262; 265–267; 437–440; 447
Z	1808–1939; 1945–1950		1
RACIĄŻ		CIECHANÓW	POLAND
B	1826–1875		202
D	1826–1875		202
M	1826–1875		202
Y	1896–1908; 1916–1939		293–295
SIERPC		PŁOCK	POLAND
B	1826–1894		203
D	1826–1894		203
M	1826–1894		203
Y	1824–1939		281–292
WYSZOGRÓD		PŁOCK	POLAND
B	1826–1873; 1875–1894		176
C	1945–1950		6
D	1826–1873; 1875–1894		176
M	1826–1873; 1875–1894		176

POZNAŃ Archives

BABIAK		KONIN	POLAND
B	1826–1859; 1882–1893		3741/1–34
D	1826–1859; 1882–1893		3441/1–34
M	1826–1859; 1882–1893		3741/1–34
BABIMOST		ZIELONA GÓRA	POLAND
C	1916–1920		314/313–315,329,1027–1029,3227
K	1835–1912		314/1049,1051–1052
X	1858–1897		314/1053
BARANÓW		KALISZ	POLAND
B	1835–1846		3573/1–13
D	1835–1846		3573/1–13
M	1835–1846		3573/1–13
BŁASZKI		SIERADZ	POLAND
B	1826–1855; 1861–1893		3742/1–3,7–8,10
D	1855–1872		3742/6,9
M	1850–1857; 1866–1867		3742,4–5
S	1861–1893; 1937–1939		805/143
BRATZ		SEE BRÓJCE	

A Army/recruit lists; **B** Birth; **C** Census; **D** Death; **E** Voter lists; **G** Immigration; **H** Holocaust; **J** Judaica; **K** Kahal; **L** Land; **M** Marriage; **N** Name changes;
O Police files; **P** Pogroms; **R** Reference; **S** School records; **T** Tax lists; **V** Divorce; **W** Occupation lists; **X** Jewish hospital; **Y** Notary records; **Z** Local government records

TOWN NAME Document Type Years	VOIVODSHIP/OBLAST (Province)	COUNTRY Zespół/Sygnatura (Poland) Fond/Opis/Delo (Belarus, Ukraine, Lithuania)
BRÓJCE	**GORZOW WIEŁKOPOLSKI**	**POLAND**
B 1847		3754/1
D 1847		3754/1
M 1847		3754/1
BUK	**POZNAŃ**	**POLAND**
C 1933–1938		4377/42
CHODZIEŻ	**PIŁA**	**POLAND**
K 1833–1865		906
S 1837–1907		1029/41–46
CZARNIKAU	**SEE CZARNKÓW**	
CZARNKÓW	**PIŁA**	**POLAND**
B 1823–1840		3575/1
D 1823–1840		3575/1
M 1823–1840		3575/1
DĄBIE	**KONIN**	**POLAND**
B 1826–1891		3743/1–67
D 1826–1891		3743/1–67
G 1918–1950		13/404–422
M 1826–1891		3743/1–67
DOBROSOLOWO	**KONIN**	**POLAND**
B 1826–1891		3621
D 1826–1891		3621
M 1826–1891		3621
GNIEZNO	**POZNAŃ**	**POLAND**
B 1823–1848		3576/1,3–11
D 1840–1848		3576/2–11
K 1926–1938		4058/1170–1175
M 1840–1847		3576/3–11
S 1819–1918		4058/600–624,1166–1168
GOŁAŃCZ	**PIŁA**	**POLAND**
K 1834–1912		338/263–266
S 1865–1870		338/586
GOLINA	**KONIN**	**POLAND**
B 1826–1830; 1832–1836; 1838; 1840–1846; 1848–1862; 1864; 1867–1870		3744/1–34,36–39
D 1826–1830; 1832–1836; 1838; 1840–1846; 1848–1862; 1864; 1866–1870		3744/1–33
M 1826–1830; 1832–1836; 1838; 1840–1846; 1848–1862; 1869		3744/1–39
GRABÓW	**KALISZ**	**POLAND**
K 1841–1907		333/268–270
GRODZISK WIEŁKOPOLSKI	**POZNAŃ**	**POLAND**
C 1797/1939		63,652
IZBICA KUJAWSKA	**WŁOCŁAWEK**	**POLAND**
B 1810–1811; 1819–1821; 1860–1865; 1882–1883; 1914–1916; 1919		3745/1,3,5,8,11–54
D 1810–1811; 1817; 1819–1821; 1860–1861; 1882–1883; 1914–1916; 1919		3745/1,4,7,10–54
M 1810–1811; 1819–1821; 1858; 1860–1865; 1882–1883; 1914–1916; 1919		3745/2,6,9,11–54
JUTROSIN	**LESZNO**	**POLAND**
K 1860–1917; 1929–1933; 1937		331/142–143; 4310/838–839
S 1889–1911		4310/240–244
KALISZ	**KALISZ**	**POLAND**
B 1809–1874		3746/1–3,6,8–21,24,27–36,39–73
D 1809–1874		3746/2,5,7–20,23,26–35,38–73
M 1809–1874		3746/2,4,8–20,22,25,27–35,37,39–73
S 1937–1939		805/145–150
KARGOWA	**ZIELONA GÓRA**	**POLAND**
K 1857–1907		314/1048,1058,1060
KĘPNO	**KALISZ**	**POLAND**
B 1825; 1827; 1830–1847		3577/1,4,7,10,13,15,18,21,24,27,30,33,36, 39,43,47, 51,55,59,63
D 1825; 1827; 1830–1847		3577/2,6,9,12,14,17,20,23,26,29,32,35,38, 42,46,50, 54,58,62,66
M 1826–1827; 1830–1831		3577/3,5,8,11,16,19,22,25,28,31,34,37,40, 44,48,52, 56,60,64
KLECKO	**POZNAŃ**	**POLAND**
K 1854–1911		4061/223–227

A Army/recruit lists; **B** Birth; **C** Census; **D** Death; **E** Voter lists; **G** Immigration; **H** Holocaust; **J** Judaica; **K** Kahal; **L** Land; **M** Marriage; **N** Name changes; **O** Police files; **P** Pogroms; **R** Reference; **S** School records; **T** Tax lists; **V** Divorce; **W** Occupation Lists; **X** Jewish hospital; **Y** Notary records; **Z** Local government records

TOWN NAME Document Type Years	VOIVODSHIP/OBLAST (Province)	COUNTRY Zespół/Sygnatura (Poland) Fond/Opis/Delo (Belarus, Ukraine, Lithuania)
KLECZEW	**KONIN**	**POLAND**
B 1808–1815; 1817; 1820–1824; 1826–1827; 1829–1881; 1883; 1886–1887; 1889; 1891–1892; 1898		3747/1–6,10–11,13,15–18,20–23,25,27,29,31, 33–34,36,38,40,42,44,46,48, 50,52,55,57–102; 3650/4,7,10
D 1809–1815; 1817; 1820–1823; 1825–1827; 1829–1831; 1866; 1883; 1887; 1889; 1891–1892; 1898		3747/2–5,8–11,13,15–18,20–23,25,27,29, 31–34,36,38,40,42,44,46,48,50,53,55,57, 59,61,63–102;3650/6,9
G 1940		4299/526
M 1809–1815; 1817; 1820–1823; 1826–1827; 1829–1831; 1866–1870; 1883; 1886–1887; 1889; 1891–1892; 1898		3747/2–5,7,10–102; 3650/5,8
T 1921–1922		4299/375–376
KŁODAWA	**KONIN**	**POLAND**
B 1826–1863; 1865–1894		3748/1–15,17,19,21–22,24,26, 28,30,32,34, 36,38,40,42,44–45, 47,49,52–53,55,57,59, 61–62,64,66,68–103
C 1933–1939; 1942		18/37
D 1826–1863; 1865–1894		3748/1–15,17,19,21–22,24,26,28,30,32,34, 36,38,40,42,44–45,47,49,52–53,55,57,59, 61–62,64,66,68–103
E 1931–1939		18/1–3,7,9,11–13
M 1826–1863; 1865–1894		3748/1–103
KOLMAR	**SEE CHODZIEŻ**	
KOŁO	**KONIN**	**POLAND**
B 1826–1893		3749/2,5,8–30,53–61,63–65,67,69,71–73, 75–83,85,87– 90,92–99
D 1825–1893		3749/1,4,7–30,53–66,68,70–73,75–77, 79–81, 83–85,87– 93,95–99
M 1826–1893		3749/3,6,8–61,63–65,68,70–77,79–81,83, 85–90,92–93, 95–99
S 1937–1939		805/157–158
KONIN	**KONIN**	**POLAND**
B 1826–1853; 1855–1856; 1858–1860; 1862–1863; 1865–1866; 1869–1874; 1882–1889; 1891–1894		3750/2–57
C 1807/1914; 1920–1923; 1932–1940		4301/244–247,395–396,430–447,510–513; 20/564–588
D 1826–1853; 1855–1856; 1858–1860; 1862–1863; 1865–1866; 1869–1874; 1882–1889; 1891–1894		3750/2–57
M 1815;1826–1853; 1855–1856; 1858–1860; 1862–1863; 1865–1866; 1869–1874; 1882–1889; 1891–1894		3750/1–57
S 1936–1939		805/159–160
KÓRNIK	**POZNAŃ**	**POLAND**
B 1811–1812		3579/1,4,6–18
D 1811–1812		3579/3,5,6–18
K 1842–1914; 1917–1934		4381/121–123,398
M 1811–1812		3579/2,6–18
S 1897–1913		4381/139,141–143
KOSTRZYN	**POZNAŃ**	**POLAND**
K 1835–1905		336/507–508
KOŹMIN	**KALISZ**	**POLAND**
B 1811–1812		3578/1
D 1811–1812		3578/3
M 1811–1812		3578/2
Z 1760–1793		4331/I/21
KRIEWIN	**SEE KRZYWIN**	
KROTOSZYN	**KALISZ**	**POLAND**
B 1817–1847		3580/1,4,7,11,14,18,22,26,30,33,36,40,43, 47
D 1817–1847		3580/3,6,10,13,17,21,25,29,32,35,39,46,50
M 1817–1847		3580/2,5,8,12,15,19,23,27,31,34,37,41,44, 48
KRZYWIN	**LESZNO**	**POLAND**
B 1825–1847		3581/1,4,6,9,12,15,18,21,24,27,30,33,36
D 1825–1847		3581/3,8,11,14,17,20,23,26,29,32,35,38
M 1825–1847		3581/2,5,7,10,13,16,19,22,25,28,31,34,37
LESZNO	**LESZNO**	**POLAND**
L 18TH CENT.		4314/I/512
T 1689; 1704–1705; 1711/1837		4314/I/512; I/596
Z 1711–1732; 1751; 1812–1821		4314/I/507; I/594
LWÓWEK	**POZNAŃ**	**POLAND**
K 1919–1933		4383/318
S 1836–1919		4383/84–87

A Army/recruit lists; **B** Birth; **C** Census; **D** Death; **E** Voter lists; **G** Immigration; **H** Holocaust; **J** Judaica; **K** Kahal; **L** Land; **M** Marriage; **N** Name changes; **O** Police files; **P** Pogroms; **R** Reference; **S** School records; **T** Tax lists; **V** Divorce; **W** Occupation lists; **X** Jewish hospital; **Y** Notary records; **Z** Local government records

TOWN NAME Document Type Years	VOIVODSHIP/OBLAST (Province)	COUNTRY Zespół/Sygnatura (Poland) Fond/Opis/Delo (Belarus, Ukraine, Lithuania)
MARGONIN	**PIŁA**	**POLAND**
S 1824–1912		1029/66
MIĘDZYCHÓD	**GORZOW WIEŁKOPOLSKI**	**POLAND**
C 1840–1858; 1870–1875; 1897–1913		313/141–143,1131–1139,1149–1150,2124
K 1834–1914		313/459–464,2117–2120,2128–2130,2133,
		2135–2136
S 1853–1873		313/3126
MIELCIESKO	**SEE MIEŚCISKO**	
MIELĘCIN	**PIŁA**	**POLAND**
B 1840–1846		3582/1–7
D 1840–1846		3582/1–7
M 1840–1846		3582/1–7
MIEŚCISKO	**PIŁA**	**POLAND**
K 1823–1913		338/267–271
MIKSTAT	**KALISZ**	**POLAND**
B 1835–1846		3583/1–10
D 1835–1846		3583/1–10
M 1835–1846		3583/1–10
MIŁOSŁAW	**POZNAŃ**	**POLAND**
S 1833–1919		339/69–72
MOSINA	**POZNAŃ**	**POLAND**
B 1835–1836		3584/1–2
D 1835–1836		3584/1–2
M 1835–1836		3584/1–2
NOWE MIASTO NAD WARTĄ	**POZNAŃ**	**POLAND**
K 1894–1918		4063/145
NOWY TOMYŚL	**POZNAŃ**	**POLAND**
K 1847–1913		315/212
OPATÓW	**KALISZ**	**POLAND**
B 1835–1846		3585/1–11
D 1835–1846		3585/1–11
M 1835–1846		3585/1–11
OSTROW WIEŁKOPOLSKI	**KALISZ**	**POLAND**
K 1834–1914		327/284,287
OSTRZESZÓW	**KALISZ**	**POLAND**
B 1835–1846		3586/1–7
D 1835–1846		3586/1–7
M 1835–1846		3586/1–7
PIŁA	**PIŁA**	**POLAND**
S 1836–1891		1029/97–100
PLESZEW	**KALISZ**	**POLAND**
B 1835–1847		3587/1–8
D 1835–1847		3587/11
M 1835–1847		3587/9
POBIEDZISKA	**POZNAŃ**	**POLAND**
K 1880–1914		329/1223–1228
S 1893–1907		4387/188–189
PODZAMCZE	**KALISZ**	**POLAND**
B 1835–1846		3588/1–9
D 1835–1846		3588/1–9
M 1835–1846		3588/1–9
POZNAŃ	**POZNAŃ**	**POLAND**
C 1830–1940		474/12001–14226; 963–12000,
		14227–15752,15754–16000
K 1845–1903		330/823
X 1929–1939		474/1898
PYZDRY	**KONIN**	**POLAND**
B 1826–1894		3751/1,3–4,6,8–30,48–81
D 1826–1894		3751/2,5A,7–30,48–81
M 1826–1894		3751/1,5–6,8–81
RASZKÓW	**KALISZ**	**POLAND**
K 1836–1858		327/291
RAWICZ	**LESZNO**	**POLAND**
K 1839–1914		331/144–146

A Army/recruit lists; **B** Birth; **C** Census; **D** Death; **E** Voter lists; **G** Immigration; **H** Holocaust; **J** Judaica; **K** Kahal; **L** Land; **M** Marriage; **N** Name changes; **O** Police files; **P** Pogroms; **R** Reference; **S** School records; **T** Tax lists; **V** Divorce; **W** Occupation Lists; **X** Jewish hospital; **Y** Notary records; **Z** Local government records

TOWN NAME Document Type Years	VOIVODSHIP/OBLAST (Province)	COUNTRY Zespół/Sygnatura (Poland) Fond/Opis/Delo (Belarus, Ukraine, Lithuania)
ROGOŹNO	**TORUŃ**	**POLAND**
B 1817/1839; 1840–1847		3589/1–6,11,14,17,20,23,26,29,32,35,38,41
D 1817/1839; 1840–1847		3589/1–5,8,10,13,16,19,22,25,28,31,34,37, 40,43
M 1817/1839; 1840–1847		3589/1–5,7,12,15,18,21,24,27,30,33,36,39, 42
RYCHWAŁ	**KONIN**	**POLAND**
B 1826–1855		3752/1–30
D 1826–1855		3752/1–30
G 1925/1939; 1945–1950		4302/16–17,119,123
M 1826–1855		3752/1–30
SARNOWA	**LESZNO**	**POLAND**
C 1858–1910		314/148
K 1816–1817		314/148A
SCHNEIDEMUHL	**SEE PIŁA**	
SCHOENLANKE	**SEE PIŁA**	
SIERAKÓW	**POZNAŃ**	**POLAND**
B 1830		3590/1–2
D 1830		3590/1–2
K 1834–1915		313/2127,2131–2132,2134
M 1830		3590/1–2
SKOKI	**POZNAŃ**	**POLAND**
K 1835–1918		338/272–274; 4066/31
SKULSK	**KONIN**	**POLAND**
B 1826–1829; 1831–1834; 1836–1846; 1848–1851; 1853–1855; 1883–1884		3753/1–46
D 1826–1829; 1831–1834; 1836–1846; 1848–1851; 1853–1855; 1883–1884		3753/1–46
M 1826–1829; 1831–1834; 1836–1846; 1848–1851; 1853–1855; 1883–1884		3753/1–46
ŚLESIN	**KONIN**	**POLAND**
B 1826–1867; 1878; 1881; 1884–1887; 1890–1891; 1894–1898		3757/1–50
D 1826–1867; 1878; 1881; 1884–1887; 1890–1891; 1894–1898		3757/1–50
G 1918–1939		25/106–116
M 1826–1867; 1878; 1881; 1884–1887; 1890–1891; 1894–1898		3757/1–50
SŁUPCA	**KONIN**	**POLAND**
B 1869–1894		3754/1–27
D 1869–1894		3754/1–11,13–27
M 1869–1894		3754/1–11,13–27
S 1937–1939		805/192–193
SOBÓTKA	**WROCŁAW**	**POLAND**
B 1846		3591/1
SOMPOLNO	**KONIN**	**POLAND**
B 1826–1829; 1833–1894		3755/1–65
D 1826–1829; 1833–1894		3755/1–65
M 1826; 1828–1829; 1833–1894		3755/1–65
ŚREM	**POZNAŃ**	**POLAND**
B 1817–1847		3592/1–2,5
D 1817–1847		3592/1–2,4
K 1919–1934		4390/706–707
M 1817–1847		3592/1–3,7–12
S 1907–1921		4390/179
SRODA WIEŁKOPOLSKA	**POZNAŃ**	**POLAND**
K 1835–1915		336/511–514
N 1878–1916		336/520–522
STAWISZYN	**KALISZ**	**POLAND**
B 1826–1865		3756/1,3
D 1826–1861		3756/2
M 1847–1854		3756/4
SWARZĘDZ	**POZNAŃ**	**POLAND**
K 1734–1792; 1823; 1825–1831; 1902–1916		4389/114–115; 906/16–17; 329/1232
S 1824–1927		4389/121–123
TRZCIANKA	**PIŁA**	**POLAND**
B 1815–1847; 1855–1908		3593/2,6
D 1815–1847; 1855–1908		3593/1,5–7
M 1815–1847; 1855–1908		3593/3,6
TUREK	**KONIN**	**POLAND**
B 1837		3758/1
D 1837		3758/1
M 1837		3758/1

A Army/recruit lists; **B** Birth; **C** Census; **D** Death; **E** Voter lists; **G** Immigration; **H** Holocaust; **J** Judaica; **K** Kahal; **L** Land; **M** Marriage; **N** Name changes; **O** Police files; **P** Pogroms; **R** Reference; **S** School records; **T** Tax lists; **V** Divorce; **W** Occupation lists; **X** Jewish hospital; **Y** Notary records; **Z** Local government records

TOWN NAME Document Type Years	VOIVODSHIP/OBLAST (Province)	COUNTRY Zespół/Sygnatura (Poland) Fond/Opis/Delo (Belarus, Ukraine, Lithuania)
UJŚCIE	**PIŁA**	**POLAND**
S 1824–1915		1029/114–116
VRONIK	**SEE WRONKI**	
WĄGROWIEC	**PIŁA**	**POLAND**
K 1826–1916		338/275–278,280–282
WANGROWITZ	**SEE WĄGROWIEC**	
WILCZYN	**KONIN**	**POLAND**
B 1827/1859		3759/1–25
D 1827/1859		3759/1–25
M 1827/1859		3759/1–25
WOLLSTEIN	**SEE WOLSZTYN**	
WOLSZTYN	**ZIELONA GÓRA**	**POLAND**
K 1698–1865		906/18–29
WONGROWITZ	**SEE WĄGROWIEC**	
WRONKI	**PIŁA**	**POLAND**
N 1832/1842		
WRZEŚNIA	**POZNAŃ**	**POLAND**
S 1832–1916		339/61–63
WYSZANÓW	**KALISZ**	**POLAND**
B 1835–1836		3594/1–2
D 1835–1836		3594/1–2
M 1835–1836		3594/1–2
ZAGÓRÓW	**KONIN**	**POLAND**
B 1826–1865; 1882; 1886–1891; 1893–1894		3760/1–35,54A–81
D 1826–1865; 1882; 1886–1891; 1893–1894		3760/1–35,54A–81
M 1826–1865; 1882; 1886–1891; 1893–1894		3760/1–81
ZDUNY	**KALISZ**	**POLAND**
D 1818–1847		3597/1–2
M 1818–1847		3597/1
ZOBTEN	**SEE SOBÓTKA**	

PRZEMYŚL Archives

TOWN NAME Document Type Years	VOIVODSHIP/OBLAST (Province)	COUNTRY
BACHÓW	**PRZEMYŚL**	**POLAND**
C 1931/1945		203/17,27,38–40
BARANÓW	**TARNOBRZEG**	**POLAND**
K 1890–1897		74/29,32
BIECZ	**KROSNO**	**POLAND**
B 1850/1937		154/1
D 1851/1874		154/2
K 1914–1916; 1922		680/20; 791/17
BIRCZA	**PRZEMYŚL**	**POLAND**
Y 1909–1911; 1934–1944		728; 1075–1080
BOLESTRASZYCE	**PRZEMYŚL**	**POLAND**
C 1935–1939; 1948		212/21–24
BRZOZÓW	**KROSNO**	**POLAND**
Y 1903–1904; 1934–1935		730; 996
BUKOWSKO	**KROSNO**	**POLAND**
K 1897; 1932–1944		154/1; 174/158
Y 1910–1919; 1929–1937		729; 955–956
BUSZKOWICE	**PRZEMYŚL**	**POLAND**
C 1932;1948		212/25–28
BUSZKOWICZKI	**PRZEMYŚL**	**POLAND**
C 1932; 1948		212/27–28
CHYRZYNA	**PRZEMYŚL**	**POLAND**
C 1931/1943		203/18,28
DACHNÓW	**PRZEMYŚL**	**POLAND**
E 1938		637/4
DĘBICA	**TARNÓW**	**POLAND**
H 1939		682/2
Y 1864–1934		77; 949–954
DOBROMIL	**LVOV**	**UKRAINE**
Y 1870–1877; 1884–1889; 1891–1913; 1919–1927; 1929–1939		78; 979–985

A Army/recruit lists; **B** Birth; **C** Census; **D** Death; **E** Voter lists; **G** Immigration; **H** Holocaust; **J** Judaica; **K** Kahal; **L** Land; **M** Marriage; **N** Name changes; **O** Police files; **P** Pogroms; **R** Reference; **S** School records; **T** Tax lists; **V** Divorce; **W** Occupation Lists; **X** Jewish hospital; **Y** Notary records; **Z** Local government records

TOWN NAME Document Type Years	VOIVODSHIP/OBLAST (Province)	COUNTRY Zespół/Sygnatura (Poland) Fond/Opis/Delo (Belarus, Ukraine, Lithuania)
DROHOBYCZKA	**PRZEMYŚL**	**POLAND**
C　1931–1950		200/19–24
DUBIECKO	**PRZEMYŚL**	**POLAND**
C　1930–1940; 1946–1950		200/25–29
D　1939–1952		200/142
Y　1874–1875; 1882–1892; 1924–1926; 1944–1949		79; 1069–1074
DUKLA	**KROSNO**	**POLAND**
Y　1924–1934		742; 1026–1027
DUŃKOWICZKI	**PRZEMYŚL**	**POLAND**
C　1930/1948		207/16–17
DYNÓW	**PRZEMYŚL**	**POLAND**
Y　1934		772; 1064–1065
FRYSZTAK	**RZESZÓW**	**POLAND**
Y　1920–1928; 1934		727; 957–958
GŁOGÓW MAŁOPOLSKI	**RZESZÓW**	**POLAND**
Y　1886–1939		80; 1128–1137
GORLICE	**NOWY SĄCZ**	**POLAND**
E　1935		791/17
L　1920–1925		791/11–14
HUCISKO NIENADOWSKIE	**PRZEMYŚL**	**POLAND**
C　1931–1939		200/30–31
ISKAŃ	**PRZEMYŚL**	**POLAND**
C　1931–1939; 1947		200/33–36
JAROSŁAW	**PRZEMYŚL**	**POLAND**
B　1867–1918		154/1
C　1939–1940		174/52
D　1865–1908		154/1–2
G　1940–1941		174/150
H　1944–1945; 1947–1949		431/124; 29/147,156
L　1944; 1946		431/107
M　1877		154/1
Y　1899; 1934–1950		81; 999–1007
JAROSŁAW REGION	**PRZEMYŚL**	**POLAND**
C　1932–1944		172–182/153–171
JASIENICA ROSIELNA	**KROSNO**	**POLAND**
K　1872; 1901; 1913		843/5
JASŁO	**KROSNO**	**POLAND**
A　1915–1918		678/7–16
E　1920/1927		790/15–17
K　1915/1927		790/64–67
JASŁO REGION	**KROSNO**	**POLAND**
C　1926		790/69
KAŃCZUGA	**PRZEMYŚL**	**POLAND**
C　1931–1944		133/23–24
KOSIENICE	**PRZEMYŚL**	**POLAND**
C　1930/1948		207/20–21
KOSZTOWO	**PRZEMYŚL**	**POLAND**
C　1931–1939		200/37–39
KROSNO	**KROSNO**	**POLAND**
Y　1928–1934		741; 1044
KRZYWCZA	**PRZEMYŚL**	**POLAND**
C　1931–1945		203/20,44–46
ŁAŃCUT	**RZESZÓW**	**POLAND**
Y　1861–1934		86; 1109–1114
LESKO	**KROSNO**	**POLAND**
B　1882–1884		154/1
LEŻAJSK	**RZESZÓW**	**POLAND**
C　1927; 1942–1943		135/61,156
D　1826–1866		154/1
E　1938–1939		135/17
G　1940–1944		135/156
H　1940–1944		135/89
L　1909–1918; 1936–1937		135/60,62

A Army/recruit lists; **B** Birth; **C** Census; **D** Death; **E** Voter lists; **G** Immigration; **H** Holocaust; **J** Judaica; **K** Kahal; **L** Land; **M** Marriage; **N** Name changes; **O** Police files; **P** Pogroms; **R** Reference; **S** School records; **T** Tax lists; **V** Divorce; **W** Occupation lists; **X** Jewish hospital; **Y** Notary records; **Z** Local government records

TOWN NAME Document Type Years	VOIVODSHIP/OBLAST (Province)	COUNTRY Zespół/Sygnatura (Poland) Fond/Opis/Delo (Belarus, Ukraine, Lithuania)
LUTOWISKA	**KROSNO**	**POLAND**
Y 1916–1917		731
MAĆKOWICE	**PRZEMYŚL**	**POLAND**
C 1930–1941		207/22–23,41,56–57,154,164
MAŁKOWICE	**PRZEMYŚL**	**POLAND**
C 1932		207/24,25,42,58,59,164
MARKOWA	**RZESZÓW**	**POLAND**
C 1931–1952		196/13,15,19–20
MIELEC	**RZESZÓW**	**POLAND**
Y 1860–1873; 1875–1905; 1907–1936		87/1240–1245
MOSTISKA	**LVOV**	**UKRAINE**
Y 1916–1918		760
MUNINA	**PRZEMYŚL**	**POLAND**
C 1937/1946		177/5,58,65,69
E 1938		177/9
NAROL	**PRZEMYŚL**	**POLAND**
E 1934–1938		189/1–2
NIENADOWA	**PRZEMYŚL**	**POLAND**
C 1931–1939		200/42
NISKO	**TARNOBRZEG**	**POLAND**
Y 1873–1934		88; 1100–1108
NIZHANKOVICHI	**LVOV**	**UKRAINE**
Y 1892–1899; 1903–1914		89; 1066–1068
OLESZYCE	**PRZEMYŚL**	**POLAND**
B 1814–1876		154/1,4
D 1814–1869		154/2
M 1860–1876		154/3
ORŁY	**PRZEMYŚL**	**POLAND**
C 1930/1941		207/26–27,43,60,61
ORZECHOWCE	**PRZEMYŚL**	**POLAND**
C 1930–1948		207/28–29,62–63
G 1931–1944		207/155,159
PILZNO	**TARNÓW**	**POLAND**
Y 1861–1934		90; 1250–1262
PRUCHNIK	**PRZEMYŚL**	**POLAND**
B 1834–1876		154/1
Y 1905–1906; 1908–1949		91; 1081–1083
PRZEDMIEŚCIE DUBIECKIE	**PRZEMYŚL**	**POLAND**
C 1932–1950		200/47–49
PRZEMYŚL	**PRZEMYŚL**	**POLAND**
A 1819–1875		129/9–16
B 1790–1827; 1853–1883		154/1,6–9,12
D 1790–1884		154/1,3–5,10,13
G 1931–1951		208/19–20,67–70,72–73,75–76,78–81
K 1791; 1799–1887		129/169–173
M 1790–1876		154/1–2
T 1819–1844		129/127–129
Y 1882–1951		92; 634; 1008–1016
PRZEMYŚL REGION	**PRZEMYŚL**	**POLAND**
C 1929–1930; 1953–1954		208/18,66,71,74,77,82
PRZEWORSK	**PRZEMYŚL**	**POLAND**
A 1795–1914		137/184–203,1186,1327
B 1815–1850		137/523
C 1910–1921		137/1318
D 1815–1850; 1913–1936		137/523,1320
E 1814–1853; 1928; 1930; 1935; 1938		137/521–522,1302–1305
H 1940–1943		137/1416
K 1782–1863; 1867; 1914		137/28,51–55,494–516,524,1173
M 1815–1850		137/523
T 1824–1863		137/517–520
X 1814–1864		137/299–301
Y 1860–1874; 1877–1935		93; 1046–1053
RADOMYŚL NAD SANEM	**TARNOBRZEG**	**POLAND**
Y 1875–1879; 1887–1923		94; 969–972

A Army/recruit lists; **B** Birth; **C** Census; **D** Death; **E** Voter lists; **G** Immigration; **H** Holocaust; **J** Judaica; **K** Kahal; **L** Land; **M** Marriage; **N** Name changes; **O** Police files; **P** Pogroms; **R** Reference; **S** School records; **T** Tax lists; **V** Divorce; **W** Occupation Lists; **X** Jewish hospital; **Y** Notary records; **Z** Local government records

TOWN NAME Document Type Years	VOIVODSHIP/OBLAST (Province)	COUNTRY Zespół/Sygnatura (Poland) Fond/Opis/Delo (Belarus, Ukraine, Lithuania)
RADYMNO	**PRZEMYŚL**	**POLAND**
B 1877		154/3
D 1877		154/3
M 1920; 1925		154/1–2
ROPCZYCE	**RZESZÓW**	**POLAND**
A 1919–1935		681/31
Y 1873–1874; 1876–1934		96; 1090–1094
ROZWADÓW	**TARNOBRZEG**	**POLAND**
K 1897		74/33
S 1890–1894		74/27
Y 1859–1893; 1915–1934		97; 1169–1173
RUSKA WIEŚ	**PRZEMYŚL**	**POLAND**
C 1931–1939		200/50
RUSZELCZYCE	**PRZEMYŚL**	**POLAND**
C 1913–1930; 1943; 1945–1957		203/22,32,49,60,69,78,87
RYMANÓW	**KROSNO**	**POLAND**
Y 1928–1933		660
RZESZÓW	**RZESZÓW**	**POLAND**
Y 1859–1943		98; 1174–1193
SANOK	**KROSNO**	**POLAND**
Y 1900–1901; 1911–1912; 1929–1934		633; 993–995
SKOPÓW	**PRZEMYŚL**	**POLAND**
C 1931/1943		203/23,33,50,61,70,79,88
SOKOŁÓW MAŁOPOSKI	**RZESZÓW**	**POLAND**
Y 1872–1873; 1875–1892; 1904–1934		101; 1056–1063
STRZYŻÓW	**RZESZÓW**	**POLAND**
Y 1873–1875; 1878–1947		102; 1246–1249
SUDOVAYA VISHNYA	**LVOV**	**UKRAINE**
Y 1894; 1897–1898; 1901–1912		99; 1040–1043
TARNOBRZEG	**TARNOBRZEG**	**POLAND**
B 1892–1909; 1916; 1918		74/30
D 1892–1909; 1916; 1918		74/30
K 1889–1898; 1916		74/26,28,31
M 1892–1909; 1916; 1918		74/30
TRÓJCZYCE	**PRZEMYŚL**	**POLAND**
C 1930/1942		207/30–31
TYCZYN	**RZESZÓW**	**POLAND**
Y 1872–1939		104; 1115–1127
TYRAWA WOŁOSKA	**KROSNO**	**POLAND**
K 1937		154/1
UJKOWICE	**PRZEMYŚL**	**POLAND**
C 1932–1933		207/32–33
ULANÓW	**TARNOBRZEG**	**POLAND**
Y 1875–1934		105; 1095–1099
USTRZYKI DOLNE	**KROSNO**	**POLAND**
Y 1894–1896		732
WALAWA	**PRZEMYŚL**	**POLAND**
C 1946–1951		212/29,45,51,70–71
WOLA KRZYWIECKA	**PRZEMYŚL**	**POLAND**
C 1930–1950		203/25,35,63,72,81,90
YAVOROW	**LVOV**	**UKRAINE**
Y 1861–1902; 1913–1915		82; 989
ZASÓW	**TARNÓW**	**POLAND**
Y 1873		106
ŻOŁYNIA	**RZESZÓW**	**POLAND**
M 1916–1922		154/1
ŻURAWICA	**PRZEMYŚL**	**POLAND**
C 1925–1951		212/52–55,59–61,63,74–75

PRZEWORSK Branch Archives

BIAŁOBOKI	**PRZEMYŚL**	**POLAND**
S 1888–1946		56/1–15,17–44

A Army/recruit lists; **B** Birth; **C** Census; **D** Death; **E** Voter lists; **G** Immigration; **H** Holocaust; **J** Judaica; **K** Kahal; **L** Land; **M** Marriage; **N** Name changes; **O** Police files; **P** Pogroms; **R** Reference; **S** School records; **T** Tax lists; **V** Divorce; **W** Occupation lists; **X** Jewish hospital; **Y** Notary records; **Z** Local government records

TOWN NAME Document Type Years	VOIVODSHIP/OBLAST (Province)	COUNTRY Zespół/Sygnatura (Poland) Fond/Opis/Delo (Belarus, Ukraine, Lithuania)
BOJANÓW	**TARNOBRZEG**	**POLAND**
C 1949		13/45–47
E 1949		13/22
T 1948; 1951		13/38–44
DĘBÓW	**PRZEMYŚL**	**POLAND**
S 1896–1948		57/1–10,17–43
GAĆ	**PRZEMYŚL**	**POLAND**
S 1884/1952		58/1–2,5–27
GŁOGOWIEC	**PRZEMYŚL**	**POLAND**
S 1885/1949		59/4–15,19–39
GNIEWCZYNA	**PRZEMYŚL**	**POLAND**
S 1888–1951		60/3–24,29–60
GORLICZYNA	**PRZEMYŚL**	**POLAND**
S 1929–1960		82/1–16
HADLE KAŃCZUCKIE	**PRZEMYŚL**	**POLAND**
S 1910–1957		79/2–10,12–41
HADLE SZKLARSKIE	**PRZEMYŚL**	**POLAND**
S 1916–1957		61/1,3–19,22–31
JAGIEŁŁA	**PRZEMYŚL**	**POLAND**
S 1893–1935		62/2–3
JAROCIN	**TARNOBRZEG**	**POLAND**
G 1945		14/35–36,39
T 1943–1954		14/6–10,54–75
JEŻOWE	**TARNOBRZEG**	**POLAND**
C 1946–1947; 1950–1951		15/35–46
G 1945–1948		15/34
T 1935–1953		15/5–7,71–123
KAMIEŃ	**RZESZÓW**	**POLAND**
A 1944; 1947–1948		16/86
C 1935–1948		16/1–9,84
E 1954		16/55,83
G 1944; 1953–1954		16/81
KRZECZOWICE	**PRZEMYŚL**	**POLAND**
S 1885–1951		63/2–15,23–46,50–57
ŁOPUSZKA MAŁA	**PRZEMYŚL**	**POLAND**
S 1893–1924; 1940–1958		64/3–28
MANASTERZ	**PRZEMYŚL**	**POLAND**
S 1896–1950		65/1–19,23–40,43–50
NISKO	**TARNOBRZEG**	**POLAND**
T 1936/1951		17/25–33,109–122
NISKO REGION	**TARNOBRZEG**	**POLAND**
C 1931–1947		17/4–15,80–82
E 1939		17/2–3
G 1932–1941; 1948–1951		17/16–18,77–79
NOWOSIELCE	**PRZEMYŚL**	**POLAND**
S 1894–1953		66/2–32,34–66
PANTALOWICE	**PRZEMYŚL**	**POLAND**
S 1886–1944		67/1–53
PRZEWORSK	**PRZEMYŚL**	**POLAND**
H 1945–1947		8/5,9–10,12
S 1921–1960		69/4–28,34–41
PRZEWORSK REGION	**PRZEMYŚL**	**POLAND**
S 1913–1953		68/7–11,15–46,52–60
RĄCZYNA	**PRZEMYŚL**	**POLAND**
S 1893–1944		83/1–48
ROZBÓRZ	**PRZEMYŚL**	**POLAND**
S 1884–1952		70/5–13,18–55
ROŻNIATÓW	**PRZEMYŚL**	**POLAND**
S 1904–1957		71/1–47
RUDNIK	**TARNOBRZEG**	**POLAND**
T 1937; 1944–1948		18/8,83–88
SIEDLECZKA	**PRZEMYŚL**	**POLAND**
S 1912–1948		72/1–12,14–18

A Army/recruit lists; **B** Birth; **C** Census; **D** Death; **E** Voter lists; **G** Immigration; **H** Holocaust; **J** Judaica; **K** Kahal; **L** Land; **M** Marriage; **N** Name changes; **O** Police files; **P** Pogroms; **R** Reference; **S** School records; **T** Tax lists; **V** Divorce; **W** Occupation Lists; **X** Jewish hospital; **Y** Notary records; **Z** Local government records

TOWN NAME Document Type Years	VOIVODSHIP/OBLAST (Province)	COUNTRY Zespół/Sygnatura (Poland) Fond/Opis/Delo (Belarus, Ukraine, Lithuania)
SIETESZ	**PRZEMYŚL**	**POLAND**
S 1902–1952		73/2–12,18–43,45–50
STANY	**TARNOBRZEG**	**POLAND**
G 1947–1951		120/13–16
T 1947–1948		120/24–29
ŚWIĘTONIOWA	**PRZEMYŚL**	**POLAND**
S 1911–1958		80/4–22
TRYŃCZA	**PRZEMYŚL**	**POLAND**
S 1915–1959		74/1–29,32–46
UBIESZYN	**PRZEMYŚL**	**POLAND**
S 1906–1953		75/1–30,33–37
UJEZNA	**PRZEMYŚL**	**POLAND**
S 1899–1950		76/1–21,23–57
ULANÓW	**TARNOBRZEG**	**POLAND**
A 1887–1927; 1935		19/8; 20/19
C 1931–1939; 1949–1950		19/5–7; 20/8–18,73
E 1949		20/72
G 1938–1939		20/20–21
T 1922–1944; 1948/1952		19/14–18,57,64; 20/22–42,102–115
WIDACZÓW	**PRZEMYŚL**	**POLAND**
S 1893–1949		77/1–4,7
WÓLKA MAŁKOWA	**PRZEMYŚL**	**POLAND**
S 1900–1956		81/1–9,12–31,34–35
ZALESIE	**PRZEMYŚL**	**POLAND**
S 1938		78/1–8,10–15

PSZCZYNA Branch Archives

TOWN NAME	VOIVODSHIP/OBLAST	COUNTRY
BIERUŃ NOWY	**KATOWICE**	**POLAND**
B 1847–1874		67/I/1–2
D 1848–1874		67/I/4–5
M 1848–1873		67/I/3
BIERUŃ STARY	**KATOWICE**	**POLAND**
H 1939–1942		55/I/717
T 1899–1924		55/I/48
IMIELIN	**KATOWICE**	**POLAND**
B 1847–1874		67/I/2
D 1848–1874		67/I/5
M 1848–1873		67/I/3
KOPCIEWICE	**KATOWICE**	**POLAND**
B 1847–1849		67/I/1
D 1848		67/I/4
MIKOŁÓW	**KATOWICE**	**POLAND**
C 1812–1847; 1863–1865; 1885–1886; 1901–1918; 1923–1938		56/I/71–73,1412,1415–1416,1422
G 1823–1847; 1862–1887; 1890–1917; 1921–1942		56/I/1416,1421,1423–1441
H 1939–1941		56/I/2041–2042
PSZCZYNA	**KATOWICE**	**POLAND**
B 1816; 1819; 1831; 1848–1874		26/I/1395,1397–1398
D 1816; 1831; 1848–1874		26/I/1395,1397–1398
H 1939–1940		26/I/3400
M 1851–1874		26/I/1397–1398
PSZCZYNA REGION	**KATOWICE**	**POLAND**
H 1941		157/I/2

PUŁTUSK Branch Archives

TOWN NAME	VOIVODSHIP/OBLAST	COUNTRY
ANDRZEJEWO	**ŁOMŻA**	**POLAND**
B 1826–1859		252
D 1826–1859		252
M 1826–1859		252
BROK	**OSTROŁEKA**	**POLAND**
B 1826–1892		135
D 1826–1892		135
M 1826–1892		135
CHORZELE	**OSTROŁEKA**	**POLAND**
B 1826/1893		229

A Army/recruit lists; **B** Birth; **C** Census; **D** Death; **E** Voter lists; **G** Immigration; **H** Holocaust; **J** Judaica; **K** Kahal; **L** Land; **M** Marriage; **N** Name changes; **O** Police files; **P** Pogroms; **R** Reference; **S** School records; **T** Tax lists; **V** Divorce; **W** Occupation lists; **X** Jewish hospital; **Y** Notary records; **Z** Local government records

TOWN NAME Document Type Years	VOIVODSHIP/OBLAST (Province)	COUNTRY Zespół/Sygnatura (Poland) Fond/Opis/Delo (Belarus, Ukraine, Lithuania)
D 1826/1893		229
M 1826–1893		229
CZYŻEW–OSADA	**ŁOMŻA**	**POLAND**
B 1826–1859		258
D 1826–1859		258
M 1826–1859		258
NASIELSK	**CIECHANÓW**	**POLAND**
B 1875–1893; 1937		116
D 1875–1893		116
M 1875–1893		116
NUR	**ŁOMŻA**	**POLAND**
B 1826/1876		264
D 1826/1876		264
M 1826/1876		264
OSTRÓW MAZOWIECKA	**OSTROŁEKA**	**POLAND**
B 1826–1892		94
D 1826–1892		94
M 1821–1829; 1831–1892		94
PRZASNYSZ	**OSTROŁEKA**	**POLAND**
B 1826–1893		106
D 1826–1893		106
M 1826–1893		106
PUŁTUSK	**CIECHANÓW**	**POLAND**
B 1875–1892		84
D 1875–1892		84
M 1875–1892		84
WYSZKÓW	**OSTROŁEKA**	**POLAND**
B 1874–1886; 1888–1892		98
D 1874–1886; 1888–1892		98
M 1874–1886; 1888–1892		98
ZARĘBY	**ŁOMŻA**	**POLAND**
B 1837–1873		273
D 1837–1873		273
M 1837–1873		273

RACIBÓRZ Branch Archives

BARANOWICE	**KATOWICE**	**POLAND**
B 1846–1859		118/1
D 1846–1859		118/1
M 1846–1859		118/1
RACIBÓRZ	**KATOWICE**	**POLAND**
B 1847–1939		3/488
D 1847–1884		3/490
M 1847–1874		3/489
RATIBOR	**SEE RACIBÓRZ**	**POLAND**
RYBNIK	**KATOWICE**	**POLAND**
C 1837–1874		78/1492–1494
RYBNIK REGION	**KATOWICE**	**POLAND**
B 1810–1874		118/1–31
D 1810–1874		118/1–31
K 1812–1911		78/1477–1483,1488–1494
M 1810–1874		118/1–31
S 1820–1900		78/1484–1487
ŻORY	**KATOWICE**	**POLAND**
C 1930–1932; 1945–1947		

RADOM Archives

BIAŁOBRZEGI	**RADOM**	**POLAND**
B 1862–1893; 1904–1939		183
D 1862–1893; 1904–1939		183
M 1862–1893; 1904–1939		183
CIEPIELÓW	**RADOM**	**POLAND**
B 1874–1894		486/1
D 1874–1894		486/1
M 1852–1853; 1874–1894		486/1

A Army/recruit lists; **B** Birth; **C** Census; **D** Death; **E** Voter lists; **G** Immigration; **H** Holocaust; **J** Judaica; **K** Kahal; **L** Land; **M** Marriage; **N** Name changes; **O** Police files; **P** Pogroms; **R** Reference; **S** School records; **T** Tax lists; **V** Divorce; **W** Occupation Lists; **X** Jewish hospital; **Y** Notary records; **Z** Local government records

TOWN NAME Document Type Years	VOIVODSHIP/OBLAST (Province)	COUNTRY Zespół/Sygnatura (Poland) Fond/Opis/Delo (Belarus, Ukraine, Lithuania)
GŁOWACZÓW	**RADOM**	**POLAND**
B 1883–1894		433/1
D 1883–1894		433/1
M 1883–1894		433/1
GNIEWOSZÓW	**RADOM**	**POLAND**
B 1826–1894		184
D 1826–1894		184
M 1826–1894		184
GOWARCZÓW	**RADOM**	**POLAND**
B 1869–1939		449
D 1867–1894; 1920–1940		449
M 1847–1913; 1920–1934		449
GROJEC	**RADOM**	**POLAND**
B 1876–1941		510/1
D 1876–1941		510/1
M 1876–1941		510/1
IŁŻA	**RADOM**	**POLAND**
B 1876–1894		443/1
D 1876–1894		443/1
M 1876–1894		443/1
KAZANÓW	**RADOM**	**POLAND**
B 1828–1864; 1866–1868; 1870–1892		185
D 1828–1864; 1866–1868; 1870–1892		185
M 1828–1858; 1878–1892		185
KLWÓW	**RADOM**	**POLAND**
B 1875–1894		76/1
D 1875–1894		76/1
M 1875–1894		76/1
KOZIENICE	**RADOM**	**POLAND**
B 1826–1894; 1925–1939		186
D 1826–1894; 1925–1939		186
M 1826–1894; 1925–1937		186
LIPSKO	**RADOM**	**POLAND**
B 1837; 1875–1894		187/1
D 1837; 1875–1894		187/1
M 1837; 1875–1894		187/1
MAGNUSZEW	**RADOM**	**POLAND**
B 1826–1839; 1842–1866; 1868–1869; 1876; 1883; 1889; 1893–1894; 1901–1902; 1905–1913; 1919–1922; 1924–1932; 1934; 1938–1939		186
D 1826–1839; 1842–1866; 1868–1869; 1876; 1883; 1889; 1893–1894; 1901–1902; 1905–1913; 1919–1922; 1924–1932; 1934; 1938–1939		188
M 1826–1839; 1842–1866; 1868–1869; 1876; 1883; 1889; 1893–1894; 1901–1902; 1905–1913; 1919–1922; 1924–1932; 1934; 1938–1939		188
MOGIELNICA	**RADOM**	**POLAND**
B 1872–1878; 1881–1894		472
D 1874–1878; 1881–1894		472
M 1871–1878; 1881–1894		472
NOWE MIASTO NAD PILICĄ	**RADOM**	**POLAND**
B 1874–1877; 1880–1882; 1887–1891		450/1
D 1874–1877; 1880–1882; 1887–1891		450/1
M 1874–1877; 1880–1882; 1887–1891		450/1
PRZYSUCHA	**RADOM**	**POLAND**
B 1869–1894		471/1
D 1869–1881; 1883–1894		471/1
M 1869–1894		471/1
PRZYTYK	**RADOM**	**POLAND**
B 1826–1939		189
D 1826–1939		189
M 1826–1918; 1921–1923; 1930–1939		189
RADOM	**RADOM**	**POLAND**
A 1842–1848; 1867–1873; 1918–1921		1
B 1826–1894		190/1
D 1826–1894		190
E 1906–1907; 1916; 1918; 1928; 1934; 1939		1; 206
G 1868–1930		1
H 1939–1943		206; 209; 331; 387
L 1865–1916; 1936; 1945		1

A Army/recruit lists; **B** Birth; **C** Census; **D** Death; **E** Voter lists; **G** Immigration; **H** Holocaust; **J** Judaica; **K** Kahal; **L** Land; **M** Marriage; **N** Name changes; **O** Police files; **P** Pogroms; **R** Reference; **S** School records; **T** Tax lists; **V** Divorce; **W** Occupation lists; **X** Jewish hospital; **Y** Notary records; **Z** Local government records

TOWN NAME Document Type Years	VOIVODSHIP/OBLAST (Province)	COUNTRY Zespół/Sygnatura (Poland) Fond/Opis/Delo (Belarus, Ukraine, Lithuania)
M 1826–1894		190
N 1821–1860		1
S 1865–1876; 1878–1912; 1929–1939		1; 123
T 1868–1914; 1916–1918		1
W 1925–1930; 1934; 1938; 1941–1942		1; 351
X 1833–1914		39; 195–196
Y 1818–1950		72–75; 77–104; 491–498
RYCZYWÓL	**RADOM**	**POLAND**
B 1826–1840; 1842–1889; 1891–1892		191
D 1826–1840; 1842–1889; 1891–1892		191
M 1826–1840; 1842–1889; 1891–1892		191
SIENNO	**RADOM**	**POLAND**
B 1874–1894		477/1
D 1874–1894		477/1
M 1874–1894		477/1
SOLEC NAD WISŁĄ	**RADOM**	**POLAND**
B 1886–1891		551/1
D 1886–1891		551/1
M 1886–1891		551/1
SZDŁOWIEC	**RADOM**	**POLAND**
B 1826–1894		192
D 1826–1894		192
M 1826–1894		192
WARKA	**RADOM**	**POLAND**
B 1873–1894		467
D 1873–1894		467
M 1873–1894		467
WOLANÓW	**RADOM**	**POLAND**
B 1826–1858; 1860–1894		193
D 1826–1858; 1860–1894		193
M 1826–1858; 1860–1894		193
ZWOLEŃ	**RADOM**	**POLAND**
B 1826–1883; 1886–1894		194
D 1826–1883; 1886–1894		194
M 1826–1883; 1886–1894		194

RADZYŃ PODLASKI Branch Archives

MIĘDZYRZEC PODLASKI	**BIAŁA PODLASKA**	**POLAND**
C 1924; 1934		24/225–227

RAWA MAZOWIECKA Branch Archives

BIAŁA RAWSKA	**SKIERNIEWICE**	**POLAND**
B 1853; 1856–1857; 1862–1868; 1871–1892		272
C 1835/1944		157/342,355,371–372,389–390,420,427, 463,476
D 1853; 1856–1857; 1862–1890		272
M 1853; 1856–1857; 1862–1890		272
BRZEZINY	**SKIERNIEWICE**	**POLAND**
D 1877–1892		
M 1877–1892		
RAWA MAZOWIECKA	**SKIERNIEWICE**	**POLAND**
B 1809/1839; 1841–1852; 1853/1862; 1865–1866; 1869–1873		45; 165
D 1809/1839; 1841–1852; 1853/1862; 1865–1866; 1869–1873		45; 165
M 1809/1839; 1841–1852; 1853/1862; 1865–1866; 1869–1873		45; 165
Y 1809–1836; 1838–1914; 1916–1946		146–147; 240–250
SKIERNIEWICE	**SKIERNIEWICE**	**POLAND**
C 1867–1939		19/12–117,132–182,191–314
Y 1873–1948		41–46; 151

RZESZÓW Archives

BŁAŻOWA	**RZESZÓW**	**POLAND**
G 1939–1941		71/38
H 1940–1944		71/38,49
L 1943–1944		71/49

A Army/recruit lists; **B** Birth; **C** Census; **D** Death; **E** Voter lists; **G** Immigration; **H** Holocaust; **J** Judaica; **K** Kahal; **L** Land; **M** Marriage; **N** Name changes;
O Police files; **P** Pogroms; **R** Reference; **S** School records; **T** Tax lists; **V** Divorce; **W** Occupation Lists; **X** Jewish hospital; **Y** Notary records; **Z** Local government records

TOWN NAME Document Type Years	VOIVODSHIP/OBLAST (Province)	COUNTRY Zespół/Sygnatura (Poland) Fond/Opis/Delo (Belarus, Ukraine, Lithuania)
CMOLAS	**RZESZÓW**	**POLAND**
C 1931		90/1–5
CZARNA	**RZESZÓW**	**POLAND**
C 1937		246/186–191
CZUDEC	**RZESZÓW**	**POLAND**
B 1940–1942		736/16
C 1935–1937; 1940–1942		736/17,20,59
D 1940–1942		736/16
H 1939–1942		736/18–20; 726/134
K 1922–1928; 1939–1942		716/1–12,9–20; 736
L 1939–1942		725/134
M 1940–1942		736/16
W 1940–1941		736/18–19
DĘBICA	**TARNÓW**	**POLAND**
A 1919–1939		518/23
C 1945		69/28
D 1937–1939; 1942–1944; 1949		518/1,28; 882/1
E 1927–1938		518/17
G 1927–1939		518/18
H 1942–1944		882/1
DUBECZNO	**CHEŁM**	**POLAND**
D 1889/1909		533/18–19
FRYSZTAK	**RZESZÓW**	**POLAND**
H 1939–1944		731/54
GALICIA REGION	**RZESZÓW**	**POLAND**
B 1880/1927		533/19; 1/2738,2741
D 1894/1909		533/19
M 1894/1909		533/19
GŁOGÓW MAŁOPOLSKI	**RZESZÓW**	**POLAND**
C 1945–1947		335/96–97
GRODZISKO DOLNE	**RZESZÓW**	**POLAND**
C 1936		248/43–55,58
KOLBUSZOWA	**RZESZÓW**	**POLAND**
C 1945–1946		332/97
L 1870–1873		416/16–17
KOBLUSZOWA GÓRNA	**RZESZÓW**	**POLAND**
A 1933–1939		390/10–11
C 1932–1949		390/1–9,13,26–49
KOMORÓW	**TARNOBRZEG**	**POLAND**
C 1933–1939		220/1
ŁAŃCUT	**RZESZÓW**	**POLAND**
A 1919–1936		29/87–95A,96
B 1883–1889		29/15–16
C 1883–1915		29/83
E 1927–1939		29/77
L 1921; 1932; 1937; 1941–1945		29/97–100,192–195
MAJDAN KRÓLEWSKI	**TARNOBRZEG**	**POLAND**
A 1918–1938		392/105–106,117–118
L 1927		392/98
MIELEC	**RZESZÓW**	**POLAND**
A 1847–1913; 1929–1932		752/36,90–914
B 1920–1935		752/89
C 1940–1943		752/117
D 1920–1935		752/89
E 1914–1930		752/88
H 1940–1943		752/117
MIELEC REGION	**RZESZÓW**	**POLAND**
C 1921–1944		765/2–3A
NIEBYLEC REGION	**RZESZÓW**	**POLAND**
B 1877; 1879–1885; 1887–1890; 1892; 1895; 1898; 1900–1904		907/3–26
D 1905–1906; 1912–1913		907/1–2
NIWISKA	**RZESZÓW**	**POLAND**
C 1931–1939		393/1–3
OLCHOWA	**RZESZÓW**	**POLAND**
E 1938		11/1

A Army/recruit lists; **B** Birth; **C** Census; **D** Death; **E** Voter lists; **G** Immigration; **H** Holocaust; **J** Judaica; **K** Kahal; **L** Land; **M** Marriage; **N** Name changes; **O** Police files; **P** Pogroms; **R** Reference; **S** School records; **T** Tax lists; **V** Divorce; **W** Occupation lists; **X** Jewish hospital; **Y** Notary records; **Z** Local government records

TOWN NAME Document Type Years	VOIVODSHIP/OBLAST (Province)	COUNTRY Zespół/Sygnatura (Poland) Fond/Opis/Delo (Belarus, Ukraine, Lithuania)
RACŁAWÓWKA	**RZESZÓW**	**POLAND**
E 1935		382/1
H 1940–1941		382/34
ROPCZYCE	**RZESZÓW**	**POLAND**
H 1940–1943		135/17–18
RUDA ŁAŃCUCKA	**RZESZÓW**	**POLAND**
C 1932–1939		269/111–123
RZESZÓW	**RZESZÓW**	**POLAND**
A 1860/1918		1/1539–1547; 1556; 1697–1698; 2723–2725
B 1866–1939 (ALPHA INDEX: 1913–1939)		533/20,44,55–57; 1/2735–2743
C 1800/1850; 1869–1910; 1921; 1935–1942		533/1,32,53,489,1497–1538,2713
D 1842–1883; 1889; 1915–1942; (ALPHA INDEX: 1935–1942)		533/18,20,42–43,50–52,58–60; 1/3774–3775
E 1925; 1939		1/105–110; 2053–2058
H 1940–1944		533/1/53; 3755
K 1858; 1882–1917; 1919–1923		533/1; 7; 2015; 2380–2384; 2471
L 1800/1850; 1940–1944; 1947		1/1488,1496,3698,3701,3755–3756; 36/498
M 1895–1942		533/2–17,21–41,45,47–49,54
N 1918–1932		533/43
Y 1940–1951		779
Z 1841–1931 (COURT RECORDS/WILLS)		533/1
RZESZÓW REGION	**RZESZÓW**	**POLAND**
A 1894–1917		313/28–50; 516/11–24
B 1939		1/2738,2741
E 1894–1917		516/11–24,32–50
SŁOCINA	**RZESZÓW**	**POLAND**
C 1931–1943		383/60–72,75–76,81–83,131–135
SOKOŁÓW MAŁOPOLSKI	**RZESZÓW**	**POLAND**
B 1825–1890; 1912		990/1–5
C 1932–1937		193/35–40
D 1877–1893		990/6
E 1939		193/34
G 1932–1937		193/35–40
STRZYŻÓW	**RZESZÓW**	**POLAND**
A 1861–1927		740/20; 71–72
TYCZYN	**RZESZÓW**	**POLAND**
B 1877–1880		884/1
S 1898–1946		180/15–62
Z 1722; 1732		255/29–30

SANDOMIERZ Branch Archives

ANNOPOL	**TARNOBRZEG**	**POLAND**
B 1856–1883		487
D 1856–1865		487
M 1856–1865		487
BOGORIA	**TARNOBRZEG**	**POLAND**
B 1826–1894		251
D 1826–1894		251
M 1826–1894		251
ĆMIELÓW	**TARNOBRZEG**	**POLAND**
C 1945		10/97
JANÓW LUBELSKI	**TARNOBRZEG**	**POLAND**
B 1883–1887		510
KLIMONTÓW	**TARNOBRZEG**	**POLAND**
B 1826–1893		171
D 1826–1877; 1880–1893		171
M 1826–1877; 1880–1893		171
KOPRZYWNICA	**TARNOBRZEG**	**POLAND**
B 1857–1858; 1882–1893		172
D 1857–1858; 1882–1893		172
M 1857–1858; 1882–1893		172
KRZESZÓW	**TARNOBRZEG**	**POLAND**
B 1854–1875; 1877–1893		378
D 1854–1874; 1877–1888		378
M 1854–1874; 1877–1893		378

A Army/recruit lists; **B** Birth; **C** Census; **D** Death; **E** Voter lists; **G** Immigration; **H** Holocaust; **J** Judaica; **K** Kahal; **L** Land; **M** Marriage; **N** Name changes; **O** Police files; **P** Pogroms; **R** Reference; **S** School records; **T** Tax lists; **V** Divorce; **W** Occupation Lists; **X** Jewish hospital; **Y** Notary records; **Z** Local government records

TOWN NAME Document Type Years	VOIVODSHIP/OBLAST (Province)	COUNTRY Zespół/Sygnatura (Poland) Fond/Opis/Delo (Belarus, Ukraine, Lithuania)
KUROZWĘKI	**TARNOBRZEG**	**POLAND**
B 1875–1894		379
D 1875–1893		379
M 1875–1887; 1889; 1892–1894		379
NISKO	**TARNOBRZEG**	**POLAND**
G 1918–1939		592
H 1943–1944		522
OPATÓW	**TARNOBRZEG**	**POLAND**
B 1831–1884; 1889–1893		44
C 1890–1941 (ALPHA INDEX: 1890–1930)		6/2
D 1831–1832; 1835–1893		44
H 1940		6/57
M 1836–1893		44
OSIEK	**TARNOBRZEG**	**POLAND**
B 1888–1941		385
D 1888–1941		385
M 1888–1941		385
OŻARÓW	**TARNOBRZEG**	**POLAND**
B 1826–1893		45
D 1826–1893		45
M 1827–1884; 1886–1893		45
POŁANIEC	**TARNOBRZEG**	**POLAND**
B 1826–1893		252
D 1826–1893		252
M 1826–1893		252
SANDOMIERZ	**TARNOBRZEG**	**POLAND**
B 1826–1893		173
C 1940; 1945		111
D 1826–1893		173
G 1939–1942		111/1988,2125
H 1940–1941		111/1809
M 1826–1893		173
STALOWA WOLA	**TARNOBRZEG**	**POLAND**
C 1939–1950		524
H 1943		524/14
STASZÓW	**TARNOBRZEG**	**POLAND**
B 1826–1894		253
D 1826–1894		253
M 1826–1894		253
TARŁÓW	**TARNOBRZEG**	**POLAND**
B 1889–1893		647
D 1889–1893		647
M 1889–1893		647
TARNOBRZEG	**TARNOBRZEG**	**POLAND**
G 1843–1948		525/80
ZAWICHOST	**TARNOBRZEG**	**POLAND**
B 1826–1894		174
D 1826–1894		174
M 1826–1894		174

SANOK Branch Archives

BALIGRÓD	**KROSNO**	**POLAND**
C 1929–1946		30/26–28
H 1944–1947		80/106
BAŻANÓWKA	**KROSNO**	**POLAND**
C 1931–1949		21/56–58
BESKO	**KROSNO**	**POLAND**
C 1931–1950		21/59–68
BRZOZÓW	**KROSNO**	**POLAND**
A 1849–1866; 1884–1918		16/81,83
E 1873; 1876; 1878; 1907; 1912; 1914; 1919; 1922; 1927–1928; 1930; 1934–1935; 1938–1939		16/18–19,378–379
S 1913		16/50
T 1778–1779		16/38
DŁUGIE	**KROSNO**	**POLAND**
C 1931–1949		21/69–70

A Army/recruit lists; **B** Birth; **C** Census; **D** Death; **E** Voter lists; **G** Immigration; **H** Holocaust; **J** Judaica; **K** Kahal; **L** Land; **M** Marriage; **N** Name changes; **O** Police files; **P** Pogroms; **R** Reference; **S** School records; **T** Tax lists; **V** Divorce; **W** Occupation lists; **X** Jewish hospital; **Y** Notary records; **Z** Local government records

TOWN NAME Document Type Years	VOIVODSHIP/OBLAST (Province)	COUNTRY Zespół/Sygnatura (Poland) Fond/Opis/Delo (Belarus, Ukraine, Lithuania)
JAĆMIERZ	**KROSNO**	**POLAND**
C 1931–1945		21/71–73,82–83
ŁUKOWE	**KROSNO**	**POLAND**
C 1921–1953		27/21–28; 30–34
ŁUPKÓW	**KROSNO**	**POLAND**
C 1931–1945		31/2–8(5)
MOKRE	**KROSNO**	**POLAND**
C 1937–1939		23/32
NOWOSIELCE	**KROSNO**	**POLAND**
C 1931–1949		21/74–75
ODRZECHOWA	**KROSNO**	**POLAND**
C 1931–1949		21/76–77
PŁONNA	**KROSNO**	**POLAND**
C 1937–1939		23/32
POSADA ZARSZYŃSKA	**KROSNO**	**POLAND**
C 1931–1949		21/84
PRZYBYSZÓW	**KROSNO**	**POLAND**
C 1937–1939		23/32
RYMANÓW	**KROSNO**	**POLAND**
G 1942–1945		46/38–41
H 1942–1945		46/38–41
RZEPEDŻ	**KROSNO**	**POLAND**
C 1937–1939		23/32
SANOK	**KROSNO**	**POLAND**
A 1869; 1874–1879; 1881–1899; 1901–1909; 1937–1939		135/570; 155/24
B 1874–1879; 1881; 1884; 1888; 1891–1894; 1897; 1902–1908; 1940		155/21
C 1918; 1927–1939		135/550–551,553–557; 574
D 1874–1879; 1881; 1884; 1888; 1891–1894; 1897; 1902–1908; 1910		155/21
G 1879; 1881–1882; 1885–1886; 1888; 1890–1894; 1897–1909		155/22
H 1938–1947		42/74
K 1893		135/231
L 1928; 1931–1939		135/572; 574
M 1874–1879; 1881; 1884; 1888; 1891–1894; 1897; 1902–1908; 1910		155/21
SMOLNIK	**KROSNO**	**POLAND**
C 1931–1945		31/2–8(6)
SOLINKA	**KROSNO**	**POLAND**
C 1934–1944		30/30
STRACHOCINA	**KROSNO**	**POLAND**
C 1931–1949		21/85–87
SUKOWATE	**KROSNO**	**POLAND**
C 1938–1943		30/29
SZCZAWNE	**KROSNO**	**POLAND**
C 1937–1939		23/32
TARNAWA GÓRNA	**KROSNO**	**POLAND**
C 1909–1952		27/33
WOLA MICHOWA	**KROSNO**	**POLAND**
C 1931–1946		31/2–8(7)
WYSOCZANY	**KROSNO**	**POLAND**
C 1937–1939		23/32
ŻARSZYN	**KROSNO**	**POLAND**
C 1945–1951		21/50–52
ZUBEŃSKO	**KROSNO**	**POLAND**
C 1932–1946		31/2–8(8)

SIEDLCE Archives

CEGŁÓW	**SIEDLCE**	**POLAND**
B 1826; 1828; 1833–1836		204/1–11
D 1827; 1829; 1833–1835		204/1–11
M 1832–1834; 1836		204/1–11
CHRUSZCZEWKA	**SIEDLCE**	**POLAND**
C 1931		74/35

A Army/recruit lists; **B** Birth; **C** Census; **D** Death; **E** Voter lists; **G** Immigration; **H** Holocaust; **J** Judaica; **K** Kahal; **L** Land; **M** Marriage; **N** Name changes; **O** Police files; **P** Pogroms; **R** Reference; **S** School records; **T** Tax lists; **V** Divorce; **W** Occupation Lists; **X** Jewish hospital; **Y** Notary records; **Z** Local government records

TOWN NAME Document Type Years	VOIVODSHIP/OBLAST (Province)	COUNTRY Zespół/Sygnatura (Poland) Fond/Opis/Delo (Belarus, Ukraine, Lithuania)
KAŁUSZYN	**SIEDLCE**	**POLAND**
B 1826–1881; 1883; 1885–1888; 1890–1891		473/1–67
D 1826–1881; 1883; 1885–1888; 1890–1891		473
M 1826–1881; 1883; 1885–1888; 1890–1891		473
KOŁBIEL	**SIEDLCE**	**POLAND**
B 1826–1837; 1854–1892		509
D 1826–1838; 1854–1892		509
M 1826–1836; 1854–1892		509
KOSÓW LACKI	**SIEDLCE**	**POLAND**
B 1827–1828; 1832–1894		185/1–91
D 1827–1828; 1832–1894		185/1–91
M 1827–1828; 1832–1894		185/1–95
LATOWICZ	**SIEDLCE**	**POLAND**
B 1827–1836		202/1–10
D 1827–1836		202/1–10
M 1827–1836		202/1–10
ŁOSICE	**BIAŁA PODLASKA**	**POLAND**
B 1829–1835; 1837–1841; 1844–1848; 1850–1860		190/1–27
D 1829–1835; 1837–1841; 1844–1848; 1850–1860		190/1–27
M 1829–1830; 1834–1841; 1844–1848; 1850–1860		190/1–27
ŁUKÓW	**SIEDLCE**	**POLAND**
B 1869–1891; 1894		602/1–9
D 1871–1883; 1885–1894		602/1–9
M 1871–1883; 1885–1894		602/1–9
MIŃSK MAZOWIECKI	**SIEDLCE**	**POLAND**
B 1826–1829; 1832–1894		201/1–65
D 1826–1829; 1832–1894		201/1–65
L 1821–1926		759/1–2448
M 1826–1829; 1832–1894		201/1–65
MOKOBODY	**SIEDLCE**	**POLAND**
B 1826–1841; 1843–1851; 1853–1860; 1862–1869		194/1–42
D 1827–1841; 1843–1851; 1853–1860; 1862; 1864–1869		194/1–42
M 1827–1836; 1838–1840; 1843–1851; 1853; 1855; 1857–1860; 1862; 1864–1868		194/1–42
MORDY	**SIEDLCE**	**POLAND**
B 1826–1833; 1835–1842; 1844–1850; 1852; 1856–1858; 1862–1863; 1867; 1870–1872; 1874; 1876–1889; 1894		196/1–46
D 1826–1833; 1835–1842; 1844–1850; 1852; 1856–1858; 1862–1863; 1867; 1870–1889; 1893–1894		196/1–46
M 1826–1830; 1832–1833; 1835–1850; 1852; 1856–1863; 1867; 1870–1872; 1874; 1876; 1878–1879; 1882; 1884–1885; 1889; 1894		196/1–46
SARNAKI	**BIAŁA PODLASKA**	**POLAND**
B 1836–1849; 1853; 1855–1858		217/1–18,31
D 1836–1849; 1853; 1855–1858		217/1–18,31
M 1836–1844; 1846–1847; 1849; 1853; 1855–1858		217/1–18,31
SEROCZYN	**SIEDLCE**	**POLAND**
B 1841; 1843–1865; 1867–1877; 1879–1881; 1883–1888; 1890–1893		219/1–48
D 1841; 1843–1865; 1867–1877; 1879–1881; 1883–1888; 1890–1893		219/1–48
M 1841; 1843–1865; 1867–1877; 1879–1881; 1883–1888; 1890–1893		219/1–48
SIEDLCE	**SIEDLCE**	**POLAND**
B 1828; 1834–1845; 1851–1852; 1856–1857; 1861–1863; 1865; 1867–1868; 1873; 1875–1877; 1885–1891; 1894		221/1–46
C 1921–1950		36/119–2356; 2362
D 1828; 1834–1845; 1851–1852; 1856–1857; 1861–1863; 1865; 1867–1868; 1873; 1875–1877; 1885–1891; 1894		221/1–46
H 1939–1944		36/83,2357,2362–2363
J 1876/1936		334/1
M 1828; 1834–1845; 1851–1852; 1856–1857; 1861–1863; 1865; 1867–1868; 1873; 1875–1877; 1885–1891; 1894		221/1–46
SIENNICA	**SIEDLCE**	**POLAND**
B 1826–1829; 1831–1836		179/1–10
D 1826–1829; 1831–1836		179/1–10
M 1826–1829; 1831–1836		179/1–10
SOKOŁÓW PODLASKI	**SIEDLCE**	**POLAND**
B 1826–1888		227/1–43,63–88
D 1826–1888		227/1–43,63–88
M 1826–1888		227/1–43,63–88

A Army/recruit lists; **B** Birth; **C** Census; **D** Death; **E** Voter lists; **G** Immigration; **H** Holocaust; **J** Judaica; **K** Kahal; **L** Land; **M** Marriage; **N** Name changes; **O** Police files; **P** Pogroms; **R** Reference; **S** School records; **T** Tax lists; **V** Divorce; **W** Occupation lists; **X** Jewish hospital; **Y** Notary records; **Z** Local government records

TOWN NAME Document Type Years	VOIVODSHIP/OBLAST (Province)	COUNTRY Zespół/Sygnatura (Poland) Fond/Opis/Delo (Belarus, Ukraine, Lithuania)
STANISŁAWÓW	**SIEDLCE**	**POLAND**
B 1826–1832; 1834–1836; 1885–1893		178/1–17
D 1826–1832; 1834–1836; 1885–1893		178/1–17
M 1826–1832; 1834–1836; 1885–1893		178/17
WĘGRÓW	**SIEDLCE**	**POLAND**
B 1826–1889		234/1–30
D 1826–1888		234/1–30
M 1826–1888		234/1–30
WODYNIE	**SIEDLCE**	**POLAND**
B 1826–1839		238/1–14
D 1826–1837; 1839		238/1–14
M 1826–1839		238/1–14

SIERADZ Branch Archives

SIERADZ	**SIERADZ**	**POLAND**
L 1931–1940		4
SZADEK	**SIERADZ**	**POLAND**
H 1940–1942		7

SKOŁYSZYN Branch Archives

BIECZ	**KROSNO**	**POLAND**
C 1930		1/27
G 1926		1/28
H 1940–1942; 1945–1946		1/40–42,90–91
L 1930		1/14
DUKLA	**KROSNO**	**POLAND**
C 1906–1927		2/2
H 1944–1949		2/55
GORLICE	**NOWY SĄCZ**	**POLAND**
A 1889–1910		3/717
C 1922		3/1003
E 1900; 1907; 1914; 1922; 1924; 1927		3/25,50,74,110,123,143,148
G 1885–1886; 1893; 1898; 1900; 1905–1906; 1910		3/715,772
K 1902–1919		945
L 1915; 1926–1927; 1949		3/146,617,895; 6/28
S 1899–1913		3/64,328
X 1907		3/296
JASŁO	**KROSNO**	**POLAND**
C 1946		7/103,123
H 1945–1946; 1949		7/97
KROSNO	**KROSNO**	**POLAND**
C 1910–1941		5/131–132
E 1927–1939		5/47
G 1900		5/129
K 1927–1936		5/84
L 1851		5/128

SŁUPSK Branch Archives

BUTOW	**SEE BYTÓW**	
MIASTKO	**SŁUPSK**	**POLAND**
B 1813–1847		70/11
D 1813–1847		70/11
M 1813–1847		70/11
RUMMELSBERG	**SEE MIASTKO**	
SŁUPSK	**SŁUPSK**	**POLAND**
B 1813–1842; 1857–1882		6/5496,5505–5506,5508
SŁUPSK REGION	**SŁUPSK**	**POLAND**
B 1874–1894		266–360
D 1874–1894		266–360
M 1874–1894		266–360
STOLP	**SEE SŁUPSK**	

A Army/recruit lists; **B** Birth; **C** Census; **D** Death; **E** Voter lists; **G** Immigration; **H** Holocaust; **J** Judaica; **K** Kahal; **L** Land; **M** Marriage; **N** Name changes; **O** Police files; **P** Pogroms; **R** Reference; **S** School records; **T** Tax lists; **V** Divorce; **W** Occupation Lists; **X** Jewish hospital; **Y** Notary records; **Z** Local government records

TOWN NAME Document Type Years	VOIVODSHIP/OBLAST (Province)	COUNTRY Zespół/Sygnatura (Poland) Fond/Opis/Delo (Belarus, Ukraine, Lithuania)

STARACHOWICE Branch Archives

CIEPIELÓW	RADOM	POLAND
B 1826–1873		162
D 1826–1873		162
M 1826–1873		162
IŁŻA	**RADOM**	**POLAND**
B 1850–1875		48
D 1850–1875		48
M 1850–1875		48
LIPSKO	**RADOM**	**POLAND**
B 1826–1874		165
D 1826–1874		165
M 1826–1874		165
OSTROWIEC ŚWIĘTOKRZYSKI	**KIELCE**	**POLAND**
B 1826–1893		216
D 1826–1893		216
M 1826–1893		216
Z 1923		214
SIENNO	**RADOM**	**POLAND**
B 1826–1873		169
D 1826–1873		169
M 1826–1873		169
STARACHOWICE	**KIELCE**	**POLAND**
Z 1940		5
TARŁÓW	**TARNOBRZEG**	**POLAND**
B 1826–1887		172
D 1826–1887		172
M 1826–1887		172

SUWAŁKI Archives

ALYTUS	ALYTUS	LITHUANIA
M 1835/1872		331
AUGUSTÓW	**SUWAŁKI**	**POLAND**
B 1850–1870(INDEX ONLY); 1903–1904 (INDEX ONLY)		12/295,308,322
C MID–19 CENT./EARLY 20TH CENT.		
D 1850–1870; 1880–1892; 1896–1897; 1903–1904		12/295,300,307–308,322
K 1809; 1890; 1897		12/92,100,102–103,108–109
L 1945–1949		313/146–147,179–180
M 1850–1870 (INDEX ONLY); 1903–1904 (INDEX ONLY)		12/295,308,322
S 1870; 1873; 1882; 1891–1892; 1897; 1902–1904		12/104–107,133–136
X 1907–1909		12/243
Y 1808–1835		220–226
Z 1807/1913		12
AUGUSTÓW REGION	**SUWAŁKI**	**POLAND**
T 1900–1911; 1913–1914		12/94–96; 23/1–15
BAKAŁARZEWO	**SUWAŁKI**	**POLAND**
B 1809–1813; 1815–1818; 1820–1822; 1826–1833; 1839–1843; 1852–1864; 1866–1867; 1870–1875; 1877–1879; 1883–1885; 1887; 1889		149/197
D 1808–1813; 1815–1821; 1823–1833; 1839–1843; 1852–1864; 1866–1867; 1870–1875; 1877–1879; 1883–1885; 1887; 1889		149; 197
M 1808–1813; 1815–1818; 1820; 1822–1823; 1826–1837; 1839–1843; 1852–1864; 1866–1867; 1870–1875; 1877–1879; 1883–1885; 1887; 1889		149; 197
BARGŁOW DWORNY	**SUWAŁKI**	**POLAND**
B 1869–1882		
D 1869/1873; 1874–1881		
M 1869/1882		
BERŹNIKI	**INCLUDED IN SEJNY**	
FILIPÓW	**SUWAŁKI**	**POLAND**
B 1808; 1821–1825; 1829–1879; 1884–1891; 1894		151; 198
D 1808–1825; 1829–1879; 1884–1891; 1894		151; 198
K 1926–1938		31/132–138,157
M 1808–1825; 1829–1877; 1884–1891; 1894		151; 198

A Army/recruit lists; **B** Birth; **C** Census; **D** Death; **E** Voter lists; **G** Immigration; **H** Holocaust; **J** Judaica; **K** Kahal; **L** Land; **M** Marriage; **N** Name changes; **O** Police files; **P** Pogroms; **R** Reference; **S** School records; **T** Tax lists; **V** Divorce; **W** Occupation lists; **X** Jewish hospital; **Y** Notary records; **Z** Local government records

TOWN NAME Document Type Years	VOIVODSHIP/OBLAST (Province)	COUNTRY Zespół/Sygnatura (Poland) Fond/Opis/Delo (Belarus, Ukraine, Lithuania)
JELENIEWO	**SUWAŁKI**	**POLAND**
B 1808–1893		152; 204
D 1808–1893		152; 204
K 1925–1926		31/144
M 1808–1893		152; 204
KRASNOPOL	**SUWAŁKI**	**POLAND**
B 1808–1826; 1828–1829; 1836/1862; 1866/1875; 1882–1885; 1894 (ALSO INCLUDED IN SEJNY)		155; 199; 207
D 1808–1826; 1828–1829; 1836/1862; 1866/1875; 1882; 1884–1885; 1894		155; 199; 207
M 1808–1826; 1828–1829; 1836/1862; 1866/1875; 1882; 1884–1885; 1894		155; 199; 207
LAZDIJAI	**LAZDIJAI**	**LITHUANIA**
B 1856–1857; 1859; 1862; 1866; 1877–1880; 1883–1884; 1889; 1894–1896; 1901; 1903–1904; 1907		200
D 1856–1857; 1859; 1862; 1866; 1877–1880; 1883–1884; 1889; 1894–1896; 1901; 1903–1904; 1907		200
M 1856–1857; 1859; 1862; 1866; 1877–1880; 1883–1884; 1889; 1894–1896; 1901; 1903–1904; 1907		200
METELIAI	**LAZDIJAI**	**LITHUANIA**
B 1808–1825		156
D 1808–1825		156
M 1808–1825		156
PRZEROŚL	**SUWAŁKI**	**POLAND**
B 1813–1825; 1827–1879; 1880/1884; 1885–1889		161; 201
D 1813–1825; 1827–1879; 1880/1884; 1885–1889		161; 201
M 1813–1825; 1827–1879; 1880/1884; 1885–1889		161; 201
PUŃSK	**SUWAŁKI**	**POLAND**
B 1808–1825; 1833–1872; 1874–1875; 1878–1882; 1884–1885; 1889		162; 202
D 1808–1825; 1833–1872; 1874–1875; 1878–1882; 1884–1885; 1889		162; 202
K 1926–1929		31/129,137
M 1808–1825; 1833–1872; 1874–1875; 1878–1882; 1884–1885; 1889		162; 202
SAKIAI	**SAKIAI**	**LITHUANIA**
B 1826–1833		332
D 1845–1851; 1867–1879		332
M 1826–1833		332
SEIRIJAI	**LAZDIJAI**	**LITHUANIA**
B 1808–1825; 1826/1856; 1857–1861; 1864–1869; 1872–1873; 1875; 1878; 1882–1883; 1887; 1890; 1893–1894; 1898; 1900–1901; 1903; 1909–1910		164; 203
D 1808–1825; 1826/1856; 1857–1861; 1864–1869; 1872–1873; 1875; 1878; 1882–1883; 1887; 1890; 1893–1894; 1898; 1900–1901; 1903; 1909–1910		164; 203
M 1808–1825; 1826/1856; 1857–1861; 1864–1869; 1872–1873; 1875; 1878; 1882–1883; 1887; 1890; 1893–1894; 1898; 1900–1901; 1903; 1909–1910		164; 203
Y 1875–1913		241–244
SEJNY	**SUWAŁKI**	**POLAND**
B 1808–1825; 1828–1829; 1836; 1838; 1840; 1844; 1847; 1849–1850; 1852; 1857–1858; 1859/1865; 1866–1875; 1880/1894		163; 207
D 1808–1825; 1826/1865; 1866–1875; 1880/1893; 1894		163; 207
K 1926–1938		31/138–143
L 1944–1949		313/155
M 1808–1826; 1828–1829; 1836; 1838; 1840; 1844; 1847/1865; 1866–1875; 1880; 1882; 1886–1887; 1889; 1893–1894		163; 207
Y 1808–1939		227–240
SUWAŁKI	**SUWAŁKI**	**POLAND**
A 1938–1939		31/205
B 1808–1825; 1826/1834; 1835–1840; 1842–1854; 1856–1888; 1891–1892		165; 204
C 1846–1867		14/208–219; 533–536; 773
D 1826/1834; 1835–1840; 1842–1854; 1856–1877; 1878/1883; 1884–1888; 1891–1892		165/204
E 1847–1867		14/208–215
K 1840–1867; 1917; 1926–1937		14/129,207–215,466,605,703–716; 31/144–148,155–156, 158,303
L 1857/1876; 1945–1949 (CONFISCATED PROPERTY)		14/89–92,94,96–104,106–113,117–119, 123–126,131–132 ,136–139,141,145,151; 313/155
M 1808–1825; 1826/1834; 1835–1840; 1842–1854; 1856–1877; 1878/1883; 1884–1893		165; 204
S 1847–1867; 1931–1937		14/208–215; 31/131
W 1812–1871; 1920–1936		31/198; 14/152–190
X 1847–1870		14/377; 27/5–20
Y 1826–1939		245–270
Z 1807–1866		14
SUWAŁKI REGION	**SUWAŁKI**	**POLAND**
T 1847; 1867; 1903–1915		14/208–215; 24/1–17
SZAKI	**SEE SAKIAI**	

A Army/recruit lists; **B** Birth; **C** Census; **D** Death; **E** Voter lists; **G** Immigration; **H** Holocaust; **J** Judaica; **K** Kahal; **L** Land; **M** Marriage; **N** Name changes;
O Police files; **P** Pogroms; **R** Reference; **S** School records; **T** Tax lists; **V** Divorce; **W** Occupation Lists; **X** Jewish hospital; **Y** Notary records; **Z** Local government records

TOWN NAME Document Type Years	VOIVODSHIP/OBLAST (Province)	COUNTRY Zespół/Sygnatura (Poland) Fond/Opis/Delo (Belarus, Ukraine, Lithuania)
VEISIEJAI	**LAZDIJAI**	**LITHUANIA**
B	1808–1825; 1840–1853; 1856–1865; 1869–1871; 1874–1875; 1879; 1884–1887; 1893; 1895; 1901–1902; 1905–1907; 1909	168; 205
D	1808–1825; 1840–1853; 1856–1865; 1869–1871; 1874–1875; 1879; 1884–1887; 1893; 1895; 1901–1902; 1905–1907; 1909	168; 205
M	1808–1825; 1840–1853; 1856–1865; 1869–1871; 1874–1875; 1879; 1884–1 887; 1893; 1895; 1901–1902; 1905–1907; 1909	168; 205
WIEJSIEJE	**SEE VEISIEJAI**	
WIŻAJNY	**SUWAŁKI**	**POLAND**
B	1808–1825; 1829–1830; 1832–1838; 1840–1842; 1844–1848; 1851–1853; 1855–1869; 1873–1874; 1877; 1879–1880; 1892	169; 206
D	1808–1825; 1829–1830; 1832–1838; 1840–1842; 1844–1848; 1851–1853; 1855–1869; 1873–1874; 1877; 1879–1880; 1892	169; 206
K	1926–1938	31/149–152
M	1808–1825; 1829–1830; 1832–1838; 1840–1842; 1844–1848; 1851–1853; 1855–1869; 1873–1874; 1877; 1879–1880; 1892	169; 206
R	1890–1939	527

SZCZECIN Archives

BANIE	**SZCZECIN**	**POLAND**
K 1839–1846		REGIERUNG STETTIN,I/10732
S 1822–1873		MAGISTRAT BAHN 168
Z 1871–1906		MAGISTRAT BAHN 170
BARLINEK	**GORZOW WIEŁKOPOLSKI**	**POLAND**
B 1847–1874		AMTSGERICHT BERLINCHEN
D 1847–1874		AMTSGERICHT BERLINCHEN
M 1847–1873		AMSTGERICHT BERLINCHEN
BERLINCHEN	**SEE BARLINEK**	
BIAŁY BÓR	**KOSZALIN**	**POLAND**
K 1843–1938		GMINY ZYDOWSKIE Z POMORZA ZACHODNIEGO 1/4
S 1820–1888		MAGISTRAT BIAŁY BÓR (BALDENBURG)/71
BOBOLICE	**KOSZALIN**	**POLAND**
K 1893–1938		GMINY ZYDOWSKIE Z POMORZA ZACHODNIEGO 5/7
CZŁUCHÓW	**SŁUPSK**	**POLAND**
K 1856–1938		GMINY ZYDOWSKIE Z POMORZA ZACHODNIEGO 8/53,53A
DABER	**SEE DOBRA**	
DEBRZNO	**SŁUPSK**	**POLAND**
K XIX CENT.		GMINY ZYDOWSKIE Z POMORZA ZACHODNIEGO 54
DOBRA	**SZCZECIN**	**POLAND**
B 1876–1891		STANDESAMIT DABER
D 1876–1891		STANDESAMIT DABER
K 1817–1846		MAGISTRAT DABER 371–374
M 1876–1885; 1887–1891		STANDESAMIT DABER
Z 1716–1843		MAGISTRAT DABER 361–370
FIDDICHOW	**SEE WIDUCHOWA**	
GOLENIÓW	**SZCZECIN**	**POLAND**
B 1848–1874		AMTSGERICHT GOLLNOW 158
D 1847–1874		AMTSGERICHT GOLLNOW 160
M 1847–1874		AMTSGERICHT GOLLNOW 159
GOLLNOW	**SEE GOLENIÓW**	
GREIFENHAGEN	**SEE GRYFINO**	
GRYFICE	**SZCZECIN**	**POLAND**
K 1831–1852		REGIERUNG STETTIN I/10734
GRYFINO	**SZCZECIN**	**POLAND**
K 1826–1854		REGIERUNG STETTIN I/10735
IŃSKO	**SZCZECIN**	**POLAND**
K 1821–1852		REGIERUNG STETTIN I/10736
KALISZ POMORSKI	**KOSZALIN**	**POLAND**
K 1856–1898		GMINY ZYDOWSKIE Z POMORZA ZACHODNIEGO 55–56

A Army/recruit lists; **B** Birth; **C** Census; **D** Death; **E** Voter lists; **G** Immigration; **H** Holocaust; **J** Judaica; **K** Kahal; **L** Land; **M** Marriage; **N** Name changes; **O** Police files; **P** Pogroms; **R** Reference; **S** School records; **T** Tax lists; **V** Divorce; **W** Occupation lists; **X** Jewish hospital; **Y** Notary records; **Z** Local government records

TOWN NAME Document Type Years	VOIVODSHIP/OBLAST (Province)	COUNTRY Zespół/Sygnatura (Poland) Fond/Opis/Delo (Belarus, Ukraine, Lithuania)
KOLBERG	**SEE KOŁOBRZEG**	
KOŁOBRZEG	**KOSZALIN**	**POLAND**
K 1803–1806		GMINY ZYDOWSKIE Z POMORZA ZACHODNIEGO 57
KOSZALIN	**KOSZALIN**	**POLAND**
K 1801–1894		GMINY ZYDOWSKIE Z POMORZA ZACHODNIEGO 58–78
ŁEBA	**SŁUPSK**	**POLAND**
G 1818; 1850–1874		MAGISTRAT ŁEBA 45–46
MASSOW	**SEE MASZEWO**	
MASZEWO	**SZCZECIN**	**POLAND**
B 1847–1888		AMTSGERICHT MASSOW 153
D 1848–1874		AMTSGERICHT MASSOW 155
M 1849–1874		AMTSGERICHT MASSOW 154
MYŚLIBÓRZ	**GORZOW WIEŁKOPOLSKI**	**POLAND**
C 1934–1943		MAGISTRAT SOLDIN 28
E 1871–1899		MAGISTRAT SOLDIN 32
NORENBERG	**SEE IŃSKO**	
PREUSSISCH FRIEDLAND	**SEE DEBRZNO**	
REGENWALDE	**SEE RESKO**	
RESKO	**SZCZECIN**	**POLAND**
C 1812		AMTSGERICHT REGENSWALDE 11/1
D 1813–1847; 1849; 1851–1894; 1935		AMTSGERICHT REGENSWALDE 11/1
M 1814–1847; 1851–1894; 1935		AMTSGERICHT REGENSWALDE 11/1
SCHIVELBEIN	**SEE ŚWIDWIN**	
SCHLOCHAU	**SEE CZŁUCHÓW**	
STARGARD SZCZECIŃSKI	**SZCZECIN**	**POLAND**
K 1870–1874; 1913–1930		MAGISTRAT STARGARD 961–962; GMINY ZYDOWSKIE POMORZA ZACHODNIEGO 79–85; REGIERUNG STETTIN I/10737, 10748–10750
Z 1766–1876		MAGISTRAT STARGARD 963–977
STETTIN	**SEE SZCZECIN**	
STRZELCE KRAJEŃSKIE	**GORZOW WIEŁKOPOLSKI**	**POLAND**
K 1907–1939		JUDISCHE GEMEINDE FRIEDEBERG NM 110/1–4
ŚWIDWIN	**KOSZALIN**	**POLAND**
E 1871–1899		MAGISTRAT SCHINELBEING 32
SWINEMUNDE	**SEE ŚWINOUJŚCIE**	
ŚWINOUJŚCIE	**SZCZECIN**	**POLAND**
K 1847–1933		GMINY ZYDOWSKIE POMORZA ZACHODNIEGO–ZBIDOR SZCZATKOW/95–132
SZCZECIN	**SZCZECIN**	**POLAND**
B 1874–1896		STANDESAMIT STETTIN
D 1874–1896		STANDESAMIT STETTIN
K 1894–1930		REGIERUNG STETTIN I/10751–10752; GMINY ZYDOWSKIE POMORZA ZACHODNIEGO 86–94
M 1874–1896		STANDESAMIT STETTIN
R 1829–1943		BIBLIOTEKA IN SZCZECIN ARCHIVES
WĘGORZYNO	**SZCZECIN**	**POLAND**
K 1904–1924		MAGISTRAT WANGERIN 71
WIDUCHOWA	**SZCZECIN**	**POLAND**
K 1840–1862		REGIERUNG STETTIN I/10733
WOLIN	**SZCZECIN**	**POLAND**
K 1875–1935		GMINY ZYDOWSKIE POMORZA ZACHODNIEGO/133–137
ZLOTÓW	**PIŁA**	**POLAND**
K 1833–1938		GMINA ZYDOWSKIE POMORZA ZACHONDNIEGO 133/137

TARNÓW Archives

CZCHÓW	**TARNÓW**	**POLAND**
B 1877–1893		

A Army/recruit lists; **B** Birth; **C** Census; **D** Death; **E** Voter lists; **G** Immigration; **H** Holocaust; **J** Judaica; **K** Kahal; **L** Land; **M** Marriage; **N** Name changes;
O Police files; **P** Pogroms; **R** Reference; **S** School records; **T** Tax lists; **V** Divorce; **W** Occupation Lists; **X** Jewish hospital; **Y** Notary records; **Z** Local government records

TOWN NAME Document Type Years	VOIVODSHIP/OBLAST (Province)	COUNTRY Zespół/Sygnatura (Poland) Fond/Opis/Delo (Belarus, Ukraine, Lithuania)
D 1877–1893		
M 1877–1893		
DĄBROWA TARNOWSKA	**TARNÓW**	**POLAND**
B 1882–1885		
TARNÓW	**TARNÓW**	**POLAND**
B 1849–1876; 1879–1899		276/USCT 1–11,37
B 1861–1895 (ALPHA INDEX)		276/USCT 12–17
B 1877–1898 (ILLEGITIMATE BIRTHS)		276/USCT 23
D 1855–1899		276/USCT 25–32
D 1850–1942 (ALPHA INDEX)		276/USCT 33–36
H 1945		15/STT49
M 1849–1899		276/USCT 18–22
M 1877–1899 (ALPHA INDEX)		276/USCT 24
W 1940–1942		214
Z 1837–1944		1
ŻABNO	**TARNÓW**	**POLAND**
B 1879; 1885–1887; 1891–1895		309/GJZ1,4
D 1886–1893		
M 1887; 1894		

TARNOWSKIE GÓRY Branch Archives

DOBRODZIEŃ	**CZĘSTOCHOWA**	**POLAND**
E 1915–1923		19/173
G 1842–1927		19/244
K 1931–1932		19/311
GUTTENTAG	**SEE DOBRODZIEŃ**	
LOBEN	**SEE LUBLINIEC**	
LUBLINIEC	**CZĘSTOCHOWA**	**POLAND**
K 1858–1907; 1918–1921; 1926–1930; 1936		3/901–904; 20/1224; 5/394,399
L 1939		5/612
S 1918–1921		20/1224
LUBLINIEC REGION	**CZĘSTOCHOWA**	**POLAND**
C 1922–1939		5/278–285,401–404
E 1929–1930; 1935; 1937–1938		5/47–65
G 1922–1939		5/401–404
Z 1936		5/399
TARNOWSKIE GÓRY	**KATOWICE**	**POLAND**
A 1856–1890		91/2356–2377,2402–2416
B 1813–1856		173/1; 91/2028
C 1817–1896; 1904–1914; 1920–1922		91/212–225,452–454,469,492,2028–2034
D 1847–1868		173/2
K 1781–1914		91/2027–2051
M 1813–1874		173/3; 91/2028
S 1845		91/1838
WIESZOWA	**KATOWICE**	**POLAND**
B 1847–1848		174/1
D 1847–1848		174/1

TOMASZÓW MAZOWIECKI Branch Archives

BĘDKÓW	**PIOTRKÓW TRYBUNALSKI**	**POLAND**
B 1826–1846		244
M 1826–1845		244
BRZEZINY	**SKIERNIEWICE**	**POLAND**
B 1808–1809; 1826–1832; 1841–1860; 1866–1886		244
D 1826–1832; 1845–1861; 1877–1886		244
M 1826–1858; 1876–1885		244
T 1865–1942		108/17,192–378,382,389–399
IINOWLODZ	**PIOTRKÓW TRYBUNALSKI**	**POLAND**
B 1811; 1826; 1828; 1830; 1832–1838; 1841–1849; 1852; 1854–1857		244
D 1811; 1826; 1828; 1830; 1832–1838; 1841–1849; 1852; 1854–1857		244
M 1811; 1826; 1828; 1830; 1832–1838; 1842–1849; 1852; 1854–1857		244
JEŻÓW	**SKIERNIEWICE**	**POLAND**
B 1826–1838; 1845–1865; 1888–1889		244
D 1828–1837; 1839–1844; 1888–1889		244

A Army/recruit lists; B Birth; C Census; D Death; E Voter lists; G Immigration; H Holocaust; J Judaica; K Kahal; L Land; M Marriage; N Name changes; O Police files; P Pogroms; R Reference; S School records; T Tax lists; V Divorce; W Occupation lists; X Jewish hospital; Y Notary records; Z Local government records

TOWN NAME Document Type Years	VOIVODSHIP/OBLAST (Province)	COUNTRY Zespół/Sygnatura (Poland) Fond/Opis/Delo (Belarus, Ukraine, Lithuania)
M 1826–1836; 1845–1884; 1888–1889		244
TOMASZÓW MAZOWIECKI	**PIOTRKÓW TRYBUNALSKI**	**POLAND**
C 1824–1942		7/1042,1070–1075,1077,1081,1089–1091, 1095,1108, 2974–3155
T 1915–1943		7/3–2505; 5/2,47,51,61,64,86,96,106,108,110,117, 134,144,149,151,154,159,161–162,165, 169,171; 174; 182; 194; 196–197; 199; 200; 204

TORUŃ Archives

BRODNICA	**TORUŃ**	**POLAND**
B 1840–1870		616/1
D 1840–1847		616/1
M 1840–1847; 1850–1874		616/1
CHEŁMNO	**TORUŃ**	**POLAND**
B 1847–1874		616/1
C 1832–1844; 1853; 1921–1939		93/1
M 1847–1874		616/1
N 1801/1812; 1845		93/1
T 1773–1920		93/1
V 1829–1830		616/1
CULM	**SEE CHEŁMNO**	
GOLUB–DOBRZYN	**TORUŃ**	**POLAND**
B 1808–1856; 1858–1876; 1878; 1881; 1885–1886; 1888–1898; 1907–1909; 1911; 1917–1918; 1922–1928; 1933		672/1
D 1808–1874; 1876; 1878; 1881; 1885–1886; 1888–1899; 1907–1909; 1911; 1916–1917; 1922–1928; 1933; 1935–1939		672/1
G 1830/1927; 1939–1942		96/1
M 1808–1876; 1878; 1881; 1885–1886; 1888–1899; 1907–1909; 1911; 1919; 1922–1928		672/1
T 1793/1919		96/1
GRAUDENZ	**SEE GRUDZIĄDZ**	
GRUDZIĄDZ	**TORUŃ**	**POLAND**
B 1834–1874		616/1
D 1837–1846; 1860–1874		616/1
M 1837–1874		616/1
ŁASIN	**TORUŃ**	**POLAND**
B 1838–1859		616/1
D 1824–1885		616/1
M 1824–1885		616/1
LUBRANIEC	**WŁOCŁAWEK**	**POLAND**
C 1850–1932		30
RADZYŃ CHEŁMIŃSKI	**TORUŃ**	**POLAND**
B 1827–1846		616/1
D 1845–1846		616/1
M 1824–1844		616/1
STRASBURG	**SEE BRODNICA**	
THORN	**SEE TORUŃ**	
TORUŃ	**TORUŃ**	**POLAND**
K 1725–1859		283/1
N 1818–1920		1/1

WARSZAWA: AGAD Archives

ALYTUS	**ALYTUS**	**LITHUANIA**
T 1811–1865		KRSW 4964–4965
AUGUSTÓW	**SUWAŁKI**	**POLAND**
T 1820–1832		KRSW 4795–4797
BAKAŁARZEWO	**SUWAŁKI**	**POLAND**
T 1811–1865		KRSW 4818–4821
BATYATYCHI	**INCLUDED IN VELIKIYE MOSTY**	
BELYY KAMEN	**LVOV**	**UKRAINE**
B 1879; 1883–1888; 1895–1897		300
BEREZHANY	**TERNOPOL**	**UKRAINE**
B 1864–1893		300
D 1870–1876; 1882–1891		300
M 1875–1876		300

A Army/recruit lists; **B** Birth; **C** Census; **D** Death; **E** Voter lists; **G** Immigration; **H** Holocaust; **J** Judaica; **K** Kahal; **L** Land; **M** Marriage; **N** Name changes;
O Police files; **P** Pogroms; **R** Reference; **S** School records; **T** Tax lists; **V** Divorce; **W** Occupation Lists; **X** Jewish hospital; **Y** Notary records; **Z** Local government records

TOWN NAME Document Type Years	VOIVODSHIP/OBLAST (Province)	COUNTRY Zespół/Sygnatura (Poland) Fond/Opis/Delo (Belarus, Ukraine, Lithuania)
BIAŁYSTOK	**BIAŁYSTOK**	**POLAND**
T 1806		2/1717B/110–144
BISKOVICHI	**INCLUDED IN SAMBOR**	
BOBRKA	**LVOV**	**UKRAINE**
B 1863–1894		300
M 1866–1876		300
BOLEKHOV	**IVANO FRANKOVSK**	**UKRAINE**
B 1877–1881; 1885–1893		300
D 1877–1884		300
Z 1612/1730		300
BOLSHOVTSY	**IVANO FRANKOVSK**	**UKRAINE**
B 1923; 1929; 1931; 1934; 1937		300
B INCLUDED IN: BURSHTYN		300
D 1923; 1929; 1934		300
M 1923; 1937		300
BORISLAV	**TERNOPOL**	**UKRAINE**
B 1878–1886; 1888–1889; 1894		300
D 1878–1894		300
D INDEX: 1878–1881		300
BORSHCHEV	**TERNOPOL**	**UKRAINE**
B 1873–1876; 1877–1885; 1886–1894		300
D 1877–1894		300
M 1846–1872; 1873–1876		300
BUCHACH	**TERNOPOL**	**UKRAINE**
B 1849–1890		300
BUDANOV	**TERNOPOL**	**UKRAINE**
B 1867–1875; 1877–1888		300
D 1877–1888		300
BUKACHEVTSY	**IVANO FRANKOVSK**	**UKRAINE**
B 1865–1876 & ALSO INCLUDED IN BURSHTYN		
D 1930; 1935; 300		
M 1930; 1932–1935		300
BURSHTYN	**IVANO FRANKOVSK**	**UKRAINE**
B 1848–1873; 1877–1891; 1923; 1935		300
D 1848–1892; 1923; 1935		300
M 1849–1876; 1923; 1935		300
CHERCHIK	**INCLUDED IN YAVOROV**	
CHERNIKHOVTSY	**INCLUDED IN ZBARAZH**	
CHERNYATIN	**INCLUDED IN GORODENKA**	
CHISHKI	**INCLUDED IN VINNIKI**	
CHMIELISKA	**INCLUDED IN SKALAT**	
CHORTKOV	**TERNOPOL**	**UKRAINE**
B 1874–1893; 1900–1901; 1921; 1926; 1934–1935		300
D 1884–1891; 1893		300
M 1923; 1927; 1930–1938		300
CHORTOVETS	**INCLUDED IN OBERTIN**	
CHUDYKOWCE	**INCLUDED IN MELNITSA PODOLSKAYA**	
CZYZOWICE	**INCLUDED IN MOSTISKA**	
DAVID GORODOK	**BREST**	**BELARUS**
C 1760; 1788		
DAVIDOV	**INCLUDED IN VINNIKI**	
DEREVNA	**GRODNO**	**BELARUS**
C 1591		
DOBROVODY	**INCLUDED IN ZBARAZH**	
DOLGE	**INCLUDED IN BORISLAV**	
DROGOBYCH	**LVOV**	**UKRAINE**
B 1877–1894		300
D 1852–1894		300
D INDEX: 1880		300
M 1877–1881; 1884–1891; 1893–1894		300
DUBLYANY	**INCLUDED IN SAMBOR**	
DUBNO	**ROVNO**	**UKRAINE**
Z 1762		300

A Army/recruit lists; **B** Birth; **C** Census; **D** Death; **E** Voter lists; **G** Immigration; **H** Holocaust; **J** Judaica; **K** Kahal; **L** Land; **M** Marriage; **N** Name changes; **O** Police files; **P** Pogroms; **R** Reference; **S** School records; **T** Tax lists; **V** Divorce; **W** Occupation lists; **X** Jewish hospital; **Y** Notary records; **Z** Local government records

TOWN NAME Document Type Years	VOIVODSHIP/OBLAST (Province)	COUNTRY Zespół/Sygnatura (Poland) Fond/Opis/Delo (Belarus, Ukraine, Lithuania)
DUNAJOW	SEE DUNAYEV	
DZVINOGRUD	LVOV	**UKRAINE**
C 1762		300
B ALSO INCLUDED IN MELNITSA PODOLSKAYA		300
FILIPKOWCE	INCLUDED IN MELNITSA PODOLSKAYA	
FILIPÓW	SUWAŁKI	**POLAND**
T 1811–1865		KRSW 4834–4837
GERMAKOVKA	INCLUDED IN MELNITSA PODOLSKAYA	
GLINNA	INCLUDED IN NAWARIYA	
GLINYANY	LVOV	**UKRAINE**
B 1860–1892		300
D 1877–1887		300
M INCLUDED IN VINNIKI		
GLUKHOVITSE	LVOV	**UKRAINE**
M INCLUDED IN VINNIKI		
GOLOGORY	LVOV	**UKRAINE**
B 1876–1881; 1883–1889; 1892–1894; 1897–1900; 1903; 1909; 1911; 1927		300
D 1877–1893; 1902; 1912; 1924–1926		300
GORDYNYA	INCLUDED IN SAMBOR	
GORODENKA	IVANO FRANKOVSK	**UKRAINE**
B 1867–1876; 1879–1891		300
D 1851–1881; 1888–1892		300
M 1856–1876		300
M PRENUPTIAL REPORTS: 1928; 1935–1936		300
GORODOK	LVOV	**UKRAINE**
B 1870–1876; 1886–1892; 1929; 1931		300
D 1933–1934; 1937		300
M 1931–1932; 1935; 1938		300
GRAJEWO	ŁOMŻA	**POLAND**
T 1823–1833		KRSW 4842
GRODNO	GRODNO	**BELARUS**
Z 1770–1789		
GUSYATIN	TERNOPOL	**UKRAINE**
B 1815–1876		300
M 1820–1876		300
GVOZDETS	IVANO FRANKOVSK	**UKRAINE**
B 1858–1876; 1936–1937; 1939		300
D 1937; 1939		300
M 1936–1937		300
HLUBOCZEK WIEŁKI	INCLUDED IN TERNOPOL	
IVANO FRANKOVSK	IVANO FRANKOVSK	**UKRAINE**
B 1864–1874; 1877–1892; 1930–1941		300
D 1863–1891		300
M 1872–1876		300
IVANOVKA	INCLUDED IN SKALAT	
KACHANOVKA	INCLUDED IN SKALAT	
KAHAJOW	INCLUDED IN NAWARIYA	
KALWARJA	MARIJAMPOLE	**LITHUANIA**
T 1820–1822; 1825–1833; 1847–1857		KRSW 4849–4858
KAMENKA BUGSKAYA	LVOV	**UKRAINE**
B 1859–1872; 1877–1881		300
D 1789–1890		300
M 1866–1876		300
KHOROSTKOV	TERNOPOL	**UKRAINE**
B 1830–1871; 1874–1886		300
KHOTIMIR	INCLUDED IN OBERTIN	
KIBARTY	SEE KYBARTAI	
KLEBANOVKA	INCLUDED IN ZBARAZH	
KOLODEYEVKA	INCLUDED IN SKALAT	
KOLOMYYA	IVANO FRANKOVSK	**UKRAINE**
B 1865–1882; 1884–1890; 1916; 1922; 1932; 1934–1939		300
D 1865–1882; 1884–1894; 1932–1939		300
M 1877–1894; 1932; 1934–1939		300

A Army/recruit lists; **B** Birth; **C** Census; **D** Death; **E** Voter lists; **G** Immigration; **H** Holocaust; **J** Judaica; **K** Kahal; **L** Land; **M** Marriage; **N** Name changes; **O** Police files; **P** Pogroms; **R** Reference; **S** School records; **T** Tax lists; **V** Divorce; **W** Occupation Lists; **X** Jewish hospital; **Y** Notary records; **Z** Local government records

TOWN NAME Document Type Years	VOIVODSHIP/OBLAST (Province)	COUNTRY Zespół/Sygnatura (Poland) Fond/Opis/Delo (Belarus, Ukraine, Lithuania)
KOMARNO	**LVOV**	**UKRAINE**
B 1888; 1903–1904; 1906		300
D 1876; 1878–1884; 1889–1891; 1893; 1895–1898; 1900; 1908–1912		300
KOPYCHINTSY	**TERNOPOL**	**UKRAINE**
B 1877–1884		300
D 1816–1876		300
M 1850–1872		300
KOROLEVKA	**IVANO FRANKOVSK**	**UKRAINE**
C 1938		300
KOSOV	**IVANO FRANKOVSK**	**UKRAINE**
B 1868–1891		300
D 1877–1891; 1909–1913		300
M 1871–1890		300
KOZLOV	**TERNOPOL**	**UKRAINE**
B 1877–1888; 1926–1928; 1937		300
D 1925–1931; 1933–1938		300
M 1937		300
KOZOVA	**TERNOPOL**	**UKRAINE**
B 1876–1893		300
KRAKOVETS	**LVOV**	**UKRAINE**
B 1877–1880; 1885–1893		300
KRAKÓW	**KRAKÓW**	**POLAND**
C 1811–1812; 1866–1888		194/903
KRIVCHE	**TERNOPOL**	**UKRAINE**
B 1830–1876		300
D 1818–1876		300
KROPEVNIK	**INCLUDED IN BORISLAV**	
KUDIRKOS NAUMIESTIS	**SAKIAI**	**LITHUANIA**
T 1825–1833		KRSW 5221–5225
KUDRINTSY	**TERNOPOL**	**UKRAINE**
B 1853–1876		300
M 1853–1876		300
KUHAJOW	**INCLUDED IN NAWARIYA**	
KUPICHVOLYA	**INCLUDED IN VELIKIYE MOSTY**	
KURNIKI	**INCLUDED IN YAVOROV**	
KUROPATNIKI	**INCLUDED IN BEREZHANY**	
KYBARTAI	**VILKAVISKIS**	**LITHUANIA**
T 1860–1867		KRSW 5163
LASZKI	**INCLUDED IN YAVOROV**	
LESIENICE	**INCLUDED IN VINNIKI**	
LESNEVICHI	**INCLUDED IN NAWARIYA**	
LIWCZE	**INCLUDED IN SOKAL**	
LUDWIKOWKA	**INCLUDED IN NAWARIYA**	
LVOV	**LVOV**	**UKRAINE**
B 1814–1837; 1857; 1863–1894; 1903; 1905–1907; 1909; 1912; 1920–1924; 1926; 1928; 1930–1931; 1935; 1937		300
D 1864–1894		300
M 1870–1894; 1908; 1920–1925; 1929–1932; 1937		300
MARIJAMPOLE	**MARIJAMPOLE**	**LITHUANIA**
T 1823–1832		KRSW 4939–4941
MELNITSA PODOLSKAYA	**TERNOPOL**	**UKRAINE**
B 1823–1890 & ALSO INCLUDED IN KUDRINTSY & KRZYWCZE		300
D 1851–1890		300
M 1908–1912		300
MIKULINTSY	**TERNOPOL**	**UKRAINE**
B 1847–1871; 1873–1894		300
D 1878–1884; 1886–1894		300
M 1877–1881; 1883–1886; 1888–1901		300
MILOSZOWICE	**INCLUDED IN NAWARIYA**	
MILYATYCHE	**INCLUDED IN NAWARIYA**	
MOSTISKA	**LVOV**	**UKRAINE**
B 1882–1888		300
M 1862–1876		300

A Army/recruit lists; **B** Birth; **C** Census; **D** Death; **E** Voter lists; **G** Immigration; **H** Holocaust; **J** Judaica; **K** Kahal; **L** Land; **M** Marriage; **N** Name changes; **O** Police files; **P** Pogroms; **R** Reference; **S** School records; **T** Tax lists; **V** Divorce; **W** Occupation lists; **X** Jewish hospital; **Y** Notary records; **Z** Local government records

TOWN NAME Document Type Years	VOIVODSHIP/OBLAST (Province)	COUNTRY Zespół/Sygnatura (Poland) Fond/Opis/Delo (Belarus, Ukraine, Lithuania)	
MOSTKI	**INCLUDED IN NAWARIYA**		
MRAZHNITSA	**INCLUDED IN BORISLAV**		
NADVORNAYA	**IVANO FRANKOVSK**		**UKRAINE**
B 1866–1884; 1903		300	
B 1884–1891		300	
D 1868–1891		300	
NARAYEV	**TERNOPOL**		**UKRAINE**
B 1876–1887		300	
NAWARIYA	**LVOV**		**UKRAINE**
B 1878; 1883–1887; 1889–1894		300	
D 1877; 1883–1894		300	
M 1878–1881; 1883–1894		300	
NESTEROV	**LVOV**		**UKRAINE**
B 1861–1894		300	
D 1870–1894		300	
M 1815–1873; 1877–1880; 1888–1892; 1927; 1937		300	
NEZVISKA	**INCLUDED IN OBERTIN**		
NIKOLAYEV	**INCLUDED IN VINNIKI**		
NOVOGRUDOK	**GRODNO**		**BELARUS**
W 1759–1859			
NOVYY YARYCHEV	**LVOV**		**UKRAINE**
B 1888–1890; 1892–1894		300	
D 1879–1883; 1889–1892		300	
M 1879; 1892		300	
NOVYYE STRELISHCHA	**LVOV**		**UKRAINE**
B 1877–1879		300	
D 1877–1884; 1888–1893		300	
M 1884–1887		300	
OBERTIN	**IVANO FRANKOVSK**		**UKRAINE**
B 1849–1874; 1877–1884		300	
D 1877–1892		300	
M 1861–1875; 1877–1889		300	
OKOPY	**TERNOPOL**		**UKRAINE**
M 1854–1876 & ALSO INCLUDED IN MELNITSA PODOLSKAYA		300	
OLESKO	**LVOV**		**UKRAINE**
B 1925–1927		300	
D 1859–1876; 1914; 1916		300	
M 1958–1875		300	
OLKHOVETS	**INCLUDED IN MELNITSA PODOLSKAYA**		
OLYKA	**VOLYNSK**		**UKRAINE**
C 18TH CENTURY		300	
OREKHOVETS	**INCLUDED IN SKALAT**		
OZMLA	**INCLUDED IN YAVOROV**		
PETROV	**INCLUDED IN OBERTIN**		
PŁOCK	**PŁOCK**		**POLAND**
Z 1939–1944		1362/II	
PODCIEMNO	**INCLUDED IN NAWARIYA**		
PODGAYTSY	**TERNOPOL**		**UKRAINE**
B 1890; INDEX ONLY: 1866–1877; 1879; 1886; 1890–1892		300	
D 1877–1880; INDEX ONLY: 1879–1882; 1884; 1887; 1899		300	
M 1847; 1877–1880; 1882; 1887–1889; 1891–1894		300	
PODSADKI	**INCLUDED IN NAWARIYA**		
PODVOLOCHISK	**TERNOPOL**		**UKRAINE**
B 1877–1889 (ALSO INCLUDED IN TERNOPOL & ZBARAZH)		300	
PORSHNA	**INCLUDED IN NAWARIYA**		
POTOCHISHCHE	**INCLUDED IN GORODENKA**		
PRZEROŚL	**SUWAŁKI**		**POLAND**
T 1826–1844		KRSW 4980–4981	
RACZKI	**SUWAŁKI**		**POLAND**
T 1821–1841		KRSW 5022–5023	
RADENITSE	**INCLUDED IN MOSTISKA**		
RAJGRÓD	**ŁOMŻA**		**POLAND**
T 1820–1833		KRSW 5029–5030	

A Army/recruit lists; **B** Birth; **C** Census; **D** Death; **E** Voter lists; **G** Immigration; **H** Holocaust; **J** Judaica; **K** Kahal; **L** Land; **M** Marriage; **N** Name changes; **O** Police files; **P** Pogroms; **R** Reference; **S** School records; **T** Tax lists; **V** Divorce; **W** Occupation Lists; **X** Jewish hospital; **Y** Notary records; **Z** Local government records

TOWN NAME Document Type Years	VOIVODSHIP/OBLAST (Province)	COUNTRY Zespół/Sygnatura (Poland) Fond/Opis/Delo (Belarus, Ukraine, Lithuania)	
RAVA RUSSKAYA	**LVOV**		**UKRAINE**
B 1845–1870		300	
D 1844–1870; 1878–1894		300	
ROGATIN	**IVANO FRANKOVSK**		**UKRAINE**
B 1859–1881; 1914; 1922; 1934; 1938–1939		300	
D 1877–1886; 1938–1939; 1938–1939		300	
M 1923; 1925; 1927; 1935; 1938–1939		300	
ROGOZNO	**INCLUDED IN YAVOROV**		
ROZDOL	**LVOV**		**UKRAINE**
B 1877–1891		300	
D 1869–1884		300	
RUDKI	**LVOV**		**UKRAINE**
B 1863–1890; 1898–1899; 1901–1902; 1904; 1910		300	
D 1867–1876; 1878–1882; 1888–1890; 1892–1897		300	
M 1883–1885; 1896; 1903		300	
RYBNIK	**INCLUDED IN BORISLAV**		
SAKIAI	**SAKIAI**		**LITHUANIA**
T 1825–1835		KRSW 5074	
SAMBOR	**LVOV**		**UKRAINE**
B 1862–1883; 1885–1894		300	
D 1868–1883; 1887–1894		300	
M 1877–1891		300	
SASOV	**LVOV**		**UKRAINE**
D 1859–1876		300	
SEIRIJAI	**LAZDIJAI**		**LITHUANIA**
T 1820–1832		KRSW 5084	
SEJNY	**SUWAŁKI**		**POLAND**
T 1823–1832; 1846/1865		KRSW 5118–5120; 5130–5131	
SEREJE	**SEE SEIRIJAI**		
SHCHIETS	**LVOV**		**UKRAINE**
B 1875; 1878; 1880–1882; 1885; 1888–1889; 1893–1894		300	
D 1878; 1881–1882; 1884; 1886; 1889		300	
M 1877–1878; 1880–1883; 1887–1890; 1893–1894		300	
SIMNAS	**ALYTUS**		**LITHUANIA**
T 1819–1837			
SKALA PODOLSKAYA	**TERNOPOL**		**UKRAINE**
B 1872–1882; 1886–1892		300	
D 1839–1892		300	
M 1923–1938		300	
SKALAT	**TERNOPOL**		**UKRAINE**
B 1859–1894		300	
D 1859–1894		300	
M 1877–1901		300	
SKHODNITSA	**INCLUDED IN BORISLAV**		
SKOLE	**LVOV**		**UKRAINE**
B 1878–1880; 1883–1894		300	
D 1877–1882; 1884–1887; 1889–1894		300	
M 1882; 1888–1894		300	
SNYATYN	**IVANO FRANKOVSK**		**UKRAINE**
M 1920–1942 (MARRIAGE ANNOUNCEMENTS)		300	
SOKAL	**LVOV**		**UKRAINE**
B 1858–1880; 1882–1894		300	
D 1831–1894		300	
M 1863–1894		300	
SOKOLNIKI	**INCLUDED IN NAWARIYA**		
SOKOLOVKA	**LVOV**		**UKRAINE**
B 1897; 1900		300	
D 1906		300	
M 1905–1906; 1910; 1912–1913; 1921–1932		300	
SOKOŁY	**ŁOMŻA**		**POLAND**
T 1827–1846		KRSW 5134	
SOLONKA	**INCLUDED IN NAWARIYA**		
SOPOCKINIE	**SEE SOPOTSKIN**		

A Army/recruit lists; **B** Birth; **C** Census; **D** Death; **E** Voter lists; **G** Immigration; **H** Holocaust; **J** Judaica; **K** Kahal; **L** Land; **M** Marriage; **N** Name changes; **O** Police files; **P** Pogroms; **R** Reference; **S** School records; **T** Tax lists; **V** Divorce; **W** Occupation lists; **X** Jewish hospital; **Y** Notary records; **Z** Local government records

TOWN NAME Document Type Years	VOIVODSHIP/OBLAST (Province)	COUNTRY Zespół/Sygnatura (Poland) Fond/Opis/Delo (Belarus, Ukraine, Lithuania)	
SOPOTSKIN	**GRODNO**		**BELARUS**
T 1822–1837		KRSW 5090	
STANISŁAWÓW	**SEE IVANO FRANKOVSK**		
STARAYA SOL	**LVOV**		**UKRAINE**
B 1892–1903		300	
STARE MIASTO	**TERNOPOL**		**UKRAINE**
B 1856–1891		300	
D 1870–1880		300	
M 1856–1876		300	
STARYAVA	**INCLUDED IN MOSTISKA**		
STARZYSKA	**INCLUDED IN YAVOROV**		
STENYATIN	**INCLUDED IN SOKAL**		
STRATIN	**IVANO FRANKOVSK**		**UKRAINE**
B 1858–1876		300	
D 1858–1876		300	
STRELISHCHA	**INCLUDED IN GORODENKA**		
STRUSOV	**TERNOPOL**		**UKRAINE**
B 1877–1890		300	
D 1871–1876		300	
M 1871; 1875		300	
STRYJ	**LVOV**		**UKRAINE**
B 1870–1872; 1875–1894; 1899		300	
D 1869–1894		300	
M 1877–1883; 1885–1894		300	
STRZELISKA NOWE	**SEE NOVYYE STRELISHCHA**		
SUWAŁKI	**SUWAŁKI**		**POLAND**
T 1822–1828; 1832–1834		KRSW 5042; 5044	
SVIRZH	**INCLUDED IN VINNIKI**		
SWIRZ	**SEE SVIRZH**		
SZCZERZEC	**SEE SHCHIRETS**		
SZCZUCZYN	**ŁOMŻA**		**POLAND**
T 1823–1830		KRSW 5094	
TARNOPOL	**SEE TERNOPOL**		
TARTAKOV	**LVOV**		**UKRAINE**
B 1858–1890; 1932; 1935		300	
D 1906; 1933–1937		300	
M 1845–1875; 1917–1921; 1932; 1934		300	
TEREBOVLYA	**TERNOPOL**		**UKRAINE**
B 1877–1891		300	
TERNOPOL	**TERNOPOL**		**UKRAINE**
B 1866–1876; 1878–1894		300	
D 1870–1876; 1878–1894		300	
K 1905–1930; 1934		300	
M 1878–1894; 1937		300	
TERPILOVKA	**INCLUDED IN ZBARAZH**		
TOLSHCHEV	**INCLUDED IN NAWARIYA**		
TORGANOVICHI	**INCLUDED IN SAMBOR**		
TROSCIANIEC	**INCLUDED IN YAVOROV**		
TURKA	**LVOV**		**UKRAINE**
B 1914–1922; 1938		300	
UGNEV	**LVOV**		**UKRAINE**
D 1853–1876		300	
M 1876		300	
ULASHKOVTSY	**TERNOPOL**		**UKRAINE**
B 1875; 1884–1885; 1889–1890; 1892		300	
D 1874–1875; 1884; 1886; 1889–1890		300	
USCIE BISKUPIE	**TERNOPOL**		**UKRAINE**
B 1831–1876 & ALSO INCLUDED IN MELNITSA PODOLSKAYA		300	
D 1831–1876		300	
VELIKIYE MOSTY	**LVOV**		**UKRAINE**
B 1861–1874; 1877–1894		300	
D 1877–1891; 1918		300	
M 1918		300	

A Army/recruit lists; **B** Birth; **C** Census; **D** Death; **E** Voter lists; **G** Immigration; **H** Holocaust; **J** Judaica; **K** Kahal; **L** Land; **M** Marriage; **N** Name changes; **O** Police files; **P** Pogroms; **R** Reference; **S** School records; **T** Tax lists; **V** Divorce; **W** Occupation Lists; **X** Jewish hospital; **Y** Notary records; **Z** Local government records

TOWN NAME Document Type Years	VOIVODSHIP/OBLAST (Province)	COUNTRY Zespół/Sygnatura (Poland) Fond/Opis/Delo (Belarus, Ukraine, Lithuania)	
VERBYANY	**INCLUDED IN YAVOROV**		
VERKHNEYE KRIVCHE	**TERNOPOL**	**UKRAINE**	
B 1830–1876		300	
D 1818–1876		300	
VERKHOVINA	**IVANO FRANKOVSK**	**UKRAINE**	
B 1877–1892		300	
VILKAVISKIS	**VILKAVISKIS**	**LITHUANIA**	
T 1823–1834		KRSW 5187–5188	
VILNIUS	**VILNIUS**	**LITHUANIA**	
L 1807/1887			
C 1811–1816			
VINNIKI	**LVOV**	**UKRAINE**	
D 1881; 1883; 1886; 1892–1894		300	
M 1883; 1885–1892		300	
VIRBALIS	**VILKAVISKIS**	**LITHUANIA**	
T 1811–1820; 1855–1860 (BUILDING LOANS)		KRSW 5148–5160	
VISHTINETZ	**SEE VISTYTIS**		
VISTYTIS	**VILKAVISKIS**	**LITHUANIA**	
T 1822–1832		KRSW 5174–5175	
VOLANKA	**INCLUDED IN BORISLAV**		
VOLKOV	**INCLUDED IN NAWARIYA**		
VOLKOVYSK	**GRODNO**	**BELARUS**	
T 1826–1828			
WARSZAWA	**WARSZAWA**	**POLAND**	
L 1804/1863		662/III	
WIEŁKIE OCZY	**PRZEMYŚL**	**POLAND**	
B 1843–1874		1481	
D 1843–1874		1481	
WIERZBOLOW	**SEE VIRBALIS**		
WISZNIEW	**INCLUDED IN BURSHTYN**		
WOLA BLAZOWSKA	**INCLUDED IN SAMBOR**		
YAGELNITSA	**TERNOPOL**	**UKRAINE**	
B 1860–1890; 1892–1897; 1902–1906; 1913; 1926–1932		300	
D 1862–1892; 1894–1895; 1900; 1905; 1907–1911; 1913; 1920–1923; 1926–1929; 1931–1932		300	
M 1874–1876; 1899–1900; 1911; 1914; 1920; 1923–1924; 1937–1938		300	
YAVOROW	**LVOV**	**UKRAINE**	
B 1848–1892; 1905–1907; 1909–1911; 1913–1936; 1938–1939		300	
D 1842–1881; 1890–1894; 1939		300	
M 1861–1876; 1913–1924; 1939		300	
ZABOLOTOW	**IVANO FRANKOVSK**	**UKRAINE**	
B 1861–1876; 1879–1882; 1888–1892		300	
D 1884–1892		300	
ZAGÓRZE	**INCLUDED IN ZALOZHTSY**		
ZAGRODKI	**INCLUDED IN SHCHERETS**		
ZALESIE	**INCLUDED IN MELNITSA PODOLSKAYA**		
ZALOZHTSY	**TERNOPOL**	**UKRAINE**	
B 1877–1890		300	
D 1823–1861; 1877; 1914		300	
D INDEX: 1877–1938		300	
M 1853; 1925–1939		300	
M INDEX: 1877–1938		300	
ZALUZE	**INCLUDED IN ZBARAZH**		
ZALUZHE	**INCLUDED IN YAVOROV**		
ZBARAZH	**TERNOPOL**	**UKRAINE**	
B 1877–1894		300	
D 1859–1893		300	
M 1859–1876		300	
ZBOROV	**TERNOPOL**	**UKRAINE**	
B 1877–1890		300	
D 1877–1886		300	
M 1921–1931		300	
ZBRIZH	**INCLUDED IN SKALA PODOLSKAYA**		

A Army/recruit lists; **B** Birth; **C** Census; **D** Death; **E** Voter lists; **G** Immigration; **H** Holocaust; **J** Judaica; **K** Kahal; **L** Land; **M** Marriage; **N** Name changes; **O** Police files; **P** Pogroms; **R** Reference; **S** School records; **T** Tax lists; **V** Divorce; **W** Occupation lists; **X** Jewish hospital; **Y** Notary records; **Z** Local government records

TOWN NAME Document Type Years	VOIVODSHIP/OBLAST (Province)	COUNTRY Zespół/Sygnatura (Poland) Fond/Opis/Delo (Belarus, Ukraine, Lithuania)
ŻELECHÓW	**SIEDLCE**	**POLAND**
T 1886–1911		ZPG/531
ZELIBOR	**INCLUDED IN BURSHTYN**	
ZHIDACHOV	**LVOV**	**UKRAINE**
B 1887–1889; 1891–1892; 1894–1895; 1897–1898; 1900–1901; 1903–1910; 1912; 1928–1929; 1931–1933		300
D 1877–1882; 1890–1895; 1897–1900; 1903; 1905–1906; 1908–1913; 1928–1933; 1935; 1938		300
M 1878; 1881; 1891–1892; 1899–1901; 1907–1909; 1913; 1928–1934		300
ZHURAVNO	**LVOV**	**UKRAINE**
B 1877–1885		300
ZNIESIENIE	**ROVNO**	**UKRAINE**
M 1870–1881; 1908; 1921–1925; 1929–1932		300
ZOLOCHEV	**LVOV**	**UKRAINE**
B 1865–1871; 1877–1891; 1893; 1899; 1904–1905		300
D 1855–1875; 1877–1892; 1894		300
M 1876; 1893; 1895; 1913; 1938		300

WARSAW Archives (Archiwum Państwówe m. Warszawy)

PŁOCK	**PŁOCK**	**POLAND**
C 1939–1942		1362/II
WARSZAWA	**WARSZAWA**	**POLAND**
B 1846–1848; 1860; 1868–1889; 1891–1894; 1908; 1911		180/I
D 1846; 1860; 1868–1889; 1891–1894; 1909		180/I
M 1826–1893		180/I
S 1852–1918		214; 216; 305; 311
Y 1808–1939		665–1660
WARSZAWA/MOKOTOW REGION	**INCLUDED IN WARSZAWA**	

WŁOCŁAWEK Archives

BRZEŚĆ KUJAWSKI	**WŁOCŁAWEK**	**POLAND**
M 1829–1833 (MARRIAGE APPLICATIONS)		
CHODECZ	**WŁOCŁAWEK**	**POLAND**
C 1850–1931		22
DOBRZYŃ NAD WISŁĄ	**WŁOCŁAWEK**	**POLAND**
B 1826–1908		563
D 1899–1936		563
M 1826–1898		563
IZBICA KUJAWSKA	**WŁOCŁAWEK**	**POLAND**
B 1866–1881; 1884; 1886–1893		563
D 1866–1881; 1884; 1886–1893		563
M 1866–1881; 1884; 1886–1893		563
KOWAL	**WŁOCŁAWEK**	**POLAND**
B 1879–1886		563
B 1839–1883 (ALPHA INDEX)		563
D 1883–1886		563
M 1885–1886 (MARRIAGE APPLICATIONS: 1821; 1863)		563
NIESZAWA	**WŁOCŁAWEK**	**POLAND**
B 1826–1903		563
D 1826–1836; 1865–1879		563
M 1826–1894		563
OSIĘCINY	**WŁOCŁAWEK**	**POLAND**
M 1867–1871; 1885–1889 (MARRIAGE APPLICATIONS)		
PIOTRKÓW KUJAWSKI	**WŁOCŁAWEK**	**POLAND**
B 1839–1852; 1859–1894		563
D 1838–1852; 1859–1896		563
M 1838–1857; 1859–1896		563
RADZIEJÓW KUJAWSKI	**WŁOCŁAWEK**	**POLAND**
B 1831–1892		
D 1826–1892		
M 1842–1844; 1854; 1858–1867 (MARRIAGE APPLICATIONS)		
M 1826–1892		

A Army/recruit lists; **B** Birth; **C** Census; **D** Death; **E** Voter lists; **G** Immigration; **H** Holocaust; **J** Judaica; **K** Kahal; **L** Land; **M** Marriage; **N** Name changes; **O** Police files; **P** Pogroms; **R** Reference; **S** School records; **T** Tax lists; **V** Divorce; **W** Occupation Lists; **X** Jewish hospital; **Y** Notary records; **Z** Local government records

TOWN NAME Document Type Years	VOIVODSHIP/OBLAST (Province)	COUNTRY Zespół/Sygnatura (Poland) Fond/Opis/Delo (Belarus, Ukraine, Lithuania)
RYPIN	**WŁOCŁAWEK**	**POLAND**
B 1808–1822; 1826–1894		563
D 1808–1822; 1826–1894		563
M 1808–1822; 1826–1894		563
WŁOCŁAWEK	**WŁOCŁAWEK**	**POLAND**
M 1872 (MARRIAGE APPLICATIONS)		563

WROCŁAW Archives

DZIERŻONIÓW	**WAŁBRZYCH**	**POLAND**
K 1654/1945		27/I
FESTENBERG	**SEE TWARDOGÓRA**	
GLATZ	**SEE KŁÓDZKO**	
KANTH	**SEE KĄTY WROCŁAWSKIE**	
KĄTY WROCŁAWSKIE	**WROCŁAW**	**POLAND**
B 1874–1877; 1886; 1888–1889; 1892–1893		556/II
D 1874–1882; 1888; 1890–1893		556/II
M 1874–1880; 1890–1893		556/II
KŁÓDZKO	**WAŁBRZYCH**	**POLAND**
D 1817–1820; 1828–1836; 1838; 1843–1844; 1847; 1875–1892		557/II
NEUMARKT	**SEE ŚRODA ŚLĄSKA**	
OELS	**SEE OLEŚNICA**	
OHLAU	**SEE OŁAWA**	
OŁAWA	**WROCŁAW**	**POLAND**
B 1874–1892		556/II
D 1874–1892		556/II
K 1809–1945		172/II
M 1874–1892		556/II
OLEŚNICA	**WROCŁAW**	**POLAND**
B 1875		556/II
D 1874–1877		556/II
M 1875–1877		556/II
SCHWEIDNITZ	**SEE ŚWIDNICA**	
ŚRODA ŚLĄSKA	**WROCŁAW**	**POLAND**
B 1880; 1883–1885; 1887–1890		556/II
C 1604; 1809–1945		172/II
M 1875; 1878; 1881–1882; 1885; 1889–1893		556/II
STRIEGAU	**SEE STRIEGAU**	
STRZEGOM	**WAŁBRZYCH**	**POLAND**
B 1874–1877; 1879–1882; 1884–1885; 1887–1889		557/II
D 1874–1878; 1881–1886; 1888–1890; 1892–1893		557/II
M 1874–1885; 1887–1892		557/II
ŚWIDNICA	**WAŁBRZYCH**	**POLAND**
B 1874–1893		557/II
D 1874–1893		557/II
M 1874–1893		557/II
TWARDOGÓRA	**WROCŁAW**	**POLAND**
B 1874–1893		556/II
D 1874–1892		556/II
M 1874–1893		556/II
WROCŁAW	**WROCŁAW**	**POLAND**
B 1874–1893		556/II
D 1874–1893		556/II
K 1604; 1809–1945		172/II
M 1874–1893		556/II
N 1604; 1809–1945		172/II
ZGORZELEC	**JELENIA GÓRA**	**POLAND**
K 1800–1945		132

ZAMOŚĆ Archives

BIŁGORAJ	**ZAMOŚĆ**	**POLAND**
B 1876–1893		209/1–18
D 1876–1893		209/1–18
M 1876–1893		209/1–18

A Army/recruit lists; **B** Birth; **C** Census; **D** Death; **E** Voter lists; **G** Immigration; **H** Holocaust; **J** Judaica; **K** Kahal; **L** Land; **M** Marriage; **N** Name changes; **O** Police files; **P** Pogroms; **R** Reference; **S** School records; **T** Tax lists; **V** Divorce; **W** Occupation lists; **X** Jewish hospital; **Y** Notary records; **Z** Local government records

TOWN NAME Document Type Years	VOIVODSHIP/OBLAST (Province)	COUNTRY Zespół/Sygnatura (Poland) Fond/Opis/Delo (Belarus, Ukraine, Lithuania)
FRAMPOL	**ZAMOŚĆ**	**POLAND**
B 1876–1893		209/1–18
D 1876–1893		209/1–18
M 1876–1892		209/1–17
GORZKÓW	**ZAMOŚĆ**	**POLAND**
B 1871–1874; 1876–1890; 1892–1893		209/1–21
D 1871–1874; 1876–1890; 1892–1893		209/1–21
M 1871–1874; 1876–1890; 1892–1893		209/1–21
GRABOWIEC	**ZAMOŚĆ**	**POLAND**
B 1876–1893		209/1–18
D 1876–1893		209/1–18
M 1876–1893		209/1–18
HORODŁO	**ZAMOŚĆ**	**POLAND**
B 1880–1890		209/1–2; 2A–2C; 3–4; 4A; 5–7
D 1880–1890		209/1–2; 2A–2C; 3–4; 4A; 5–7
M 1880–1890		209/1–2; 2A–2C; 3–4; 4A; 5–7
HRUBIESZÓW	**ZAMOŚĆ**	**POLAND**
B 1870; 1875–1885; 1887–1893		209/00; 0; 0A; 1; 1A; 2–6; 6A; 7–20
D 1870; 1875–1884; 1887–1893		209/00; 0; 0A; 1; 1A; 2–6; 6A; 7–20
M 1870; 1875–1884; 1887–1893		209/00; 0; 0A; 1; 1A; 2–6; 6A; 7–20
IZBICA	**ZAMOŚĆ**	**POLAND**
B 1873–1874; 1876–1893		209/1–20
D 1862; 1876–1893		209/1–20
M 1873–1874; 1876–1893		209/1–20
JARCZÓW	**ZAMOŚĆ**	**POLAND**
B 1876–1892		209/1–17
D 1876–1892		209/1–17
M 1876–1892		209/1–17
JAROSŁAWIEC	**ZAMOŚĆ**	**POLAND**
B 1881–1886; 1889; 1891–1893		209/1–10
D 1881–1886; 1889; 1891–1893		209/1–10
M 1881–1886; 1889; 1891–1893		209/1–10
JÓZEFÓW	**ZAMOŚĆ**	**POLAND**
B 1876–1882; 1884–1885; 1887–1893		209/1–16
D 1876–1877; 1879; 1881–1882; 1884–1885; 1887–1893		209/1–2,4,6–16
M 1876–1881–1882; 1884–1885; 1887–1890; 1892–1893		209/1,6–13; 15–16
KOMARÓW	**ZAMOŚĆ**	**POLAND**
B 1873–1891		209/O; OA; OB; 1–16
D 1873–1891		209/O; OA; OB; 1–16
M 1873–1891		209/O; OA; OB; 1–16
KRASNOBRÓD	**ZAMOŚĆ**	**POLAND**
B 1874; 1876–1878; 1881–1893		209/1–16
D 1874; 1876–1878; 1881–1893		209/1–16
M 1874; 1876–1878; 1881–1893		209/1–16
S 1926–1927; 1934–1935		12/404–406
KRASNYSTAW	**CHEŁM**	**POLAND**
B 1871–1872		209/1–2
C 1907–1951		22
D 1871–1872		209/1–2
M 1871–1872		209/1–2
Y 1876–1924		103–106/171
Z 1916–1944		22
KRYŁÓW	**ZAMOŚĆ**	**POLAND**
B 1876–1880; 1882–1883; 1885–1890; 1892		209/1–14
D 1876–1880; 1882–1883; 1885–1890; 1892		209/1–14
M 1876–1880; 1882–1883; 1885–1890; 1892		209/1–14
ŁASZCZÓW	**ZAMOŚĆ**	**POLAND**
B 1876–1877; 1879–1882; 1884–1889; 1891–1893		209/1–15
D 1876–1877; 1879–1882; 1884–1889; 1891–1893		209/1–15
M 1876–1877; 1879–1882; 1884–1889; 1891–1893		209/1–15
SZCZEBRZESZYN	**ZAMOŚĆ**	**POLAND**
B 1876–1893		209/1–18
D 1876–1893		209/1–18
M 1876–1893		209/1–18
S 1927–1937		12/511
Y 1824–1954		107–116

A Army/recruit lists; **B** Birth; **C** Census; **D** Death; **E** Voter lists; **G** Immigration; **H** Holocaust; **J** Judaica; **K** Kahal; **L** Land; **M** Marriage; **N** Name changes; **O** Police files; **P** Pogroms; **R** Reference; **S** School records; **T** Tax lists; **V** Divorce; **W** Occupation Lists; **X** Jewish hospital; **Y** Notary records; **Z** Local government records

TOWN NAME Document Type Years	VOIVODSHIP/OBLAST (Province)	COUNTRY Zespół/Sygnatura (Poland) Fond/Opis/Delo (Belarus, Ukraine, Lithuania)
TARNOGÓRA	**ZAMOŚĆ**	**POLAND**
B 1871–1872		209/1–2
D 1871–1872		209/1–2
M 1871–1872		209/1–2
TARNOGRÓD	**ZAMOŚĆ**	**POLAND**
B 1877–1881; 1883–1893		209/1–16
D 1877–1881; 1883–1893		209/1–16
M 1877–1881; 1883–1893		209/1–16
TOMASZÓW LUBELSKI	**ZAMOŚĆ**	**POLAND**
B 1869–1893		209/OA; OB; OC; 1–9; 9A; 10–20
C 1890–1949		24
D 1876–1893		209/OD; 1–9; 9A; 10–15; 17; 19–20
M 1866–1893		209/1–15,17–20
T 1927–1952		24
Y 1810–1936		117–126
Z 1892–1950		24
TUROBIN	**ZAMOŚĆ**	**POLAND**
B 1870–1871; 1876–1889; 1891–1893		209/1–18
D 1870–1871; 1876–1889; 1891–1893		209/1–18
M 1870–1871; 1876–1889; 1891–1893		209/1–18
TYSZOWCE	**ZAMOŚĆ**	**POLAND**
B 1876–1893		209/1–15
D 1876–1893		209/1–15
M 1876–1877; 1879–1893		209/1–15
Y 1927–1934		127–130/1–38
UCHANIE	**ZAMOŚĆ**	**POLAND**
B 1866; 1876–1880 (SEE ALSO: JAROSŁAWIEC)		209/0–3
D 1866; 1876–1880 (SEE ALSO: JAROSŁAWIEC)		209/0–2
M 1866; 1876–1879 (SEE ALSO: JAROSŁAWIEC)		209/0–2
WYSOKIE	**ZAMOŚĆ**	**POLAND**
B 1876; 1879; 1882–1891		209/1–12
D 1876; 1879; 1882–1891		209/1/12
M 1876; 1879; 1882–1891		209/1–12
ZAMOŚĆ	**ZAMOŚĆ**	**POLAND**
B 1866–1890		209/1; 4; 6–7; 10
C 1880–1951		25
D 1876–1890		209/3; 9; 11
M 1865–1888		209
S 1926–1939		12; 576–579
T 1937–1948		9
Y 1810–1824; 1873–1939		131–146
Z 1821–1939		25
ŻÓŁKIEWKA	**ZAMOŚĆ**	**POLAND**
B 1871–1880		209/1–10
D 1871–1880		209/1–10
M 1871–1880		209/1–10

ŻARY Branch Archives

SORAU	**SEE ŻARY**	
SZPROTAWA	**ZIELONA GÓRA**	**POLAND**
Z 1812–1861		1
ŻAGAŃ	**ZIELONA GÓRA**	**POLAND**
L 1897–1944		119
ŻARY	**ZIELONA GÓRA**	**POLAND**
L 1865–1940		90

ZIELONA GÓRA Archives (located in Stary Kisielin)

GŁOGÓW	**LEGNICA**	**POLAND**
Z 1582/1858		13
KARGOWA	**ZIELONA GÓRA**	**POLAND**
Z 1824/1945		356
KOŻUCHÓW	**ZIELONA GÓRA**	**POLAND**
B 1847–1875		138/288–290
D 1847–1875		138/288–290
L 1864–1945		185

A Army/recruit lists; **B** Birth; **C** Census; **D** Death; **E** Voter lists; **G** Immigration; **H** Holocaust; **J** Judaica; **K** Kahal; **L** Land; **M** Marriage; **N** Name changes; **O** Police files; **P** Pogroms; **R** Reference; **S** School records; **T** Tax lists; **V** Divorce; **W** Occupation lists; **X** Jewish hospital; **Y** Notary records; **Z** Local government records

TOWN NAME Document Type Years	VOIVODSHIP/OBLAST (Province)	COUNTRY Zespół/Sygnatura (Poland) Fond/Opis/Delo (Belarus, Ukraine, Lithuania)
M 1847–1875		138/288–290
SZLICHTYNGOWA	**LESZNO**	**POLAND**
B 1835–1847		132
D 1835–1847		132
M 1835–1847		132
Z 1820–1931		361
SZPROTAWA	**ZIELONA GÓRA**	**POLAND**
G 1813–1845		
WSCHOWA	**LESZNO**	**POLAND**
B 1838		124
D 1838		124
M 1838		124
Z 1793–1841		363
ZIELONA GÓRA	**ZIELONA GÓRA**	**POLAND**
K 1834/1908		CITY ACTS OF ZIELONA GÓRA
L 1865–1945		

ŻYRARDÓW Branch Archives (temporarily located in Kutno)

GRODZISK MAZOWIECKI	**WARSZAWA**	**POLAND**
B 1826–1882		280
D 1826–1882		280
M 1826–1882		280
MSZCZONÓW	**SKIERNIEWICE**	**POLAND**
B 1826–1869; 1872; 1875–1877		25
D 1826–1869; 1872; 1875–1877		25
M 1826–1869; 1872; 1875–1877		25
NADARZYN	**WARSZAWA**	**POLAND**
B 1826–1874		180
D 1826–1874		180
M 1826–1874		180
WISKITKI	**SKIERNIEWICE**	**POLAND**
B 1826–1887		63
D 1826–1887		63
M 1826–1887		63
ŻYRARDÓW	**SKIERNIEWICE**	**POLAND**
B 1886–1887		308
D 1886–1887		308
M 1886–1887		308

ŻYWIEC Branch Archives

BIERNA	**BIELSKO BIAŁA**	**POLAND**
C 1931		5/2
CZERNICHÓW	**BIELSKO BIAŁA**	**POLAND**
C 1934–1939		9/7
JORDANÓW	**NOWY SĄCZ**	**POLAND**
G 1888–1896; 1934–1938		27/120–121
Z 1806; 1825; 1872–1876; 1939; 1942–1943; 1945–1946		27/10–11,119–220,226,237,262,273
ŁODYGOWICE	**BIELSKO BIAŁA**	**POLAND**
C 1934		5/3–10
ŁODYGOWICE REGION	**BIELSKO BIAŁA**	**POLAND**
L 1925		5/1
MAKÓW PODHALAŃSKI	**BIELSKO BIAŁA**	**POLAND**
A 1914–1919; 1927–1937		28/3,24–25
C 1937		28/20–21
E 1934–1939		28/73
G 1933–1938		28/18,22–23
K 1940		28/37
L 1945; 1947–1948		28/60,64
W 1941–1942		28/56
MOSZCZENICA	**NOWY SĄCZ**	**POLAND**
C 1934–1939		9/8
OCZKÓW	**BIELSKO BIAŁA**	**POLAND**
C 1934–1939		9/9

A Army/recruit lists; **B** Birth; **C** Census; **D** Death; **E** Voter lists; **G** Immigration; **H** Holocaust; **J** Judaica; **K** Kahal; **L** Land; **M** Marriage; **N** Name changes; **O** Police files; **P** Pogroms; **R** Reference; **S** School records; **T** Tax lists; **V** Divorce; **W** Occupation Lists; **X** Jewish hospital; **Y** Notary records; **Z** Local government records

TOWN NAME Document Type Years	VOIVODSHIP/OBLAST (Province)	COUNTRY Zespół/Sygnatura (Poland) Fond/Opis/Delo (Belarus, Ukraine, Lithuania)
PEWEL MAŁA C 1931; 1934–1939	**BIELSKO BIAŁA**	**POLAND** 9/3–4,10
PIETRZYKOWICE C 1934	**BIELSKO BIAŁA**	**POLAND** 5/11–13/VOL.1–3
PRZYŁĘKÓW C 1934–1939	**BIELSKO BIAŁA**	**POLAND** 9/11
RADZIECHOWY G 1931–1939	**BIELSKO BIAŁA**	**POLAND** 13/1
RAJCZA G 1931	**BIELSKO BIAŁA**	**POLAND** 8/1
RYCERKA DOLNA G 1945–1946	**BIELSKO BIAŁA**	**POLAND** 8/13–16,VOL.1–2
RYCHWAŁD C 1931	**BIELSKO BIAŁA**	**POLAND** 3/3
SPORYSZ C 1931–1940	**BIELSKO BIAŁA**	**POLAND** 9/6,13
SPORYSZ REGION C 1931 L 1935–1939	**BIELSKO BIAŁA**	**POLAND** 9/5 9/19
ŚWINNA C 1934–1939	**BIELSKO BIAŁA**	**POLAND** 9/14–15,VOL. 1–2
TRZEBINIA C 1934–1939	**BIELSKO BIAŁA**	**POLAND** 9/16–18
ZWARDOŃ G 1945–1946	**BIELSKO BIAŁA**	**POLAND** 8/18
ŻYWIEC A 1884; 1886–1899; 1912; 1915; 1917; 1919–1925 G 1915–1931 L 1932	**BIELSKO BIAŁA**	**POLAND** 14/1; 1/34–35 1/86 13/42
ŻYWIEC REGION C 1939–1940; 1945–1947	**BIELSKO BIAŁA**	**POLAND** 17/5; 15/148; 13/42

Jasło. Świątynia izraelicka

▮ *Synagogue in Jasło, pre-Holocaust* 2

A Army/recruit lists; **B** Birth; **C** Census; **D** Death; **E** Voter lists; **G** Immigration; **H** Holocaust; **J** Judaica; **K** Kahal; **L** Land; **M** Marriage; **N** Name changes; **O** Police files; **P** Pogroms; **R** Reference; **S** School records; **T** Tax lists; **V** Divorce; **W** Occupation lists; **X** Jewish hospital; **Y** Notary records; **Z** Local government records

ARCHIVAL HOLDINGS INDEXED BY REPOSITORY
Jewish Historical Institute

by Miriam Weiner

TOWN NAME Document Type Years	VOIVODSHIP/OBLAST (Province)	COUNTRY Zespół /Sygnatura (Poland) Fond/Opis/Delo (Belarus, Ukraine, Lithuania)

WARSZAWA - Jewish Historical Institute

ALEKSANDRÓW KUJAWSKI	**WŁOCŁAWEK**	**POLAND**
C 1919/1939		105
E 1919/1939		105
K 1919/1939		105
T 1919/1939		105
BĘDZIN	**KATOWICE**	**POLAND**
C 1939		212-213
H 1939–1943		212-213
BIAŁA PODLASKA	**BIAŁA PODLASKA**	**POLAND**
H 1941–1942 (RESIDENT BOOKS OF 3,000 JEWS SENT TO GHETTO IN MIĘDZYRZEC)		
BIAŁYSTOK	**BIAŁYSTOK**	**POLAND**
H 1939–1942		204
BIERUTÓW	**WROCŁAW**	**POLAND**
C 1810/1908		PROVINCE: ŚLĄSK
D 1851–1908		
K 1810/1908		PROVINCE: ŚLĄSK
Z 1810/1908		PROVINCE: ŚLĄSK
BRESLAU	**SEE WROCŁAW**	
BRZEG	**OPOLE**	**POLAND**
D 1937		
E 1742/1937		PROVINCE: ŚLĄSK
K 1742/1937		PROVINCE: ŚLĄSK
S 1742/1937		PROVINCE: ŚLĄSK
T 1742/1937		PROVINCE: ŚLĄSK
Y 1742/1937		PROVINCE: ŚLĄSK
Z 1742/1937		PROVINCE: ŚLĄSK
BRZEŚĆ KUJAWSKI	**WŁOCŁAWEK**	**POLAND**
C 1909–1939		105
E 1909–1939		105
K 1909–1939		105
T 1909–1939		105
BYDGOSZCZ	**BYDGOSZCZ**	**POLAND**
C 1838/1939		104; 224
E 1838/1939		104; 224
K 1838/1939		104; 224
T 1838/1939		104; 224
Y 1838-1939		104; 224
BYTOM	**KATOWICE**	**POLAND**
Z 1814; 1835; 1855		PROVINCE: ŚLĄSK
CHODECZ	**WŁOCŁAWEK**	**POLAND**
C 1919/1939		105
E 1919/1939		105
K 1919/1939		105
T 1919/1939		105
CHOJNÓW	**LEGNICA**	**POLAND**
K 1846/1922		PROVINCE: ŚLĄSK
Z 1846/1922		PROVINCE: ŚLĄSK
CZĘSTOCHOWA	**CZĘSTOCHOWA**	**POLAND**
C 1930–1938		113
H 1940–1943 (LIST OF 4,700 CAMP WORKERS IN HASAG LABOR CAMP)		207,212

A Army/recruit lists; **B** Birth; **C** Census; **D** Death; **E** Voter lists; **G** Immigration; **H** Holocaust; **J** Judaica; **K** Kahal; **L** Land; **M** Marriage; **N** Name changes;
O Police files; **P** Pogroms; **R** Reference; **S** School records; **T** Tax lists; **V** Divorce; **W** Occupation lists; **X** Jewish hospital; **Y** Notary records; **Z** Local government records

TOWN NAME Document Type Years	VOIVODSHIP/OBLAST (Province)	COUNTRY Zespoł /Sygnatura (Poland) Fond/Opis/Delo (Belarus, Ukraine, Lithuania)
DOBRODZIEŃ	**CZĘSTOCHOWA**	**POLAND**
K 1825/1929		PROVINCE: ŚLĄSK
S 1825/1929		PROVINCE: ŚLĄSK
Y 1825/1929		PROVINCE: ŚLĄSK
Z 1825/1929		PROVINCE: ŚLĄSK
DZIAŁOSZYCE	**KIELCE**	**POLAND**
B 1829/1846		
D 1829/1846		
M 1829/1846		
DZIERŻONIÓW	**WAŁBRZYCH**	**POLAND**
G 1812/1912		PROVINCE: ŚLĄSK
T 1812/1912		PROVINCE: ŚLĄSK
FALENICA	**WARSZAWA**	**POLAND**
K 1940–1943		212
FRANKENSTEIN	**SEE ZĄBKOWICE**	
GLIWICE	**KATOWICE**	**POLAND**
B 1812–1847		107
D 1847–1870		107
E 1812/1939		107; 112
K 1812/1939		107; 112
L 1812/1939		107; 112
S 1812/1939		107; 112
Y 1812/1939		107; 112
Z 1812/1939		107; 112
GŁOGÓW	**LEGNICA**	**POLAND**
D 1796; 1828/1850		PROVINCE: ŚLĄSK
M 1796; 1828/1850		PROVINCE: ŚLĄSK
GNIEZNO	**POZNAŃ**	**POLAND**
K 1917–1918		
GORZÓW ŚLĄSKI	**CZĘSTOCHOWA**	**POLAND**
C 1796/1934		PROVINCE: ŚLĄSK
D 1934		
K 1796/1934		PROVINCE: ŚLĄSK
M 1860–1863		
S 1796/1934		PROVINCE: ŚLĄSK
T 1796/1934		PROVINCE: ŚLĄSK
Y 1796/1934		PROVINCE: ŚLĄSK
Z 1796/1934		PROVINCE: ŚLĄSK
GRODKÓW	**OPOLE**	**POLAND**
E 1880/1936		PROVINCE: ŚLĄSK
K 1880/1936		PROVINCE: ŚLĄSK
GROSS STREHLITZ	**SEE STRZELCE OPOLSKIE**	
GRUDZIĄDZ	**TORUŃ**	**POLAND**
K 1847		114
GRUENBERG	**SEE ZIELONA GÓRA**	
IZBICA KUJAWSKA	**WŁOCŁAWEK**	**POLAND**
C 1919/1939		105
E 1919/1939		105
K 1919/1939		105
T 1919/1939		105
JASŁO	**KROSNO**	**POLAND**
K 1940–1943		212
JĘDRZEJÓW	**KIELCE**	**POLAND**
K 1940–1943		212
KAMIENNA GORA	**JELENIA GÓRA**	**POLAND**
K 1908/1939		PROVINCE: ŚLĄSK
W 1908/1939		PROVINCE: ŚLĄSK
KARGOWA	**ZIELONA GÓRA**	**POLAND**
K 1834/1891		PROVINCE: POZNAŃ
T 1834/1891		PROVINCE: POZNAŃ
KŁÓDZKO	**WAŁBRZYCH**	**POLAND**
K 1805/1916		PROVINCE: ŚLĄSK
T 1805/1916		PROVINCE: ŚLĄSK
KLUCZBORK	**OPOLE**	**POLAND**
E 1840/1918		PROVINCE: ŚLĄSK

A Army/recruit lists; **B** Birth; **C** Census; **D** Death; **E** Voter lists; **G** Immigration; **H** Holocaust; **J** Judaica; **K** Kahal; **L** Land; **M** Marriage; **N** Name changes; **O** Police files; **P** Pogroms; **R** Reference; **S** School records; **T** Tax lists; **V** Divorce; **W** Occupation lists; **X** Jewish hospital; **Y** Notary records; **Z** Local government records

TOWN NAME Document Type Years	VOIVODSHIP/OBLAST (Province)	COUNTRY Zespół /Sygnatura (Poland) Fond/Opis/Delo (Belarus, Ukraine, Lithuania)
K 1840/1918		PROVINCE: ŚLĄSK
S 1840/1918		PROVINCE: ŚLĄSK
Y 1840/1918		PROVINCE: ŚLĄSK
Z 1840/1918		PROVINCE: ŚLĄSK
KOŃSKIE	**KIELCE**	**POLAND**
K 1940–1943		212
KOWAL	**WŁOCŁAWEK**	**POLAND**
C 1919/1939		105
E 1919/1939		105
K 1919/1939		105
T 1919/1939		105
KOŹLE	**OPOLE**	**POLAND**
A 1908/1938		PROVINCE: ŚLĄSK
X 1908/1938		PROVINCE: ŚLĄSK
Z 1908/1938		PROVINCE: ŚLĄSK
KOŹMIN	**KALISZ**	**POLAND**
B 1821		
C 1801/1872		PROVINCE: POZNAŃ
S 1801/1872		PROVINCE: POZNAŃ
T 1801/1872		PROVINCE: POZNAŃ
KOŻUCHÓW	**ZIELONA GÓRA**	**POLAND**
K 1883–1884		PROVINCE: ŚLĄSK
KRAKÓW	**KRAKÓW**	**POLAND**
A 1701/1939		101
C 1701/1939		101
D 1903–1929 (REQUESTS FOR PERMISSION TO BURY)		101
E 1701/1939		101
H 1940–1941 (INCLUDES APPLICATIONS FOR RESIDENCY: 19,500 DOCUMENTS WITH PHOTOS)		206
K 1701/1939		101; 107; 109; 212
M 1897–1929		101
S 1701/1939		101
T 1701/1939		101
X 1701/1939		101
Z 1701/1939		101
KROTOSZYN	**KALISZ**	**POLAND**
D 1846/1938		PROVINCE: POZNAŃ
LESZNO	**LESZNO**	**POLAND**
Z 1807/1936		PROVINCE: POZNAŃ
LEWIN BRZESKI	**OPOLE**	**POLAND**
K 1902/1939		PROVINCE: ŚLĄSK
T 1902/1939		PROVINCE: ŚLĄSK
ŁÓDŹ	**ŁÓDŹ**	**POLAND**
H 1939–1945 (INCLUDES LIST OF 8,000 SURVIVORS)		205
LUBIEŃ KUJAWSKI	**WŁOCŁAWEK**	**POLAND**
C 1919/1939		105
E 1919/1939		105
K 1919/1939		105
T 1919/1939		105
LUBLIN	**LUBLIN**	**POLAND**
H 1939–1945 (INCLUDES LIST OF 3,000 JEWS IN CONCENTRATION CAMP IN LUBLIN WITH PHOTOS)		208
K 1940–1943		212
L 1940–1941 (3,000 NAMES OF PROPERTY OWNERS)		
LUBLIN REGION	**LUBLIN**	**POLAND**
L 1940 (CONFISCATION OF PROPERTY)		
LUBRANIEC	**WŁOCŁAWEK**	**POLAND**
C 1919/1939		105
E 1919/1939		105
K 1919/1939		105
T 1919/1939		105
LVOV	**LVOV**	**UKRAINE**
H 1940–1942		212
LVOV / ZNIESIENIE DIST.	**LVOV**	**UKRAINE**
D 1914		
MIĘDZYBÓRZ	**KALISZ**	**POLAND**
T 1877–1878		PROVINCE: ŚLĄSK

A Army/recruit lists; **B** Birth; **C** Census; **D** Death; **E** Voter lists; **G** Immigration; **H** Holocaust; **J** Judaica; **K** Kahal; **L** Land; **M** Marriage; **N** Name changes; **O** Police files; **P** Pogroms; **R** Reference; **S** School records; **T** Tax lists; **V** Divorce; **W** Occupation lists; **X** Jewish hospital; **Y** Notary records; **Z** Local government records

TOWN NAME Document Type Years	VOIVODSHIP/OBLAST (Province)	COUNTRY Zespół /Sygnatura (Poland) Fond/Opis/Delo (Belarus, Ukraine, Lithuania)
NAMYSŁÓW	**OPOLE**	**POLAND**
K 1851/1889		PROVINCE: ŚLĄSK
NEUSALZ	**SEE NOWA SÓL**	
NOWA SÓL	**ZIELONA GÓRA**	**POLAND**
D 1878–1927		PROVINCE: ŚLĄSK
K 1877/1937		PROVINCE: ŚLĄSK
NYSA	**OPOLE**	**POLAND**
K 1816/1856		PROVINCE: ŚLĄSK
Z 1816/1856		PROVINCE: ŚLĄSK
OLEŚNICA	**WROCŁAW**	**POLAND**
D 1812		PROVINCE: ŚLĄSK
E 1812/1920		PROVINCE: ŚLĄSK
K 1812/1920		PROVINCE: ŚLĄSK
M 1812		PROVINCE: ŚLĄSK
T 1812/1920		PROVINCE: ŚLĄSK
Y 1812/1920		PROVINCE: ŚLĄSK
Z 1812/1920		PROVINCE: ŚLĄSK
OLESNO	**CZĘSTOCHOWA**	**POLAND**
E 1854/1897		PROVINCE: ŚLĄSK
K 1854/1897		PROVINCE: ŚLĄSK
S 1854/1897		PROVINCE: ŚLĄSK
Y 1854/1897		PROVINCE: ŚLĄSK
OPOLE	**OPOLE**	**POLAND**
P 1846/1905		PROVINCE: ŚLĄSK
PLESZEW	**KALISZ**	**POLAND**
C 1785/1846		PROVINCE: POZNAŃ
S 1785/1846		PROVINCE: POZNAŃ
PODGÓRZE	**KRAKÓW**	**POLAND**
A 1893/1936		102
C 1893/1936		102
E 1893/1936		102
K 1893/1936		102; 108
T 1893/1936		102
Y 1893/1936		102
Z 1893/1936		102
POLAND (COUNTRY)	**WARSZAWA**	**POLAND**
G 1935–1937 (IMMIGRATION TO PALESTINE)		115
H 1945–1946 (ALPHA LIST OF 250,000 SURVIVORS)		
POZNAŃ	**POZNAŃ**	**POLAND**
K 1700–1938		116
PRZEDECZ	**KONIN**	**POLAND**
C 1919/1939		105
E 1919/1939		105
K 1919/1939		105
T 1919/1939		105
RADOM	**RADOM**	**POLAND**
K 1940-1943		212
REICHENBACH	**SEE DZIERŻONIÓW**	
SAGAN	**SEE ŻAGAŃ**	
SCHWIEBUS	**SEE ŚWIEBODZIN**	
ŚRODA ŚLĄSKA	**WROCŁAW**	**POLAND**
C 1807/1891		PROVINCE: ŚLĄSK
K 1807/1891		PROVINCE: ŚLĄSK
T 1807/1891		PROVINCE: ŚLĄSK
Y 1807/1891		PROVINCE: ŚLĄSK
Z 1807/1891		PROVINCE: ŚLĄSK
STASZÓW	**TARNOBRZEG**	**POLAND**
K 1940–1943		212
STRZEGOM	**WAŁBRZYCH**	**POLAND**
K 1842/1930		PROVINCE: ŚLĄSK
T 1842/1930		PROVINCE: ŚLĄSK
STRZELCE OPOLSKIE	**OPOLE**	**POLAND**
K 1855/1920		PROVINCE: ŚLĄSK
Y 1855/1920		PROVINCE: ŚLĄSK
Z 1855/1920		PROVINCE: ŚLĄSK

A Army/recruit lists; B Birth; C Census; D Death; E Voter lists; G Immigration; H Holocaust; J Judaica; K Kahal; L Land; M Marriage; N Name changes; O Police files; P Pogroms; R Reference; S School records; T Tax lists; V Divorce; W Occupation lists; X Jewish hospital; Y Notary records; Z Local government records

TOWN NAME Document Type Years	VOIVODSHIP/OBLAST (Province)	COUNTRY Zespół /Sygnatura (Poland) Fond/Opis/Delo (Belarus, Ukraine, Lithuania)
SWARZĘDZ	**POZNAŃ**	**POLAND**
K 1781/1851		PROVINCE: POZNAŃ
T 1781/1851		PROVINCE: POZNAŃ
Z 1781/1851		PROVINCE: POZNAŃ
ŚWIEBODZIN	**ZIELONA GÓRA**	**POLAND**
K 1934–1935		PROVINCE: ŚLĄSK
SYCÓW	**KALISZ**	**POLAND**
D 1886–1903		
E 1846/1914		PROVINCE: ŚLĄSK
K 1846/1914		PROVINCE: ŚLĄSK
T 1846/1914		PROVINCE: ŚLĄSK
X 1846/1914		PROVINCE: ŚLĄSK
Y 1846/1914		PROVINCE: ŚLĄSK
TERNOPOL	**TERNOPOL**	**UKRAINE**
L 1881–1939		110
S 1881–1939		110
X 1881–1939		110
Y 1881–1939		110
TOSZEK	**KATOWICE**	**POLAND**
K 1831/1877		PROVINCE: ŚLĄSK
TRACHENBERG	**SEE ŻMIGRÓD**	
TWARDOGÓRA	**WROCŁAW**	**POLAND**
C 1937		PROVINCE: ŚLĄSK
WAŁBRZYCH	**WAŁBRZYCH**	**POLAND**
K 1853/1928		PROVINCE: ŚLĄSK
T 1853/1928		PROVINCE: ŚLĄSK
W 1853/1928		PROVINCE: ŚLĄSK
Z 1853/1928		PROVINCE: ŚLĄSK
WARSAW	**WARSZAWA**	**POLAND**
H 1939–1942 (INCLUDES LIST OF 13,000 DEATHS IN WARSAW GHETTO)		201
K 1857–1878; 1940–1943		212
WIELOWIEŚ	**KATOWICE**	**POLAND**
D 1838–1852		
K 1838/1926		PROVINCE: ŚLĄSK
WITKÓW	**ZAMOŚĆ**	**POLAND**
K 1820–1868		
WITKOWO	**KONIN**	**POLAND**
B 1823–1829		PROVINCE: POZNAŃ
WŁOCŁAWEK	**WŁOCŁAWEK**	**POLAND**
K 1919–1939		105/113
WŁOSZCZOWA	**KIELCE**	**POLAND**
K 1940–1943		212
WOHLAU	**SEE WOŁÓW**	
WOŁCZYN	**OPOLE**	**POLAND**
B 1833–1838		
D 1833–1838		
E 1833/1926		PROVINCE: ŚLĄSK
K 1833/1926		PROVINCE: ŚLĄSK
T 1833/1926		PROVINCE: ŚLĄSK
W 1833/1926		PROVINCE: ŚLĄSK
Y 1833/1926		PROVINCE: ŚLĄSK
Z 1833/1926		PROVINCE: ŚLĄSK
WOŁÓW	**WROCŁAW**	**POLAND**
K 1858/1885		PROVINCE: ŚLĄSK
Z 1858/1885		PROVINCE: ŚLĄSK
WROCŁAW	**WROCŁAW**	**POLAND**
C 1794/1939		103
D 1816; 1831–1893		103
E 1794/1939		103
K 1794/1939		103; 105
L 1794/1939		103
S 1794/1939		103
T 1794/1939		103
W 1794/1939		103
X 1794/1939		103
Y 1794/1939		103

A Army/recruit lists; **B** Birth; **C** Census; **D** Death; **E** Voter lists; **G** Immigration; **H** Holocaust; **J** Judaica; **K** Kahal; **L** Land; **M** Marriage; **N** Name changes; **O** Police files; **P** Pogroms; **R** Reference; **S** School records; **T** Tax lists; **V** Divorce; **W** Occupation lists; **X** Jewish hospital; **Y** Notary records; **Z** Local government records

TOWN NAME Document Type Years	VOIVODSHIP/OBLAST (Province)	COUNTRY Zespół /Sygnatura (Poland) Fond/Opis/Delo (Belarus, Ukraine, Lithuania)
Z 1794/1939		103
WSCHOWA	**LESZNO**	**POLAND**
K 1827/1938		PROVINCE: POZNAŃ
S 1827/1938		PROVINCE: POZNAŃ
Y 1827/1938		PROVINCE: POZNAŃ
Z 1827/1938		PROVINCE: POZNAŃ
ZĄBKOWICE	**WAŁBRZYCH**	**POLAND**
K 1860/1928		PROVINCE: ŚLĄSK
S 1860/1928		PROVINCE: ŚLĄSK
Y 1860/1928		PROVINCE: ŚLĄSK
Z 1860/1928		PROVINCE: ŚLĄSK
ZABRZE	**KATOWICE**	**POLAND**
K 1870/1934		107/159
ŻAGAŃ	**ZIELONA GÓRA**	**POLAND**
C 1855/1930		PROVINCE: ŚLĄSK
K 1855/1930		PROVINCE: ŚLĄSK
S 1855/1930		PROVINCE: ŚLĄSK
Y 1855/1930		PROVINCE: ŚLĄSK
Z 1855/1930		PROVINCE: ŚLĄSK
ZARĘBY	**ŁOMŻA**	**POLAND**
B 1808–1939		
D 1808–1939		
M 1808–1939		
ZIELONA GÓRA	**ZIELONA GÓRA**	**POLAND**
E 1804/1916		PROVINCE: ŚLĄSK
K 1804/1916		PROVINCE: ŚLĄSK
Y 1804/1916		PROVINCE: ŚLĄSK
Z 1804/1916		PROVINCE: ŚLĄSK
ŻMIGRÓD	**WROCŁAW**	**POLAND**
K 1860/1935		PROVINCE: ŚLĄSK
Y 1860/1935		PROVINCE: ŚLĄSK
Z 1860/1935		PROVINCE: ŚLĄSK
ZOLOCHEV	**LVOV**	**UKRAINE**
D 1912–1916		
ŻYCHLIN	**PŁOCK**	**POLAND**
C 1918–1939		106/111
K 1918–1939		106/111
T 1918–1939		106/111

▌ *Konin, Jewish cemetery, pre-1941(destroyed)*   3

A Army/recruit lists; B Birth; C Census; D Death; E Voter lists; G Immigration; H Holocaust; J Judaica; K Kahal; L Land; M Marriage; N Name changes;
O Police files; P Pogroms; R Reference; S School records; T Tax lists; V Divorce; W Occupation lists; X Jewish hospital; Y Notary records; Z Local government records

ARCHIVAL HOLDINGS INDEXED BY REPOSITORY
Urząd Stanu Cywilnego - Warszawa Śródmieście

by Miriam Weiner

TOWN NAME	OBLAST (Province)	COUNTRY
Document Type Years		Zespół /Sygnatura (Poland) Fond/Opis/Delo (Belarus, Ukraine, Lithuania)

WARSZAWA - USC WARSZAWA ŚRÓDMIEŚCIE

BELYY KAMEN	**LVOV**		**UKRAINE**
B	1893–1903	1017	
D	1886–1913	1017	
BEREZHANY	**TERNOPOL**		**UKRAINE**
B	1894–1942	983	
D	1892–1922	983	
M	1877–1942	983	
BOBRKA	**LVOV**		**UKRAINE**
B	1895–1940	933	
D	1915–1940	933	
BOGORODCHANY	**IVANO FRANKOVSK**		**UKRAINE**
B	1919–1931; 1936	1049	
D	1919–1931; 1936	1049	
M	1921–1930; 1936	1049	
BOLEKHOV	**IVANO FRANKOVSK**		**UKRAINE**
B	1894–1898; 1901–1924; 1934–1940	1027	
D	1891–1940; 1942	1027	
M	1877–1906; 1917–1940	1027	
BOLSHOVTSY	**IVANO FRANKOVSK**		**UKRAINE**
B	1901–1942	1035	
D	1901–1935; 1941–1942	1035	
M	1901–1924; 1928–1939	1035	
BORISLAV	**LVOV**		**UKRAINE**
B	1895–1937; 1939	935	
D	1895–1898; 1900–1939	936	
M	1886–1906; 1908–1925; 1927–1939	936	
BORSHCHEV	**TERNOPOL**		**UKRAINE**
B	1895–1940	975	
D	1895–1942	975	
M	1877–1941	975	
BRODY	**LVOV**		**UKRAINE**
D	1941–1942	981	
BUCHACH	**TERNOPOL**		**UKRAINE**
B	1891–1942	986	
D	1900–1915; 1917–1942	986	
M	1907–1939	986	
BUDANOV	**TERNOPOL**		**UKRAINE**
B	1889–1896; 1898–1908; 1910–1942	1008	
D	1889–1914; 1918–1934	1008	
BUKACHEVTSY	**IVANO FRANKOVSK**		**UKRAINE**
B	1909–1941	1036	
D	1909–1942	1036	
M	1906–1936; 1939	1036	
BURSHTYN	**IVANO FRANKOVSK**		**UKRAINE**
B	1892–1912; 1915–1941	1037	
D	1893–1942	1037	
M	1878–1939	1037	
CHORTKOV	**TERNOPOL**		**UKRAINE**
B	1894–1935	988	
D	1891–1942	988	

A Army/recruit lists; **B** Birth; **C** Census; **D** Death; **E** Voter lists; **G** Immigration; **H** Holocaust; **J** Judaica; **K** Kahal; **L** Land; **M** Marriage; **N** Name changes; **O** Police files; **P** Pogroms; **R** Reference; **S** School records; **T** Tax lists; **V** Divorce; **W** Occupation lists; **X** Jewish hospital; **Y** Notary records; **Z** Local government records

TOWN NAME Document Type Years	OBLAST (Province)	Zespół /Sygnatura (Poland) Fond/Opis/Delo (Belarus, Ukraine, Lithuania)
M 1886–1942		988
DOBROMIL	**LVOV**	**UKRAINE**
B 1886–1925		937
M 1915–1940		937
DROGOBYCH	**LVOV**	**UKRAINE**
B 1895–1939; 1941		938
D 1895–1896; 1898–1937; 1939; 1942		938
M 1895–1897; 1899–1905; 1907–1916; 1918–1934; 1936–1939; 1941–1942		938
DUNAYEV	**TERNOPOL**	**UKRAINE**
B 1924–1934		996
D 1924–1934		996
M 1924–1934		996
GALICH	**IVANO FRANKOVSK**	**UKRAINE**
B 1923–1931		1033
D 1923–1936		1033
M 1923–1931		1033
GLINYANY	**LVOV**	**UKRAINE**
B 1893–1942		997
D 1887–1923; 1934–1942		997
D 1853–1933 (INDEX)		997
M 1877; 1899; 1902; 1907; 1909–1911; 1915–1940		997
GOLOGORY	**LVOV**	**UKRAINE**
B 1898–1942		1018
D 1894–1942		1018
M 1877–1939; 1942		1018
GORODENKA	**IVANO FRANKOVSK**	**UKRAINE**
B 1892–1940		1028
D 1893–1940		1028
D 1889–1940 (ALPHA INDEX)		1028
M 1878–1940		1028
GORODOK	**LVOV**	**UKRAINE**
B 1893–1901; 1903–1942		939
D 1890–1942		939
M 1915–1939		939
GRIMAYLOV	**TERNOPOL**	**UKRAINE**
B 1919–1936		1001
D 1919–1936		1001
M 1905–1931		1001
GVOZDETS	**IVANO FRANKOVSK**	**UKRAINE**
B 1920–1942		1030
D 1936–1942		1030
D 1920–1928 (ALPHA INDEX)		1030
M 1879–1942		1030
IVANO FRANKOVO	**LVOV**	**UKRAINE**
B 1916–1940		940
D 1916–1942		940
M 1918–1940		940
IVANO FRANKOVSK	**IVANO FRANKOVSK**	**UKRAINE**
B 1893–1941		1043
D 1892–1939		1043
M 1889–1939; 1941–1942		1043
M 1857–1900 (ALPHA INDEX)		1043
JANÓW	**LVOV**	**UKRAINE**
B SEE: IVANO FRANKOVO		
B 1898–1942		1009
D 1877–1939; 1941–1942		1009
M 1886–1939		1009
KAMENKA BUGSKAYA	**LVOV**	**UKRAINE**
B 1893–1942		990
B 1877–1942 (INDEX)		990
D 1891–1941		990
M 1878–1942		990
M 1877–1942 (INDEX)		990
KHODOROV	**LVOV**	**UKRAINE**
B 1914–1926		934
D 1926–1940		934

A Army/recruit lists; **B** Birth; **C** Census; **D** Death; **E** Voter lists; **G** Immigration; **H** Holocaust; **J** Judaica; **K** Kahal; **L** Land; **M** Marriage; **N** Name changes;
O Police files; **P** Pogroms; **R** Reference; **S** School records; **T** Tax lists; **V** Divorce; **W** Occupation lists; **X** Jewish hospital; **Y** Notary records; **Z** Local government records

TOWN NAME Document Type Years	OBLAST (Province)	COUNTRY Zespół /Sygnatura (Poland) Fond/Opis/Delo (Belarus, Ukraine, Lithuania)
M 1877–1909; 1914–1939		934
KHOROSTKOV	**TERNOPOL**	**UKRAINE**
B 1886–1940		992
KOLOMYYA	**IVANO FRANKOVSK**	**UKRAINE**
B 1895–1915; 1919–1942		1031
D 1898–1928; 1931–1942		1031
M 1895–1902; 1904–1906; 1908–1915; 1916; 1921–1924; 1926; 1928–1939		1031
KOMARNO	**LVOV**	**UKRAINE**
B 1878–1903; 1905–1940		962
D 1905; 1915–1942		962
M 1877–1914; 1916–1939		962
KOPYCHINTSY	**TERNOPOL**	**UKRAINE**
B 1885–1896; 1901–1928		991
D 1889–1933		991
M 1879–1938		991
KOSOV	**IVANO FRANKOVSK**	**UKRAINE**
B 1892–1922; 1927–1937		1032
D 1892–1927		1032
M 1891–1929		1032
KOZLOV	**TERNOPOL**	**UKRAINE**
B 1889–1941		1005
D 1886–1942		1005
KOZOVA	**TERNOPOL**	**UKRAINE**
B 1894–1940		984
D 1891–1940		984
M 1877–1940		984
KRAKOVETS	**LVOV**	**UKRAINE**
B 1909–1940		944
D 1889–1940		944
M 1877–1939		944
LISETS	**IVANO FRANKOVSK**	**UKRAINE**
B 1920–1931		1036
D 1919–1931		1036
M 1919–1931		1036
LVOV	**LVOV**	**UKRAINE**
B 1895–1939; 1941		927
D 1895–1939; 1942		927
D 1895–1906; 1913–1918; 1935–1937 (ALPHA INDEX)		927
M 1895–1939; 1924–1929 (ALPHA INDEX)		927
MARINOPOL	**IVANO FRANKOVSK**	**UKRAINE**
B 1922–1931; 1936		1035
D 1922–1931; 1936		1035
M 1922–1931; 1936		1035
MELNITSA PODOLSKAYA	**TERNOPOL**	**UKRAINE**
B 1891–1941		976
D 1890–1942		976
M 1877–1939		
MIKULINTSY	**TERNOPOL**	**UKRAINE**
B 1895–1898; 1900; 1902–1925; 1927		1006
D 1895; 1900–1910; 1914–1920; 1922–1925; 1928–1940		1006
M 1901–1914; 1917–1930; 1935; 1937–1940; 1942; 1933–1934 (ALPHA INDEX)		1006
MONASTYRISKA	**TERNOPOL**	**UKRAINE**
B 1924–1939		987
D 1918–1940		987
M 1918–1942		987
MOSTISKA	**LVOV**	**UKRAINE**
B 1889–1909		974
M 1877–1938		974
NADVORNAYA	**IVANO FRANKOVSK**	**UKRAINE**
B 1892–1938		1034
D 1892–1940; 1942		1034
M 1890–1939; 1942		1034
NARAYEV	**TERNOPOL**	**UKRAINE**
B 1887–1939		985
D 1877–1935		985
M 1877–1939		985

A Army/recruit lists; **B** Birth; **C** Census; **D** Death; **E** Voter lists; **G** Immigration; **H** Holocaust; **J** Judaica; **K** Kahal; **L** Land; **M** Marriage; **N** Name changes; **O** Police files; **P** Pogroms; **R** Reference; **S** School records; **T** Tax lists; **V** Divorce; **W** Occupation lists; **X** Jewish hospital; **Y** Notary records; **Z** Local government records

TOWN NAME Document Type Years	OBLAST (Province)	COUNTRY Zespół /Sygnatura (Poland) Fond/Opis/Delo (Belarus, Ukraine, Lithuania)
NAWARIYA	**LVOV**	**UKRAINE**
B 1895; 1901–1922; 1924–1938		930
D 1901; 1909–1918; 1920–1938		930
M 1895; 1898–1903; 1905–1908; 1911–1938		930
NESTEROV	**LVOV**	**UKRAINE**
B 1895–1899; 1901–1910; 1912–1930; 1932; 1934–1940		973
D 1895–1897; 1899–1932; 1936–1942		973
M 1893–1898; 1900–1939		973
NIKOLAYEV	**LVOV**	**UKRAINE**
M 1938–1939		1046
NOVYY YARYCHEV	**LVOV**	**UKRAINE**
B 1896; 1900; 1902–1903; 1906–1912; 1914–1915;1917–1936		929
D 1899–1907; 1909; 1911–1913; 1915; 1922; 1927; 1932; 1934; 1936		929
M 1897; 1913–1914; 1916–1921; 1924–1929; 1934–1935		929
NOVYYE STRELISHCHA	**LVOV**	**UKRAINE**
B 1899–1940		935
D 1894–1942		935
M 1894–1939		935
OBERTIN	**IVANO FRANKOVSK**	**UKRAINE**
B 1891–1941		1029
D 1893–1940; 1848–1912 (ALPHA INDEX)		1029
M 1890–1942		1029
OLESKO	**LVOV**	**UKRAINE**
B 1877–1942		1019
D 1877–1942		1019
M 1878–1940		1019
OZERNYANY	**TERNOPOL**	**UKRAINE**
D 1915–1942		1024
M 1877–1939		1024
OZERYANY	**INCLUDED IN BORSHCHEV**	
PEREMYSHLYANY	**LVOV**	**UKRAINE**
B 1902–1909; 1924–1942		998
D 1908–1942		998
M 1877–1913; 1920–1939		
PODGAYTSY	**TERNOPOL**	**UKRAINE**
B 1896; 1898–1899; 1902; 1906–1908; 1930–1934		995
D 1896–1900; 1904–1925		995
M 1899–1901; 1906; 1910; 1911–1921		995
PODKAMEN	**TERNOPOL**	**UKRAINE**
B 1900–1942		982; 1038
D 1921–1942		982
M 1914–1915; 1920–1939		982
PODVOLOCHISK	**TERNOPOL**	**UKRAINE**
B 1889–1942		1002
D 1920–1922		1002
M 1883–1942		1002
POMORYANY	**LVOV**	**UKRAINE**
B 1918–1942		1014
D 1919–1941		1014
M 1923–1939		1014
PROBEZHNAYA	**TERNOPOL**	**UKRAINE**
B 1890–1936		994
D 1938		994
RAWA RUSSKA	**LVOV**	**UKRAINE**
B 1892–1912; 1920–1925		960
D 1895–1925		960
M 1877–1935		960
ROGATIN	**IVANO FRANKOVSK**	**UKRAINE**
B 1898–1922; 1931–1939		1039
D 1899–1942		1039
M 1908–1912; 1923; 1925; 1927; 1935; 1938–1939		1039
ROZDOL	**LVOV**	**UKRAINE**
B 1892–1942		1047
D 1884–1942		1047
M 1903–1938		1047

A Army/recruit lists; **B** Birth; **C** Census; **D** Death; **E** Voter lists; **G** Immigration; **H** Holocaust; **J** Judaica; **K** Kahal; **L** Land; **M** Marriage; **N** Name changes; **O** Police files; **P** Pogroms; **R** Reference; **S** School records; **T** Tax lists; **V** Divorce; **W** Occupation lists; **X** Jewish hospital; **Y** Notary records; **Z** Local government records

TOWN NAME	OBLAST (Province)	COUNTRY
Document Type Years		Zespół /Sygnatura (Poland) Fond/Opis/Delo (Belarus, Ukraine, Lithuania)

RUDKI	**LVOV**		**UKRAINE**
B	1890–1923; 1932–1939		963
D	1877–1940		963
M	1877–1939		963
SAMBOR	**LVOV**		**UKRAINE**
B	1895–1909; 1911–1942		967
D	1895–1915; 1920–1940		967
M	1892–1940		967
SASOV	**LVOV**		**UKRAINE**
B	1888–1913; 1921–1942		1020
D	1879–1913; 1921–1940		1020
M	1884–1912; 1922–1939		1020
SHCHERETS	**LVOV**		**UKRAINE**
B	1895–1899; 1901; 1903–1904; 1906–1915; 1917–1925; 1927–1930		931
D	1896–1897; 1900–1903; 1905–1926; 1928; 1930–1932; 1934–1935		931
M	1896–1898; 1900		931
SKALA PODOLSKAYA	**TERNOPOL**		**UKRAINE**
B	1893–1939		979
D	1893–1900; 1912–1941		979
M	1882–1940; 1882–1913 (INDEX)		979
SKALAT	**TERNOPOL**		**UKRAINE**
B	1895–1896; 1898–1942		1003
D	1895–1942		1003
M	1902–1939		
SKOLE	**LVOV**		**UKRAINE**
B	1895–1942		1044
B	1900–1909 (ALPHA INDEX)		1044
D	1895–1942		1044
D	1898; 1901; 1904–1905 (ALPHA INDEX)		1044
M	1895–1940; 1942		1044
SNYATYN	**IVANO FRANKOVSK**		**UKRAINE**
B	1918–1940		1040
B	1863–1915 (SUPPLEMENTAL REGISTRATIONS)		1040
D	1917–1928		1041
M	1905–1914; 1920–1940; 1942; 1862–1909 (SUPPLEMENTAL REGISTRATIONS)		1041
SOKAL	**LVOV**		**UKRAINE**
B	1895–1911; 1914–1915; 1917–1919; 1922–1942		969
D	1895–1935; 1937–1939		969
M	1895–1909; 1911–1942		969
SOKOLOVKA	**LVOV**		**UKRAINE**
B	1877–1900; 1910–1913; 1920–1927		1021
D	1877–1916; 1921–1931		1021
M	1877–1916; 1922–1934		1021
SOLOTWINA	**IVANO FRANKOVSK**		**UKRAINE**
B	1916–1931		1048
D	1916–1931		1048
M	1919–1931 & ALSO INCLUDED IN KOLOMYYA		1048
STANISLAWÓW	**SEE IVANO FRANKOVSK**		
STARE MIASTO	**TERNOPOL**		**UKRAINE**
B	1892–1903		995
D	1884–1895		995
M	1877–1907		995
STARYY SAMBOR	**LVOV**		**UKRAINE**
B	1910–1940		968
D	1896–1942		968
M	1908–1940		968
STOYANOV	**TERNOPOL**		**UKRAINE**
M	1901–1913; 1931–1939		1000
STRUSOV	**TERNOPOL**		**UKRAINE**
B	1890–1933		1010
D	1877–1933		1010
M	1877–1939		1010
STRYJ	**LVOV**		**UKRAINE**
B	1895–1939; 1895; 1906 (ALPHA INDEX)		1045
D	1895–1940		1045
M	1895–1942		1045

A Army/recruit lists; **B** Birth; **C** Census; **D** Death; **E** Voter lists; **G** Immigration; **H** Holocaust; **J** Judaica; **K** Kahal; **L** Land; **M** Marriage; **N** Name changes; **O** Police files; **P** Pogroms; **R** Reference; **S** School records; **T** Tax lists; **V** Divorce; **W** Occupation lists; **X** Jewish hospital; **Y** Notary records; **Z** Local government records

TOWN NAME Document Type Years	OBLAST (Province)	COUNTRY Zespół /Sygnatura (Poland) Fond/Opis/Delo (Belarus, Ukraine, Lithuania)
M 1895–1896 (ALPHA INDEX)		1045
SUDOVAYA VISHNYA	**LVOV**	**UKRAINE**
B 1901–1939; 1941		954
D 1915–1939; 1941		954
M 1915–1939		954
SVIRZH	**LVOV**	**UKRAINE**
B 1895–1942		998
D 1877–1942		999
M 1878–1940		999
TARTAKOV	**LVOV**	**UKRAINE**
B 1891–1936; 1938–1940		970
D 1877–1905; 1908–1910; 1912; 1914–1930; 1932–1939		970
M 1877–1904; 1906–1915; 1917–1930; 1932–1935		970
TEREBOVLYA	**TERNOPOL**	**UKRAINE**
B 1892–1940		1011
D 1912–1938		1011
M 1877–1914; 1917–1940		1011
TERNOPOL	**TERNOPOL**	**UKRAINE**
B 1895–1899; 1901–1918; 1920–1939; 1876–1941		1007
D 1895–1918; 1920–1928; 1931–1939		1007
M 1895–1914; 1917–1931; 1933; 1936–1939		1007
TOLSTOYE	**TERNOPOL**	**UKRAINE**
B 1868–1920; 1922–1939		1004
D 1924–1934		1004
M 1890–1939		1004
TURKA	**LVOV**	**UKRAINE**
B 1914–1942		971
D 1915–1935		971
M 1916–1937		972
UGNEV	**LVOV**	**UKRAINE**
B 1889–1898; 1903–1935		961
D 1877–1925		961
M 1882–1931		961
ULASHKOVTSY	**TERNOPOL**	**UKRAINE**
B 1895		1025
D 1896; 1898–1900		1025
VELIKIYE MOSTY	**LVOV**	**UKRAINE**
B 1895–1915; 1917–1940		972
D 1892–1934; 1931–1939 (ALPHA INDEX)		972
M 1879–1918; 1920–1938		
VERKHOVINA	**IVANO FRANKOVSK**	**UKRAINE**
B 1877–1927		1033
D 1884–1918		1033
M 1891–1911; 1914–1936		1033
VINNIKI	**LVOV**	**UKRAINE**
B 1898–1901; 1904; 1907–1921; 1931–1932; 1934–1937		932
D 1895; 1897; 1899; 1902–1903; 1908–1914; 1916–1828; 1931–1934; 1936; 1938		932
M 1895–1901; 1904–1908; 1910–1913; 1915; 1917–1926; 1928–1929; 1933–1938		932
YAGELNITSA	**TERNOPOL**	**UKRAINE**
B 1891–1933; 1934; 1937–1938		989
D 1891–1933		989
M 1877–1939		989
YAVOROV	**LVOV**	**UKRAINE**
B 1893–1941		943
D 1895–1942		943
M 1877–1937		943
ZABOLOTOV	**IVANO FRANKOVSK**	**UKRAINE**
B 1908–1911		1042
D 1893–1919		1042
M 1896–1931		1042
ZALOZHTSY	**TERNOPOL**	**UKRAINE**
B 1902–1923; 1925–1942		1015
D 1877–1942		1015
M 1914–1939		1015
ZAVALOV	**TERNOPOL**	**UKRAINE**
B 1870–1914		1023

A Army/recruit lists; **B** Birth; **C** Census; **D** Death; **E** Voter lists; **G** Immigration; **H** Holocaust; **J** Judaica; **K** Kahal; **L** Land; **M** Marriage; **N** Name changes; **O** Police files; **P** Pogroms; **R** Reference; **S** School records; **T** Tax lists; **V** Divorce; **W** Occupation lists; **X** Jewish hospital; **Y** Notary records; **Z** Local government records

TOWN NAME Document Type Years	OBLAST (Province)	COUNTRY Zespół /Sygnatura (Poland) Fond/Opis/Delo (Belarus, Ukraine, Lithuania)
ZBARAZH	**TERNOPOL**	**UKRAINE**
B 1895–1912; 1914–1942		1013
D 1908–1911		1013
M 1876–1942		1013
ZBOROV	**TERNOPOL**	**UKRAINE**
B 1890–1925; 1936–1942		1016
D 1886–1934		1016
M 1907–1935		1016
ZHIDACHOV	**LVOV**	**UKRAINE**
B 1890–1942; 1855–1941 (ALPHA INDEX)		1054
D 1919–1942		1054
M 1915–1939		1054
ZHOVTEN	**IVANO FRANKOVSK**	**UKRAINE**
B 1923–1931		1034
D 1923–1931		1034
M 1923–1931		1034
ZHURAVNO	**LVOV**	**UKRAINE**
D 1877–1900 (ALPHA INDEX)		1055
ZOLOCHEV	**LVOV**	**UKRAINE**
B 1892–1908; 1910–1942		1022
D 1893–1896; 1898–1937		1022
M 1877–1912; 1916–1938		1022

■ *Lutowiska Jewish cemetery, 1997*

4

A Army/recruit lists; **B** Birth; **C** Census; **D** Death; **E** Voter lists; **G** Immigration; **H** Holocaust; **J** Judaica; **K** Kahal; **L** Land; **M** Marriage; **N** Name changes; **O** Police files; **P** Pogroms; **R** Reference; **S** School records; **T** Tax lists; **V** Divorce; **W** Occupation lists; **X** Jewish hospital; **Y** Notary records; **Z** Local government records

Poznań, old market square, 1920 — 1

Bielsko (Bielitz), 1920 — 2

Bielsko-Biała, c. 1918 — 3

Skierniewice, ul. Koszarowa, 1915 — 4

The language of the publication is shown in ( ) at the end of the bibliographic entry, as follows:

(F)	French	(P)	Polish
(G)	German	(R)	Russian
(H)	Hebrew	(Y)	Yiddish

All other books are in English. If a publication is in both English and another language, then (E) is added at the end of the bibliographic entry to show that the book has an English section.

GENERAL

Abramovitch, Raphael. *The Vanished World*. New York: Forward Association, 1947.

Abramsky, Chimen, Maciej Jachimczyk, and Antony Polonsky. *The Jews in Poland*. Oxford: Blackwell, 1986.

Bader, Gershom. *Draysig doyres yiden in Poylen* (Thirty Generations of Jews in Poland). New York: Orion Press, 1927. (Y)

Bałaban, Majer. *Di yidn in Poyln* (The Jews in Poland). Vilna: B. Kletskin, 1930. (Y)

————. *Studia historyczne* (Historical Studies). Warsaw: M. S. Fried, 1927. (P)

————. *Zabytki historyczne Żydów w Polsce* (The Jewish Historic Landmarks of Poland). Warsaw: Warszawskie Zjednoczone Zakłady Graficzne "Spółdruk," 1929. (P)

Borwicz, Michael. *1000 Years of Jewish Life in Poland*. Paris: Centre D'Études Historiques, 1955. (E, F)

Brocke, Michael. *Beter und Rebellen: Aus 1000 Jahren Judentum in Polen* (The Pious and the Rebels: 1000 Years of Jews in Poland). Frankfurt: Deutscher Koordinierungsrat der Gesellschaften für Christlich-Jüdische Zusammenarbeit, 1983. (G)

Dąbrowska, Danuta, and Abraham Wein. *Pinkas ha-kehilot: entsiklopediyah shel ha-yishuvim le-min hivasdam ve-`ad le-ahar shoat milhemet ha-`olam ha-sheniyah-Polin* (Encyclopaedia of Jewish Communities–Poland). Vols. 1–4. Jerusalem: Yad Vashem, 1976–1989. (H)

Dobroszycki, Lucjan, and Barbara Kirshenblatt-Gimblett. *Image Before My Eyes: A Photographic History of Jewish Life in Poland, 1864–1939*. New York: Schocken, 1977.

Ertel, Rachel. *Le Shtetl: La bourgade juive de Pologne de la tradition à la modernité* (The Jewish Small Town in Poland from Tradition to Modernity). Paris: Payot, 1982. (F)

Poznań (Posen), 1916   5

Ropczyce, market square, c. 1917   6

Poznań (Posen), 1916   7

Mława, town square, 1915   8

Fuks, Marian. *Polish Jewry: History and Culture*. Warsaw: Interpress, 1982. (E)

Goren, Natan. *Yahadut Lita* (The Jews of Lithuania). Tel Aviv: Hotsa'at Am Ha-Sefer, 1960. (H)

Gruber, Ruth Ellen. *Upon the Doorposts of Thy House: Jewish Life in East-Central Europe, Yesterday and Today*. New York: John Wiley & Sons, 1994.

Halpern, Israel. *Bet Yisrael be-Polin mi-yamim rishonim ve-'ad li-yemot ha-ḥurban* (The House of Israel in Poland from the Earliest Times to the Time of its Destruction). 2 vols. Jerusalem: Youth Department of the Zionist Organization, 1948–1953. (H)

Hertz, Aleksander. *The Jews in Polish Culture*. Evanston, IL: Northwestern University Press, 1988.

Horowitz, Hirsch. *Le-toledot ha-kehilot be-Polin* (The History of the Jewish Communities in Poland). Jerusalem: Mosad Harav Kook, 1978. (H)

Lewin, Isaac. *The Jewish Community of Poland*. New York: Philosophical Library, 1985.

Lowenthal, Ernst. *Juden in Preussen* (Jews in Prussia). Berlin: D. Reimer, 1981. (G)

Matwijowska, Krystyna. *Z historii ludności żydowskiej w Polsce i na Śląsku* (From the History of the Jewish Population in Poland and in Silesia). Wrocław: Wydawnictwo Universytetu Wrocławskiego, 1994. (P)

Michalewicz, Jerzy. *Żydowskie okręgi metrykalne i Żydowskie gminy wyznaniowe w galicjidoby autonomicznej* (Jewish Metrical Regions and Jewish Relgious Communities in Galicia). Kraków: Księgarnia Akademicka, 1995. (P, E)

Opalski, Magdalena. *Poles and Jews: A Failed Brotherhood*. Hanover, NH: University Press of New England, 1992.

Paluch, Andrzej K. *The Jews in Poland*. Kraków: Research Center on Jewish History and Culture in Poland, 1992.

Piszczek, Radosław. *Preserving Traces of Jewish Culture in Poland: For the Living and the Dead*. Warsaw: Krajowa Agencja Wydawnicza, 1988.

Pogonowski, Iwo Cyprian. *Jews in Poland: A Documentary History*. New York: Hippocrene Books, 1993.

Polish Association in Great Britain. *Jews in Poland (Yesterday and Today)*. London: The White Eagle Press, 1968.

Polonsky, Antony. *From Shtetl to Socialism*. London: Littman Library of Jewish Civilization, 1993.

Porter, Ruth, and Nili Kadari. *Journey to Poland: In Search of a Vanished World*. Tel Aviv: Beth Hatefutsoth, 1990.

Rosman, Moshe. *Polin: The Jews of Eastern Europe: History and Culture*. Tel Aviv: Open University, 1991.

Rubin, Eli. *700 Years of Jewish Life in Poland*. London: W. & G. Foyle, 1944.

Schall, Jakób. *Historja Żydów w Polsce, na Litwie i Rusi* (History of the Jews in Poland, Lithuania and Russia). Lwów: Polska Niepodległa, 1934. (P)

Schoenfeld, Joachim. *Jewish Life in Galicia Under the Austro-Hungarian Empire and in Reborn Poland 1898–1939*. Hoboken, NJ: Ktav, 1985.

Schwartz, Rosaline, and Susan Milamed. *From Alexandrovsk to Zyrardow: A Guide to YIVO's Landsmanshaftn Archive*. New York: YIVO, 1986.

Weinryb, Bernard D. *Texts and Studies in the Communal History of Polish Jewry*. New York: American Academy for Jewish Research, 1951.

PRE–WORLD WAR I

Agnon, S. J., and Ahron Eliasberg. *Das Buch von den polnischen Juden* (The Book of the Polish Jews). Berlin: Jüdischer Verlag, 1916. (G)

Bałaban, Majer. *Dzieje Żydów w Galicyi i w Rzeczypospolitej Krakowskiej 1772–1868* (History of the Jews in Galicia and in the Commonwealth of Kraków, 1772–1868). Lwów: Księgarnia Polska, 1916. (P)

———. *Skizzen und Studien zur Geschichte der Juden in Polen* (Sketches and Studies in the History of the Jews in Poland). Berlin: Louis Lamm, 1911. (G)

Baron, Salo W. *A Social and Religious History of the Jews*. Vol. 16: *Poland–Lithuania 1500–1650*. 2nd ed. New York: Columbia University Press, 1976.

Brann, Marcus. *Geschichte der Juden in Schlesien* (History of the Jews of Silesia). Breslau: W. Jacobsohn, 1896. (G)

Brawer, Abraham Yaakov. *Galitsiyah vi-yehudeha* (Galicia and Its Jews). Jerusalem: Mosad Bialik, 1956. (H)

Cała, Alina. *Asymilacja Żydów w Królestwie Polskim (1864–1897)* (The Assimilation of the Jews in the Kingdom of Poland [1864–1897]). Warsaw: Państwowy Instytut Wydawniczy, 1989. (P)

Cygielman, Shmuel Arthur. *Yehude Polin ve-Lita `ad shenat 408 (1648): mevo'ot u-mekorot mevo'arim* (The Jews of Poland and Lithuania Until 408 [1648]). Jerusalem: Zalman Shazar Center for Jewish History, 1991. (H)

Synagogue in Nasielsk, undated sketch (burned at end of 19th century)   9

Synagogue in Janowiec, 1916 (since destroyed)   10

Suwałki, market square, c. 1917   11

Synagogue in Ostrołęka, early 20th century (since destroyed)   12

Synagogue in Szczebrzeszyn, post-1945   13
(reconstructed for different purpose)

Synagogue in Szczebrzeszyn, pre-1939   14

Synagogue in Szydłów, undated (renovated)   15

Dubnow, Simon M. *History of the Jews in Russia and Poland from the Earliest Times Until the Present Day.* 3 vols. Philadelphia: Jewish Publication Society, 1918. Reprint, 2 vols. New York: Ktav, 1975.

Eisenbach, Arthur. *The Emancipation of the Jews in Poland, 1780–1870.* Oxford: Blackwell, 1991.

Eisenbach, Artur. *Z dziejów ludności żydowskiej w Polsce w XVIII i XIX wieku* (The History of the Jewish Population in Poland in the Eighteenth and Nineteenth Centuries). Warsaw: Państwowy Instytut Wydawniczy, 1983. (P)

Feldstejn, Hermann. *The Poles and the Jews.* Chicago: Polish Young Men's Publishing Co., 1915.

Fettke, Dieter. *Juden und Nichtjuden im 16. und 17. Jahrhundert in Polen: Soziale und ökonimische Beziehungen in Responsen polnischer Rabbiner* (Jews and Non-Jews in the Sixteenth and Seventeenth Centuries in Poland: Social and Economic Relations in the Responsa of the Polish Rabbis). Frankfurt-am-Main: Verlag Peter Lang, 1986. (G)

Finkielstein, Leo. *Megilat Polin* (Scroll of Poland). Buenos Aires: Central Farband of Polish Jews in Argentina, 1947. (Y)

Frenk, Azriel Nathan. *Ha-`ironim veha-yehudim be-Polin: masah histori* (Burghers and Jews in Poland: Historical Study). Warsaw: ha-Misrad le-hotsa'at sifrut ve-`itonut she-`al yad ha-Histadrut ha-Tsiyonit be-Polin, 1921. (H)

Gelber, N. M. *Die Juden und der polnische Aufstand 1863* (The Jews in the Polish Uprising of 1863). Vienna: R. Lowit, 1923. (G)

Goldberg, Jacob. *Jewish Privileges in the Polish Commonwealth: Charters of Rights Granted to Jewish Communities in Poland-Lithuania in the Sixteenth to Eighteenth Centuries, Critical Edition of Original Latin and Polish Documents with English Introductions and Notes.* Jerusalem: Israel Academy of Sciences and Humanities, 1985.

Hagen, William W. *Germans, Poles and Jews: The Nationality Conflict in the Prussian East, 1772–1914.* Chicago: University of Chicago Press, 1980.

Halperin, Israel. *Pinkas Va'ad Arba' Aratsot* (The Records of the Council of the Four Lands 1580–1792). Jerusalem: Bialik Institute, 1945. (H)

Häusler, W. *Das galizische Judentum in der Habsburgermonarchie (1772–1848)* (Galician Jewry under the Habsburg Monarchy [1772–1848]). Munich: R. Oldenbourg, 1979. (G)

Heppner, Aron, and Isaac Herzberg. *Aus Vergangenheit und Gegenwart der Juden und der jüdischen Gemeinden in der Posener Landen* (From the Past and Present of the Jews and Jewish Congregations in Poznań Region). 2 vols. Bromberg and Koschmin, Germany: Selbstverlag der Verfasser, 1904-1931. (G)

Hirschberg, Isidor. *Verzeichnis sämmtlicher naturalisirten Israeliten im Grossherzogthum Posen* (Comprehensive Lists of Jews Granted Citizenship in the Grand Duchy of Posen). Bromberg, Germany: I. Hirschberg, 1836. (G)

Synagogue in Parzęczew, pre-1939 (since destroyed) 16

Synagogue in Przedbórz, pre-Holocaust (since destroyed) 17

Synagogue in Siemiatycze, pre-1939 (reconstructed) 18

Synagogue in Lubraniec, pre-1939 (reconstructed) 19

Hirschhorn, S. *Di geshikhte fun yidn in Poyln 1788–1914* (The History of Jews in Poland 1788–1914). Warsaw: Levin-Epstein Bros., 1923. (Y)

Horn, Maurycy. *Regesty dokumentów i ekscerpty z metryki koronnej do historii Żydów w Polsce 1697–1795. T. I.: Czasy saskie (1697–1763); T. II.: Rządy Stanisława Augusta (1764–1795, Część I: 1764–1779)* (Summaries of Records and Excerpts of the Crown Registry Relating to the History of the Jews in Poland, 1697–1795. Vol. 1: The Saxon Era [1697–1763]; Vol. 2: The Reign of Stanisław August [1764–1795, Part 1: 1764–1779]). Warsaw: Ossolineum, 1984. (P)

———. *Żydzi na Rusi Czerwonej w XVI i w pierwszej połowie XVII w* (The Jews in Ruthenia in the Sixteenth Century and the First Half of the Seventeenth Century). Warsaw: Państwowe Wydawnictwo Naukowe, 1975. (P)

Horodezky, Samuel A. *Shelosh me'ot shanah shel yahadut Polin* (Three Hundred Years of Polish Jewry). Tel Aviv: Dvir, 1946. (H)

Horowitz, Hirsch. *Le-toledot ha-kehilot be-Polin* (The History of the Jewish Communities in Poland). New York: Research Institute of Religious Jewry, 1969. (H)

Hundert, Gershon. *Security and Dependence: The Jews of One Private Town in the Polish Commonwealth.* Tel Aviv: Tel Aviv University, 1983.

Hundert, Gershon David. *The Jews in a Polish Private Town: The Case of Opatow in the Eighteenth Century.* Baltimore: Johns Hopkins University Press, 1992.

Kaźmierczyk, Adam. *Materiały źródłowe do dziejów Żydów w księgach grodzkich dawnego województwa krakowskiego z lat 1674–1696* (Documents Relating to Jewish History in the Municipal Records from the Kraków Province in the Years 1674–1696). Kraków: Universitas, 1995. (P)

Leszczyński, Anatol. *Sejm Żydów Korony 1623–1764* (Jewish Parliament in the Kingdom of Poland 1623–1764). Warsaw: Jewish Historical Institute, 1994. (P)

Levitats, Isaac. *The Jewish Community in Russia, 1772–1844.* New York: Columbia University Press, 1943.

———. *The Jewish Community in Russia, 1844–1917.* Jerusalem: Posner, 1981.

Lipschitz, Jacob Lippman. *Zikhron Ya'akov: historiyah yehudit be-Rusyah ve-Polin shenot 520–656, 1760–1896* (Jewish History in Russia and Poland, 1760–1896). Kowno-Sloboda: N. Lifshits, 1924–1930. (H)

Litman, Jacob. *The Economic Role of the Jews in Medieval Poland: The Contribution of Yitzhak Schipper.* Lanham, MD: University Press of America, 1984.

Luft, Edward David. *The Naturalized Jews of the Grand Duchy of Posen in 1834 and 1835.* Atlanta: Scholars Press, 1987.

Synagogue in Żółkiewka, undated (destroyed)   20

Synagogue in Kurów, pre-1939 (since destroyed)   21

Synagogue in Działoszyce, 1950   22

Synagogue in Pińczów, pre-1939 (since destroyed)   23

Mahler, Raphael. *Toledot ha-yehudim be-Polin 'ad me'ah ha-19* (History of the Jews in Poland Until the 19th Century). Merhavia, Israel: Hakibutz Ha-Artsi Ha-Shomer Ha-Tsa'ir, 1946. (H)

————. *Yidn in amolikn Poyln* (The Jews in Old Poland). Warsaw: Idisz Buch, 1958. (Y)

Mark, Bernard. *Di geshikhte fun Yidn in Poyln* (History of the Jews in Poland). Warsaw: Wydawnictwo "Idisz Buch," 1957. (Y)

Maser, Peter, and Adelheid Weiser. *Juden in Oberschlesien* (The Jews in Upper Silesia). Berlin: Gebr. Mann Verlag, 1992. (G)

Meisl, Josef. *Geschichte der Juden in Polen und Rusland* (History of the Jews in Poland and Russia). Berlin: C.A. Schwetschke & Sohn, 1921–1925. (G)

Opalski, Magdalena. *The Jewish Tavern-Keeper and his Tavern in Nineteenth Century Polish Literature.* Jerusalem: Center for Research in the History and Culture of Polish Jews and the Zalman Shazar Center, 1986.

Polonsky, Anthony, et al. *The Jews in Old Poland, 1000–1795.* London: Tauris, 1993.

Rosman, Murray Jay. *The Lords' Jews: Magnate-Jewish Relations in the Polish-Lithuanian Commonwealth During the Eighteenth Century.* Cambridge, MA: Harvard University Press for the Center for Jewish Studies, 1990.

Shulman, Nisson E. *Authority and Community: Polish Jewry in the Sixteenth Century.* Hoboken, NJ: Ktav, 1986.

Teimanas, David B. *L'Autonomie des communautés juives en Pologne au XVI et XVII si»cles* (The Autonomy of the Jewish Communities in Poland in the Sixteenth and Seventeenth Centuries). Paris: Jouve & Cie., 1933. (F)

Weinryb, Bernard D. *The Jews of Poland: A Social and Economic History of the Jewish Community in Poland from 1100 to 1800.* Philadelphia: Jewish Publication Society, 1982.

————. *Neueste Wirtschaftsgeschichte der Juden in Russland und Polen: von der 1. Polnischen Teilung bis zum Tode Alexanders II (1772–1881)* (Recent Economic History of the Jews in Russia and Poland [1772–1881]). 2nd ed. Hildesheim-New York: G. Olms, 1972, revision of 1934 edition. (G, E)

Wettstein, Feivel Hirsch. *Le-korot ha-yehudim be-Polin uvi-yeḥud be-Kraka, mi-shenat 1096 'ad shenat 1587* (History of the Jews in Poland and Particularly in Kraków from 1096 to 1587). Jerusalem, 1968. (H)

Wischnitzer, Mark. *A History of Jewish Crafts and Guilds.* New York: Jonathan David, 1965.

Zarchin, Michael Moses. *Jews in the Province of Posen.* Philadelphia: Jewish Publication Society, 1939.

Synagogue in Józefów, pre-1939 (destroyed)   24

Synagogue in Kępno, pre-1945 (renovated)   25

Synagogue in Łaszczów, pre-1939   26

Żydzi w Małopolsce: studia z dziejów osadnictwa i życia społecznego (Jews in Little Poland: Studies on the History of Settlement and Social Life). Przemyśl: Południowo-Wschodni Instytut Naukowy w Przemyślu, 1991. (P)

BETWEEN THE WARS

Brandes, Leon. "Der rekhtlekher matsev fun yidn in Poyln tsvishn beyde velt-milkhomes" (The Legal Status of Jews in Poland Between the Two World Wars). *YIVO Bleter* 42 (1962): 147–186. (Y)

Fishman, Joshua A. *Studies on Polish Jewry 1919–1939: The Interplay of Social, Economic and Political Factors in the Struggle of a Minority for its Existence (Shtudyes vegn Yidn in Poyln, 1919–1939)*. New York: YIVO, 1974. (E,Y)

Glicksman, William M. *In the Mirror of Literature: The Economic Life of the Jews in Poland as Reflected in Yiddish Literature (1914–1939)*. New York: Living Books, 1966.

————. *Jewish Social Welfare Institutions in Poland as Described in Memorial (Yizkor) Books (Studies in Jewish Communal Activity)*. Philadelphia: M. E. Kalish Folkshul, 1976.

Gutman, Yisrael, *et al. The Jews of Poland Between Two World Wars*. Hanover, NH: University Press of New England, 1989.

Heller, Celia S. *On the Edge of Destruction: Jews of Poland Between the Two World Wars*. 2nd ed. Detroit: Wayne State University Press, 1994.

Kugelmass, Jack, and Jonathan Boyarin. *From A Ruined Garden: The Memorial Books of Polish Jewry*. New York: Schocken, 1983. Reprint, New York: Columbia University Press, 1997.

Lewin, Isaac, and Nahum Michael Gelber. *A History of Polish Jewry During the Revival of Poland*. New York: Shengold Publishers, 1990.

Marcus, Joseph. *Social and Political History of the Jews in Poland, 1919–1939*. New York: Mouton, 1983.

Memoirs of Jewish Poland—1932: Photographs: Nachum Tim Gidal. Tel Aviv: Beth Hatefutsoth, 1984.

Mendelsohn, Ezra. *The Jews of East Central Europe Between the World Wars*. Bloomington: Indiana University Press, 1983.

Polonsky, Antony. *Polin-Studies in Polish Jewry, Vol. 8: Jews in Independent Poland 1918–1939*. London: The Littman Library of Jewish Civilization, 1994.

Rothschild, Joseph. *East Central Europe Between the Two World Wars*. Seattle: University of Washington Press, 1974.

Synagogue in Szczekociny, pre-1939 (storage room) 27

Synagogue in Szydłów, c. 1913 (reconstructed) 28

Synagogue in Inowłódz, pre-1939 (reconstructed) 29

Holocaust memorial in Staszów Jewish cemetery, 1996 30

Schipper, Ignancy, A. Tartakower, A. Hafftka, and Isaac Lewin, et al., eds. Żydzi w Polsce odrodzonej (The Jews in Reborn Poland). 2 vols. Warsaw: Nakładem Wydawnictwa "Żydzi w Polsce Odrodzonej," 1932 and 1934. (P)

Shakked, Shlomit. Poland: Aperture to a World Laid Waste. Tel Aviv: Eretz Israel Museum, 1988.

Spizman, Leib. Khalutsim in Poyln: antologye fun der khalutsisher bavegung. (Pioneers in Poland: Anthology of the Chalutz Movement). 3 vols. New York: Research Institute of the Labor Zionist Movement, 1959. (Y)

Tamir, Nachman. Polish Jewry Before the Holocaust. New York: Herzl Press, 1983.

Tencer, Golda. And I Still See Their Faces: Images of Polish Jews. Warsaw: Shalom Foundation, 1996. (E,P)

Vinecour, Earl. Polish Jews: The Final Chapter. New York: New York University Press, 1977.

Vishniac, Roman. Polish Jews: A Pictorial Record. New York: Schocken, 1965.

⸻. Roman Vishniac. New York: Grossman Publishers, 1974.

⸻. A Vanished World. New York: Farrar, Straus & Giroux, 1983.

Wieviorka, Annette, and Yitzhok Niborski. Les livres du souvenir: memoriaux juifs de Pologne (Yizkor Books: Jewish Memorials of Poland). Paris: Editions Gallimard/Julliard, 1983. (F)

Wiles, Timothy. Poland Between the Wars, 1918–1939. Bloomington: Indiana University Polish Studies Center, 1989.

Wolf, Lucien. The Legal Sufferings of the Jews in Russia: A Survey of Their Present Situation and a Summary of Laws. London: T. Fisher Unwin, 1912.

Żebrowski, Rafał. Dzieje Żydów w Polsce: wybór tekstów źródłowych, 1918–1939 (History of Polish Jewry: Selected Documents, 1918–1939). Warsaw: Żydowski Instytut Historyczny, 1993. (P)

⸻. Po-Lin: Kultura Żydów polskich w XX wieku (Poland: Culture of Polish Jewry in the Twentieth Century). Warsaw: Amarant, 1993. (P)

HOLOCAUST

Apenszlak, Jacob. The Black Book of Polish Jewry: An Account of the Martyrdom of Polish Jewry Under the Nazi Occupation. New York: The American Federation for Polish Jews in Cooperation with the Association of Jewish Refugees and Immigrants from Poland, 1943.

Apenszlak, Jacob, and Moshe Polakiewicz. Armed Resistance of the Jews in Poland. New York: American Federation for Polish Jews, 1944.

Kraków deportations, March 3, 1941   31

Concentration camp in Płaszów, 1943–1945   32

Jews of Kraków en route to ghetto, March 3, 1941   33

Majdanek death camp, guard towers, 1994   34

Arad, Yitzhak. *Belzec, Sobibor, Treblinka, The Operation Reinhard Death Camps.* Bloomington: Indiana University Press, 1987.

————. *The Pictorial History of the Holocaust.* Jerusalem: Yad Vashem; and New York: Macmillan, 1990.

Barkai, Meyer. *The Fighting Ghettos.* Philadelphia: J. B. Lippincott Co., 1962.

Berenstein, Tatiana. *Eksterminacja Żydów na ziemiach polskich w okresie okupacji hitlerowskiej: zbiór dokumentów* (Extermination of Jews in Poland During the Nazi Occupation: Selected Documents). Warsaw: Żydowski Instytut Historyczny, 1957. (P)

Council for the Preservation of Monuments to Resistance and Martyrdom. *Scenes of Fighting and Martyrdom Guide: War Years in Poland 1939–1945.* Warsaw: Sport i Turystyka Publications, 1968.

Czech, Danuta. *Auschwitz Chronicle 1939–1945.* New York: Henry Holt, 1990.

Davies, Norman, and Antony Polonsky, eds. *Jews in Eastern Poland and the USSR, 1939–1946.* Houndmills, Basingstoke, Hampshire: Macmillan, in association with the School of Slavonic and East European Studies, University of London, 1991.

Debski, Jerzy, *et al.*, eds. *Death Books from Auschwitz: Remnants.* Birkenau: State Museum of Auschwitz-Birkenau, 1993.

Eisenbach, Artur. "Operation Reinhard—Mass Extermination of the Jewish Population in Poland." *Polish Western Affairs* 3, no. 1 (1962): 80–124.

Engel, David. *Facing a Holocaust: The Polish Government-in-Exile and the Jews, 1943–1945.* Chapel Hill, NC: University of North Carolina Press, 1993.

————. *In the Shadow of Auschwitz: The Polish Government-in-Exile and the Jews, 1939–1942.* Chapel Hill, NC: University of North Carolina Press, 1987.

The Extermination of Polish Jewry: Album of Pictures. Berlin: Prepared for the American Joint Distribution Committee, 1946.

Falstein, Louis. *Martyrdom of Jewish Physicians in Poland.* New York: Exposition Press, 1963.

Friedman, Philip. *Martyrs and Fighters: The Epic of the Warsaw Ghetto.* New York: Praeger, 1954.

————. *Zagłada Żydów polskich w okresie okupacji niemieckiej 1939–1945* (The Destruction of Polish Jews During the German Occupation, 1939–1945). Monachium (Munich): Nakł. Federacji Żydów Polskich, 1947. (P)

Auschwitz-Birkenau crematoria, 1994　　35

Treblinka death camp, c. 1988　　36

Holocaust memorial at Majdanek, c. 1980s　　37

Gutman, Yisrael, ed. *Encyclopedia of the Holocaust.* 4 vols. New York: Macmillan, 1990.

Gutman, Yisrael, and Shmuel Krakowski. *Unequal Victims: Poles and Jews During World War Two.* New York: Holocaust Library, 1986.

Hellman, Peter. *The Auschwitz Album: A Book Based Upon an Album Discovered by a Concentration Camp Survivor.* New York: Random House, 1981.

Huberband, Shimon. *Kiddush Hashem—Jewish Religious and Cultural Life in Poland During the Holocaust.* Hoboken, NJ: Ktav, 1987.

Kasdan, Chaim Solomon. *Lerer-yisker-bukh* (Teacher Memorial Book). New York: Zydowski Centralna Organizacja Szkolna, 1952–1954. (Y)

Katz, Alfred. *Poland's Ghettos at War.* New York: Twayne, 1970.

Klibański, Bronia. "The Underground Archives of the Bialystok Ghetto Founded by Mersik and Tenenbaum." *Yad Vashem Studies* 2 (1958): 295–330.

Krakowski, Shmuel. *The War of the Doomed: Jewish Armed Resistance in Poland* (1942–1944). Jerusalem: Yad Vashem, 1984.

Meirtchak, Benjamin. *Jewish Military Casualties in the Polish Army in World War II.* 3 vols. Tel Aviv: World Federation of Jewish Fighters, Partisans and Camp Inmates, 1994–1996.

Mogilansky, Roman. *Ghetto Anthology.* Los Angeles: American Congress of Jews from Poland and Survivors of Concentration Camps, 1985.

Mokotoff, Gary. *How to Document Victims and Locate Survivors of the Holocaust.* Teaneck, NJ: Avotaynu, 1995.

Pinchuk, Ben-Zion. *Shtetl Jews Under Soviet Rule: Eastern Poland on the Eve of the Holocaust.* Oxford: Blackwell, 1990.

Prekerowa, Teresa. *Zarys dziejów Żydów w Polsce w latach 1939–1945* (A Brief History of Polish Jewry in the Years 1939–1945). Warsaw: Wydawnictwo Uniwersytetu Warszawskiego, 1992. (P)

Ringelblum, Emmanuel. *Polish-Jewish Relations During the Second World War.* Jerusalem: Yad Vashem, 1974.

Scharf, Rafael F., comp., and Willie George, photog. *In the Warsaw Ghetto Summer 1941.* New York: Aperture, 1993.

Schepansky, Israel. *Luaḥ ha-shoah shel yahadut Polin* (Holocaust Calendar of Polish Jewry). New York: I. Schepansky, 1974. (H)

Shpizman, Leib. *Di yidn in Natsi-Poyln* (The Jews in Nazi Poland). New York: Yidisher Kemfer, 1942. (Y)

Main gate to Kraków ghetto, 1941–1943   38

Synagogue in Widawa, c. 1950
(only walls remain in a new structure)   39

Synagogue in Strzyżów, c. 1967   40

Synagogue in Sejny, 1987   41

State Museum of Auschwitz-Birkenau. *Death Books from Auschwitz*. 3 vols. Munich: KG Saur, 1995.

Świebocka, Teresa. *Auschwitz: A History in Photographs*. Warsaw: Państwowe Muzeum Oswiecim-Brzezinka, 1993.

Taffet, Gerszon. *Zagłada Żydostwa polskiego, album zdjęć* (Extermination of Polish Jews, Album of Pictures). Łódź: Centralna zydowska Komisja historyczna w Polsce, 1945. (P)

Tec, Nechama. *When Light Pierced the Darkness. Christian Rescue of Jews in Nazi-Occupied Poland*. New York: Oxford University Press, 1986.

Tenenbaum, Joseph. *Underground—The Story of a People*. New York: Philosophical Library, 1952.

Trunk, Isaiah. *Judenrat*. New York: Macmillan, 1972.

Umińska, Apolonia, and Natalia Aleksiun-Mądrzak. *Inwentarz zbioru "Pamiętniki Żydów" 1939–1945. Archiwum Żydowskiego Instytutu Historycznego* (Inventory of the Collection "Memoirs of Jews" 1939–1945. Archives of the Jewish Historical Institute.) Warsaw: Jewish Historical Institute, 1994. (P)

United States Holocaust Memorial Museum. *Historical Atlas of the Holocaust*. New York: Simon & Schuster and Macmillan, 1996.

The Warsaw Ghetto: The 45th Anniversary of the Uprising. Warsaw: Interpress Publishers, 1988.

Wroński, Stanisław, and Maria Zwolakowa. *Polacy-Żydzi 1939–1945* (Poles and Jews 1939–1945). Warsaw: Książka i Wiedza, 1971. (P)

Zuckerman, Yitzhak. *A Surplus of Memory: Chronicle of the Warsaw Ghetto Uprising*. Trans. and ed. by Barbara Harshav. Berkeley: University of California Press, 1993.

Zuckerman, Yitzhak, and Moshe Basok. *Sefer milḥamot ha-getaot* (The Book of the Fighting Ghettos). Tel Aviv: Ha Kibuts Ha Me'uḥad, 1954. (H)

POST–WORLD WAR II

Banas, Josef. *The Scapegoats: The Exodus of the Remnants of Polish Jewry*. New York: Holmes & Meier, 1979.

Dobroszycki, Lucjan. *Survivors of the Holocaust in Poland: A Portrait Based on Jewish Community Records 1944–1947*. Armonk, NY: M. E. Sharpe, 1994.

Gutman, Yisrael. *Ha-yehudim be-Polin aḥare milḥemet ha-`olam ha-sheniyah* (The Jews in Poland After World War II). Jerusalem: Zalman Shazar Center for the Furtherance of the Study of.Jewish History, 1985. (H)

Synagogue in Dąbrowa Tarnowska, 1994 42

Synagogue in Dąbrowa Tarnowska, 1994 43

Synagogue in Stawiski, pre–1945 44

Synagogue in Raków (sketch), c. 1915 45

Irwin-Zarecka, Iwona. *Neutralizing Memory: The Jews in Contemporary Poland*. New Brunswick, NJ: Transaction Publishers, 1989.

Niezabitowska, Małgorzata. *Remnants: The Last Jews of Poland*. New York: Friendly Press, 1986.

Register of Jewish Survivors in Poland: List of Jews in Poland (58,000 Names). 2 vols. Jerusalem: The Jewish Agency for Palestine, Search Bureau of Missing Relatives, 1945.

Strauss-Marko, Shlomo. *Di geshikhte fun yidishn yishev in nokhmilkhomedikn Poyln* (The History of the Jewish People in Poland After the War). Tel Aviv: Strauss-Marko, 1987. (Y)

Surviving Jews in Lublin. New York: World Jewish Congress, n.d.

BIBLIOGRAPHIES

Baker, Zachary M. *Bibliography of Eastern European Memorial (Yizkor) Books*. New York: Jewish Genealogical Society, 1992.

Bałaban, Majer. *Bibliografia historii Żydów w Polsce i w krajach ościennych za lata 1900–1930* (Bibliography of the History of the Jews in Poland and in Neighboring Lands: Works Published During the Years 1900–1930). Jerusalem: World Federation of Polish Jews, 1978. (P)

Glikson, Paul. *Preliminary Inventory of the Jewish Daily and Periodical Press Published in the Polish Language: 1832–1982*. Jerusalem: Hebrew University Institute on Jewish Studies, 1983.

Hundert, Gershon David, and Gershon C. Bacon. *The Jews in Poland and Russia: Bibliographical Essays*. Bloomington: Indiana University Press, 1984.

Judaica: bibliografia publikacji polskich za lata 1980–1986 (Judaica: Bibliography of Polish Publications in the Years 1980–1986). Warsaw: Żydowski Instytut Historyczny, 1987. (P)

Lerski, Jerzy J., and Halina T. Lerski. *Jewish-Polish Coexistence, 1772–1939: A Topical Bibliography*. New York: Greenwood Press, 1986.

Muszyńska, Katarzyna. *Bibliographies of Polish Judaica*. Kraków: Research Center of Jewish History and Culture in Poland, 1993.

Pilarczyk, Krzysztof. *Przewodnik po bibliografiach polskich judaików* (Guide to Bibliographies of Polish Judaica). Kraków: Research Center of Jewish History and Culture in Poland, 1992. (P)

Szeintuch, Yechiel. *Preliminary Inventory of Yiddish Dailies and Periodicals Published in Poland Between the Two World Wars*. Jerusalem: Center for Research on the History and Culture of Polish Jews at Hebrew University, 1986.

Józefów, Jewish cemetery, c. 1959   46

Sokołów Małopolski, Jewish cemetery, c. 1980   47

Lutomiersk, Jewish cemetery, undated (destroyed)   48

Szydłów, Jewish cemetery, 1957   49

Teller, A., H. Volovici, and H. Assouline. *Guide to the Sources for the History of the Jews in Poland in the Central Archives.* Jerusalem: Central Archives for the History of the Jewish People, Hebrew University of Jerusalem, Center for Research on the History and Culture of Polish Jews, 1988.

Zeichner, Dvora, and A. Szechter. *Bibliography of Hebrew and Yiddish Publications in Poland Since 1944.* Jerusalem: Hebrew University of Jerusalem, 1987.

CEMETERIES

Alter, Avraham Mordecai. *Be-darke Polin ha-avelut: sipurah shel Polin ha-ḥarevah* (In the Paths of Poland's Mourning: The Story of Destroyed Poland). Jerusalem: Merkaz le-ḥeker he-ḥasidut ve-maḥshevet Yisrael, 1987. (H)

Bak, Maria. "Cmentarze żydowskie w województwie opolskim" (Jewish Cemeteries in the Opole Province). *BŻIH* 4/128 (1983): 119–122. (P)

Bałaban, Majer. *Historia Żydów w Krakowie i na Kazimierzu 1304–1868* (History of the Jews in Kraków and Kazimierz 1304–1868). 2 vols. Kraków: "Nadzieja" Towarzystwo ku Wspieraniu Chorej Młodzieży Żydowskiej Szkół Średnich i Wyższych w Krakowie, 1931–1936. (P)

———. *Die Judenstadt von Lublin* (The Jewish Town in Lublin). Berlin: Jüdischer Verlag, 1919. (G)

———. *Przewodnik po żydowskich zabytkach Krakowa* (Guide to Jewish Historic Landmarks in Kraków). Kraków: Nakładem Stowarzyszenia "Solidarność-B'nei B'rith," 1935. (P)

———. *Zabytki historyczne Żydów w Polsce* (The Jewish Historic Landmarks of Poland). Warsaw: Warszawskie Zjednoczone Zakłady Graficzne "Spółdruk," 1929. (P)

Bartosz, Adam. "Najstarsze dokumenty do historii cmentarza żydowskiego w Tarnowie" (The Oldest Documents Concerning the History of the Jewish Cemetery in Tarnów). *BŻIH* 2/106 (1978): 111–114. (P)

———. *Żydowskie zabytki województwa tarnowskiego* (Jewish Landmarks in the Province of Tarnów). Tarnów: Muzeum Okręgowe w Tarnowie, 1989. (P)

Bergman, Eleonora. "Góra Kalwaria: The Impact of a Hasidic Cult on the Urban Landscape of a Small Polish Town." *Polin: A Journal of Polish-Jewish Studies* 5 (1990): 3–24.

Borwicz, Michael. *1000 Years of Jewish Life in Poland.* Paris: Centre D'Études Historiques, 1955. (E, F)

Izbica Kujawska, Jewish cemetery, 1929   50
(since destroyed)

Brilling, Bernhard. "Mittelaeterliche jüdische Grabsteine aus Schlesien (Breslau-Brieg)" (Medieval Jewish Gravestones from Silesia). In *Theokratia, Jahrbuch des Institutum Judaicum Delitzschianum* I (1967–1969). Leiden: E. J. Brill, 1970, pp. 88–96. (G)

Burchard, Przemysław. *Pamiątki i zabytki kultury żydowskiej w Polsce* (Landmarks and Monuments of Jewish Culture in Poland). Warsaw: P. Burchard, 1990. (P)

Domańska, Hanna. "Mój dom będzie zwany domen modlitwy" (My House Will Be Called the House of Prayer). *Kalendarz Żydowski* (1991–1992): 78–100. (P)

Duda, Eugeniusz. *A Guide to Jewish Cracow*. Warsaw: Jewish Information and Tourist Bureau, 1992.

————. *Krakowskie judaica* (Kraków Judaica). Warsaw: Wydawnictwo PTTK "Kraj," 1991. (P)

Rymanów, Jewish cemetery, 1994   51

Einhorn, Ignacy. "Halacha-pień judaizmu" (Halakha-Jewish Law, The Stem of Judaism). *Kalendarz Żydowski* (1990–1991): 76–85. (P)

Faryna-Paszkiewicz, Hanna, Piotr Paszkiewicz, and Monika Krajewska. *Cmentarze żydowskie w Warszawie* (The Jewish Cemeteries in Warsaw). Warsaw: PWN, 1992. (P)

Fijałkowski, Paweł, and Stefan Rakowski. *Ludzie i zabytki: Żydzi na ziemiach polskich* (People and Monuments: Jews in the Polish Land). Warsaw: Bau-Help, 1992. (P)

Friedberg, Bernhard. *Luḥot zikaron* (The Rabbis of Kraków, Her Wise Men and Elders). Drohobycz: A. H. Zupnik, 1897. (H)

Frysztak, Jewish cemetery, 1993   52

Fuks, Marian. *Polish Jewry: History and Culture*. Warsaw: Interpress, 1982.

Gostyński, Zalman. *Des pierres racontent* (Shteyner dertseyln) (Stones Recount). Paris: Union des Juifs Originaires de l'Europe de l'Est, 1973. (F, Y)

Gruber, Ruth Ellen. *Jewish Heritage Travel: A Guide to Central and Eastern Europe*. New York: Wiley, 1994.

Gruber, Samuel, and Phyllis Myers. *Survey of Historic Jewish Monuments in Poland*. New York: Jewish Heritage Council, World Monuments Fund, 1995.

Hondo, Leszek. *Epitafia i symbolika żydowskiego cmentarza w Tarnowie* (Epitaphs and Symbolism of the Gravestones at the Jewish Cemetery in Tarnów). Tarnów: Komitet Opieki nad Zabytkami Kultury Żydowskiej w Tarnowie, n.d. (P)

Hondo, Leszek, Dariusz Rozmus, and Andrzej Witek. *Cmentarz żydowski w Pilicy: Rys historyczny i materialy inwentaryzacyjne* (The Jewish Cemetery in Pilica: Historical Sketch and Inventory). Kraków: Jagiellonian University, 1995. (P)

Lesko, Jewish cemetery, undated   53

Tyczyn, Jewish cemetery, 1995   54

Zawiercie, Jewish cemetery, 1986   55

Korczyna, Jewish cemetery, 1993   56

Ciechanowiec, a few tombstones from Jewish   57
cemetery in front of Agricultural Museum, 1994

Ignatowski, Grzegorz. "Początki i dzieje nowego cmentarza żydowskiego w Łodzi" (The Beginnings and History of the "New" Jewish Cemetery in Łódź). BŻIH 3–4/143–144 (1987): 59–70. (P)

Jagielski, Jan. "Kamieniom powierzamy pamięć ich męki i unicestwienia" (To Stones We Entrust the Memory of Their Suffering, Torture and Annihilation). Kalendarz Żydowski (1990–1991): 151–154. (P)

———. "Zabytki żydowskie w katalogu zabytków sztuki w Polsce" (Jewish Landmarks in the Catalog of Monuments of Art in Poland). BZIH 3–4/135–136 (1985): 143–153. (P)

Jevnin, Samuel. Sefer naḥalat 'olamim (The Eternal Inheritance). Warsaw: Y. Goldman, 1882. (H)

Kagan, Joram. Hippocrene Insiders' Guide to Poland's Jewish Heritage. New York: Hippocrene, 1992.

Kerz, Izaak. Szkice z dziejów gminy Zydowskiej oraz cmentarza w Łodzi (Sketches from the Annals of the Jewish Community and the Cemeteries of Łódź). Łódź: Oficyna Bibliofilów, 1996. (P)

Krajewska, Monika. "Cmentarze żydowskie w Polsce: nagrobki i epitafia" (Jewish Cemeteries in Poland: Gravestones and Epitaphs). 57 Polska Sztuka Ludowa 1–2 (1989): 27–44. (P)

———. "Ha-semalim al matsevot ha-kevarim ha-yehudiim be-Polin" (Symbols on Jewish Tombstones in Poland). Gal-Ed 9 (1986): 175–192. (H)

———. "Świadkiem niech będzie ten kamień" (May the Witness be This Stone). Kalendarz Żydowski (1986–1987): 206–210. (P)

———. "Symbolika nagrobków żydowskich—obraz religii i tradycji" (Jewish Tombstone Symbols—A Reflection of Religion and Tradition). In Bernard Wodecki, ed., Religia i kultura żydowska: Materiały z sesji judaistycznej (Jewish Religion and Culture: Papers from the Judaica Session). Pieniężno: Muzeum Misyjno-Etnograficzne, 1986, pp. 114–122. (P)

———. "Symbolika płaskorzeźbna na cmentarzach żydowskich w Polsce" (Symbolism of Reliefs in Jewish Cemeteries in Poland). Polska Sztuka Ludowa 47/1–2 (1989): 45–59. (P)

———. A Time of Stones. Warsaw: Interpress, 1983.

———. A Tribe of Stones: Jewish Cemeteries in Poland. Warsaw: Polish Scientific Publishers, 1993.

Krajewska, Monika, and Jan Jagielski. "Opracowanie dotyczące zabytków cmentarzy żydowskich w Polsce" (Regarding Jewish Cemeteries and Monuments in Poland). In Bernard Wodecki, ed., Religia i kultura żydowska: Materiały z sesji judaistycznej (Jewish Religion and Culture: Papers from the Judaica Session). Pieniężno: Muzeum Misyjno-Etnograficzne, 1986, pp. 123–126. (P)

Opatów, Jewish cemetery, 1991   58

Staszów, Jewish cemetery, 1996   59

Jarosław, Jewish cemetery, 1994   60

Krajewski, Stanisław. "Przykłady epitafiów hebrajskich na cmentarzach żydowskich w Polsce" (Examples of Hebrew Inscriptions in Jewish Cemeteries in Poland). *Polska Sztuka Ludowa* 47/1–2 (1989): 60–62. (P)

Kroszczor, Henryk. *Cmentarz żydowski w Warszawie* (Jewish Cemetery in Warsaw). Warsaw: Państwowe Wydaw. Naukowe, 1983. (P)

Łagiewski, Maciej. *Macewy mówią* (Tombstones Speak). Wrocław: Zakład Narodowy imienia Ossolińskich, 1991. (P)

———. *Stary cmentarz żydowski we Wrocławiu* (The Old Jewish Cemetery in Wrocław). Wrocław: Muzeum Architektury, 1986. (P)

Levy, A. *Jüdische Grabmalkunst in Osteuropa* (The Art of Jewish Tombs). Berlin: Verlag Pionier, 1923. (G)

Mahler, Ozjasz. *Przewodnik po żydowskich zabytkach Krakowa* (Guide to Jewish Landmarks in Kraków). Kraków: Nakład własny, 1931. (P)

Mansfeld, Boguslaw. "Cmentarz żydowski w Lubaczowie" (The Jewish Cemetery in Lubaczow). BŻIH 3–4/123–124 (1982): 109–114. (P)

Map of Jewish Heritage in Poland. Warsaw: National Tourism Promotion Agency, 1995.

Map of Judaics in Poland. Warsaw: Wydawnictwa Geologiczne, 1991.

Maser, Peter, and Adelheid Weiser. *Juden in Oberschlesien* (Jews in Upper Silesia). Berlin: Gebr. Mann Verlag, 1992. (G)

Morawski, Karol. *Przewodnik historyczny po cmentarzach warszawskich* (Historical Guide to the Warsaw Cemeteries). Warsaw: PTTK, 1989. (P)

Murzyn, Natalia. *Cisza co z nieba spływa: cmentarz żydowski w Katowicach* (Silence That Flows from Heavens: Jewish Cemetery in Katowice). Katowice: Muzeum Historii Katowic, 1994. (P)

Museum of Ethnography and Folklore. *Polish Synagogues and Cemeteries and Their Destruction*. Tel Aviv: Museum of Ethnography and Folklore, 1971.

Muszyńscy Danuta and Lech. "Cmentarze żydowskie" (Jewish Cemeteries). *Kalendarz Żydowski* (1991–1992): 169–187. (P)

Muzeum Historyczne m. Krakowa. *Bóżnice i cmentarze w Polsce południowo-wschodniej: katalog wystawy* (Synagogues and Cemeteries in Southeastern Poland: Catalog of the Exhibition). Kraków: Muzeum Historyczne m. Krakowa, 1986. (P)

Nissenbaum, Sh. B. "Evreiskie nadgrobnye pamyatniki goroda Lublina (XVI–XIX v.)" (Jewish Gravestones in Lublin [Sixteenth–Nineteenth Centuries]. In *Evreiskaia Starina*. St. Petersburg: St. Petersburg Jewish Historical and Ethnographic Society, 1913, pp. 1–32. (R)

Żywiec, Jewish cemetery, 1991   61

Jasło, Jewish cemetery, 1994   62

Szydłowiec, Jewish cemetery, 1959   63

Lutowiska, Jewish cemetery, 1997   64

Penkalla, Adam. "Cmentarz żydowski w Przytyku" (Jewish Cemetery in Przytyk). BŻIH 1–2/129–130 (1984): 175–182. (P)

———. "Gmina i cmentarz żydowski w Ożarowie" (Jewish Community and Cemetery in Ożarów). BŻIH 2/110 (1979): 53–68. (P)

Podgarbi, Bronisław. *Cmentarz żydowski w Łodzi* (The Jewish Cemetery in Łódź). Łódź: Artus, 1990. (P)

Prager, Moshe. *Le-ot ule-`ed; pinkas zikaron le-vate `almin she-nehersu ve-hulelu bi-shenot ha-shoah* (For a Sign and a Witness: A Memorial Book of the Cemeteries That Were Destroyed and Desecrated in the Holocaust Years). Tel Aviv: Ḥevrah Kaddisha, 1973. (H)

Przysuskier, Leon. *Cmentarze żydowskie w Warszawie* (The Jewish Cemeteries in Warsaw). Warsaw: Wieczność, 1936. (P)

Pukaczewski, Andrzej. *Hortus Iudaeorum: Cmentarz żydowski w Łodzi* (Garden of the Jews: The Jewish Cemetery in Łódź). Łódź: Wydawnictwo Łódzkie, 1992. (P)

Rosenstein, Neil. *Polish Jewish Cemeteries*. Elizabeth, NJ: Computer Center for Jewish Genealogy, 1983.

Rożek, Michał. *Żydowskie zabytki krakowskiego Kazimierza* (Jewish Monuments of Kraków's Kazimierz). Kraków: Oficyna Cracovia, 1990. (P)

Schipper, Ignacy. *Cmentarze żydowskie w Warszawie* (The Jewish Cemeteries in Warsaw). Warsaw: Maor, 1938. (P)

Schwartzman, Arnold. *Graven Images: Graphic Motifs of the Jewish Gravestone*. New York: Harry N. Abrams, 1993.

Stary cmentarz żydowski w Łodzi: dzieje i zabytki (The Old Jewish Cemetery in Łódź). Łódź: Wydawnictwo Sport i Turystka, 1989. (P)

They Lived Among Us: Jewish Heritage in Poland. Warsaw: National Tourism Promotion Agency, 1995.

Trzciński, Andrzej. "Polichromia nagrobków na cmentarzach żydowskich w Polsce Południowo-Wschodniej" (Tombstone Polychromes in Jewish Cemeteries in South-Eastern Poland). *Polska Sztuka Ludowa* 47/1–2 (1989): 63–64. (P)

———. *The Traces of Monuments of Jewish Culture in the Lublin Region*. Lublin: Wojewódzki Ośrodek Informacji Turystycznej, 1989. (E)

Vinecour, Earl. *Polish Jews: The Final Chapter*. New York: New York University Press, 1977.

Wiśniewski, Tomasz. *Jewish Rare Series* (photographs reprinted onto postcards, 1,000 per series). Białystok: T. Wiśniewski, 1992.

Żelechów, Jewish cemetery, 1982   65

Synagogue in Rymanów (ruins), 1994   66

Synagogue in Żarki, c. 1960   67

Synagogue in Żarki, 1989   68

Zawidzka, Iwona. *Cmentarz żydowski w Wiśniczu* (The Jewish Cemetery in Wiśnicz). Bochnia, Poland: Muzeum im. St. Fischera, 1987. (P)

———. *Miejsce święte dla wszystkich żyjących, czyli rzecz o cmentarzu żydowskim w Bochni* (Holy Place for the Living: Jewish Cemetery in Bochnia). Bochnia, Poland: Muzeum im. St. Fischera, 1992. (P)

Zielinski, Jacek Antoni, and Lucyna Krakowska. *Ta'arukhat matsevot bet-ha-kevarot ha-yehudi be-Shidlovtsah* (Exhibition of Tombstones of the Jewish Cemetery in Szydłowiec). Tel Aviv: Israel Museum of Ethnography and Folklore, 1963–1964. (H)

Zunz, Jehiel Mattathias. `*Ir ha-tsedek: toldot rabane `ir Kraka* (City of Justice: History of the Kraków Rabbinate). Lemberg (Lwów): Verlag d. Verfassers, 1874. (H)

SYNAGOGUES

Aronson, Chil. "Wooden Synagogues in Poland." *Menorah Journal* 25 (1937): 326–332.

Balaban, Majer. "Bóżnice obronne na wschodnich kresach Rzeczypospolitej" (Fortified Synagogues in the Eastern Border Regions of the Republic). In *Studia Historyczne*. Warsaw: M. S. Fried, 1927, pp. 93–99. (P)

———. *Die Judenstadt von Lublin* (The Jewish Town of Lublin). Berlin: Jüdischer Verlag, 1919. (G)

———. *Dzieje Żydów w Krakowie i na Kazimerzu: 1304–1868* (History of the Jews in Kraków and Kazimierz, 1304–1868). 2 vols. Kraków: "Nadzieja" Towarzystwo ku Wspieraniu Chorej Młodzieży Żydowskiej Szkół Średnich i Wyższych w Krakowie, 1931 and 1936. (P)

———. *Przewodnik po żydowskich zabytkach Krakowa* (Guide to Jewish Historic Landmarks in Kraków). Kraków: Stowarzyszenie Solidarność B'nai B'rith, 1935. (P)

———. "Wehrhafte Synagogen in den öestlichen Randgebieten der pölnischen Republik" (Functioning Synagogues in the Eastern Part of the Polish Republic). *Menorah* 6/7 (June 1927): 369–376. (G)

———. *Zabytki historyczne Żydow w Polsce* (Historic Monuments of Polish Jews). Warsaw: Warszawskie Zjednoczone Zakłady Graficzne "Spółdruk," 1929: 45–105. (P)

Baranowski, Jerzy. "O zabytkowej bóżnicy w Tykocinie" (The Ancient Synagogue in Tykocin). BŻIH 34 (1960): 158–170. (P)

Baranowski, Jerzy. "Synagoga w Chmielniku" (The Synagogue in Chmielnik). BŻIH 36 (1960): 95–106. (P)

Baranowski, Jerzy, and Henryk Jaworowski. "Historia i rozwój przestrzenny synagogi w Piotrkowie Trybunalskim" (History and Development of the Synagogue in Piotrków Trybunalski). BŻIH 57 (1966): 121–133. (P)

Synagogue in Lesko, c. 1990   69

Synagogue in Tykocin   70
(preserved as a Jewish museum)

Synagogue in Tykocin   71

Baranowski, Zofia and Jerzy Baranowski. "Dzielnica żydowska i synagoga w Zamościu" (The Jewish Quarter and Synagogue in Zamość). BŻIH 63 (1967): 39–56. (P)

Bartosz, Adam. "Synagoga Nowa w Tarnowie" (New Synagogue in Tarnów). BŻIH 3–4/147–148 (1988): 185–196. (P)

———. *Tarnowskie Judaica* (Tarnów Judaica). Warsaw: Wydawnictwo PTTK "Kraj," 1992. (P)

———. *Żydowskie zabytki województwa tarnowskiego* (Jewish Monuments in Tarnów Province). Tarnów: Muzeum Okręgowe w Tarnowie, 1989. (P)

Bartyś, J. "Materiały do budownictwa drewnianego i do struktury społeczno-zawodowej ludności żydowskiej w Strykowie w XVIII wieku" (Materials Concerning the Wooden Architecture and the Social and Professional Structure of the Jewish Population in Stryków in the Eighteenth Century). BŻIH 11–12 (1954): 89–96. (P)

Bergman, Eleonora. "The Function of Synagogues in the PRL, 1988." Polin: A Journal of Polish–Jewish Studies 5 (1990): 40–49.

———. "Góra Kalwaria: The Impact of a Hasidic Cult on the Urban Landscape of a Small Polish Town." Polin: A Journal of Polish–Jewish Studies 5 (1990): 3–24.

———. "Ślady kultury żydowskiej na Mazowszu" (Traces of Jewish Culture in the Mazowsze Region of Warsaw). Ośrodek Dokumentacji Zabytków, Zespół Badań Regionalnych Warszawy i Mazowsza 1 (1993): 16–40. (P)

———. *Synagogi w Polsce* (Synagogues of Poland). Warsaw: Spotkania z zabytkami, 1990. (P)

Bergman, Eleonora, and Ryszard Brykowski. "Drewniana synagoga - z problematyki badań nad drewnianą architekturą sakralną w Polsce" (The Wooden Synagogue: Problems in the Study of Wooden Ecclesiastic Structures in Poland). Ochrona Zabytków 1–2 (1983). (P)

Bersohn, Mathias. "Einiges über die alten Holzsynagogen in Polen" (Remarks on the Ancient Wooden Synagogues of Poland). Mitteilungen der Gesellschaft für jüdische Volkskunde 8 (1901); 14 (1904). (G)

———. *Kilka słów o dawniejszych bożnicach drewnianych w Polsce* (A Few Words About the Old Wooden Synagogues in Poland). Kraków: Drukarnia "Czasu" Kluczyckiego i spółki, 1895–1903. (P)

Borwicz, Michael. *1000 Years of Jewish Life in Poland*. Paris: Centre D'Études Historiques, 1955. (E,F)

Breyer, Alois. *Holzsynagogen in Polen* (Wooden Synagogues in Poland). Baden bei Wien: Buchhandlung "Sohar," 1934. (G)

Synagogue in Nowy Korczyn, 1957 (now ruins)   72

Synagogue in Kazimierz Dolny, 1991   73

Synagogue in Kazimierz Dolny, 1916   74

Synagogue in Kazimierz Dolny, c. 1955   75

Breyer, Alois, Max Eisler, and Max Grunwald. "Holzsynagogen in Polen" (Wooden Synagogues in Poland). *Menorah* 3/4 (March/April 1932): 113–132. (G)

Burchard, Przemysław. *Pamiątki i zabytki kultury żydowskiej w Polsce* (Landmarks and Monuments of Jewish Culture in Poland). Warsaw: P. Burchard, 1990. (P)

Busch, Ralf. "Synagoge und Kultgerat Osteuropäischen Judentum" (Synagogues and Cultic Objects of East European Jewry). In Brocke, Michael, *Beter und Rebellen Aus 1000 Jahren Judentum in Polen* (The Pious and the Rebels: 1000 Years of Jews in Poland). Frankfurt: Deutscher Koordinierungsrat der Gesellschaften für Christlich-Jüdische Zusammenarbeit, 1983. (G)

Buxton, David Roden. *The Wooden Churches of Eastern Europe: An Introductory Survey*. Cambridge: Cambridge University Press, 1981.

Bystrowski, Cezary, et al. *Tykocińskie impresje* (Impressions of Tykocin). Tykocin: Supraśl, 1994. (P)

Cempla, Joseph. *Avne kodesh: seride bate keneset be-Polin* (Holy Stones: Remnants of Synagogues in Poland). Tel Aviv: Dvir, 1959. (H)

Cohn, Jacob. *Geschichte der Synagogen Gemeinde Kattowitz* (History of the Synagogue of the Katowice Community). Katowice: Buch-und Kunstdr. J. Herlitz, 1990. (G)

Dąbrowska, Danuta, and Abraham Wein. *Pinkas ha-kehilot: entsiklopediyah shel ha-yishuvim le-min hivasdam ve-`ad le-aḥar shoat milḥemet ha-`olam ha-sheniyah, Poland* (Encyclopedia of Jewish Communities from Their Founding Until After the Second World War, Poland). Vols. 1–4. Jerusalem: Yad Vashem, 1976–1989. (H)

Dawidowicz, David. "Al teḥiyah emunatit yehudit aḥat be-Polin" (On One Jewish Religious Revival in Poland). *Gazit* 106/11–12 (1947): 42–47. (H)

———. *Bate keneset be-Polin ve-ḥurbenam* (The Synagogues of Poland and Their Destruction). Jerusalem: Mosad Harav Kook and Yad Vashem, 1960. (H)

———. "Bate keneset ha-`atikim be-Polin" (The Old Synagogues of Poland). *Gazit* 94/6 (1943): 19–23. (H)

———. "Bate keneset mivtsariim be-Polin" (The Fortified Synagogues of Poland). *Gazit* 107–108, nos. 5–6 (1947): 42–48; 113–114, nos. 7–8 (1948): 41–42; 115–116, nos. 9–10 (1948): 41–48; 129–130, nos. 9–10 (1950): 36–40. (H)

———. *Omanut ve-omanim be-vate keneset shel Polin* (Art and Artists in Polish Synagogues). Tel Aviv: Hakibbutz Hameuchad, 1982. (H)

———. *Shuln in Poyln* (Sinagogas en Polonia [Synagogues in Poland]). Buenos Aires: Unión Central Israelita Polaca en la Argentina, 1961. (Y)

Synagogue in Kraśnik, 1924 (now ruins) 76

Synagogue in Goniądz, pre-1945 (since destroyed) 77

Synagogue in Goniądz, pre-1945 (since destroyed) 78

———. *Tsiyure-kir be-vate keneset be-Polin* (Wall Paintings in Polish Synagogues). Jerusalem: Bialik Institute, 1968. (H)

DeBreffny, Brian. *The Synagogue*. New York: Macmillan, 1978.

Dobroszycki, Lucjan, and Barbara Kirshenblatt-Gimblett. *Image Before My Eyes: A Photographic History of Jewish Life in Poland Before the Holocaust*. New York: Schocken, 1977.

Dobrzycki, Jerzy. *Stara bóżnica kazimierska* (The Old Synagogue of Kazimierz). Kraków: Muzeum Historyczne Miasta Krakowa, 1965. (P)

Domańska, Hanna. "Mój dom będzie zwany domen modlitwy" (My House Will Be Called the House of Prayer). *Kalendarz Żydowski* (1991–1992): 78–100. (P)

———. "Synagogi postępowe w Gdańsku i Sopocie, ich budowa, zagłada, upamiętnienie" (Progressive Synagogues in Gdańsk and Sopot, Their Construction, Destruction and Commemoration). *Kalendarz Żydowski* (1994–1995): 33–42. (P)

Duda, Eugeniusz. *From the History and Culture of Jews in Cracow: Guide to the Permanent Exhibition in the Old Synagogue*. Kraków: Historical Museum of Kraków, 1986.

———. *A Guide to Jewish Cracow*. Warsaw: Jewish Information and Tourist Bureau, 1992. (E)

Fijałkowski, Paweł. "Żydzi w Polsce środkowej w XV–XVIII w. Dzieje i kultura" (Jews in Central Poland from the Fifteenth to the Eighteenth Century, Their History and Culture). *Kalendarz Żydowski* (1990–1991): 16–23. (P)

Fijałkowski, Paweł, and Stefan Rakowski. *Ludzie i zabytki: Żydzi na ziemiach polskich* (People and Monuments: Jews in the Land of Poland). Warsaw: Bau-Help, 1992. (P)

Fuks, Marian. *Polish Jewry History and Culture*. Warsaw: Interpress, 1982. (E)

Gloger, Zygmunt. "Bóżnica w Nasielsku" (Synagogue in Nasielsk). *Kłosy* 8 (1879). (P)

———. "Bóżnica w Wysokiem Mazowieckiem" (Synagogue in Wysokie Mazowieckie). *Kłosy* 19, no. 471 (1874). (P)

Gostyński, Zalman. *Des pierres racontent* (Shteyner dertseyln) (Stones Recount). Paris: Union des Juifs Originaires de L'Europe de l'Est, 1973. (F, Y)

Grotte, Alfred. *Alte schlesische Judenfriedhofe (Breslau und Dyherrnfurth)* (Old Jewish Cemeteries [Breslau and Brzeg Dolny]). Berlin: Verlag Guido Hackebeil, 1927. (G)

Synagogue in Łęczyca, pre-1945 (since destroyed)   79

Synagogue in Kurów, pre-1939 (since destroyed)   80

Synagogue in Opatów, 1933 (destroyed after 1945)   81

————. *Deutsche, böhmische und pölnische Synagogentypen vom XI bis Anfang XIX Jahrhunderts* (German, Bohemian and Polish Synagogues from the Eleventh to the End of the Nineteenth Centuries). Berlin: Der Zirkel Architektur-Verlag, 1915. (G)

————. *Synagogenspuren in Schlesischen Kirchen* (Traces of Synagogues in the Churches of Silesia). Breslau (Wroclaw): M. and H. Marcus, 1937. (G)

Gruber, Ruth Ellen. *Jewish Heritage Travel: A Guide to Central and Eastern Europe.* New York: Wiley, 1995.

Gruber, Samuel, and Phyllis Myers. *Survey of Historic Jewish Monuments in Poland.* New York: Jewish Heritage Council, World Monuments Fund, 1995.

Guterman, Alexander. *Me-hitbolelut li-leumiyut: perakim be-toledot bet ha-keneset ha-gadol ha-sinagogah be-Varshah 1806–1943* (From Assimilation to Nationalism: Chapters in the History of the Warsaw Great Synagogue 1806–1943). Jerusalem: Carmel Publishing House, 1993. (H)

Huberman, Ida. *Tikrot metsuyarot be-vate keneset me-'ets bi-derom-mizraḥ Polin* (Painted Ceilings in the Wooden Synagogues in Southeastern Poland). Tel Aviv: Tel Aviv University, 1979. (H)

Jagielski, Jan. "Zabytki żydowskie w katalogu zabytków sztuki w Polsce" (Jewish Landmarks in the Catalogue of Art Monuments in Poland). BŻIH 3–4/135–136 (1985): 143–153. (P)

Kagan, Joram. *Hippocrene Insiders' Guide to Poland's Jewish Heritage.* New York: Hippocrene, 1992.

Kalendarz Żydowski-Almanach (Jewish Calendar and Almanac). Warsaw: Związek Religijny Wyznania Mojżeszowego w PRL, 1989–1990, 1991–1992. (P)

Kandel, Dawid. "Bożnica w Pińczowie" (Synagogue in Pinczów). *Kwartalnik poświęcony badaniu przeszłości Żydów w Polsce,* 1/2 (1912): 28–35. (P)

————. "Bożnica w Sandomierzu" (Synagogue in Sandomierz). *Kwartalnik poświęcony badaniu przeszłosci Żydów w Polsce,* 1/1 (1912): 10–23. (P)

————. "Bożnica w Stepaniu" (Synagogue in Stepan). *Kwartalnik poświęcony badaniu przeszłości Żydów w Polsce,* 1/3 (1912): 37–46. (P)

Kaufmann, David. "Die Kunst in den Holzsynagogen Polens" (Art in the Wooden Synagogues of Poland). *Gesammelte Schriften von David Kaufmann* 1 (1908), 96–103. (G)

Krautheimer, Richard. *Bate keneset bi-yeme ha-benayim* (Synagogues of the Middle Ages). Jerusalem: Bialik Institute, 1994. (H)

Synagogue in Zawichost, c. 1930 (since destroyed) 82

Synagogue in Biała Rawska, pre-1939 83
(now a fire station)

Synagogue in Biała Rawska, pre-1939 84

Synagogue in Biała Rawska, pre-1939 85

Krinsky, Carol Herselle. *Synagogues of Europe: Architecture, History, Meaning*. New York: Architectural History Foundation, 1985: 53–56 and 200–235.

Kroszczor, Henryk. "Wielka synagoga na Placu Tłomackiem" (The Great Synagogue at Tłomacki Square). BŻIH 3/95 (1975): 3–16. (P)

Krupiński, Andrzej B. *Dawna synagoga Nowosądecka* (The Old Synagogue in Nowy Sącz). Nowy Sącz: Muzeum Okręgowe w Nowym Sączu, 1985. (P)

———. *Zabytki urbanistyki i architektury województwa tarnowskiego* (Urban and Architectural Landmarks and Monuments in Tarnów Province). Warsaw: Wydawnictwo PTTK "Kraj," 1989. (P)

Kubiak, A. "Zabytkowa architektura żydowska w Polsce" (The Architecture of Jewish Landmarks in Poland). BŻIH 2–3/6–7 (1953): 122–170. (P)

Landsberger, Franz. *A History of Jewish Art*. Cincinnati: The Union of American Hebrew Congregations, 1946.

Lechowski, Andrzej. *Przewodnik po wystawach muzeum w Tykocinie* (Guide to the Museum Exhibits in Tykocin). Białystok: Okręgowe Muzeum w Białymstoku, 1987. (P)

Ludwikowski, Leszek. *Stara bóżnica na Kazimierzu w Krakowie* (The Old Synagogue in the Kazimierz District of Kraków). Kraków: Muzeum Historyczne m. Krakowa, 1981. (P)

Lukomski, George K. "Jewish Architecture in Poland." *Journal of Royal Institute of British Architects*, 3rd series, 41/14 (June 1934): 748–753.

———. *Jewish Art in European Synagogues (From the Middle Ages to the Eighteenth Century)*. London/New York: Hutchinson, 1947.

———. "Synagogues of Eastern Europe." *The Architectural Review* (May 1945): 139–148.

———. "The Wooden Synagogues of Eastern Europe." *Burlington Magazine* (Jan. 1935): 14–21.

Mahler, Ojasz. *Przewodnik po żydowskich zabytkach Krakowa* (A Guidebook of Jewish Landmarks in Kraków). Kraków: Nakład Własny, 1936. (P)

Małkowska, Ewa. *Synagoga na Tłomackiem* (The Synagogue on Tłomackie Street). Warsaw: Wydawnictwo Naukowe PWN, 1991. (P)

Map of Jewish Heritage in Poland. Warsaw: National Tourism Promotion Agency, Poland, 1995.

Map of Judaica in Poland. Warsaw: Wydawnictwa Geologiczne, 1991.

Maser, Peter, and Adelheid Weiser. *Juden in Oberschlesien* (Jews in Upper Silesia). Berlin: Gebr. Mann Verlag, 1992. (G)

Synagogue in Nowe Miasto nad Pilicą, 86
pre-1939 (since destroyed)

Synagogue in Chęciny, pre-1945 87

Synagogue in Krzepice, pre-1939 (ruins) 88

Meek, H. A. *The Synagogue*. London: Phaidon Press, 1995.

Mokłowski, Kazimierz. "Bóżnice drewniane i meczety" (Wooden Synagogues and Mosques). *Sztuka Ludowa w Polsce* (1903): 424–443. (P)

Museum of Ethnography and Folklore. *Polish Synagogues and Cemeteries and Their Destruction*. Tel Aviv: Museum of Ethnography and Folklore, 1971.

Muzeum Historyczne m. Krakowa. *Bóżnice i cmentarze w Polsce południowo-wschodniej: Katalog wystawy* (Synagogues and Cemeteries in Southeastern Poland: Exhibition Catalog). Kraków: Muzeum Historyczne m. Krakowa, 1986.

Pakentreger, Aleksander. "Identyfikacja i rekonstrukcja inskrypcji starohebrajskich i aramejskich w Synagodze Wielkiej w Tykocinie" (Identification and Reconstruction of Old Hebrew and Aramaic Epitaphs in the Grand Synagogue in Tykocin). BŻIH 3–4/123–124 (1982): 99–108. (P)

Penkalla, Adam. "Synagoga i Gmina w Szydłowie" (The Synagogue and the Community of Szydłów). BŻIH 1–2/121–122 (1982): 57–70. (P)

Penkalla, Adam. "Synagoga w Klimontowie (województwo tarnobrzeskie)" (The Synagogue in Klimontów [Tarnobrzeg Province]). BŻIH 4/116 (1980): 45–56. (P)

Penkalla, Adam. "Zespół synagogalny w Ciepielowie (województwo radomskie)" (The Synagogue Complex in Ciepielów [Radom Province]). BŻIH 1–2/145–146 (1988): 145–146; 2 (1988): 115–124. (P)

———. "Zespół synagogalny w Tarłowie (województwo tarnobrzeskie)" (Synagogue Complex in Tarłów [Tarnobrzeg Province]). BŻIH 2/150 (1989): 85–94. (P)

Penkalla, Adam, and Jerzy Szczepański. "Synagoga w Kielcach" (The Synagogue in Kielce). BŻIH 4/120 (1981): 53–58. (P)

Piechotka, Maria and Kazimierz Piechotka. "Aron ha-kodesz w bóżnicach polskich: Ewolucja formy między XVI i początkiem XIX wieku" (The Holy Ark in Poland's Synagogues: The Evolution of Forms Between the Sixteenth and Beginning of the Nineteenth Centuries). In Andrzej K. Paluch, *The Jews in Poland*. Vol. 1. Kraków: Jagiellonian University, 1992. (P)

———. *Bóżnice drewniane* (Wooden Synagogues). Warsaw: Wydawnictwo Budownictwo i Architektura, 1957. (P)

———. *Bramy nieba–bóżnice drewiane w dawnej Rzeczpospolitej* (The Gates of Heaven: Wooden Synagogues in the old Polish Commonwealth). Warsaw: Krupski i S-ka, 1996. (P)

Synagogue in Łęczna, c. 1965   89

Synagogue in Łańcut, c. 1952   90

Synagogue in Łańcut, 1990 (now a museum) 91

———. "Polichromie polskich bóżnic drewnianych" (Polichromies of Polish Wooden Synagogues). *Polska Sztuka Ludowa* 47, nos. 1–2 (1989): 65–87. (P)

———. "Polish Synagogues in the Nineteenth Century." *Polin: A Journal of Polish-Jewish Studies* 2 (1987): 179–198.

———. *Wooden Synagogues*. Warsaw: Arkady, 1959.

Pinkerfeld, Yaakov. *Bi-shevile omanut yehudit* (In the Pathways of Jewish Art). Merḥavia, Israel: Ha-Shomer Ha-Tsair, 1957. (H)

Rejduch-Samkowa, Izabella. "Sztuka żydowska w Polsce w. XVII i XVIII w." (Jewish Art in Poland in the Seventeenth and Eighteenth Centuries). In *Żydzi w dawnej Rzeczypospolitej*, 1991: 321–343. (P)

Rożek, Michał. *Żydowskie zabytki krakowskiego Kazimierza* (Jewish Monuments of Kraków's Kazimierz). Kraków: Oficyna Cracovia, 1990. (P)

Sandel, Jozef G. "Żydowska sztuka kulturowa (Jewish Folk Art)." In *Straty wojenne zbiorów polskich w dziedzinie rzemiosła artystycznego* 2. Warsaw: MKIS, 1953. (P)

Schwarz, Hans-Peter. *Die Architektur der Synagoge* (The Architecture of the Synagogue). Frankfort am Main: Klett-Cotta, 1988. (G)

Szampanier, Dora. *Bate ha-keneset be-tif'artam uve-ḥurbanam* (*Synagogues in Glory and in Ruins*. Haifa: Karmel Print, 1991. (H, E).

Szczęk, Stanisław. "Odbudowa synagogi w Rymanowie" (Restoration of the Synagogue in Rymanów). *Materiały Muzeum Budownictwa Ludowego w Sanoku* 28 (1984). (P)

Szyszko-Bohusz, Adolf. "Materiały do architekury bóżnic w Polsce" (Documents Regarding Synagogue Architecture in Poland). In *Prace Komisji do Badań Historii Sztuki w Polsce* (Publication of the Commission for the Study of Art History in Poland). Vol. 4, no. 1. Kraków: Polish Academy of Science and Learning, 1927. (P)

They Lived Among Us: Jewish Heritage in Poland. Warsaw: National Tourism Promotion Agency, 1995.

Trzciński, Andrzej. *A Guide to Jewish Lublin and Surroundings*. Warsaw: Jewish Information and Tourist Bureau, 1991. (E)

———. *The Traces of Monuments of Jewish Culture in the Lublin Region*. Lublin: Wojewódzki Ośrodek Informacji Turystycznej, 1989. (E)

Urban, K. *Pfarrer: Die katholische Kirche und die Synagoge in Czieschowa* (The Catholic Church and the Synagogue in Cieszowa). Oppeln, Germany, 1911. (G)

Synagogue in Przemyśl, c. 1952 (since destroyed)   92

Synagogue in Kutno, pre-1939 (since destroyed)   93

Synagogue in Kutno, interior, pre-1939   94

Synagogue in Węgrów, 1915 (since destroyed)   95

Verbin, Moshe. *Bate keneset mi-`ets be-Polin ha-kedumah* (Wooden Synagogues of Old Poland). Ramat Gan, Israel: Culture and Art Authority, 1988. (H)

————. *Wooden Synagogues of Poland in the Seventeenth and Eighteenth Centuries.* Herzliya, Israel: Herzliya Museum, 1990.

Vinecour, Earl. *Polish Jews: The Final Chapter.* New York: New York University Press, 1977.

Wierzbicki Yeshbutsky, "Bóżnica w Jabłonowie nad Prutem" (A Synagogue in Jabłonów nat Prutem). In *Sprawozdania Komisji dla badania historii sztuki* (Report by the Commission of Art History) 4/2, 1891. Kraków: Polish Academy of Science. (P)

Wigoder, Geoffrey. *The Story of the Synagogue.* Tel Aviv: Beth Hatefutsoth, 1986.

Wischnitzer, Rachel. "Mutual Influences Between Eastern and Western Europe in Synagogue Architecture from the Twelfth to the Eighteenth Centuries." *YIVO Annual of Jewish Social Science* II–III (1947–1948): 25–68.

Wischnitzer-Bernstein, Rachel. *The Architecture of European Synagogues.* Philadelphia: Jewish Publication Society, 1964.

————. "Synagogen im ehemaligen Königreich Polen" (Synagogues in the Former Kingdom of Poland). In S. J. Agnon and Ahron Eliasberg, *Das Buch von den pölnischen Juden.* Berlin: Jüdischer Verlag, 1916, 87–105. (G)

Wiśniewski, Tomasz. *Heartland of the Jewish Life: Synagogues and Jewish Communities in the Białystok Region.* Białystok: David, 1992. (E,P)

————. *Jewish Rare Series* (photographs made into postcards, 1,000 prints in series). Białystok: T. Wiśniewski, 1992.

Wooden Synagogues in Poland: Catalogue of Exhibition with Illustrations. Tel Aviv: Tel Aviv Museum, 1941.

Yargina, Zoya. *Wooden Synagogues.* Moscow: Image Publishing House, 1993.

Zajczyk, Szymon. "Architektura barokowych bóżnic murowanych w Polsce" (Polish Baroque Brick Synagogue Architecture). *Biuletyn Naukowy Zakładu Architektury Polskiej Historii Sztuki Politechniki Warszawskiej* 4 (1933): 106–195. (P)

————. "Architektura bóżnic barokowych w Polsce" (Synagogue Architecture of the Baroque Era in Poland). *Biuletyn naukowy wydawany przez Zakład Architektury Polskiej Historii Sztuki Politechniki Warszawkiej* 59/1 (1932): 186–195. (P)

————. "Bóżnica w Kępnie" (The Synagogue in Kępno). *BŻIH* 43–44 (1962): 63–83. (P)

————. "Bóźnice drewniane na terenie województwa białostockiego" (Wooden Synagogues in the Province of Białystok.) In *Województwo białostockie: przeszłość i zabytki* (The Province of Białystok: Its Past and Its Monuments). Białystok: Lechja, 1929. (P)

Zilbersztejn, Sara. "Postępowa Synagoga na Daniłowiczowskiej w Warszawie" (Progressive Synagogue at Daniłowiczowska Street in Warsaw). BŻIH 74 (1970): 31–57. (P)

GENEALOGY

Barthel, Stephen S., and Daniel Schlyter. "Using Prussian Gazetteers to Locate Jewish Religious and Civil Records in Poznan." *Avotaynu*, vol. 6, no. 2 (Summer 1990): 12–13.

Beider, Alexander. *A Dictionary of Jewish Surnames from the Kingdom of Poland*. Teaneck, NJ: Avotaynu, 1996.

————. "Jewish Surnames in the Kingdom of Poland." *Avotaynu*, vol. 10, no. 2 (Summer 1994): 15–19.

Bussgang, Fay Vogel. "Census Records and City Directories in the Kraków Archives." *Avotaynu*, vol. 12, no. 2 (Summer 1996): 27–28.

Chorzempa, Rosemary A. *Morbus Why and How our Ancestors Died: A Genealogist's Dictionary of Terms Found in Vital Records with Descriptions of the Diseases as They Relate to the Health of Our Ancestors*. Chicago: Polish Genealogical Society of America, 1991.

Cymbler, Jeffrey K. "Polish-Jewish Genealogical Research—A Primer." *Avotaynu*, vol. 9, no. 2 (Summer 1993): 4–12.

Frazin, Judith R. *A Translation Guide to 19th-Century Polish-Language Civil-Registration Documents*. 2nd ed. Northbrook, IL: The Jewish Genealogical Society of Illinois, 1989.

The Galitizianer. Vols. 1–. Gesher Galicia Special Interest Group, 1993–.

Hoffman, William F. *Polish Surnames: Origins and Meanings*. Chicago: Polish Genealogical Society of America, 1992.

A Journal of Jewish Genealogical Information from the Kielce and Radom Special Interest Group. Vols. 1–. Kielce and Radom Special Interest Group, 1997–.

Korwin, Ludwik. *Szlachta polska pochodzenia żydowskiego* (Polish Gentry of Jewish Origin). Bonn: Institut für angewandte Sozialgeschichte, 1985. (P)

Luft, Edward D. "Jewish Genealogical Research in Poland." *Avotaynu*, vol. 5, no. 2 (Summer 1989): 8–10.

————. "More on Polish-Jewish Genealogical Research." *Avotaynu*, vol. 10, no. 1 (Spring 1994): 12–13.

Synagogue in Maciejów, pre–1939   100

Synagogue in Wieluń, 1927   101

Synagogue in Tarnogród, undated (now ruins)   102

Synagogue in Chmielnik, pre-1939 (now ruins)   103

"Polish-Jewish Records at the Genealogical Society of Utah." *Avotaynu*, vol. 2, no. 1 (Jan. 1986): 5–17.

Reychman, Kazimierz. *Szkice genealogiczne* (Genealogical Sketches). Warsaw: F. Hoesick, 1936. (P)

Shea, Jonathan D. *Russian Language Documents from Russian Poland*. New Britain, CT: J. Shea, 1985. Reprint, Orem, UT: Genealogy Unlimited, 1989.

Shea, Jonathan D., and William F. Hoffman. *Following the Paper Trail: A Multilingual Translation Guide*. Teaneck, NJ: Avotaynu, 1994.

Silverman, Marlene, ed. *Landsmen*. Washington, D.C.: Suwalki-Lomza Interest Group for Jewish Genealogists, 1990–.

Skowronek, Jerzy. "Jewish Genealogical Research in Polish Archives." *Avotaynu*, vol. 10, no. 2 (Summer 1994): 5–8.

Volovici, Hanna. "Polish Sources at the Central Archives for the History of the Jewish People." *Avotaynu*, vol. 10, no. 2 (Summer 1994): 21–22.

PERIODICALS

Avotaynu: The International Review of Jewish Genealogy. Teaneck, NJ: Avotaynu, 1985–.

Biuletyn Żydowskiego Instytutu Historyczynego w Polsce (BŻIH) (Bulletin of the Jewish Historical Institute in Poland). Warsaw: Jewish Historical Institute, 1950–. (P)

Bleter far geszichte (Bleter far geshikhte/Pages of History: Quarterly Bulletin of the Jewish Historical Institute in Poland). Vols. 1– . 1948– . Warsaw: Żydowski Instytut Historyczny (Jewish Historical Institute) (P)

Gal-Ed: Studies on the History of the Jews in Poland. Nos.1–. 1962–. Tel Aviv: "Gal-Ed," Society for Historical Research of Polish Jewry Founded by Tel-Aviv University–Diaspora Research Institute and the World Federation of Polish Jews. (H, E)

Polin: A Journal of Polish-Jewish Studies. Vols. 1–. 1986–. Oxford: Basil Blackwell Institute for Polish-Jewish Studies.

Yad Vashem Studies (on the European Jewish Catastrophe and Resistance II), edited by Shaul Esh. Jerusalem: Yad Vashem, 1958– .

YIVO Annual of Jewish Social Science. Vols. 1–. 1946–. New York: Yiddish Scientific Institute–YIVO.

YIVO Bleter, Monthly of the Yiddish Scientific Institute. Vols. 1–. 1931–. Wilno-New York: Yiddish Scientific Institute/YIVO Institute for Jewish Research. (Y)

COLLECTED BIOGRAPHIES

Bader, Gershom. *Medinah va-ḥakhameha; toldot kol ha-ḥakhamim veha-sofrim be-Galitsyah mi-yemot Mendelson 'ad ha-yom* (A Land and Its Sages: The History of the Sages and Writers in Galicia from the Days of Mendelssohn Until Today). New York: National Booksellers, 1934. (H)

Bersohn, Mathias. *Słownik biograficzny uczonych Żydów polskich XVI, XVII i XVIII wieku* (Biographical Dictionary of Jewish Scholars in Poland in the Sixteenth, Seventeenth and Eighteenth Centuries). Warsaw: P. Laskauer, 1905. (P)

Elior, Rachel, et al. *Tsadikim ve-anshe ma'aseh: meḥkarim ba-ḥasidut Polin* (Righteous and Great Men: Studies in Polish Hasidism). Jerusalem: Mosad Harav Kook, 1994. (H)

Falstein, Louis. *Martyrdom of Jewish Physicians in Poland*. New York: Exposition Press, 1963.

Fater, Issachar. *Yidishe muzik in Poyn tsvishn beyde velt-milkhomes* (Jewish Music in Poland Between the Two World Wars). Tel Aviv: World Federation of Polish Jews, 1970. (Y)

Friedberg, Bernhard. *Luḥot zikaron: ha'atakot me-avne ha-matsevot bi-sedeh ha-kevarot be-ir Krako im toldot ḥakhme ha-ir u-gedoleha* (Tables of Memory: Copies of Tombstones in Kraków Cemeteries, With a History of the City's Wise Men and Elders). Drohobycz, Poland: A. H. Zupnik, 1897. (H)

Getter, Norbert. *Orędownicy równości obywatelskiej w Polsce* (Defenders of Citizens' Equality in Poland). Lwów: Lwowski Instytut Wydawniczy, 1939. (P)

Jevnin, Samuel. *Sefer naḥalat `olamim* (The Eternal Inheritance). Warsaw: Y. Goldman, 1882. (P)

Kasdan, Hayim Solomon. *Lerer-yisker-bukh* (Teachers Memorial Book). New York: Zydowski: Centralna Organizacja Szkolna, 1952–1954. (Y)

Lowenthal, Ernst G. *Juden in Preussen: Biographisches Verzeichnis, ein Repräsentativer Querschnitt* (The Jews in Prussia: A Biographical Register, a Representative Cross-Section). Berlin: D. Reimer, 1981. (G)

Mieses, Mateusz. *Christliche Polen jüdischer Abstammung (Polacy-chrześcijanie pochodzenia żydowskiego)* (Christian Poles of Jewish Origin). Warsaw: Verlag M. Fruchtman, 1939. (G,P)

Schipper, Ignacy. *Żydzi w Polsce Odrodzonej* (Jews in Reborn Poland). Warsaw: Nakładem Wydawnictwa "Żydzi w Polsce Odrodzonej," 1936. (P)

Wunder, Meir. *Meorei-Galicia (Luminaries of Galicia): Encyclopedia of Galician Rabbis and Scholars*. Vol. 1. Jerusalem: Makhon le-hantsahat Yahadut Galitsyah, 1978–. (H)

Zunz, Jehiel Mattathias. *`Ir ha-tsedek (Gecshichte der Krakauer Rabbinat)* (History of the Kraków Rabbinate). Lemberg (Lwów): Verlag d. Verfassers, 1874. (H)

Synagogue in Zwoleń, early 1900s (since destroyed)   104

Ustrzyki Dolne, Jewish cemetery, 1961   105

Synagogue in Przysucha, undated (abandoned)   106

Synagogue in Klimontów, c. 1952 (renovated)   107

Synagogue in Sokołów Małopolski, 1994 108
(now a cultural center)

Synagogue in Poryck, pre-1945 109

Synagogue in Kuźnica Białostocka, pre-1945 110
(since destroyed)

Lubaczów, Jewish cemetery, c. 1963 111

FILMS

A Time to Gather Stones Together. Washington, D.C.: Documentaries International Film and Video Foundation, 1993 (distributed by Ergo Media, Inc., under new title: *Routes to Roots: Rediscovering Jewish Poland and Ukraine*).

At the Crossroads: Jews of Eastern Europe Today. Rudavsky and Strom Productions, 1989 (distributed by Arthur Canton Films).

Diamonds in the Snow. Mira Reym Binford, 1994 (distributed by The Cinema Guild).

Image Before My Eyes. New York: YIVO, 1980 (distributed by Ergo Media, Inc.).

The Jews of Poland: Five Cities. Jerusalem: Spielberg Jewish Film Archives, 1988 (distributed by Ergo Media, Inc.).

The Last Chapter, Ben-Lar Productions, 1946.

Łódź Ghetto. The Jewish Heritage Project, 1989 (distributed by Acorn Media Publishing).

Not Like Sheep to the Slaughter: The Story of the Białystok Ghetto. Israel Film Service, 1990 (distributed by Ergo Media, Inc.).

Pilgrimage of Remembrance: Jews in Poland Today. Yaron Shemer Assoc., 1991 (distributed by Ergo Media, Inc.).

Polish Judaics. Warsaw: Polish Tourist Information Centre and Sportfilm Warszawa Stadion Dziesięciolecia, c. 1990 (can be purchased at the Jewish Historical Institute).

Shtetl. Marian Marzyński, 1996 (distributed by Log In Enterprises).

The Story of Chaim Rumkowski and the Jews of Łódź. Peter Cohen, 1982 (distributed by The Cinema Guild).

The Warsaw Ghetto. London: BBC, 1969 (distributed by Social Studies School Services).

The Warsaw Ghetto Uprising. Ghetto Fighters' House at Kibbutz Lohamei Hagetaot, 1993 (distributed by Ergo Media, Inc.).

GAZETTEERS

Chajes, Saul. "Nemen fun Galitsishe erter in yidish: mekoyrim un inem folks-loshn" (Place Names of Galicia in Jewish Sources and in Modern Yiddish). *YIVO Bleter* 7, no. 3 (1934): 229–249, 286. (Y)

Cohen, Chester G. *Shtetl Finder.* Los Angeles: Periday Company, 1980. Reprint, Bowie, MD: Heritage Books, 1989.

Poznań, Jewish cemetery, c. 1990   112

Szczucin Jewish cemetery, 1994   113

Synagogue in Nowy Korczyn, 1936 (abandoned)   114

Synagogue in Sochaczew, early 1900s   115
(since destroyed)

Halpern, Israel. "Shemot geografiim shel Polin" (Polish Geographical Names in Hebrew Sources). *Leshonenu* 4 (1932): 233–240. (H)

Kagan, Berl. *Sefer ha-prenumerantn-Hebrew Subscription Lists: With an Index to 8,767 Jewish Communities in Europe and North Africa.* New York: Library of the Jewish Theological Seminary of America and Ktav Publishing House, 1975.

Lenius, Brian J. *Genealogical Gazetteer of Galicia.* 2nd ed. Anola, Canada: B. Lenius, 1993.

Mahler, Raphael. "Jewish Place-Names in Old Poland." *Reshumot* 5 (1953): 146–161. (H)

Mokotoff, Gary, and Sallyann Amdur Sack. *Where Once We Walked: A Guide to the Jewish Communities Destroyed in the Holocaust.* Teaneck, NJ: Avotaynu, 1991.

————. *WOWW Companion: A Guide to the Communities Surrounding Central & Eastern European Towns.* Teaneck, NJ: Avotaynu, 1995.

Stankiewicz, Edward. "Yiddish Place Names in Poland." In Uriel Weinreich, ed., *Field of Yiddish: Studies in Language, Folklore and Literature.* (Second collection). The Hague: Mouton, 1965, pp. 158–181.

FILM DISTRIBUTORS

ACORN MEDIA PUBLISHING, 7910 Woodmont Ave. #350, Bethesda, MD 20814

ARTHUR CANTON FILMS, 1501 Broadway #403, New York, NY 10036

BEN-LAR PRODUCTIONS, 311 West 24th Street, New York, NY 10011

THE CINEMA GUILD, 1697 Broadway #506, New York, NY 10019

ERGO MEDIA, INC., 668 American Legion Drive, P.O. Box 2037, Teaneck, NJ 07666

JEWISH HISTORICAL INSTITUTE, ul. Tłomackie 3/5, 00-090 Warsaw, Poland

LOG IN ENTERPRISES, 4 La Rue Road, Spencer, NY 14883

NATIONAL TOURISM PROMOTION AGENCY, 9 Mazowiecka Str., 00-052 Warsaw, Poland

SOCIAL STUDIES SCHOOL SERVICE, 10200 Jefferson Blvd., Culver City, CA 90232

POSTCARD DISTRIBUTOR

TOMASZ WIŚNIEWSKI, Box 351, 15-001 Bialystok, Poland

▌ Holocaust memorial at Treblinka death camp, 1975   116

▌ Memorial wall constructed from tombstone fragments (remains of cemetery behind), Kazimierz Dolny, 1990   117

POLISH STATE ARCHIVES ADDRESS LIST

The following list of archives was provided by the administrative offices of the Polish State Archives. A few *oddział* archives are not represented in the archival inventories (Chapter 7), primarily because they do not have material relevant to the focus of this book. The Polish State Archives is in the process of restructuring its system, which has resulted in the recent consolidation of some smaller branch archives and the establishment of new district archives. Therefore, material that was previously reported to be in a specific archives may now be in the process of being moved to its new location. For example, the *oddział* archives in Będzin were closed and all documents were moved to the district archives in Katowice.

Key:	**Archiwum Państwowe**	District Archives under jurisdiction of the Polish State Archives in Warsaw
	Oddział	Branch of District Archive
	Zamek (in address)	Castle

ADMINISTRATIVE OFFICES
and CENTRAL ARCHIVES

Naczelna Dyrekcja Archiwów Państwowych
(Chief Administrative Offices of the State Archives)
00-950 Warszawa
skr. poczt. 1005
ul. Długa 6

T(elephone)/**F**(ax)

831-3206 T
831-7563 F

Archiwum Główne Akt Dawnych (AGAD)
00-263 Warszawa
ul. Długa 7

831-5491 T
831-1608 F

AGAD Archives, ul. Długa 7, Warszawa, 1996,   1
a division of the Polish State Archives

Archiwum Akt Nowych (AAN)
02-103 Warszawa
ul. Hankiewicza 1

22-52-45 T
23-00-42 F

Archiwum Dokumentacji Mechanicznej (ADM)
00-202 Warszawa
ul. Świętojerska 24

831-1736 T
831-1736 F

ARCHIWA PAŃSTWOWE
and ODDZIAŁ ARCHIVES

Archiwum Państwowe w Białymstoku
15-950 Białystok
Rynek Kościuszki 4

43-56-55 T
43-56-03 F

Oddział w Łomży
18-400 Łomża
ul. Legionów 36

16-49-39 T

Archiwum Państwowe w Bydgoszczy
85-009 Bydgoszcz
ul. Dworcowa 65

22-96-76 T
22-35-11 F

Oddział w Inowrocławiu
88-100 Inowrocław
ul. Narutowicza 58

57-64-44 T

Archiwum Państwowe w Częstochowie
42-200 Częstochowa
ul. Rejtana 13

63-82-31 T
63-89-31 T

Archiwum Państwowe w Elblągu
z siedzibą w Malborku
82-200 Malbork
skr. poczt. 94
Zamek

72-24-56 T

Plaque at entrance to AGAD Archives in Warsaw   2
(formerly Raczynski Palace, constructed 1702–1704)

Archiwum Państwowe w Gdańsku
80-958 Gdańsk
skr. poczt. 401
ul. Wały Piastowskie 5

31-74-63 T
31-83-66 T
31-83-66 F

Archiwum Państwowe w Kaliszu
62-800 Kalisz
ul. Złota 43   57-35-91   T/F

Archiwum Państwowe w Katowicach
40-145 Katowice 33
skr. poczt. 1   58-25-46   T
ul. Józefowska 104   58-38-31   F

Oddział w Bielsku-Białej
43-300 Bielsko-Biała
ul. Słowackiego 80/82   12-26-14   T

Oddział w Cieszynie
43-400 Cieszyn
ul. Śrutarska 28   52-06-47   T

Oddział w Gliwicach
44-100 Gliwice
ul. Zygmunta Starego 8   31-44-40   T

Oddział w Oświęcimiu
32-603 Oświęcim
Muzeum Państwowe
Blok 1   43-12-37   T

Oddział w Pszczynie
43-200 Pszczyna
ul. Brama Wybrańców 2
Zamek   110-35-60   T

Oddział w Raciborzu
47-400 Racibórz
ul. Opolska 10   415-24-72   T

Oddział w Tarnowskich Górach
42-600 Tarnowskie Góry
ul. Gliwicka 5   185-25-54

Oddział w Żywcu
34-300 Żywiec
ul. Świętokrzyska 50a   61-28-17   T

Archiwum Państwowe w Kielcach
25-953 Kielce   344-38-20   T
ul. Warszawska 17   368-10-69   F

Oddział w Jędrzejowie
28-300 Jędrzejów
ul. Reymonta 12   61-996   T

Oddział w Pińczowie
28-400 Pińczów
ul. Buska 32   72-002   T

Oddział w Sandomierzu
27-600 Sandomierz
ul. Żydowska 4   832-25-09   T

Oddział w Starachowicach
27-210 Starachowice
ul. Hutnicza 14   55-07   T

Archiwum Państwowe w Koszalinie
75-950 Koszalin
skr.poczt.149   42-26-22   T
ul.M.Skłodowskiej-Curie 2

Oddział w Słupsku
76-200 Słupsk
ul. W. Lutosławskiego 17   42-23-27   T

▌ *Archives in Rzeszów, 1993*   3

▌ *Archives in Wrocław, 1996*   4

▌ *Archives in Białystok, 1996*   5

▌ *Archives in Łódź, 1996*   6

Oddział w Szczecinku 78-400 Szczecinek ul. Parkowa 3	40-463	T
Archiwum Państwowe w Krakowie 30-960 Kraków ul. Sienna 16	21-37-33 22-40-94 21-35-44	T T F
Oddział w Bochni 32-700 Bochnia ul. Proszowska 54	22-107	T
Oddział w Nowym Sączu 33-300 Nowy Sącz ul. Nawojowska 43	20-659	T
Oddział w Nowym Targu 34-400 Nowy Targ ul. Bor 10	63-548	T
Oddział w Tarnowie 33-101 Tarnów ul. Chemiczna 16	33-06-21	T
Archiwum Państwowe w Lesznie 64-100 Leszno ul. Bolesława Chrobrego 32	20-30-01	T
Archiwum Państwowe w Lublinie 20-950 Lublin skr. poczt. 113 ul. Jezuicka 13	532-8071 532-3537	T
Oddział w Chełmie 22-100 Chełm ul. Siedlecka 4	64-23-22	T
Oddział w Kraśniku 23-210 Kraśnik ul. Kardynała Wyszyńskiego 2	825-66-14	T
Oddział w Radzyniu Podlaskim 21-300 Radzyń Podlaski ul. Międzyrzecka 2 (Zamek)	52-00-70	T
Archiwum Państwowe w Łodzi 90-950 Łódź skr. poczt. 36 pl. Wolności 1	32-02-02 32-62-01 32-02-11	T T F
Oddział w Pabianicach 95-200 Pabianice ul. Gdańska 6	15-38-38	T
Oddział w Sieradzu 98-200 Sieradz ul. POW 5	271-642	T
Archiwum Państwowe w Olsztynie 10-521 Olsztyn skr. poczt. 39 ul. Partyzantów 18	527-60-96 535-92-72	T F
Oddział w Mrągowie 11-700 Mrągowo ul. Królewiecka 55	27-05	T
Oddział w Nidzicy 13-100 Nidzica skr. poczt. 16 ul. Jagiełły 2A	625-33-14	T

■ *Archives in Kraków, 1996*　　　　7

■ *Archives in Lublin, 1996*　　　　8

■ *Archives in Pińczów, a branch archive*　　9
of AP Kielce, 1995

Archiwum Państwowe w Opolu		
45-016 Opole	54-55-36	T
skr. poczt. 356	54-40-75	T
ul. Zamkowa 2	54-21-12	F
Oddział w Brzegu		
49-300 Brzeg		
ul. Bolesława Chrobrego 31	16-33-17	T
Oddział w Nysie		
48-300 Nysa		
ul. Biskupa Jarosława 11	33-41-13	T
Archiwum Państwowe w Piotrkowie Trybunalskim		
97-300 Piotrków Trybunalski		
ul. Toruńska 4	49-69-71	T/F
Oddział w Tomaszowie Mazowieckim		
97-200 Tomaszów Mazowiecki		
ul. Spalska 120	24-65-70	T
Archiwum Państwowe w Płocku		
09-400 Płock		
ul. Kazimierza Wielkiego 9B	62-24-91	T
Oddział w Kutnie		
99-300 Kutno		
ul. Zamkowa 4	53-39-81	T
Oddział w Łęczycy		
99-100 Łęczyca		
ul. Belwederska 38	29-27	T
Archiwum Państwowe w Poznaniu		
60-967 Poznań		
skr. poczt. 546	52-46-01	T
ul. 23 Lutego 41/43	51-73-10	F
Oddział w Gnieźnie		
62-200 Gniezno		
ul. Zielony Rynek 12	26-18-17	T
Oddział w Koninie		
62-500 Konin		
ul. 3 Maja 78	42-92-77	T
Oddział w Pile		
64-920 Piła		
skr. poczt. 231		
ul. Śniadeckich 31	12-31-89	T
Archiwum Państwowe w Przemyślu		
37-700 Przemyśl	70-62-71	T
ul. Lelewela 4	70-76-34	F
Oddział w Przeworsku		
37-200 Przeworsk		
ul. Rynek 1	48-73-18	T
Archiwum Państwowe w Radomiu		
26-600 Radom	362-11-59	T
ul. Rynek 1	362-11-50	F
Archiwum Państwowe w Rzeszowie		
35-959 Rzeszów	32-684;32-670	T
ul. Bożnicza 2	38-304	F
Ośrodek Badań Historii Żydów		
Oddział AP w Rzeszowie	32-670	T
35-959 Rzeszów		
ul. Bożnicza 2		

Tour group of Jewish researchers in Lublin Archives, 1991   10

Shelves of documents in Lublin Archives, 1989   11

Gloria Resin researching her family history in the Sandomierz Archives, a branch archive of AP Kielce   12

Oddział w Sanoku
38-500 Sanok
Rynek 10 — 31-999 — T

Oddział w Skołyszynie
38-242 Skołyszyn — 96 — T

Archiwum Państwowe w Siedlach
08-110 Siedlce
ul. Biskupa Ignacego Świrskiego 2 — 22-574 — T

Archiwum Państwowe w Suwałkach
16-400 Suwałki
ul. Kościuszki 69 — 66-21-67 — T

Oddział w Ełku
19-300 Ełk
ul. Kąpielowa 1 — 10-25-04 — T

Archiwum Państwowe w Szczecinie
70-410 Szczecin
ul. Św. Wojciecha 13 — 33-50-02 T / 33-50-18 T / 33-67-70 F

Oddział w Gorzowie Wielkopolskim
66-400 Gorzów Wielkopolski
ul. Grottgera 24/25 — 22-79-68 — T

Oddział w Płotach
73-310 Płoty
ul. Zamkowa 2 — 51-351 — T

Oddział w Stargardzie Szczecińskim
73-110 Stargard Szczeciński
ul. Basztowa 2 — 77-56-76 — T

Archiwum Państwowe w Toruniu
87-100 Toruń
pl. Rapackiego 4 — 24-754 T / 10-129 F

Oddział w Grudziądzu
86-300 Grudziądz
ul. J. Włodka 15 — 25-915 — T

Oddział we Włocławku
87-800 Włocławek
ul. Skorupki 4 — 32-28-57 — T/F

Archiwum Państwowe m.st. Warszawy
00-270 Warszawa
ul. Krzywe Koło 7 — 831-18-03 T / 831-00-46 T / 831-37-31 F

Oddział w Działdowie
13-200 Działdowo
ul. Jagiełły 31 — 21-64 — T

Oddział w Górze Kalwarii
05-530 Góra Kalwaria
ul. Ks. Z.Sajny 1 — 727-3149 — T

Oddział w Łowiczu
99-400 Łowicz
ul. 3 Maja 1 — 37-39-86 — T

Oddział w Mławie
06-500 Mława
ul. Narutowicza 3 — 54-33-09 — T

Oddział w Nowym Dworze Mazowieckim
05-100 Nowy Dwór Mazowiecki
ul. Kościuszki 1 — 775-2723 — T

Archives in Skołyszyn, a branch archive of AP Rzeszów 13

Archives in Gdańsk, c. 1996 14

Archives in Siedlce, c. 1996 15

Archives in Kielce, c. 1996 16

Oddział w Otwocku 05-400 Otwock ul. Górna 7	779-3871	T
Oddział w Pułtusku 06-100 Pułtusk ul. Zaułek 22	34-97	T
Oddział w Rawie Mazowieckiej 96-200 Rawa Mazowiecka ul. Kościuszki 5	35-51	T
Oddział w Żyrardowie (temporarily in Kutno) 99-300 Kutno ul. Zamkowa 4	53-39-81	T
Archiwum Państwowe we Wrocławiu 50-215 Wrocław ul. Pomorska 2	21-81-01 21-81-38 22-83-95	T T F
Oddział w Jeleniej Górze 58-500 Jelenia Góra ul. Podwale 27	752-42-08	T
Oddział w Kamieńcu Ząbkowickim 57-230 Kamieniec Ząbkowicki pl. Kościelny 4	17-35-40	T
Oddział w Legnicy 59-220 Legnica ul. Piastowska 22	29-350	T
Oddział w Lubaniu 59-800 Lubań ul. Bankowa 6	722-23-00	T
Oddział w Wałbrzychu (in Boguszów) 58-370 Boguszów-Gorce ul. Poniatowskiego 57	44-94-49	T
Archiwum Państwowe w Zamościu 22-400 Zamość skr. poczt. 136 ul. Moranda 4	39-23-35	T
Archiwum Państwowe w Zielonej Górze 66-002 Stary Kisielin ul. Pionierów Lubuskich 53	27-25-88 20-96-95	T F
Oddział w Wilkowie Wilkowo 66-200 Świebodzin (temporary location)	81-17-25	T
Oddział w Żarach 68-200 Żary pl. Kardynała Wyszyńskiego 2	74-32-34	T

Source: *Archiwa w Polsce: Informator Adresowy.* Warszawa: Naczelna Dyrekcja
Archiwów Państwowych, 1996.

INTERNET URL FOR THE POLISH STATE ARCHIVES

<http://ciuw.warman.net.pl/alf/archiwa/doc1.eng.html>

Tarnów Archives, a branch archive of AP Kraków,   17
1994

Maciej Dudek, director of Tarnów Archives, a   18
branch archive of AP Kraków, shows Miriam
Weiner examples of documents, 1994

Archives in Piotrków Trybunalski, 1996   19

Archives in Bochnia, a branch archive of   20
AP Kraków, 1995

INDEX TO POLISH STATE ARCHIVES BY LOCALITY

Archive Location (city)	Archiwum Państwowe (District Archive)	Page no.
Białystok	Białystok	294
Bielsko Biała	Katowice	295
Bochnia	Kraków	295
Boguszów	Wrocław	*
Brzeg	Opole	*
Bydgoszcz	Bydgoszcz	295
Chełm	Lublin	*
Cieszyn	Katowice	296
Częstochowa	Częstochowa	297
Działdowo	Warszawa	298
Elbląg[1]	Elbląg	298
Ełk	Suwałki	298
Gdańsk	Gdańsk	298
Gliwice	Katowice	300
Gniezno	Poznań	*
Góra Kalwaria	Warszawa	300
Gorzów Wielkopolski	Szczecin	301
Grudziądz	Toruń	*
Inowrocław	Bydgoszcz	301
Jędrzejów	Kielce	302
Jelenia Góra	Wrocław	303
Kalisz	Kalisz	303
Kamieniec Ząbkowicki	Wrocław	*
Katowice	Katowice	305
Kielce	Kielce	308
Konin	Poznań	*
Koszalin	Koszalin	309
Kraków	Kraków	309
Kraśnik	Lublin	311
Kutno	Płock	311
Łęczyca	Płock	311
Legnica	Wrocław	311
Leszno	Leszno	311
Łódź	Łódź	301
Łomża	Białystok	317
Łowicz	Warszawa	319
Lubań	Wrocław	*
Lublin	Lublin	319
Malbork	See Elbląg	
Mława	Warszawa	330
Mrągowo	Olsztyn	*
Nidzica	Olsztyn	*
Nowy Dwór Mazowiecki	Warszawa	330
Nowy Sącz	Kraków	331
Nowy Targ	Kraków	*
Nysa	Opole	*

Archive Location (city)	Archiwum Państwowe (District Archive)	Page no.
Olsztyn	Olsztyn	332
Opole	Opole	334
Oświęcim	Katowice	335
Otwock	Warszawa	336
Pabianice	Łódź	336
Piła	Poznań	336
Pińczów	Kielce	336
Piotrków Trybunalski	Piotrków Tryb.	338
Płock	Płock	339
Płoty	Szczecin	*
Poznań	Poznań	339
Przemyśl	Przemyśl	344
Przeworsk	Przemyśl	347
Pszczyna	Katowice	349
Pułtusk	Warszawa	349
Racibórz	Katowice	350
Radom	Radom	350
Radzyń Podlaski	Lublin	352
Rawa Mazowiecka	Warszawa	352
Rzeszów	Rzeszów	352
Sandomierz	Kielce	354
Sanok	Rzeszów	355
Siedlce	Siedlce	356
Sieradz	Łódź	358
Skołyszyn	Rzeszów	358
Słupsk	Koszalin	358
Starachowice	Kielce	359
Stargard Szczeciński	Szczecin	*
Stary Kisielin	See Zielona Góra	
Suwałki	Suwałki	359
Szczecin	Szczecin	361
Szczecinek	Koszalin	*
Tarnów	Kraków	362
Tarnowskie Góry	Katowice	363
Tomaszów Mazowiecki	Piotrków Tryb.	363
Toruń	Toruń	364
Wałbrzych	Wrocław	*
Warszawa	Warszawa	364, 372
Wilkowo	Zielona Góra	*
Włocławek	Toruń	372
Wrocław	Wrocław	373
Zamość	Zamość	373
Żary	Zielona Góra	375
Zielona Góra[2]	Zielona Góra	375
Żyrardów[3]	Warszawa	376
Żywiec	Katowice	376

[1]The Elbląg branch archives are located in Malbork
[2]The Zielona Góra branch archives are located in Stary Kisielin
[3]The Żyrardów branch archives are located in Kutno

* These archives are not included in the inventories (did not respond to survey or do not have relevant material)

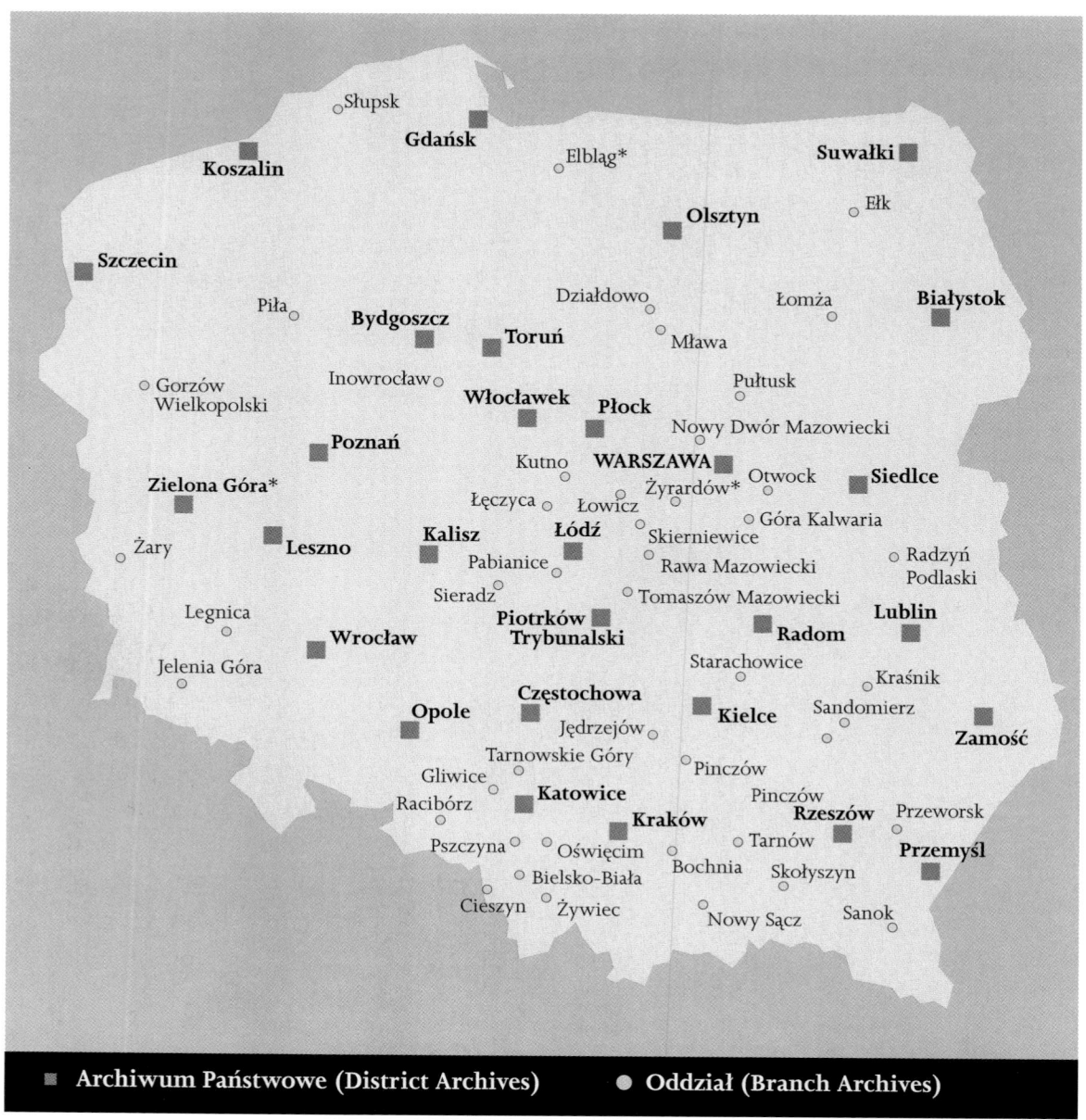

Archiwum Państwowe (District Archives) ● Oddział (Branch Archives)

Location of Polish State Archives Included in Repository Inventory *Map 13*

* The Elbląg branch archives are located in the town of Malbork.
  The Zielona Góra archives are located in the town of Stary Kisielin.
  The Żyrardów branch archives are temporarily located in the town of Kutno and housed with the
  Kutno branch archives.

ARCHIVE CLOSINGS SCHEDULED FOR LATE 1997

Przeworsk archives will close and documents will be sent to the Przemyśl archives.
Brzeg archives will close and documents will be sent to the Opole archives.
Pabianice archives will close and documents will be sent to the Łódź archives.
Działdowo archives will close and documents will be sent to the Mława archives.

PLACE-NAME VARIANTS IN EASTERN GALICIA
(refers only to localities included in archival inventories)

Polish	Russian	Ukrainian
Biały Kamień	Belyj Kamen	Bilyj Kamin'
Bóbrka	Boberka	Bibrka
Bohorodczany	Bogorodchany	Bohorodchany
Bolechów	Bolekhov	Bolekhiv
Bołszowce	Bolshovtsy	Bilshovtsy
Borszczów	Borshchev	Borshchiv
Borysław	Borislav	Boryslav
Brody	Brody	Brody
Brzeżany	Berezhany	Berezhany
Buczacz	Buchach	Buchach
Budzanów	Budanov	Budaniv
Bukaczowce	Bukachevtsy	Bukachivtsi
Bursztyn	Burshtyn	Burshtyn
Chocimierz	Khotmir	Khotmir
Chodorów	Khodorov	Khodoriv
Chorostków	Khorostkov	Khorostkiv
Czortków	Chortkov	Chortkiv
Czortowiec	Chortovets	Chortovets
Dobromil	Dobromil	Dobromyl'
Drohobycz	Drogobych	Drohobych
Dunajow	Dunayev	Dunaiv
Gliniany	Gliniany	Hliniany
Gołogóry	Gologory	Holohory
Gródek Jagielloński	Gorodok	Horodok
Grzymałów	Grimaylov	Hrymaliv
Gwoździec	Gvozdetz	Hvizdets
Halicz	Galich	Halych
Horodenka	Gorodenka	Horodenka
Husiatyn	Gusyatin	Husiatyn
Jagielnica	Yagelnitsa	Yagol'nitsa
Janów Trembowelski	Ivanovka	Ivanivka
Jaryczów Nowy	Novyj Yarychev	Yarychiv Novyj
Jaworów	Yavorov	Iavoriv
Jezierna	Ozernaya	Ozerna
Jezierzany	Ozeryany	Ozeryany
Jezupol	Zhovten	Yezupil
Kamionka Strumiłowa	Kamenka Bugskaya	Kam'ianka Buz'ka
Kołomyja	Kolomyia	Kolomyia
Komarno	Komarno	Komarno
Kopyczyńce	Kopychintsy	Kopychyntsi
Kosów	Kosov	Kosiv
Kozłów	Kozlov	Kozliv
Kosowa	Kozova	Kozova
Krakowiec	Krakovets	Krakovets
Kropiwnik Stary	Kropevnik	Kropiwnik Stary
Krzywcze	Verkhneye Krivche	Kryvche

PLACE-NAME VARIANTS IN EASTERN GALICIA
(refers only to localities included in archival inventories)

Polish	Russian	Ukrainian
Kudryńce	Kudrintsy	Kudryntsi
Lwów	Lvov	Lviv
Łysiec	Lisets	Lysets
Marjampol	Marinopol	Marinopil
Mielnica	Melnitsa Podolskaya	Melnitsa
Mikołajów	Nikolayev	Mikolaiv
Mikulińce	Mikulintsy	Mikulyntsi
Monasterzyska	Monastyriska	Monastyryska
Mosty Wielkie	Velikiye Mosty	Mosty Velyki
Mościska	Mostiska	Mostyska
Mraźnica	Mrazhnitsa	Mraznitsya
Nadwórna	Nadvornaya	Nadvirna
Narajów	Narayev	Naraiv
Nawarja	Navarya	Navariya
Obertyn	Obertin	Obertyn
Okopy	Okopy	Okopy
Olchowiec	Olkhovets	Olkhovets
Olesko	Olesko	Olesko
Podhajce	Podgatysy	Pidhajtsi
Podkamień	Podkamen	Pidkamin
Podwołoczyska	Podvolochisk	Pidvolochyska
Pomorzany	Pomoryany	Pomoryany
Probużna	Probezhnaya	Probizhna
Przemyślany	Peremyshlyany	Peremyshlyany
Rawa Ruska	Rava Russkaya	Rava Ruska
Rohatyn	Rogatin	Rohatyn
Rozdół	Rozdol	Rozdil
Rudki	Rudki	Rudky
Sądowa Wisznia	Sudovaya Vishnya	Sudova Vyshnya
Sambor	Sambor	Sambir
Sasów	Sasov	Sasiv
Schodnica	Skhodnitsa	Skhidnitsya
Skała Podolska	Skala Podolskaya	Skala Podolskaya
Skałat	Skalat	Skalat
Skole	Skole	Skole
Śniatyn	Snyatyn	Snyatyn
Sokal	Sokal	Sokal
Sokołówka	Sokolovka	Sokolivka
Sołotwina	Solotvina	Solotvina
Stanisławów	Ivano-Frankovsk	Ivano Frankivs'k
Stara Sól	Staraya Sol	Stara Sil
Stare Miasto	Staroye Misto	Starye Misto
Stary Sambor	Staryi Sambor	Staryj Sambir
Stojanów	Stoyanov	Stoyaniv
Stratyn	Stratyn	Stratyn
Strusów	Strusov	Strusiv
Stryj	Stryj	Stryj

PLACE-NAME VARIANTS IN EASTERN GALICIA
(refers only to localities included in archival inventories)

Polish	Russian	Ukrainian
Świrz	Svirzh	Svirzh
Szczerzec	Shchirets	Shchyrets
Tarnopol	Ternopol	Ternopil'
Tartaków	Tartakov	Tartakiv
Touste	Tolstoye	Tovste
Trembowla	Terebovlya	Terebovlya
Turka	Turka	Turka
Uhnów	Ugnev	Uhniv
Ułaszkowce	Ulashkovtsy	Ulashkivtsi
Winniki	Vinniki	Wynnyky
Żabie	Verkhovina	Verkhovina
Zabłotów	Zabolotov	Zabolotiv
Załoźce	Zalozhtsy	Zaliztski
Zawałów	Zavalov	Zavaliv
Zbaraż	Zbarazh	Zbarazh
Zborów	Zborov	Zboriv
Złoczów	Zolochev	Zolochiv
Żółkiew	Nesterov	Zhovka
Żurawno	Zhuravno	Zhuravno
Żydaczów	Zhidachov	Zhydachiv

NOTE: Because German was one of the administrative languages of the Austro-Hungarian Empire, a small number of localities in the above list, principally large cities, were also known by German versions of the place names—for example, Lwów (Lemberg) and Stanisławów (Stanislau).

▌ Lviv, Plac Bernardyński, c. 1917 (the church in center now houses the Lviv Historical Archives)   1

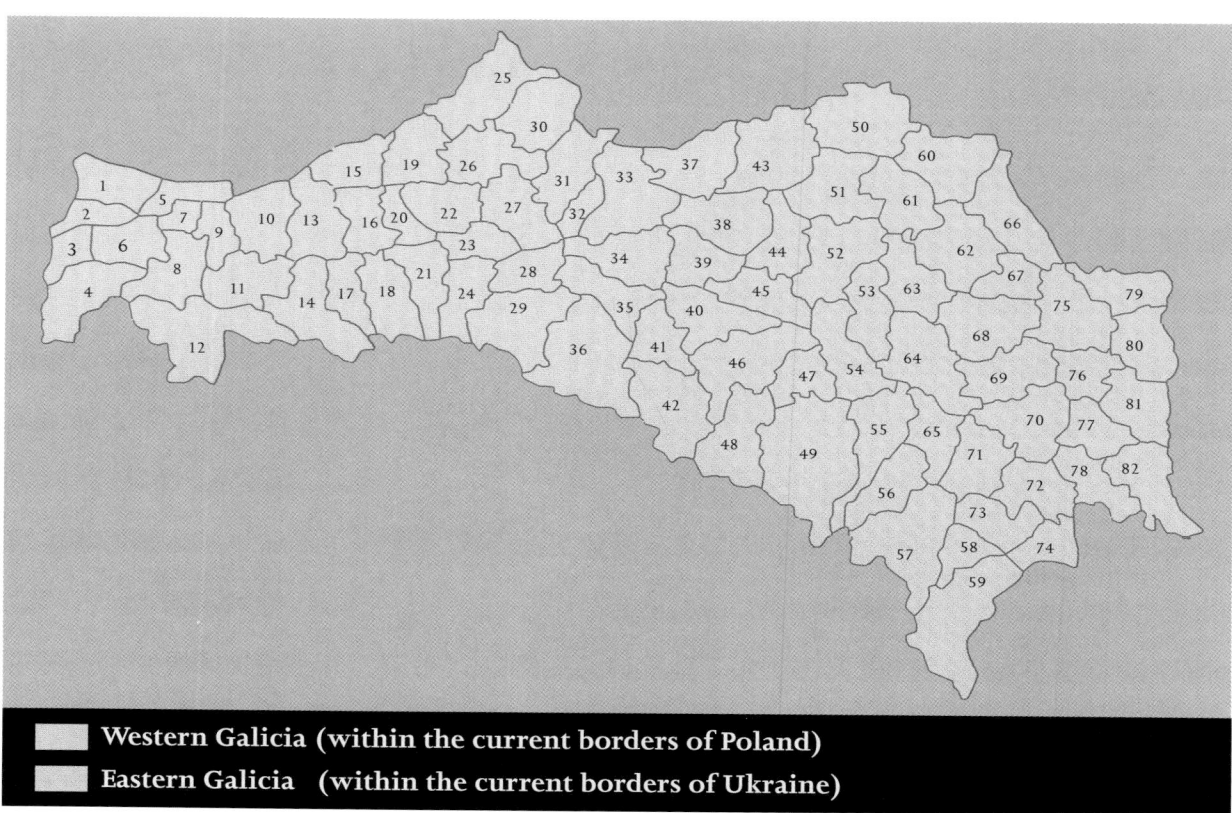

Western Galicia (within the current borders of Poland)

Eastern Galicia   (within the current borders of Ukraine)

Galicia: Administrative Districts, 1906–1914

Map 14

MAP KEY					
Biała	3	Kolbuszowa	26	Rudki	45
Bóbrka	53	Kolomyja	73	Rzeszów	27
Bochnia	10	Kosów	59	Sambor	40
Bohorodczany	56	Kraków	5	Sanok	29
Borszczów	82	Krosno	24	Skałat	80
Brody	66	Lańcut	31	Skole	48
Brzesko	13	Limanowa	11	Śniatyn	74
Brzeżany	68	Lisko	36	Sokal	50
Brzozów	28	Lwów	52	Stanislawów	65
Buczacz	70	Mielec	19	Stary Sambor	41
Chrzanów	1	Mościska	39	Stryj	47
Cieszanów	37	Myślenice	8	Stryżów	23
Czortków	77	Nadwórna	57	Tarnobrzeg	25
Dąbrowa	15	Nisko	30	Tarnopol	75
Dobromil	35	Nowy Sącz	14	Tarnów	16
Dolina	49	Nowy Targ	12	Tłumacz	71
Drohobycz	46	Oświęcim	2	Trembowla	76
Gorlice	18	Peczeniżyn	58	Turka	42
Gródek Jagielloński	44	Pilzno	20	Wadowice	6
Grybów	17	Podgórze	7	Wieliczka	9
Horodenka	72	Podhayce	69	Zaleszczyki	78
Husiatyn	81	Przemyśl	34	Zbaraż	79
Jarosław	33	Przemyślany	63	Zborów	67
Jasło	21	Przeworsk	32	Złoczów	62
Jaworów	38	Radziechów	60	Żółkiew	51
Kalusz	55	Rawa Ruska	43	Żydaczów	54
Kamionka Strumiłowa	61	Rohatyn	64	Żywiec	4
		Ropczyce	22		

Source: Lenius, Brian J. *Genealogical Gazetteer of Galicia*. 2nd ed. Anola, Manitoba, Canada: B. Lenius, 1993.

SURVIVING JUDAICA FROM GALICIA

▌ Judaica Exhibition in Museum Okręgowe in Rzeszów (formerly Western Galicia)   2

▌ Display of Jewish books at the Jewish History Research Center in the Rzeszów Archives, 1990   3

GENERAL GLOSSARY

Aleja (al.) (P)	Avenue
Bimah (H)	Platform in the synagogue from which the Torah is read during services
Chevra Kadisha (H/Y)	Burial society
Council of the Four Lands	*See* Vaad Arba Aratzot
Gmina (P)	Local administrative district
Guberniya (R)	Province (geographic district) within the Kingdom of Poland (from 1844 to World War I); the term was also used in the former Russian Empire
Hasid (pl. Hasidim) (H/Y)	Follower of disciples of Pietist movement founded by Israel Ba'al Shem Tov in the second half of the eighteenth century
Haskalah (H/Y)	Jewish Enlightenment, a movement that sought to spread modern European culture among Jews from the late eighteenth to the late nineteenth centuries
Judenrat (G)	Jewish Council selected by the Nazis
Landsmanshaftn (H/Y)	Organization of Jews from the same town or region
Kahal (H/Y)	Jewish community council
Kehillah (H/Y)	Jewish community
Klezmer (Y)	A group of musicians who traveled from village to village in Eastern Europe playing traditional music at various events and celebrations. *Klezmer* music was played on trumpets, clarinets, flutes, bugles, violins, cellos and drums
Księgi duchowne (P)	Community books
Księgi metrykalne (P)	Registers of births, deaths and marriages (commonly known as metrical books)
Małżeństwo (P)	Marriage
Mensch (Y)	An honorable, decent person worthy of respect and admiration
Miasto (pl. Miasta) (P)	Town
Mikvah, Mikveh (H/Y)	Jewish ritual bath
Misnaged (pl. Misnagdim) (H)	An opponent of Hasidism
Nowa, Nowe, Nowy (P)	New
Oblast (R)	Current administrative district (province) where town is located
Pinkas (pl. Pinkassim) (H/Y)	Jewish register books
Plac (P)	Square (as in town square or plaza)
Powiat (P)	County
Rynek	Market square
Shtetl (H/Y)	Small town
Shtibel (pl. Shtiblekh) (H/Y)	Small prayer house, generally Hasidic
Stary, Stara, Stare (P)	Old
Starosta (P)	Provincial administration
Tsaddik (pl. Tsaddikim) (H/Y)	A pious, righteous man; often refers to a Hasidic charismatic leader; also known as *rebbe* or leader
ulica (ul.) (P)	Street
Urodzenie (P)	Birth
Urząd Stanu Cywilnego (P)	Registrar's office of local vital records registration (within the last 100 years)
Vaad Arba Aratzot (H/Y)	Council of the Four Lands (Jewish National Council)
Voivodship (P)	Current administrative district (province) where town is located
Yizkor book	Memorial book published by survivors from a particular town or region
Zgon (pl. zgony) (P)	Death

LEGEND:

(G)	German
(H)	Hebrew
(P)	Polish
(Y)	Yiddish

HOLOCAUST GLOSSARY

Concentration camps (Konzentrationslager; KL)
Places of incarceration in which people were detained without regard to due process and the legal norms of arrest and detention. The extensive German camp system also included labor camps, transit camps, prisoner-of-war camps and extermination camps.

Extermination camps
The six killing centers—Chełmno, Bełżec, Sobibór, Treblinka, Auschwitz-Birkenau and Majdanek—established by the Germans in occupied Poland.

Generalgouvernement (General Government)
A territory in central and southern Poland established after the defeat of Poland in September 1939; it had a German civilian administration.

Ghetto
An enclosed district of a city where the Germans forced the Jewish population to live under conditions of severe crowding and deprivation. Ghettos were established in Poland, the Baltic states, the Soviet Union, the Protectorate of Bohemia and Moravia, and Hungary.

Greater Germany
A term referring to Germany and its annexed territories. It came into common German usage after the incorporation of Austria in 1938.

Protectorate of Bohemia and Moravia
A German protectorate established after the partition of Czechoslovakia in 1939, in violation of the Munich Agreement.

Reichskommissariat Ostland
A territory established after the German invasion of the Soviet Union in June 1941. It encompassed Lithuania, Latvia, Estonia, most of Belorussia and part of northeastern Poland, and had a German civilian administration.

Reichskommissariat Ukraine
A territory established after the German invasion of the Soviet Union in June 1941. It encompassed part of eastern Poland and most of the Ukraine, as far east as the area around the cities of Kiev and Dnepropetrovsk, and had a German civilian administration.

Sonderkommando
A prisoner forced-labor detachment assigned to work in the killing area of an extermination camp.

Source: *Historical Atlas of the Holocaust* by the United States Holocaust Memorial Museum. Copyright © 1996 by Yechiam Halevy. (New York: Macmillan Publishing USA, a Simon & Schuster Company).

Polski

The Polish Alphabet

Printed	Cursive
A a	*A a*
Ą ą	*Ą ą*
B b	*B b*
C c	*C c*
Ć ć	*Ć ć*
D d	*D d*
E e	*E e*
Ę ę	*Ę ę*
F f	*F f*
G g	*G g*
H h	*H h*
I i	*I i*
J j	*J j*
K k	*K k*
L l	*L l*
Ł ł	*Ł ł*
M m	*M m*
N n	*N n*
Ń ń	*Ń ń*
O o	*O o*
Ó ó	*Ó ó*
P p	*P p*
R r	*R r*
S s	*S s*
Ś ś	*Ś ś*
T t	*T t*

Printed	Cursive	Printed	Cursive
U u	*U u*	Z z	*Z z*
W w	*W w*	Ź ź	*Ź ź*
Y y	*Y y*	Ż ż	*Ż ż*

Polish is one of the Slavic languages that use the Roman alphabet, not the Cyrillic, largely because writing came to the Poles by way of Roman Catholic rather than Greek Orthodox clergy. The letters *q*, *v*, and *x* are not used in Polish, and the distinctly Polish characters *ą, ć, ę, ł, ń, ó, ś, ź* and *ż* are considered separate letters of the alphabet, each following its unmodified counterpart (*ą* after *a*, *ć* after *c*, and so on). The *ą, ę, ń,* and *y* never appear initially and thus are seldom capitalized; but since documents sometimes highlight words by spelling them out in upper-case letters, it seems best to show all upper-case forms, even those rarely seen.

The basic vowels of Polish are much as in the Romance languages: *a* is like the *a* in "father," *e* like that in "let," *i* like that in "machine," *o* somewhat like that in "hot," *u* like the *oo* in "book," and *y* like the short *i* sound in "hit." The vowel *ó* is pronounced exactly the same as Polish *u*, and some words are spelled either way (*Jakób* vs. *Jakub*, for example). The nasal vowel *ą* sounds like English "*own*" with the *n*-sound never quite finished, but before *b* or *p* it sounds more like *om* in "home." The nasal *ę* is generally pronounced like *en* in "m*en*," again without quite finishing the *n*-sound; before *b* or *p* it sounds more like *em* in "m*em*ory," and in some positions it loses its nasal quality. But generally pronouncing *ą* like *on* (*om*) and *ę* like *en* (*em*) will approximate the correct sound. Polish does not distinguish between long and short vowels.

The *i* is special because it often follows consonants as a sign of softening; thus Poles pronounce *ne* as somewhat like "neh," but *nie* more like "nyeh." The consonants *ć, ń, ś,* and *ź* are spelled that way only when they precede other consonants; before vowels they're spelled *ci, ni, si,* and *zi*. In either case they are pronounced, respectively, more or less like soft *ch* (as in "*ch*eese"), *ni* (as in "o*ni*on"), *sh* (as in "*sh*eep") and the sound of the *s* in "plea*s*ure." In a word like *cicho* (quiet, quietly) the *i* not only softens the *c* to a *ch*-sound, it also supplies the first syllable's vowel.

Many consonants are pronounced much as in English, but the *l* is more like that in "*l*eaf" than that in "hi*ll*," and the *r* is lightly trilled, as in Italian. Polish *h* and *ch* are pronounced the same, a little harsher than an initial *h* in English but not quite so guttural as *ch* in German "Ba*ch*." Polish *w* sounds like English *v* and Polish *ł* is pronounced like English *w* (all of which explains how "Lech Wałęsa" can come out sounding like "Lekh Vawensa"). The *c* is pronounced like a combined *ts* (e. g., English "knigh*ts*"), the *g* is always as in "*g*one" (never as in "*g*ym"), and the *j* is always pronounced like *y* in "*y*ield." The *s* is pronounced as it is in English "*s*oon," and *z* is pronounced as in "*z*ebra" (but remember the softened pronunciation of *ci, ni, si,* and *zi*).

The *cz, rz, sz* combinations are similar to *ć, ź,* and *ś*, respectively, but are articulated differently; *ż* is pronounced the same as *rz*. The combination *dź* or *dzi* sounds like an English *j* in "*j*ail." In Polish the accent almost always falls on the next-to-last syllable of any given word. Mastering certain sound combinations can be difficult for non-Poles, but once you do master them you'll find Polish words are pronounced exactly as they're spelled!

Source: Shea, Jonathan D., and William F. Hoffman. *Following the Paper Trail: A Multilingual Translation Guide.* New Milford, CT: Language & Lineage Press, 1991.

Русский

The Russian Alphabet

Printed	Cursive	English
А а	$\mathcal{A}a$	a
Б б	$\mathcal{B}d$	b
В в	$\mathcal{B}b$	v
Г г	$\mathcal{T}_{i}$	g
Д д	$\mathcal{D}g$	d
Е е	$\mathcal{E}e$	ye
Ё ё	$\ddot{\mathcal{E}}\ddot{e}$	yo
Ж ж	$\mathcal{K}\mathcal{K}$	zh
З з	$3z$	z
И и	$\mathcal{U}u$	i
Й й	$\breve{\mathcal{U}}\breve{u}$	y
К к	$\mathcal{K}\kappa$	k
Л л	$\mathcal{L}\lambda$	l
М м	$\mathcal{M}\mathcal{M}$	m
Н н	$\mathcal{H}\mu$	n
О о	$\mathcal{O}o$	o
П п	$\mathcal{T}n$	p
Р р	$\mathcal{P}p$	r
С с	$\mathcal{C}c$	s
Т т	$\mathcal{T}m$	t
У у	$\mathcal{Y}y$	u
Ф ф	$\mathcal{F}\phi$	f
Х х	$\mathcal{X}x$	kh
Ц ц	$\mathcal{U}u$	ts
Ч ч	$\mathcal{C}v$	ch

Printed	Cursive	English	Printed	Cursive	English
Ш ш	$\mathcal{U}\mu$	sh	- Ь	-ь	—
Щ щ	$\mathcal{U}\mu\mu$	shch	Э э	$\mathcal{Э}э$	e
- Ъ	- ъ	—	Ю ю	$\mathcal{HO}ю$	yu
- Ы	- ы	—	Я я	$\mathcal{Я}я$	ya

Russian is one of several Slavic languages that use the Cyrillic alphabet (others are Belarusian, Bulgarian, Macedonian, Serbian, and Ukrainian). There are minor variations in the form of the Cyrillic alphabet used in other Slavic languages; the alphabet shown here is that used in modern Russian. Pre-1917 Russian documents also used the characters **i**, equivalent to modern **и**, and **ѣ**, equivalent to modern **е**.

Even a superficial glance at the Cyrillic alphabet reveals that it is not totally foreign. When Cyril tried to devise a way of writing Slavic sounds, he borrowed extensively from the Greek alphabet and also modified some characters to represent distinctively Slavic phonemes. A few sounds were so foreign to Greek that characters were borrowed from other sources, e. g., ש and צ from Hebrew to make **ш** and **ц**, representing the *sh* and *ts* sounds.

Besides the printed and cursive forms, italic letters appear in documents. Even after one becomes familiar with the normal printed forms, a few italic forms can be puzzling, e. g., *т, д, г*, but the answer is simple: some italic forms are derived from their cursive equivalents. So *т* = т, *д* = д (∂ and *g* are both acceptable cursive forms of д), *г* = г, and so on.

Russian vowels are like those of other European languages — **а** = *a* as in "*f*ather," **э** = *e* as in "l*e*t," **и** = *i* as in "mach*i*ne," **о** = a sound somewhere between the *o*'s in "*O*ct*o*ber," and **у** = *u* as in "r*u*de" — but **а, э, ы, о** and **у** follow what are termed "hard" consonants, while the forms **я, е, и, ё** and **ю** follow consonants that are "softened" or palatalized. The basic distinction is illustrated by the word **нет** ("no"), pronounced "nyet" because the *e* vowel follows a palatalized *n* — a word pronounced like English "net," with a hard n, would be spelled **нэт**. This is why one often sees **я** transcribed as *ya,* **ё** as *yo,* and so on; the vowels are written differently to reflect the hard or soft quality of the consonants they follow. Standard Russian pronunciation gives full value only to vowels in accented syllables, and the farther the vowel is from the stress the less distinctly it is pronounced: **молоко** (milk), accented on the last syllable, is not pronounced like "mo-lo-KO" but more like "muh-lah-KO."

The table at left shows approximate English equivalents of the sounds represented by Russian consonants, but more must be said. The letter **г** does generally sound like the English *g* in "go," but at the end of words it can sound like *k*, and in the declensional suffixes -ого, -его, and archaic -яго and -аро it sounds like English *v*. The letter **ж** (often rendered in English as "zh") sounds like *s* in English "pleasure." The **ч** sounds like the *ch* in "*ch*urch," the **ш** sounds like the *sh* in "*sh*eet," and **щ** is *sh* and *ch* run together, as in the name "Khru*shch*ev."

Of the letters with no English equivalents given, the **x** is pronounced like *ch* in German "Ba*ch*" or Scottish "lo*ch*," **ъ** signifies that the preceding consonant is not softened or palatalized, **ь** shows that it is softened or palatalized, and **ы** represents a unique sound somewhat like the *y* in "ver*y*."

Source: Shea, Jonathan D., and William F. Hoffman. *Following the Paper Trail: A Multilingual Translation Guide.* New Milford, CT: Language & Lineage Press, 1991.

𝕯𝖊𝖚𝖙𝖘𝖈𝖍   The German Alphabet

Roman	Fraktur	Cursive
A a	𝕬 a	*Cursive*
B b	𝕭 b	
C c	ℭ c	
D d	𝕯 d	
E e	𝕰 e	
F f	𝕱 f	
G g	𝕲 g	
H h	ℌ h	
I I	𝕴 i	
J j	𝕵 j	
K k	𝕶 k	
L, l	𝕷 l	
M m	𝕸 m	
N n	𝕹 n	
O o	𝕺 o	
P p	𝕻 p	
Q q	𝕼 q	
R r	𝕽 r	
S s	𝕾 ſ s	
T t	𝕿 t	
U u	𝖀 u	
V v	𝖁 v	
W w	𝖂 w	
X x	𝖃 x	
Y y	𝖄 y	
Z z	𝖅 z	

Roman	Fraktur	Cursive
Ä ä	𝕬 ä	
Ö ö	𝕺 ö	
Ü ü	𝖀 ü	
ß	ß	
ch	ch	
sch	ſch	
ck	ck	
tz	tz	

The rather intimidating typeface known in German as *Fraktur* was generally used in Germany until before World War II, but has since been replaced in common usage by the alphabet familiar to us. Even in the modern Roman-based alphabet there are a few modified letters used for special sounds in German, and these are listed on the right-hand side of the chart: *ä* (a-umlaut), *ö* (o-umlaut), *ü* (u-umlaut) and *ß* (eszet). The other letter combinations (*ch, sch, ck,* and *tz*) are shown because their printed or cursive forms can be hard to recognize; but they are not regarded as separate characters and do not affect alphabetical order. Note also the alternate forms of lower-case s in *Fraktur* and cursive: ſ and ∫ are the usual forms, s and ß are used at the end of words or at dividing spots in compound words. We've all seen similar usage in older English-language documents such as the Declaration of Independence, where the letters that look like uncrossed *f*'s are actually *s*'s.

German cursive script can be as intimidating as the printed *Fraktur*. Consider 𝒢𝑒𝓈𝓊𝓃𝒹𝒽𝑒𝒾𝓉, a familiar expression to most Americans—it looks like a series of angular scrawls, but it's "Gesundheit," what you say when someone sneezes! Any combination of *n* (e), *r* (c), *m* (m), *n* (n), *u* (u), *v* (v), and *w* (w) can be frustrating to decipher, especially if the penmanship is sloppy. The best approach is to identify the easier letters, such as *b*, *h*, *a*, and *v*; distinguish ∫ (s) and *f* (h) by their extending above and below the other letters; then start counting up-and-down strokes and trying to match them with problem letters. Hints: *u* (u) should always have that little curve over it, and *v* (v) and *w* (w) end with tailing curves that are usually discernable. Your odds improve if you have a limited list of candidate words to choose from; if you've inferred that the word in question might refer to a parent, *Mutter* can suddenly go from "M—r" to *Mutter*, "mother." So a good dictionary can help a lot with deciphering written words.

Source: Shea, Jonathan D., and William F. Hoffman. *Following the Paper Trail: A Multilingual Translation Guide.* New Milford, CT: Language & Lineage Press, 1991.

Chapter/Section picture number	Credit
TABLE OF CONTENTS	
Title photo	Jerzy Langda & PAN
1	Photographer unknown
FOREWORD	
1	Arnold Kramer
ACKNOWLEDGMENTS	
1	Maria Skowronek
2–4	Miriam Weiner
5	Mariola Jeziak
INTRODUCTION	
Title photo	AP Kraków
1, 3	PAN
2, 4	Miriam Weiner
5	H. Poddębski & PAN
6	AP Suwałki
7	Chuck Fishman
CHAPTER 1	
Title photo, 8	AP Kraków
1	AP Katowice (in Gliwice)
2–4	M. Weiner Archives
5	Judaica Foundation
6–7	AP Lublin
9	AP Rzeszów
CHAPTER 2	
Title photo, 1, 3	M. Weiner Archives
2	PAN
4–5	Chuck Fishman
6	J. Sobieniak
7	Robert Waszkiewicz
8	Jan Jagielski
Będzin	
1	L. Surowiec & KAW
2–3, 9	Jeffrey K. Cymbler
4, 8	J. Cymbler Archives
5	Jan Jagielski
6	J. Nowicki & PAN
7	S. Jakubowski & KAW
10	D. Braverman Archives
11	W. Zieliński & KAW
Białystok	
1	Marjorie Goldberg
2–5, 7, 18	Miriam Weiner
9, 13	M. Weiner Archives
6, 8	Jan Jagielski
10, 12, 14, 16–17	T. Wiśniewski Archives
11, 15	J. Tymiński & KAW

Chapter/Section picture number	Credit
Chełm	
1, 6	M. Weiner Archives
2	PAN
3	P. Krassowski & KAW
4	Miriam Weiner
5	Chuck Fishman
Częstochowa	
1, 6, 10	M. Weiner Archives
2–3	Monika Krajewska
4, 8	D. Braverman Archives
5	Alter Kacyzna[1]
7, 13	M. Brenner Archives
9, 12	PTIC
11	K. Jabłoński & KAW
Gdańsk	
1	Piotr Kulikowski
2	Jan Jagielski
3	PAN
4	P. Krassowski & KAW
Kalisz	
1	JHI Archives
2–3	J. Jagielski Archives
4, 5, 9	Jan Jagielski
6	M. Weiner Archives
7	J. Malinowski & KAW
8	A. Araszkiewicz & KAW
Kielce	
1, 4, 8–9, 12–14	M. Weiner Archives
2, 5–6	Jan Jagielski
3	PAN
7	Steve Lipman
10	A. Karczewski & KAW
11	P. Krassowski & KAW
Kraków	
1, 6, 10	Miriam Weiner
2, 4, 16–17, 20	Look Pol 1989
3	PTIC
5, 8	Jerzy Langda & PAN
7, 22	Paul Petroff
9	S. Zbadyński & NTPA
11	Jan Jagielski
12–14, 18	M. Weiner Archives
15	H. Pawlak & KAW
19, 24	M. Brenner Archives
21, 23	Wojciech Gorgolewski & Center for Jewish Culture
Łódz	
1–2	ARA "Telegraph"
3–4, 11–15, 17–18, 20–22	M. Weiner Archives
5–10	Jan Jagielski
16, 19	L. Surowiec & KAW
23	W. Małek & "Gwarant"

[1]Abramovitch, Raphael. *The Vanished World*. New York: Forward Association, 1947.

ABBREVIATIONS
AP   Archiwum Państwowe
JHI   Jewish Historical Institute
KAW   Krajowa Agencja Wydawnica
NTPA   National Tourism Promotion Agency
PAN   Instytut Sztuki Polskiej Akademii Nauk
USC   Urząd Stanu Cywilnego (local town halls)
WMF   World Monuments Fund

LEGEND

Example: Miriam Weiner = photographer credit
M. Weiner Archives = private collection
(primarily antique postcards)

Chapter/Section picture number	Credit
Łomża	
1	M. Bronarski & KAW
2, 5	M. Weiner Archives
3–4	Jan Jagielski
Lublin	
1, 10–11, 13, 15–17, 20	M. Weiner Archives
2	PAN
3, 7, 9	Miriam Weiner
4–5	Jan Jagielski
6	Marjorie Goldberg
8	B. Łopieński & NTPA
12	J. Tymiński & KAW
14	Chuck Fishman
18	A. Stelmach
19	E. Baranowska & KAW
Międzyrzec Podlaski	
1	PAN
2–5	Mariola Jeziak
Nowy Sącz	
1	T. Hermańczyk & P AN
2–3	Miriam Weiner
4	M. Weiner Archives
5	J. Żak & KAW
Otwock	
1	M. Weiner Archives
2–5	Jan Jagielski
6	Z. Żyburtowicz & KAW
7	A. Ruckgaber & KAW
Piotrków Trybunalski	
1–2	Jan Jagielski
3	M. Weiner Archives
4	J. Tymiński & KAW
Płock	
1	P. Kulikowski/Bau-Help
2, 6	M. Brenner Archives
3, 5	Michael Brenner
4	A. Karczewski & KAW
Przemyśl	
1	Chuck Fishman
2	J. Jagielski Archives
3	M. Weiner Archives
4	J. Siudecki & KAW
5	Miriam Weiner
Radom	
1	M. Kirschenbaum Archives
2, 8	Miriam Weiner
3–4	Jan Jagielski
5, 10	Stephen Dubner
6	J. Śmiałowski & KAW
7, 9, 11–15	A. Lipson Archives
16	M. Weiner Archives

Chapter/Section picture number	Credit
Radomsko	
1	J. Cymbler Archives
2	K. Jabłoński & KAW
3	Jeffrey K. Cymbler
4	Michael Brenner
5	M. Weiner Archives
6	A. Stelmach & KAW
Rzeszów	
1	T. Hermańczyk & PAN
2, 5	Jan Jagielski
3	M. Weiner Archives
4	J. Makarewicz & KAW
Siedlce	
1	J. Jagielski Archives
2–3, 5	Jan Jagielski
4	M. Weiner Archives
6	W. Stasiak & KAW
Sosnowiec	
1, 3	D. Braverman Archives
2	Yizkor Book[1]
4	Monika Krajewska
5	A. Ładno & KAW
Tarnów	
1, 6, 8–10	M. Weiner Archives
2, 4	Susan Reisler & WMF
3, 5, 13	Sam Gruber & WMF
7	J. Jagielski Archives
11	J. Makarewicz & KAW
12	R. Dutkiewicz & KAW
Tomaszów Mazowiecki	
1	J. Jagielski Archives
2	Ewa Kozłowska & PAN
3	Monika Krajewska
4	Jan Jagielski
5	J. Tymiński & KAW
6	M. Weiner Archives
7	K. Kaczyński & KAW
Warszawa	
1	A. Kossobudzki & NTPA
2, 8	Archer Trade
3, 6	Andrzej Marzec & NTPA
4, 17–19, 21–22, 25–26, 29–30, 33–34	M. Weiner Archives
	M. Weiner Archives
5, 7, 11, 14	JHI
9, 16	K. Wojciewski & NTPA
10, 32, 37	Miriam Weiner
12, 15	Jan Jagielski
13, 24	Paul Petroff
23	S.R. Sadowski & KAW
27	P. Krassowski & KAW
20, 28	K. Jablóński & KAW
31	Hotel Bristol
35–36, 38	Monika Krajewska

[1]Geshur, Meier Shimon. *Sefer Sosnovits veha-sevivah be-Zaglembyah* (*Book of Sosnowiec and the Surrounding Region in Zaglebie*). 2 vols. Tel Aviv: Sosnowiec Societies in Israel, the United States, France and Other Countries, 1973–1974. (H, Y)

Chapter/Section picture number	Credit
Włocławek	
1	K. Piechotka Archives
2	Jan Jagielski
3–4	W. Stasiak & KAW
5	M. Weiner Archives
6	Z. Kalinowski & PAN
Wrocław	
1–2	Chuck Fishman
3	Jan Jagielski
4	JHI
5	M. Weiner Archives
6	S. Jabłońska & KAW
7	PAN
Zamość	
1, 5	L. Surowiec & KAW
2	H. Poddębski & PAN
3	Ryszard Bogdziewicz
4, 7–9	PAN
6	M. Weiner Archives
CHAPTER 3	
Title photo, 1	Mariola Jeziak
2	Miriam Weiner
3	AP Piotrków Trybunalski
4, 9, 15	AP Kielce (in Pinczów)
5	AP Siedlce
6	AP Kielce (in Sandomierz)
7, 11, 16	AP Kraków
8, 19, 21, 23, 25	AP Lublin
10	AP Kraków (in Nowy Sącz)
12	AP Kraków (in Tarnów)
13	AP Białystok
14	AP Przemyśl
17	AP Płock
18	AP Rzeszów
20	AP Łódź
22	AP Katowice
24	AP Bydgoszcz (in Inowłocławek)
CHAPTER 4	
Title photo, 1–2, 13	Miriam Weiner
3, 5, 10, 12	USC Rejowiec
4, 7–9,11	USC Nowy Sącz
6	USC Jarosław
14–16	USC Warsaw Śródmieście
17	T. Przypkowski & PAN
18–19	PAN
CHAPTER 5	
Title photo, 1, 3–4, 6–12	JHI
2	P. Sonnenburg
5	Miriam Weiner
CHAPTER 6	
Title photo, 8	Jan Jagielski
1, 26–28	Bruce Liebowitz
2–4	AP Kraków
5–7, 9–10	Majdanek Museum Archives
11, 23–25	Miriam Weiner
12–14, 16–20	Auschwitz-Birkenau Archives
15	M. Weiner Archives
21–22	Mariola Jeziak

Chapter/Section picture number	Credit
CHAPTER 7	
Title photo	AP Białystok
1	Miriam Weiner
2	J. Jagielski Archives
3	M. Weiner Archives
4	Joan Krotenberg
Appendix 1	
1–8, 11, 97, 113	M. Weiner Archives
9, 12, 14–15, 18–21, 23–24, 26–27,	PAN
29, 44, 48, 50, 77–80, 93–94, 100,	PAN
103–104, 110, 115	PAN
10, 28, 74	K. Kłos & PAN
13, 53	C. Olszewski & PAN
16–17, 25, 83–85, 87	S. Zajaczyk & PAN
22	E. Dobrowolski & PAN
30, 51, 54, 56, 59, 66, 108	Mariola Jeziak
31– 33, 38	AP Kraków
34–35, 57	Marjorie Goldberg
36	W. Stasiak & KAW
37	Majdanek Museum Archives
39	M. Kwiczala & PAN
40, 67	T. Hermańczyk & PAN
41	Fundacja Pogranicze Sejny
42–43, 52, 58, 60, 62, 70–71, 73	Miriam Weiner
45	S. Stępniewski & PAN
46–47, 63, 98	Witalis Wolny & PAN
49, 75, 89	J. Szandomirski & PAN
55, 68	Jeffrey K. Cymbler
61	Yale Reisner
62, 116	Chuck Fishman
64	Joan Krotenberg
65, 112	Jan Jagielski
69	K. Wojciewski & NTPA
72	V. Król & PAN
76, 95, 114	H. Poddębski & PAN
81–82	A. Oles & PAN
86, 106	M. Moraczewska & PAN
88	T. Przypkowski & PAN
90	Ewa Kozłowska & PAN
91	Barbara Blicharski
92	K. Oz & PAN
96	S. Deptuszewski & PAN
99	Harold Kaiman
101	A. Bochnak & PAN
102	S. Sempoliński & PAN
105	L. Święcki & PAN
107	T. Przypkowski & PAN
109	J. Bułhak & PAN
111	K. Wolski & PAN
117	Samuel Gruber & WMF
Appendix 2	
1, 7, 9, 13, 18, 20	Mariola Jeziak
2–3, 10–12, 17	Miriam Weiner
4	AP Wrocław
5	AP Białystok
6, 8, 15, 19	Polish State Archives
14	AP Gdańsk
16	J. Dąbrowski & AP Kielce
Appendix 3	
1	M. Weiner Archives
2	M. Wideryński
3	Miriam Weiner
Appendix 6	
1	Kraków Archives
2	Miriam Weiner

ADDRESSES OF INSTITUTIONS, FIRMS AND ORGANIZATIONS LISTED ABOVE

CENTER FOR JEWISH CULTURE, ul. Batory 12, 31-135 Kraków, POLAND

FUNDACJA POGRANICZE SEJNY, ul. J. Piłsudskiego 37, 16-500 Sejny, POLAND

INSTYTUT SZTUKI POLSKIEJ AKADEMII NAUK, ul. Długa 26/28, 00-950 Warszawa, POLAND

JEWISH HISTORICAL INSTITUTE, ul. Tłomackie 3/5, 00-090 Warsaw, POLAND

JUDAICA FOUNDATION OF POLAND, ul. Meiselsa 17, 31-058 Kraków, POLAND

KRAJOWA AGENCJA WYDAWNICZA, ul. Wilcza 46, 00-679 Warszawa, POLAND

NATIONAL TOURISM PROMOTION AGENCY, 9 Mazowiecka Str., 00-052 Warsaw, POLAND

UNIA HOTEL, Aleje Racławickie 12, 20-037 Lublin, POLAND

WORLD MONUMENT FUND, 949 Park Avenue, New York, NY 10028

COPYRIGHT OF PHOTOGRAPHS

All photographs are owned and/or copyrighted by the named photographer or institution.

MAP CREDITS

Maps 1, 3, 7	*Encyclopaedia Judaica* and Keter Publishing House Jerusalem Ltd.
Maps 9, 10, 11, 12, Map Glossary	*Historical Atlas of the Holocaust* by the United States Holocaust Memorial Museum. Copyright © 1996 by Yechiam Halevy (New York: Macmillan Publishing USA, a Simon & Schuster Company).
Map 14	*Genealogical Gazetteer of Galicia*, 2nd ed., by Brian J. Lenius (Anola, Manitoba, Canada: B. Lenius, 1993).

MAP GRAPHICS

Adaptation of maps	Dorcas Gelabert and Stephen Freeman
Maps 4, 5, 8, 13, 14	Stephen Freeman
Maps 2, 6	Dorcas Gelabert and Stephen Freeman

One page of photographs from an album in the Kraków Archives depicting deportations to the Kraków ghetto (Podgórze District), 1942   1

Judaica exhibition, Rzeszów Archives (former synagogue), 1990

2